IMAGES
of America

SURRY COUNTY

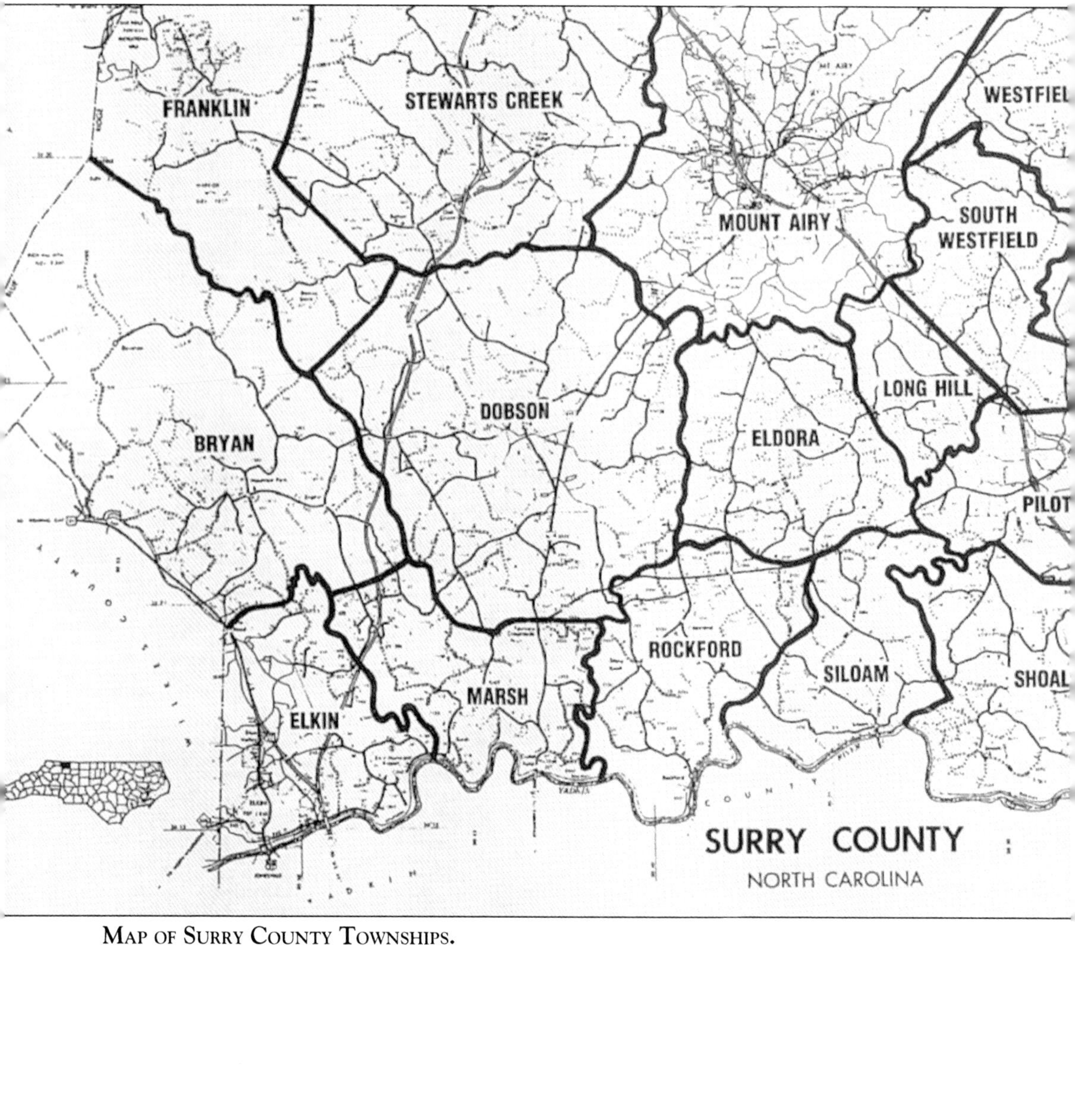

MAP OF SURRY COUNTY TOWNSHIPS.

IMAGES
of America

SURRY COUNTY

Carolyn Boyles, Wilma Hiatt,
and the Surry County Genealogical Association

ARCADIA
PUBLISHING

ISBN 978-0-7385-0640-1

Published by Arcadia Publishing
Charleston, South Carolina

Printed in the United States of America

Library of Congress Catalog Card Number: 00-106898

For all general information contact Arcadia Publishing at:
Telephone 843-853-2070
Fax 843-853-0044
E-mail sales@arcadiapublishing.com
For customer service and orders:
Toll-Free 1-888-313-2665

Visit us on the Internet at www.arcadiapublishing.com

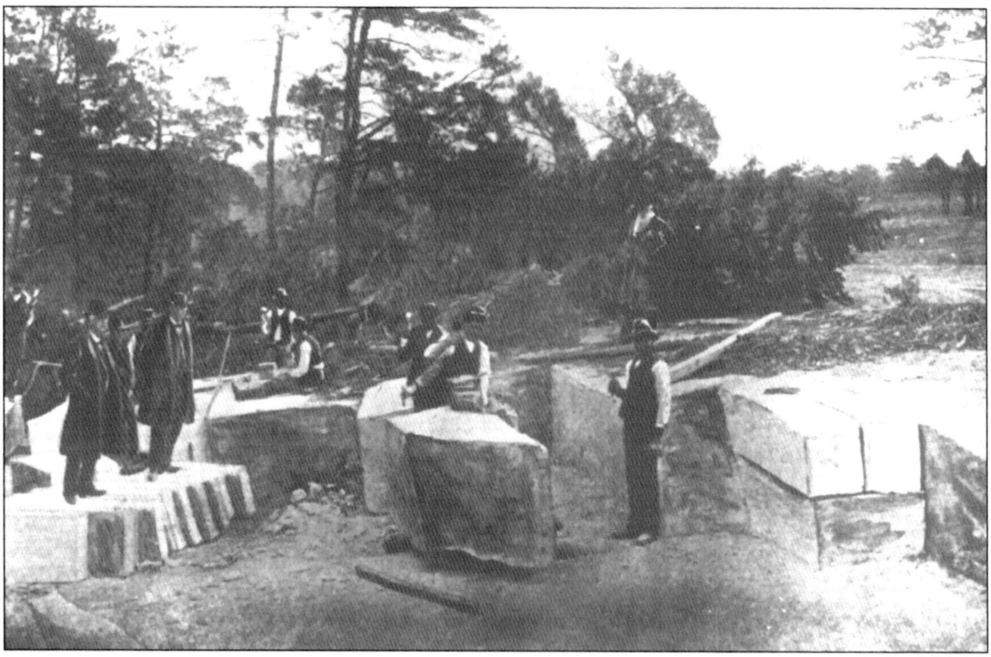

GRANITE QUARRY IN FLAT ROCK. North Carolina Granite Corporation, located in the community of Flat Rock, is the largest open-faced quarry in the world. The quarry was first owned by Thomas Smith, who purchased the property in 1780. It is not known how long the quarry has been worked, but it was mentioned as early as 1775 by the Moravians in Salem. There are many buildings in Mount Airy made of granite; hence, Mount Airy is called "the Granite City." (Courtesy of Ruth Minick.)

Contents

Acknowledgments 6

Introduction 7

1. Bryan Township 9

2. Dobson Township 17

3. Eldora and Long Hill Townships 25

4. Elkin and Marsh Townships 37

5. Franklin Township 51

6. Mount Airy Township 59

7. Pilot Township 69

8. Rockford Township 79

9. Shoals and Siloam Townships 89

10. Stewart's Creek Township 105

11. South Westfield and Westfield Townships 115

ACKNOWLEDGMENTS

The Surry County Genealogical Association (SCGA) began to focus on the possibility of a Surry County pictorial history late in 1999 after Cindy Casey of the Forsyth County Genealogical Society spoke to our group. We would like to thank Cindy for presenting the idea to us, sharing invaluable information, and for the enthusiasm she extended to us to go forward with this project.

SCGA member Esther Johnson got us started by contacting many of the contributors of photographs. Esther is relentless in her endeavor, and we thank her for her support all through the project. A book committee was formed and we thank all of its members for taking time out of their busy schedules to attend our many meetings. The members of the book committee were Wilma Hiatt (chairman), Carolyn Boyles, Judy Cardwell, Esther Johnson, Teresa Smith, Carlos Surratt, and Peggy Wall. These individuals also made contacts to gather photographs for the book.

After the group was formed, Carolyn Boyles agreed to be our editor, and we thank her immensely for her many hours spent on the project. Her knowledge and computer capabilities have certainly enhanced the quality of the book. When Carolyn became a member of the committee, she surely didn't realize she would undertake the job as editor. Working closely with Carolyn in the last phase of the book, Wilma Hiatt did a lot of the legwork bringing all the pieces together for Carolyn. We thank her and Agee Hiatt (her husband), for their support and help during these last busy weeks.

A special thanks to Norma Bowen, Emma Boyles, Andy Bryant, Dennis "Bud" Cameron, Donald Davis, Hester Jackson, Mildred Matthews, Ruth Minick, Ann Stewart, and Agnes Well for their support and for just being there ready to help when needed. Their efforts were very important in the completion of the book. Most of all, we thank the many contributors of photographs who are listed after each image. We couldn't have done it without you.

The association greatly appreciates the cooperation of everyone who submitted photographs and regrets being unable to use them all due to limited space.

—Surry County Genealogical Association

INTRODUCTION

On the eastern slopes of the Blue Ridge Mountains, at the meeting of the North Carolina and Virginia borders, is a bountiful place. With the beautiful tree-covered blue ridge as its backdrop, there lies below it valleys, hills, woodlands, and pleasant fields. Riverlets of pure water spring forth from mountain headwaters and meander through the hills and valleys forming creeks by the score and flowing into rivers by the names of Mitchell, Fisher, and Ararat. These languid rivers flow across the land until each, in its time and place, enters the ambling Yadkin River, marking this good land's southern boundary. The eastern boundary is marked by that magnificent sentinel known as Pilot Mountain, whose wooded slopes rise upward until its nearly bald pinnacle touches God's beautiful sky. Then traveling along the northern boundary, the Virginia line, one traverses ridges and mountains back to Fishers Peak in the blue ridge. Here is a place of singular beauty.

For over two and a quarter centuries, this lovely place has been known as Surry County, a good place to live, work, worship, and play. This pictorial history reminds us of those who lived here in the late nineteenth and the first half of the twentieth centuries. Nearly everyone pictured in this book is gone now, but they and their contemporaries helped make Surry the wonderful place it is today. They created farms and towns, and established homes, churches, and the communities we value today. We are indebted to those who have lived before us, and this book will help to remind us of those who passed this way.

The mode and manner of living today is far removed from the scenes preserved on these pages. Older folks may remember those simpler times, but the younger generation can't imagine how different things are today. For instance, a hundred years ago there were no paved roads. The roads that did exist were poor, and fording creeks and rivers was normal. Railroads to Mount Airy and Elkin were built in the last quarter of the nineteenth century, but, for the most part, people traveled over rough roads on mule or horseback or by wagons pulled by mules or oxen. In the pictures that follow, you will see some of the early motorized vehicles.

In nearly every home could be found two books: *Blum's Almanac* and the Holy Bible. Both were used. The first was helpful in planting gardens and crops and a host of other things; people believed in doing things by the signs of the moon and the planets. The second book was to live by—it was God's instruction book for us. Table grace and reading the Bible as a family were daily practices.

Nearly every family had at least one milk cow, a hog pen, and chicken coop. The milk cow provided milk, buttermilk, and butter. In the late fall of the year, the hogs were killed for sausage, bacon, pork chops, tenderloin, livermush, and other things that the family would have eaten through the year, as well as the lard used for cooking. Nearly all this meat had to be salt- or smoke-cured or canned since there was no means of refrigeration. Chickens laid eggs and were also served fried on the table. Almost all of the food a family would eat was raised on the farm. To supplement the meat for the table, wild game was hunted and used for cooking in different ways.

Today a number of people raise gardens, but they aren't as large or as necessary as they were in earlier days. From the garden one obtained vegetables; however, when they weren't in season, they weren't available. Thus canning and preserving vegetables was a necessary task in supplying the table for the rest of the year. Canned beans, peas, corn, hominy, sauerkraut, tomatoes, pickled beets, and cucumbers were all important to the family. Potatoes, turnips, apples, and pears were kept in cellars or in pits covered with dirt to keep them from going bad. Berries, grapes, and other fruits were canned or made into preserves. Crops raised at the turn of the century included corn, wheat, and other grains, as well as cane, cotton, and tobacco.

On average, families were larger than they are today, and three generations might live together. The preparation of meals, which were eaten around the kitchen table, was slow, hot, and hard work. There was no running water—springs and wells provided water. Most of the family's clothing was made by the women in the family. Houses were lit by candles or oil lamps, and heat was generated by a fireplace or a wood stove in the kitchen. An outhouse was used by those who had them and the woods by those who didn't. Baths in a tub happened just once a week; the rest of the week you just wiped off what was dirty.

By the 1920s, houses in town had indoor toilets, some kind of electric lighting, and, in some cases, telephones, but it wasn't until the 1930s that electricity was available in rural communities. And it wasn't until the 1920s that many cars were seen in the county.

Things have changed a lot over the years, and some things are decidedly better. Educational opportunities are much better in our modern schools than the one-room schools of a century ago. Medicine and health care are much better today than they once were—cemeteries reveal the high number of deaths that occurred among children and young mothers in the days of long ago. Two things that have remained fundamental in the lives of Surry County residents are a strong sense of family and the role of the church and spiritual life. Today the family unit might look different from the family of 100 years ago, but a sense of the importance of family and home remain strong. The church also retains a special place in people's lives—you can't travel far in Surry County and not find at least one church.

This pictorial history of previously unpublished photographs is divided into chapters that focus on townships. The division of counties into townships was a result of the North Carolina's adoption of the Constitution in 1868. Originally there were 11 townships; now there are 15. The county map shows the current township divisions, and readers will notice that some neighboring townships have been combined for the purposes of this book. The table of contents will direct you to the pages where the different township groupings begin.

The community thanks the Surry County Genealogical Association for making this pictorial history a reality. Thanks, also, to all who made pictures available for inclusion. Hopefully this will begin a continuing effort toward an even more complete pictorial history in the future.

Enjoy this visual retrospective of Surry County. Share it with friends. Buy copies for family members. Books go out of print, but every home having a dog-eared copy years from now will count it a treasure. May this word to the wise be sufficient.

—Dennis W. "Bud" Cameron
Register of Deeds

One

Bryan Township

Bryan Township lies in the western part of Surry County and borders Wilkes and Alleghany Counties. Mitchell's River, South Fork, and Christian Creeks run through the township. Among the communities in the area are Mountain Park, Devotion, State Road, and Zephyr. The churches include State Road Primitive Baptist (the site of a historical marker), Mountain Park Baptist, Mitchell's River Primitive Baptist (established in 1785), Rocky Ford Baptist, Mount Pleasant Baptist, and Grassy Creek Methodist. Gum Orchard Baptist, located in Zephyr, was established in 1865. Some of the schools in the township's history include Bryan, Hickory Springs, Mountain Park, Union Hill, and Zephyr. The one-room schoolhouses of Flat Branch, Good Springs, Liberty, Mitchell's River, Rocky Ford, and Possum Trot were consolidated into Mountain Park.

Kapp's Mill on Mitchell's River was a large operation believed to have been started in 1872 and is a typical example of a gristmill that was accompanied by a general store, a blacksmith shop, and a post office. One lady recalls that her mother's first store-bought shoes were purchased at Kapp's Mill for 10¢, a price that was covered by bartering eggs. But the shoes were mismatched—one top was made of leather and the other of cloth. Kapp's Mill became an early social center for the surrounding area.

The R.J. Reynolds's estate at Devotion greatly boosted the economy in the 1930s by employing a large number of people. Wages at that time were $1 a day for a man's labor and $2 for a man, his team, and his wagon.

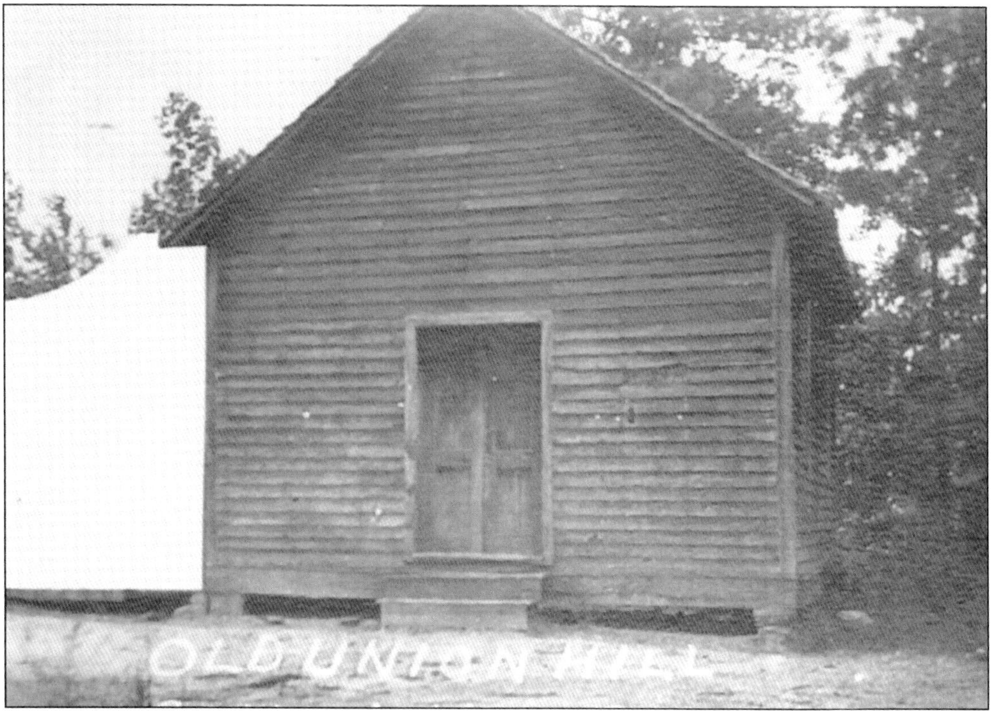

UNION HILL SCHOOL. Union Hill was an early schoolhouse in Bryan Township. (Courtesy of Annie Lee Gentry.)

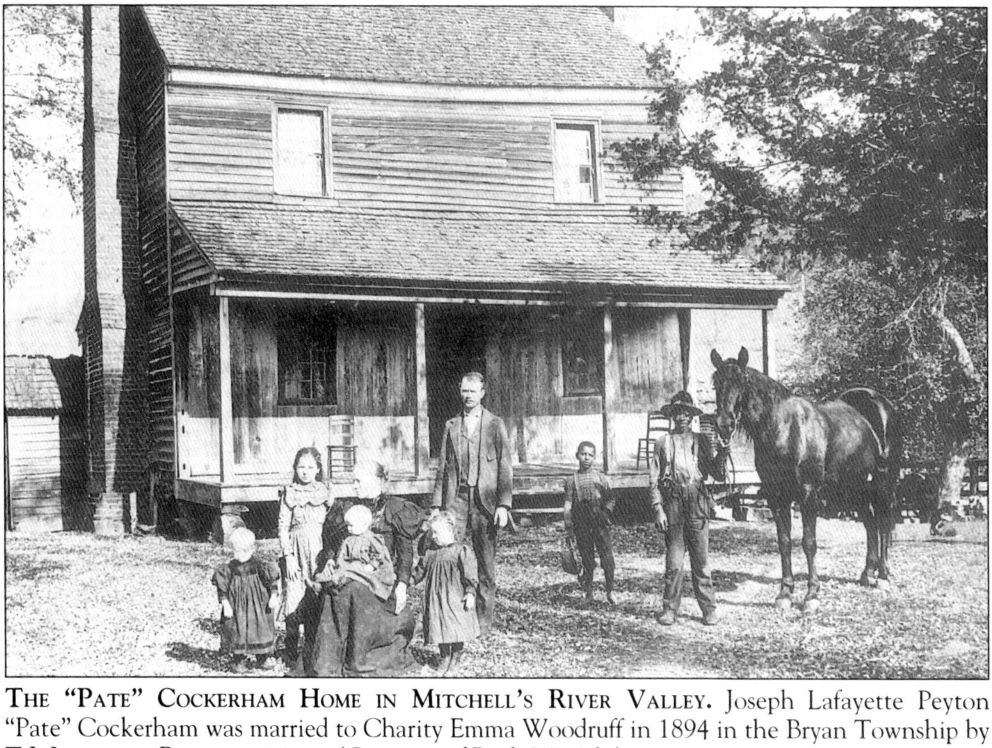

THE "PATE" COCKERHAM HOME IN MITCHELL'S RIVER VALLEY. Joseph Lafayette Peyton "Pate" Cockerham was married to Charity Emma Woodruff in 1894 in the Bryan Township by T.J. Lawson, a Baptist minister. (Courtesy of Ruth Minick.)

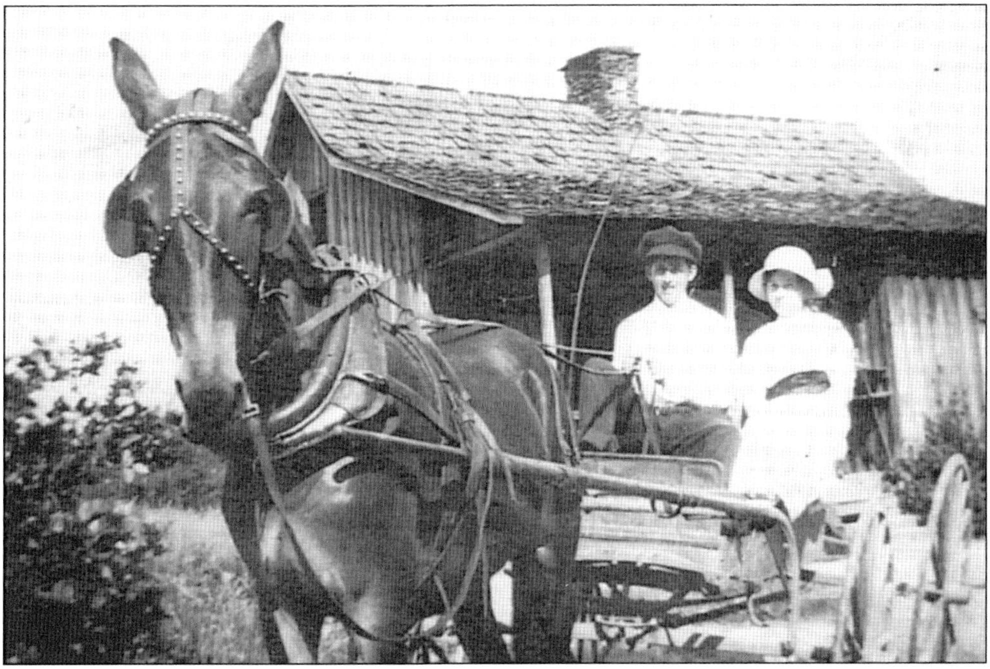

JOHN'S LITTLE MULE "ALICE." John Frank Nixon takes his sister Annie for a Sunday afternoon ride, c. 1916. (Courtesy of Annie Lee Gentry.)

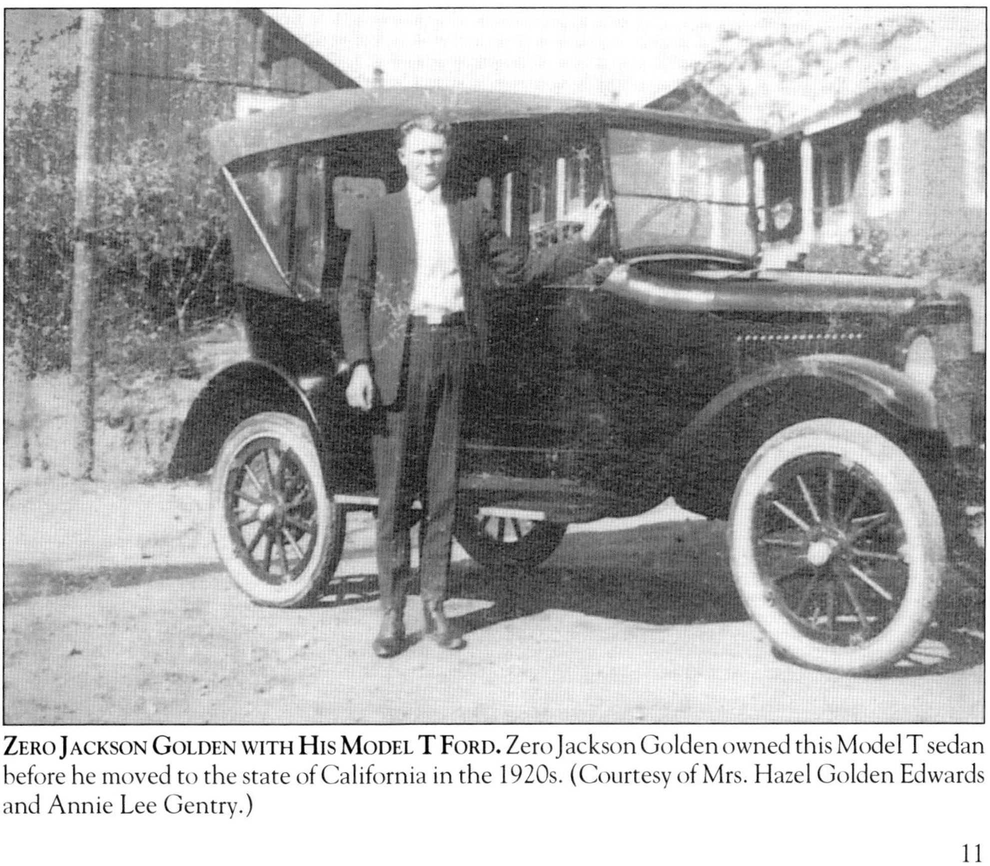

ZERO JACKSON GOLDEN WITH HIS MODEL T FORD. Zero Jackson Golden owned this Model T sedan before he moved to the state of California in the 1920s. (Courtesy of Mrs. Hazel Golden Edwards and Annie Lee Gentry.)

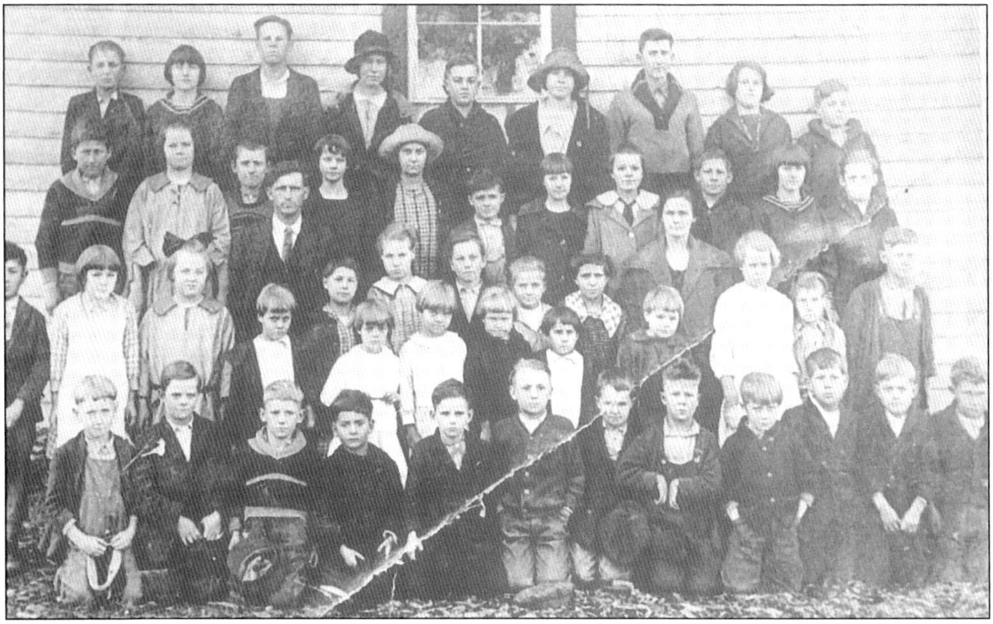

ZEPHYR SCHOOL CLASS IN 1923–1924. Teachers Walter Calloway and Flarence Wall taught at this one-room school. Pictured, from left to right, are the following: (first row) Charles Willey, Gaither Wall, Archie Melton, Bryant Smith, DeWitt Collins, Wheeler Bowers, Fred Melton, Walter Hayes, unidentified, unidentified, Wade Eldridge, and Windell Smith; (second row) Martha Welborn, Edna Wall, Alice Wall, Kathryn Tucker, unidentified, and Pearl Bowers; (third row) Edd Welborn, Mary Lee Holyfield, Bessie Eldridge, ? Hayes, Emma Laster, Rufus Wall, unidentified, Cleta Welborn, Onia Bryant, Virgie Laster, and unidentified; (fourth row) Coley Melton, Pearl Eldridge, Clearence Melton, Virgie Wall, Thelma Smith, John Melton, Edna Melton, Pansy Haynes, unidentified, Mary Melton, and Heber Mounce; (fifth row) Pholey Snow, Hettie Melton, Coy Mayes, Empress Mounce, Lee Eldridge, Bertha Bryant, Paul Melton, Vertie Holyfield, and Gilmer Eldridge. (Courtesy of Emily Southard.)

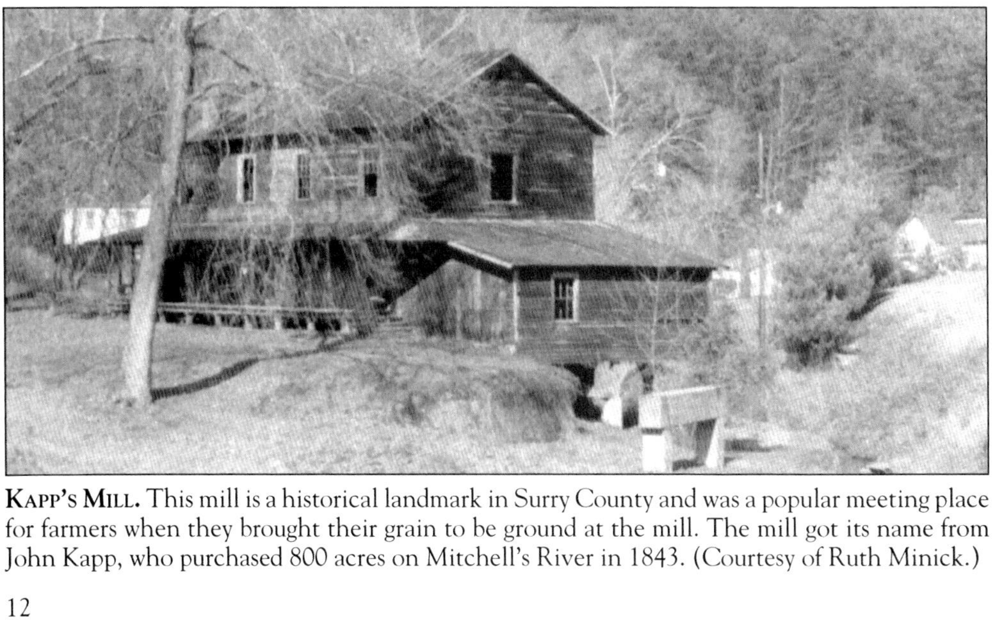

KAPP'S MILL. This mill is a historical landmark in Surry County and was a popular meeting place for farmers when they brought their grain to be ground at the mill. The mill got its name from John Kapp, who purchased 800 acres on Mitchell's River in 1843. (Courtesy of Ruth Minick.)

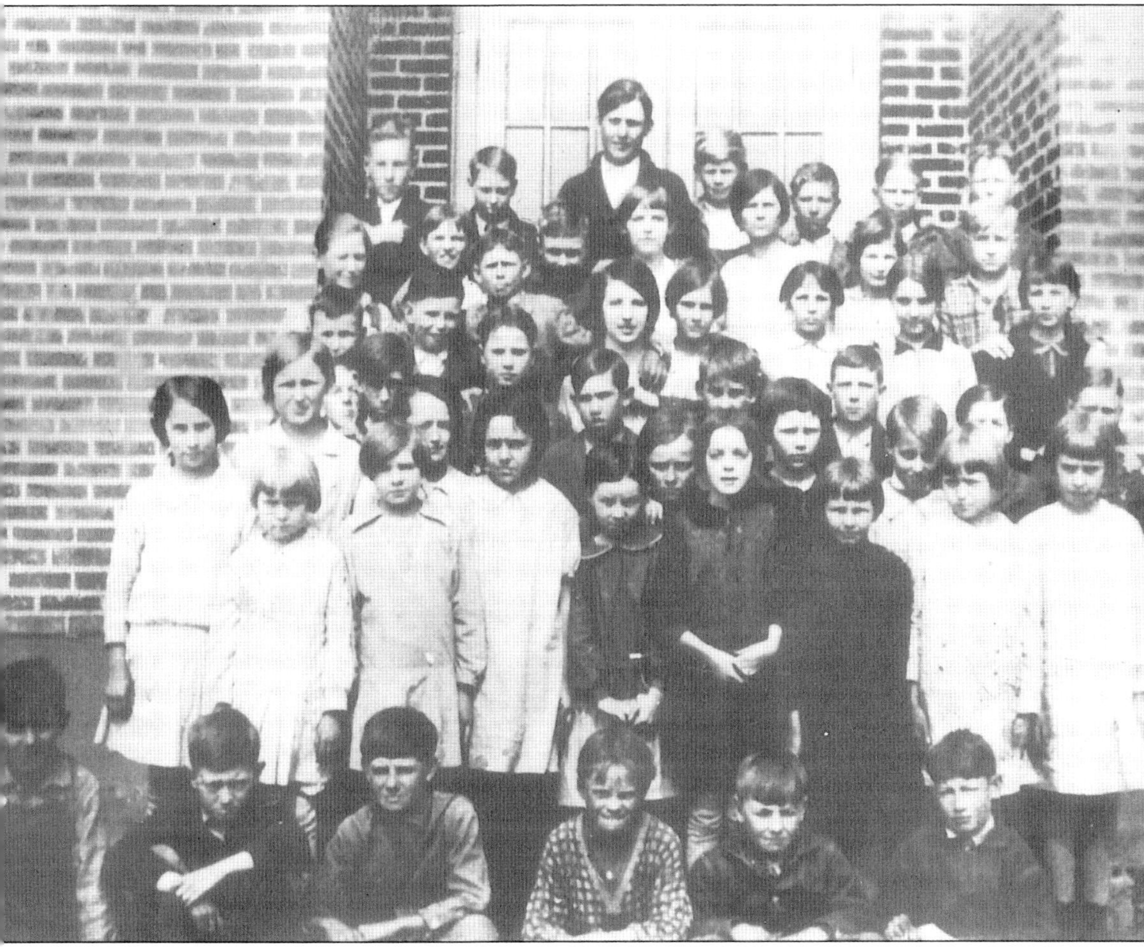

Zephyr School Class in 1927–1928. All one-room schools were consolidated into a new brick building, c. 1927. Before the days of electricity, the building was equipped with a "Delco" battery, which furnished water from the well to the school and provided for indoor restrooms. Mr. Walt Burguess was in charge of the maintenance of the system. Pictured, from left to right, are the following: (first row) Oscar Stanley, Andrew Snow, Jack Swift, Spencer White, Reece Bowers, and Ray Wall; (second row) Mary Welborn, Helen Snow, Lillian Southard, Lillian Dockery, Fairy Dobbins, Edna Wall, Kathryn Tucker, Mary Snow, and unidentified; (third row) Mary Lee Holyfield, Martha Welborn, Roy Stanley, Jack Swift, Reid Willey, Homer Smith, and unidentified; (fourth row) Judge Fowler and Artis Stanley (two little boys); (fifth row) George Willey, DeWitt Collins, Hardin Wall, Miss Thelma Smith (teacher), Ollie Mae Key, Mary Southard, Florence Haynes, and Vera Baker (sister to the teacher); (sixth row) Tom Bill Draughn, Garvey Southard, Spurgeon Southard, Philip Southard, Nillie Isaac, Versie Swift, Nell Wall, and Laura Nance; (seventh row) Richard Osborne, Daniel Boone McHaffy, Clarence Melton, Quiller Laster, unidentified, Grier Michael, and unidentified. (Courtesy of Emily Southard.)

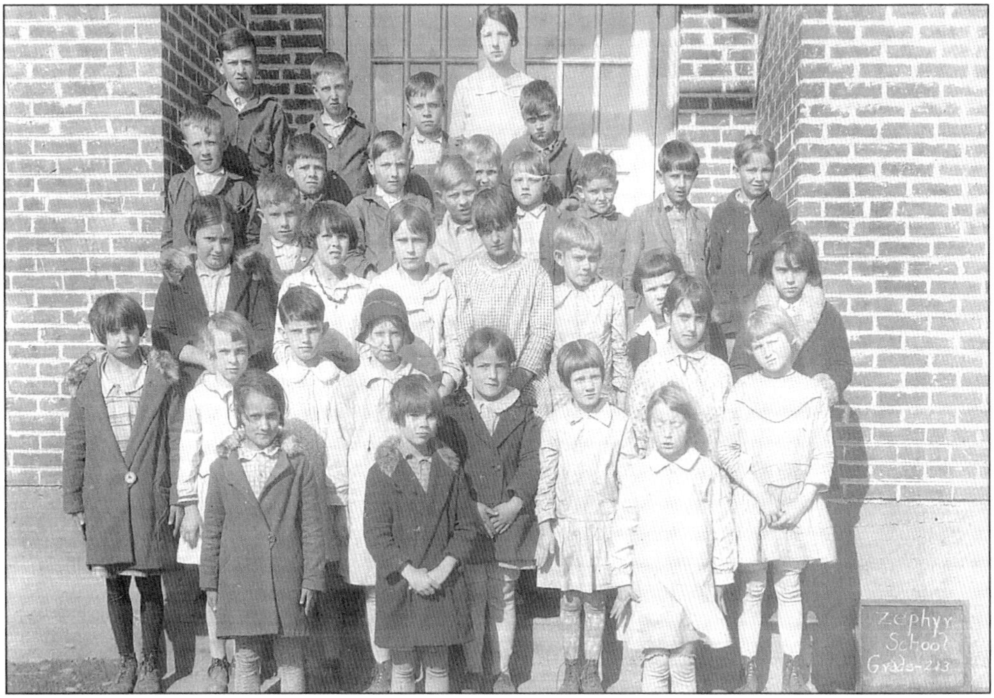

Zephyr Second and Third Grade Class, 1928. Pictured, from left to right, are the following: (first row) Ruby Welborn, Gladys Collins, and Sarah Draughn; (second row) Versie Collins, Hazel Mounce, Judy Ellis, Elsie Draughn, Minnie Bowers, Madgelene Southard, Ona Laster, and Kate Wall; (third row) Ruby Hiatt, Edith Collins, Stella Mounce, Mary Isaac, Dorothy Southard, Emily Holder, and "Duck" Wright; (fourth row) Morrison Snow, Beauford Laster, Raymond Holder, Reece Bowers, Quilla Laster, Robert Snow, Hardin Wall, Clarence Southard, Artis Stanley, and Garvey Golden; (fifth row) Roger Holder, Wilbour Southard, Quentin Holder, Miss Thelma Baker (teacher), and Hubert Hayes. (Courtesy of Emily Southard.)

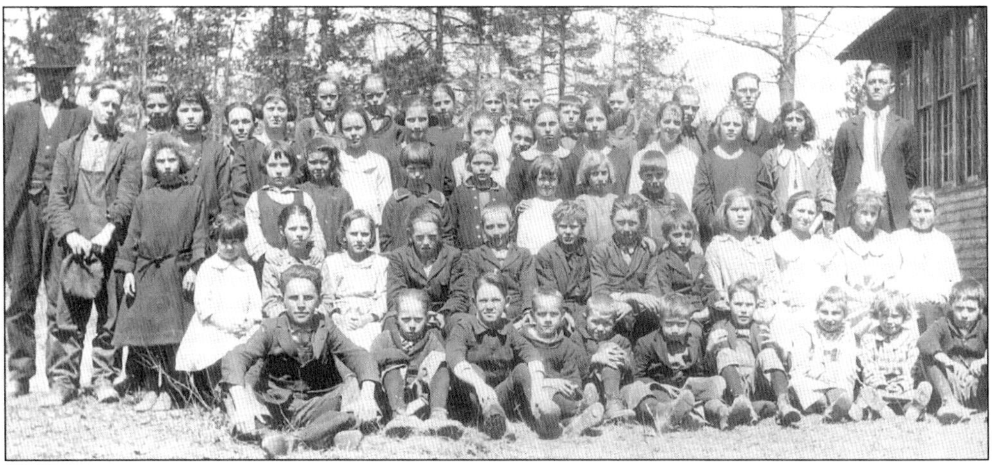

Liberty School Group, c. 1920s. This school was located on Liberty School Road near Mountain Park. The teacher on the right is Claude M. Harris, but the students are unidentified except for the name of Frank "Bill" Haynes. Reverend Walter Calloway and Lee Black were also teachers at Liberty School. (Courtesy of Annie Lee Gentry.)

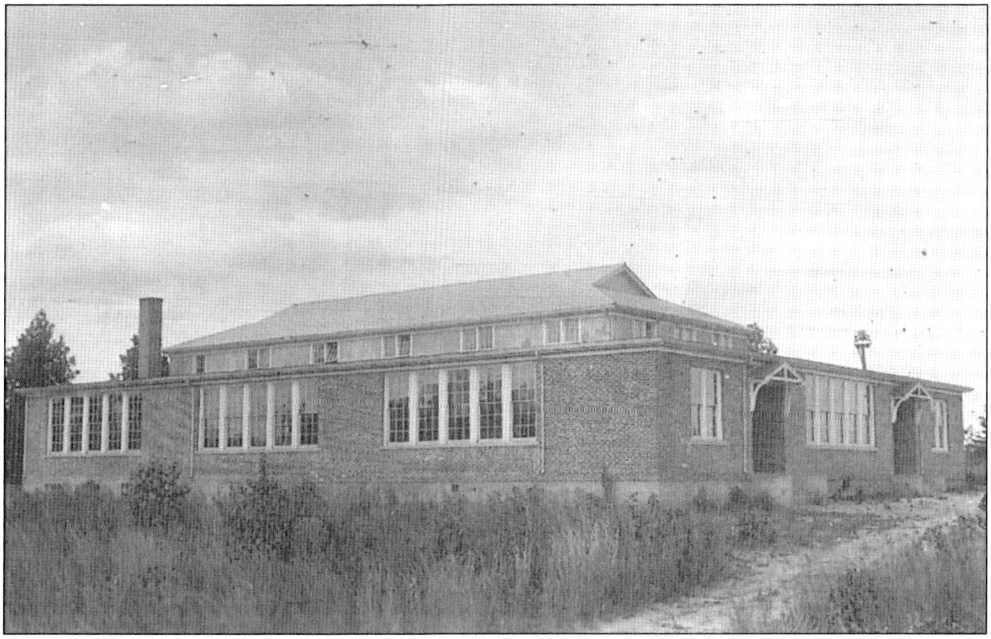

BRYAN SCHOOL. This school was located north of Mountain Park at the intersection of Union Hill and Kapps Mill Road. Grades one through seven were housed in this brick building, which served as a school until about 1932. After the closing of Mountain Park College, the grade school was relocated to Mountain Park to the former college campus. Teachers at the school included Claude Harris, Paul Lewis, Elizabeth Joyce, DeEtte Cockerham, Sally Woodruff, Spencer Norman, and Livingston Williams. (Courtesy of Annie Lee Gentry.)

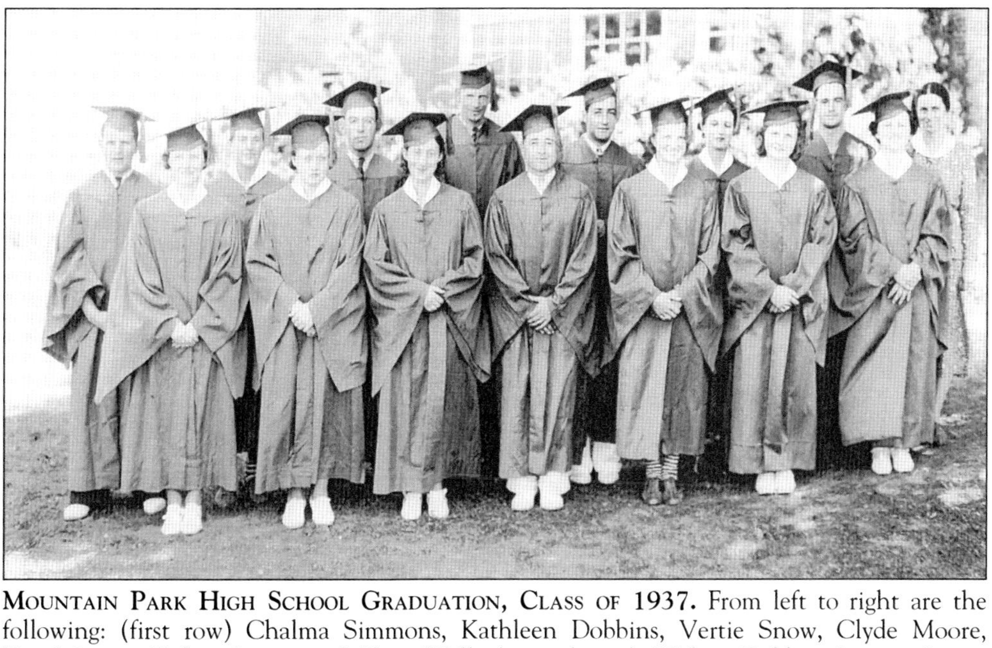

MOUNTAIN PARK HIGH SCHOOL GRADUATION, CLASS OF 1937. From left to right are the following: (first row) Chalma Simmons, Kathleen Dobbins, Vertie Snow, Clyde Moore, Hazel Lowe, Helen Snow, and Elsie Wall; (second row) Walter Golden, Juanita Lowe, Adrian Nixon, Bill Swift, Kemp Walker, Minnie Williams, Dan Norman, and Mrs. Baldwin (teacher). (Courtesy of Vertie Coe.)

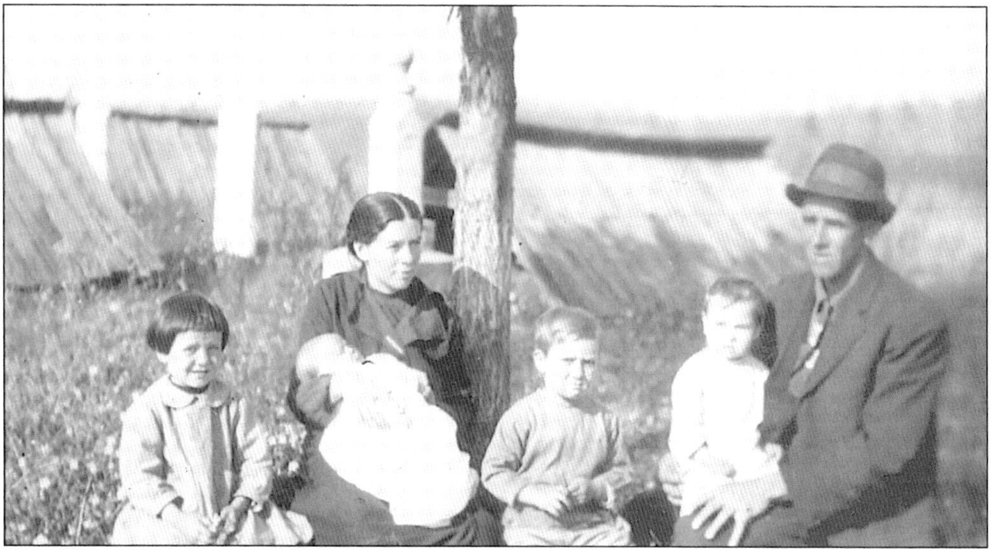

Jones-Cockerham Family Cemetery. These A-frame grave shelters are made of wooden shingles and would protect the graves for many years. Visiting the cemetery are W. Verlin Holder and wife, Bessie, with four of their ten children, who are, from left to right, Phosie, baby Quentin, Fred, and Roger. (Courtesy of Emily Southard.)

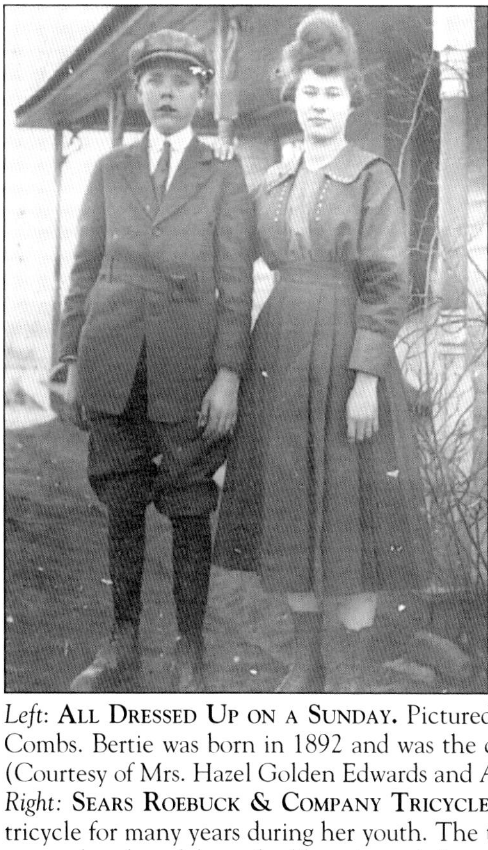

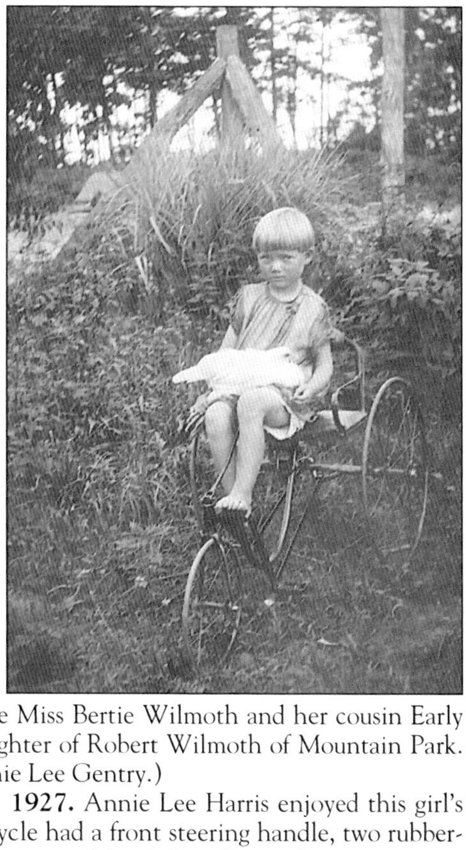

Left: **All Dressed Up on a Sunday.** Pictured are Miss Bertie Wilmoth and her cousin Early Combs. Bertie was born in 1892 and was the daughter of Robert Wilmoth of Mountain Park. (Courtesy of Mrs. Hazel Golden Edwards and Annie Lee Gentry.)
Right: **Sears Roebuck & Company Tricycle, c. 1927.** Annie Lee Harris enjoyed this girl's tricycle for many years during her youth. The tricycle had a front steering handle, two rubber-covered push pedals, and rubber-rimmed tires. (Courtesy of Annie Lee Gentry.)

Two

Dobson Township

Dobson Township is in the center of Surry County and is named for the county seat, Dobson, which is in the center of the county as the law requires. Big Fisher River flows into the township from the west and joins Little Fisher River from the north. Beaver Creek, Pigeon Roost Creek, Cody Creek, King's Creek, Chapmans Creek, and Burrus Creek all flow into the Yadkin River. The highest place in Dobson Township is Turner Mountain, now the site of several broadcast towers. The town of Dobson has the highest elevation of any town in Surry County at 1,275 feet above sea level.

Early churches in the area included Old Fisher River Baptist, Central View Baptist, Cross Roads Baptist, Dobson Baptist, Salem Fork Christian, and Salem Fork Baptist. In 1900, the schools in the Dobson Township were New Hope, Wrights, Hanes, Piney Grove, Edmonds, Vernon, Center, Caves, Keyfield, Salem Fork, Dobson, Judville, and Stanley. But in the year 2000, the schools located in Dobson are Dobson Elementary, Central Middle School, Surry Central High, and Surry Community College.

All county government agencies are located in the town of Dobson, including the sheriff's department, social services, agriculture, jail, health and welfare, county manager, school superintendent, fire department, and the county courthouse, which houses the register of deeds, the clerk of court, and the tax and mapping departments.

It is estimated that there are around 20,000 people in Dobson during the day and a little over 1,100 at night. The saying goes that few people who live in the town of Dobson work in Dobson and those that work in Dobson live elsewhere in the county.

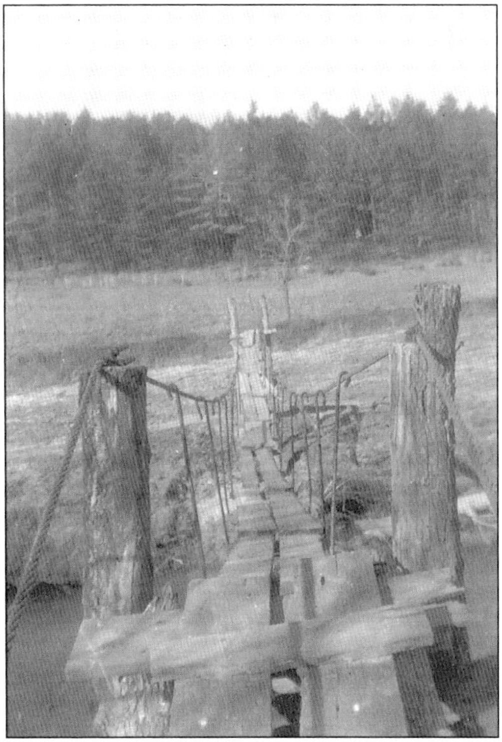

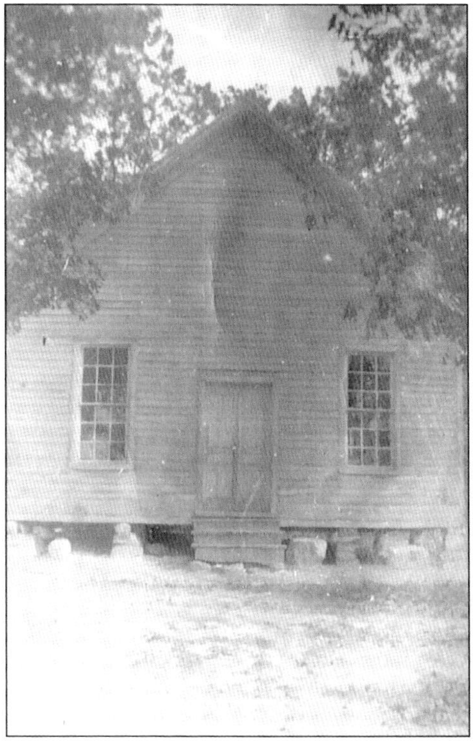

Left: **FOOTBRIDGE.** This swinging footbridge is located near the Fisher's River Primitive Baptist Church near Dobson. (Courtesy of Jasper B. Brindle.)
Right: **FISHER'S RIVER PRIMITIVE BAPTIST CHURCH NEAR DOBSON.** The exact date of this church's organization is not known, but records show that the church was holding regular monthly meetings as early as 1808. (Courtesy of Jasper B. Brindle.)

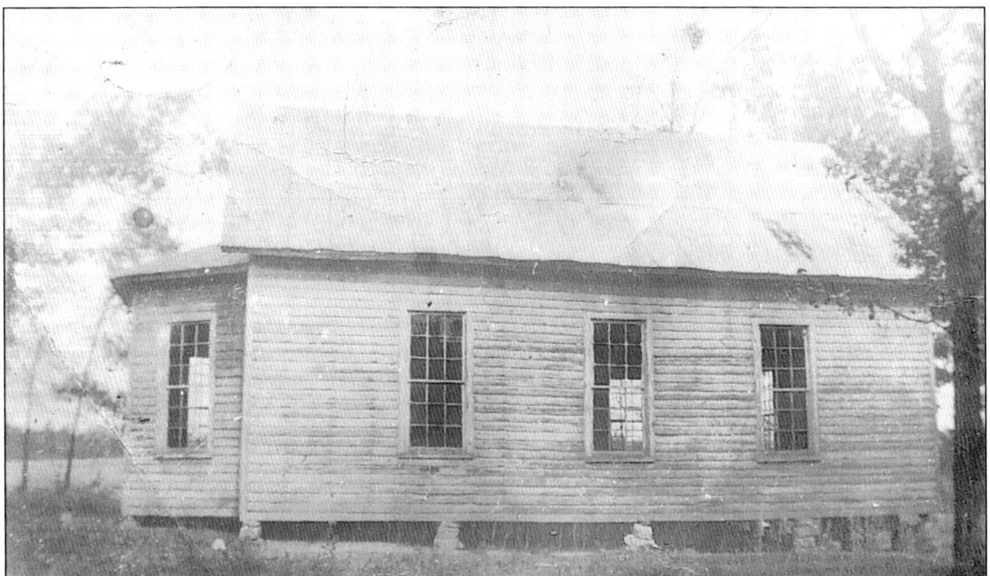

ANOTHER VIEW OF FISHER'S RIVER PRIMITIVE BAPTIST CHURCH. (Courtesy of Jasper B. Brindle.)

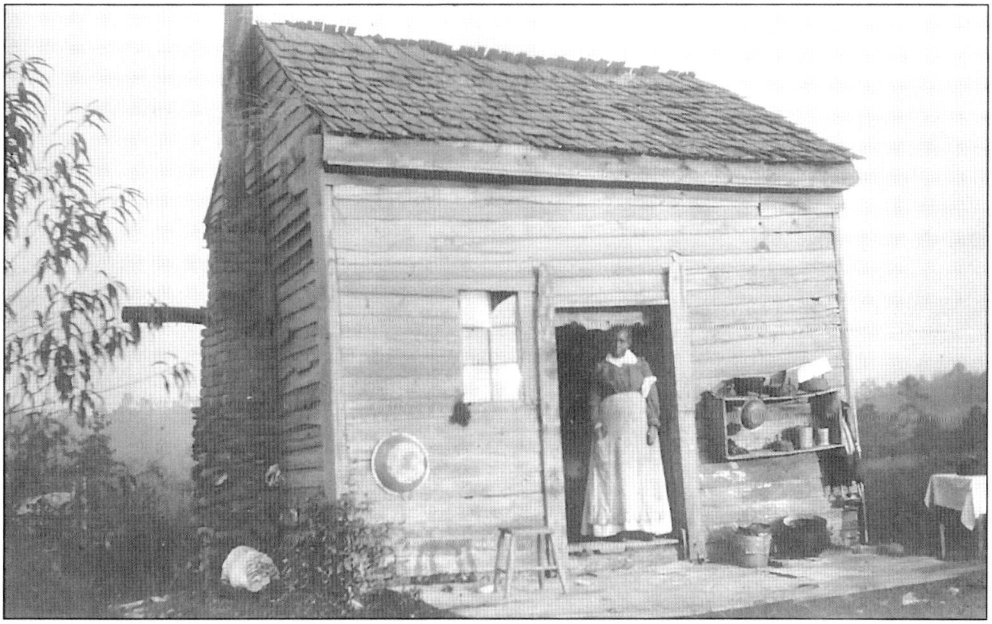

The Residence of Aunt Lucy. Aunt Lucy arrived in Dobson with the Waugh family, who had come from the Waughtown community in Winston-Salem. In early census records she was listed as mulatto, named Lucy Waugh, and was a member of the household of the Waugh and Freeman families. (Courtesy of Ruth Minick.)

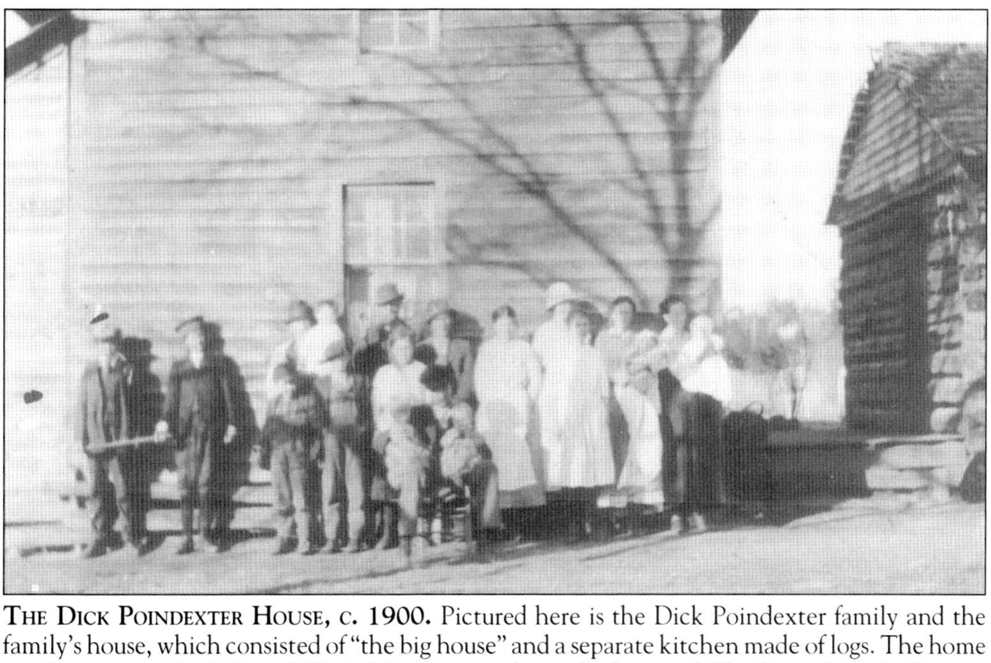

The Dick Poindexter House, c. 1900. Pictured here is the Dick Poindexter family and the family's house, which consisted of "the big house" and a separate kitchen made of logs. The home was later owned by J.C. and Kizzie Hutchens and was the home of Charlie and Vissie Beamer for several years. Later a covered breezeway was built to connect the two buildings. (Courtesy of Mildred Matthews.)

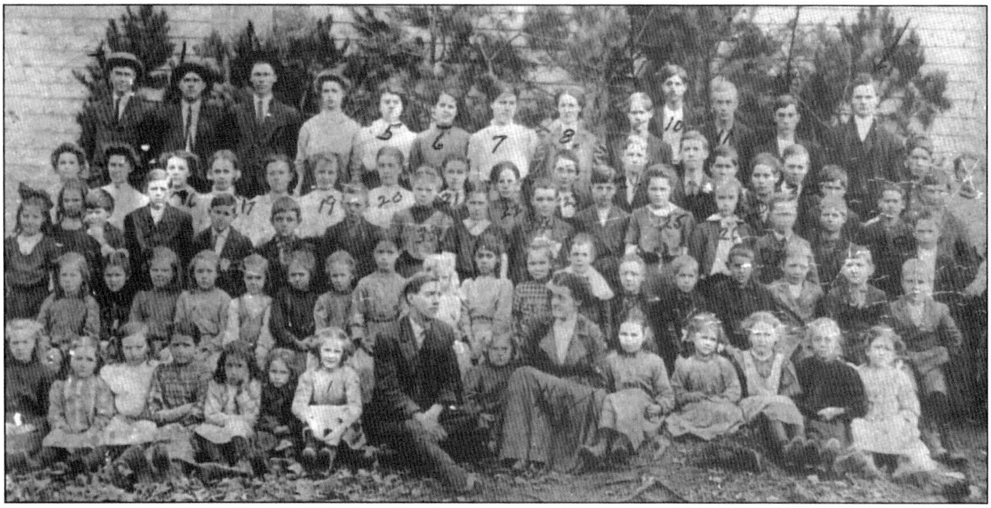

ATKINS SCHOOL STUDENTS, C. 1912. From left to right are the following: (first row) Nora Holyfield, unidentified, Lela Edmonds, Ethel Bullin, Tricia Atkins, Ethel Atkins, Levora Holyfield, Walter Combs (teacher), Mae Lundy, Ila Stanley (teacher), Pearl Shinault O'Neal, Minnie Shinault Boyles, Sudie Moser, Letha Hill, and Lucy Whitaker; (second row) Lucy Key, Alma Harbour, Lula Key, Lema Holyfield, Rosie Loflen, Minnie Atkins, Betty Evans, Metta Evans Shinault, unidentified, Ida Moser, Bessie Doss, Lloyd Doss, Coley Fowler, Hadley Harbour, Elbert Bullin, Virgil Doss, Wiley Whitaker, and Mallory Bullen; (third row) Pearl Atkins, Sallie Atkins, Willie McKinney, Johnny Holyfield, Esker Harbour, George Southern, Oscar Moser, Bertha Bullin, Bessie Cooper, Earnest Collins, Clinton Atkins, Gracie Edmonds, Minnie Loflin, Virgil Doss, unidentified, Luther Bullin, and unidentified; (fourth row) Mary Holifield Moser, Eulala Harbour Wilmoth, Bessie Holyfield, Ester (Mae) O'Neal Hardy, Daisy Holyfield Miller, Maggie Southern Badgett, Dora Moser, Nanie Collins, Lina Atkins, McKinley Doss, Walter Key, Carl Evans, unidentified, John Atkins, Dallas Moser, Gurney Atkins, Luther Bullin, unidentified, and Bertha Atkins; (fifth row) Joby Collins, Mallory Harbour, Jesse Moser, Bertha Southern Gunter, Pearl Harbour Snow, Lillie Holyfield Stanley, Eunice Moser, Sarah Doss, Sam Atkins, Arthur Atkins, Will Moser, Will Hill, and Ben O'Neal. (Courtesy of Peggy Ring and Melva Greene.)

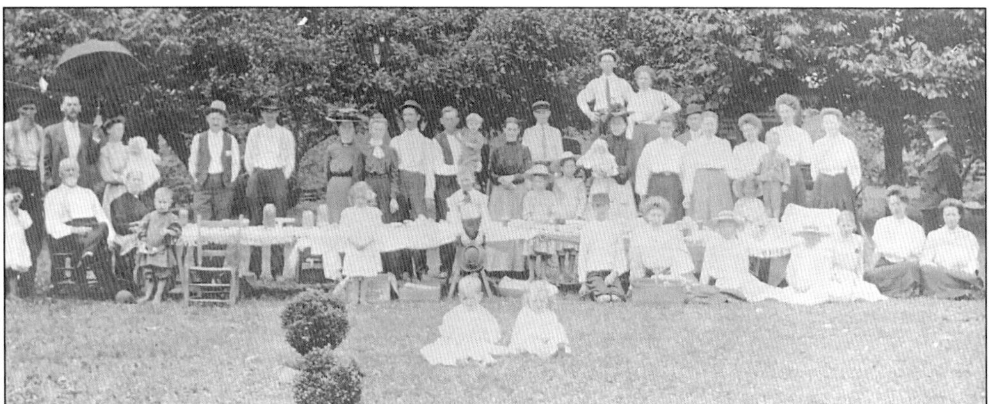

BIRTHDAY DINNER AT THE HENRY BEAMER HOMEPLACE, 1915. The older man and woman seated at the left end of the table are Henry and Kathryn Cockerham Beamer. The others pictured are some of their children, grandchildren, great-grandchildren, friends, and neighbors. (Courtesy of Mildred Matthews.)

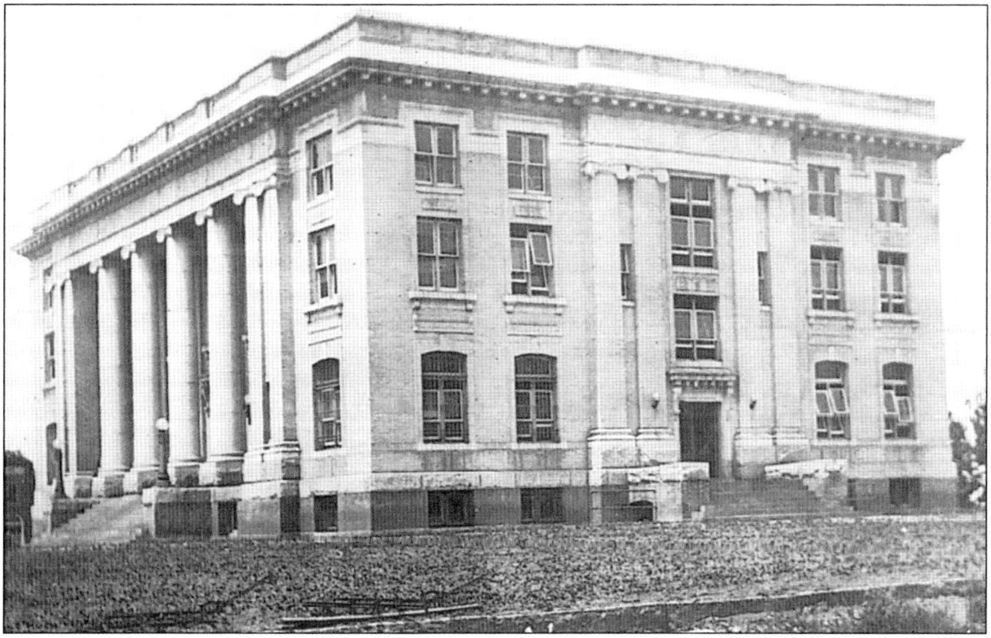

Surry County Courthouse in Dobson, c. 1920–1930. This old picture postcard shows the Surry County courthouse as it once was. The courthouse was completed in 1917 and replaced the 1851 courthouse that had stood at the same spot. The renovation of 1972 added space on both sides, and the columns on the west side were removed at that time. (Courtesy of Annie Lee Gentry.)

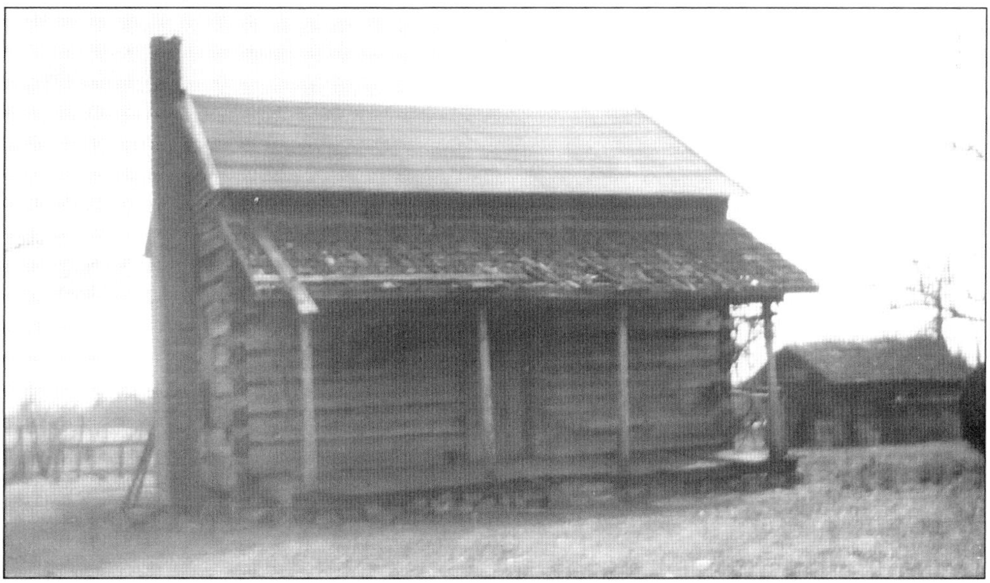

Henry Beamer Homeplace in Dobson, c. 1937. The Henry and Kathryn Beamer homeplace was located near the Crossroads Baptist Church, and they lived here from c. 1870 to c. 1924. The Beamers had 14 children, who were all born and raised at this house. Their children were Henry Edward, Willie Y., Eugene, Richard Brady, Mary Alice, Meshack Franklin, Nancy Ellen, Elizabeth Parks, Peter Wilson, Thurzia Lodene, Jacob C., Clyde Dixie, Rachel Catherine, and Charlie Mosley Beamer. (Courtesy of Mildred Matthews.)

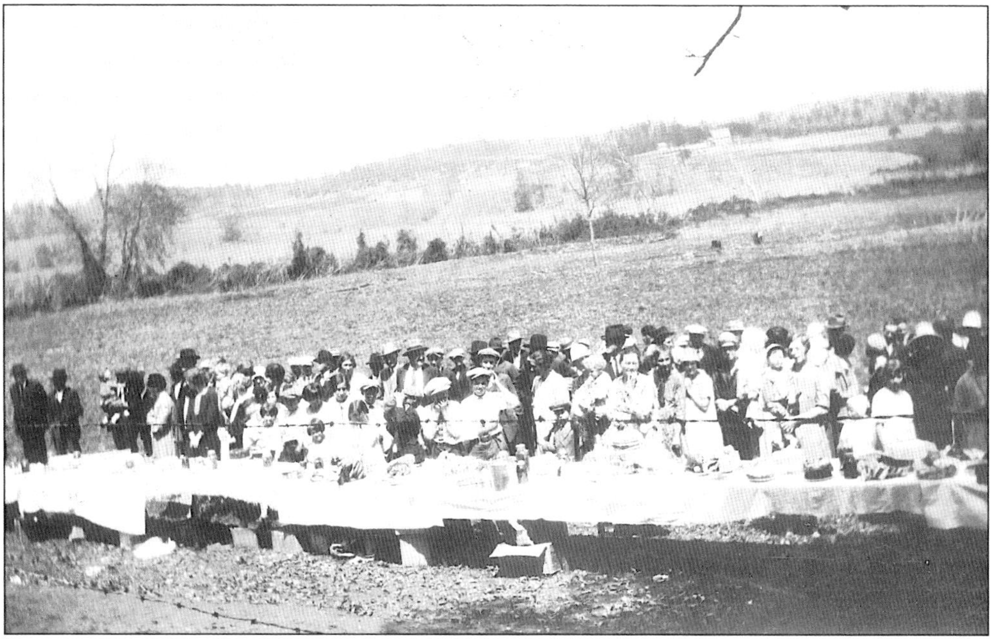

Scene in the Salem Fork Community. A birthday dinner is enjoyed at Frank Llewellyn's homeplace on White Dirt Road in the Salem Fork community. Frank Llewellyn was the Surry County clerk of court in the 1930s. (Courtesy of Paul Riggs.)

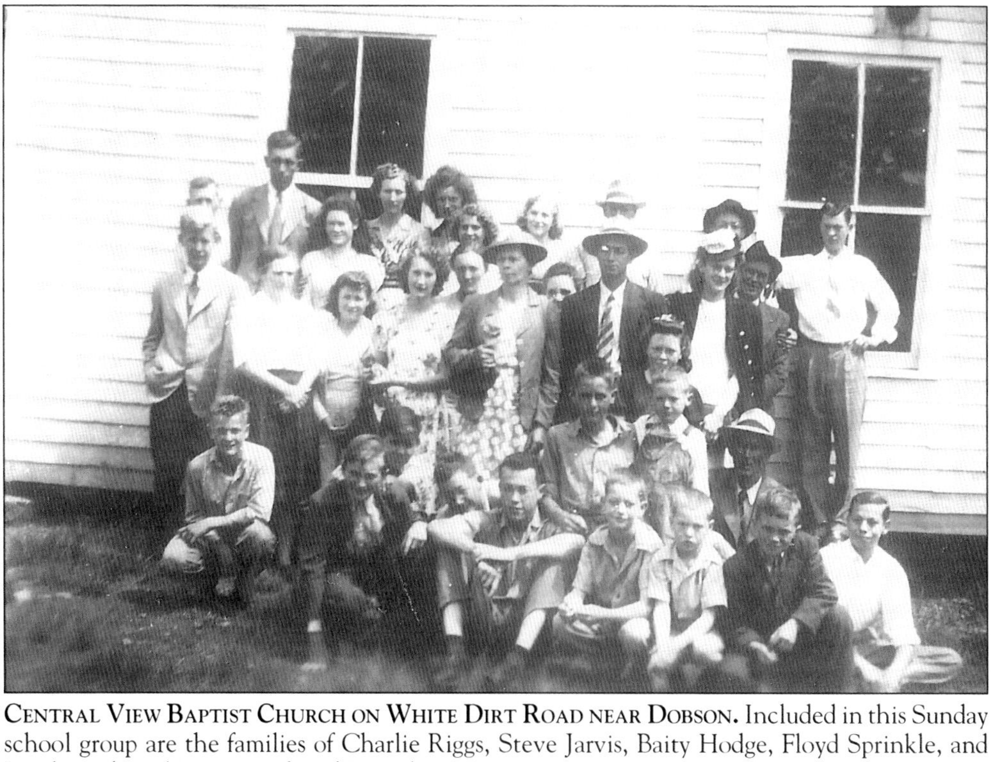

Central View Baptist Church on White Dirt Road near Dobson. Included in this Sunday school group are the families of Charlie Riggs, Steve Jarvis, Baity Hodge, Floyd Sprinkle, and Frank Hodges. (Courtesy of Paul Riggs.)

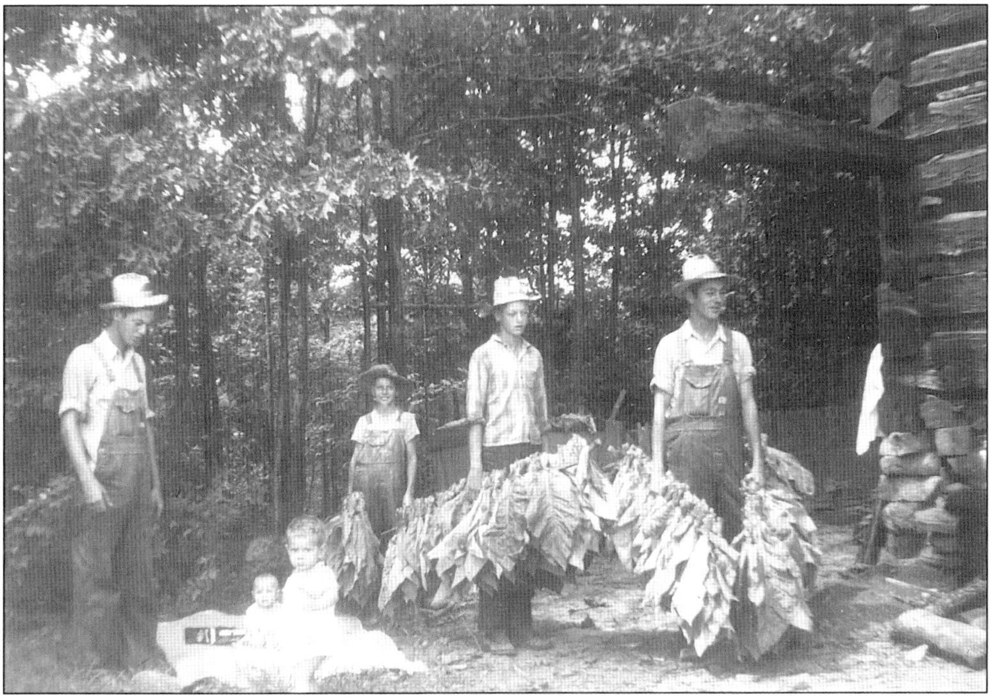

Barning Tobacco in the Salem Fork Community. Paul Riggs talks to the children on the quilt while Monroe Riggs, Fred Riggs, and Ray Riggs put the tobacco in the barn. The tobacco from the field has been twined on sticks. (Courtesy of Paul Riggs.)

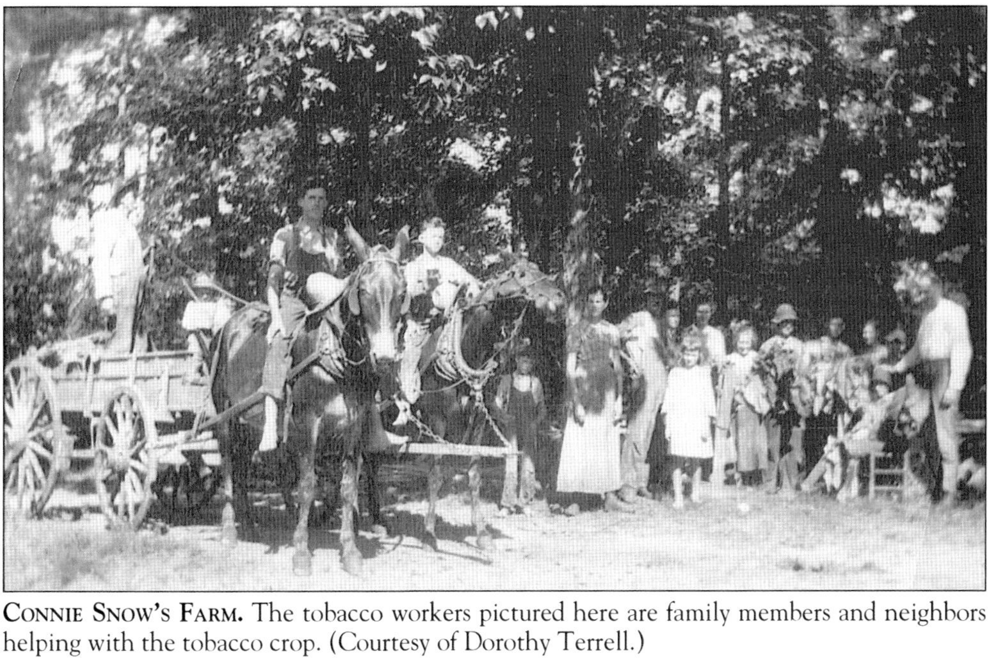

Connie Snow's Farm. The tobacco workers pictured here are family members and neighbors helping with the tobacco crop. (Courtesy of Dorothy Terrell.)

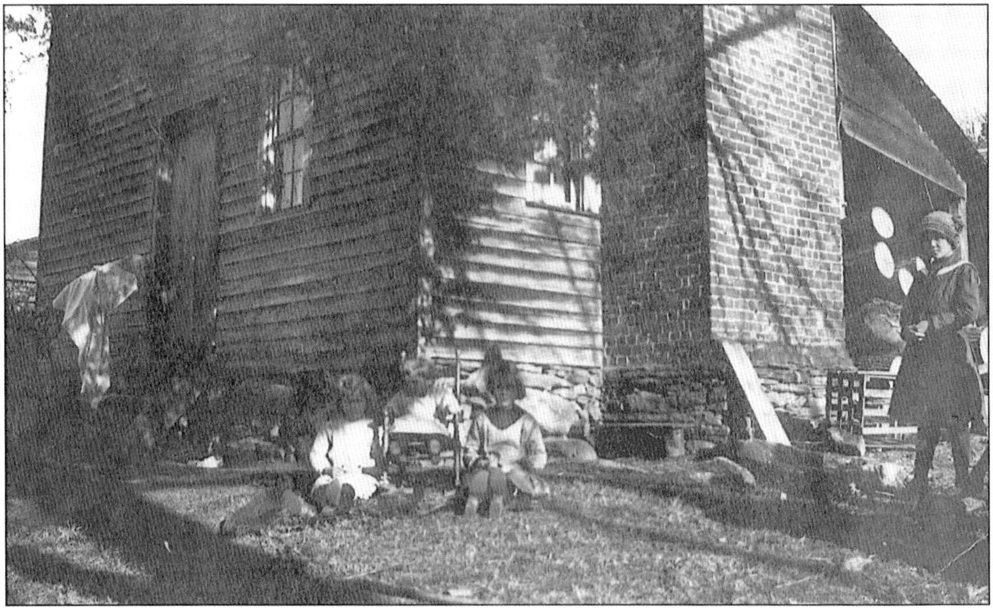

Time for a Photograph. With their eyes on the photographer, these children are pictured behind the "old house" on their grandfather Jordan Snow's farm. Pictured, from left to right, are Dorothy Snow, Garland Snow, Thelma Snow, and ? Hemmings. (Courtesy of Dorothy Terrell.)

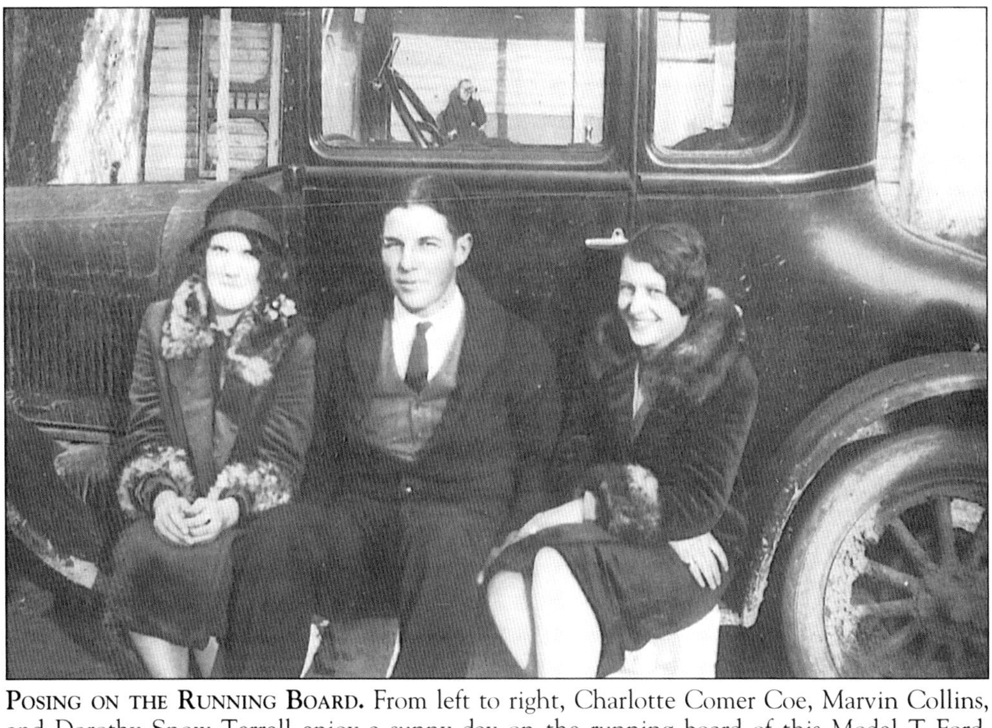

Posing on the Running Board. From left to right, Charlotte Comer Coe, Marvin Collins, and Dorothy Snow Terrell enjoy a sunny day on the running board of this Model T Ford. (Courtesy of Dorothy Terrell.)

Three

Eldora and Long Hill Townships

The Ararat River runs between the townships of Eldora and Long Hill, which are in the southern part of Surry County. Whittier Creek is located in the Eldora Township, and Stony Creek, in Long Hill Township. Stony Creek rises in east Surry County and flows southwest into the Ararat River.

Some of the early schools in the Eldora Township were Ash Hill, Ball Knob, Corinth, Dunnigan, Eldora, Ivy Hill, Jones, Key, and Union. Ararat School was in Long Hill at one time but was purchased by Cynthia Sudol and moved into the Eldora Township. In the early 1960s, Eldora Elementary was closed and it became a part of Copeland Elementary School. Some early churches in Eldora included Blackwater Methodist Church, Bryant Memorial, Little Mountain, Mt. Vine Methodist, and Rock Hill. Early settlers in the Eldora area included the following families: the Badgetts, the Chiltons, the Joneses, the Keys, the Lawrences, the Mills, the Taylors, and the Tuckers.

The name Long Hill was derived from the long hills that lead down to the Ararat River in the region. In fact, there was a long hill to travel to get anywhere in the community. Long Hill School was on top of a hill that is now called the Ararat-Longhill Road. Ararat is also a town located in Long Hill and was the location of the train depot when the railroad came in the 1880s. Some early families in the area were the Ashburns, the Bryants, the Chiltons, the Davises, the Keys, the Needhams, and the Peeles, and there was an early general store in the Ararat community operated by Samuel Fulk, who later established a hardware store in Pilot Mountain. There was also Key's Store, and a little later, Bryant's Store, which also served as a post office. Forkner's tobacco factory was also located in Ararat. Needham's Mill could be found on the Old Hollow Road, and on Flat Shoals Creek was the Armstrong Mill, which ground wheat and corn. Some of the early churches in Long Hill included Ararat Friends, Bryant Methodist, New Hope Methodist, Simmons Grove, and Stony Creek Primitive Baptist.

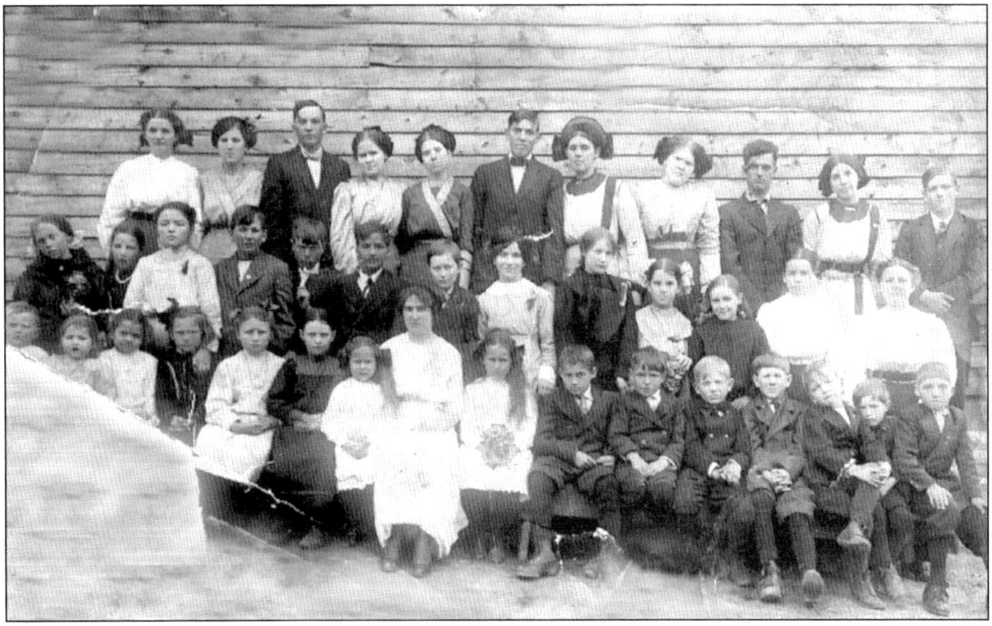

Key School Students, c. 1914. Key School (Ash Hill or Ball Knob) was located in the Eldora Township, and this photograph could have been made on the last day of the school year. Two of the students appear to have gifts, perhaps for the teachers or a close friend. From left to right are the following: (first row) Brady Jones, Elvie Simmons, Levie Simmons, Esie Key, Lillian Simpson, Molly Johnson, Terrell Riddle, unidentified teacher, Myrtle Terrell Johnson, Jacob Simmons, Dave Terrell, Herman Simpson, Gene Bennett, unidentified, unidentified, and Brady Danley; (second row) Pearl Simpson, Hattie Key, Bessie Simpson, Hobert Simpson, Howard Terrell, Dewey Simpson, Calab Johnson, Annie Simpson, unidentified, Maude Bennett, Ellen Bullen, and Nora Simmons; (third row) Nonnie Simmons, Pearl Bennett, Oliver Gaberial Key, Nina Terrell Key, Effie Bennett, Walter Terrell, Bertie Johnson, Prissy Armstrong, Johnnie Simmons, Mollie Johnson, and Bud Simpson. (Courtesy of Opal Edmonds and Melva Greene.)

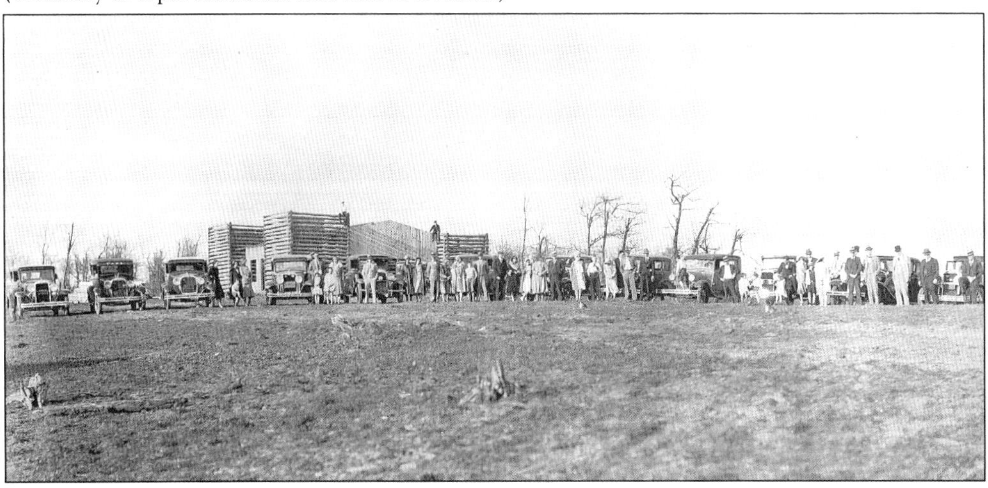

Barn-Raising, c. 1930. This photograph was found among the papers of Samuel Jacob Badgett, who was born in the Eldora Township. Note the taxi that is second from the left. (Courtesy of Lee Roy and Minerva Hicks.)

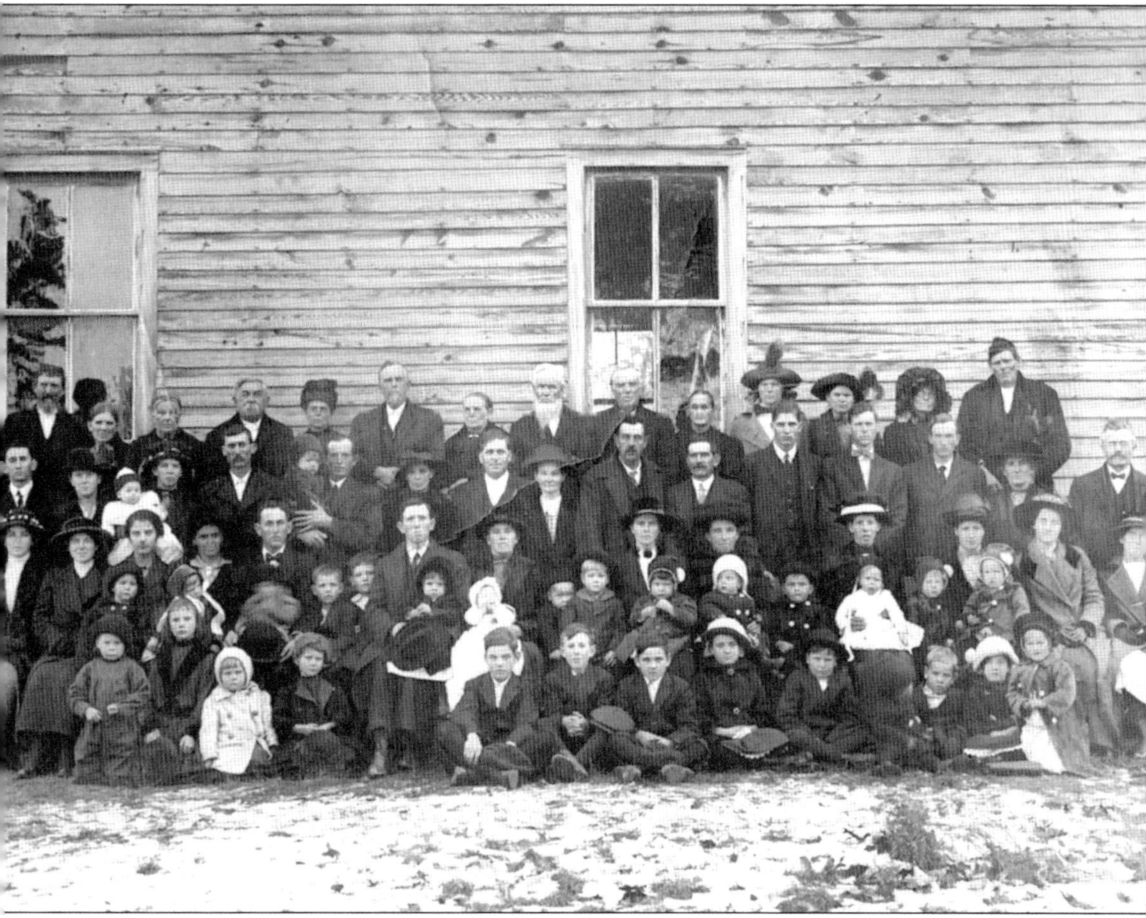

Key Family Reunion at Union Primitive Baptist Church, 1914. Pictured, from left to right, are the following: (first row) Ernest Mosley, Lela Gardner, Ila Ferguson, Maude Ferguson, Herman Badgett, Gene Bennett, Chester Badgett, Elsie Badgett Harbor, Aubrey Marsh, Oscar Badgett, Bertha Badgett, and Gracie Bryant; (second row) children Elmer Mosley, Clarence Key, Lawrence Key, Doris Key, Alton Key, Georgia Bryant's boys, Myrtle Marsh Nichols, Elbert Badgett, Alton Marsh, Lottie Stanley, Ila Stanley, and Oscar Key in Bessie Key's arms; (third row) Lottie Badgett, Pearl Bennett, Bertha Butner, Mary Badgett, Mildred Key in Mary's arms, Rich Ferguson, Claude in Rich's arms, Gabriel Key, Emma Key, Mecie Marsh, Susie Badgett, Josie Stanley, Bessie Key, Cora Taylor, and Maude Bennett; (fourth row) Bloom Denny, Betty Ferguson, Lucy Mosley, Sid Mosley, Stacy Mosley, Jasper Key, Cora Key, Davis in Cora's arms, Alva Bryant, Georgia Bryant, Charlie Badgett, Joel Key, Esker Key, Jethro Stanley, Robert Key, Betty Bryant, and Thomas Bryant; (fifth row) Billy Bennett, Pheobe Bennett, Lydia Badgett, Nick Badgett, Mattie Hickman, G.O. Key, Sarah Key, William Key, King Key, Lucy Key, Lucy Fulk, Georgia Fulk, Laura Fulk, and Jacob Fulk. (Courtesy of Paul Key and Melva Green.)

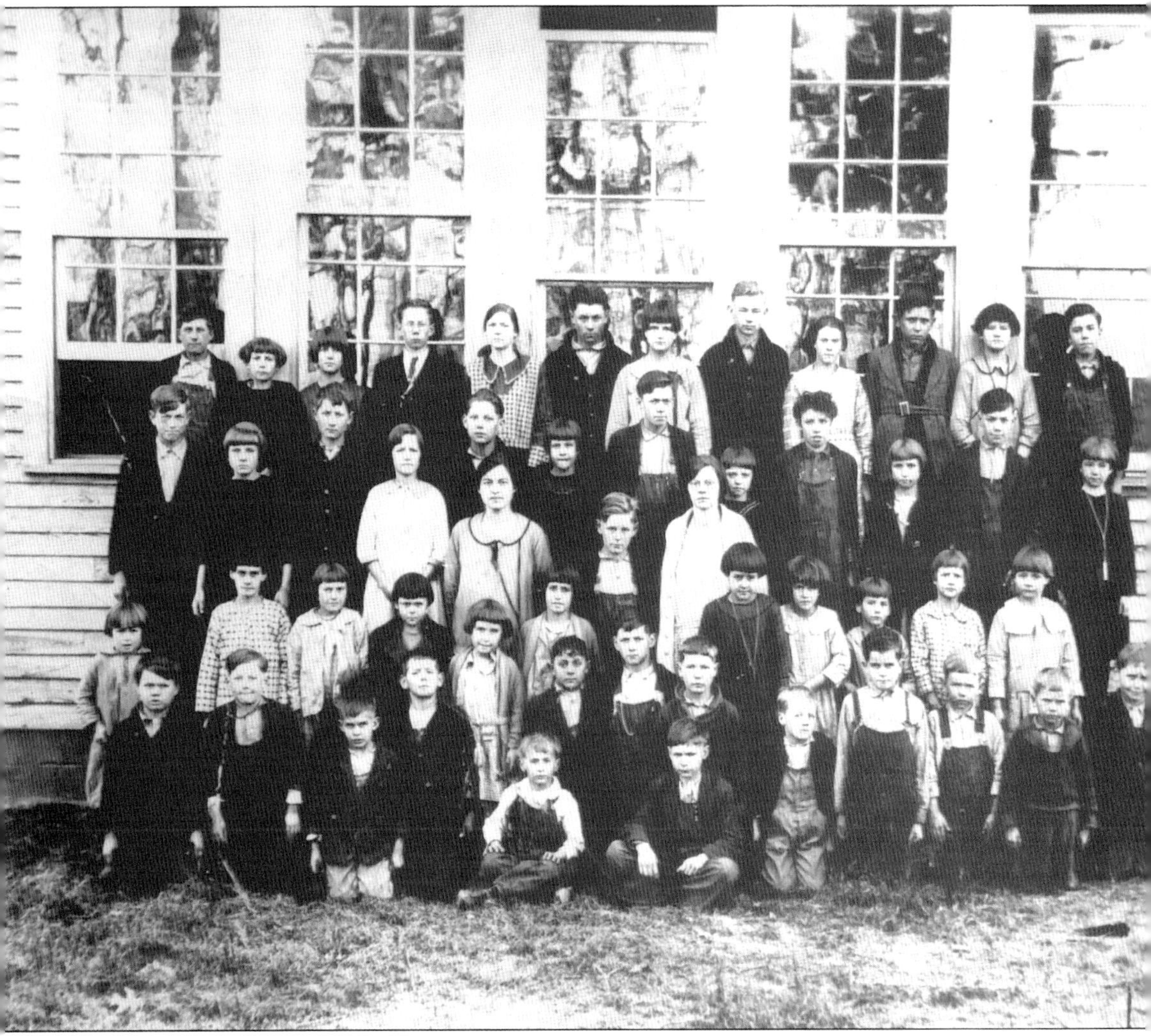

CORINTH SCHOOL STUDENTS, 1924. Grades one through eight are shown in this photograph. From left to right are the following: (first row) Dillard Reid, Clinton Davis, Claude Coe, Clinton Moseley, Loyd Key, Elmer Patterson, Woodrow Evans, Fred Key, Otis Evans, Porter Riddle, Ralph Ring, Hassell Key, and Webster Moser; (second row) Blanche Key, Josie Coe, Sadie Wall, Evelyn Patterson, Ethel Southern, Ruth Southern, Stacy Whitaker, May Riddle, Tessie Moseley, Stella Reid, and Myrtle Evans; (third row) Alex Shinault, Ruby Key, Ernest Evans, Opal Evans, unidentified, Ruth Riddle, Lawrence Branch, Olla Peel, Luther Peel, Nonnie Wood, Web Branch, Littie Ring, Alice Chilton, unidentified, and Inez Paisley; (fourth row) Charles Davis, Stacy Moseley, Thelma Reid, Ernest Moseley, Lillie Moser, Jack Evans, Alice Riddle, Willie Ring, Ila Coe, Lacy Whitaker, Anna Wall, and Floyd Harbour. (Courtesy of Tessie Moseley Patterson and Melva Greene.)

WILLIAM S. KEY IN HIS CASKET. In 1888, at age 68, William S. Key left his home in Eldora Township to visit relatives out West. He traveled by train to Weston, Oregon, where Hezekiah Key lived. He spent Thanksgiving with the family, developed pneumonia, and died on December 6, 1888. According to Irene Padgett's book *Key Is My Name*, he was buried in Weston. A picture was made of him in his casket and sent home to his widow and family in Surry County. (Courtesy of Betsy Davis.)

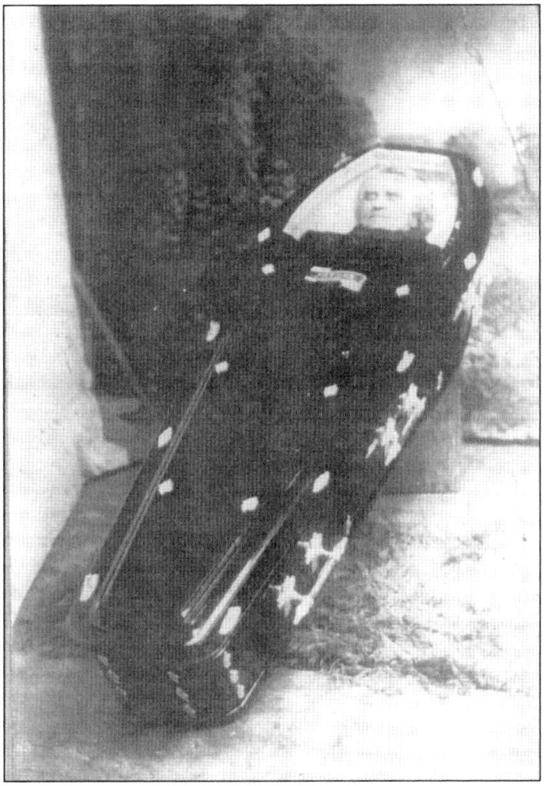

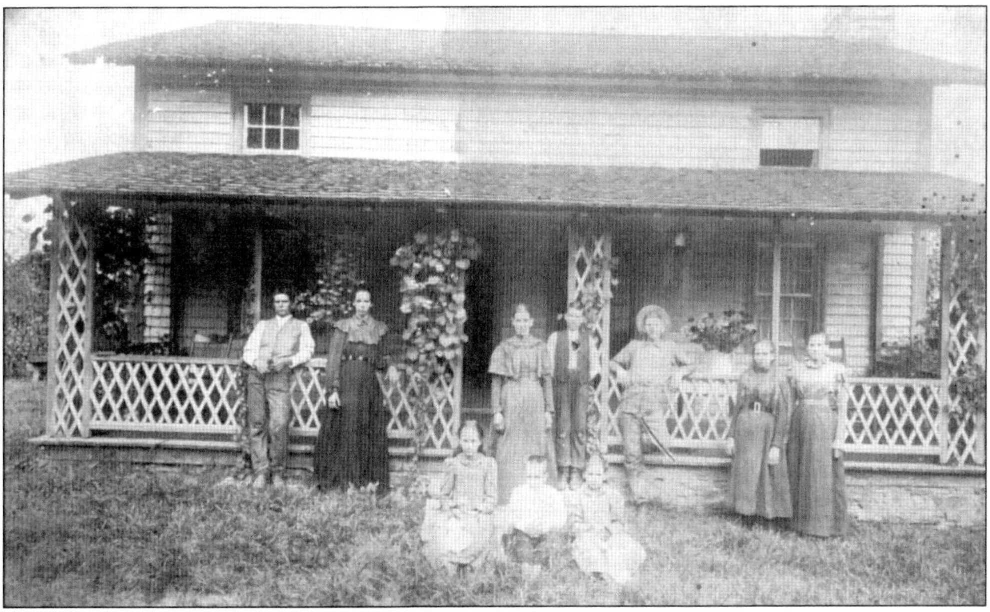

FAMILY OF RUSSELL R. KEY, C. 1896. Russell R. Key (1846–1896) died at age 50, leaving nine children at home. Pictured at their home in the Eldora Township are his wife and 9 of their 12 children. Pictured, from left to right, are the following: (front row) Betty Key, Sid Key, and Ida Key; (back row) Joel Key, Anna Key, Roseanne Boaz Denny Key (mother), Gabriel Key, Charlie Key, Emma Key, and Ellen Key. (Courtesy of Betsy Davis.)

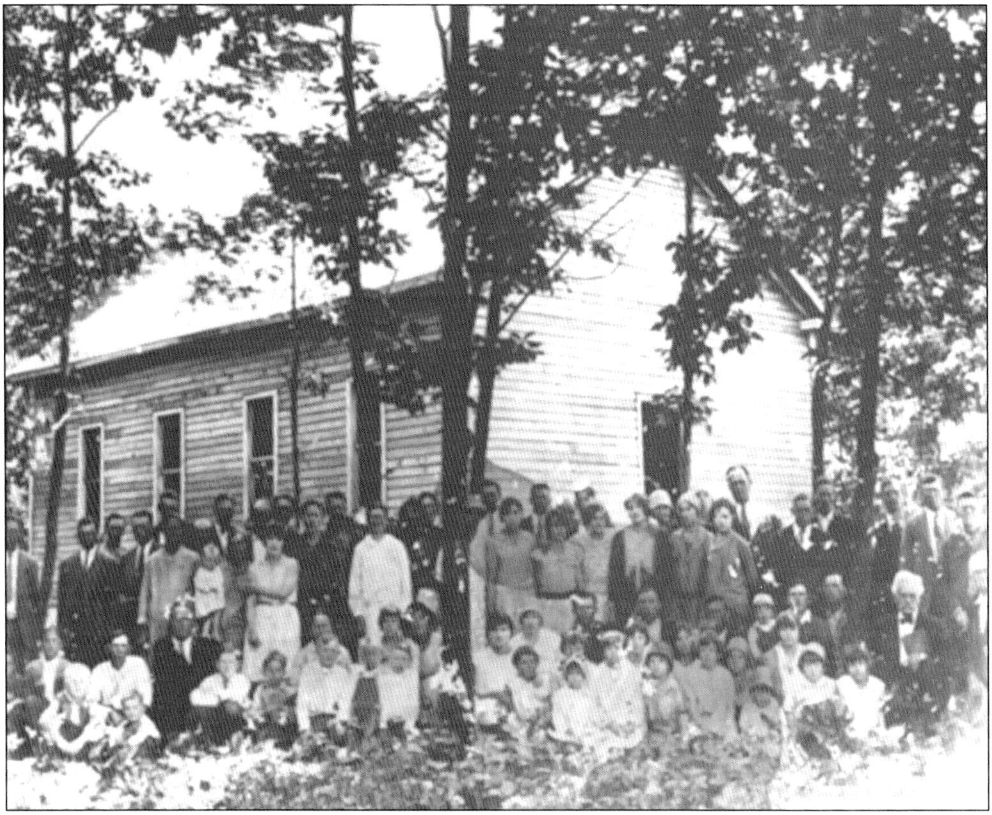

BLACKWATER METHODIST CHURCH GROUP. Blackwater Methodist Church was built about 1928 with lumber from Union School. The school was located on the present site of Union Primitive Baptist Church in Eldora Township. Pictured, from left to right, are the following: (first row) Wayne Hayes, Paul Johnson, unidentified, Curtis Danley, Ralph Venable, Garnet Danley, Alma Hayes, Esther Brown, Marie Brown, Stella O'Neal, Ida Hutson, ? Hutson, Lola Venable Denny, Thelma Goins, Stella Hutson, Myrtle Johnson, and Vena Johnson Bennett; (second row) Ellis Danley, Brady Hutson, Ott Hayes, Albert Hutson, Ada Hutson, Tilda Dalton, Etta Danley, Clearcy Hutson, Treva Johnson, and Ethel Johnson Sawyer; (third row) Edna Hutson, Willie Hutson, Preston Johnson, Hardin Brown, Murphy Hutson holding baby Vance, William Tolbert, Thomas Bryant (pastor), and Andrew Danley; (fourth row) Henry Mayes, Floyd Danley, Berkley Danley, Velna Venable Quesinberry, Stella Venable, Irene McCraw, Lula Danley Simpson, Myrtle Terrell Johnson, Alma Key Danley, ? Armstrong, George Tolbert, unidentified, Thomas Moore, and Morgan Wall; (fifth row) John Danley, Berkley Danley, Willie Johnson, Clinton Moore, Monroe Hutson, Walter O'Neal, Perry Danley, unidentified, unidentified, Melinda Moore, John Hutchens, Harvey Johnson, unidentified, Beulah Moore, Minnie Moore, and unidentified. (Courtesy of Roby Venable and Melva Greene.)

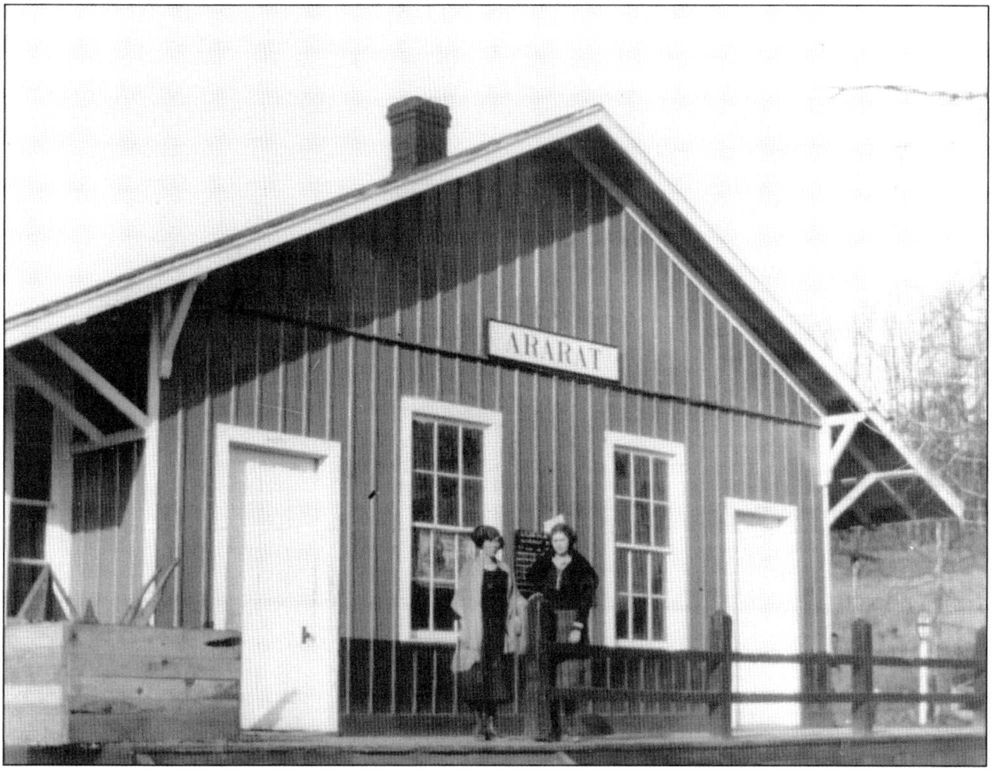

Ararat Train Depot in Long Hill Township, c. 1920s. The Forkner and Bryant families were among the first to settle in Ararat. Robert Forkner (1849–1900) was the first depot agent in Ararat, and his home was located on the hill opposite the depot. The Reverend Thomas Bryant was a Methodist minister in Ararat and also served as a depot agent. (Courtesy of Joyce Brown and Christine Shelton.)

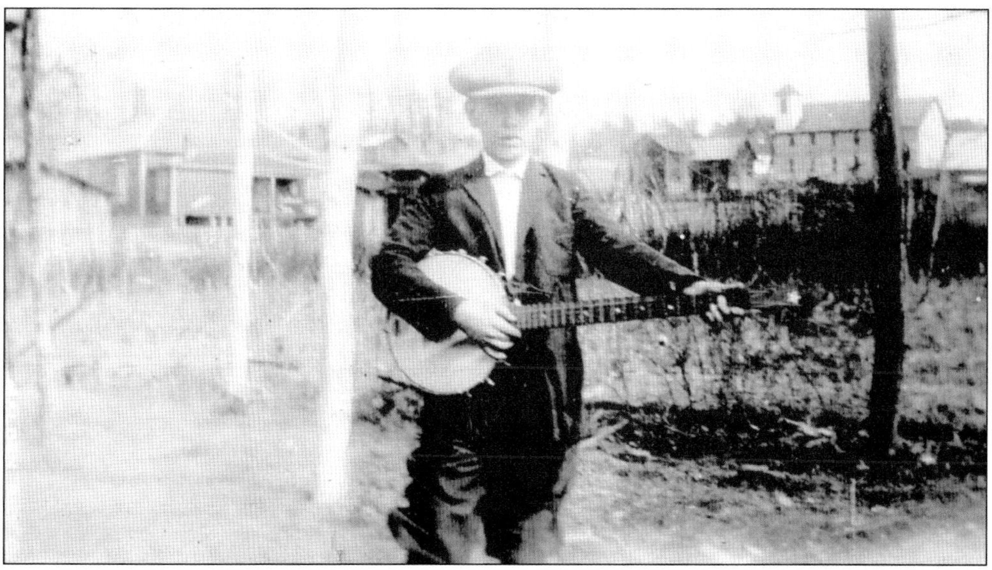

Banjo Player. The young banjo player is unidentified. In the background is Ellis Mills's house (left) and Bryant Memorial Church (right). (Courtesy of the Bryant family.)

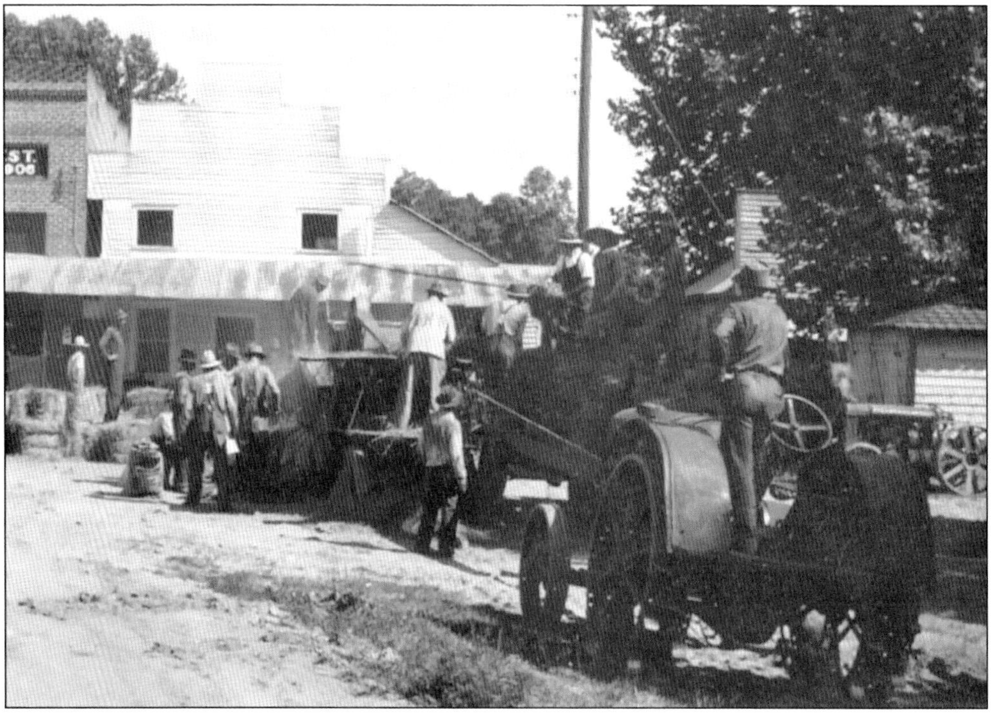

Baling Hay. Hay is baled in front of the Bryant Store (left) and Key Store (right) in Ararat. (Courtesy of the Bryant family.)

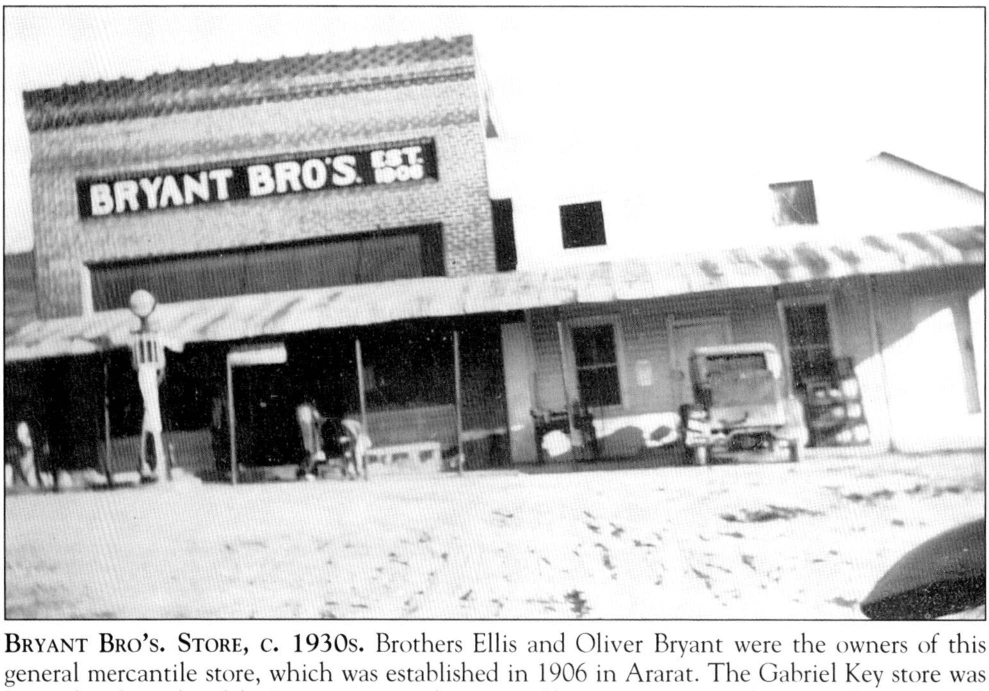

Bryant Bro's. Store, c. 1930s. Brothers Ellis and Oliver Bryant were the owners of this general mercantile store, which was established in 1906 in Ararat. The Gabriel Key store was located to the right of the Bryant store and was out of business in 1931. The post officeand a doll sock factory were located behind the Bryant store at one time. (Courtesy of the Bryant family.)

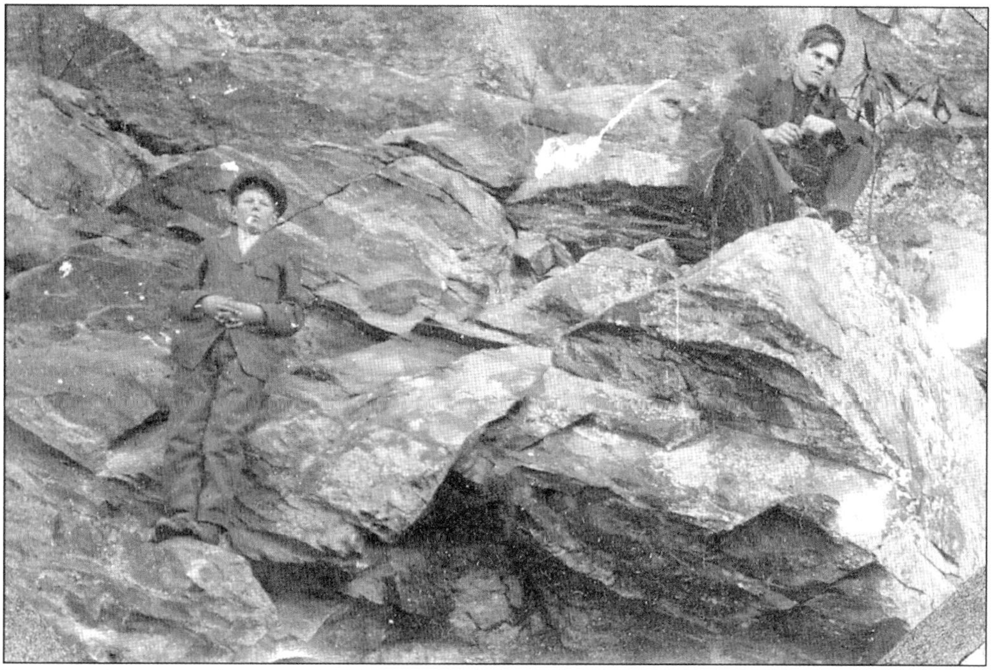

Buzzard Rock in Ararat. A favorite Sunday afternoon pastime was going out to Buzzard Rock. Charlie Driver (right) is pictured with an unidentified friend. The railroad track ran right by the rock and the train would stop at the water tank that was located nearby. (Courtesy of the Bryant family.)

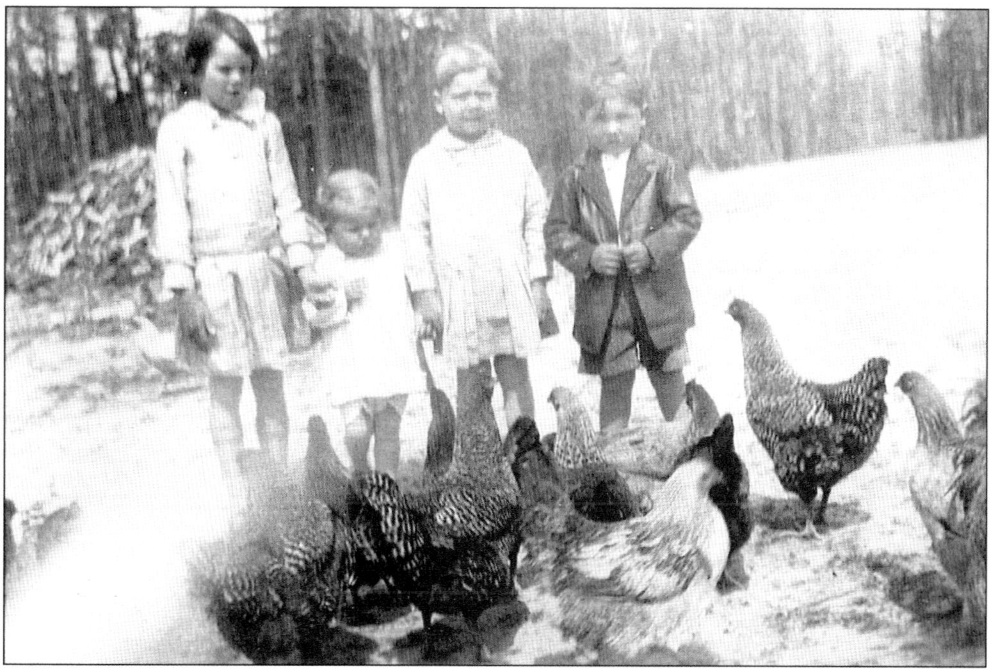

Playing with the Dominiques, c. 1930. Pictured, from left to right, are Martha Needham, Lucille Tilley, Louise Tilley, and Milton Davis at the home of Jim Davis. (Courtesy of Ruth Tolbert.)

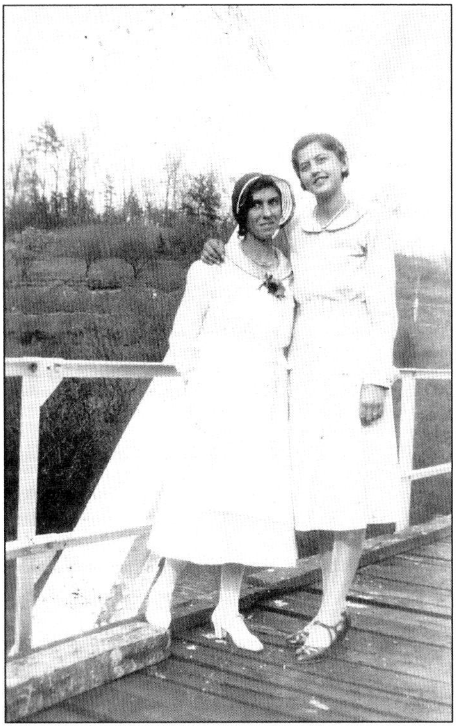

Bridge in Ararat, c. 1932. Standing on the Ararat bridge are Annie Beck (left) and Leola Atkins Key (right). (Courtesy of Ruth Tolbert.)

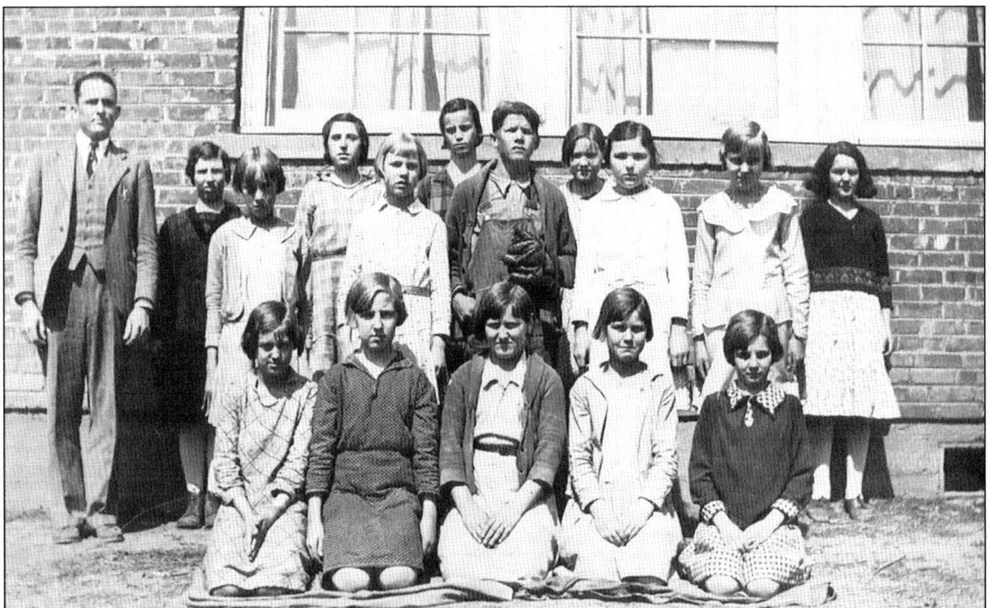

Long Hill School Class, 1932. This school was located on Ararat Road and burned in February 1934. These members of the fifth grade class, from left to right, are as follows: (first row) Tracy Simmons, Ruby Simmons, Mellie Willard, Dorothy Frances, and Cloyce Key; (second row) Ralph Hunt (teacher), Alice Welch, Hazel Needham, Nanny Ashburn, Lucille Hudson, Mary Ruth Fulk, Claude Cook, Nonnie Simmons, Ruth Marion, Dorothy Redman, and Ela Branch. (Courtesy of Dorothy Chilton.)

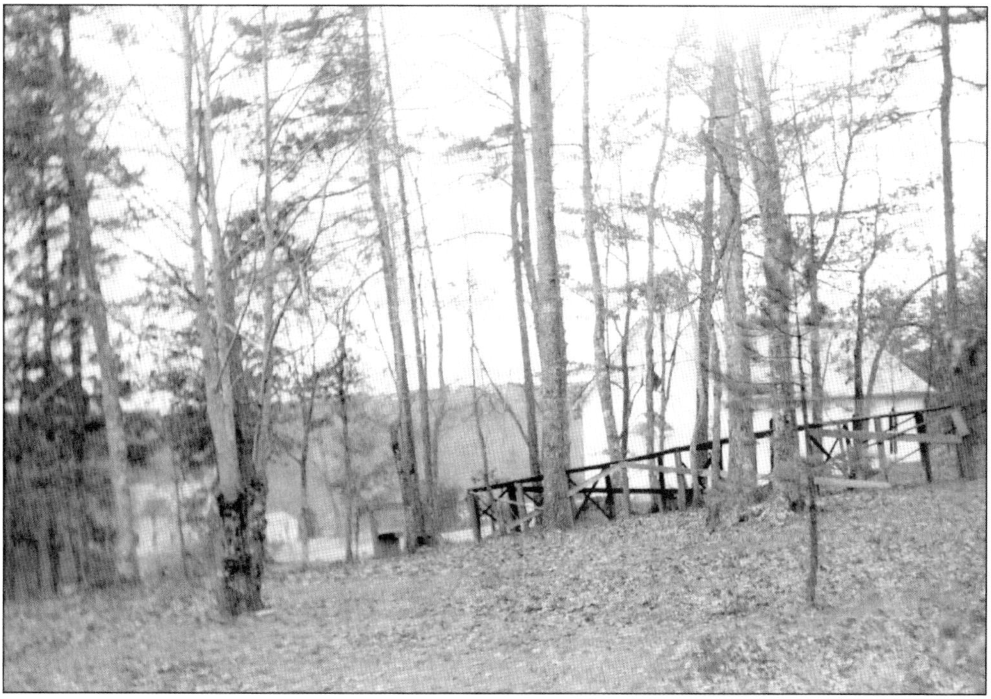

ARARAT FRIENDS MEETING. On June 20, 1924, the Ararat Monthly Meeting was "set off" from Pine Hill and became a part of the Surry Quarterly Meeting. (Courtesy of the Bryant family.)

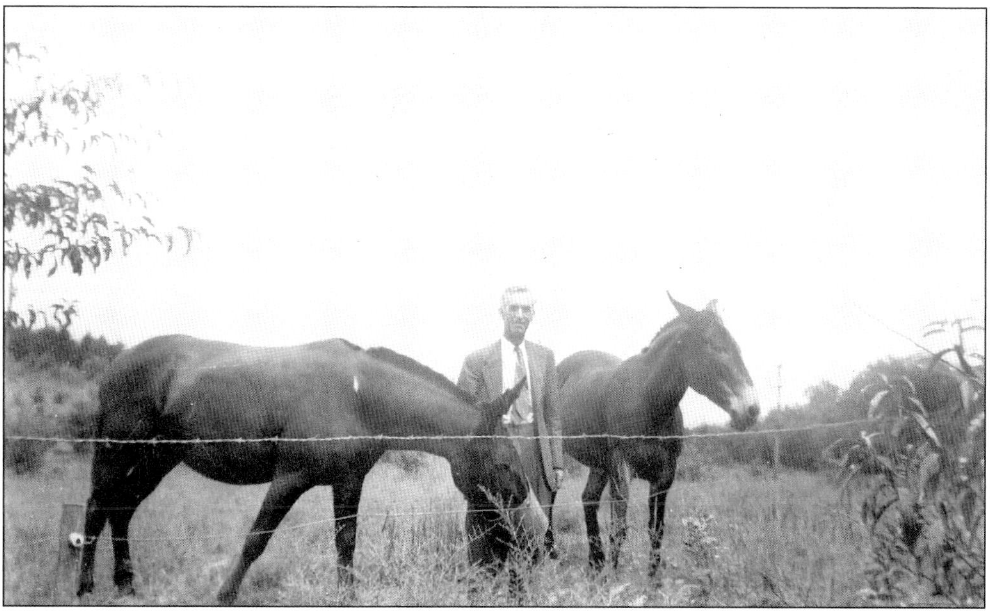

REVEREND J.W. CHILTON, C. 1940. Pictured here is Reverend J.W. Chilton, a Baptist minister, in the pasture of his farm showing off his mules. Reverend Chilton was the son of James and Rebecca Bryant Chilton. He married Rosa E. Boyles, the daughter of J.R. and Sallie Bennett Boyles, on February 18, 1900, in the Longhill Township at the home of J.R. Boyles. (Courtesy of Dorothy Chilton.)

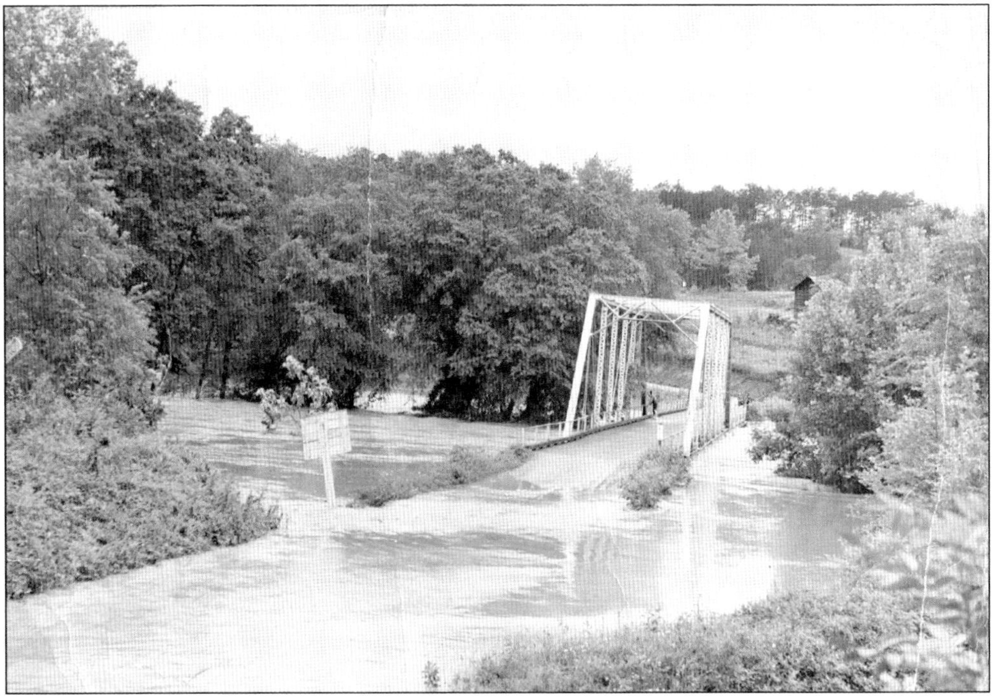

Bridge over the Ararat River. Pictured here is the bridge located over the Ararat River during the 1940 flood. (Courtesy of Joyce Fulk.)

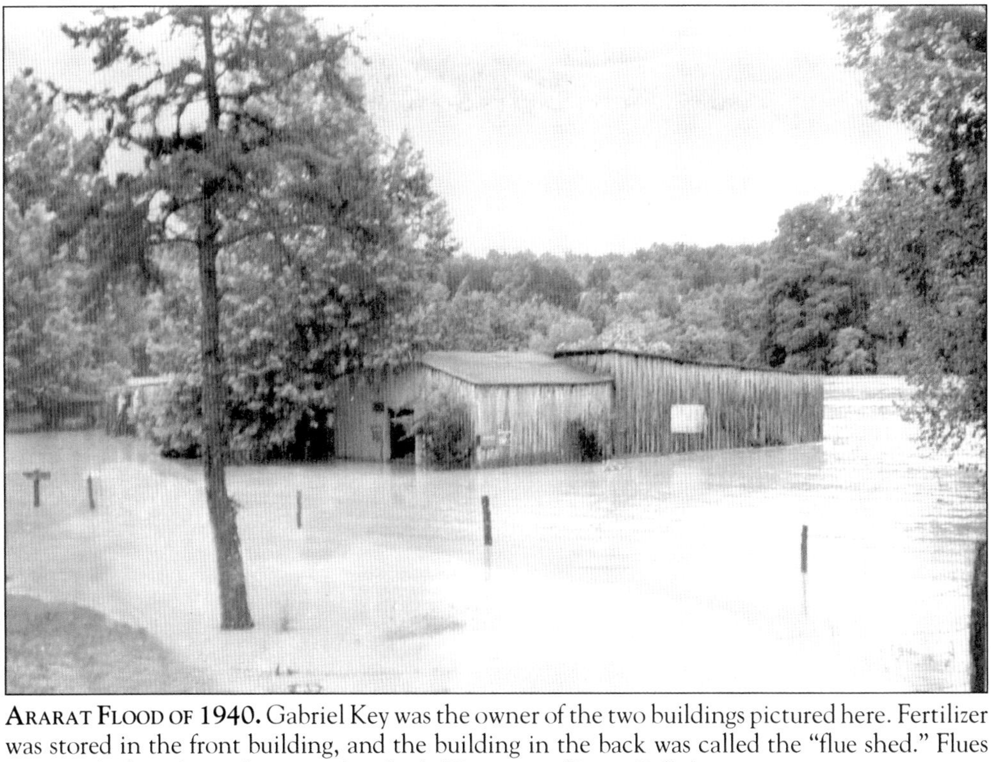

Ararat Flood of 1940. Gabriel Key was the owner of the two buildings pictured here. Fertilizer was stored in the front building, and the building in the back was called the "flue shed." Flues were made for tobacco barns in this shed. (Courtesy of Joyce Fulk.)

Four

Elkin and Marsh Townships

The Elkin and Marsh Townships are located in southwest Surry County. The Yadkin River is their southern border, and Mitchell's River divides the two townships. Fertile "bottom land" may be found next to the Yadkin River.

The town of Elkin lies in Elkin Township near the Wilkes County line and was named for the Elkin Creek, which flows through the town to the Yadkin River. Some early schools in the area were Canebrake, Oak Ridge, and Rock Spring. Early churches included Elkin Presbyterian, Galloway Memorial Episcopal Chapel, Elkin First Baptist, and Elkin Methodist. Early settlers in this area included families with the surnames Bryan, Kimbrough, Hill, Yates, Martin, Gwyn, Chatham, Hughes, Davis, Kerby, Speer, Shores, and Allen. Several old iron works were started in this area, and the bridge over the Yadkin River between Elkin and Jonesville (now in Yadkin County) had a 210-foot span, the longest suspension bridge in the world at that time. The bridge was torn down in 1913. The first post office was established in Elkin on June 4, 1856, with Richard R. Gwyn as postmaster. The town was incorporated on March 5, 1889.

There are no established towns in Marsh Township; however, three large communities are within its boundaries: Fairview, Crutchfield, and Little Richmond. Burch is a small community located near the Yadkin River, and a former post office here was established on August 25, 1853, with Thomas B. Roberts as the postmaster. Burch is commonly referred to as Burch Station since it is where trains pass through. Bear Creek and Snow Creek are two of the most commonly known creeks that flow in Marsh Township. Some of the area's early schools were Cheny and Mulberry, and early churches were Bear Creek and Mount Hermon. Early settlers in this area included the families of Horn, Lewis, Riggs, Stewart, Bradley, Howard, Baker, and Davis.

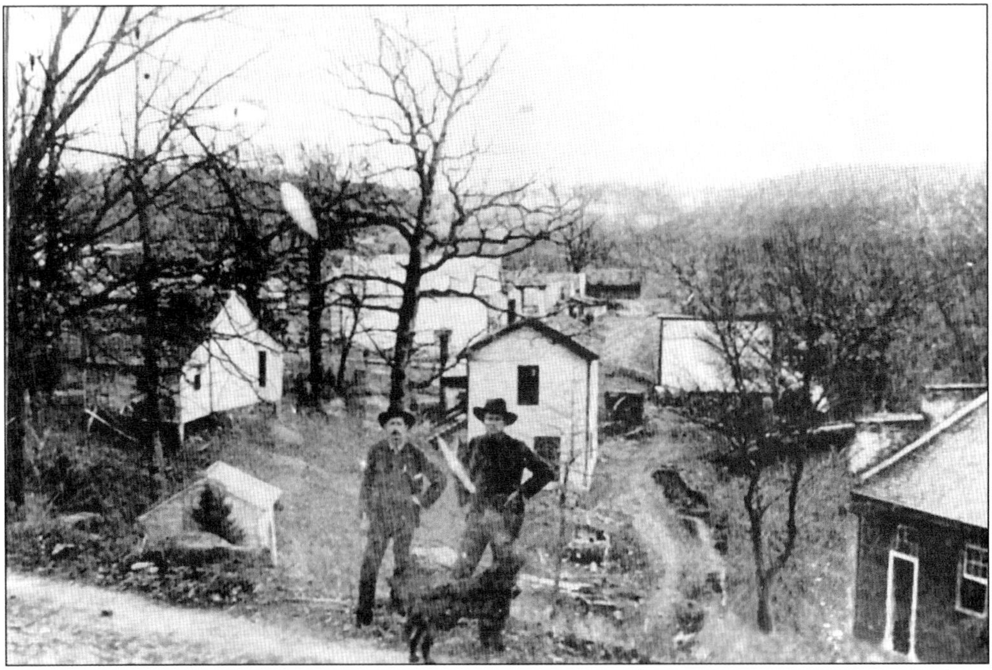

FRONT STREET IN ELKIN, C. 1890. The photographer who took this image was looking south from Virginia Road when he photographed these two men with their dog. (Courtesy of Emily Southard.)

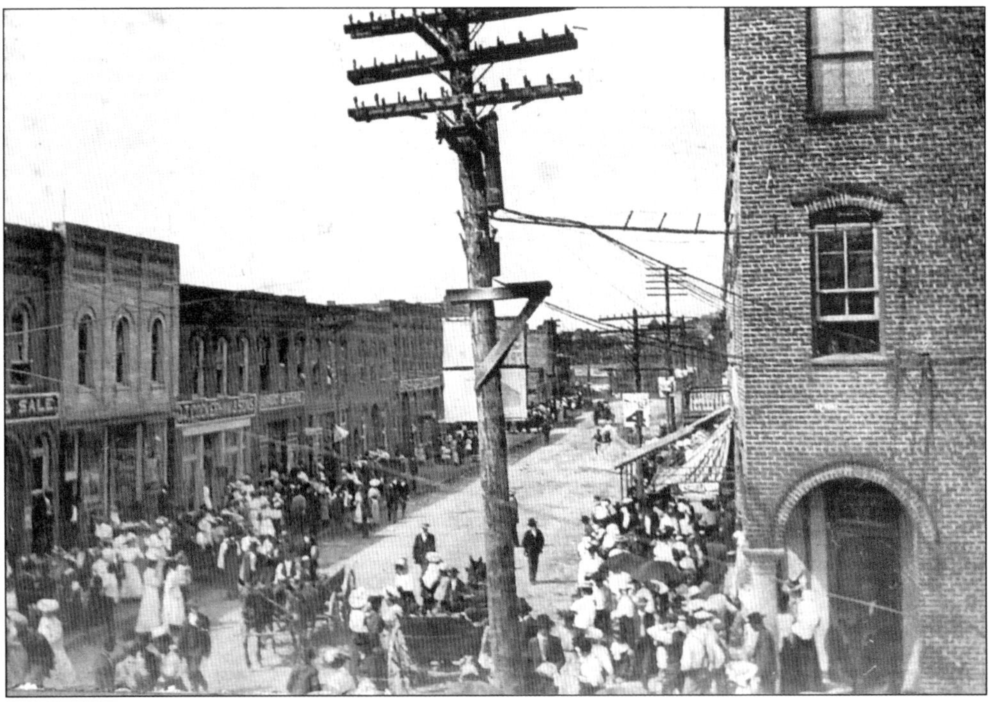

ELKIN, C. 1909. Most of the residents here appear to be dressed in their finery and gathered in groups to socialize. Perhaps they are waiting for some special event to take place in downtown Elkin. (Courtesy of Mary Marsh.)

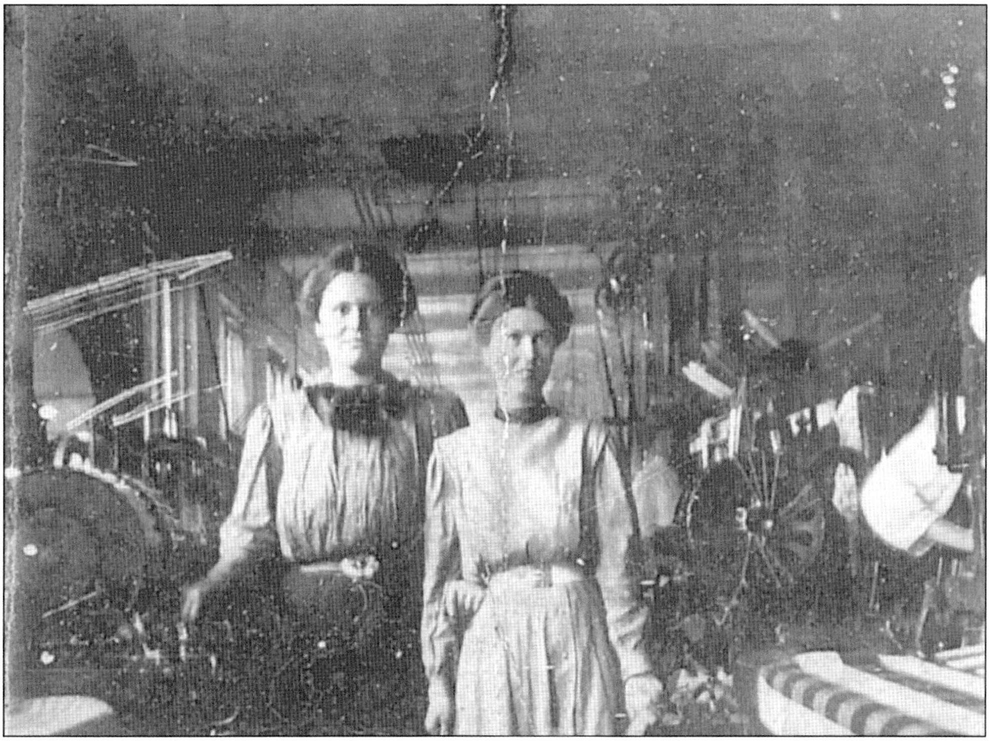

CHATHAM MILL, 1909. Cora Pinnix and Laura Hanks are seen here in the weave room at Chatham Mill. (Courtesy of Mary Marsh.)

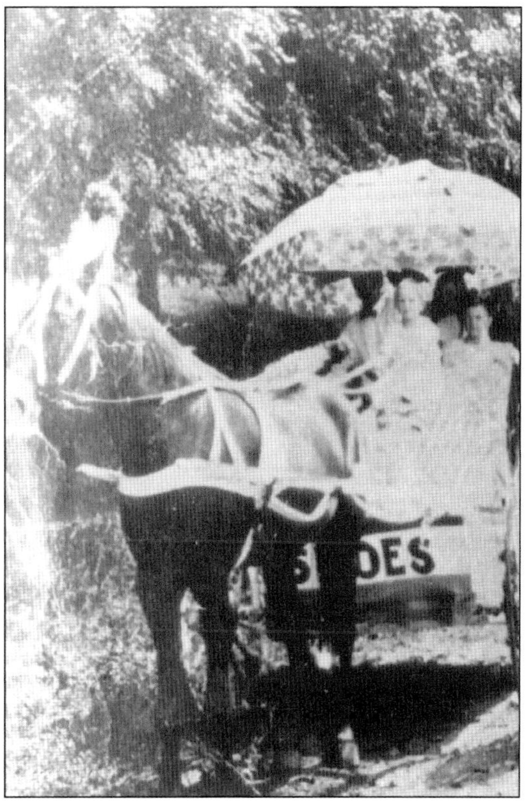

JULY 4, 1910 PARADE. This Fourth of July parade shows the float of D.J. Cockerham & Sons. Daniel Jasper Cockerham (1841–1917) was the owner of the business in Elkin. (Courtesy of Jim Cockerham.)

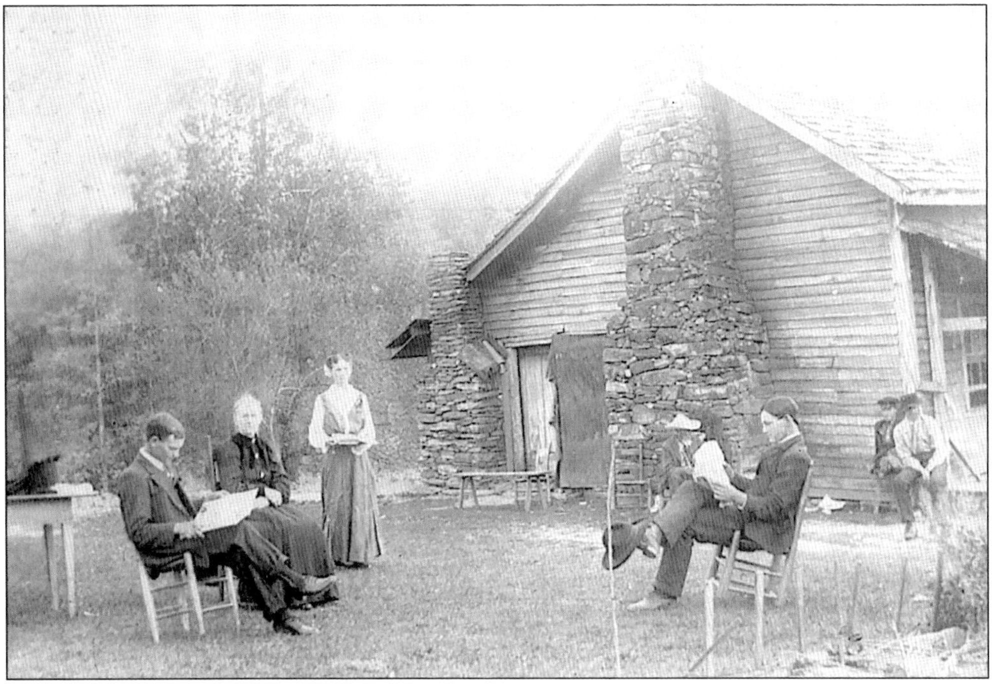

A Leisure Afternoon, c. 1915. The homeplace of Mrs. Celia Ann Mosley Guyer (born in 1853) was located in the Poplar Springs community. Pictured, from left to right, are Robert Guyer, Celia Mosley Guyer Williams, daughter Lillie (standing), and Windom Guyer. Nat Williams (the man with beard near rock chimney) and two unidentified young men are pictured in the background. (Courtesy of Mrs. Hazel Golden Edwards and Annie Lee Gentry.)

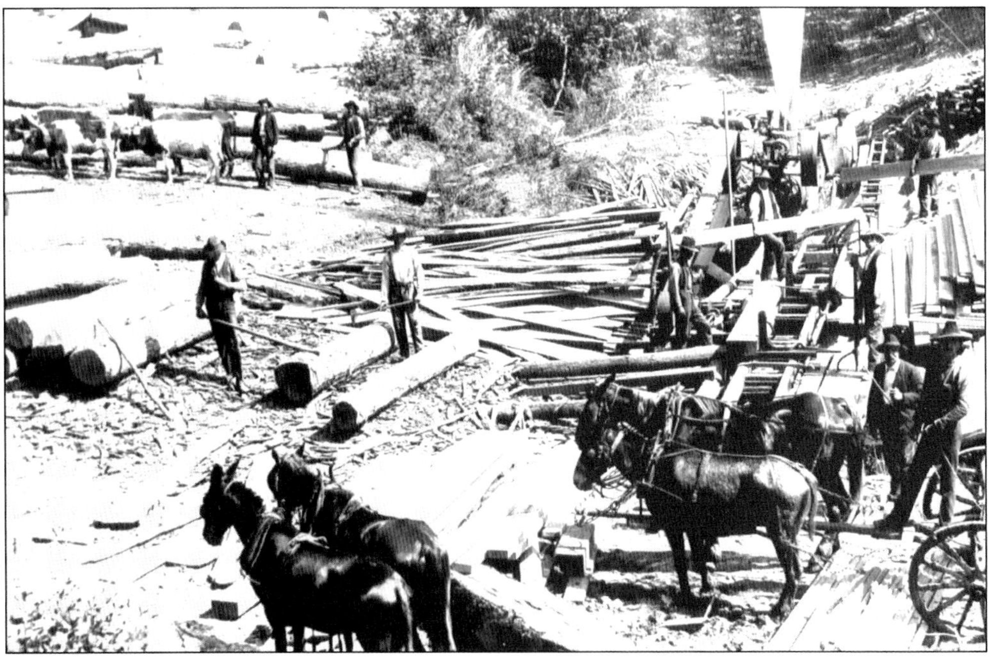

W.B. Minick and Brother Lumber Mill. This lumber mill was located in Elkin and burned in June 1917. (Courtesy of Ruth Minick.)

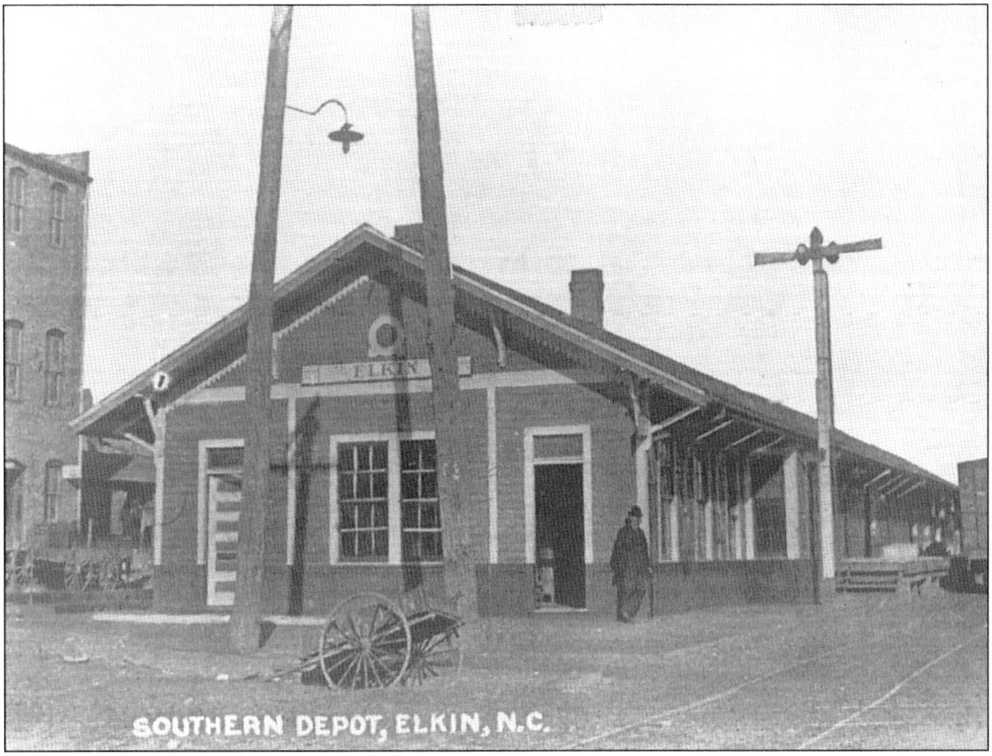

SOUTHERN DEPOT IN ELKIN. (Courtesy of the Elkin Historical Society.)

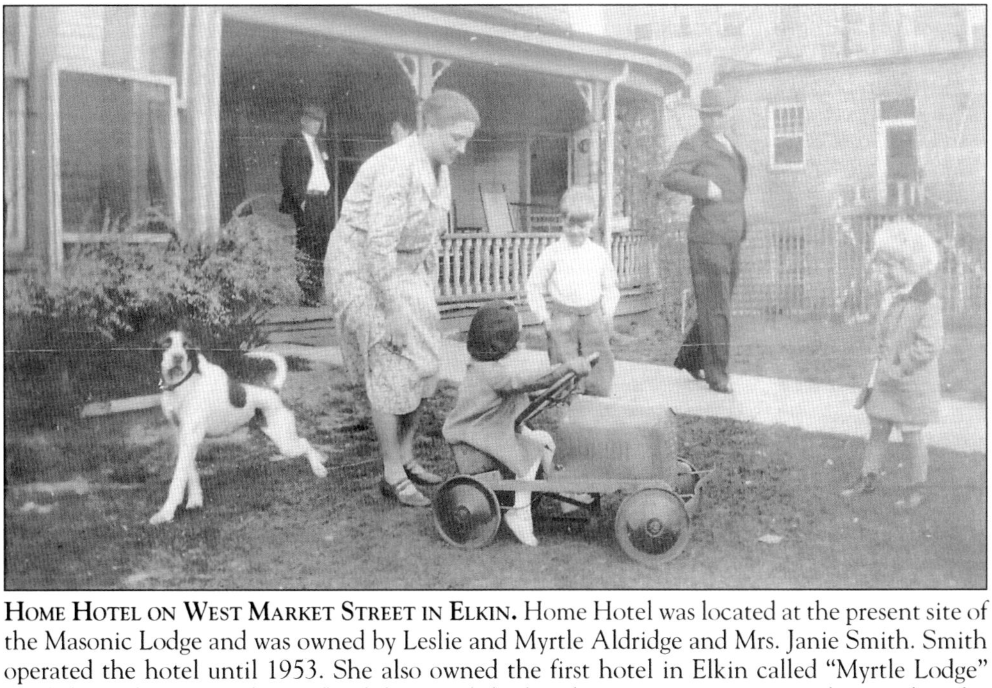

HOME HOTEL ON WEST MARKET STREET IN ELKIN. Home Hotel was located at the present site of the Masonic Lodge and was owned by Leslie and Myrtle Aldridge and Mrs. Janie Smith. Smith operated the hotel until 1953. She also owned the first hotel in Elkin called "Myrtle Lodge" until the early 1920s, when a flood destroyed the hotel. Many prominent people stayed in the Home Hotel, which was located beside Hotel Elkin (right). (Courtesy of Mary Aldridge.)

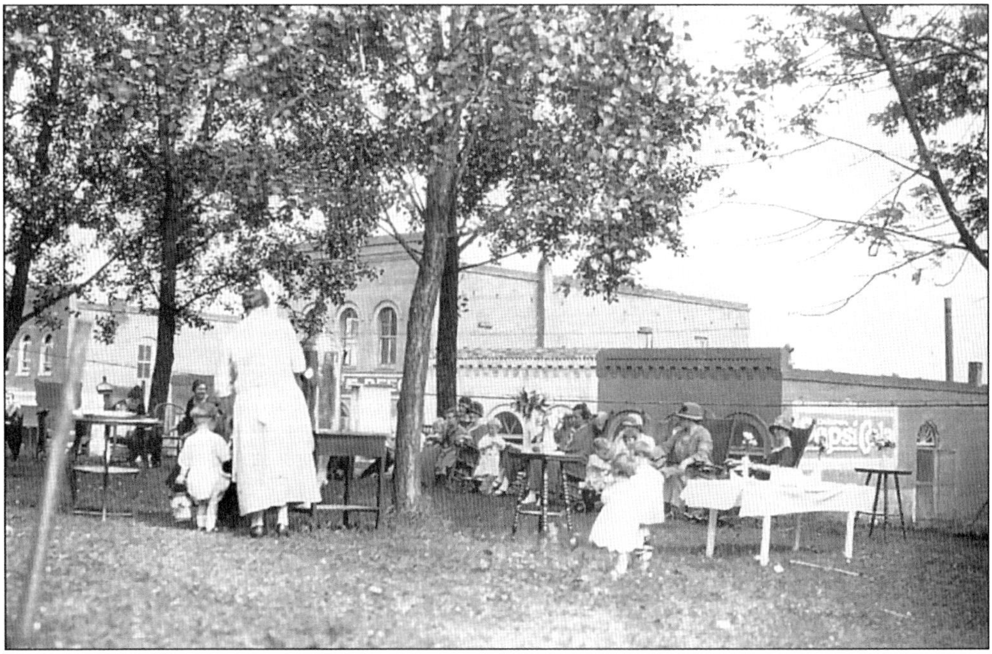

MAIN STREET IN ELKIN, c. 1925. Eugene Aldridge was three years old at this birthday party in a park on Main Street. Northwestern Agency is located here, across the street from the old Mosley and Reece business. (Courtesy of Mary Aldridge.)

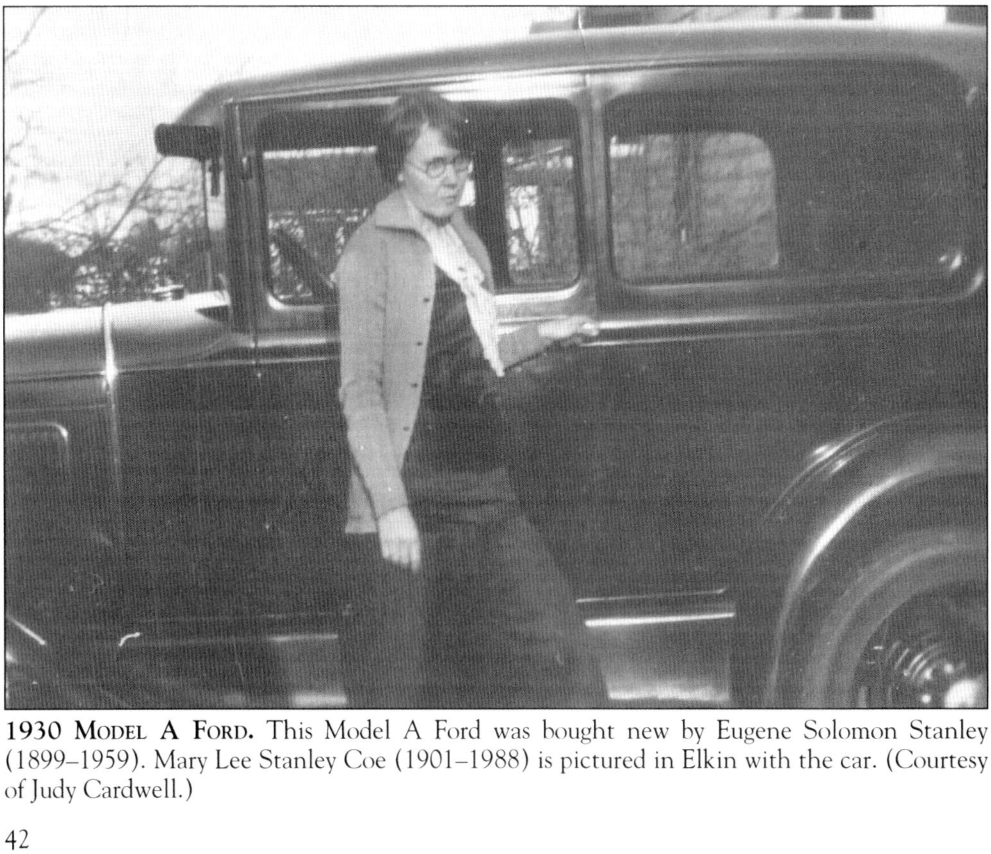

1930 MODEL A FORD. This Model A Ford was bought new by Eugene Solomon Stanley (1899–1959). Mary Lee Stanley Coe (1901–1988) is pictured in Elkin with the car. (Courtesy of Judy Cardwell.)

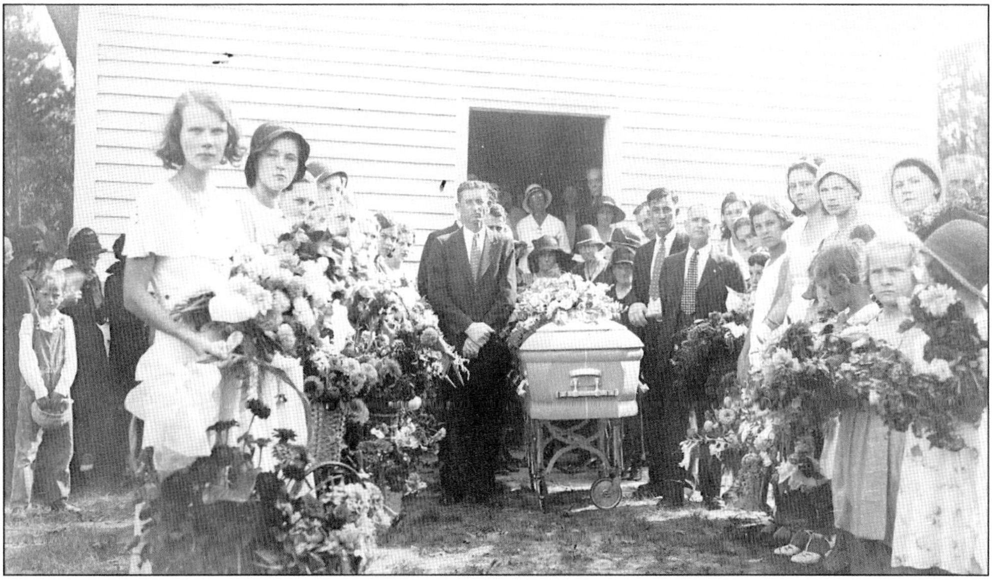

FUNERAL OF MELISSA GUYER CROUSE AT EBENEZER METHODIST CHURCH, 1932. From left to right are pallbearers Sid Hudspeth, Doc Steel, and Dave Masten. Some of the young ladies holding flowers are Beulah Lawrence, Savannah Guyer, Betty Mae Masten, Reba Steel, Lola Hudspeth, Grace Masten, and Maudie Hudspeth. (Courtesy of Emma H. Boyles.)

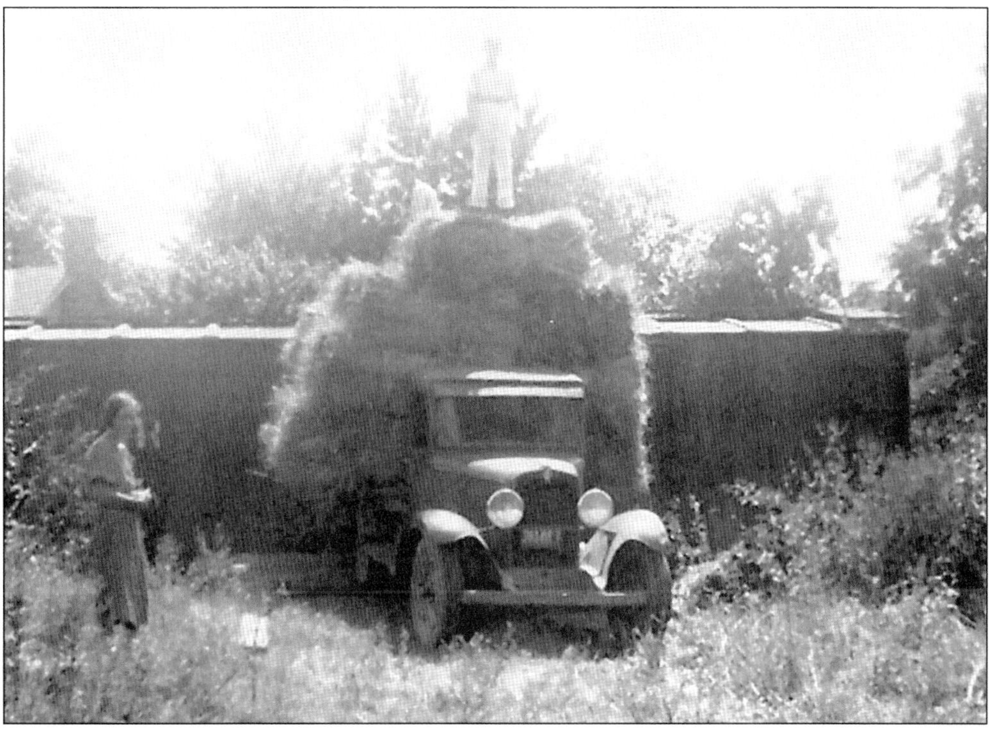

LOADING STRAW ON THE BOXCAR, 1933. The load of straw is being shipped to Benjamin T. Crump and Company in Richmond, Virginia. Pictured on top of the straw is Sidney Hudspeth, and to his left is his brother John Hudspeth. The straw was used to make horse collars. (Courtesy of Emma H. Boyles.)

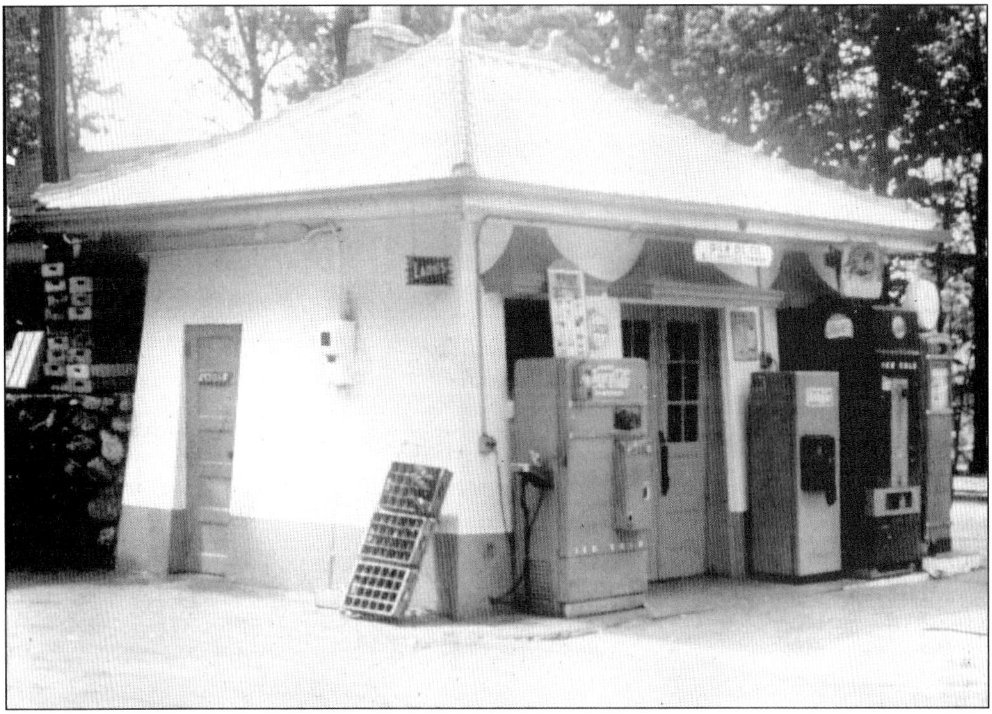

G & B Oil Company. Pictured here is the original headquarters of G & B Oil Company, located on North Bridge Street in Elkin. The structure was built in the 1920s. (Courtesy of G & B Energy, Inc.)

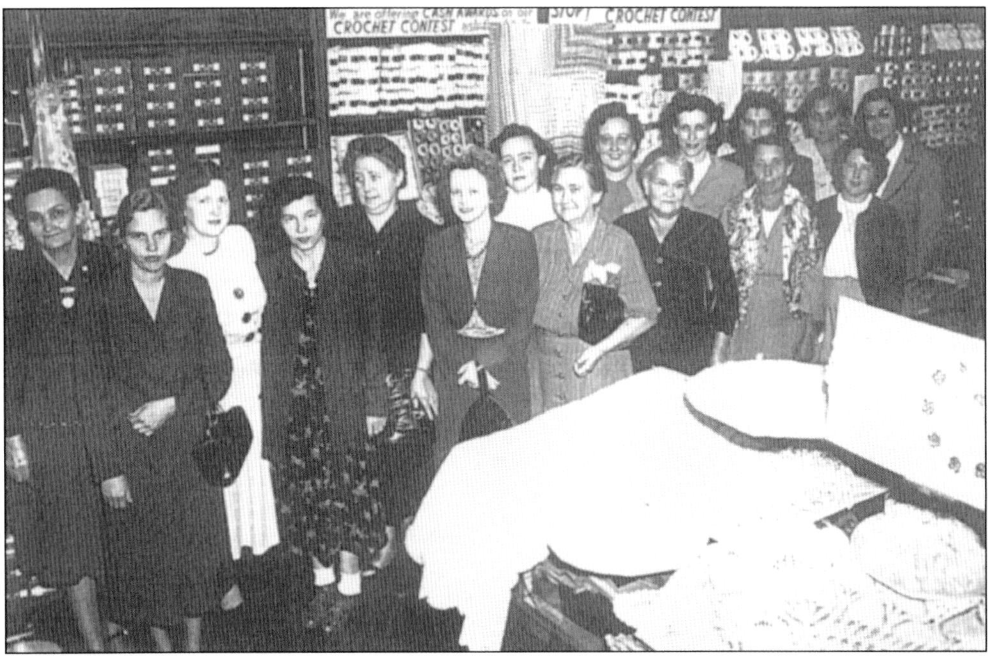

Crochet Contest, c. 1936. Cash awards were given to the winners of this crochet contest held at Mr. Walker's Five & Dime store at Elkin. Issie Mayes, a contestant, is pictured eighth from the left. (Courtesy of Avis Schuyler.)

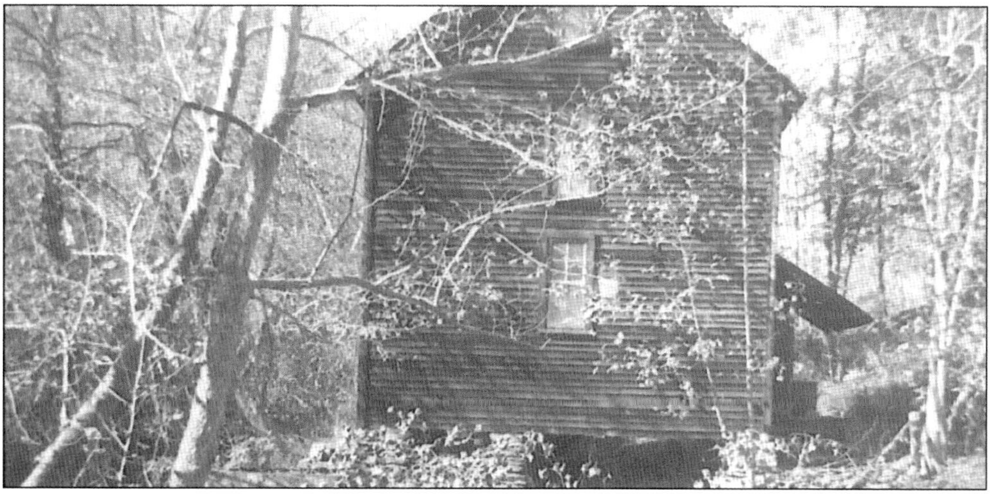

Joe Layne's Mill near Little Richmond. Farmers far and near would take their wheat, corn, oats, barley, rye, etc. to the mill to be ground for home use and to feed farm animals. (Courtesy of Mildred Matthews.)

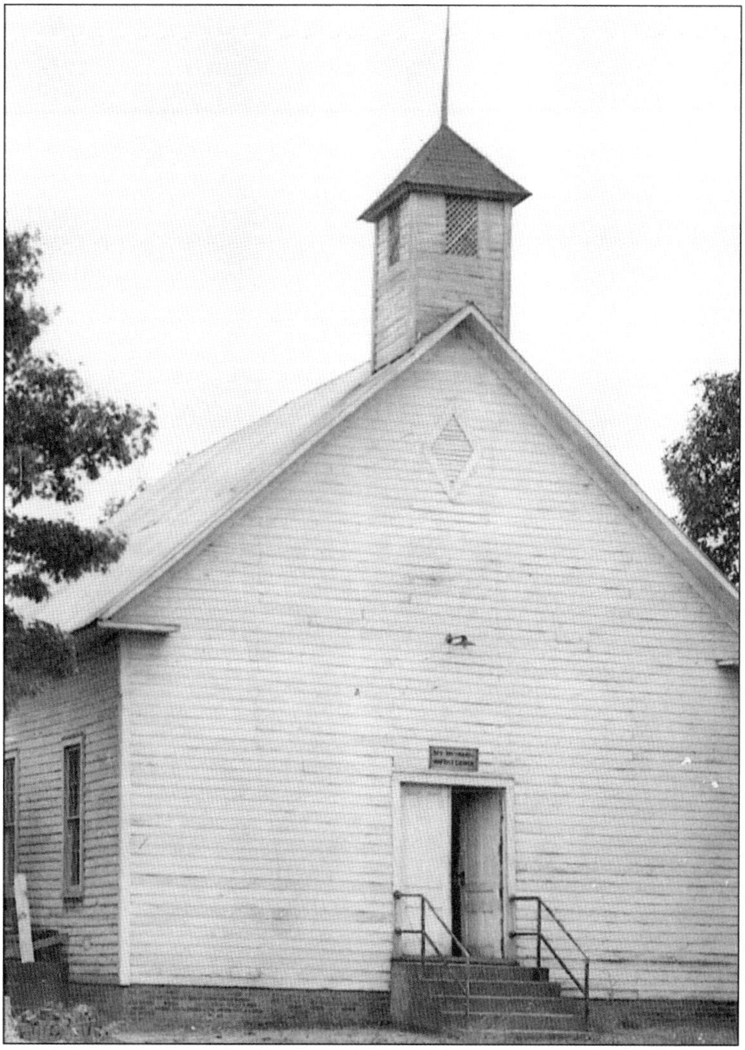

Mount Hermon Baptist Church in Marsh Township. Mount Hermon Baptist Church is near the community of Crutchfield and originated in 1891 from the church known as Baptist Church of Christ. (Courtesy of Hessie Stanley.)

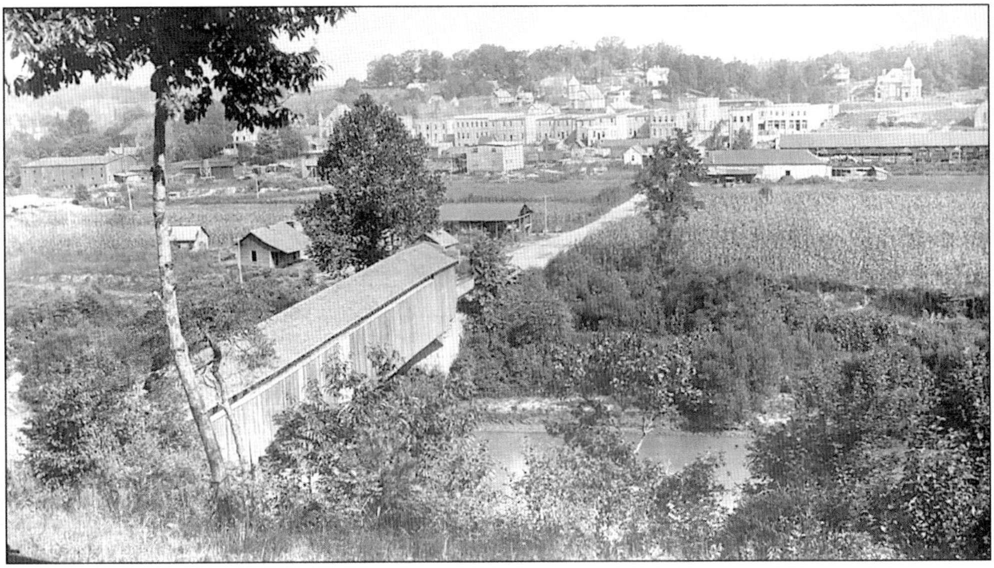

Bridge Street Located in Elkin. Looking north from the Jonesville side of the Yadkin River, one can see Bridge Street in 1907. Notice the covered bridge over the Yadkin River. (Courtesy of the Elkin Historical Society.)

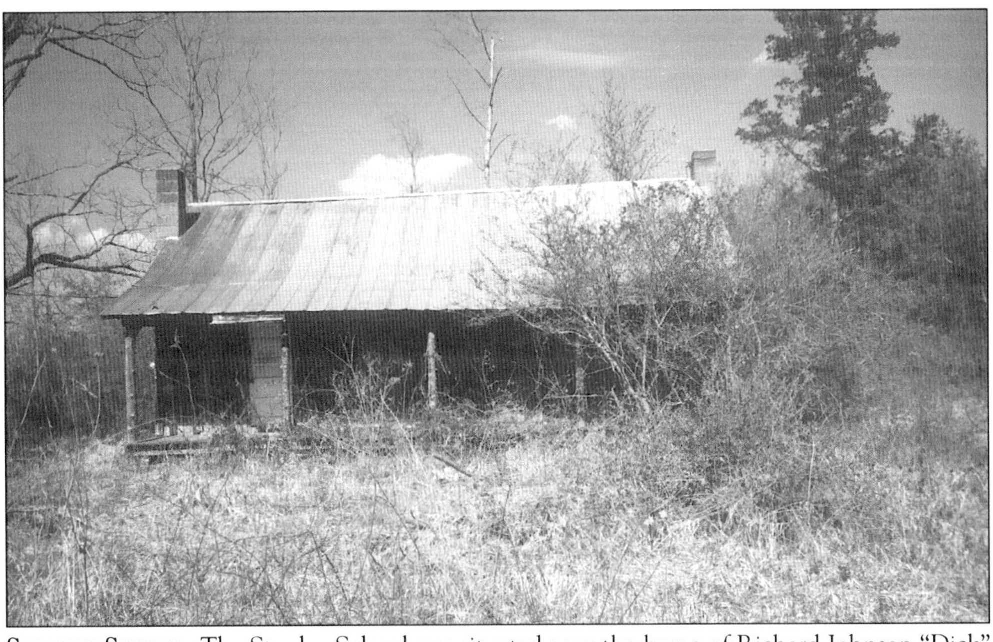

Stanley School. The Stanley School was situated near the home of Richard Johnson "Dick" and Elizabeth Baker Stanley near Bear Creek Baptist Church. R.J. Stanley was a teacher and a magistrate, and he taught at the Stanley School, *c.* 1890. The building was used as a residence for many years before it was torn down. (Courtesy of Mildred Matthews.)

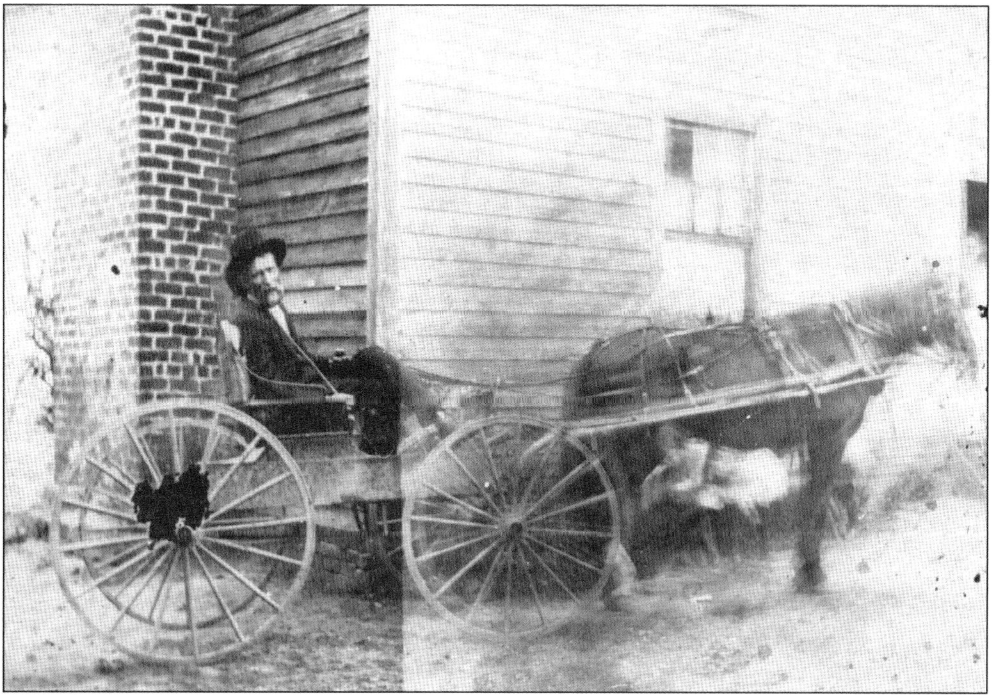

LEONARD "LEN" BRAY OUTSIDE HIS HOME, 1895. Len Bray (1851–1926), the son of Lewis Bray, was married to Rebecca Chaney. (Courtesy of Judy Cardwell.)

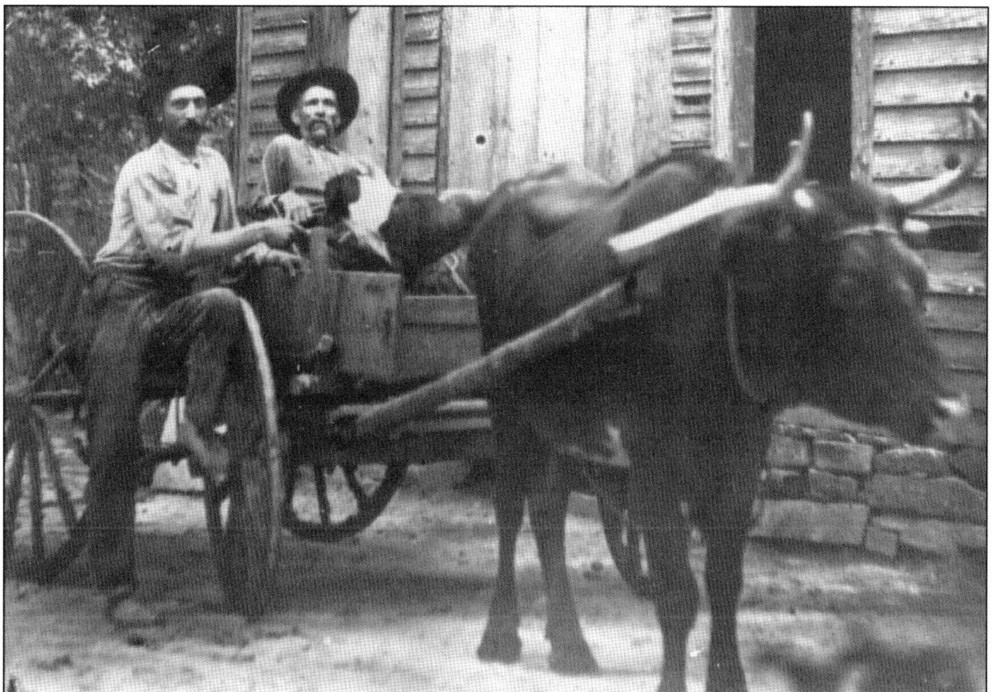

"OLD BUCK," C. 1900. The steer "Old Buck" provides transportation for Henry Poindexter "Deck" Bray (1853–1930) and Leonard Bray (1851–1926). (Courtesy of Judy Cardwell.)

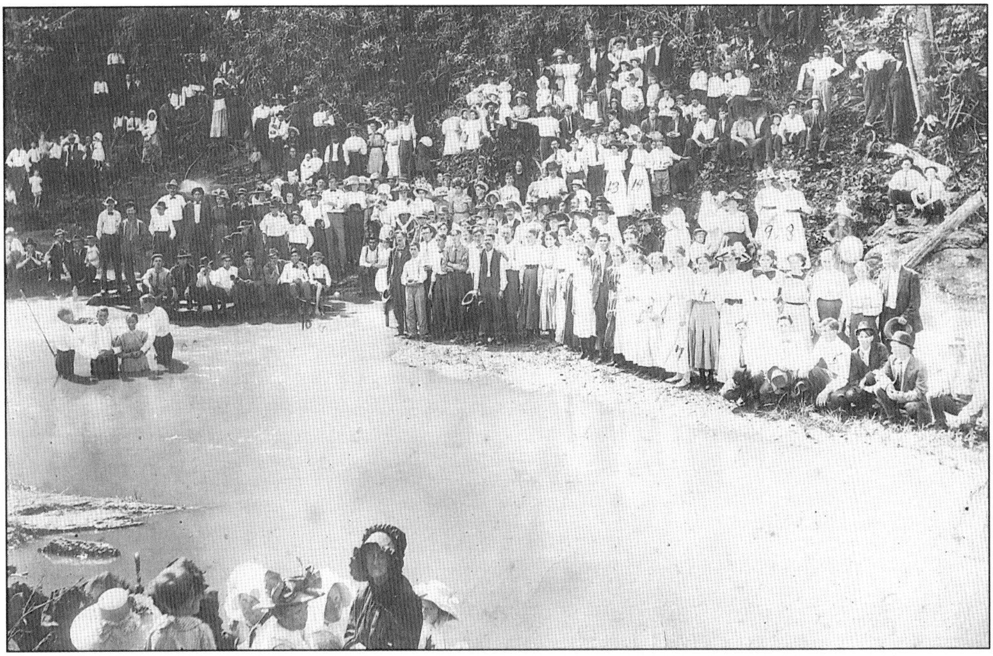

A Union Cross Baptist Church Baptism, 1910. Minister L.B. "Brack" Murry and assistant Jones Carter baptize Solomon and Ada Cockerham Stanley in Snow Creek behind the home of Charlie Dobbins. Others are waiting to be baptized. Pictured third from the left is W. Verlin Holder, age 19; next to him is Talmadge Dockery, wearing a hat and dark suit. In the foreground is Christana Holder dressed in a black bonnet and dress. Facing Mrs. Holder is her granddaughter Savanah Holder. (Courtesy of Emily Southard.)

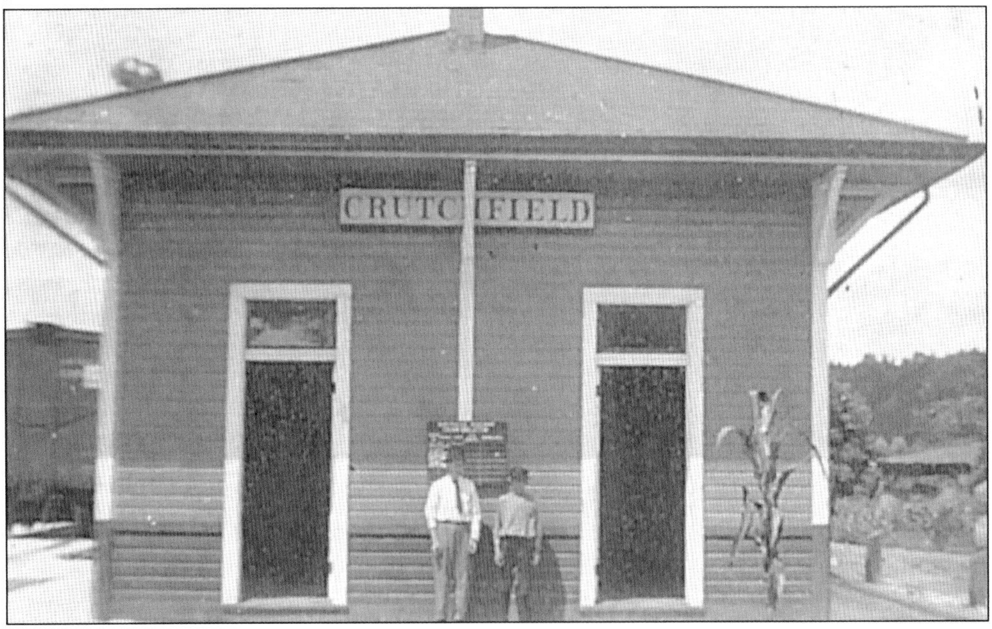

Crutchfield Depot. The Crutchfield Depot was named in honor of Will Crutchfield. The mail would come on the train to Crutchfield, and Arvil Speer would pick up the mail and deliver it to Boonville and Yadkinville. (Courtesy of Mary Aldridge.)

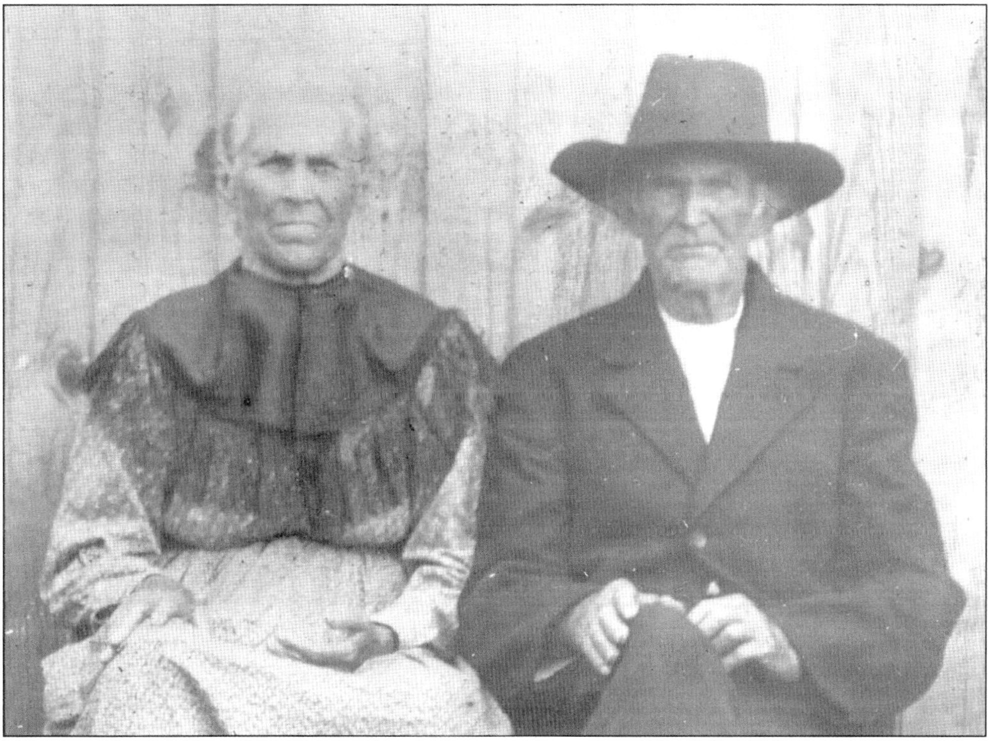

EARLY SETTLERS IN THE BEAR CREEK COMMUNITY. Laticia "Lettie" Stanley Poindexter and William "Bill" Poindexter lived near Bear Creek Baptist Church. Lettie was the daughter of Jesse and Sally Wilmoth Stanley. The couple's children were John, Willie, Richard, Sarah, L.C., and M.M. Poindexter. (Courtesy of Mildred Matthews.)

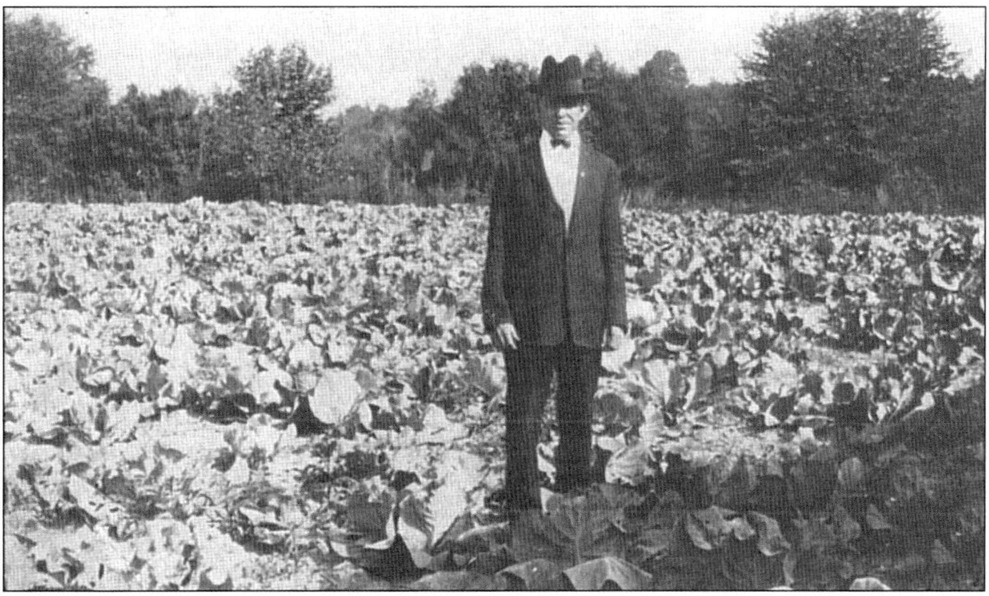

REVEREND SCALES DRAUGHN. Reverend Draughn lived in Crutchfield and was the pastor of the Siloam Baptist Church, Fairview Baptist Church, and others. He appears to be dressed for church rather than for working in his cabbage patch. (Courtesy of Frances Snow.)

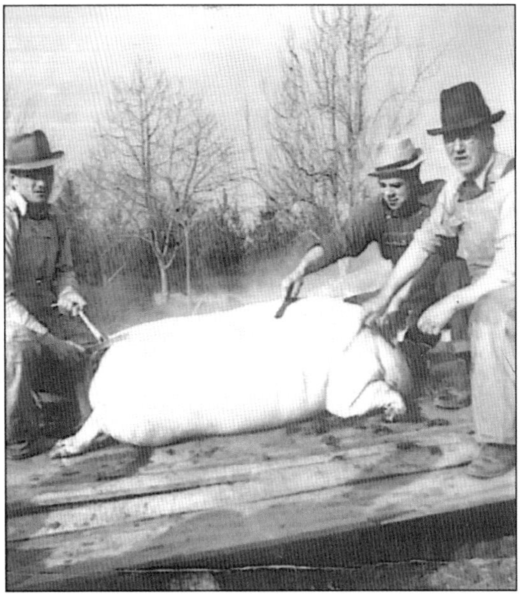

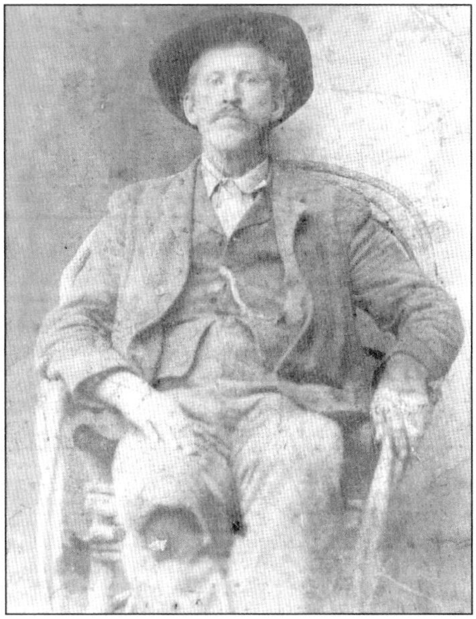

Left: **DRESSING PORK.** Phillip Southard, Raymond Holder, and J.R. "Buck" Baker are seen here on the Holder farm. (Courtesy of Emily Southard.)
Right: **NAMED FOR THE PIONEER DANIEL BOONE.** Daniel Boone Stanley (1847–1927), the son of Jesse and Sally Wilmoth Stanley, was married to Fannie Jane White. They lived in the Bear Creek community and had eight children: Thomas, Cleve, Harrison, Sally Bet, Sis, Verlie, Ernest, and William "Bill" Stanley. (Courtesy of H.C. Stanley and Mildred Matthews.)

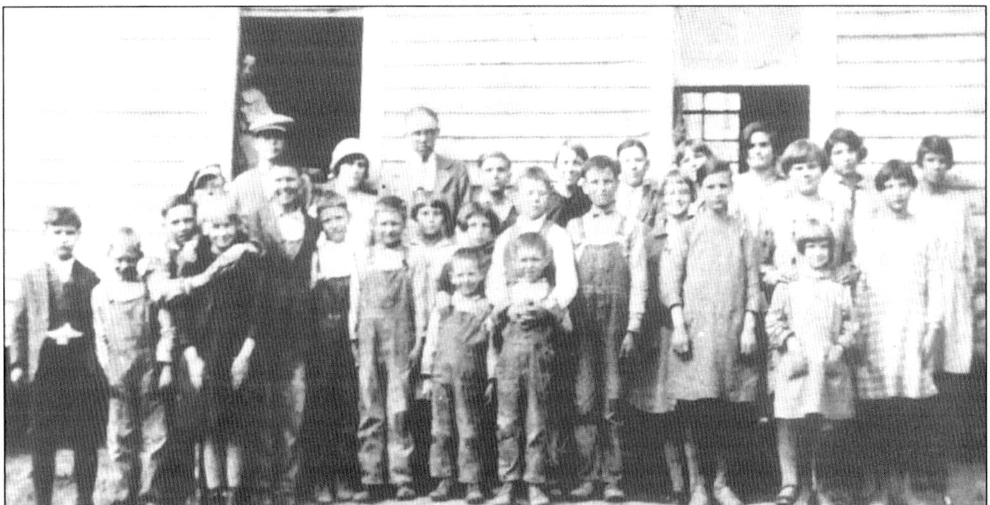

MULBERRY SCHOOL STUDENTS, C. 1926. Mulberry School was located off Poplar Springs Road on Joe Layne Mill Road. Pictured here, from left to right, are the following: (first row) Ralph Renegar, Garvey Southard, Spurgeon Southard, Laura Nance, Hilton Southard, unidentified, Wilber Southard, Ollie Mae Key, Mary Southard, Kernie Mounce, Miles Anthony, Millie Anthony, Lillian Southard, Ruth Mounce, and Lixie Marion; (second row) Floyd Stanley (with cap), Avery Marshall (tall with cap), Sallie Bunker (teacher), Mr. DeBorde (teacher), King Key, Ima Southard, Avery Cockerham, Virginia Draughn, unidentified, Lillie Mounce, Grace Marion, and unidentified. (Courtesy of Emily Southard.)

Five

Franklin Township

Franklin Township is located in northwest Surry County, and both Skull Camp Mountain (with an altitude of 2,082 feet) and Warrior Mountain (with an altitude of 1,850 feet) are located within the township. Ramey Creek rises in the northwest and flows east into Roaring Fork, which flows southwest into Fisher River. Beaverdam Creek rises in the north and flows southeast into Little Fisher River. The township is bordered on the north by Grayson County, Virginia, and on the west by Allegheny County, North Carolina.

In the early 1800s, the Skull Camp post office served the area, which included such communities as Lowgap, Ladonia, and Roaring Gap. Lowgap, named from a nearby low gap in the Blue Ridge Mountains, was the home of Governor Jesse Franklin and the township was named for the Franklin family. T.N. Woodruff started a well-known evergreen business in Lowgap named W.M. Woodruff's Son and Company. The business provided Galax leaves and ferns, with which to make wreaths, to florists all over the United States. The first case of prepared Galax leaves was sold on October 22, 1920.

Some early schools located in the area were Oak Grove, Roaring Gap, Lowgap, Ladonia, and McMickell, and early churches included Flat Top Primitive Baptist, Mountain View Baptist, Roaring Gap Baptist, and Ladonia Baptist. Some of the earliest known settlers included the following families: Williams, Franklin, Davis, Hughes, and Phillips. The Camp Raven Knob Scout Reservation is located south of Lowgap and covered 15 acres when it was formed in 1950. It was owned by the Old Hickory Council, Boy Scouts of America. Raven Knob Pond was on an unnamed tributary of Fisher River. Scouts now enjoy Lake Sobotta at Camp Raven Knob.

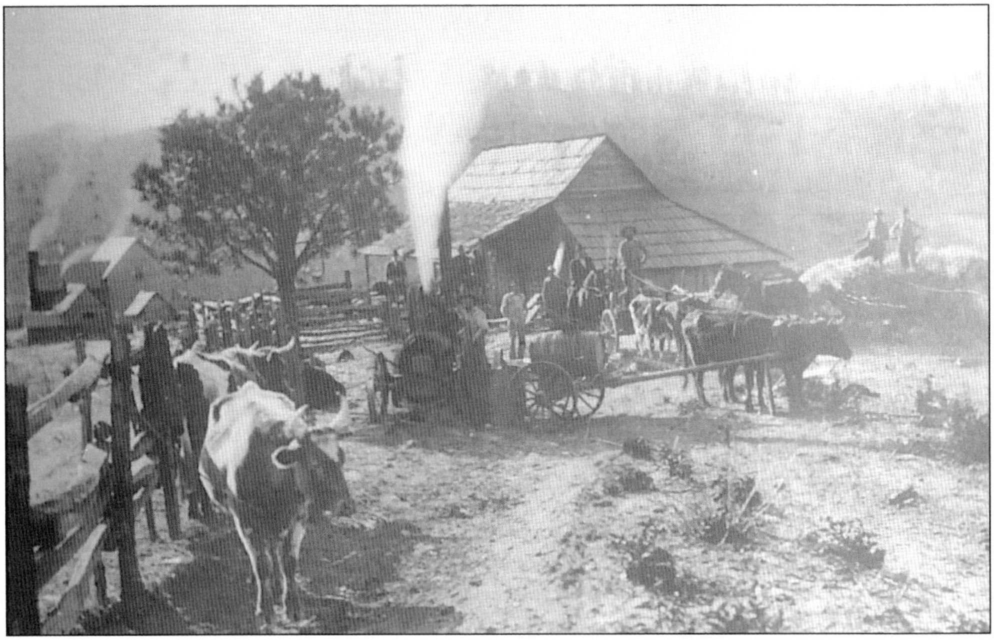

George Ramey's Home at Lowgap. Pictured on the wagon with steers is Cooper Bartley, on the horse is Daniel Ramey, and between them is George Ramey. Hezekiah Bartley (to the left of the steam) is on the fence and Aleck Bartley is firing the boiler. Corn is being cut and blown up in the barn loft with the wood-burning steam engine. The feed cutter had a pipe to run cut corn up in the barn loft. Daniel Ramey owned the outfit and the oxen in the photograph. (Courtesy of Stella Carrico.)

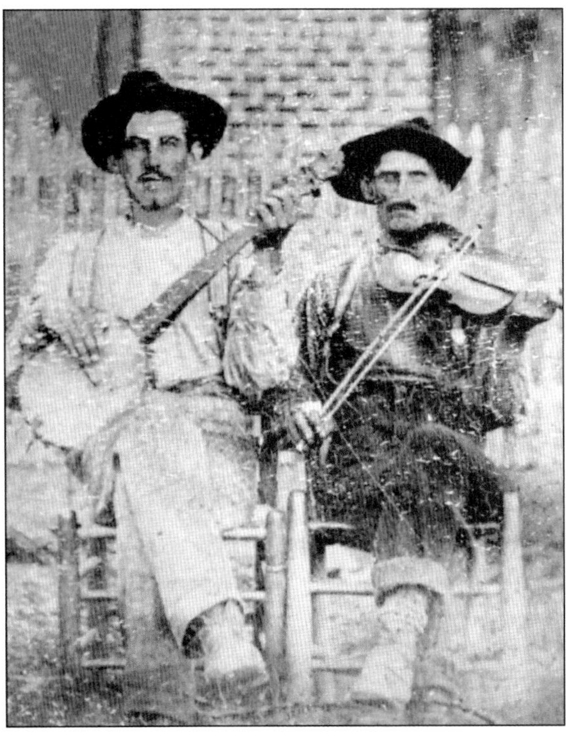

Music Makers. Pictured before 1904 are Friel Galyean with his banjo and Houston Galyean with his fiddle. (Courtesy of Teresa Smith.)

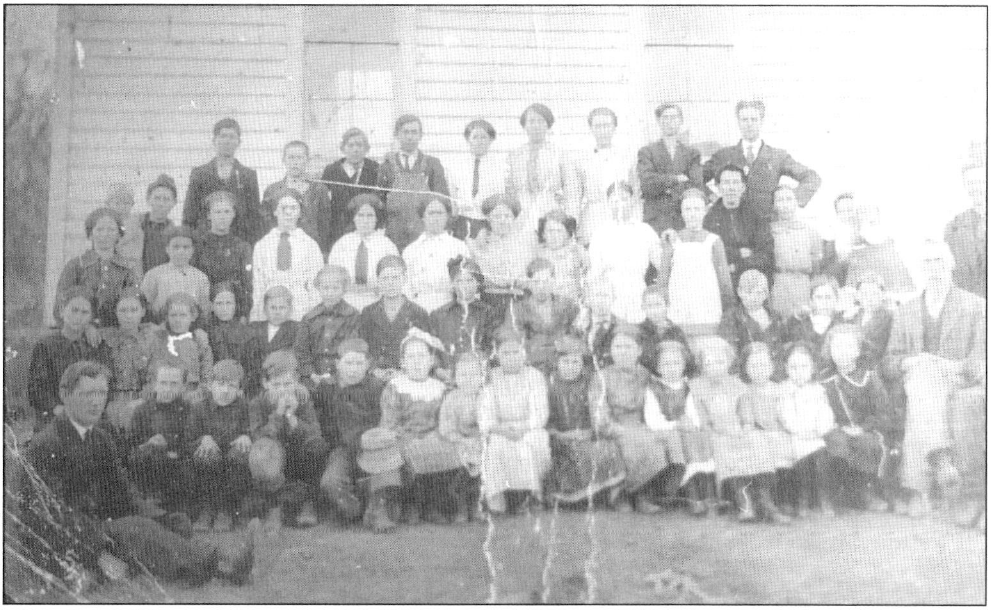

Roaring Gap School Students, 1911. Teacher Ike Frost is seated at left. School committee members seated at right are Hezekiah Bartley, Louis Hice, and Creed Evans (standing). Pictured, from left to right, are the following: (first row) Oscar Goodson, Clyde Bartley, Isaac Johnson, Pate Hice, Dora Dickens, Alice Todd, Elmer Todd, Kate Brannock, Grace Murphy, Pearl Poole, Rhoda Poole, Vanessa Carson, and Ida Johnson; (second row) Esther Goodson, Bertha Hice, Pearl Doby, Bertha Goodson, Ambrose Dickens, Dora Thompson, Phinneas Evans, Emma Johnson, Claude Moncus, Faris Evans, Fred Murphy, Jarvie Goodson, Kyle Bartley, Mack Bartley, and Bina Doby; (third row) Lela Johnson, Betty Moncus, Minnie Dickens, Elsie Bartley, Callie Goodson, May Johnson, Ethel Ramey, Ina Doby, Mattie Bartley, Sadie Poole, Caroline Brannock Ramey, Betty Bartley, Minnie Ann Murphy, and Vera Murphy; (fourth row) Julson Doby (18 months old) in the arms of his mother, Lucinda Brannock Doby, Roby Johnson, Guy Murphy, George Bartley, Isom Bartley, Mattie Doby, Blanche Bartley Ramey, Bessie Bartley Ramey, Guy Bartley, and Charlie Hodge. (Courtesy of Stella Carrico.)

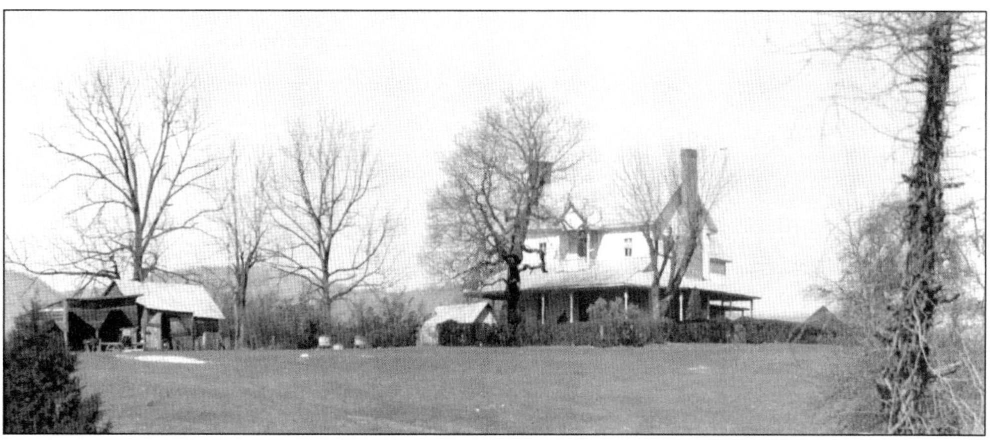

Jesse Franklin Home at Lowgap. This house belonging to Jesse Franklin, governor of North Carolina in 1820 and 1821, was demolished in 1968. A graveyard was located just beyond the building on the left. (Courtesy of Ruth Minick.)

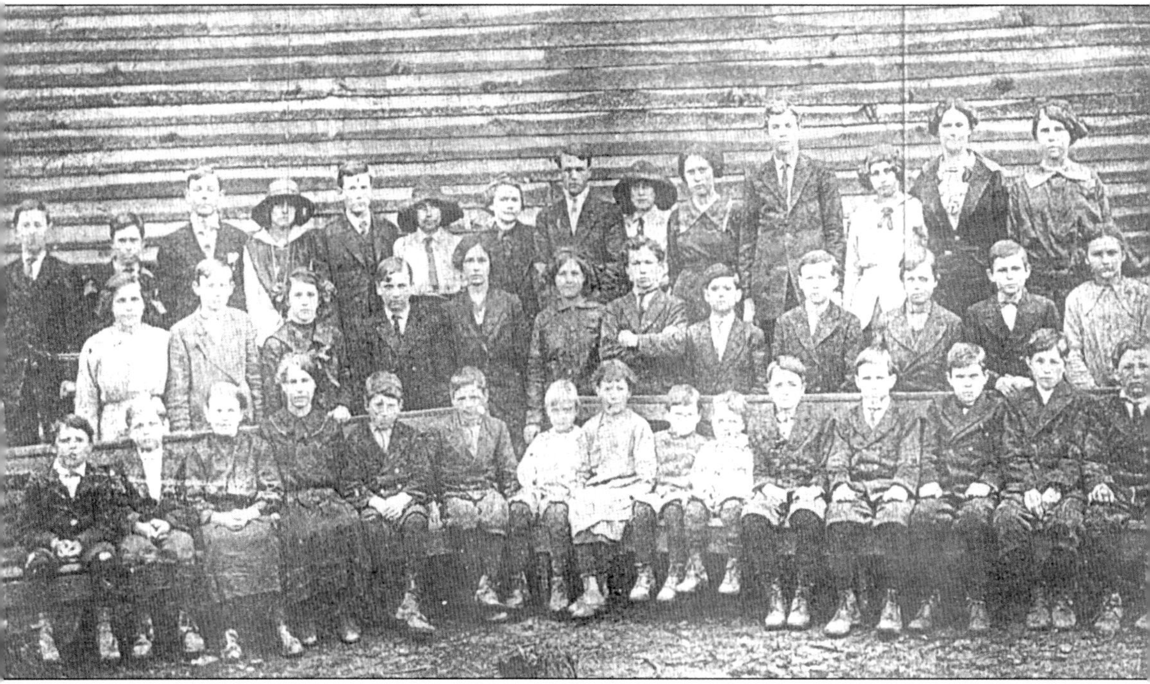

LOWGAP SCHOOL STUDENTS, 1914. Pictured, from left to right, are the following: (first row) Farmer Lowe, Banks Todd, Imer (Beamer) Thompson, Ida (Ramey) Sexton, Odie Ramey, Kemp Ramey, Glenn Doyle, Ann (Ramey) Adams, Curtis Gentry, Howard Doyle, Tinsley Galyean, Lynwood Gentry, Garner Ramey, Brady Simcox, and Mack Todd; (second row) Nannie (Johnson) Bartley, Cosby Davis, Lizzie (Gentry) Lowe, Duncan Lowe (teacher), Ethel (Lowe) Cockerham, Ennice (Todd) Goodson, Beeker Lowe, Willie Carico, Dixie Lowe, Dixie Ramey, Boyd Ramey, and Hallie (Carson) Winesett; (third row) Sherman Beamer, Lonnie Johnson, Dexter Davis, Elizabeth (Woodruff) Cross, Verlin Gentry, Gusta (Todd) Bartley, Mrs. Sarah (Cox) Lowe (teacher's mother), Porter Lowe, Thelma (Woodruff) Lowe, Lela Cockerham, Schylar Ramey, Inez (Todd) Lowe, Margie (Dickens) Hodges, and Arvenia (Lowe) Sutherland. (Courtesy of Diane Niston.)

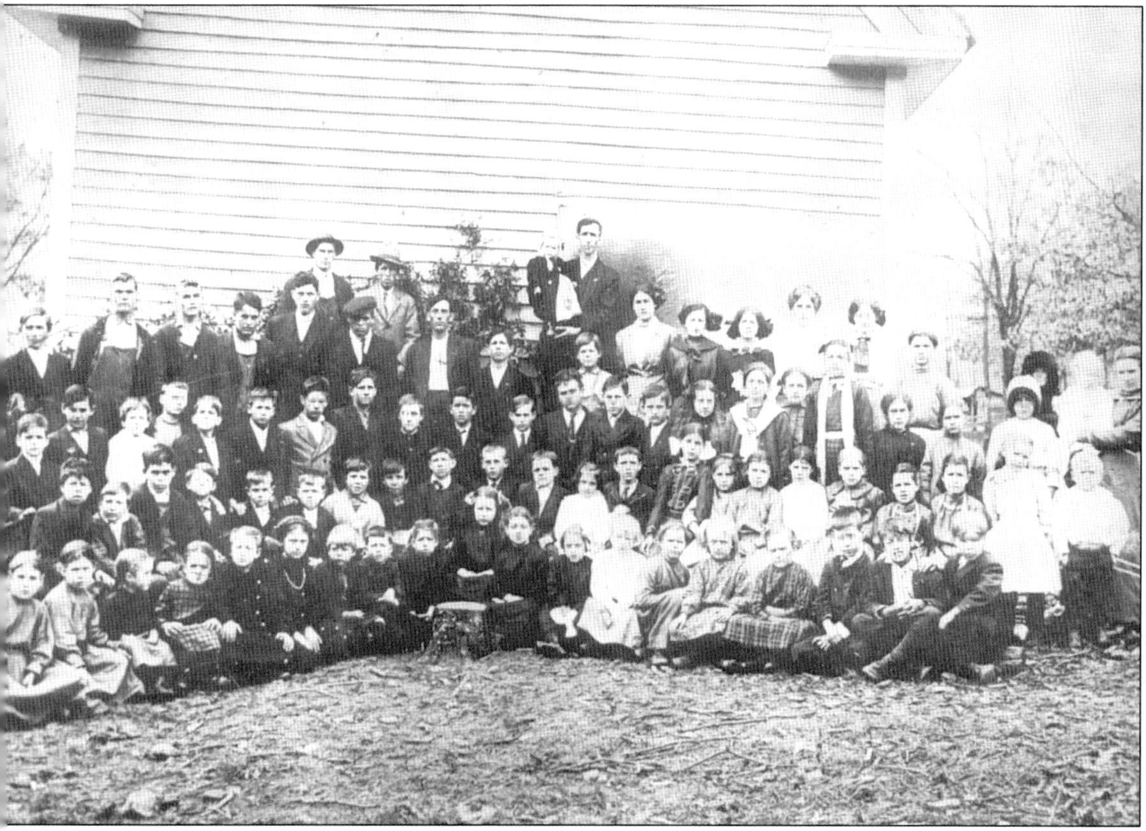

Oak Grove School Class, c. 1914. Oak Grove School was in the Roaring Gap community in Lowgap. Pictured, from left to right, are the following: (first row) Ima Crouse, Lola Ramey, Thelma Lowe, Linnie Lowe, Mamie Galyean, Texa Wilson, Bertie Richardson, Boyd Dickens, Margie Richardson, Minnie Galyean, Edna Bedsaul, Pearl Bedsaul, Ila Taylor, Emma Norman, Nella Galyean, Bertha Lowe, Skyler Dickens, Oscar Ramey, and Levi Richardson; (second row) Kilen Richardson, Letcher Brown, Fred Lowe, Luther Galyean, Coy Kirby, Roy Kirby, Mack Crouse, Isom Richardson, Porter Dickens, Kemper Lowe, Carmon Lowe, Vera Lowe, Theodore Lowe, Attice Dickens, Ollie Brown, Mattie Ramey, Zora Richardson, Gracie Smith, Levina Lowe, and Crissie Lowe; (third row) Felton Creed, Jay Simmons, Paul Taylor, Guy Norman, Brady Smith, Ivers Galyean, Greely Dickens, Johnnie Richardson, Ivan Payne, Marvin Galyean, Raleigh Creed, Harvey Lowe, Eather Galyean, Sterling Lowe, Mared Galyean, Laura Lowe, Lola Lowe, Linnie Lowe Holderfield, Ada Norman, Eva Richardson, Jane Lowe (in background), Launa Lowe, and Ida Lowe; (fourth row) Sanders Lowe, Ike Norman, Clemmons Norman, Audy Lowe, Kester Lowe, Claud Lowe, Bascom Lowe, Corby Lowe, Oscar Donathan, Essie Simmons, Ona Galyean, Lorena Galyean, Lottie Lowe, Ophelia Kirby, and Tilda Norman; (fifth row) Elmer Lowe, Kelly Lowe (teacher), Gene Schuyler, and daughter Helen. (Courtesy of Avis Schuyler.)

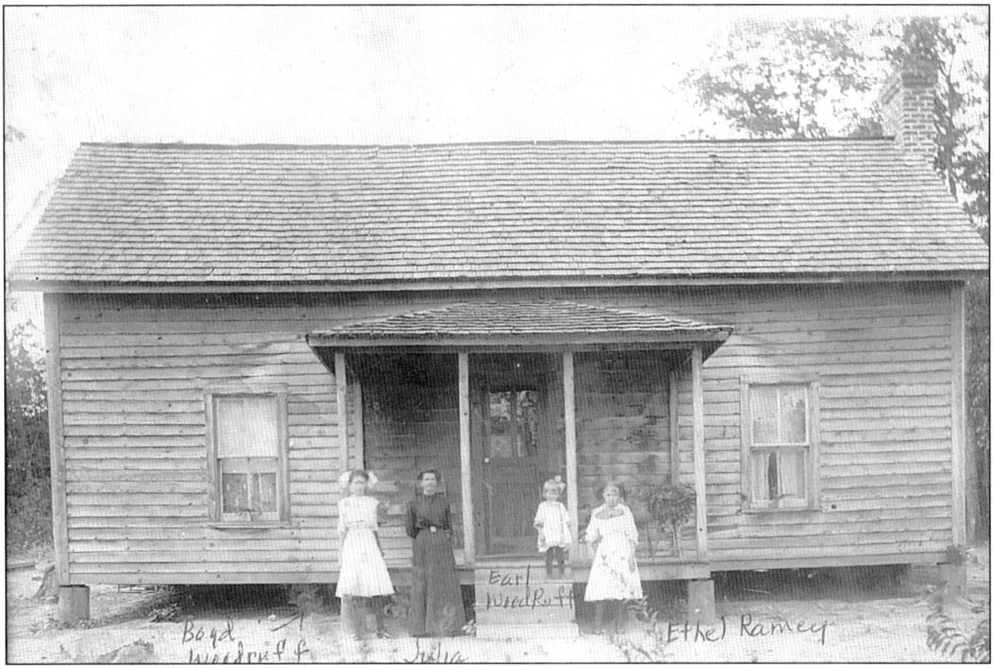

WOODRUFF HOME. From left to right are Boyd Woodruff, Julia Woodruff, Earl Woodruff, and Ethel Ramey. Julia Woodruff's home (before it burned) was located on the site where Stella R. Carrico's house now stands. (Courtesy of Stella Carrico.)

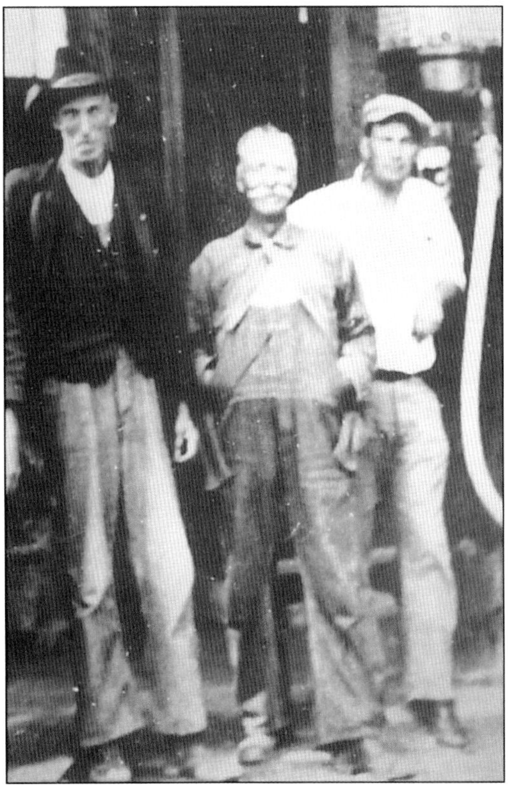

GUY DICKEN'S STORE. Pictured, from left to right, in front of the store are Charlie Jarrell (1874–1943), Bennett Sanders Lowe (1872–1956), and Frazier Golding (1906–1955). (Courtesy of Teresa Smith.)

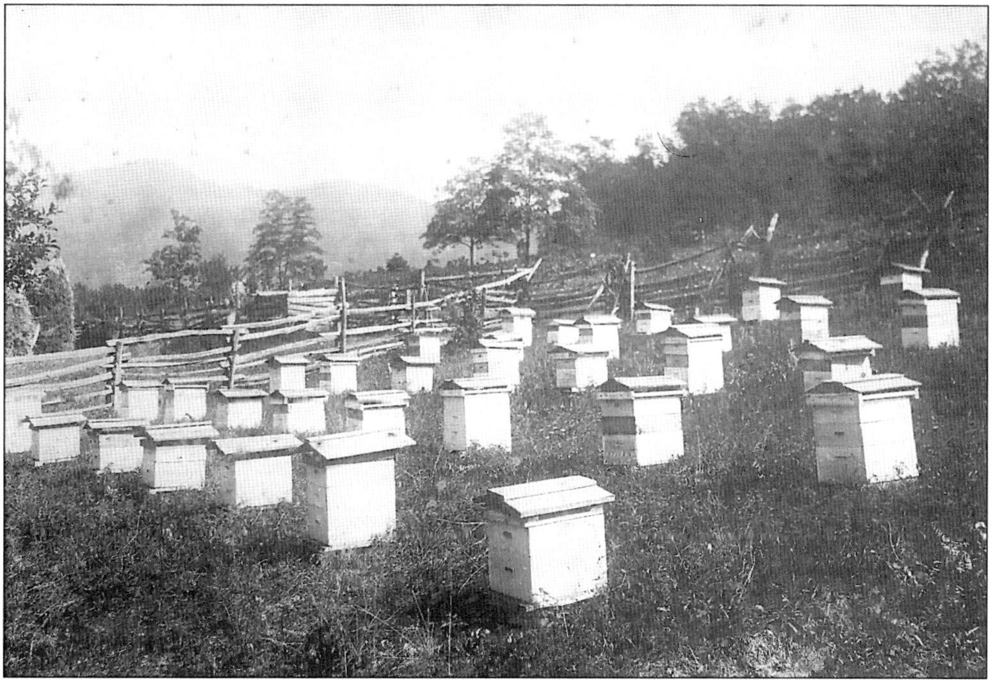

Beehives on the Property of Layfette Galyean. Sourwood honey is the most popular honey that beekeepers hope to harvest. The mountains of Surry County are a good location to find sourwood. (Courtesy of Avis Schuyler.)

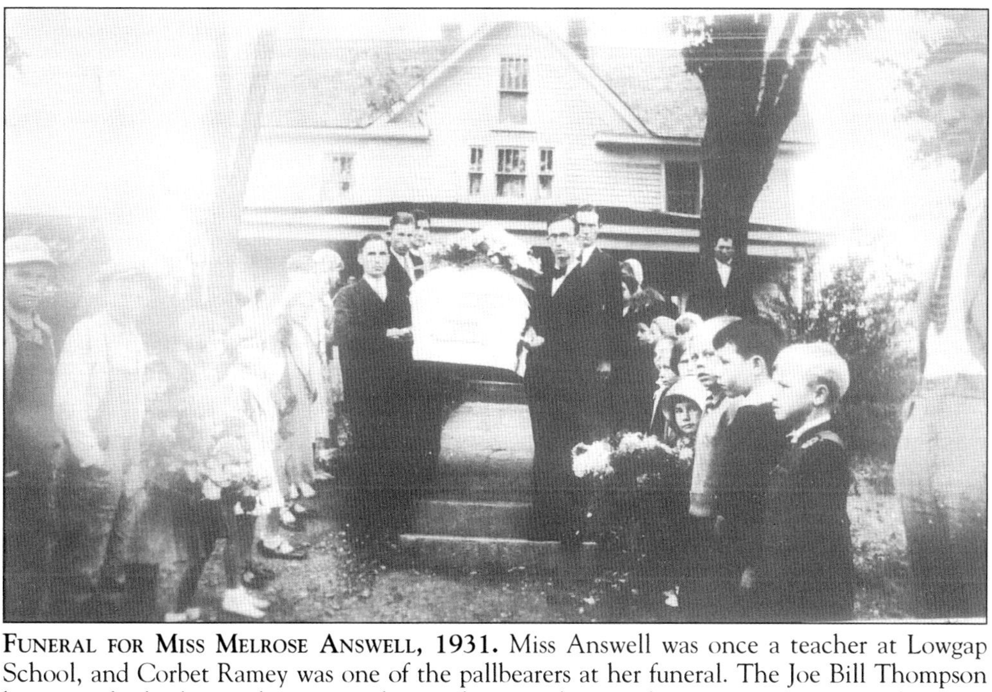

Funeral for Miss Melrose Answell, 1931. Miss Answell was once a teacher at Lowgap School, and Corbet Ramey was one of the pallbearers at her funeral. The Joe Bill Thompson house in the background was a residence where teachers in the Lowgap community boarded. (Courtesy of Avis Schuyler.)

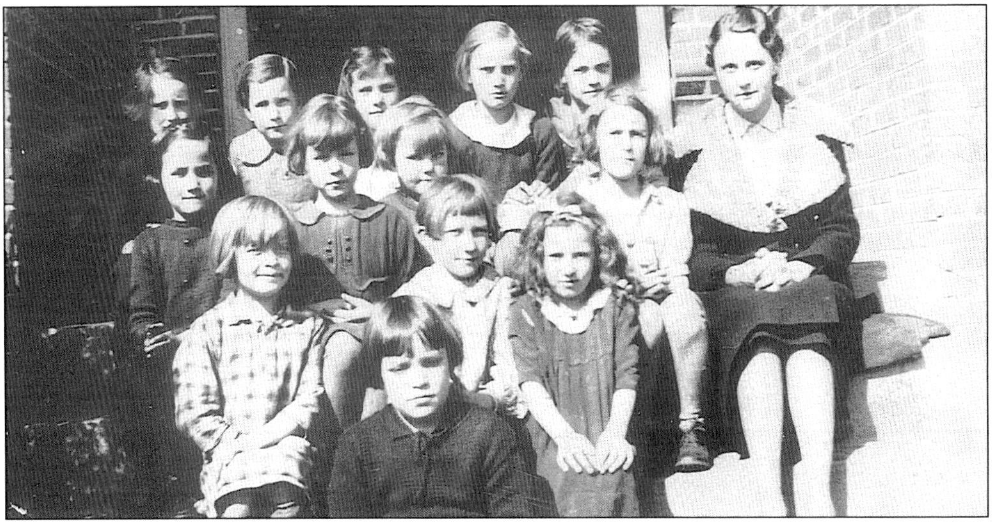

Lowgap Elementary School, c. 1935. The members of this second grade class are pictured, from left to right, as follows: (first row) Ruby Dell Lowe; (second row) Vera Norman, Polly Worrell, and Jackie Golding; (third row) Peggy Lowe, Edith Mayes, Ruby Hawks, Eula Mae Galyean, and Nell Armfield Folger (teacher); (fourth row) Sybil Nichols, Dorothy Joyce, Foy Lee Hodges, Pearl Norman, and Lou Ella Lowe. (Courtesy of Diane Niston.)

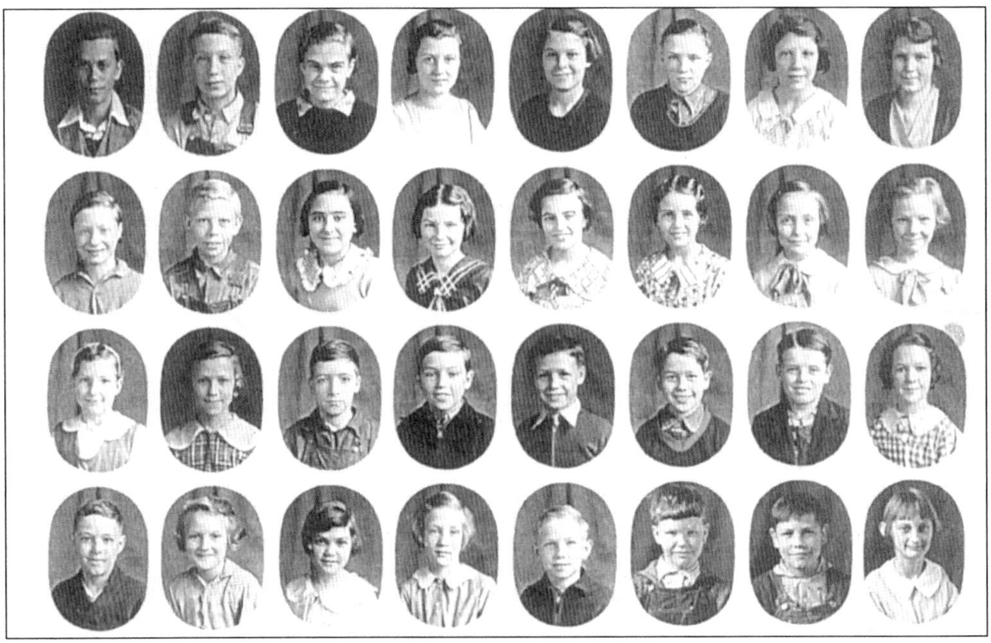

Fourth Grade Class at Lowgap School, 1935. Pictured, from left to right, are the following: (first row) Kenny Roberts, Lillian Thompson, Sena Norman, Eva Mayes, Edgar Mayes, Eldean Hodges, Jesse Harrold, and Elizabeth Bartley; (second row) Ethel Callaway, Retha Brannock, Bill Joyce, Ralph Thompson, Bob Lowe, Basil Stewart, Ford Rudy Ramey, and Alma Ward; (third row) Doris Johnson, Elbert Ford Ramey, Helen Sexton, Ida Lee Ramey, Nadine Creed, May Nell Lowe, Johnsie Hayes, and Nina Rose Wagoner; (fourth row) Elmer Brannock, Alan Johnson, Cena Lowe, Allie Galyean, Mildred Galyean, Elvin Golding, Blanche Lowe, and Ruby Hodges. (Courtesy of Ethel Smith.)

Six

Mount Airy Township

The Mount Airy Township is located in the northeastern part of Surry County and is bordered on the north by Patrick and Carroll Counties in Virginia. The Ararat River flows through the township, as well as such creeks as Faulkner's, Johnson's, Lovill's, Osborns, Paul's, Renfro, Rocky, Seed Cane, and Stewart's.

Mount Airy and the vicinity were first called "The Hollows" by earlier settlers and mapmakers because of its location in hollows between ridges on the east, Pilot Mountain on the south, and the Blue Ridge on the north and west. The town of Mount Airy was thought to have been named "Mount Airy" after an early plantation. However, a 1749 map by Jefferson-Frye states that an early landowner named "Mount" was in the region of Buck Shoals, south of the city limits.

The Moravians began to preach in "The Hollows" as early as 1764. One of the early churches was Stuart's Creek Primitive Baptist Church, which was first known as Forkner's Church when it was established c. 1794. The church was also referred to as "Old Hollow."

In 1877, the first shovel of dirt was turned to bring the railroad into Mount Airy, and 11 years later in 1888, the train rolled into the station at Mount Airy. Also located in the township are the communities of Bannertown, Flat Rock, Salem, Sheltontown, Slate Mountain, Sulphur Springs, Toast, and White Plains. Flat Rock is the site of the world's largest open-faced granite quarry. Some early schools in the area include Salem, McBride, Greenhill, Franklin, Key, and Nichols.

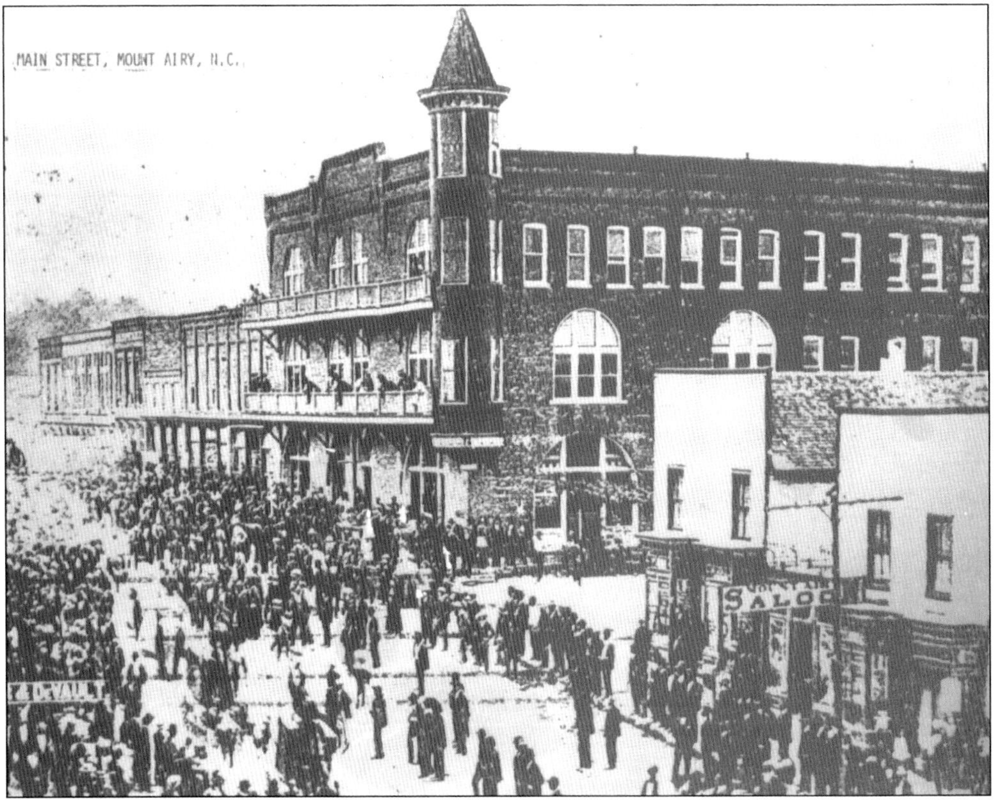

BLUE RIDGE HOTEL, C. 1895. Blue Ridge Hotel (1892–1965) was located on Main Street in Mount Airy. Pictured here is Main Street in a view looking south. The streets were full of people waiting for the circus that was coming to town. (Courtesy of Ruth Minick.)

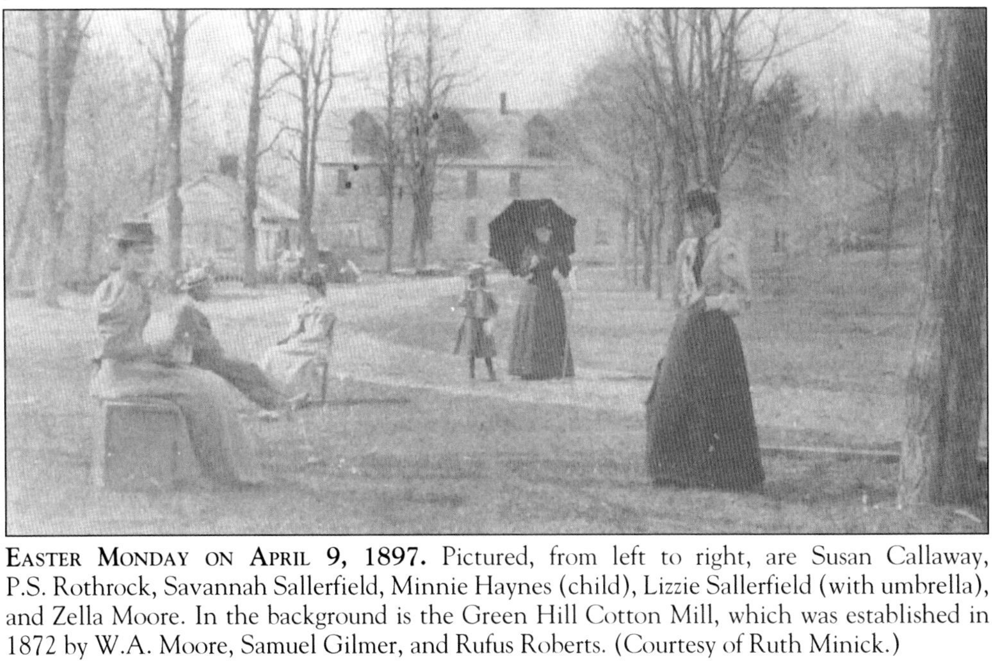

EASTER MONDAY ON APRIL 9, 1897. Pictured, from left to right, are Susan Callaway, P.S. Rothrock, Savannah Sallerfield, Minnie Haynes (child), Lizzie Sallerfield (with umbrella), and Zella Moore. In the background is the Green Hill Cotton Mill, which was established in 1872 by W.A. Moore, Samuel Gilmer, and Rufus Roberts. (Courtesy of Ruth Minick.)

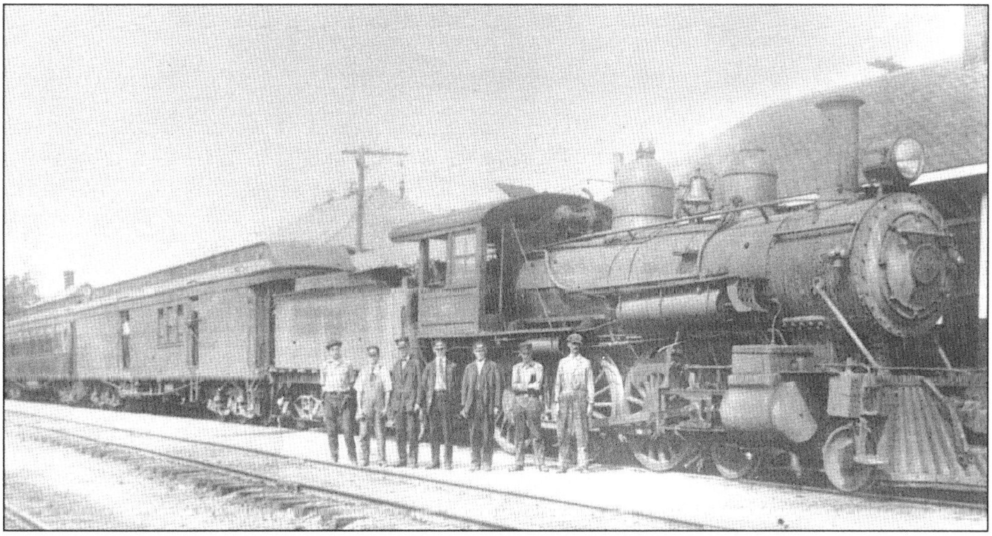

Atlantic & Yadkin Passenger Train, 1900. In 1877, a railroad to link the Blue Ridge Mountains to Wilmington, North Carolina, was planned and would be called the Cape Fear & Yadkin Valley Railroad. Eleven years after the first shovel of dirt was turned, the train arrived in Mount Airy on May 28, 1888. It took 12 hours for the train to travel from Fayetteville, North Carolina, on a trial run to Mount Airy. Pictured here, from left to right, are "Big Fox" (baggage master), unidentified (mail clerk), Hunk Folger (conductor), ? Stout (brakeman), unidentified, Johnny Martin (fireman), and Jim Tensel (engineer). (Courtesy of Carl Talley and Ruth Minick.)

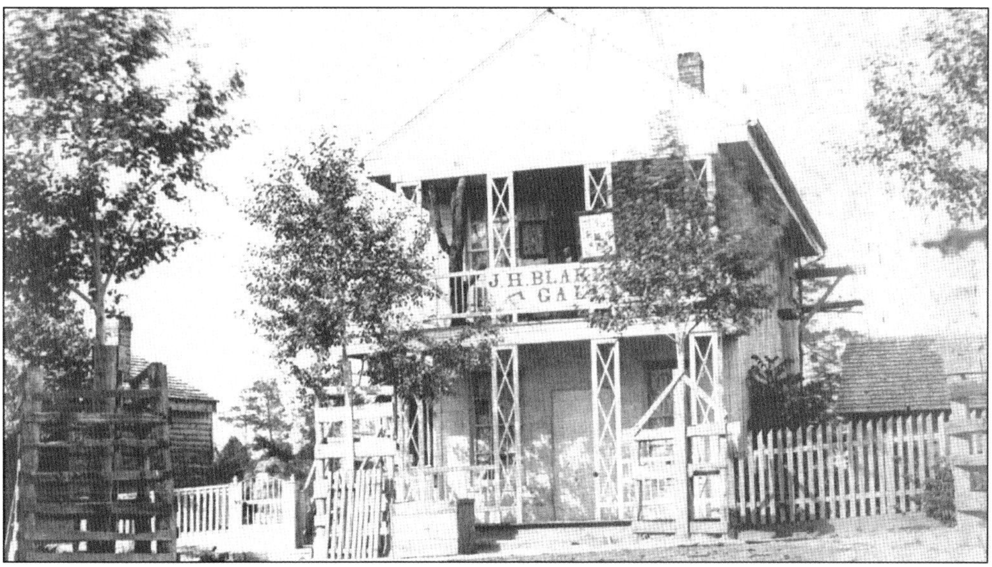

J.H. Blakemore's Photograph Gallery in Mount Airy. J.H. Blakemore was a well-known photographer in Mount Airy whose photographs have been recognized throughout the area since the Civil War. His most notable was an image of the famous Siamese Twins. In the 1890s, comments were made about him taking flashlight photographs. In other words, he was going to make pictures in the night as well as in the day. Blakemore was also a member of a local cornet band and orchestra. His gallery was located on Main Street near the opera house on the south side where the old Belk building was located. (Courtesy of Ruth Minick.)

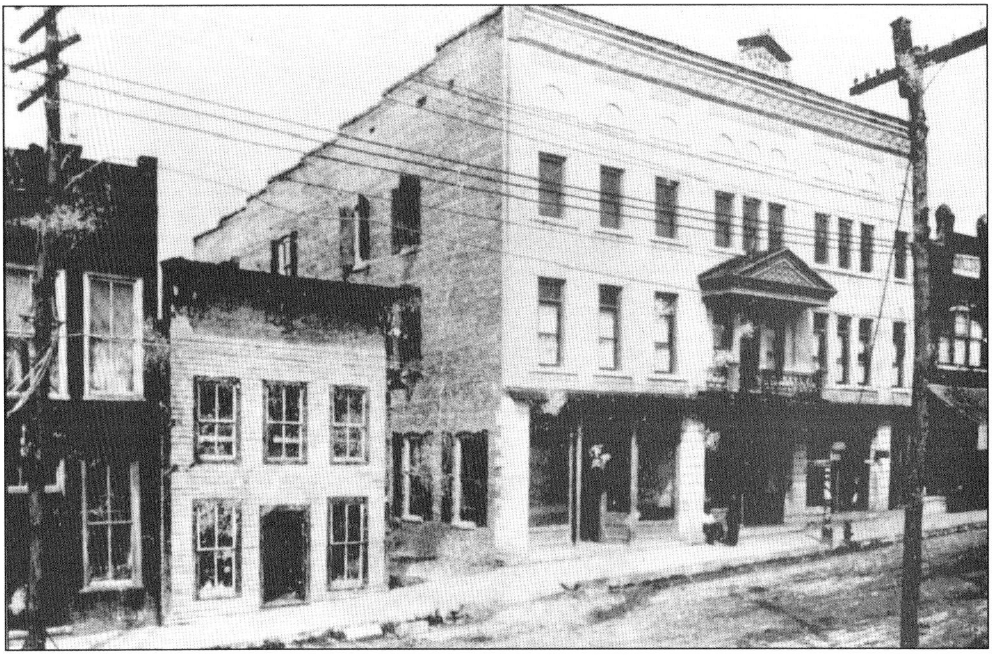

Banner Building, c. 1904. This photograph was taken looking west on Main Street in Mount Airy. During 1913–1914, the Commercial Club and the Chamber of Commerce were located on the second floor of the Banner Building, and the third floor held the Masonic Hall, Junior Order Hall, and the Mystic Circle Hall. The building was located several doors away from the present-day Snappy Lunch, a popular restaurant. (Courtesy of Ruth Minick.)

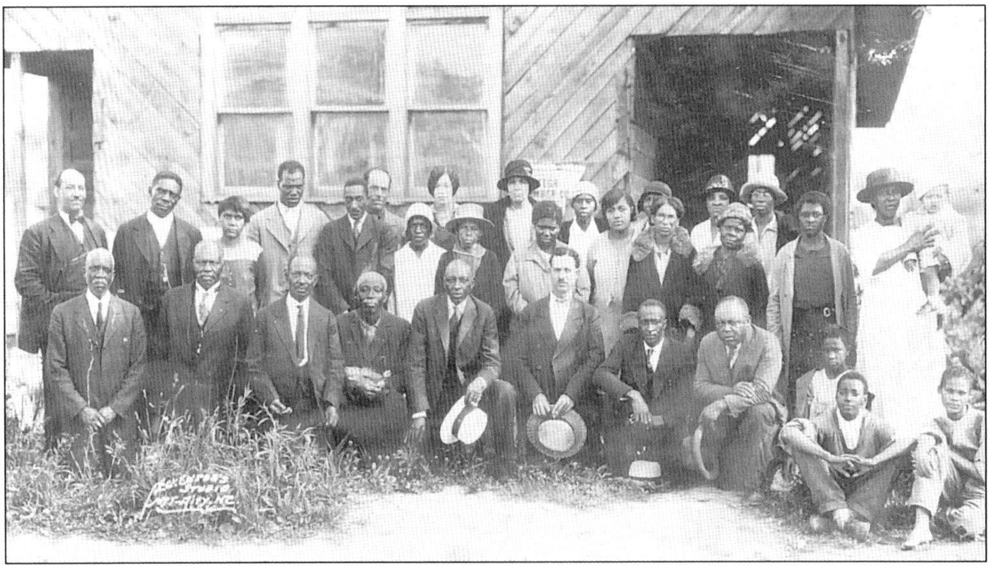

Zion Baptist Church on Old Virginia Street in Mount Airy. Members of the congregation pose with their guests. Some of those seen here are Sonny Leonard, Charlie Valentine, J.R. Mathis, Will Tucker, Miss Nell Hughes, Josh Hubbard, Mrs. Ellen Hines, Miss Mozell Mathis, Mrs. Lillie Bunker, Mrs. Mary Cockerham, Mrs. Sarah Leonard holding Sonny Tucker, Christina Farrell, Mrs. Farrell, Martha Conrad, and Mrs. Nora Glover. (Courtesy of Ruth Minick.)

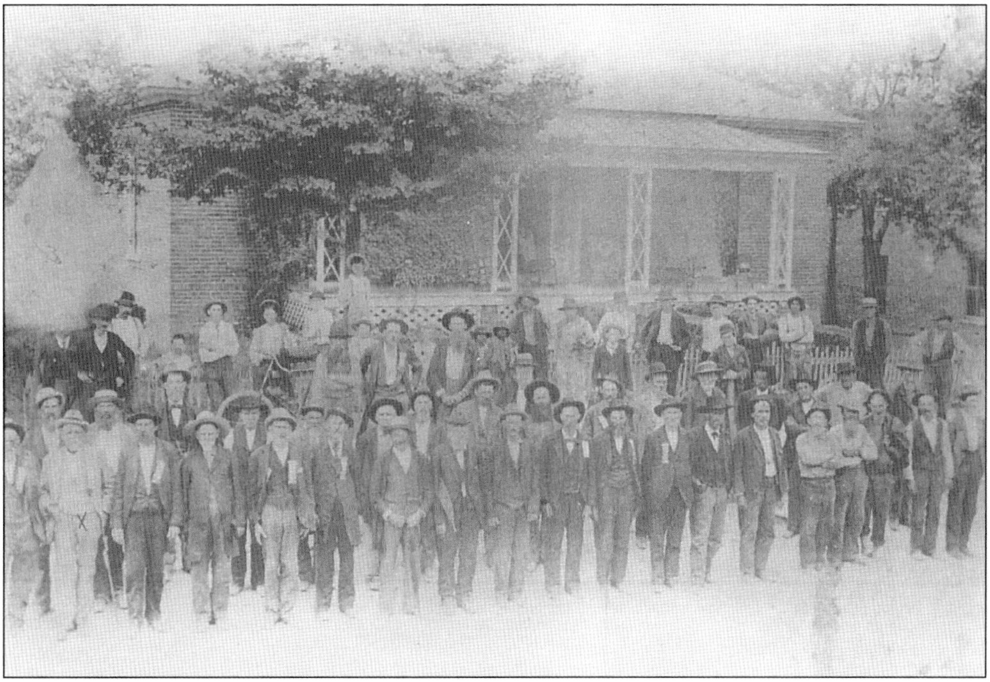

Confederate Reunion in Mount Airy. The Jesse Moore house (in the background) was built in 1867 and stood until 1919 in the center of town on Main Street, just north of Lamm Drug Store on the same side of the street. (Courtesy of Ruth Minick.)

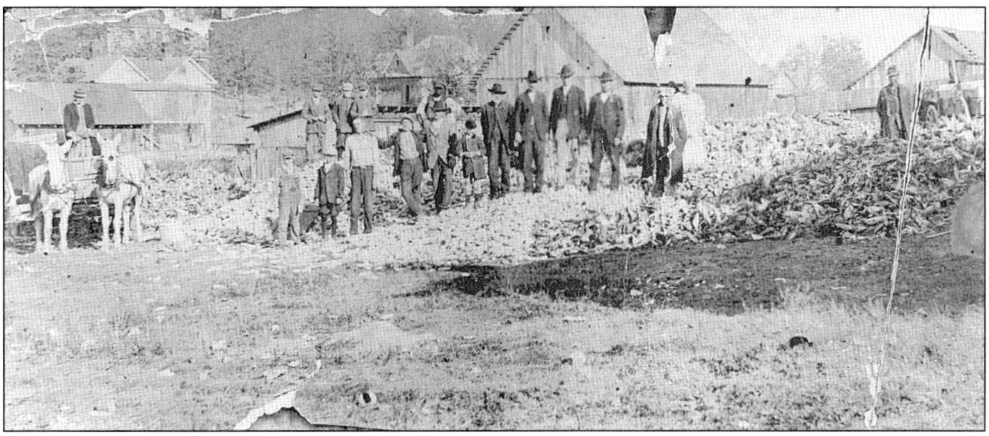

Charlie Webb's Corn Harvest, c. 1917. Charlie Webb rented a farmhouse on Orchard Street in Mount Airy and moved there from Cana, Virginia, along with his brother Enoch after 1912. Their father, Anderson Alexander Webb, still lived at Cana but came down to help harvest the corn. Corn was planted in the bottomland on the Ararat River two blocks east of the Mount Airy Post Office. At harvest time, the corn was brought through town on short wagons to Charlie's house. Enoch Webb is in the wagon, and the two tallest men dressed in black in the center are Anderson Webb and Charlie Webb. (Courtesy of Mary Columbine.)

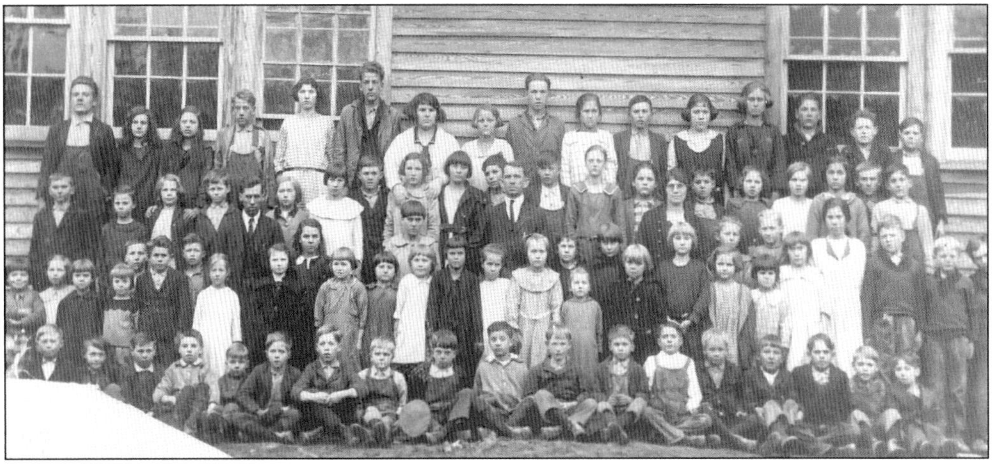

Sheltontown Elementary School Students, c. 1922. Pictured, from left to right, are the following: (first row) unidentified, Lester Love, Robert Hall, Archie Kirkman, Grady Kirkman, Hersie Love, Earl Watson, Dennis Hiatt, Carlis Kirkman, Carlis Scott, Hasten Kirkman, Romney Noah, Tobe Kirkman, Treva Kirkman, Dewey Inman, Joe Durham, Vester Inman, Garney Love, and Hersey Kirkman; (second row) Annie Hiatt, Lizzie Bennett, unidentified, Clemmie Kirkman, Roy Kirkman, unidentified, Wilford Lawrence, Erma Inman, Lillie Mae Taylor, Ola Forest, Elsie McMillion, Louisa Durham, ? Durham, unidentified, ? Stevens, Ella Kirkman, Gladys Inman, Florence Hall, Alverta Chaney, unidentified, Versie Shelton, ? Adkins, Beatrice Coe, Viola Hall, Della Kirkman, Elva Kirkman, Ellen Hiatt, May Stevens, Elsie Kirkman, George Lewis, unidentified, and unidentified; (third row) J. Van Collins, Kathie Kirkman, Jessie Snoddy, Vance Watson, Alvis Love (teacher), Annie Mae Kirkman, Lemora Noah, Harvey Johnson, Geneva Samuels, Ellie Stevens, James C. Hiatt, Willie Blair (teacher), Grady Adkins, Eva Noah, Stella Hiatt, Alma Wall (teacher), Vestal Hiatt, Jeanetta Lawrence, Thelma Kirkman, Bessie Adkins, Coy Kirkman, and Dink Kirkman; (fourth row) Walter Adkins, Ethel Jessup, Delphia Lawrence, Herbert Snoddy, Zelphia Kirkman, Marvin Snoddy, Etta Hiatt, Lettie Kirkman, Jim Johnson, Mary Lee Durham, Orby Kirkman, Pearl Hiatt, Bessie Love, Carter Shelton, Roscoe Inman, and Cecil Kirkman. (Courtesy of Don Hiatt and Wilma Hiatt.)

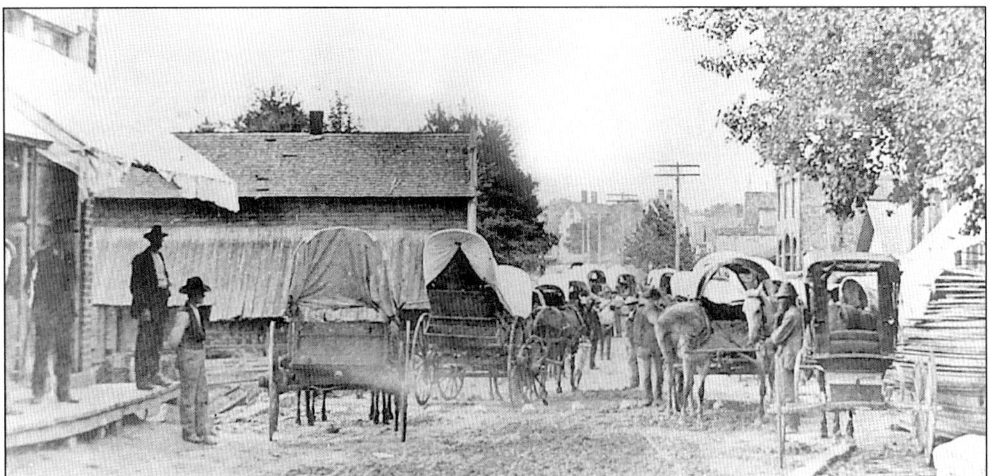

Mount Airy Looking North, Early 1900s. This photo was taken from just north of Oak Street in Mount Airy. Note the wooden walkways. (Courtesy of Ruth Minick.)

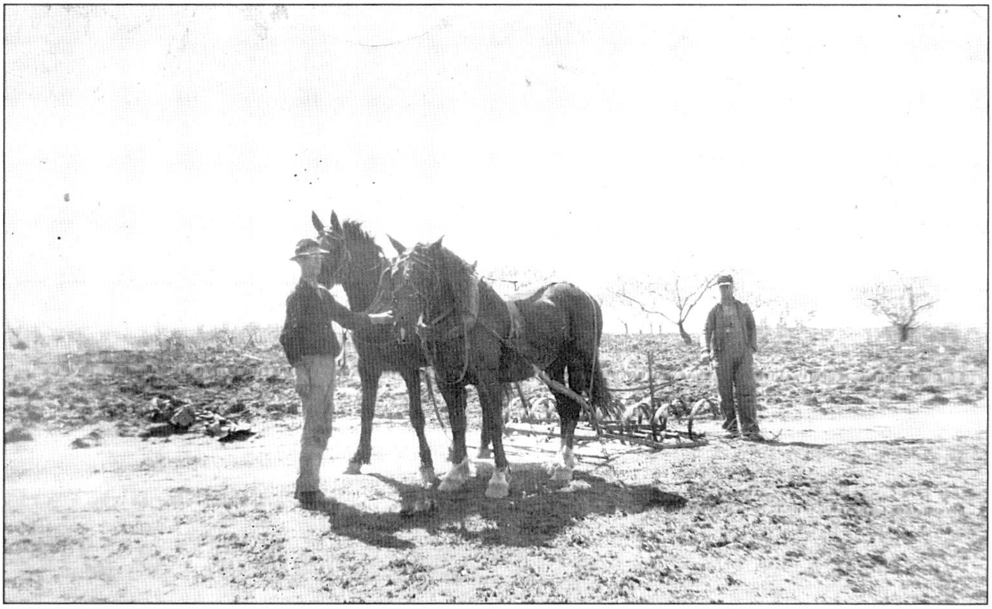

Ready for a Day's Work. R.S. Johnson appears to be talking to the horses while Leonard Draughn is behind the harrow ready for work in the White Plains community. (Courtesy of Robert Johnson.)

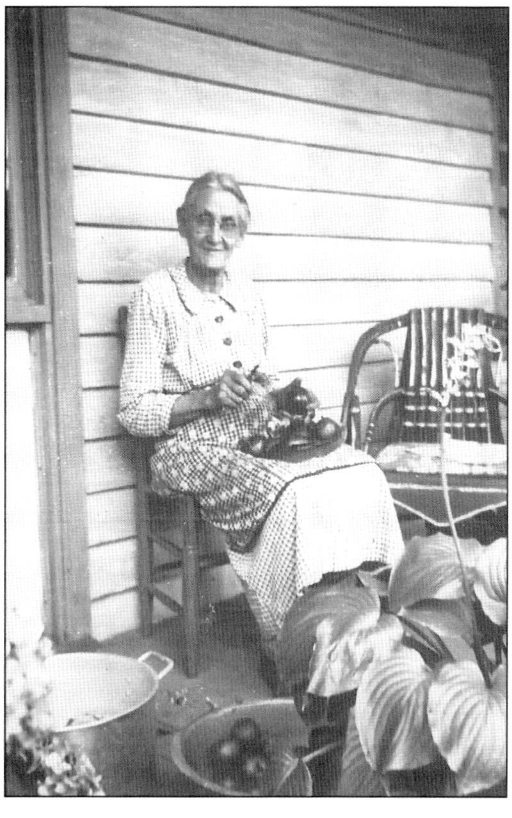

Paulina Combs Sumner Peeling Apples. Women sitting on their cane-bottomed chairs on the porch or under the shade trees while peeling apples was a familiar sight in rural Surry County. Paulina, the daughter of Saint Clair and Sarah Combs, died in 1947 at the age of 88. (Courtesy of Robert Johnson.)

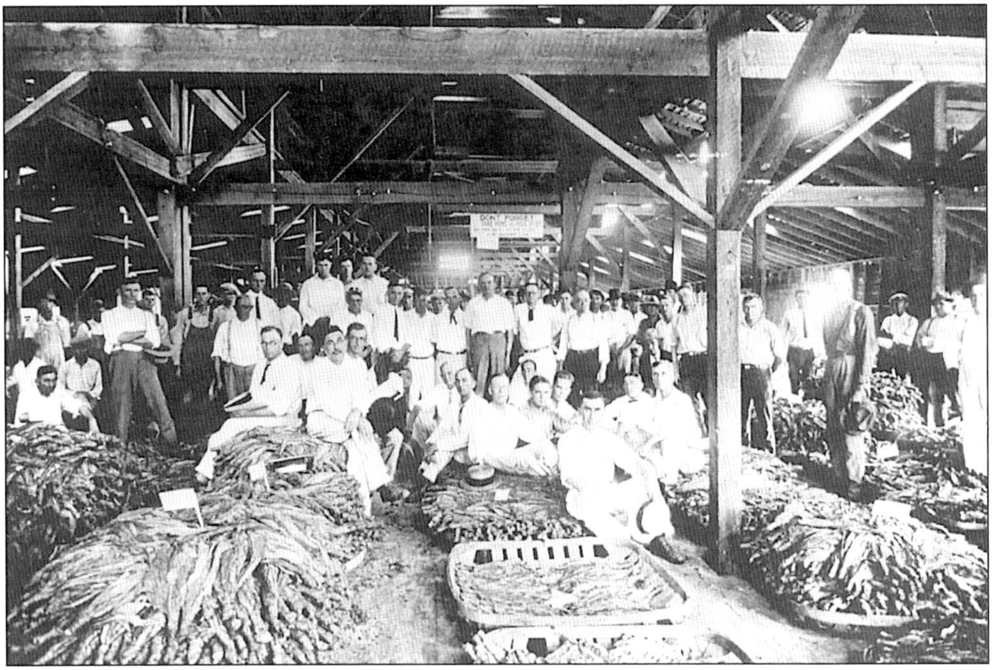

The Farmer's Union Warehouse. The Farmer's Union Warehouse was located on Franklin Street in Mount Airy on the site of the Masonic Temple. In the foreground is Girder Jarrell (holding hat), the president of the corporation and warehouse manager. On the left (sitting on a bale of tobacco) is his brother Alton Jarrell, holding books in his hand. Standing at the extreme right is Austen Snow and to his left is Frank Coalson (holding hat). (Courtesy of Wilma Hiatt.)

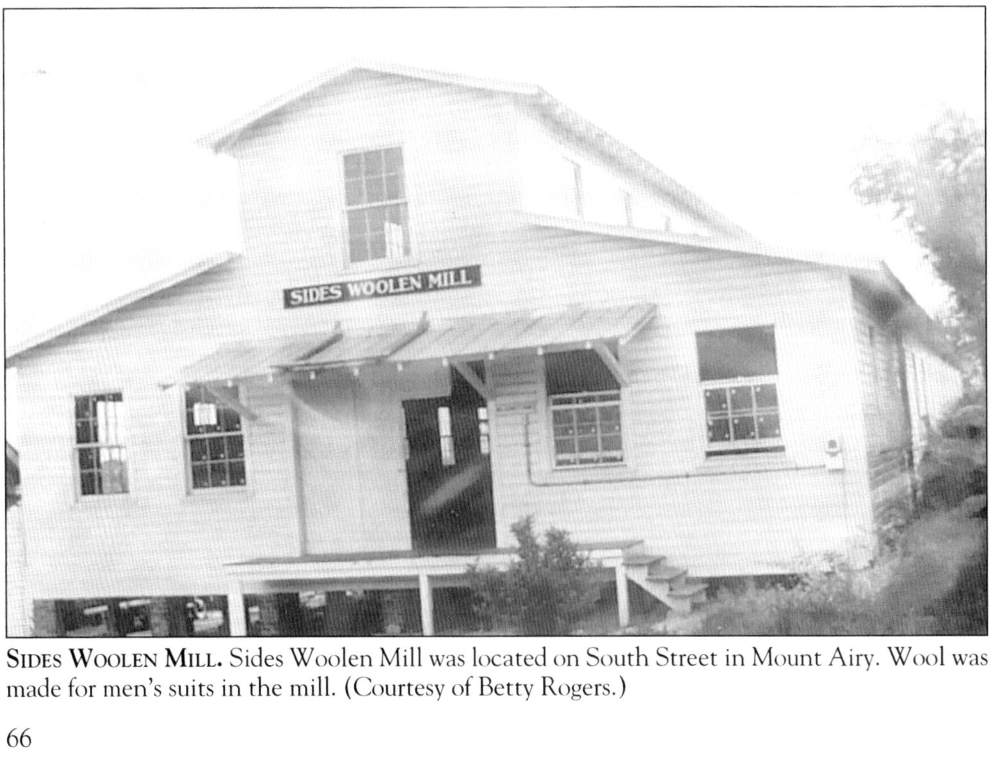

Sides Woolen Mill. Sides Woolen Mill was located on South Street in Mount Airy. Wool was made for men's suits in the mill. (Courtesy of Betty Rogers.)

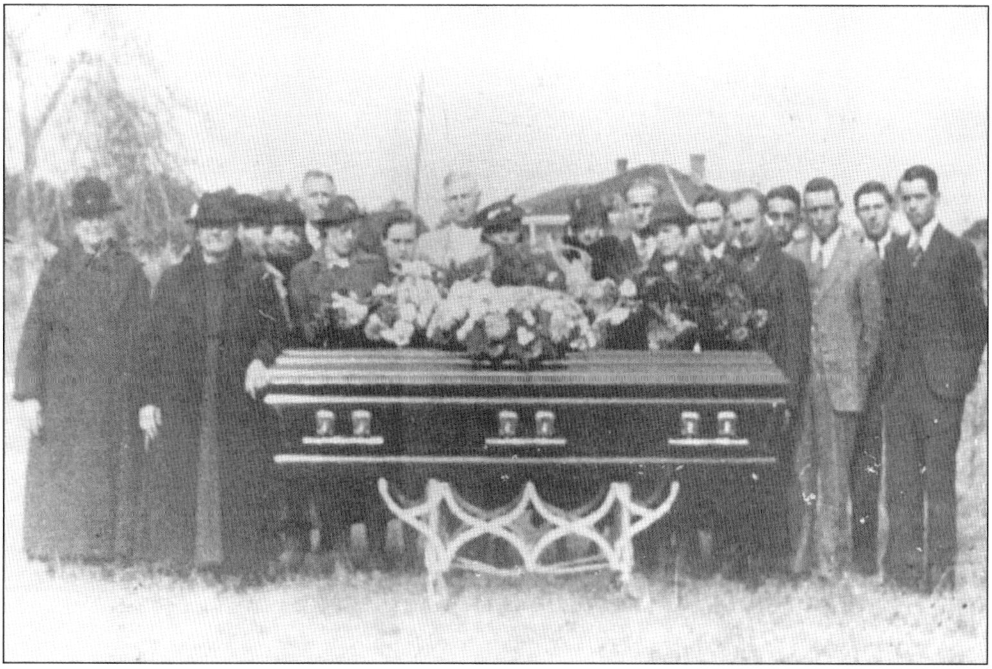

FUNERAL IN MOUNT AIRY, 1936. Talitha Katherine Cockerham Beamer's coffin is surrounded by her children and grandchildren. She lived with her husband, Henry Beamer, at the Henry Beamer place and raised 14 children. She was buried at the Beamer graveyard near Crossroads Baptist Church. (Courtesy of Mildred Beamer.)

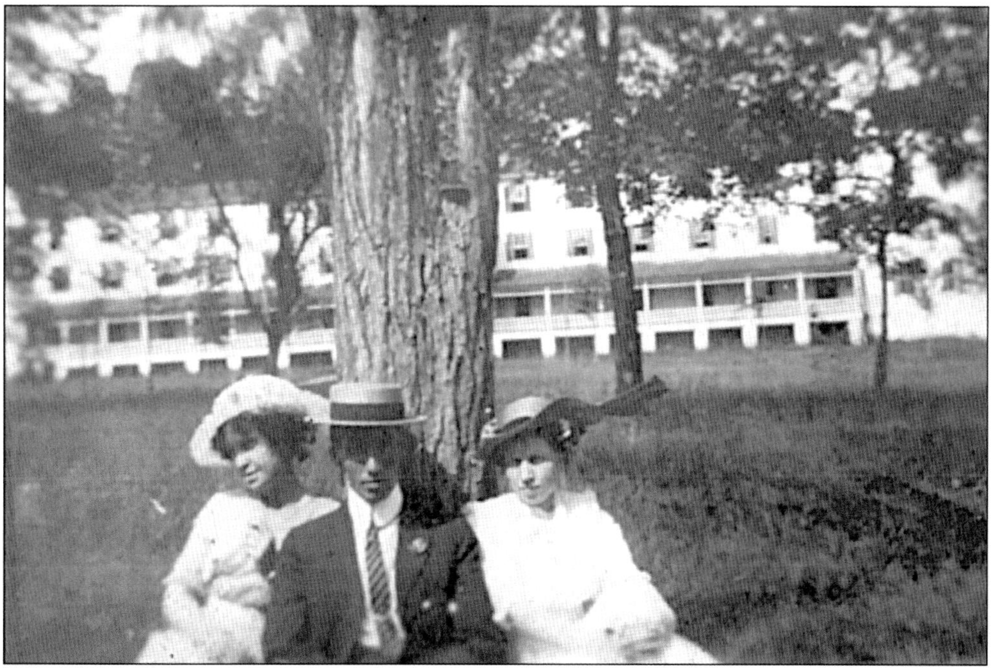

VISITORS AT THE WHITE SULPHUR SPRINGS HOTEL. Pictured, from left to right, are Isabel Saunders, R.S. (Bob) Johnson, and Margie Sumner relaxing on the lawn of the hotel. (Courtesy of Robert Johnson.)

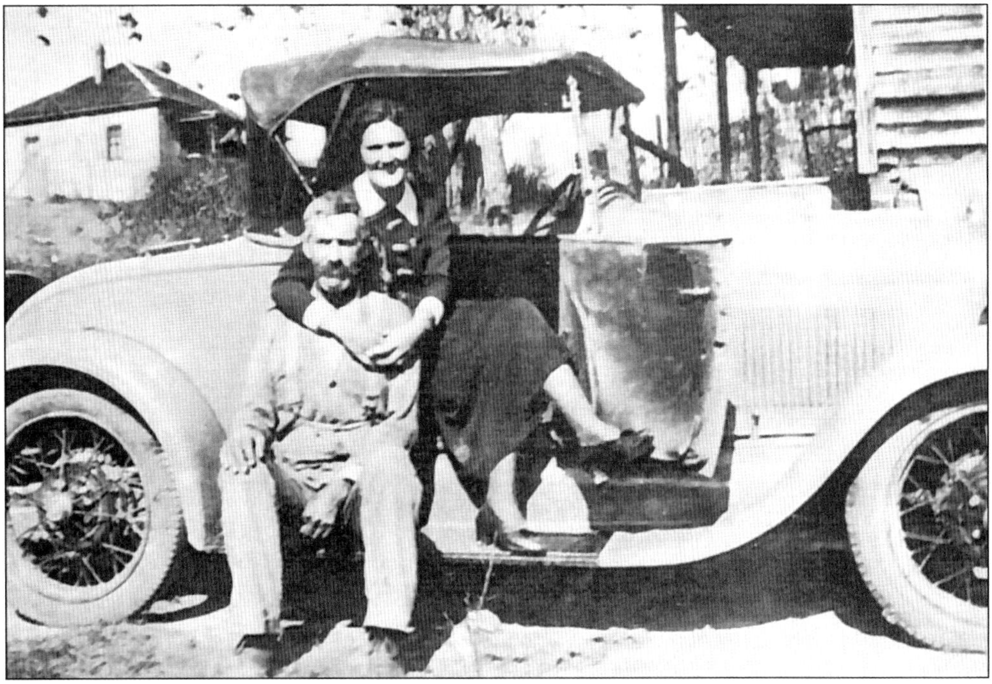

Father and Daughter. Alex Slate and daughter Margie Slate Beverly are pictured on Frank Street (off Riverside Drive) in Mount Airy in the 1930s. (Courtesy of Barbara Wilcox.)

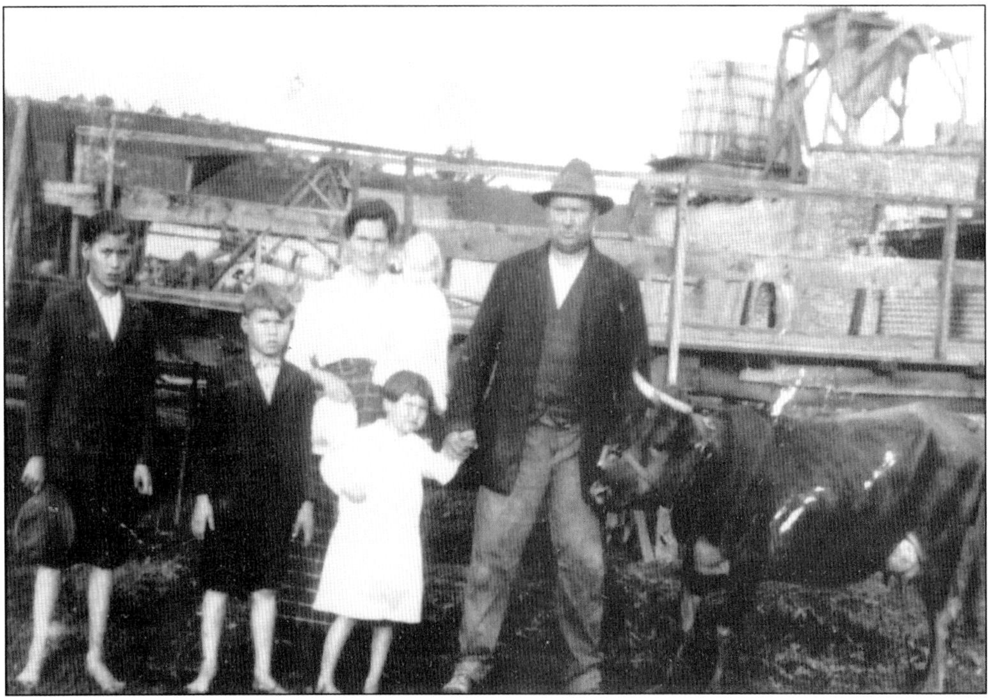

Trip to the Stockyard. Having just bought a cow at the stockyard, George King is seen here with his family: his wife, Etta Belle Combs King, and their children, from left to right, Paul, Bill, Ida Mae, and Albert (baby). (Courtesy of Barbara Wilcox.)

Seven

Pilot Township

Located on the east side of Surry County, Pilot Township is bordered on the north by South Westfield and Long Hill Townships, on the west by Eldora and Siloam Townships, on the south by Shoals Township, and on the east by Stokes County. The Ararat River forms the western boundary of the Pilot Township. The only town within the township is Pilot Mountain.

There has been a settlement along Tom's Creek, near Pilot Mountain, for well over 200 years, and records dating back to 1761 document the existence of early settlers. The hamlet had been called Hog Wallow, Tom's Creek, and Pilotville, before the name Pilot Mountain was adopted. The year 1888 brought the completion of the railroad, which ushered in a period of growth and prosperity in the community. The depot and Depot Street were the center of business and social life at that period in time.

The establishment of Trinity Academy, in 1892, a missionary effort of Trinity College (Duke University), drew even more families to town, and some of the newcomers established businesses while others bought land for farming. The town, which incorporated in 1889, bought the academy from Trinity College in 1900.

A number of businesses and homes were destroyed by fires in 1899 and 1919, but the town rebuilt and continued to prosper. About 1912, Job Hiatt, who ran a gristmill on Tom's Creek, began selling electric power to the citizens between the hours of 4 a.m. and 10 p.m. A whistle would sound early in the morning to indicate that power was on, and again in the evening to signal that it was off.

The area has experienced many changes over the past century, but excellent schools and a good standard of living continue to attract families to the community.

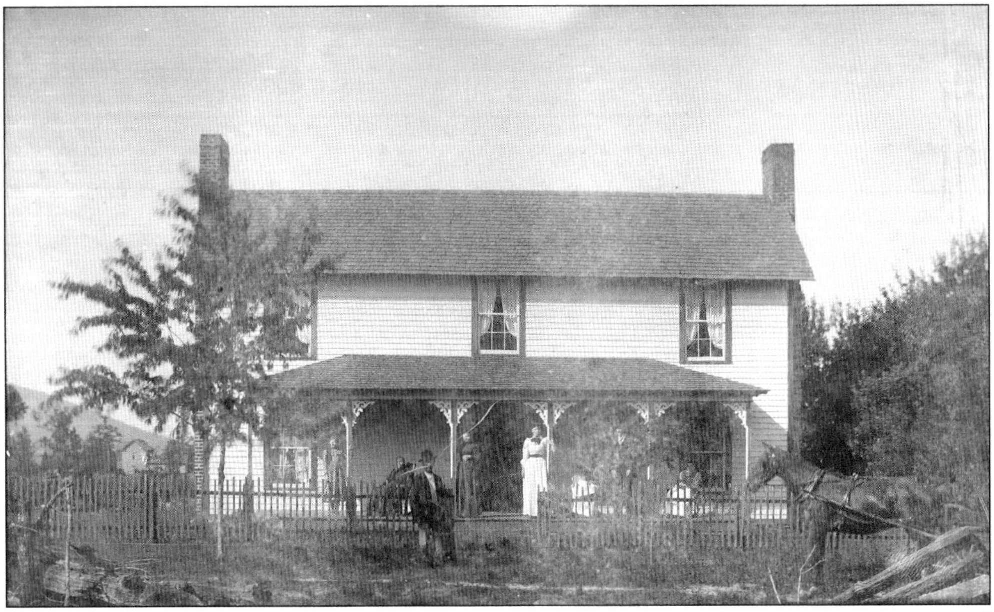

JOHN FRANCIS STEPHENS HOME ON WEST MAIN STREET IN PILOT MOUNTAIN, C. 1890. Pictured standing in front of the home is James Monroe Napier. This home was later renovated by Mrs. Lawson (Mattie) Trotter. (Courtesy of the Charles H. Stone Library Archives.)

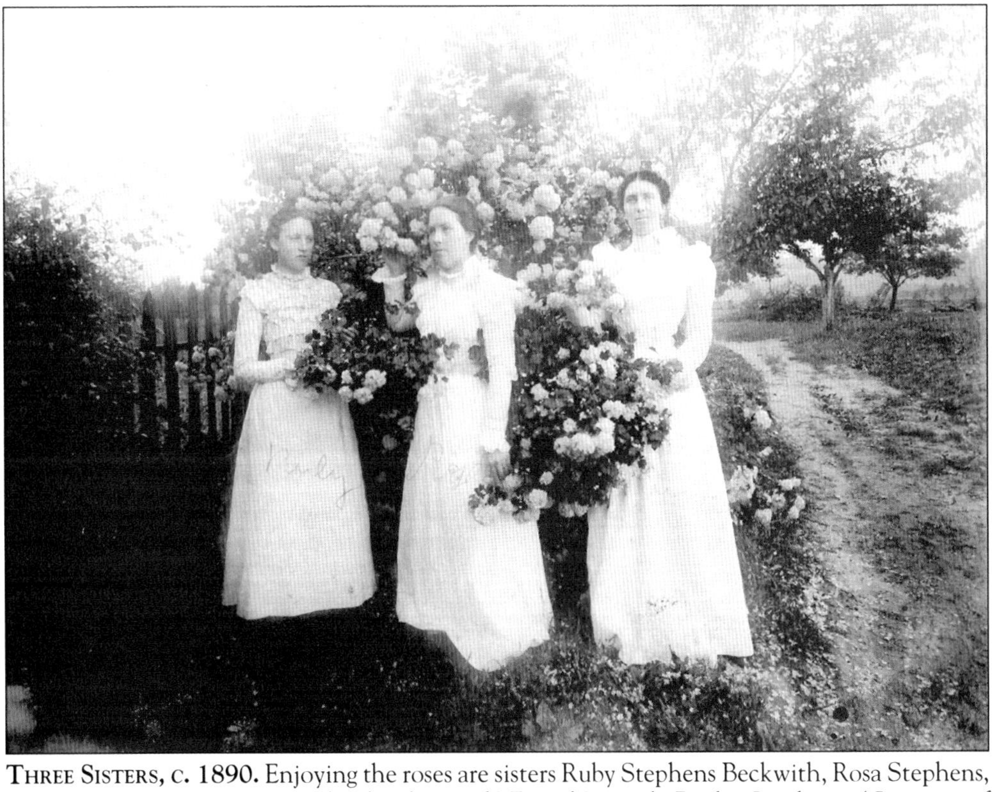

THREE SISTERS, C. 1890. Enjoying the roses are sisters Ruby Stephens Beckwith, Rosa Stephens, and Eunice Stephens Napier, the daughters of J.F. and Lucinda Boyles Stephens. (Courtesy of the Charles H. Stone Library Archives.)

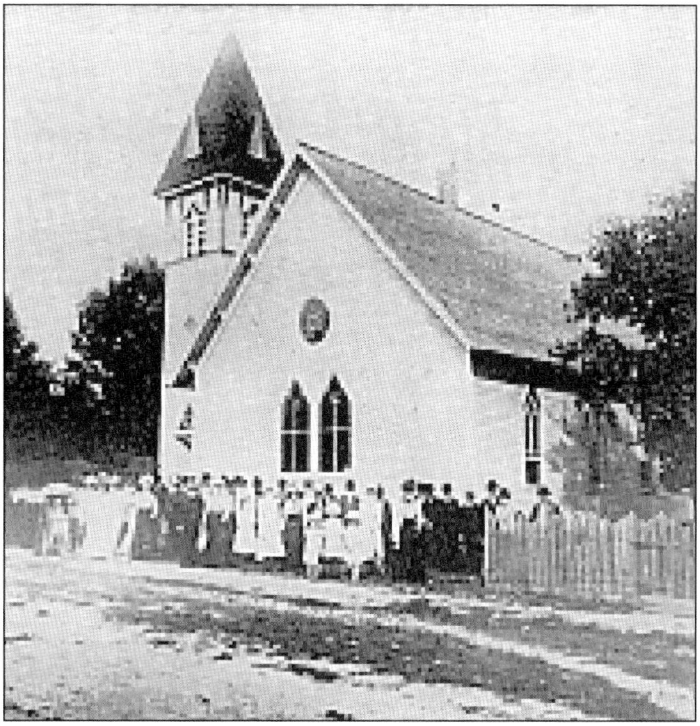

Pilot Mountain Methodist Church on Stephens Street, c. 1910. (Courtesy of First United Methodist Church.)

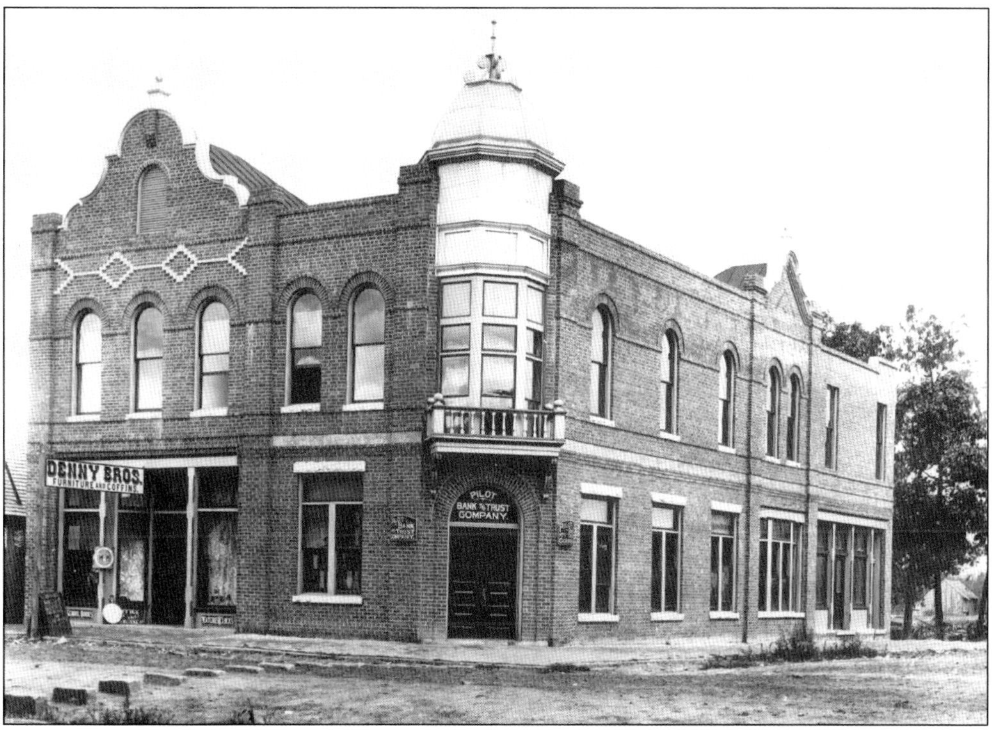

Business on Main Street, 1910. This handsome building was the home of Denny Brothers Furniture and Coffins and the Pilot Bank and Trust Company, which later became the Bank of Pilot Mountain. At one time the upstairs was used as an infirmary. (Courtesy of Bob Thomas.)

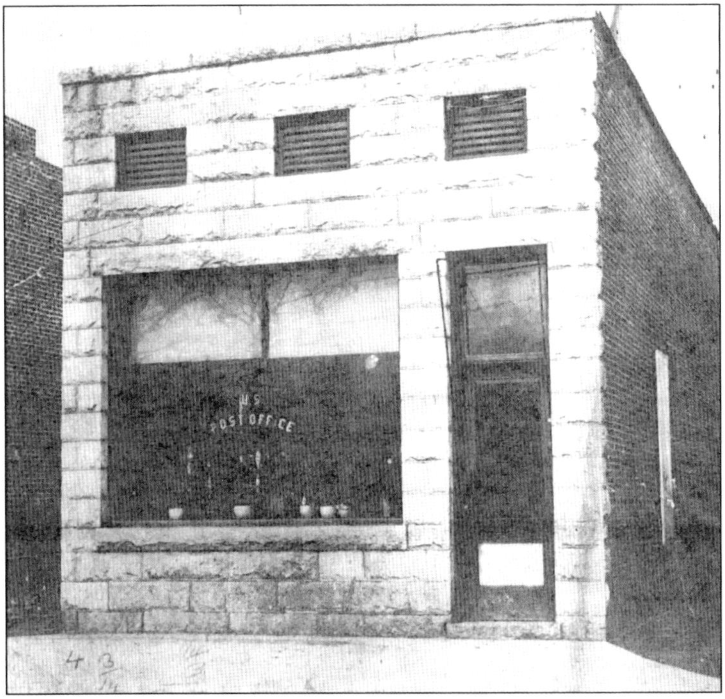

Post Office on Main Street in Pilot Mountain Prior to 1920. Originally built to house the post office, this structure eventually became Farmer's Bank, which was chartered in October 1920. Today, it is the office of attorney Edward N. Swanson. (Courtesy of Carolyn Boyles.)

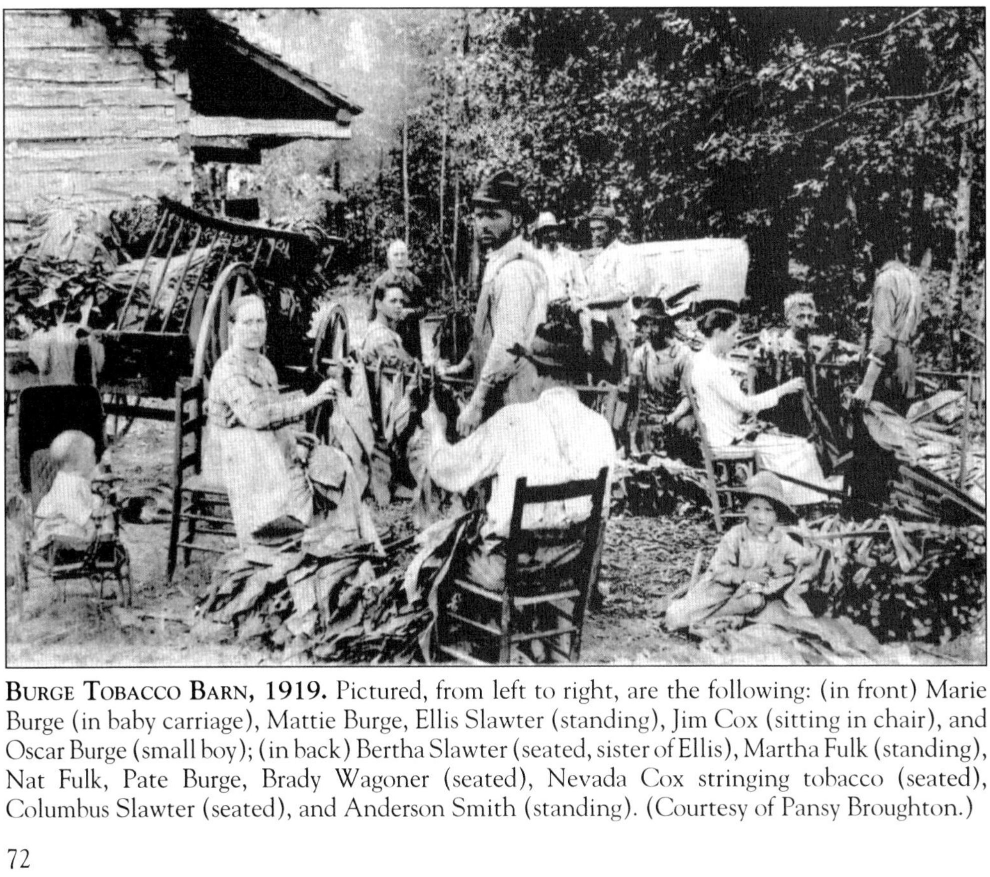

Burge Tobacco Barn, 1919. Pictured, from left to right, are the following: (in front) Marie Burge (in baby carriage), Mattie Burge, Ellis Slawter (standing), Jim Cox (sitting in chair), and Oscar Burge (small boy); (in back) Bertha Slawter (seated, sister of Ellis), Martha Fulk (standing), Nat Fulk, Pate Burge, Brady Wagoner (seated), Nevada Cox stringing tobacco (seated), Columbus Slawter (seated), and Anderson Smith (standing). (Courtesy of Pansy Broughton.)

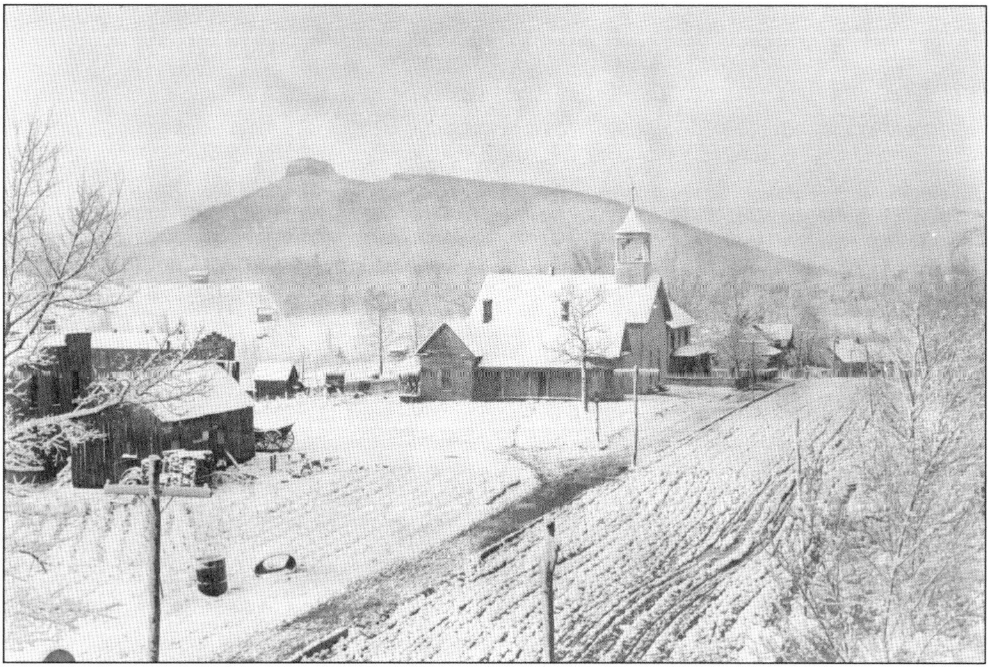

A Pilot Mountain Snow Scene on Depot Street Prior to 1910. The first house is the Christie Needham home, next is Pilot Mountain Baptist Church and the Fowler home. These three buildings burned on March 12, 1919. From the center to the right are Hill's Livery Stable and the jail. (Courtesy of Homer and Gayle Vaughn.)

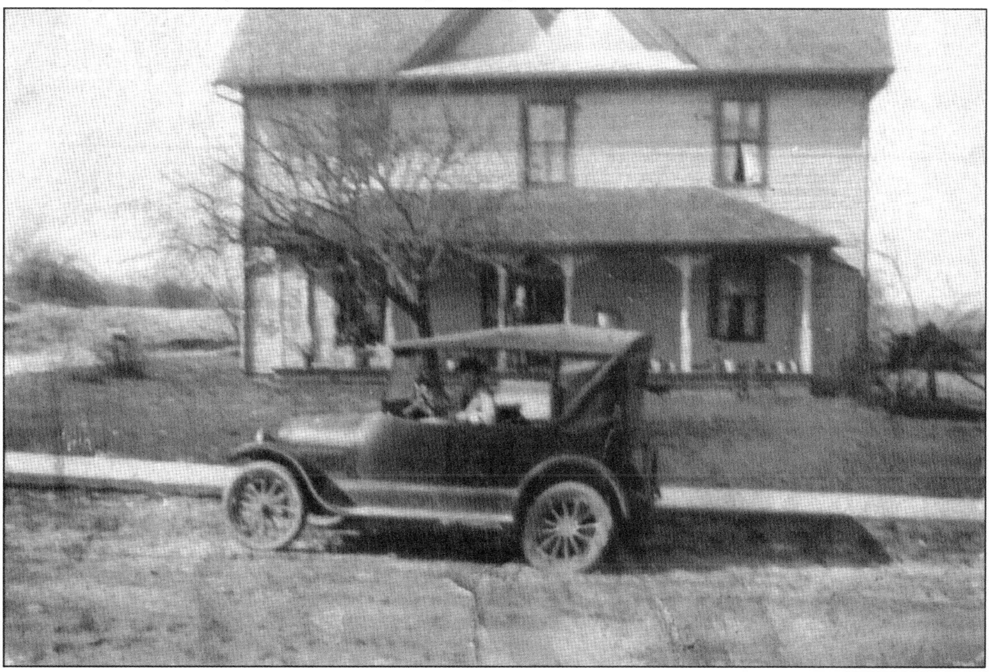

W.F. Boyles Home, c. 1920. The W.F. Boyles home, built about 1870, is located on Main Street in Pilot Mountain. This photograph was taken before the building's renovation in 1924. The car is a four-cylinder Buick touring car. (Courtesy of Carolyn Boyles.)

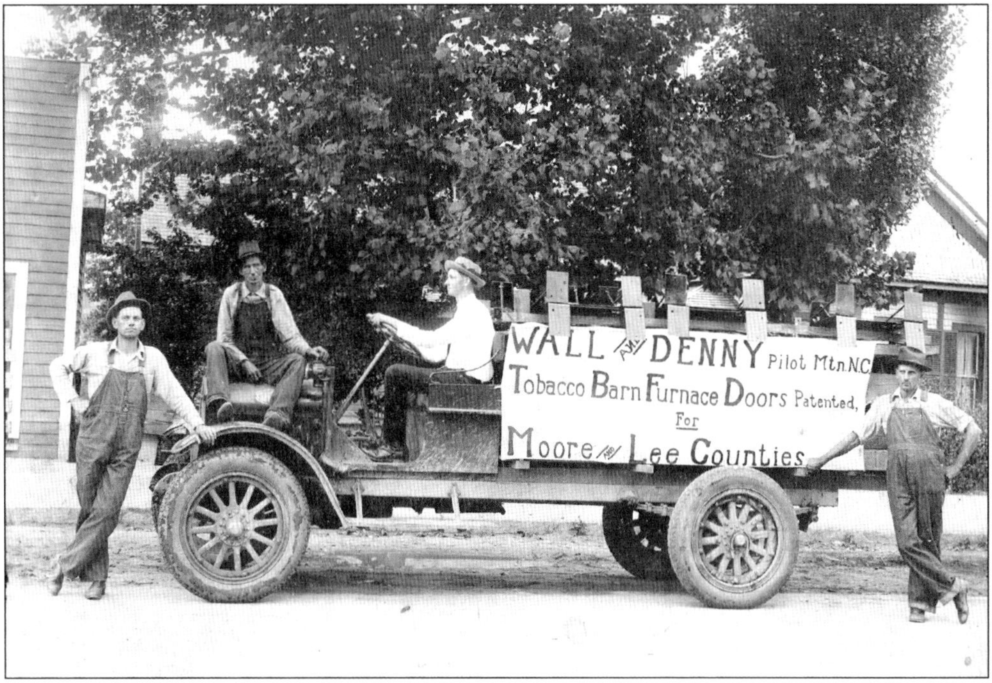

Wall and Denny of Pilot Mountain. Thirty-three sets of tobacco barn furnace doors are being delivered to Moore and Lee Counties. From left to right are Porter Wall, Mr. Shropshire (blacksmith), Frank Swanson, and J. Willis Denny. This photograph was taken on Main Street in Pilot Mountain. (Courtesy of Martin Wall.)

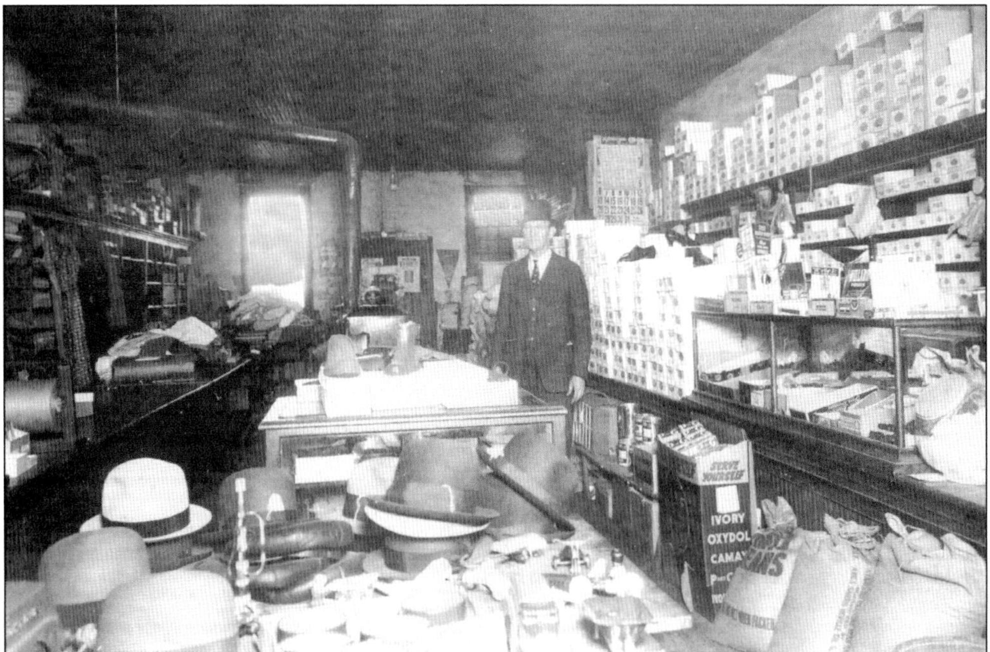

W.F. Boyles Store, 1925. W.F. Boyles (1882–1965) is pictured inside his general mercantile store on Main Street in Pilot Mountain. (Courtesy of Johnnie Mae Boyles.)

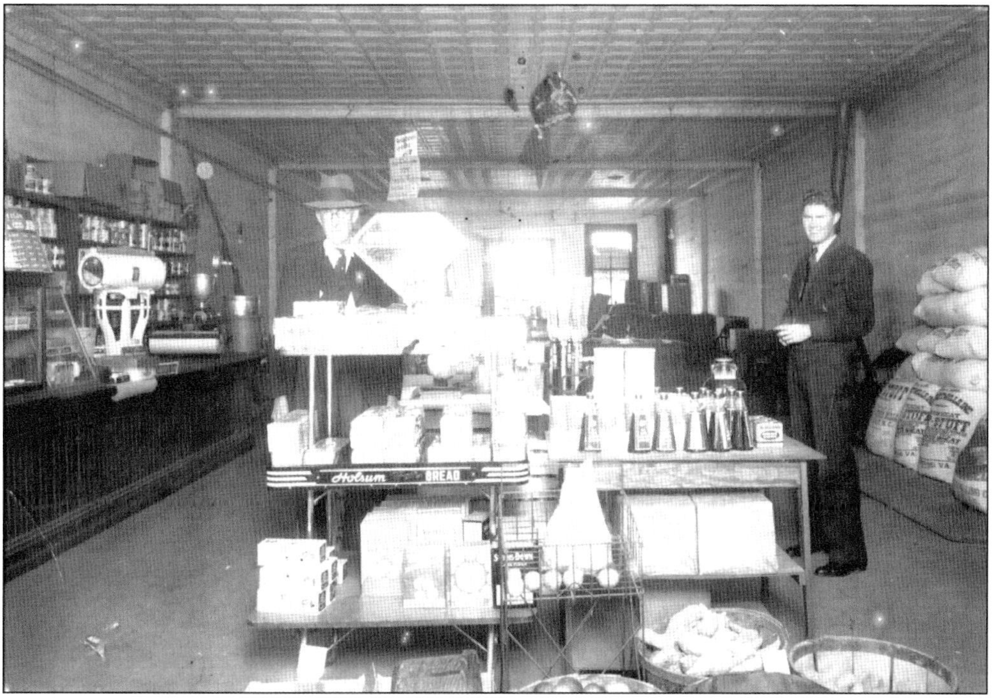

JARRELL'S GROCERY, C. 1936. James B. Jarrell and his son-in-law Glenn Stone are pictured here inside Jarrell's Grocery on Main Street. (Courtesy of Ruth Jarrell Stone.)

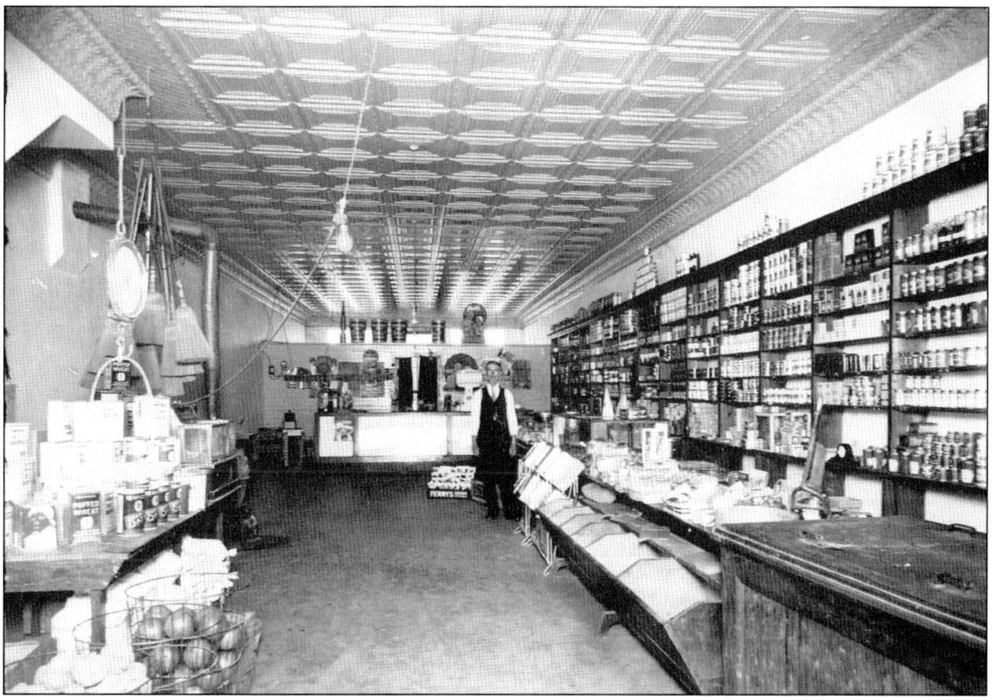

GENERAL MERCANTILE STORE. Joseph Henry Smith is pictured in his store in 1935. The building is now occupied by Bakersmith Antiques and Collectibles. (Courtesy of Emily Nelson Martin.)

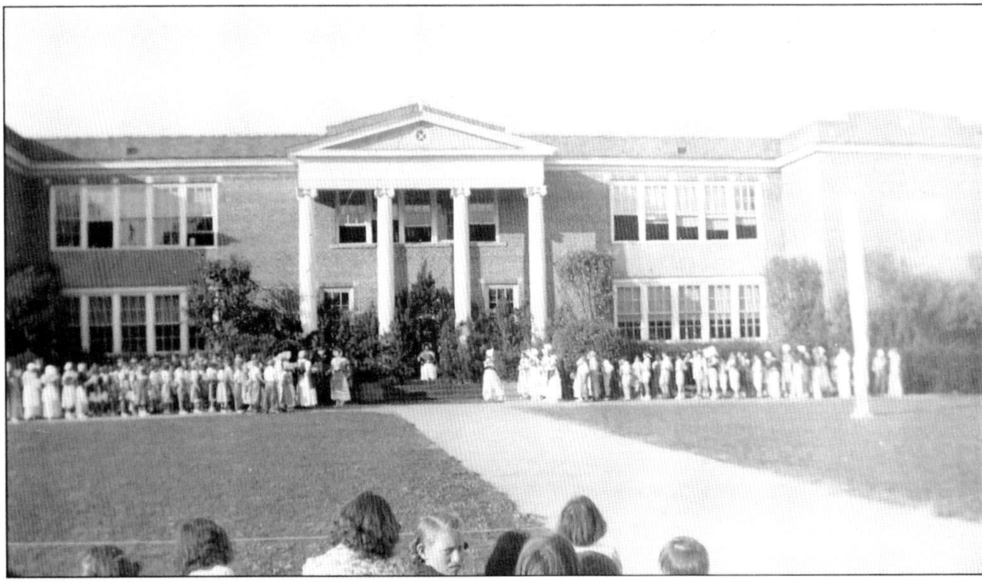

Pilot Mountain School. The annual May Day celebration was held on May 4, 1939. This building, constructed in 1924, housed all school grades, until a six-room annex was built in 1938. The Pilot Mountain Auditorium Restoration Committee is actively working to preserve this landmark. (Courtesy of Bob Thomas.)

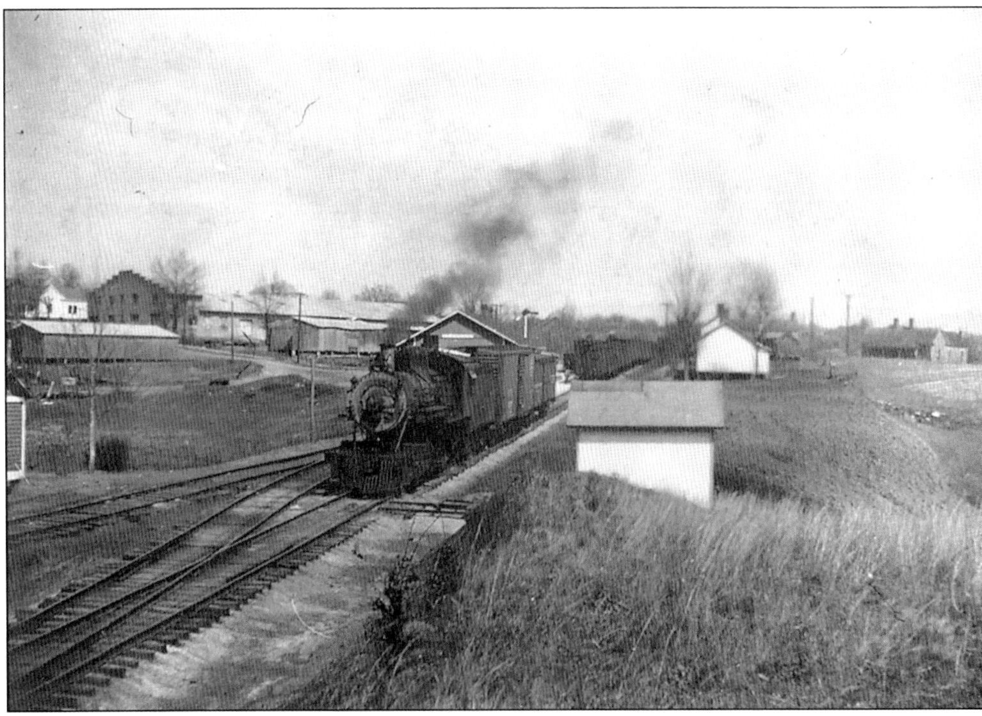

A Train Pulling Away from the Pilot Mountain Depot, c. 1930. (Courtesy of Carolyn Boyles.)

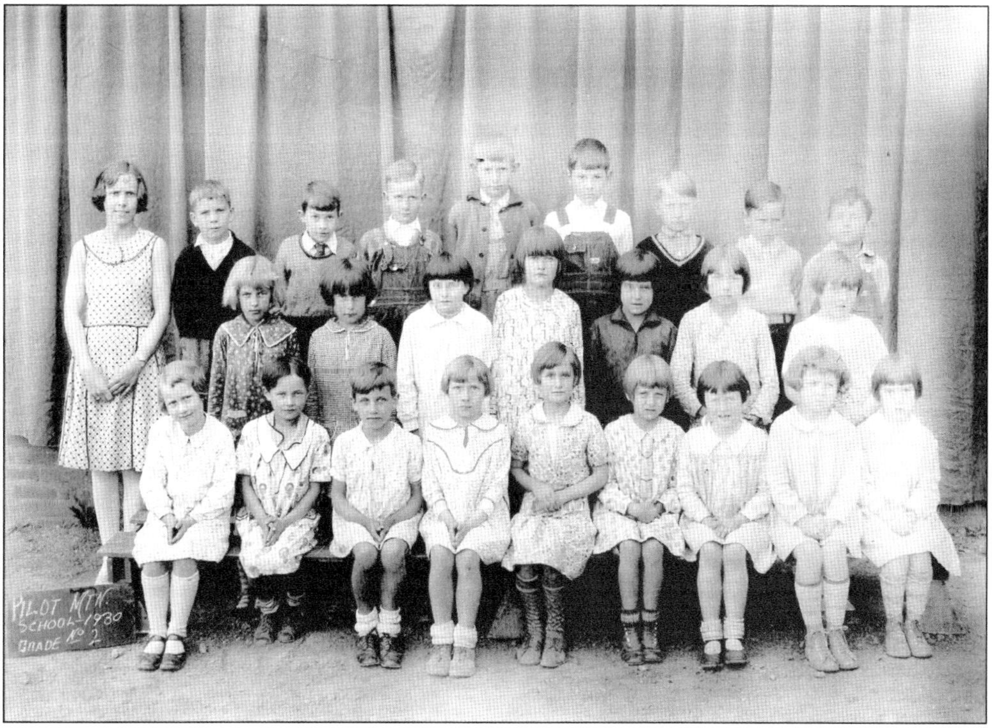

SECOND GRADE CLASS AT PILOT MOUNTAIN SCHOOL, 1930. Pictured, from left to right, are the following: (first row) Joanne Kirkman, Katy Lynch, Sara Wilson, Virginia Childress, Jacquelene Boyles, Marion Cooke, Willie Mae Jessup, Eugenia Fulk, and Mattie Mae Fulk; (second row) Miss Ethel Snow, unidentified, unidentified, Mary Elizabeth Johnson, Clara Brown, Tommie Butner, unidentified, and Mary Lois Gordon; (third row) Jack Boyles, Sammy Fowler, Simpson Nelson, unidentified, Joe Simmons, Raymond Boaz, R.B. McDaniel, and Tommy Macon. (Courtesy of Bob Thomas.)

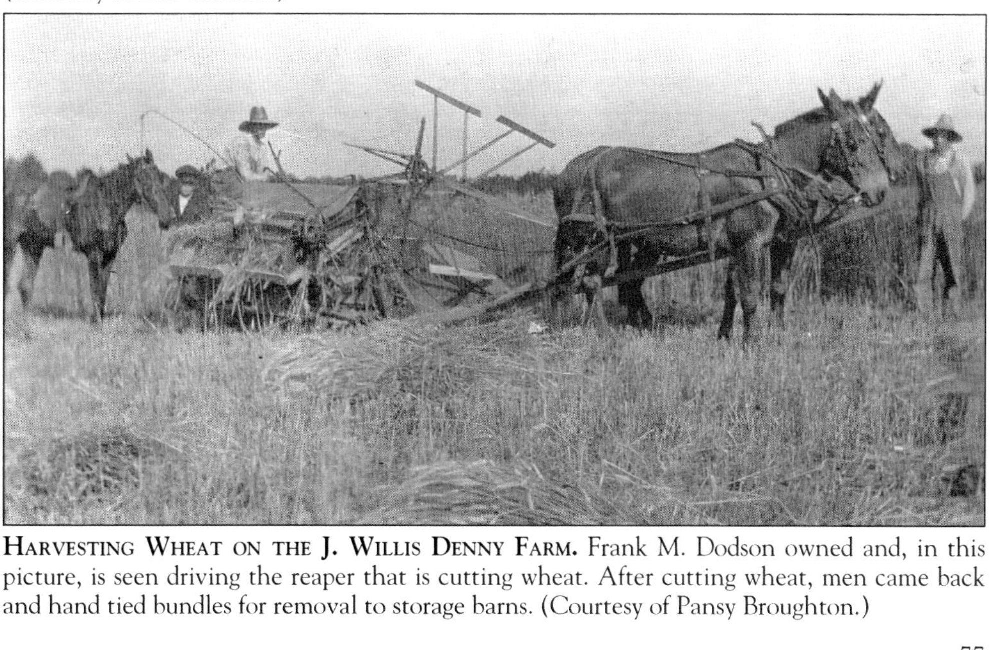

HARVESTING WHEAT ON THE J. WILLIS DENNY FARM. Frank M. Dodson owned and, in this picture, is seen driving the reaper that is cutting wheat. After cutting wheat, men came back and hand tied bundles for removal to storage barns. (Courtesy of Pansy Broughton.)

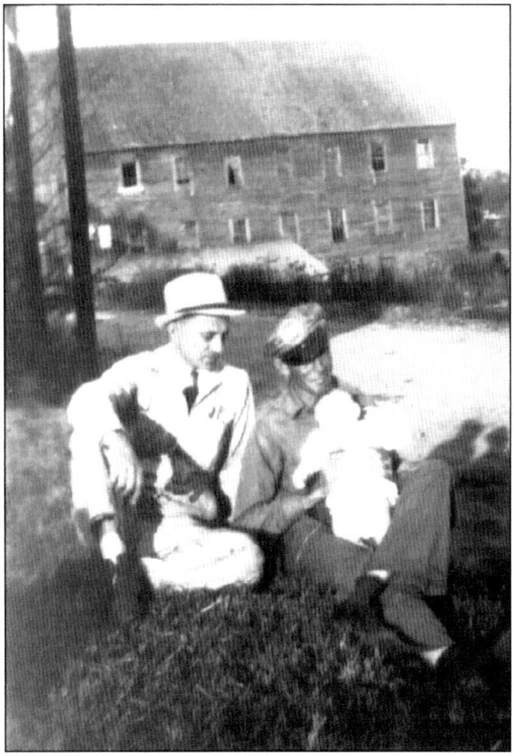

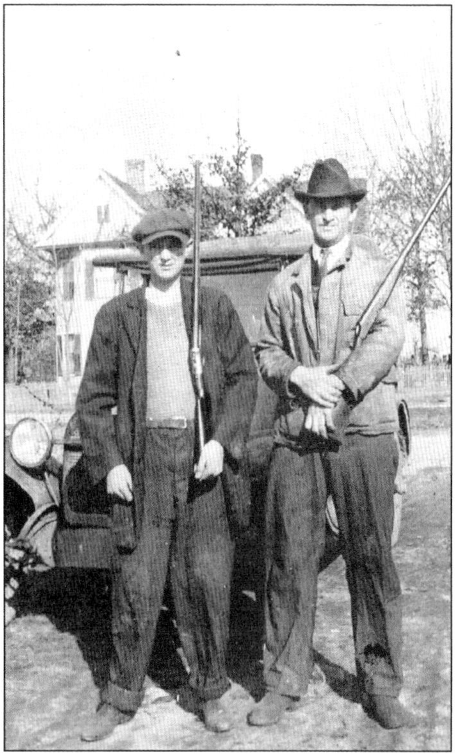

Left: **THE OLD RED FACTORY, C. 1935.** Roscoe Boaz, Paul Latham, and his daughter Louise Latham pose for this photograph near the "Old Red Factory," one of seven plug tobacco factories that operated in Pilot Mountain. (Courtesy of Carolyn Boyles.)
Right: **HUNTING ON THANKSGIVING DAY, C. 1920.** Pictured here are Walter Boyles (right) and his cousin Ovid Boyles. The O.N. Swanson home is in the background. (Courtesy of Carolyn Boyles.)

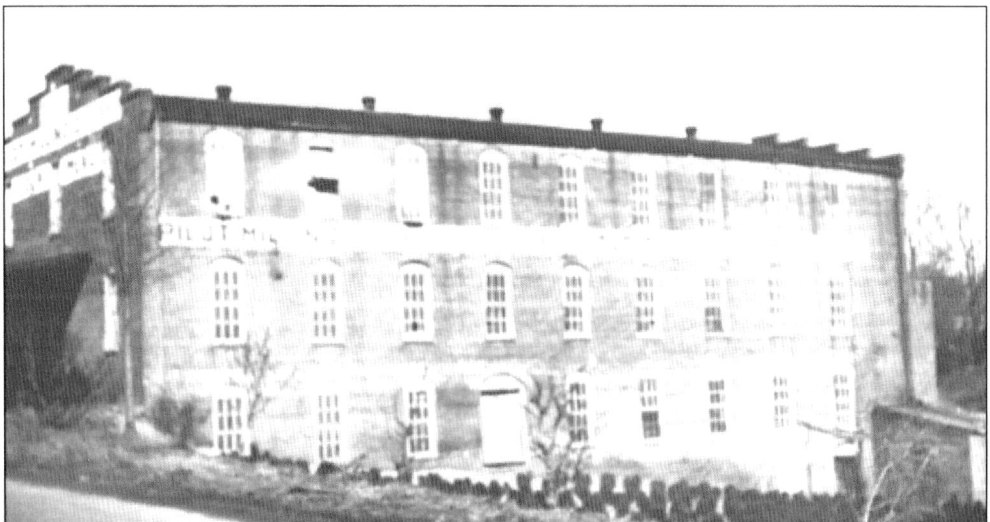

PILOT MILLING COMPANY ON DAVIS STREET, C. 1940. This building originally housed the Dodson Brothers Tobacco Factory. (Courtesy of Lenice Johnson.)

Eight

Rockford Township

Rockford Township is located in south central Surry County and is bordered on the south by Yadkin County. In 1789, a committee was appointed to select a new site for the county seat of Surry County, which at that time still included the southern portion that is now Yadkin County. The committee agreed upon a place on the north side of the Yadkin River that contained 53 acres that could be purchased from Thomas and Moses Ayers. The town was called Rockford, named for the white rock ford in the river. The first order of business was to lay out roads to Rockford and to build a jail and a courthouse. The jail was a two-story whitewashed wooden building; the upstairs was reserved for debtors and the downstairs for criminals. Soon after the founding of the town in 1795, Moses Ayers was given permission to start a ferry. Rockford remained the county seat until 1850, when Yadkin County was formed from Surry County with the Yadkin River as its northern boundary. The county seat was then removed to Dobson. However, court continued to be held in Rockford for three years until the new courthouse in Dobson was completed. Some of the early schools in the township included Stony Knoll, Poplar Springs, and Harbour. Among the early churches were Rockford Baptist and Rockford Methodist.

Many notable men of the day visited Rockford, which was known not only for its governmental status, but also for its hotels, stores, churches, and schools. There were teachers, doctors, ministers, and lawyers, as well as a blacksmith, a forge, a tinsmith, and a tannery. There was also a brick kiln, which furnished bricks for the building of stores and homes. Many of the old historic structures remain intact in Rockford—some are privately owned and others are owned by the Rockford Preservation Society.

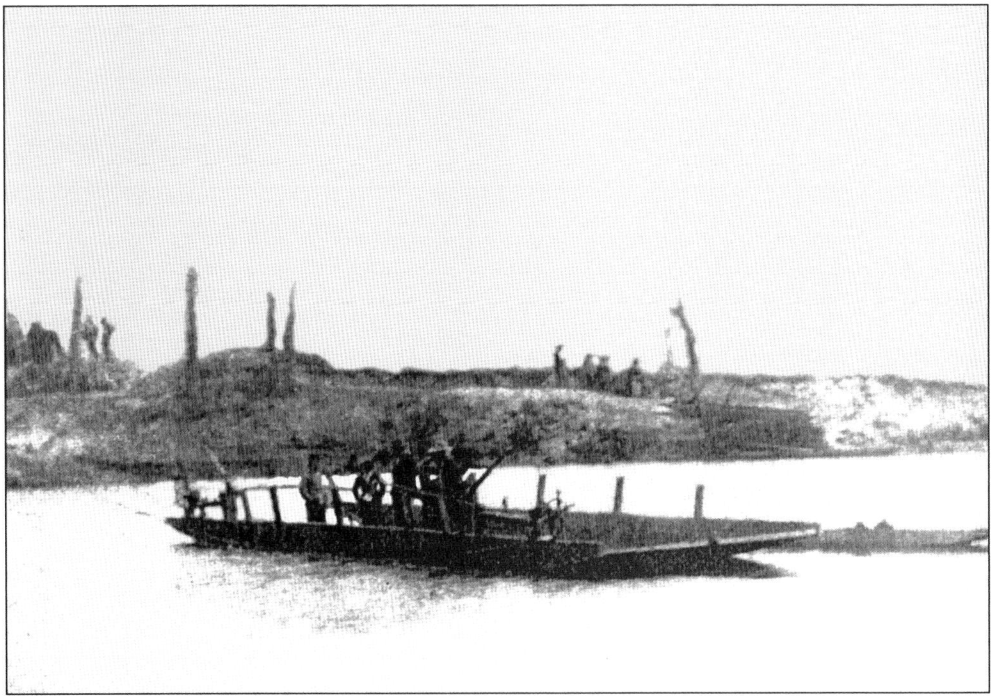

ROCKFORD FERRY, 1916. Pictured here is the ferry moving across the Yadkin River. (Courtesy of Judy Cardwell.)

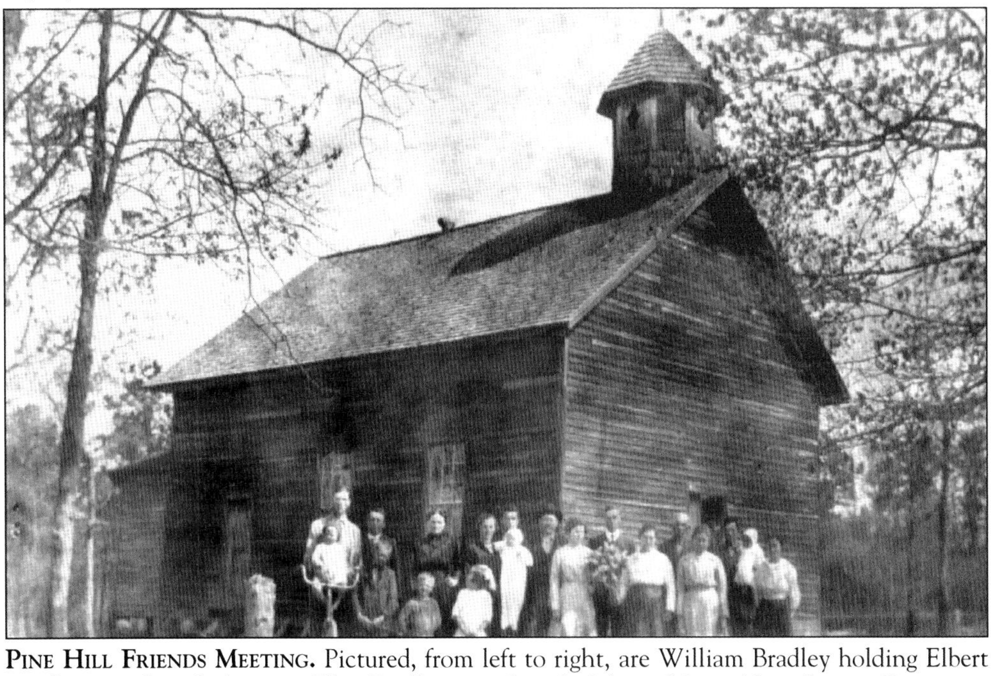

PINE HILL FRIENDS MEETING. Pictured, from left to right, are William Bradley holding Elbert Bradley, unidentified man, Ellis Bradley, unidentified boy, Mary Alice Logan Patterson, unidentified girl, Etta Patterson Ring holding Cecil Ring, Irvin Ring, Wright Ashburn, Ella Patterson, Esker Patterson, Julia Whitaker Patterson, unidentified man and woman, Jasper Patterson holding James Patterson, and Emma Jones Patterson. (Courtesy of Melva Greene.)

Out in the Corn Field. Samuel Edward Banner (1870–1959) is pictured here with his first wife, Milly Ada Brinkley (1870–1910). Sam Banner ran a country store in the Stony Knoll community but lost the store during the Depression. He was also a well-known janitor at Copeland School. The family lived in a house that once served as a schoolhouse. (Courtesy of Judy Cardwell.)

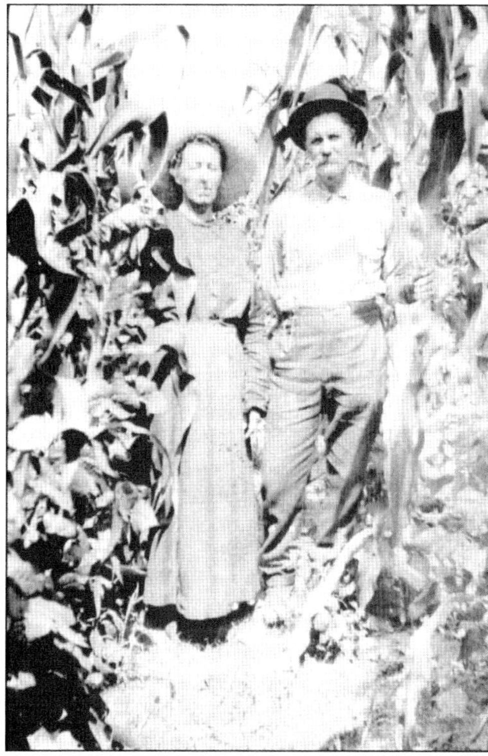

Grant-Burrus Hotel in Rockford. This hotel was operated by Reuben Grant and John G. Burrus in its early years. (Courtesy of Ruth Minick.)

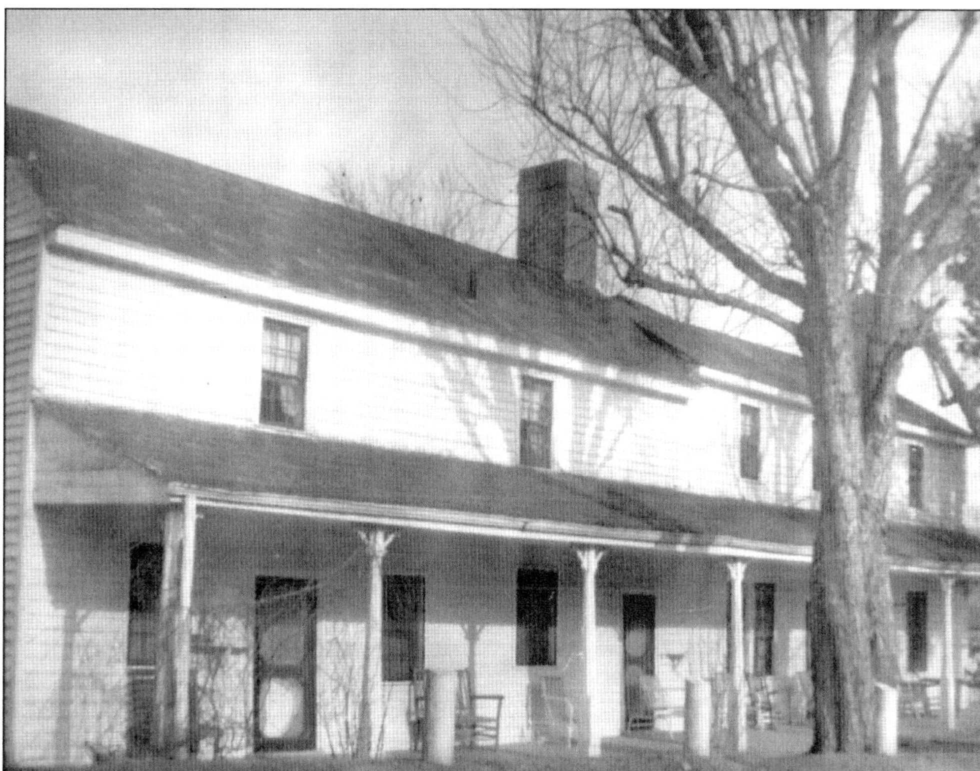

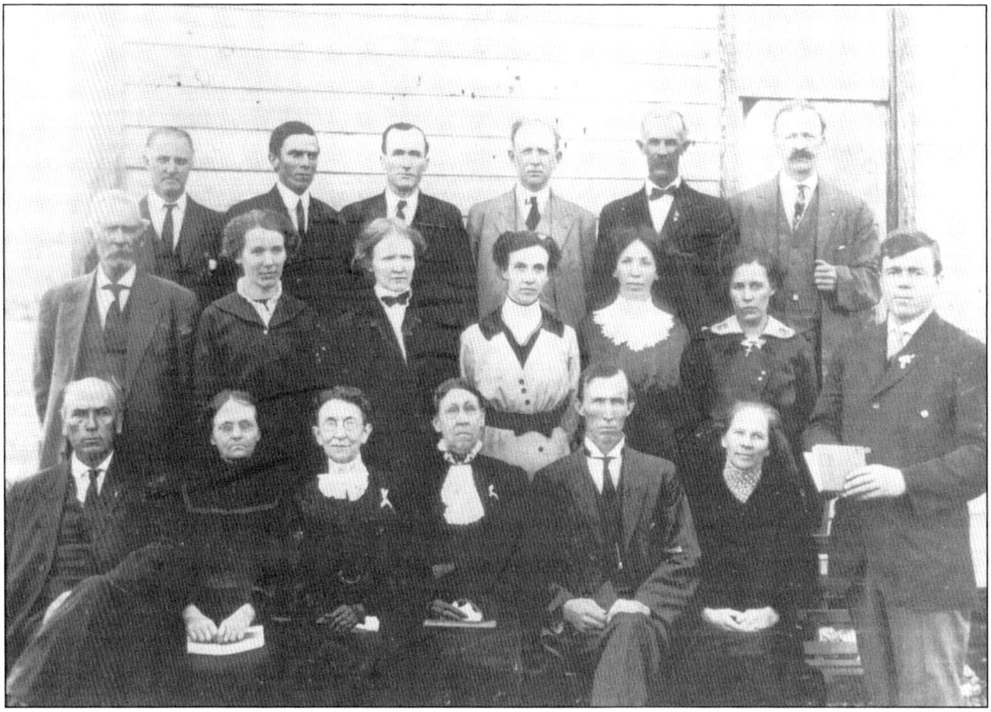

BIBLE SCHOOL IN ROCKFORD. Pictured, from left to right, are the following: (first row) Bob Burrus and wife Molly, Callie Thore and sister Cornelia Nixon, Reverend George Burrus, Mary Etta Burrus, and unidentified teacher (standing); (second row) John Burrus, Viola Burrus, Molly Jane Burrus (sister to the preacher), Lucy Davenport, Luela Davenport, and unidentified; (third row) unidentified, Romie Burrus, Charlie Davis, Brona Holyfield, Yancy Davenport, and Johnny Dunn. (Courtesy of Marthalene Davis.)

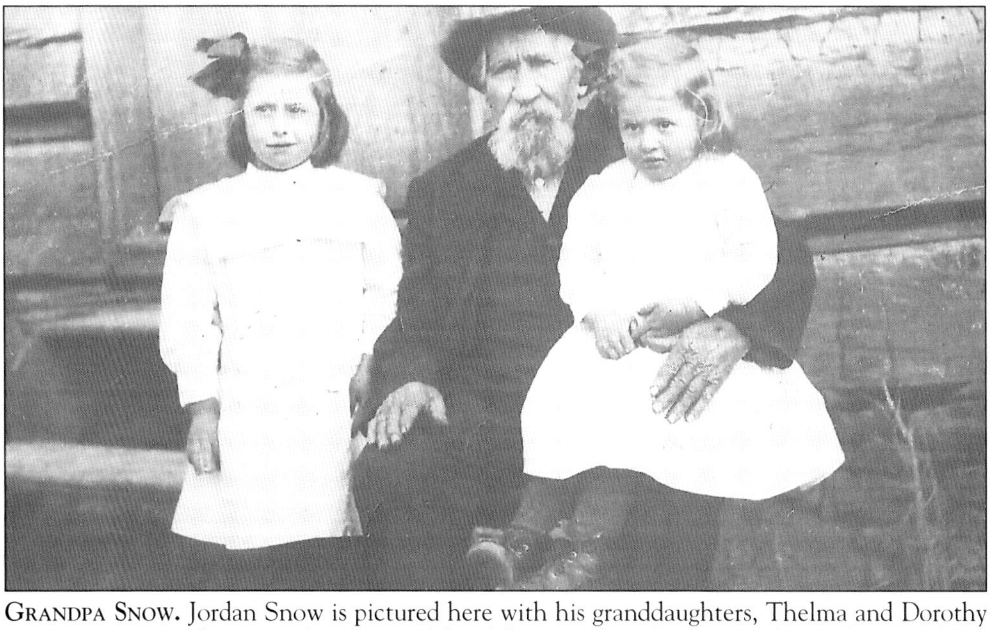

GRANDPA SNOW. Jordan Snow is pictured here with his granddaughters, Thelma and Dorothy Snow, *c.* 1913. Jordan Snow (1829–1930) lived for 101 years. (Courtesy of Dorothy Terrell.)

Dr. William Polk Dobson II (1842–1923). Dr. Dobson was well known in the towns of Rockford and Dobson, the latter of which was named for William Polk Dobson, a lawyer, large landholder, and a man of affairs. He was also a cousin of President James K. Polk and one of those who spoke at the nominating convention. He died in 1846. (Courtesy of Marthalene Davis.)

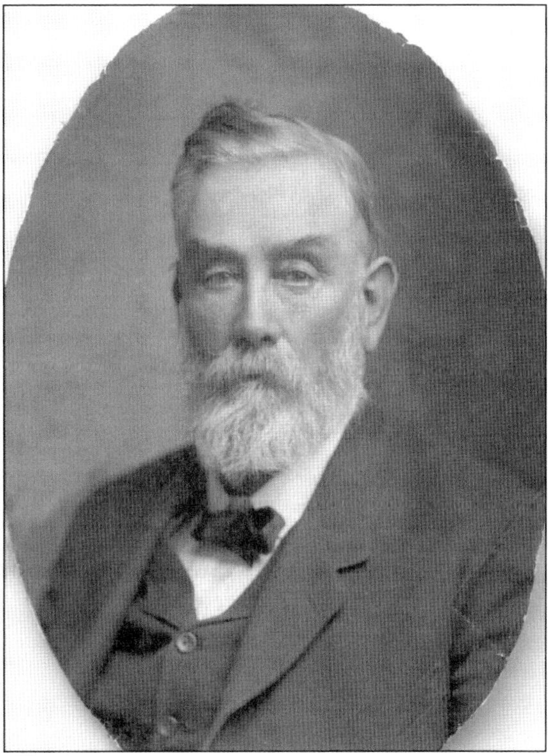

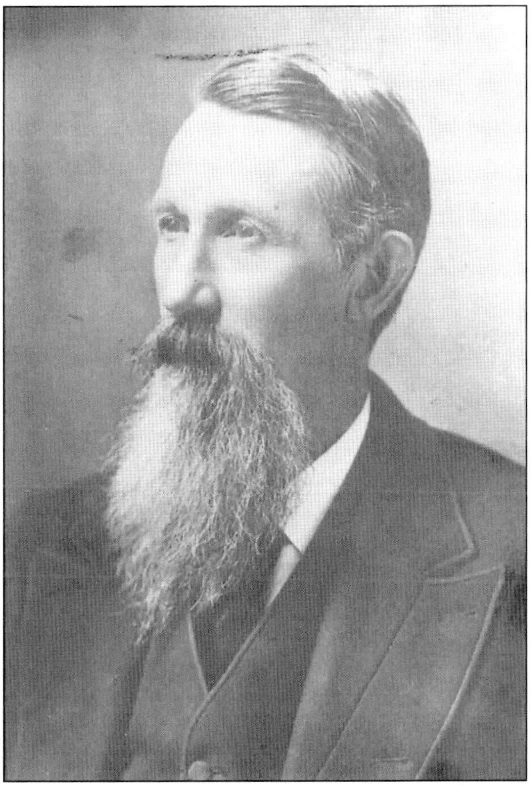

Unsuccessful Bid for Governor. Dr. Tyre York (1836–1916) was born in Rockford and was the son of Mark and Nancy Gadberry York. In 1884, York ran for governor of North Carolina on the Republican ticket but did not win. He was a member of Congress from Wilkes County, North Carolina. (Courtesy of Jim Cockerham.)

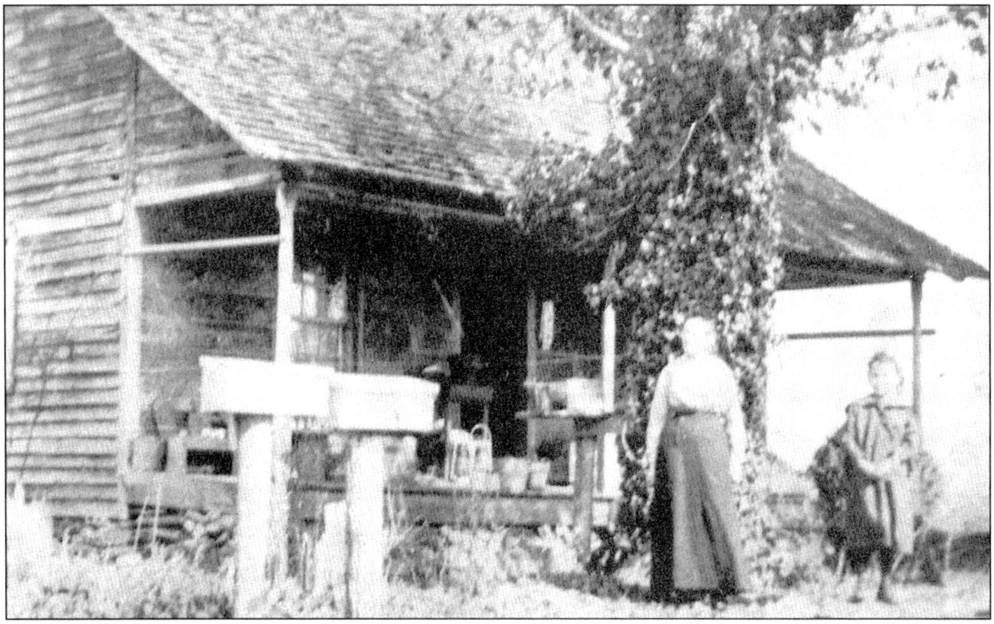

Former Butcher Post Office. Lucinda Doss Butcher (1850–1938) and a grandchild stand in front of her home, which held the town's post office, in the Butcher community in 1922. Lucinda was the wife of John William Butcher (1852–1922). According to the *Yadkin Valley News* on August 24, 1893, the name of the post office at Butcher, North Carolina, was changed to Stony Knoll, and Mr. W.M. McDowell was appointed the postmaster to succeed Mr. J.W. Butcher. (Courtesy of Jim Cockerham.)

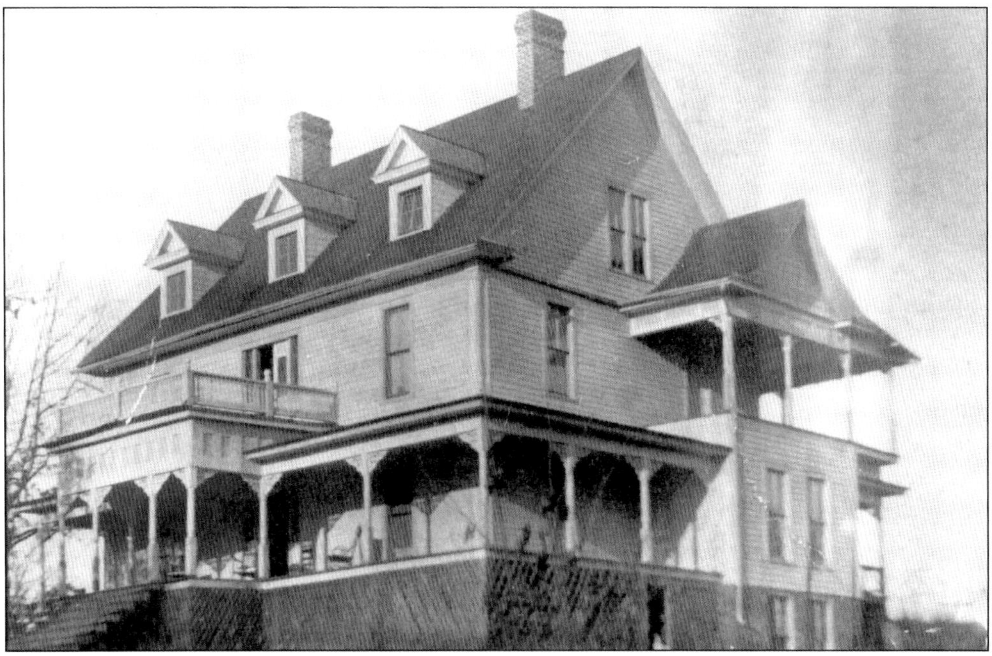

J.D. Hamlin House. This house was completed in 1904 and was later the home of the C.A. Houck Sr. family and the birthplace of all of the Houck children. (Courtesy of Marthalene Davis.)

BOHANAN MILL. The Bohanan Mill was located on the south side of the Yadkin River in Surry County. This location is now in Yadkin County. (Courtesy of Marthalene Davis.)

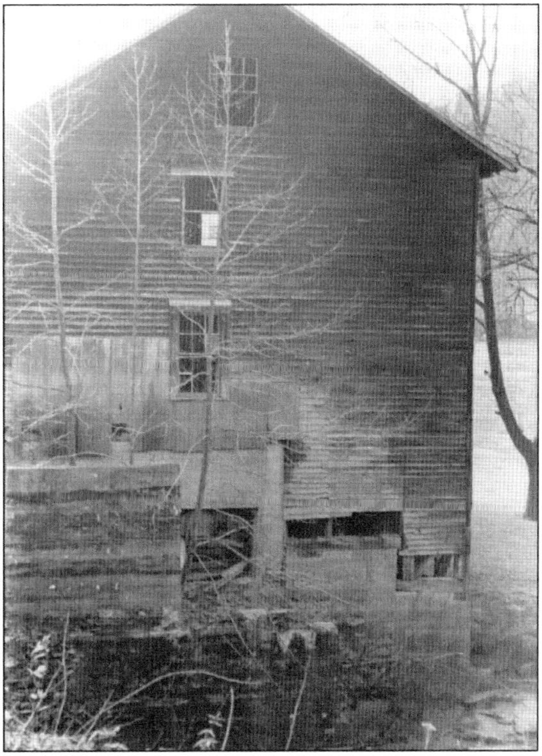

COPELAND SCHOOL CLASS, 1924. From left to right are Harvey Hiatt, Clayton Smith, Howard Taylor, Alton Harbour, Fred Davis, and Arthur Graham, teacher. (Courtesy of Marthalene Davis.)

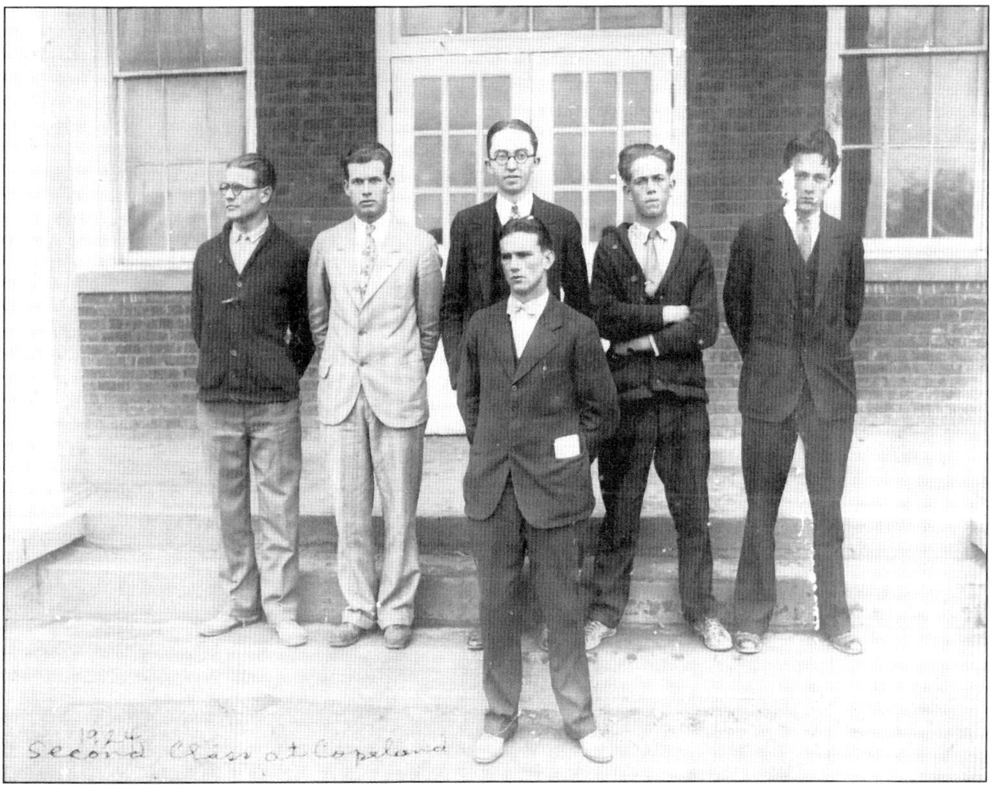

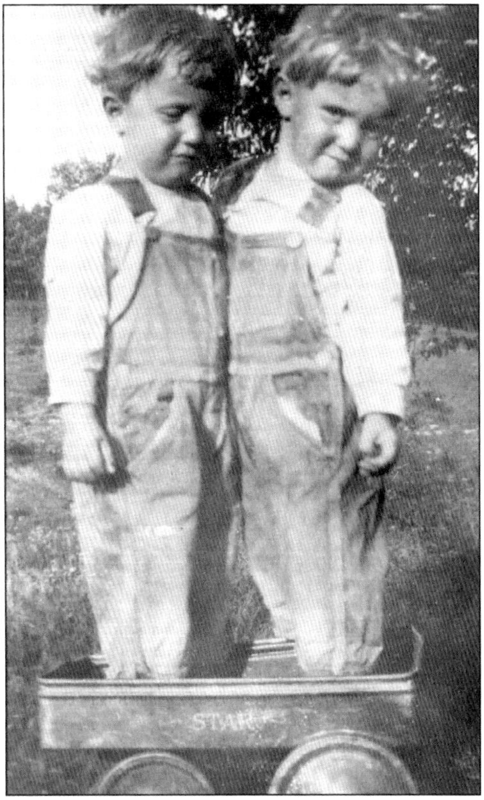

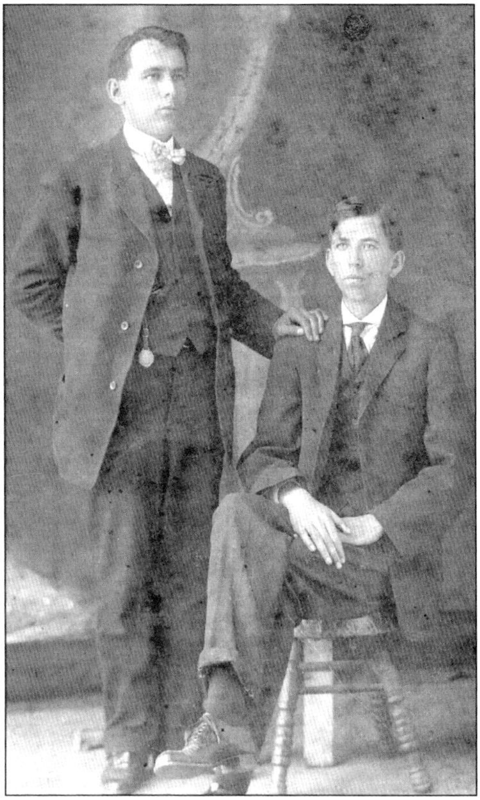

Left: **STAR WAGON, 1928.** Twins John and Jim Stanley were born on December 24, 1925, the sons of Eugene S. Stanley and Mary Lee Coe. (Courtesy of Judy Cardwell.)
Right: **BLAND BROTHERS.** Frank Bland and Dallas Bland (seated) were responsible for starting the Bland Piano Company. These men grew up in Rockford. (Courtesy of Marthalene Davis.)

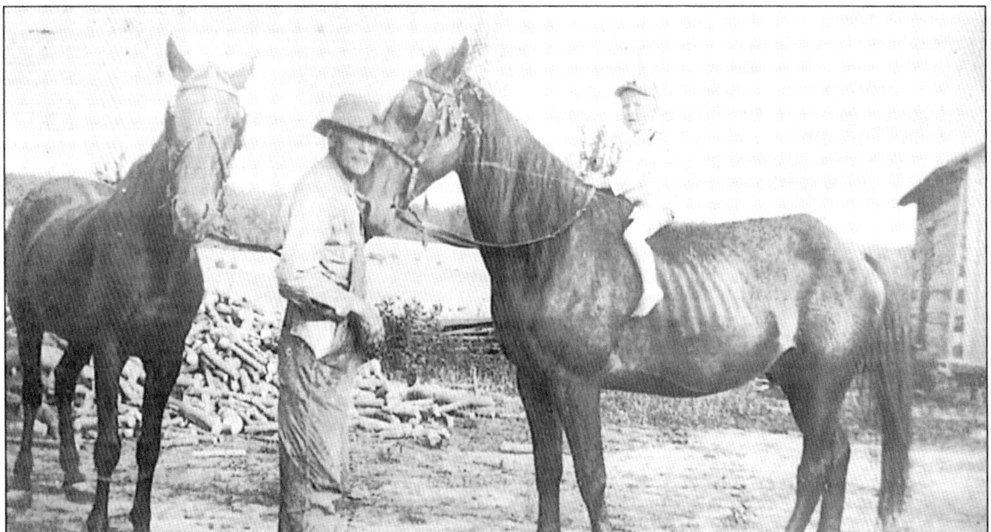

TAKING AN EARLY MORNING RIDE. John Terrell and his grandson Bruce Johnson are pictured here with mules. (Courtesy of Dave Terrell.)

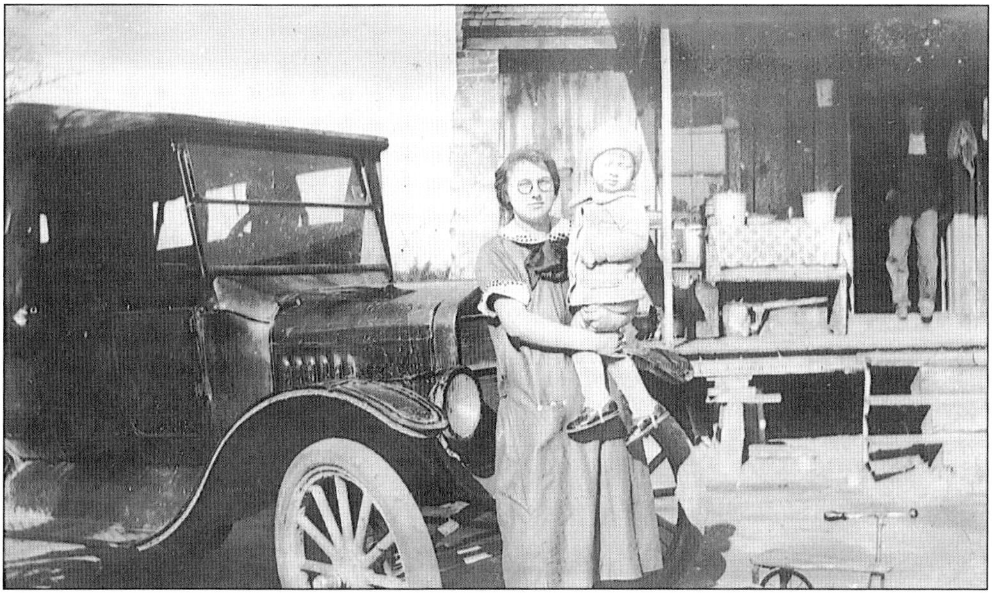

Josie and the Model T Ford. Josie Simpson holds a child while a gentleman watches from the doorway on the porch. (Courtesy of Dorothy Terrell.)

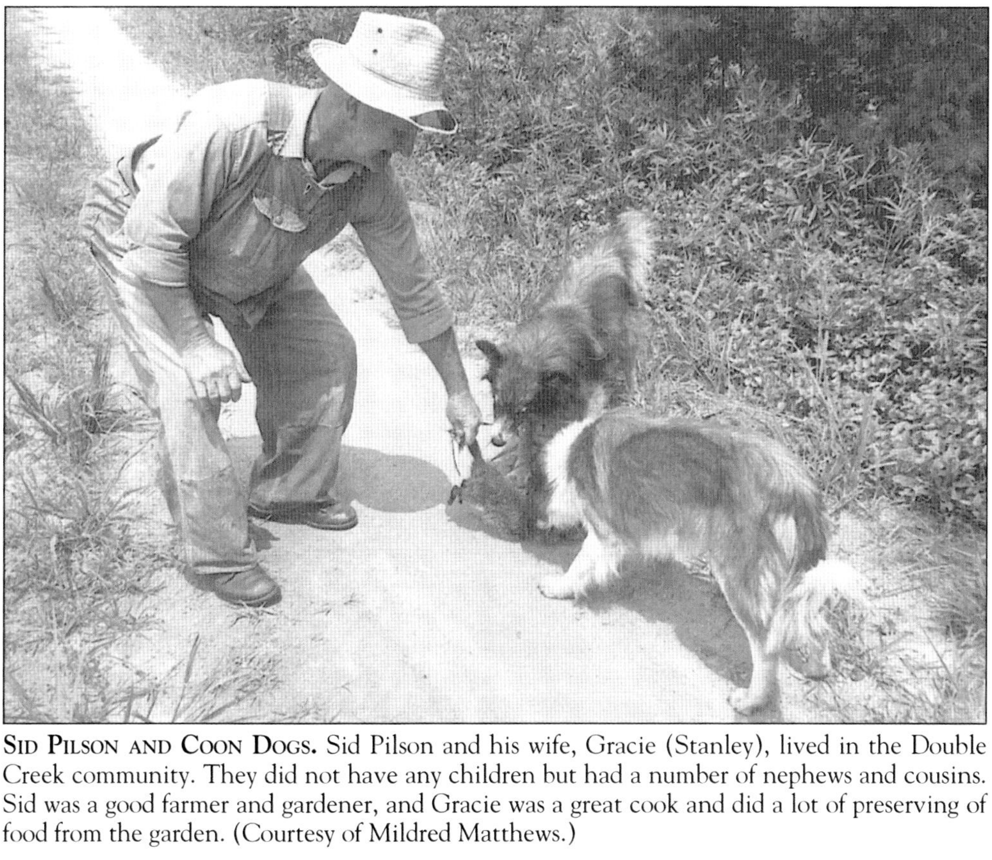

Sid Pilson and Coon Dogs. Sid Pilson and his wife, Gracie (Stanley), lived in the Double Creek community. They did not have any children but had a number of nephews and cousins. Sid was a good farmer and gardener, and Gracie was a great cook and did a lot of preserving of food from the garden. (Courtesy of Mildred Matthews.)

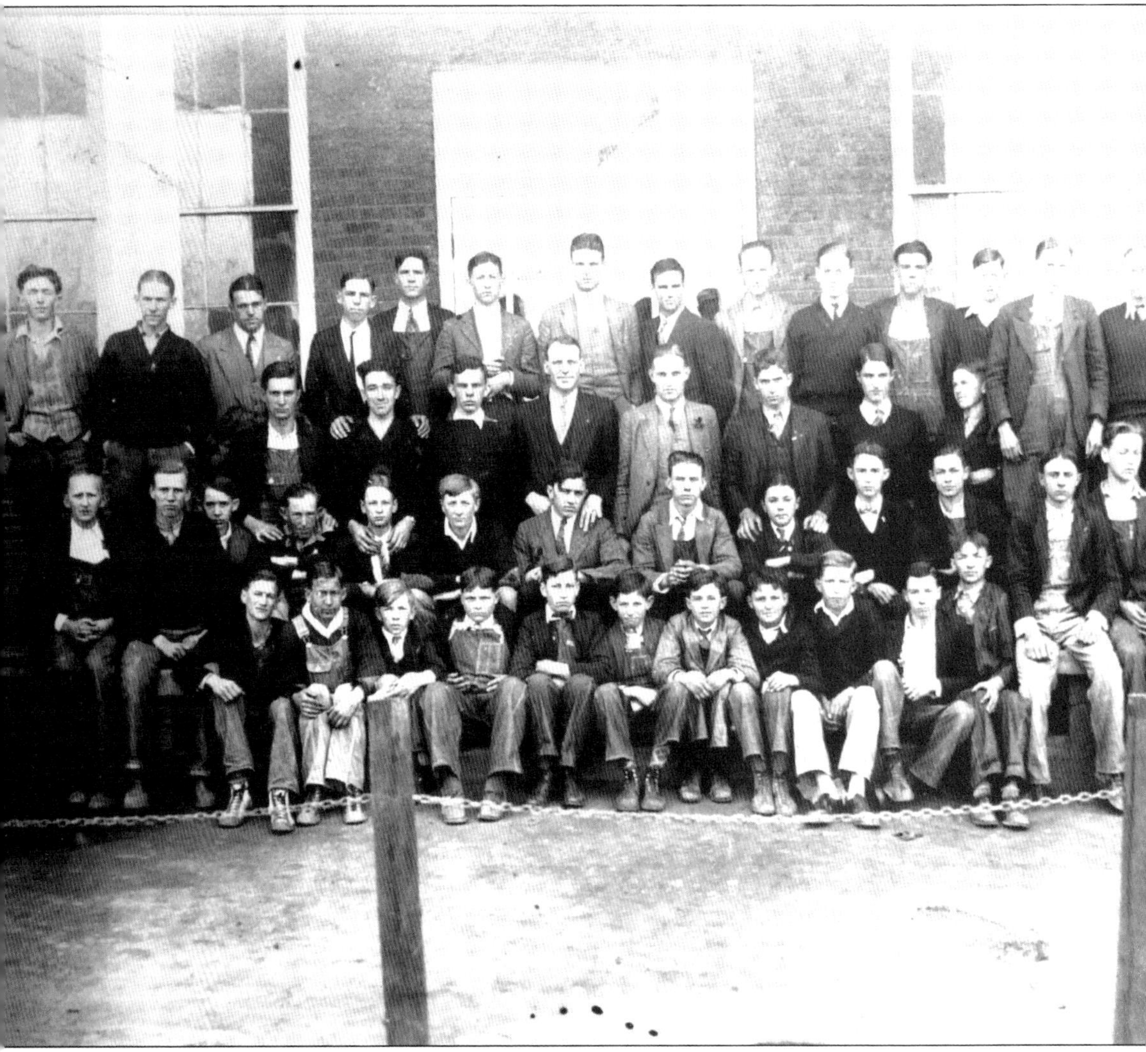

Copeland School Boys, 1930. Pictured, from left to right, are the following: (first row) Carl Snow, Paul Flynn, Ralph Atkins, Robert Snow, Glenn Snow, Walter Perkins, Hal Brigg, Theaford Simpson, Lamon Bruner, Glenn Venable, and Cecil Atkins; (second row) Clete Snow, Ervin Key, Carlton Fulk, Gray Anthony, George Snow, Kermit Watson, Willie Simmons, unidentified, Robert Johnson, Clarence Fulk, Howard Tucker, Elmer Patterson, and Richard Shackerford; (third row) unidentified, Claude Simpson, Jerry Marion, Marion Chilton, Woodrow Matthews, Wade Snow, Paul Snow, and Sam Key; (fourth row) unidentified, Ralph Snow, C.G. Kirkman, James Cook, Landrous Stanley, Frank Jones, Davis Key, Arthur Graham (principal), Manley Stanley, Aubrey Snow, Paul Key, Monroe Hardy, Warren Coe, and Bob Martin. (Courtesy of Melva Greene.)

Nine

Shoals and Siloam Townships

The Shoals and Siloam Townships are located in the southeastern part of the county with the Yadkin River as their southern boundary. The Ararat River flows between the two townships. Horne Creek and Grassy Creek are located in the Shoals Township and flow into the Yadkin River.

The community of Shoals originated in 1867, when several families settled there to farm the rich bottomlands. A huge flat rock and loose stones in the Yadkin River made a good fording place. These shoals measured 2 miles in length. A family named Bean settled there and the ford became known as Bean Shoals Ford, later shortened to Shoals, and was mentioned as early as 1819 in a survey of the rivers of North Carolina. The first post office at Shoals was established on March 23, 1891, with Boyle E. Moser as the postmaster. Among the early schools in the township were Brown, Fairview, and Pilot View. The Missionary Baptist Church of Bean Shoals was organized in 1867, though its name was changed to Shoals Baptist in 1943. Before 1880, Shoals Methodist Church was operated as a mission of the Mt. Zion Church.

Located on the banks of the Yadkin River, the town of Siloam was originally part of the holdings of Morgan Bryant, but in 1771, the land was sold by Bryant to Samuel Freeman. The Old Siloam Methodist Church, established in 1808, was named for the Pool of Siloam in the Bible. It became the religious, educational, and social center of the community, and the name was eventually given to the settlement. The Siloam Baptist Church began in 1899. A post office was established in Siloam on February 3, 1837, with Micajah Reeves as postmaster, and it remained there until 1890, when the railroad came through. The Siloam Academy opened about 1892, and other early schools included Douglas, Stanford, and Poplar Springs. Some of the early families in the area included the Atkinsons, the Cundiffs, the Hardys, the Marions, the Snows, and the Whitakers.

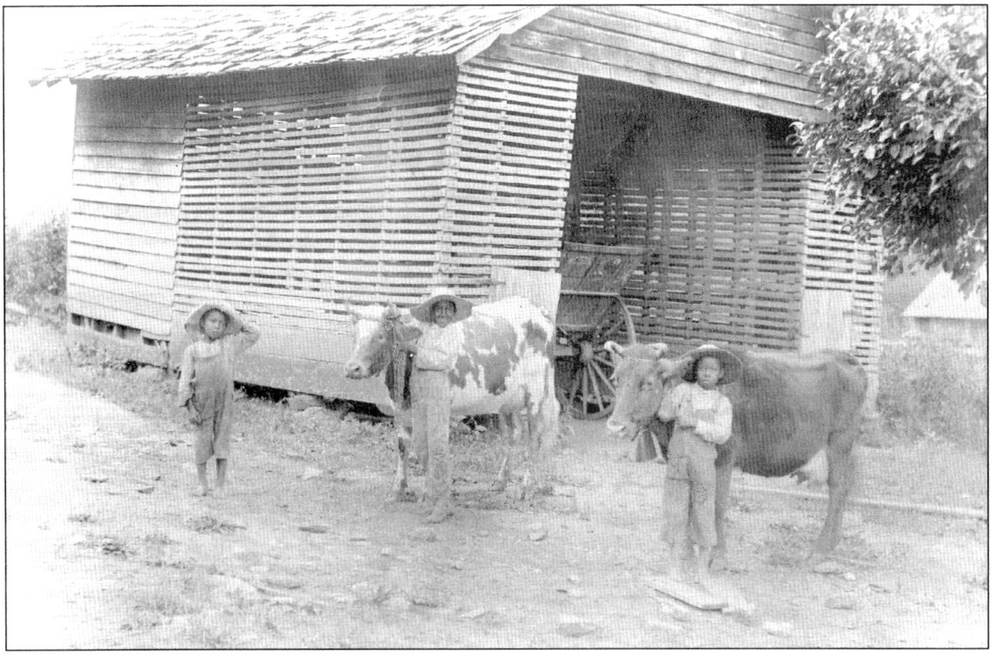

Corn Crib at Horne Creek Farm before 1910. The children pictured here are thought to be some of the Hauser family's neighbors. (Courtesy of Horne Creek Farm.)

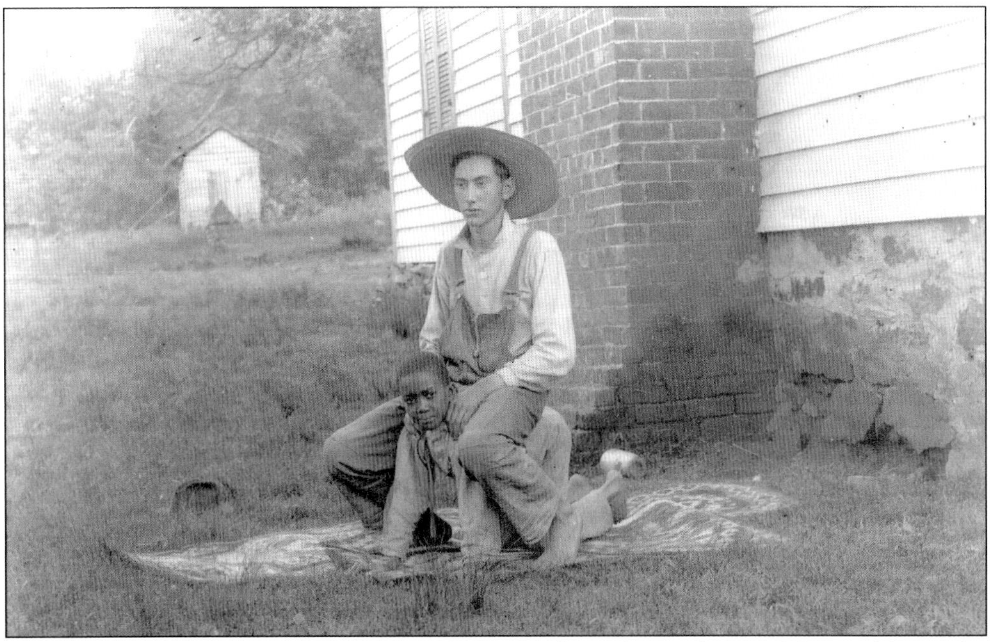

Play Time at the Hauser Farm. One of the Hauser boys plays with one of the neighbors, who is thought to be one of the Sawyer family children. (Courtesy of Horne Creek Farm.)

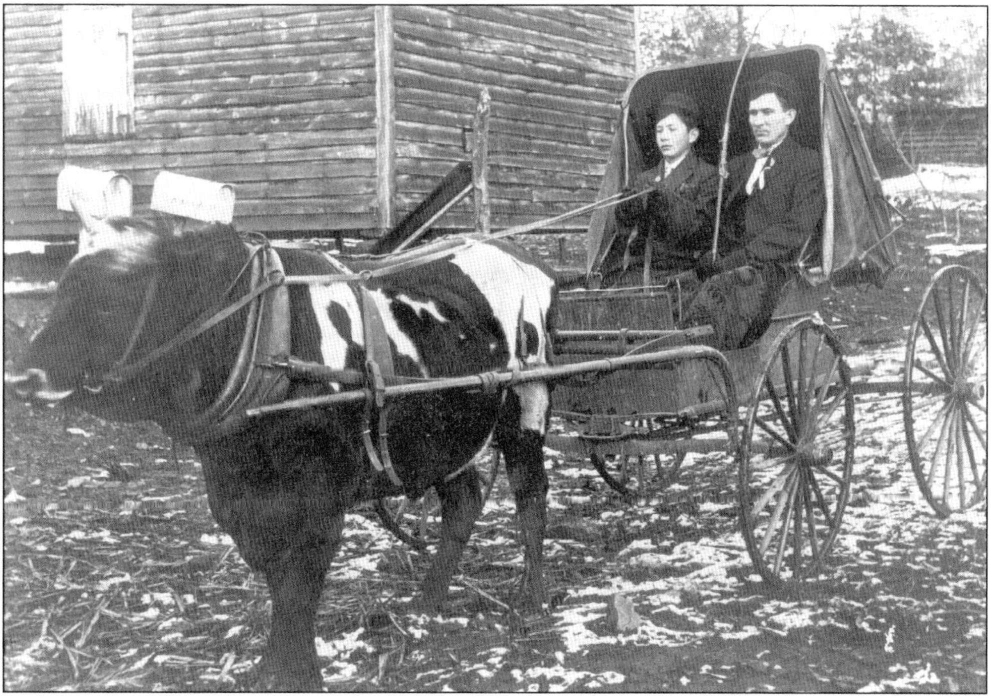

Squire and Robert Hauser on the Hauser Farm before 1910. (Courtesy of Horne Creek Farm.)

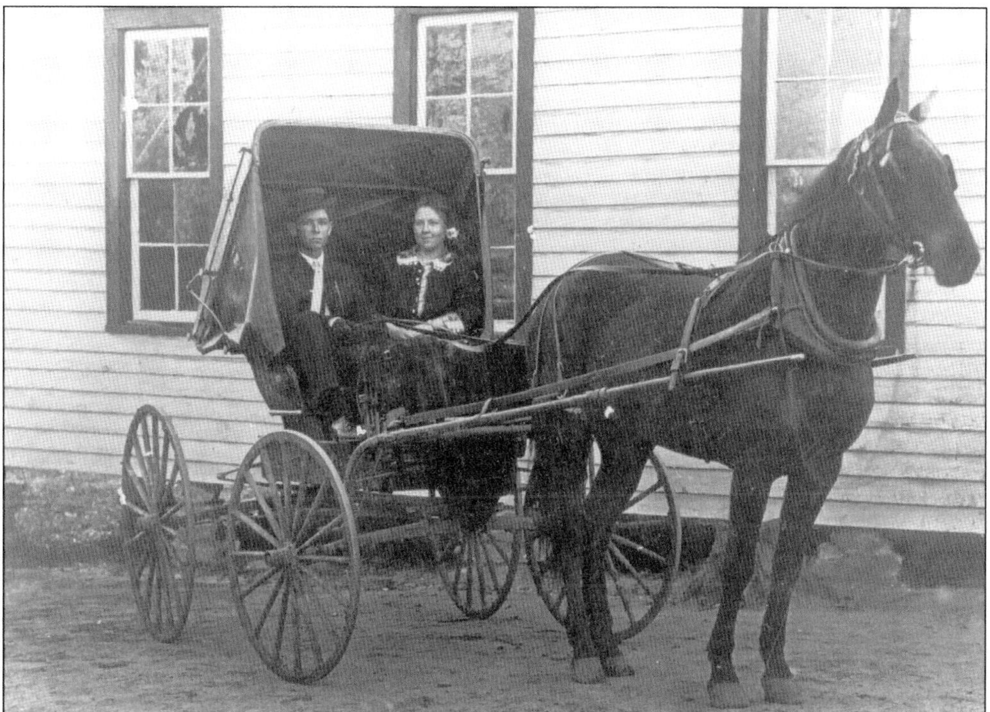

Taking an Afternoon Ride. John Allen and his sister Laura are pictured in the buggy outside Mt. Zion Church before 1915. (Courtesy of Clarence Allen.)

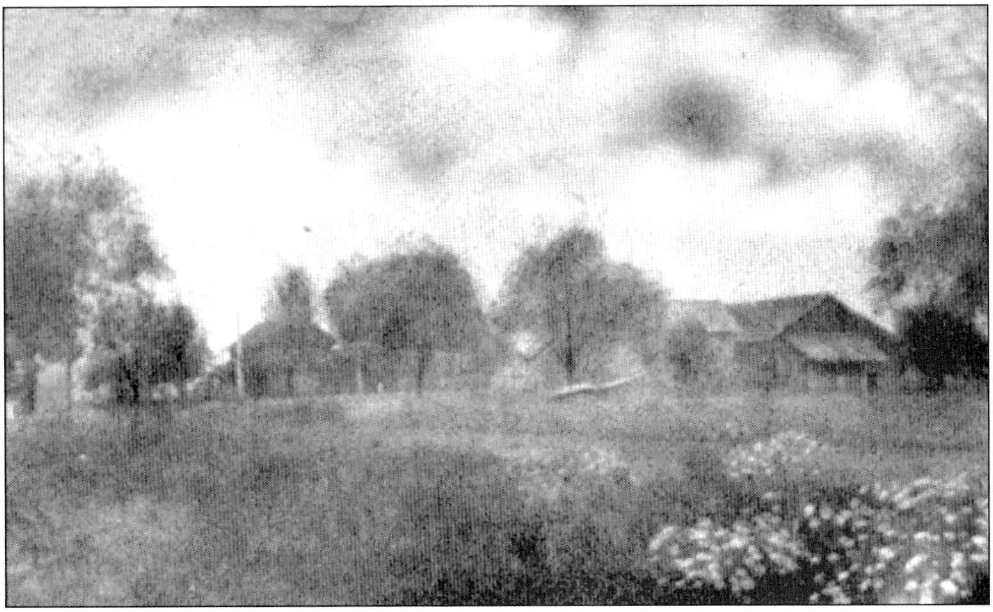

The James and Matilda Barber Farm in Shoals. The log buildings pictured, from left to right, are the fruit and vegetable dry house, the two-story house built in 1870, the wash house, the well house (located at the back corner of the house), the corn crib, the cow barn, and the double-crib feed barn. (Courtesy of Inez Jessup.)

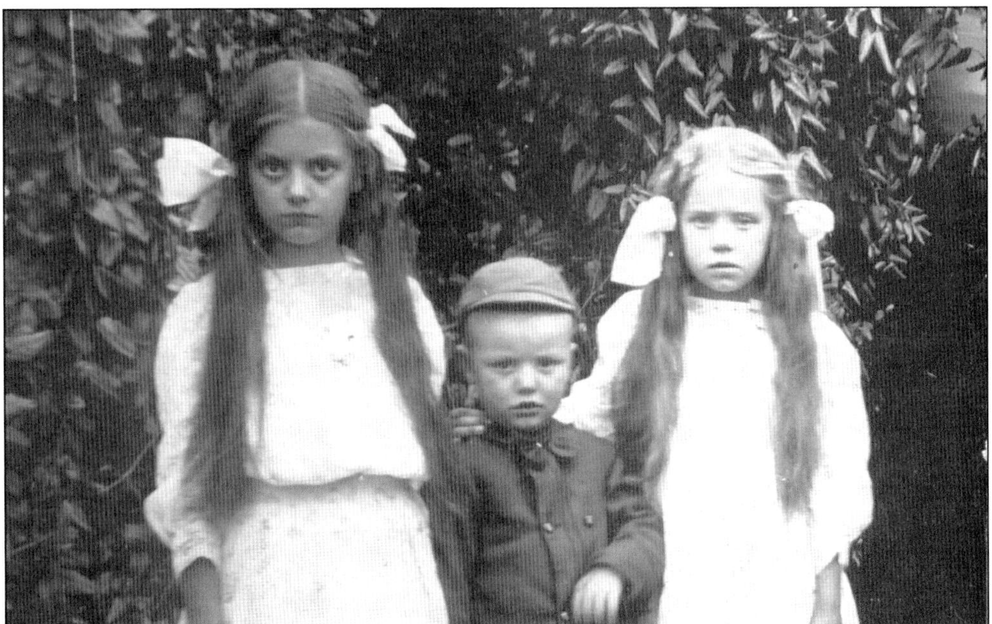

The Children of Henry Harrison and Carrie Lula Scott Bowen. From left to right are Roxie Bowen Roth, Robert "Bob" Bowen, and Viola Bowen Flynn. Roxie was born in Shoals in 1901 and served eight years on the Surry County Board of Commissioners as the representative of Elkin during the 1960s. (Courtesy of Lib Marion.)

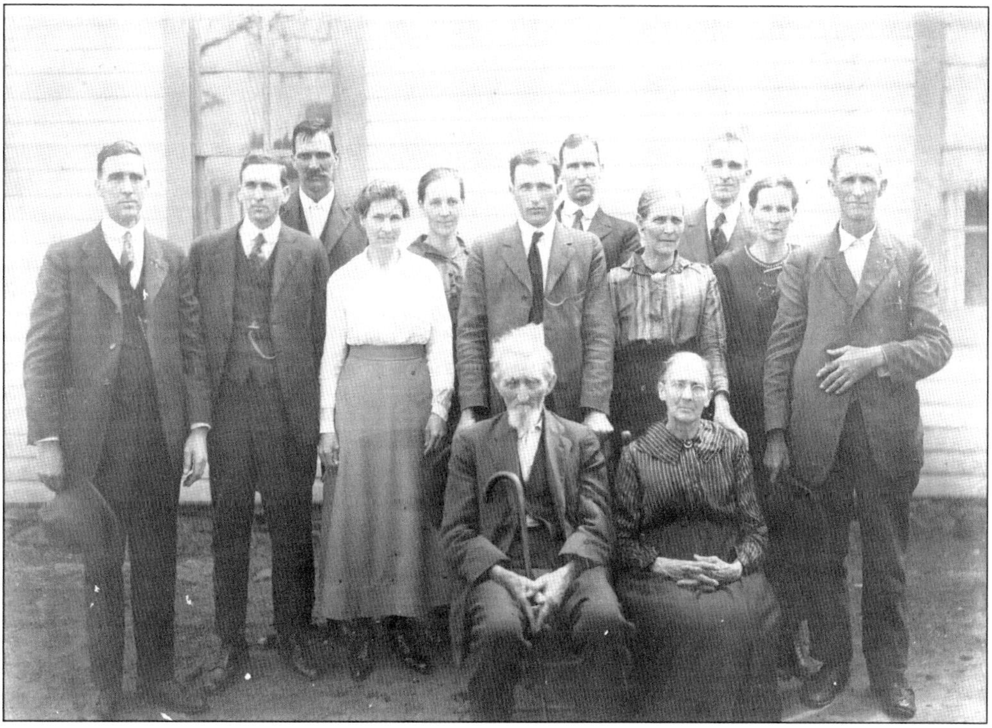

Caudle Family, Early 1900s. Seated in front are William and Parmella Pulliam Caudle, and behind them are their children, who are, from left to right, Ed, Ulysses, Jim, Annie, Effie, Early, Jack, Becky, Arch, Martha, and Will. (Courtesy of Jack Westmoreland.)

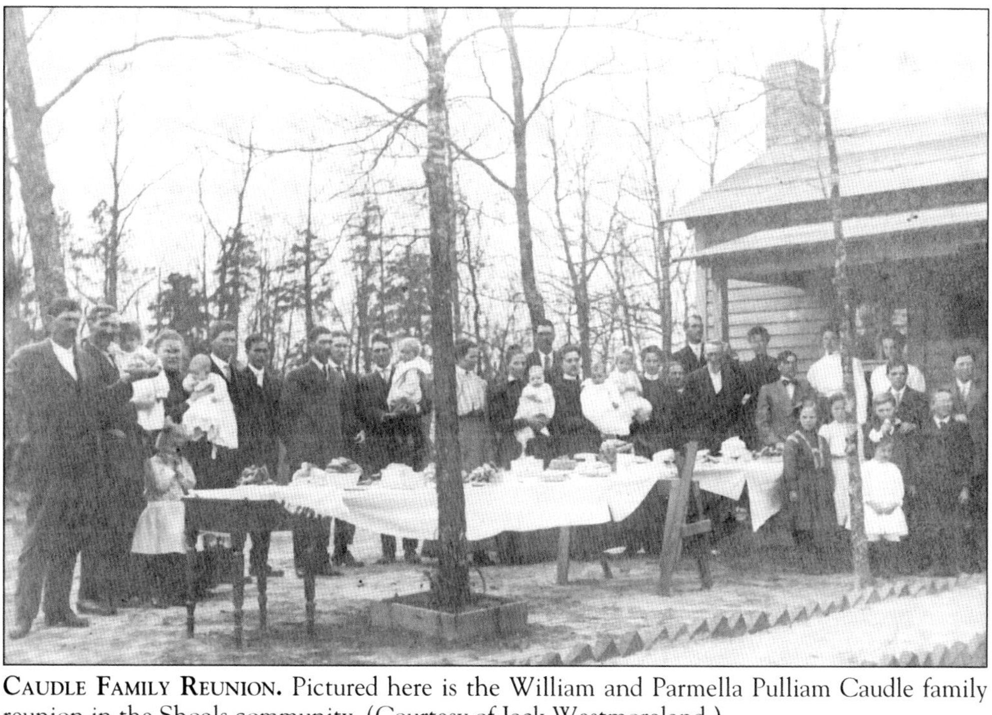

Caudle Family Reunion. Pictured here is the William and Parmella Pulliam Caudle family reunion in the Shoals community. (Courtesy of Jack Westmoreland.)

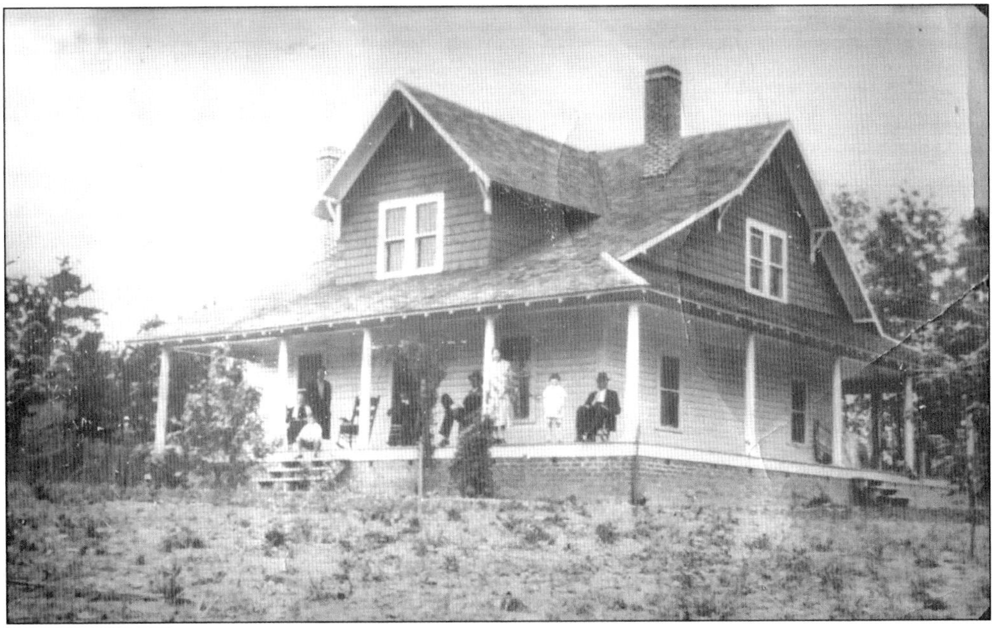

WESTMORELAND HOME, 1930. The home was built in 1927. Sitting on the porch steps is Roger Jackson Westmoreland, and behind him, from left to right, are Charlotte Kreeger Hauser, Mrs. Raleigh Hunter, unidentified, Reverend Raleigh Hunter, Annie Westmoreland, Billy Westmoreland Needham, and Joseph Westmoreland. (Courtesy of Jack Westmoreland.)

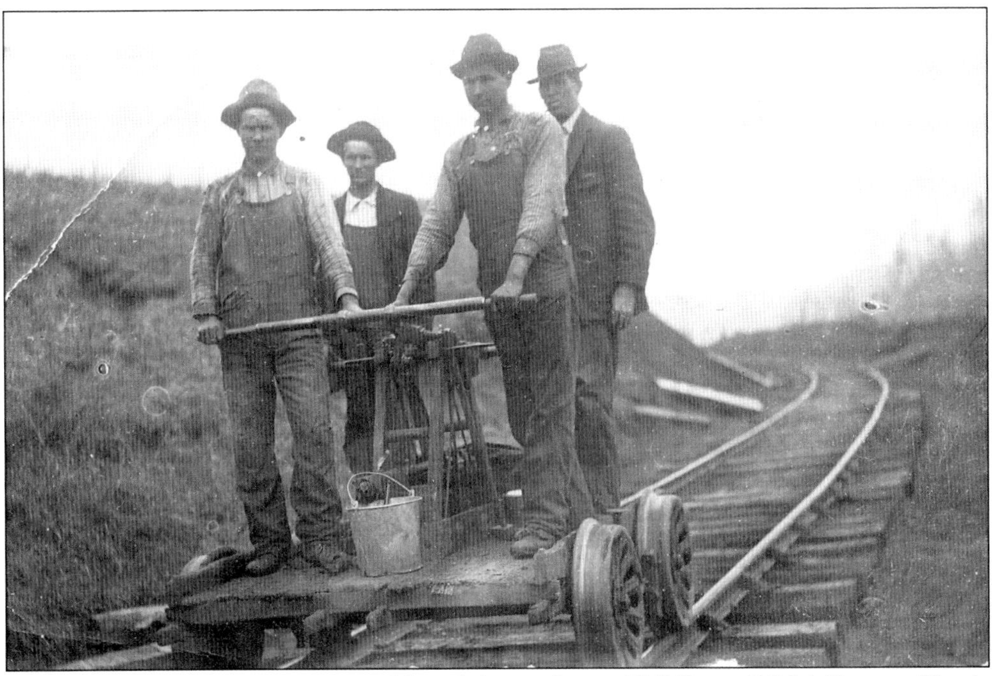

SHOALS RAILROAD STATION. Pictured from left to right are Will Kiger, Bill McKinney, Claude Douglas, and Joseph Westmoreland, who worked for the railroad for 23 years. A store and post office were also located at the railroad station. (Courtesy of Jack Westmoreland.)

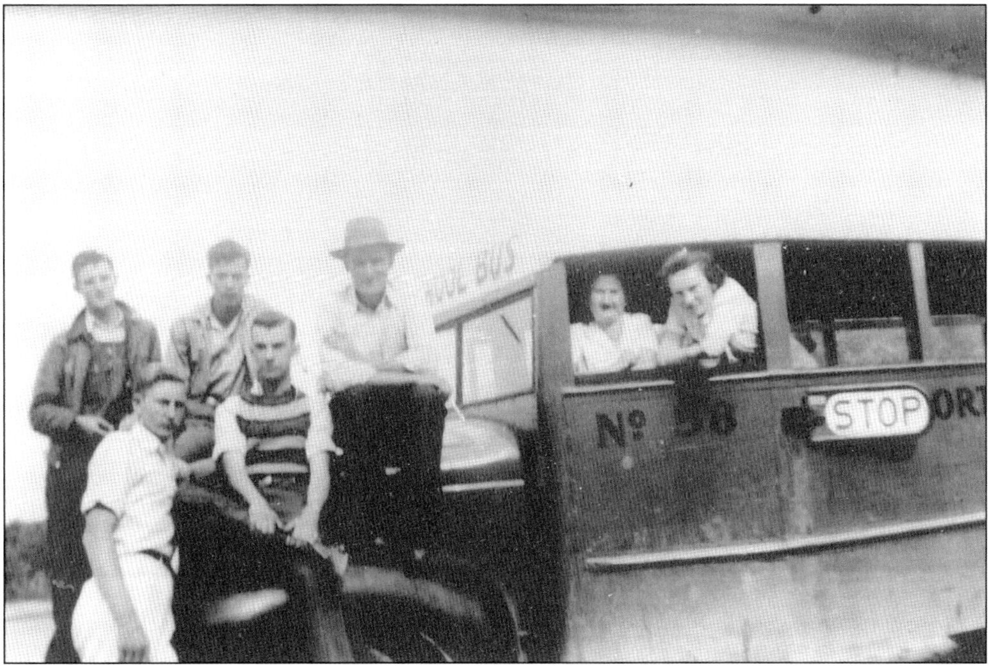

SHOALS SCHOOL BUS. Pictured, from left to right, are Hoyt Inman, Jim Fowler, Jack Westmoreland, Zane Caudle, and Dean Matthews. Inside the bus are Agnes Wright (left) and Ellen Hauser (right). (Courtesy of Jack Westmoreland.)

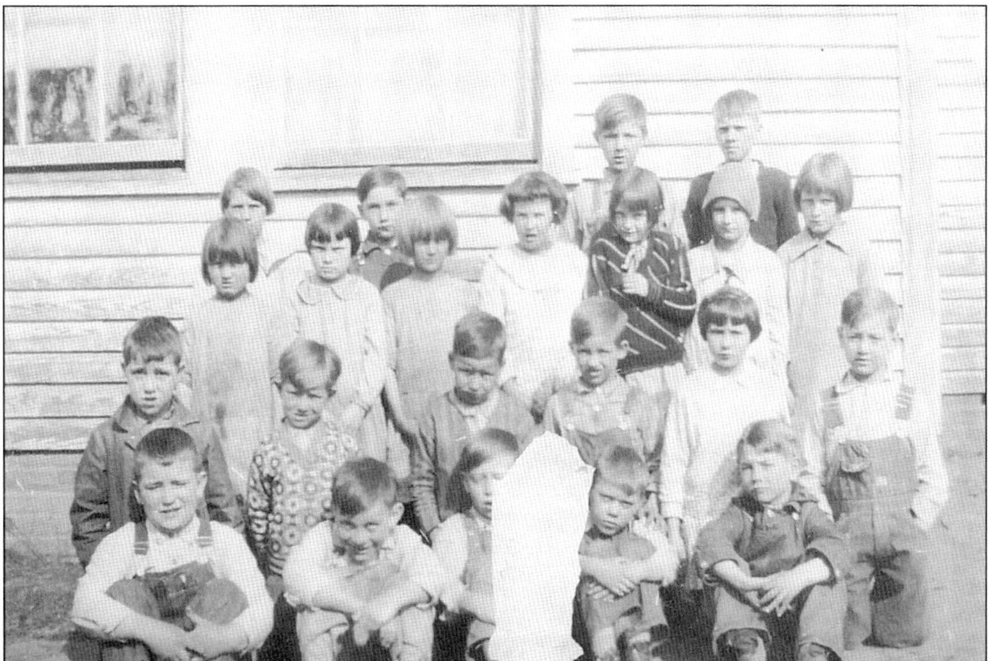

SHOALS SCHOOL CLASS, c. 1930. On the first row are, from left to right, Jack Westmoreland, Carl Hauser, and Albert Butner. The other students are unidentified. (Courtesy of Jack Westmoreland.)

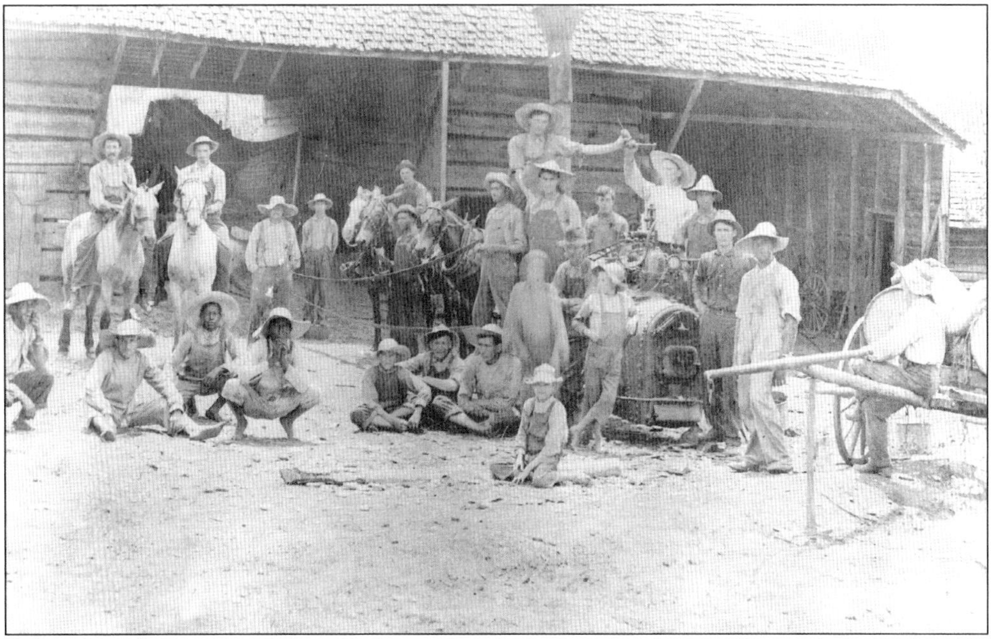

Hauser Farm before 1910. A work group is pictured in front of the double-crib feed barn. (Courtesy of Horne Creek Farm.)

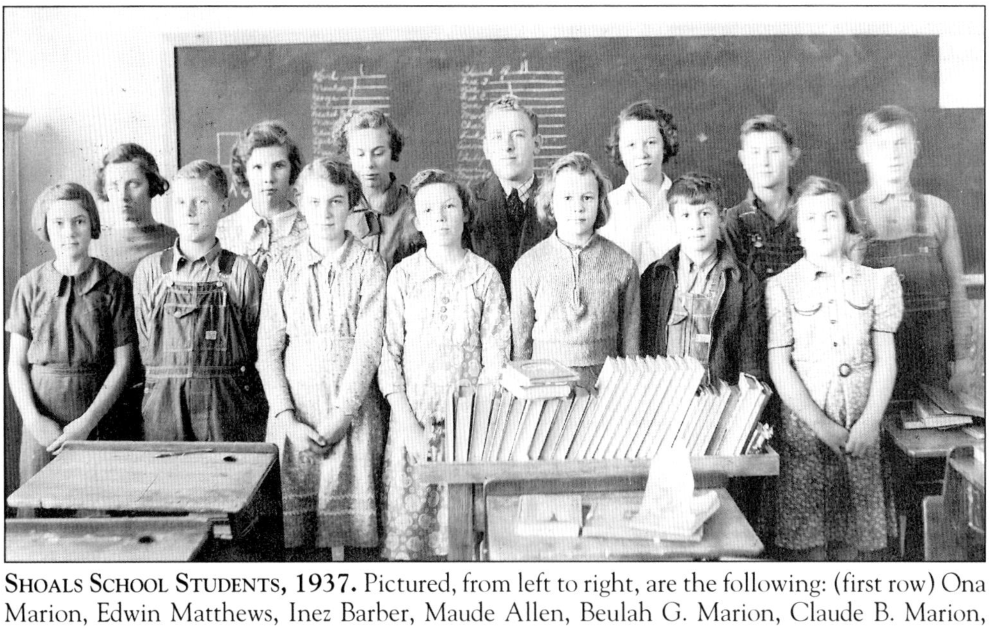

Shoals School Students, 1937. Pictured, from left to right, are the following: (first row) Ona Marion, Edwin Matthews, Inez Barber, Maude Allen, Beulah G. Marion, Claude B. Marion, and Margaret Marion; (second row) Erroll Owen, Opal Allen, Myrtle Fain, Shirley Ramey (teacher), Margaret Brim, Buford Caudle, and Luther Fulton. (Courtesy of Inez Jessup.)

Siloam Store, c. 1910. A.C. Snow and Oscar Snow are pictured in front of the store they operated in Siloam. (Courtesy of Frances Snow.)

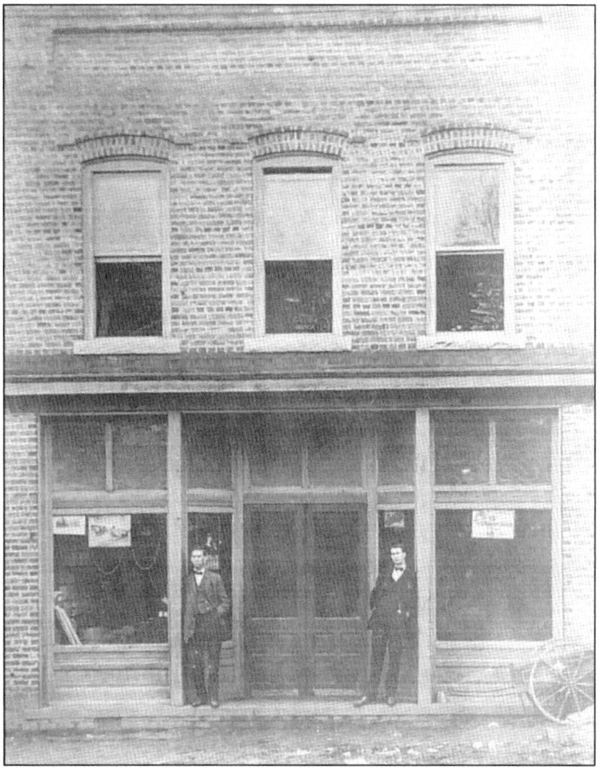

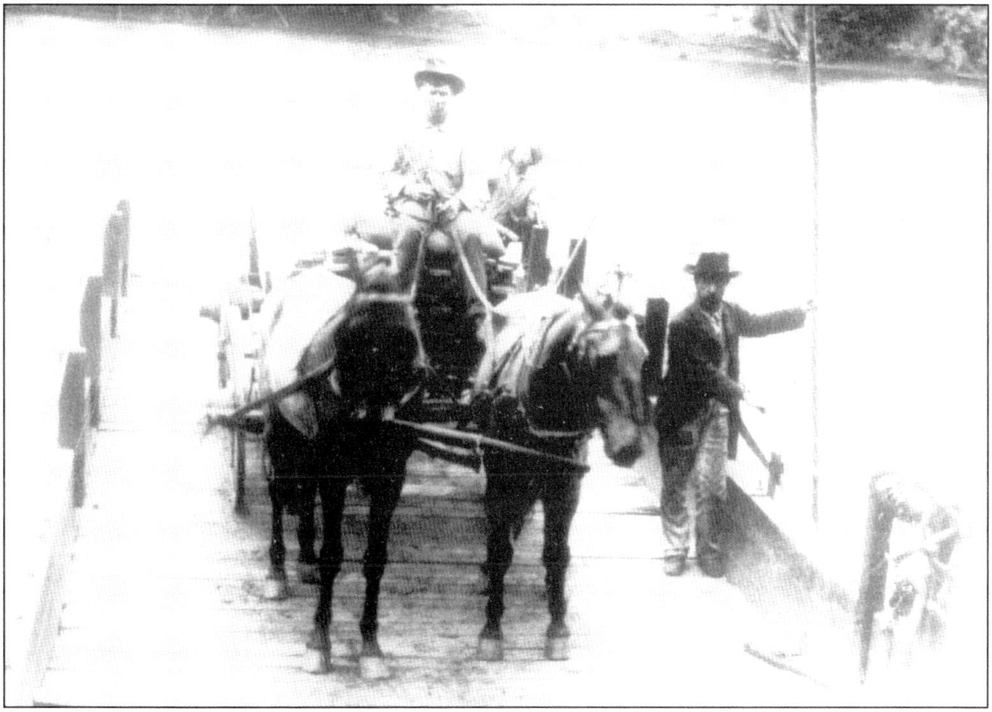

Hall's Ferry on the Yadkin River at Siloam. Hall's ferry was in operation in Siloam as late as the 1930s. (Courtesy of Irma Robertson of Yadkin County and Horne Creek Farm.)

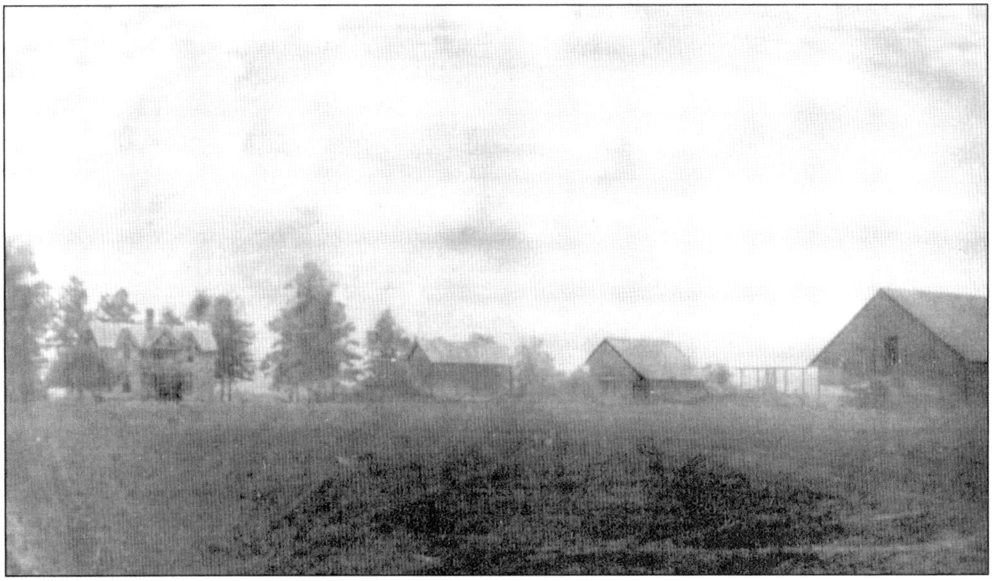

Paul Snow Farm, c. 1930. The Paul Snow farm is located on Hogan Creek Road. (Courtesy of Carole Simpson.)

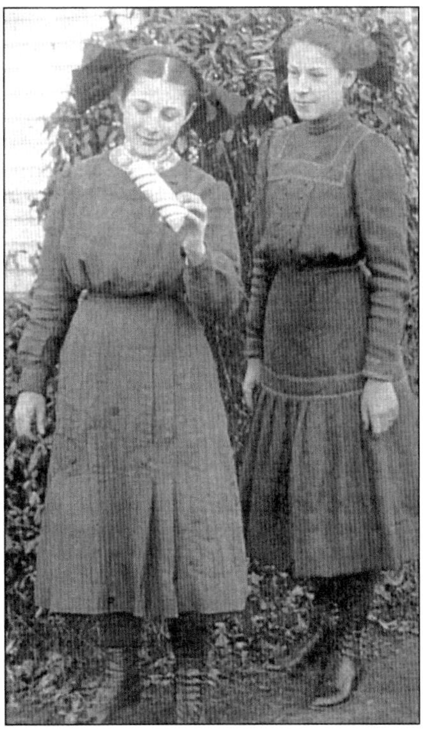

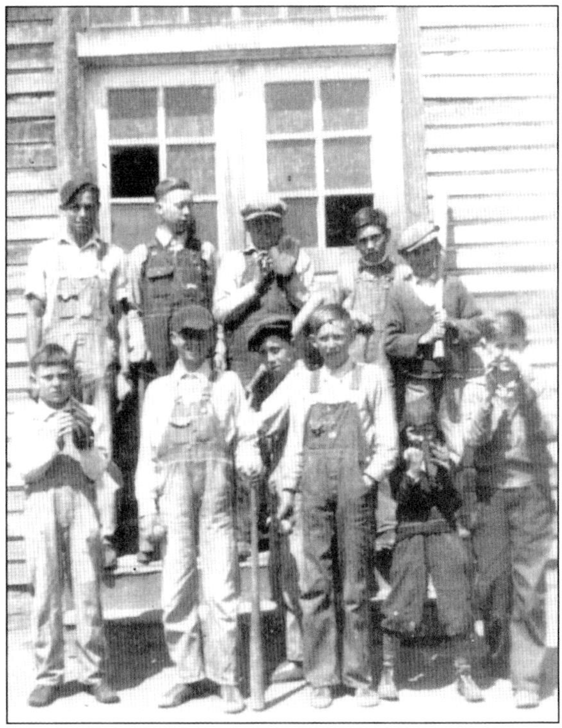

Left: **Young Friends.** Pictured here are Jennie Apperson (right) and an unidentified friend. (Courtesy of Frances Snow.)
Right: **Ball Players at the Old Shoals School, c. 1934.** From left to right are the following: (first row) Carl Hauser, Roby McCollum, Sam Scott Jr., Carl Scott, Billy Hicks, and Buford Caudle; (second row) Raymond Harvey, Albert Butner, Jack Westmoreland, unidentified, and unidentified. (Courtesy of Carl and Reba Scott.)

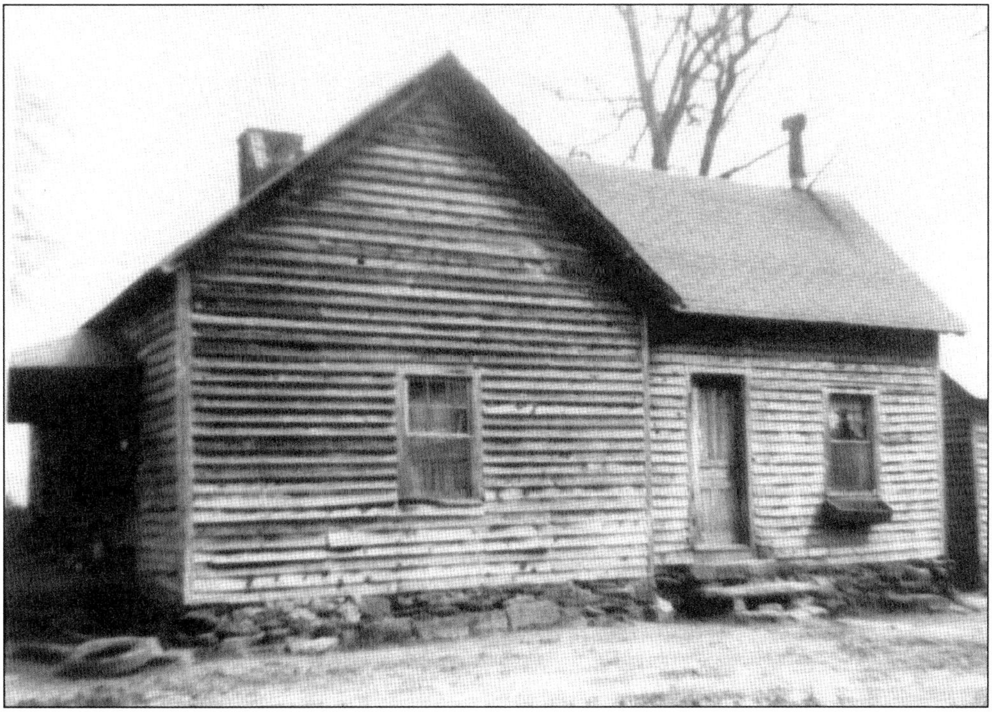

HARRISON PATTERSON HOMEPLACE. The Patterson homeplace is located on Stanford Church Road in Siloam. (Courtesy of Carole Simpson.)

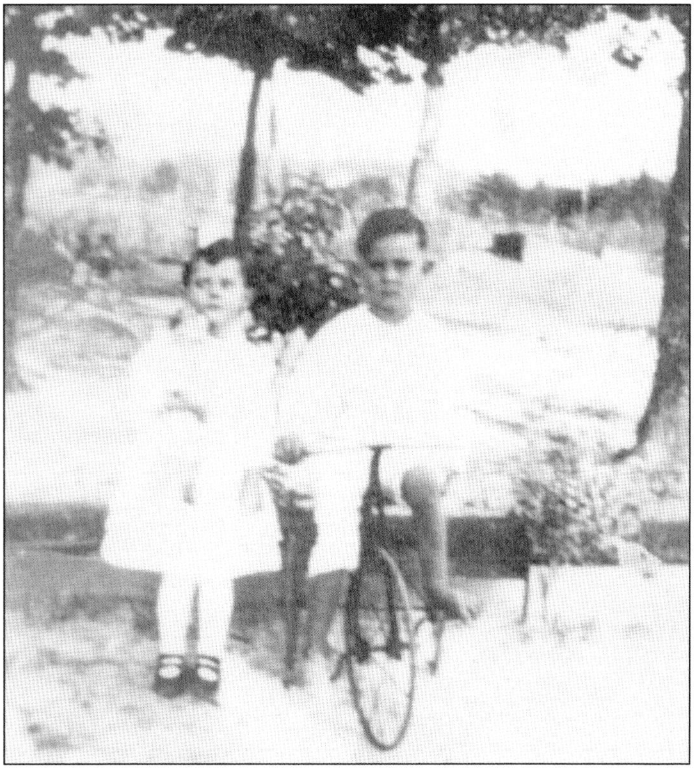

SUMMER PASTIME. Evelyn Patterson, with Elma Patterson, is waiting patiently to ride his tricycle. (Courtesy of Carole Simpson.)

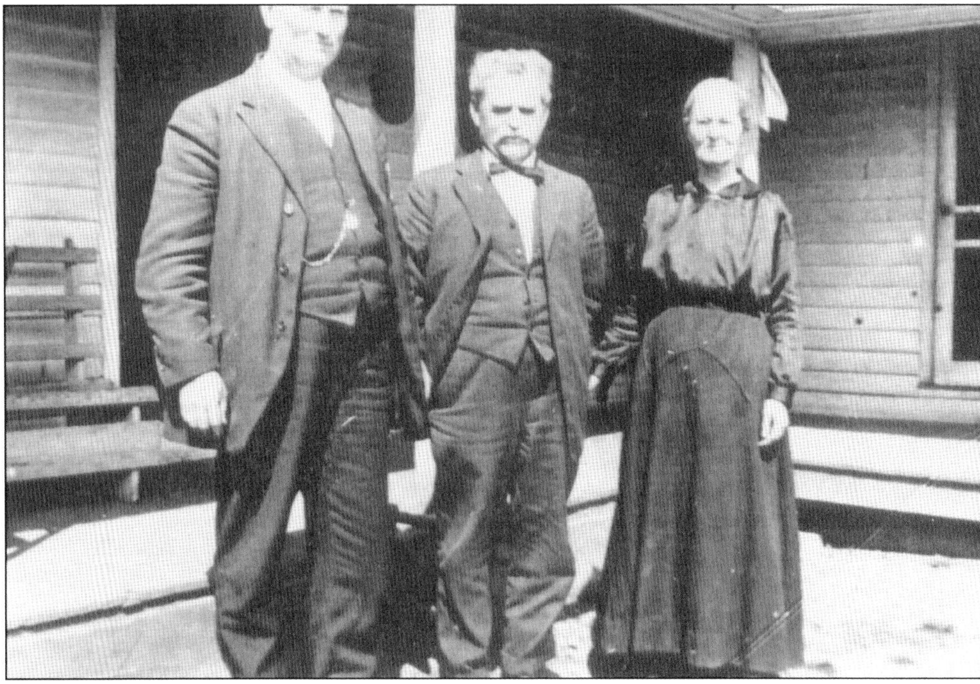

Hardy Homeplace. The Hardy homeplace is located in the Siloam community. Pictured here are, from left to right, Ira Bowman, John Hardy, and his wife, Emma Hardy. (Courtesy of Carole Simpson.)

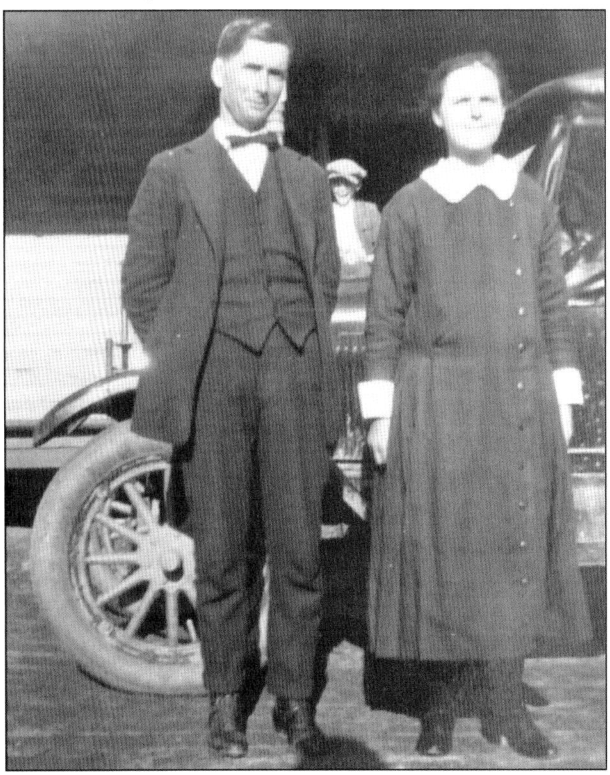

Delfaw and Minnie Snow. The Snows were prosperous farmers in the Siloam Township and well known for their lovely home and progressive attitudes. (Courtesy of Carole Simpson.)

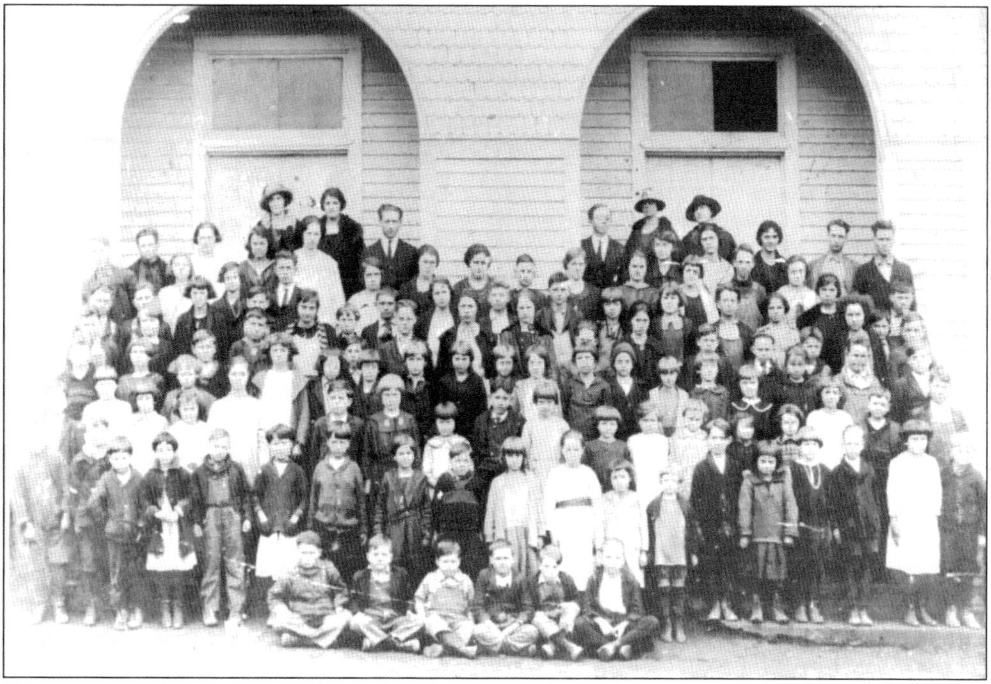

Siloam Academy, c. 1923. Siloam Academy was a public school in Siloam. The teachers who are identified on the back row include Nina Robertson Miller, Lela Hardy, Maggie Miller, and Pamelia Hall Davanport. (Courtesy of Carole Simpson.)

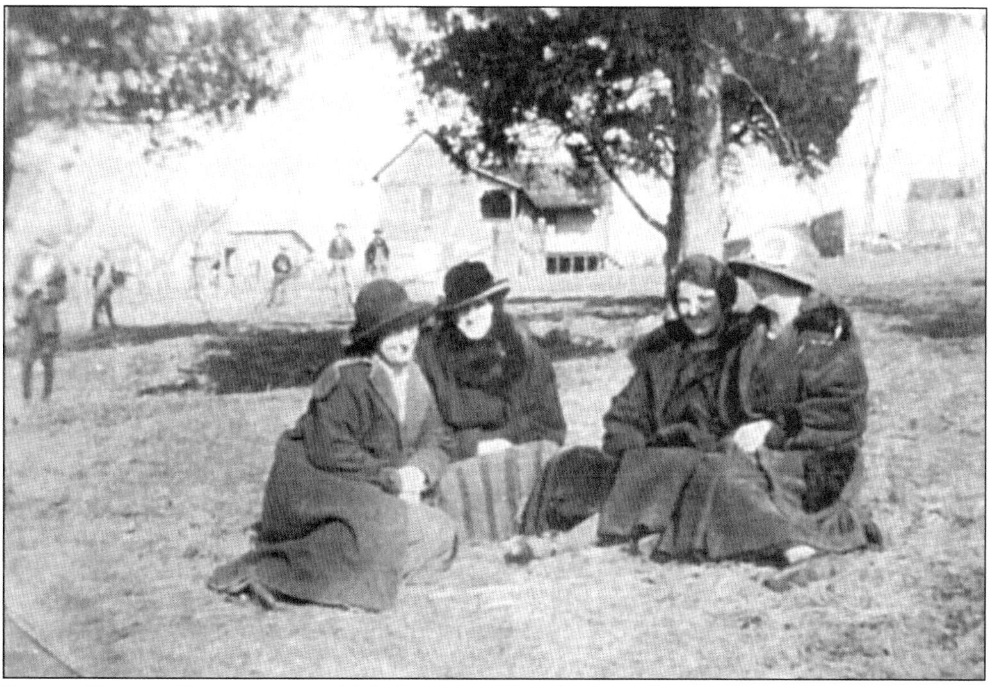

Siloam School Teachers, c. 1924. Seated on the playground at recess are, from left to right, Pamelia Hall Davenport, Nina Robertson Miller, Lela Hardy, and Maggie Miller. (Courtesy of Frances Snow.)

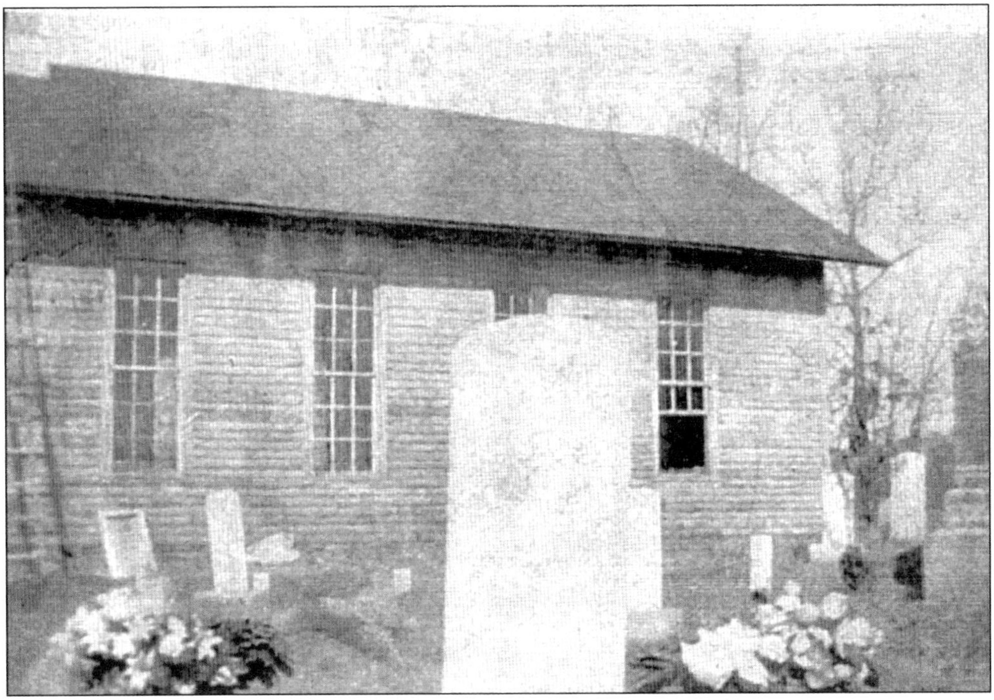

CEMETERY AT THE OLD SILOAM CHURCH. (Courtesy of Frances Snow.)

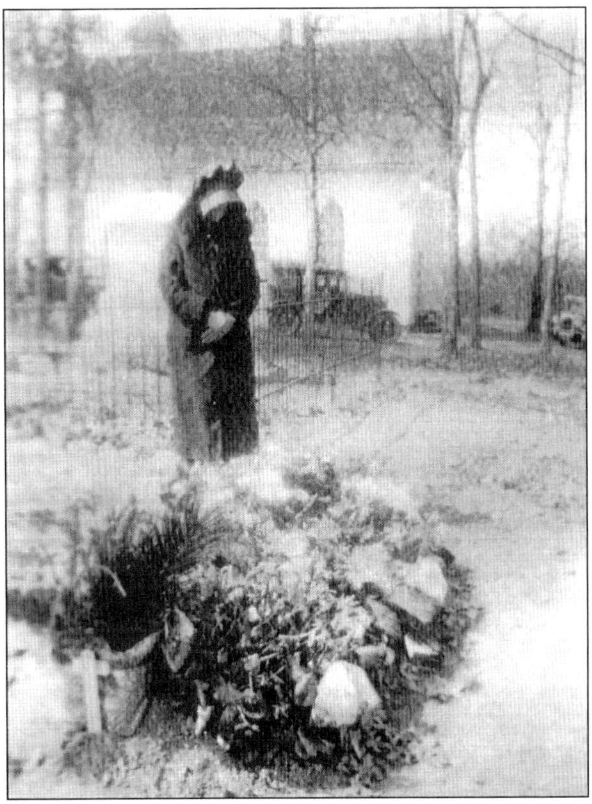

SILOAM BAPTIST CHURCH, 1928. Emma Hardy is pictured here visiting her husband's grave. (Courtesy of Frances Snow.)

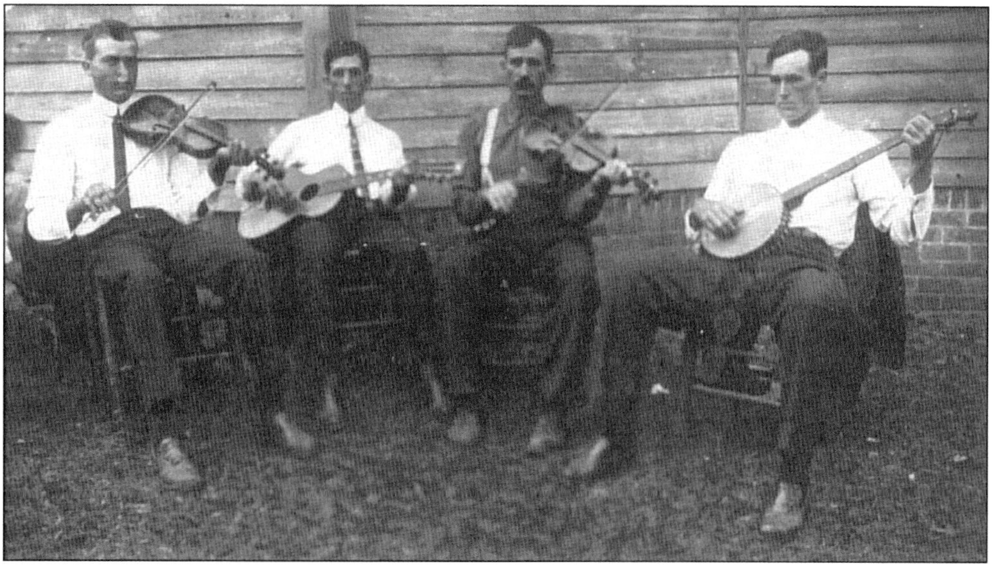

Fiddler's Convention. Surry County has a rich traditional music history. Many well-known musicians who play old-time mountain music are still playing at the local fiddler's conventions. The new Blue Ridge Music Center being built on the Blue Ridge Parkway will overlook Round Peak in Surry County. (Courtesy of Frances Snow.)

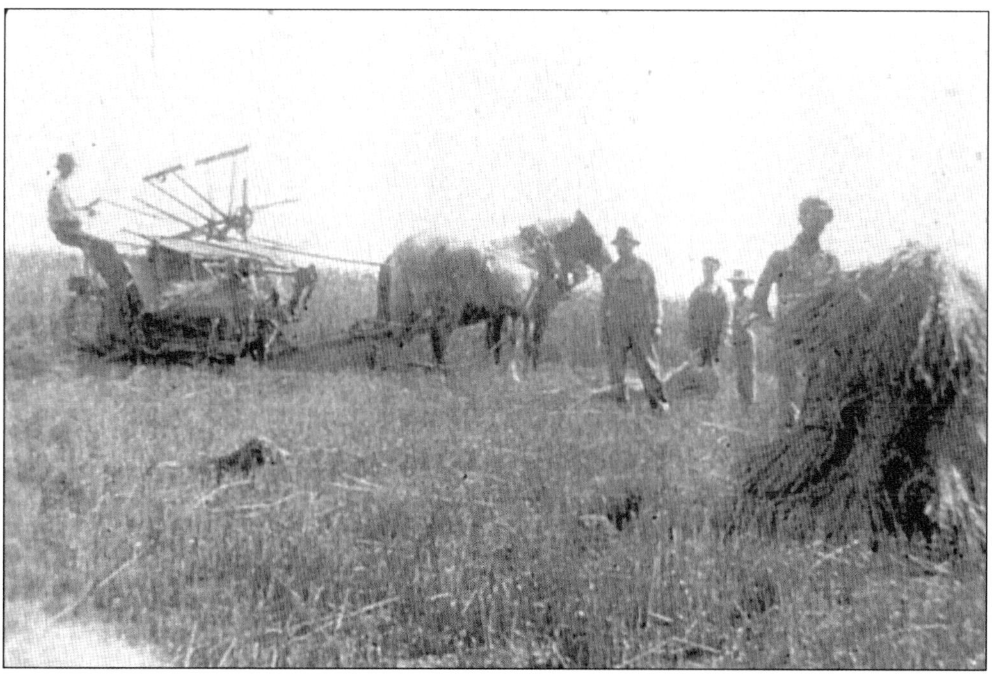

Harvesting Wheat. A.C. Snow is on the horse-drawn machine. (Courtesy of Frances Snow.)

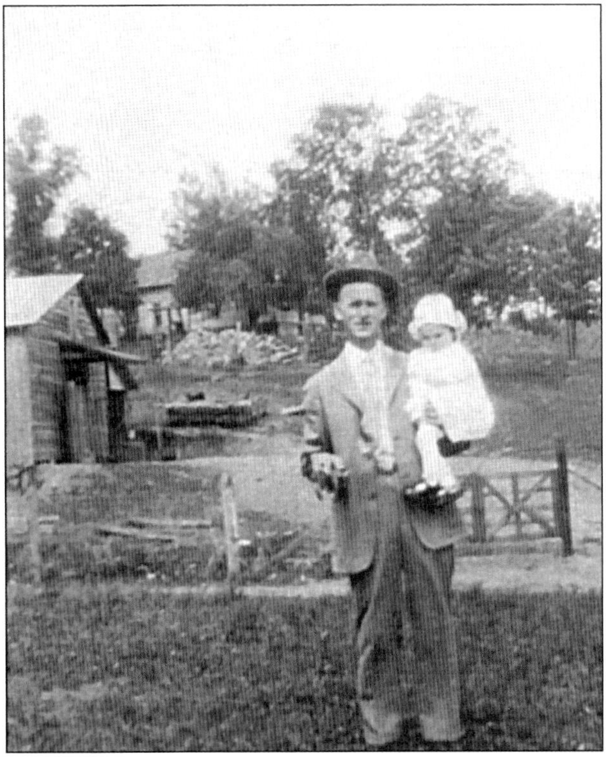

LIVERY STABLES IN SILOAM, c. 1923. F.E. "Ed" Snow and his daughter Jessie are pictured here all dressed up. The livery stables are in the background. (Courtesy of Frances Snow.)

RESTING A BIT. Mrs. John Hardy and Mrs. Samuel Atkinson sit on the grounds of the Siloam Baptist Church, *c.* 1940. The cemetery is shown in the background. (Courtesy of Frances Snow.)

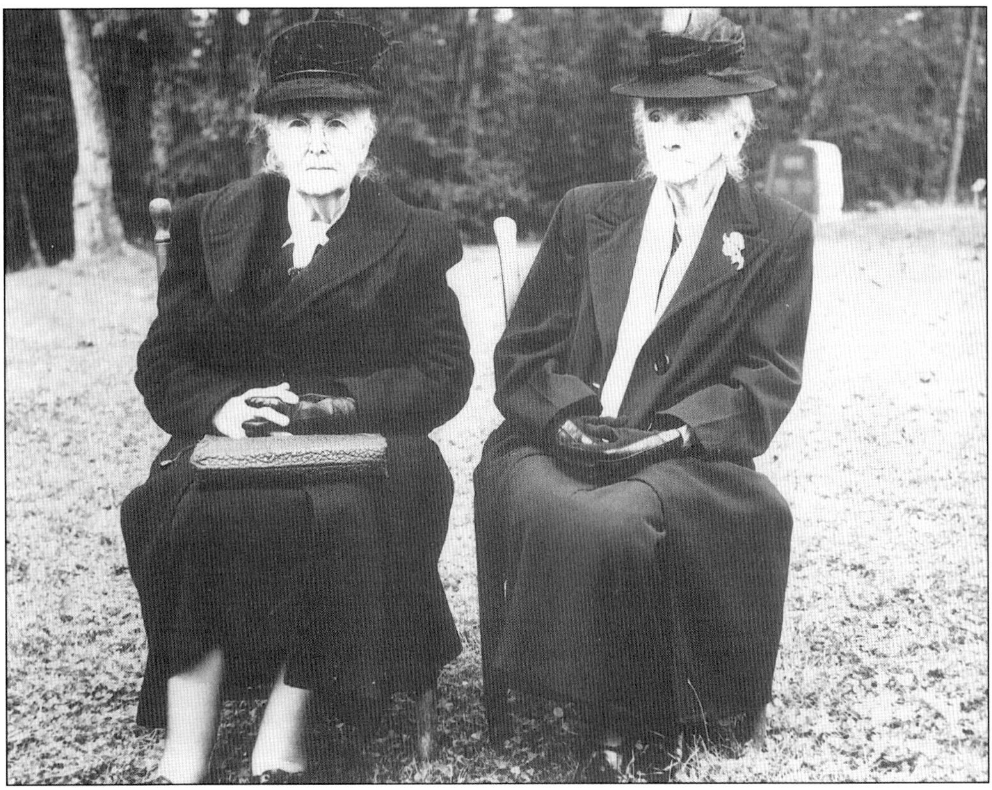

Ten

Stewart's Creek Township

Stewart's Creek Township is located in the northern part of the county. And the creek for which it is named, Stewart's Creek, rises in Virginia and flows southeast into Surry County and enters the Ararat River. Paul's Creek, which is about 14 miles long, also rises in Virginia, flows south through this township, and enters Stewart's Creek. Little Fisher River rises in Virginia and flows into the Fisher River.

Fisher's Peak (at an altitude of 3,609 feet) is in Stewart's Township and was named for Colonel Daniel Fisher who was in charge of surveying the line between Virginia and North Carolina. He took the line across the top of the peak; legend has it that the exertion killed him and he was buried on top of the peak. Round Peak Mountain (with an altitude of 2,094 feet) is located between Camp Creek and Little Fisher River, and Buck Mountain (with an altitude of 1,805 feet) is located between Fulcher Mountain and Round Peak Mountain.

Communities in the township include Crooked Oak, Beulah, Pine Ridge, Round Peak, and Laurel Springs. Some early schools in the area were Antioch, Beamer, Imogene, Ivy Green, and Zion Hill, and early churches included Beulah Methodist Episcopal Church South (established in the 1880s), Hebron Methodist Episcopal, Zion Methodist Episcopal Church South (established in 1885), Zion Hill Primitive Baptist Church (established in 1878 and sometimes called Crooked Oak), and Round Peak Primitive Baptist Church (established in 1825 by Elder Silas Jones). Early families in the area had such surnames as Barker, Bledsoe, Cockerham, Davis, Easley, Gallion, Golding, Hawks, Holder, Lowe, Norman, Snow, Stewart, Taliafero, and Tucker.

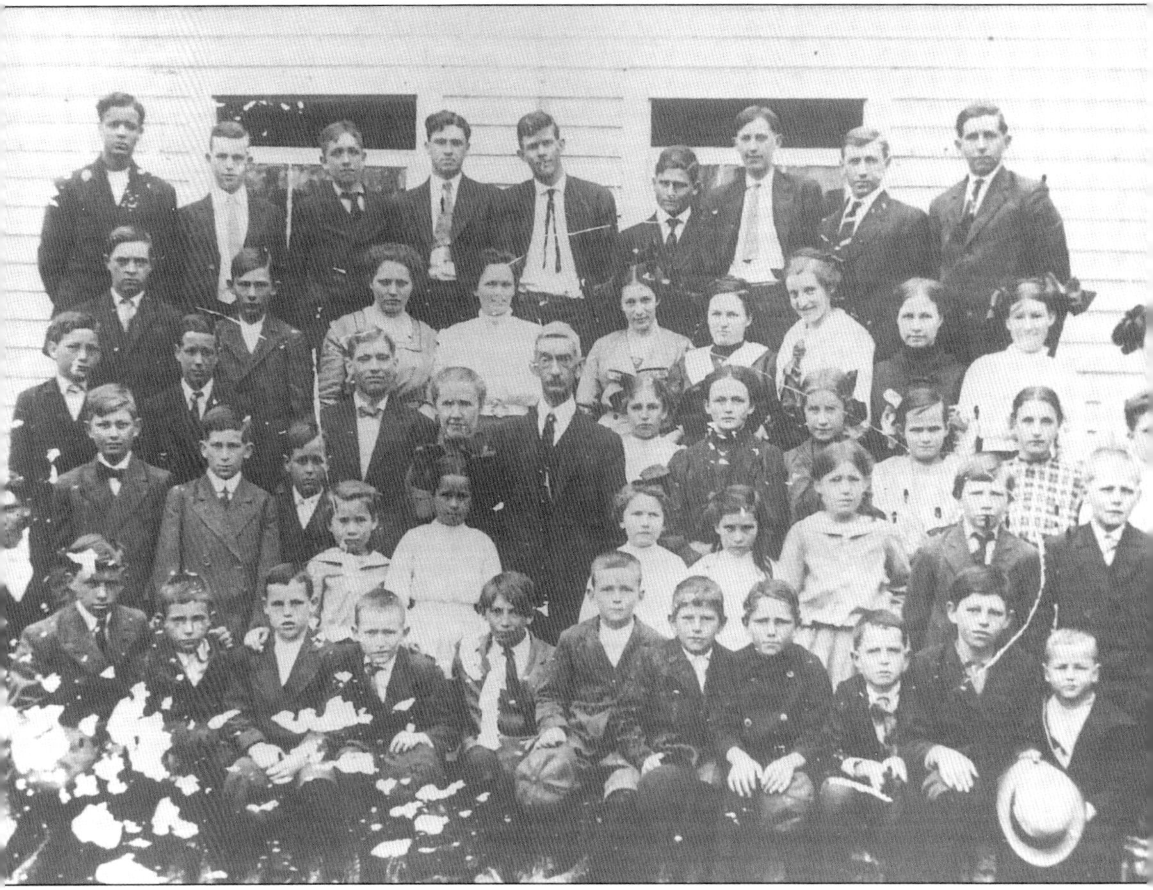

ANTIOCH SCHOOL STUDENTS, C. 1910. Pictured, from left to right, are the following: (first row) Ray Felts, unidentified, Raymond Allred, Rush Johnson, Dewey Collins, Carl Sparger, unidentified, Charlie Collins, unidentified, Kemp Reece, and unidentified; (second row) Samson Collins, Terry Beamer, Frank Johnson, George Younger, Mary Beamer, Sallie Younger, and the rest of the row is unidentified; (third row) Harrison Younger, Nathan Draughn, unidentified, Mary Bet East, Superintendent Cundiff, unidentified, Lucille Sparger, unidentified, Edna East, Margie Johnson, and Alice Allred; (fourth row) unidentified, unidentified, Mary Seal, Foy Johnson, Helen Sparger, Mary East, Mary Johnson, unidentified, and Annie Allred; (fifth row) Petis Younger, Caleb Allred, unidentified, ? Draughn, Guy Sparger, Benton Seal, Jess Gwyn, Tom East, and John Gwyn. The identifications were made in 1990 by Terry Beamer, age 90. (Courtesy of Gerald Collins.)

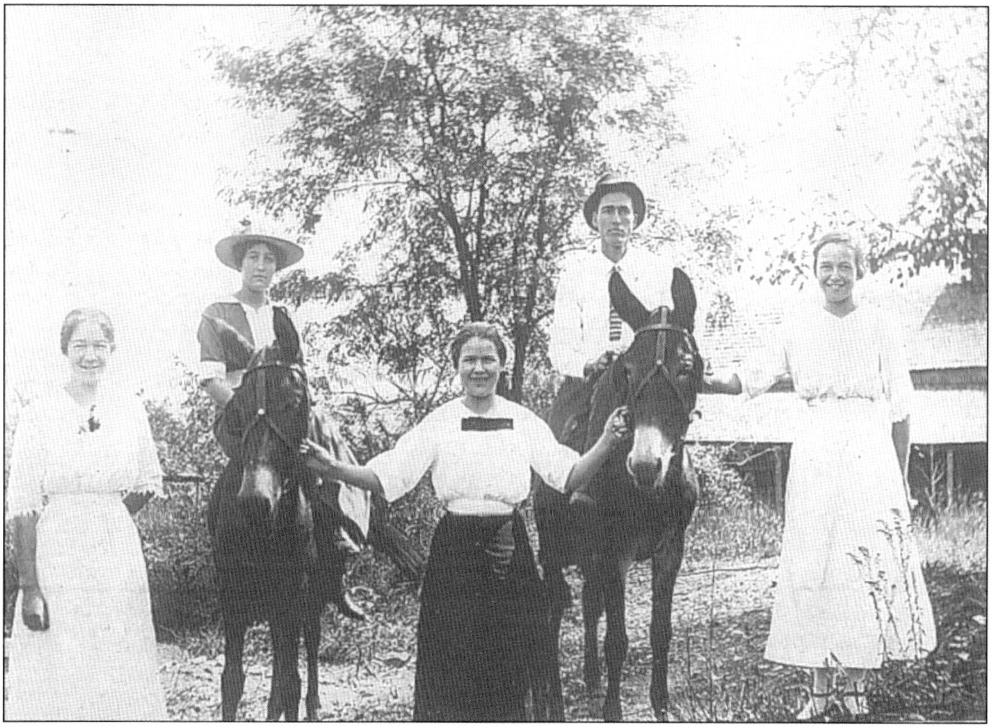

An Afternoon in 1917. From left to right are Dora Nixon, Jane Nixon, Vertie Nixon, Lester Nixon, and Zephyr Nixon. Lester Nixon died in World War I. (Courtesy of Janie Draughn.)

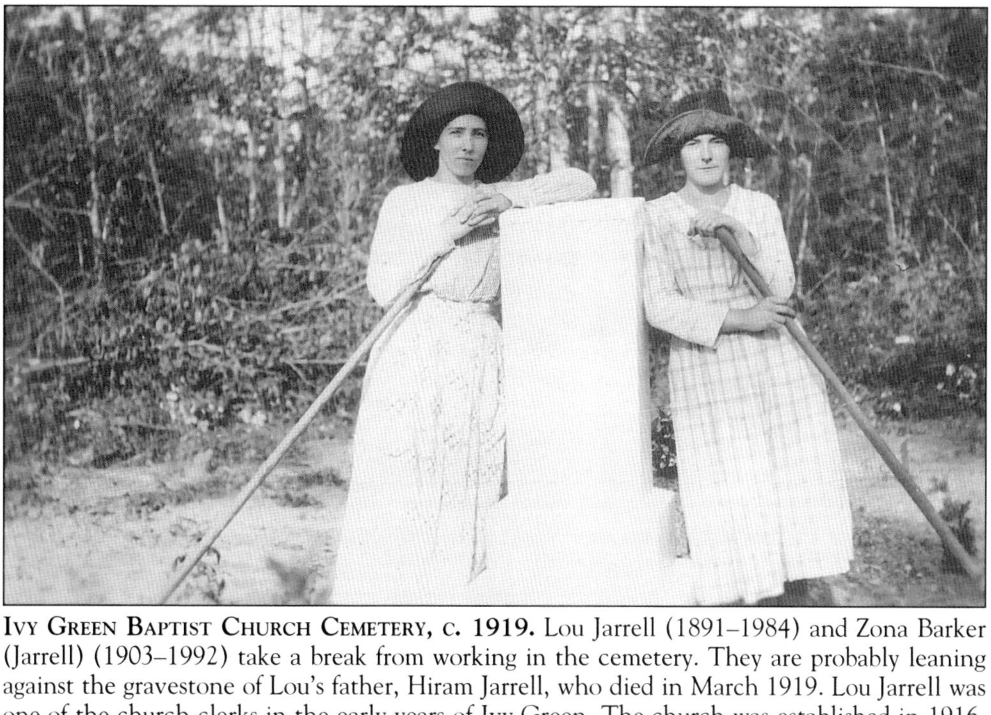

Ivy Green Baptist Church Cemetery, c. 1919. Lou Jarrell (1891–1984) and Zona Barker (Jarrell) (1903–1992) take a break from working in the cemetery. They are probably leaning against the gravestone of Lou's father, Hiram Jarrell, who died in March 1919. Lou Jarrell was one of the church clerks in the early years of Ivy Green. The church was established in 1916. (Courtesy of Wilma Hiatt.)

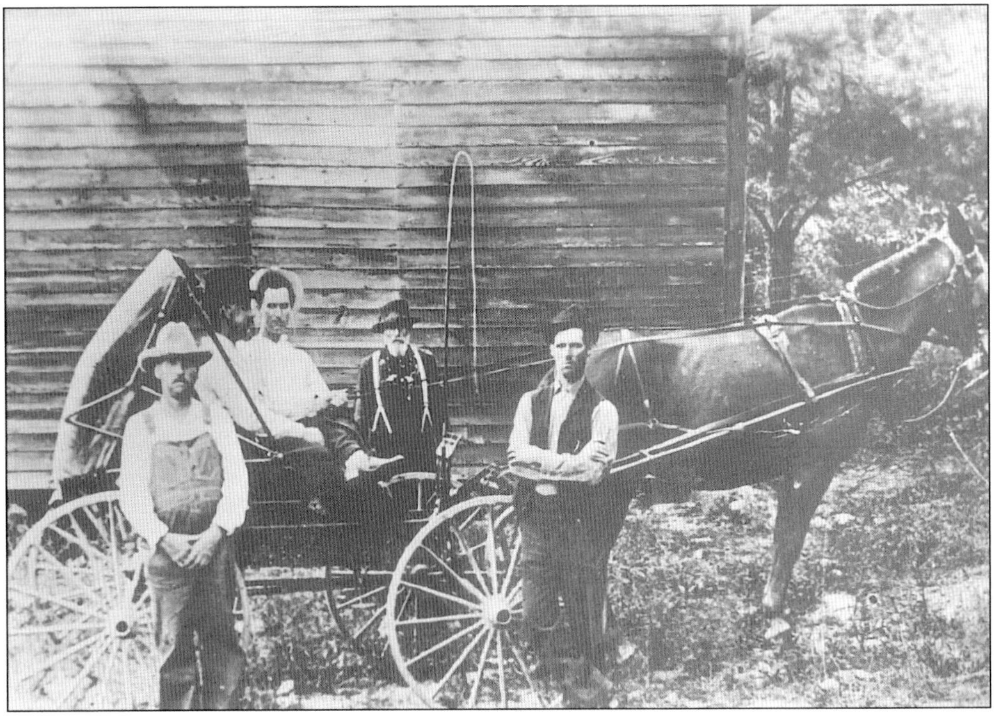

HORSE AND BUGGY USED TO CARRY MAIL. Pictured here is a style of buggy that was used to carry mail in the Stewart's Creek Township. (Courtesy of Wilma Hiatt.)

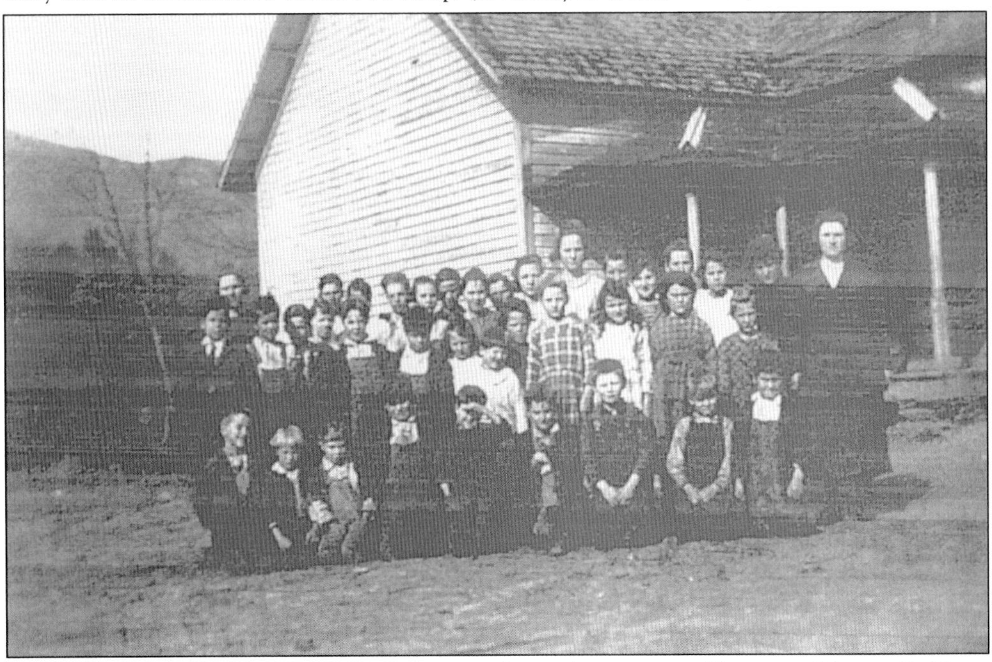

IVY GREEN SCHOOL STUDENTS, 1920. Among the students pictured here are Glenna Golding, Alex Burcham, Nina Stewart, Vera Snow Patterson, Evaline Burcham, Indy Ward, Ada Leftwich, Nonnie Snow, Grover Holder, Rayburn Snow, and teacher Grace Easter. (Courtesy of Teresa Smith.)

IVY GREEN CHURCH AND ROUND PEAK MASONIC LODGE. Ivy Green Baptist Church is located on Old Lowgap Road in the Round Peak community of Surry County. The deed for the church property was recorded in 1913, and an organizational meeting was held on October 16, 1916. In March 1929, a windstorm destroyed the church but the congregation immediately voted to rebuild on the same property. The church was responsible for the first floor and the Masonic Lodge for the second floor. (Courtesy of Teresa Smith.)

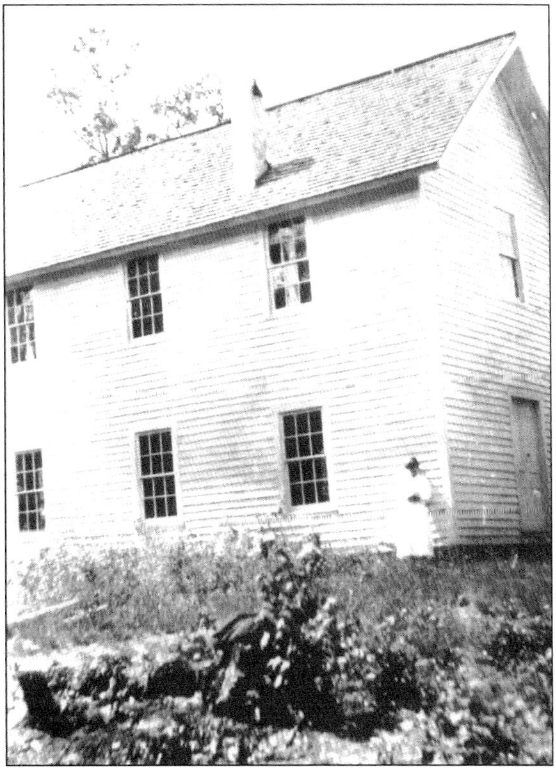

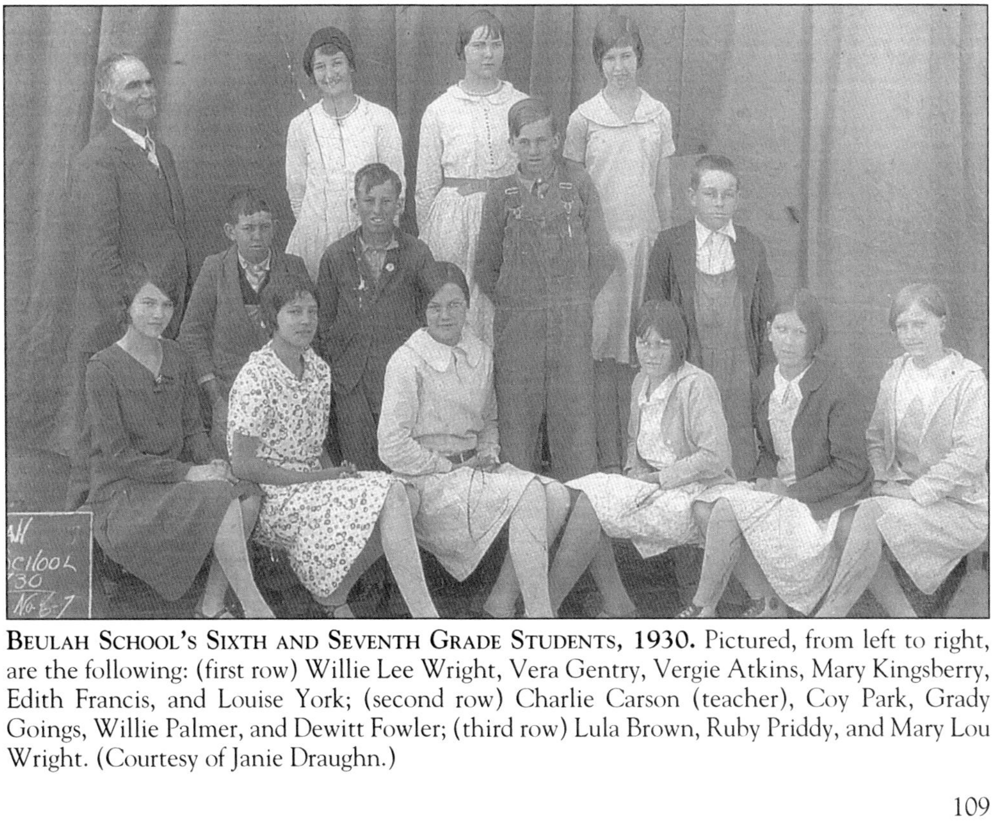

BEULAH SCHOOL'S SIXTH AND SEVENTH GRADE STUDENTS, 1930. Pictured, from left to right, are the following: (first row) Willie Lee Wright, Vera Gentry, Vergie Atkins, Mary Kingsberry, Edith Francis, and Louise York; (second row) Charlie Carson (teacher), Coy Park, Grady Goings, Willie Palmer, and Dewitt Fowler; (third row) Lula Brown, Ruby Priddy, and Mary Lou Wright. (Courtesy of Janie Draughn.)

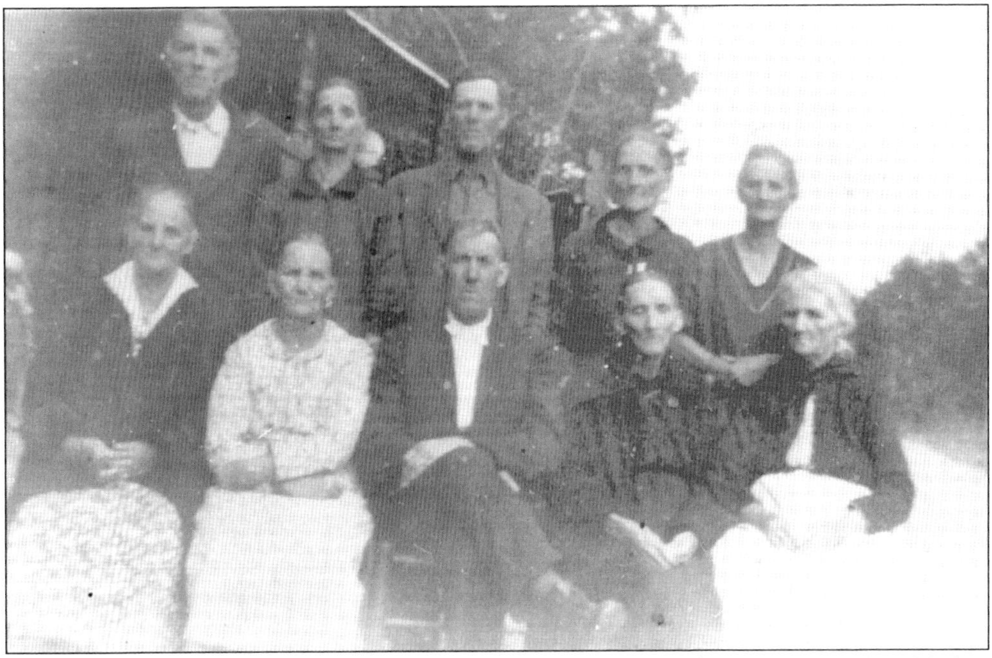

GOLDING FAMILY. From left to right are the following: (first row) Mary Payne, Ann Hodge, Tom Golding, Betty Snow, and Jane Payne; (second row) Fraizer Golding, Dina Surratt, Bogie Golding, Ada Sutphin, and Lonie Scott. (Courtesy of Carlos Surratt.)

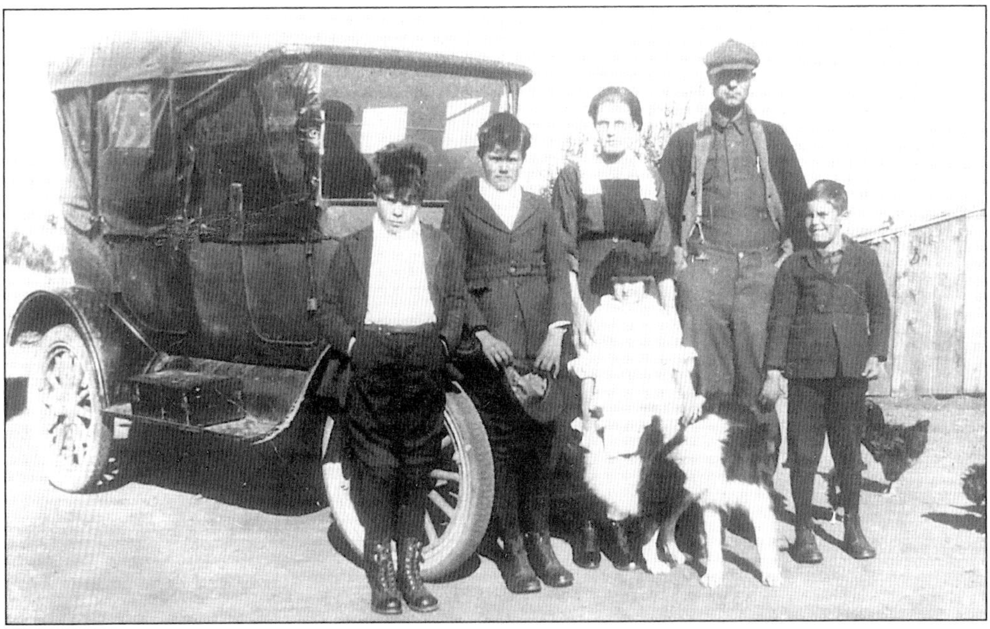

SAM HOLDER FAMILY TRAVELS TO NEW MEXICO. The Sam Holder family lived in the Pine Ridge community and was one of many families in Surry County to travel out West. This photograph was taken just before they left for New Mexico in 1922; they returned to Surry County in 1924. Pictured, from left to right, are Woodrow Holder, Grover Holder, Vivian Barker Holder, Sam Holder, and youngest son Harl Holder. Daughter Alice Holder is standing in front of her mother. (Courtesy of Wilma Hiatt.)

RASSIE ALL DRESSED UP, 1930. Mrs. Rassie Southern Watson looks too dressed up to put corn in the slatted corn crib behind her. (Courtesy of Helen Johnson.)

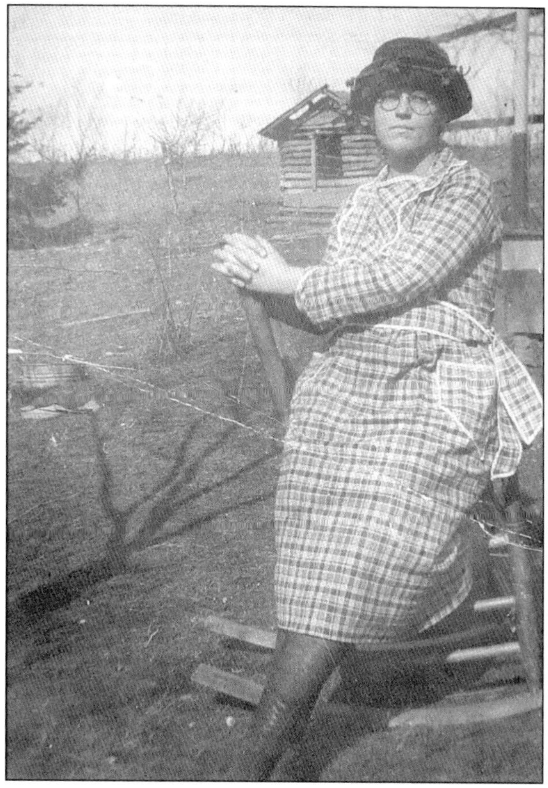

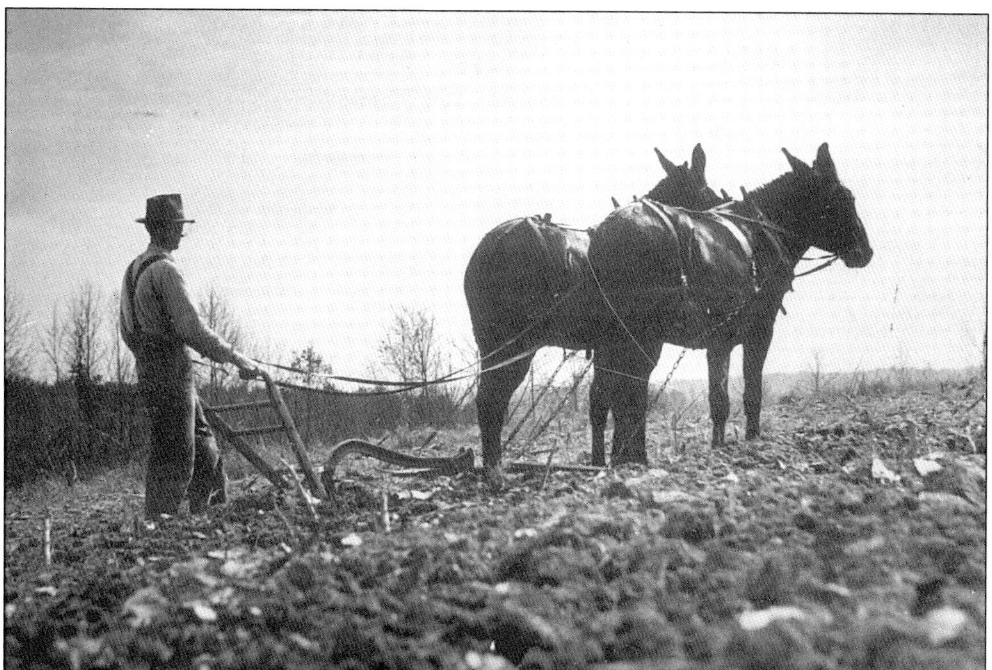

THE SPRING PLOWING SEASON. Vestal Watson is pleased to see Roda and Kate pulling the turning plow. He is preparing for another crop during 1931. (Courtesy of Helen Johnson.)

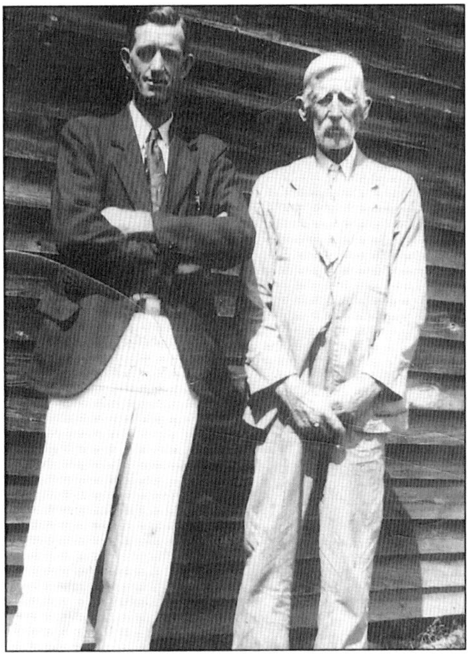

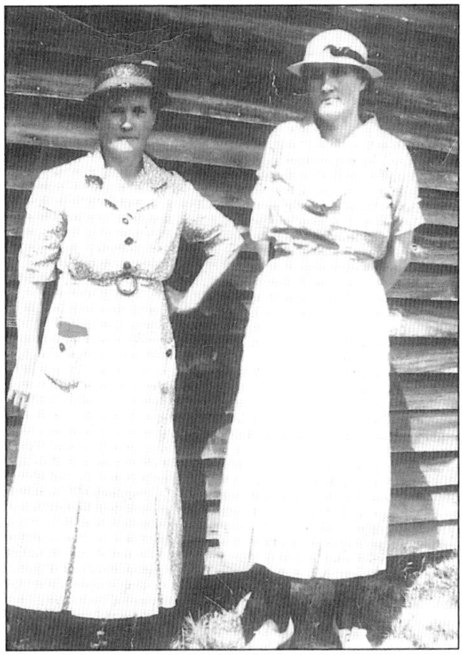

Left: **CHURCH ELDERS.** Elder S.T. "Sam" Atkinson (left) and his father, Elder William "Bill" Atkinson (right), appear here at the old Round Peak Primitive Baptist Church, *c.* 1936. (Courtesy of Jack McKinney.)
Right: **PAYNE SISTERS.** Rene Payne Sutphin (left) and her sister Cindy Payne McKinney (right) are pictured at the old Round Peak Primitive Baptist Church, *c.* 1936. (Courtesy of Jack McKinney.)

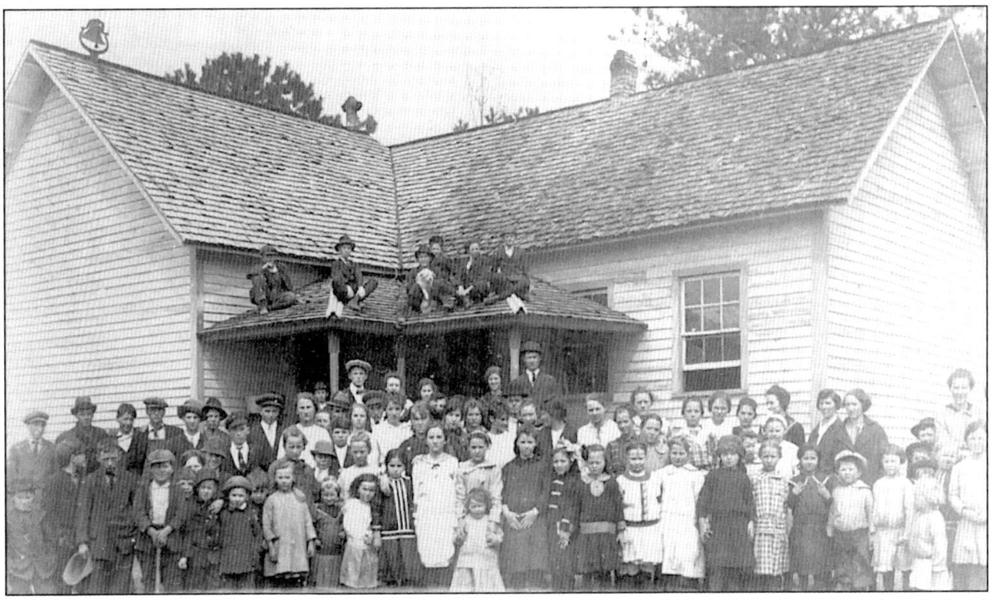

IVY GREEN SCHOOL, C. 1908. Pictured here are sisters Lou and Evie Jarrell (second and third from the left) standing on the porch with other students. Note the dog on the roof of the school. The Everett Holder homeplace near Ivy Green Church was previously the site of Ivy Green School. (Courtesy of Teresa Smith.)

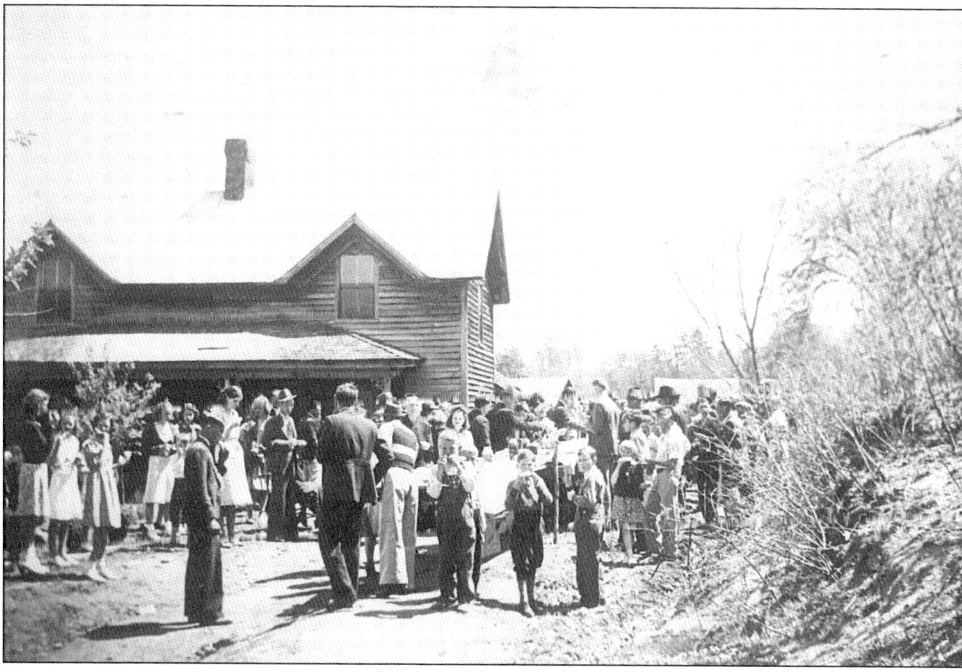

HOME OF WILLIAM AND DRUCILLA SEAL. Family members gather for a reunion in this photograph. William Samuel Seal (1865–1962) was the son of William Earp and Nancy Fountain Jarrell Seal. William's wife, Drucilla McHone Seal, was the daughter of Newel and Polly McHone and was 100 years old when she died in 1971. (Courtesy of Helen Johnson.)

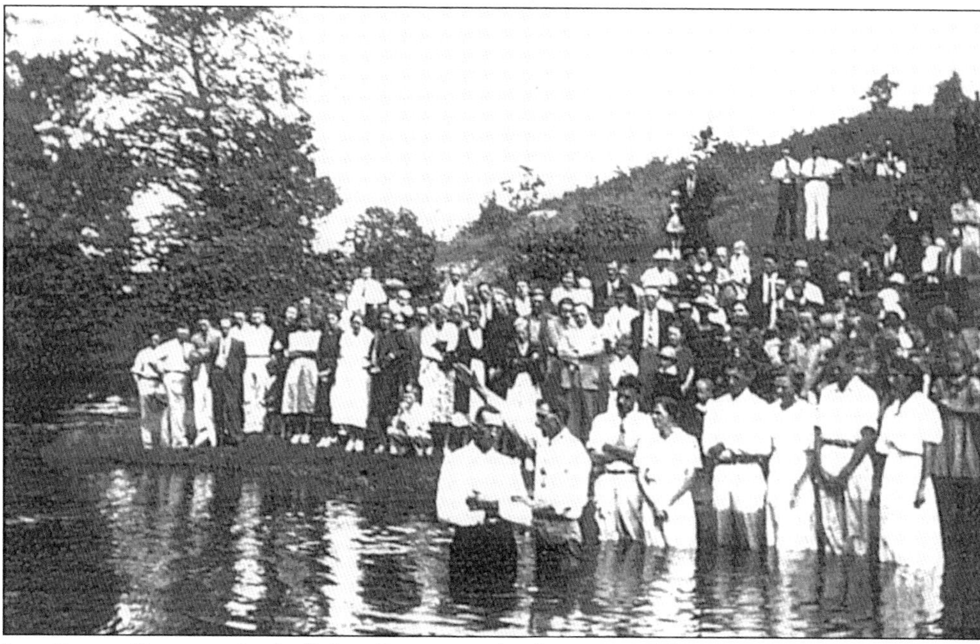

IVY GREEN BAPTISM. Little Fisher River was the location of the Ivy Green Baptist Church baptism in 1938. Pictured, from left to right, are Edgar J. Smith, Reverend Albert Gilley, Garner Moore, Beatie Moore, Charlie Fulk, Imogene Fulk, Oren Jarrell, and Treva Stewart (standing in the water). (Courtesy of Ethel Smith.)

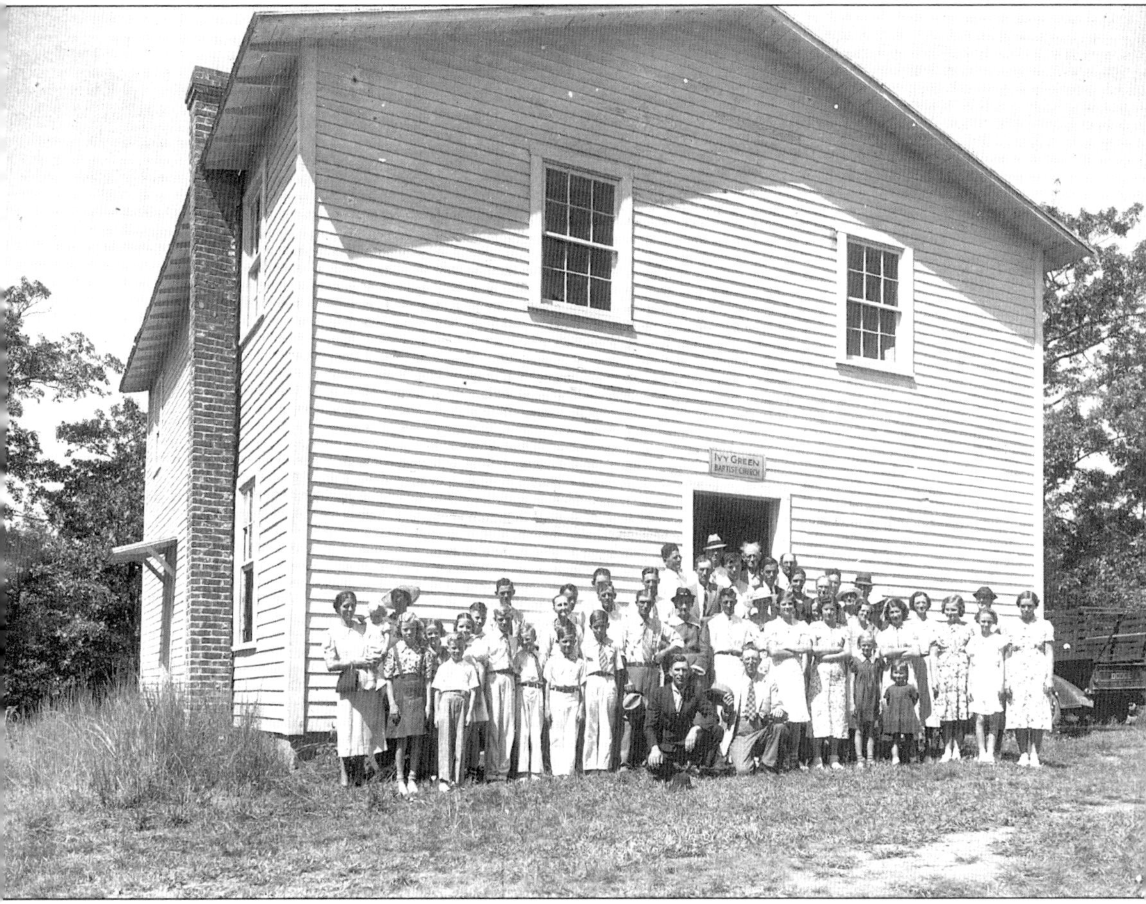

IVY GREEN BAPTIST CHURCH, 1938. Pictured in this photograph are Zona Barker Jarrell, Wilma Lee Jarrell, Laura Stewart, Mary Rose Jarrell, Betty Jo Jarrell, Rudolph Jarrell, Mary Katherine Tickle, Junior Tickle, Oren V. Jarrell, unidentified, Clellan Jarrell, Marvin Sutphin, Missouri Calloway, Fred Thompson, Jack Seal, Sid Jarrell, Ralph Thompson, Charlie Fulk, Luther Tickle, Benton Seal, Drucilla Seal, J. Albert Gilley, Dan Calloway, Wesley Seal, Clarence Hawks, Alfred Moore, Dave Turney, Alphonso Thompson, Lizzie Seal, J.A. Henson, Sam Seal, Effie Thompson, Mabel Tickle, Mary Jane Tickle, Garner Moore, Hazel Tickle, Beatie Moore, Ed Woodruff, Emogene Jarrell Fulk, Josifae Jarrell, Josie Seal, Treva Stewart Hodges, Mary Ruth Thompson, Cordia Holder Woodruff, Ethel Calloway Smith, Evie Jarrell, Bernelle Jarrell Rich, and Pauline Thompson. (Courtesy of Wilma Hiatt.)

Eleven

South Westfield and Westfield Townships

The South Westfield Township lies in eastern Surry County, and the Westfield Township lies in the more northeastern portion of the county, just north of South Westfield. Both townships are bordered on the east by Stokes County, North Carolina, and on the west by Mount Airy Township.

Stony Creek and Tom's Creek flow south through the South Westfield Township and enter the Ararat River. The Chinquapin Creek rises in western Stokes County and flows through South Westfield, where it enters Tom's Creek. Among the early schools located in South Westfield were Cooks, Hill, Simmons Grove, and Taylor.

Westfield is one of the oldest settlements in the county and grew up around a Quaker mission established there in 1760. The community was first known as Tom's Creek but was renamed Westfield in 1786 because it was a western missionary field for the New Garden Quakers. Some of the names associated with the original membership of Westfield Monthly Meeting are Ballard, Beales/Beals, Beeson, Bond, Bryant, Burris, Carr, Carson, Davis, Frazier, Grigg, Hart, Hiatt, Jackson, Jessop, Jones, Mackiney, Pinson, Puckett, Reece, Simmons, Sumner, and White. Mount Herman Methodist Episcopal Church was organized in 1829. Some of the early schools in Westfield included Albion, Brim, Hollow Springs, Knob, and Love. Chestnut Ridge is located here between the Rutledge Creek, which rises in the township and flows southeast into the Ararat River and the head of Big Creek. Archies Creek flows east into Stokes County, where it enters the Dan River.

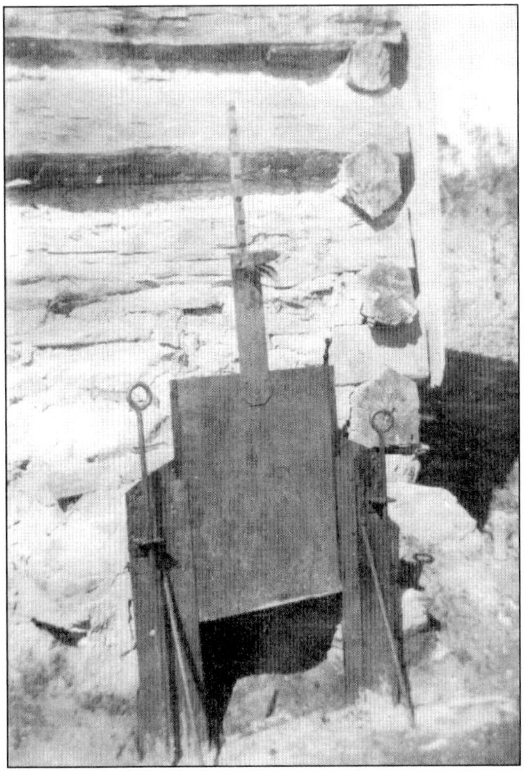

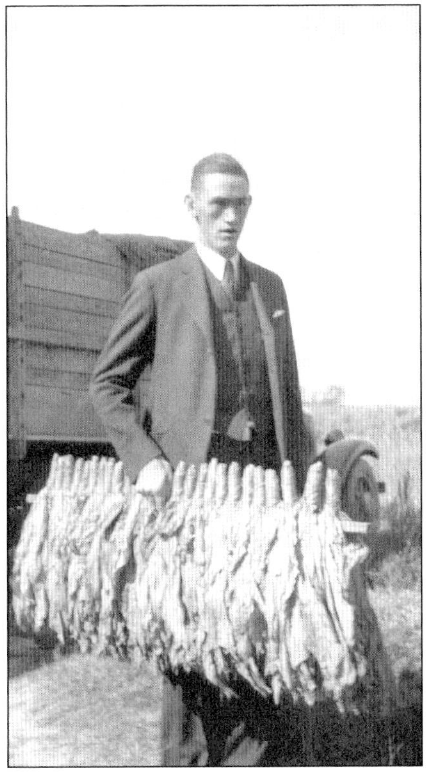

Left: **TOBACCO FLUE AT BARN.** This particular model of a wood burner for curing tobacco was manufactured by Wall and Denny of Pilot Mountain. (Courtesy of Martin Wall.)
Right: **TYING TOBACCO.** Frank Johnson never wanted anyone else to tie his tobacco. (Courtesy of Lenice Johnson.)

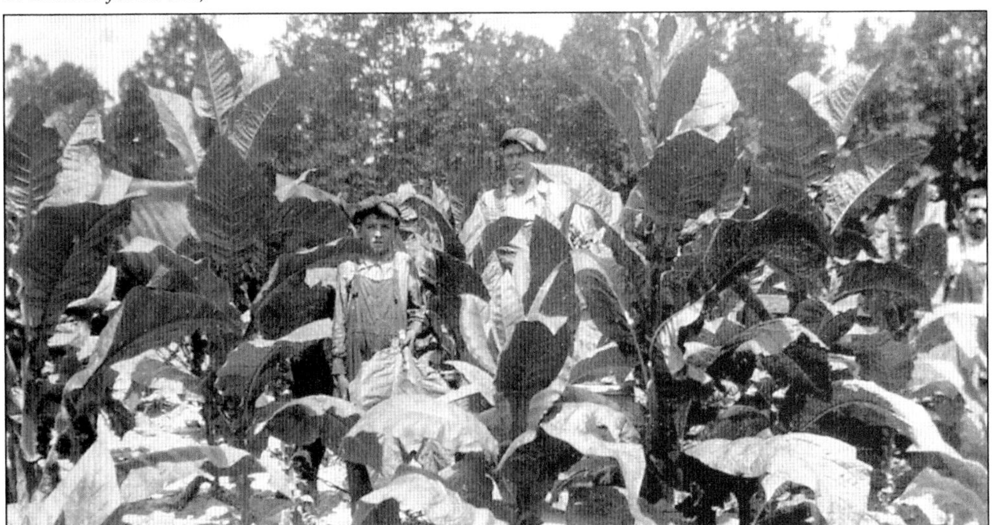

FULLY GROWN TOBACCO. This tobacco is taller than the workers harvesting the crop. Pictured, from left to right, are Raymond Johnson, Levi Johnson, and George Johnson. Tobacco plants grow well with careful cultivation, proper soil conditions, sunlight, and rain and can be 2 to 8 feet in height. (Courtesy of Nellie Benge.)

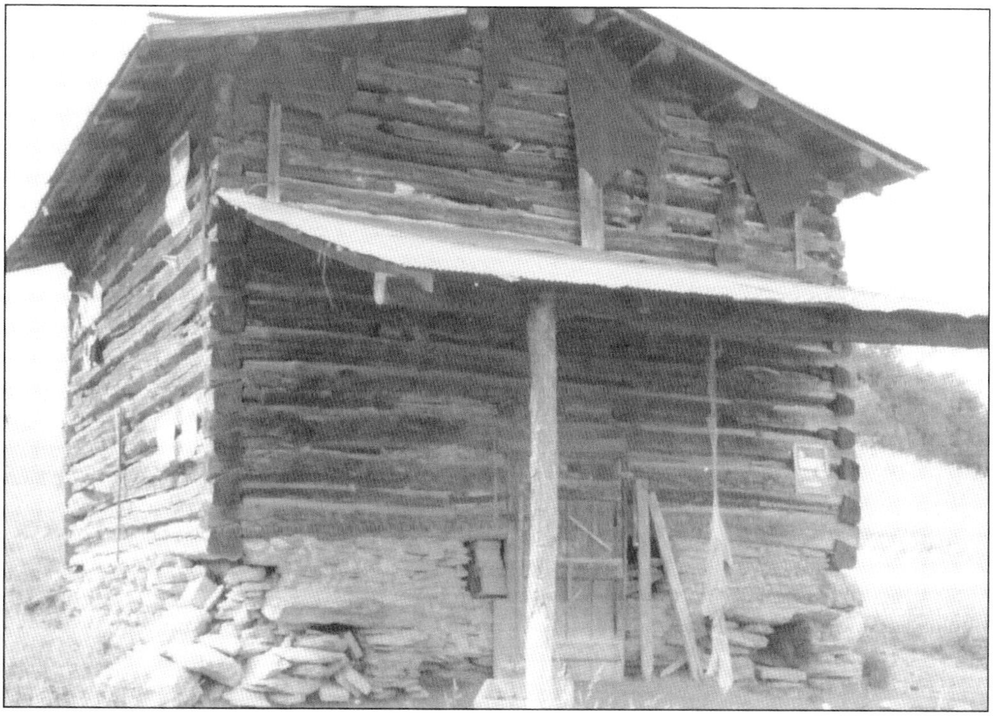

Tobacco Barn. Tobacco barns, such as this one, are still scattered throughout Surry County. (Courtesy of Stella Carrico.)

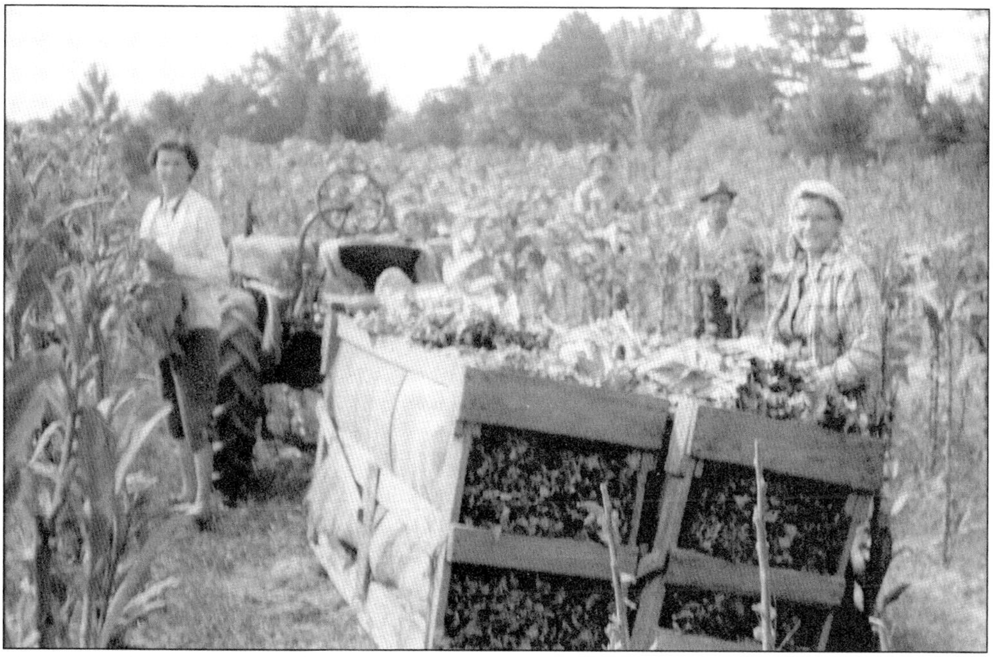

Tobacco Harvest. Pictured, from left to right, are Milner Rogers, Coonie Rogers, Raymond Johnson, and Lenice Holt Johnson as they work in their tobacco crop. The tobacco plant is related to many well-known flowers and vegetables that include the petunia, the garden pepper, the tomato, and the eggplant. (Courtesy of Lenice Johnson.)

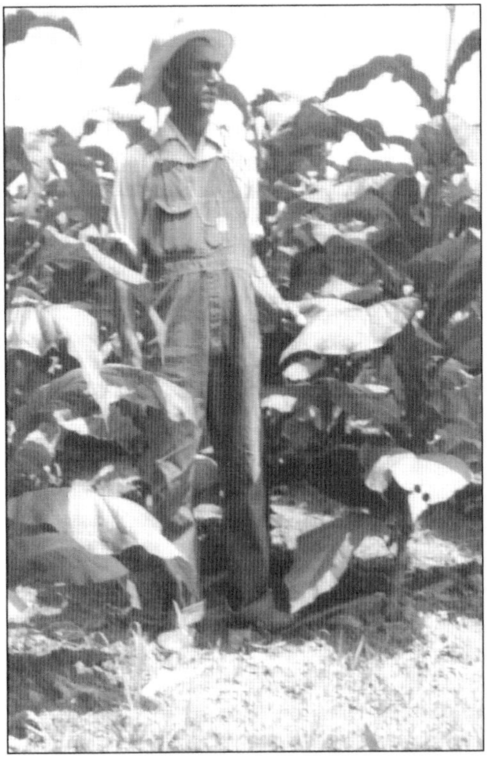

Frank Johnson in His Tobacco Patch. Tobacco plants are planted in well-fertilized fields. (Courtesy of Lenice Johnson.)

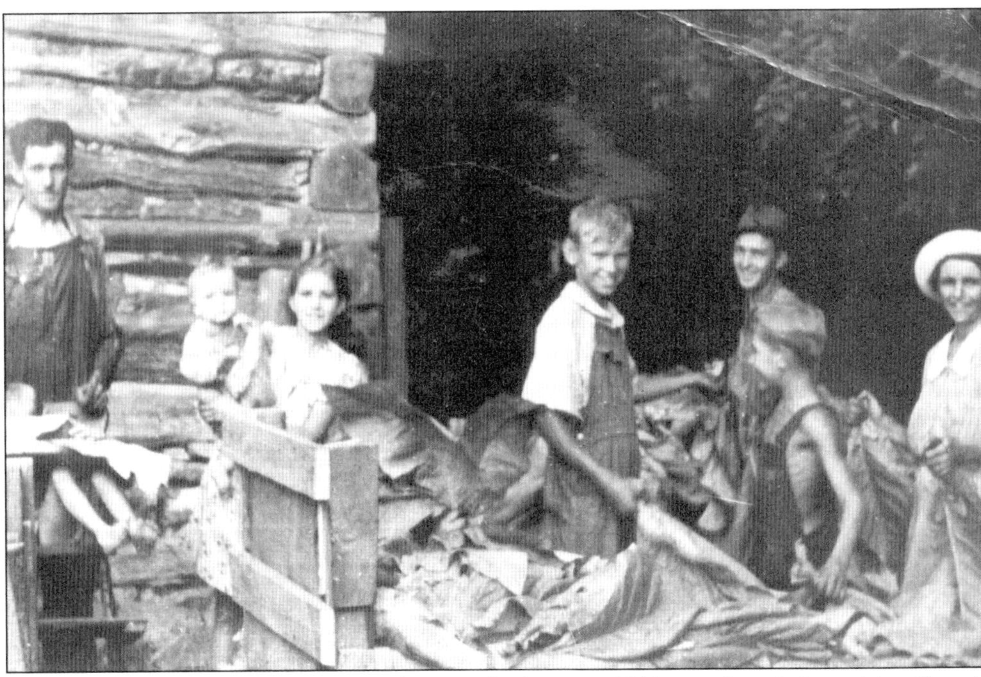

From the Fields to the Barn. Working at the barn, c. 1940, are, from left to right, Coonie Rogers, Wayne Rogers (in chair), Eldon Rogers, Nellie Rogers Benge, Graham Tilley, Raymond Johnson, Boyce Rogers, and Milner Rogers. Tobacco is hung in the barn for drying. (Courtesy of Nellie Benge.)

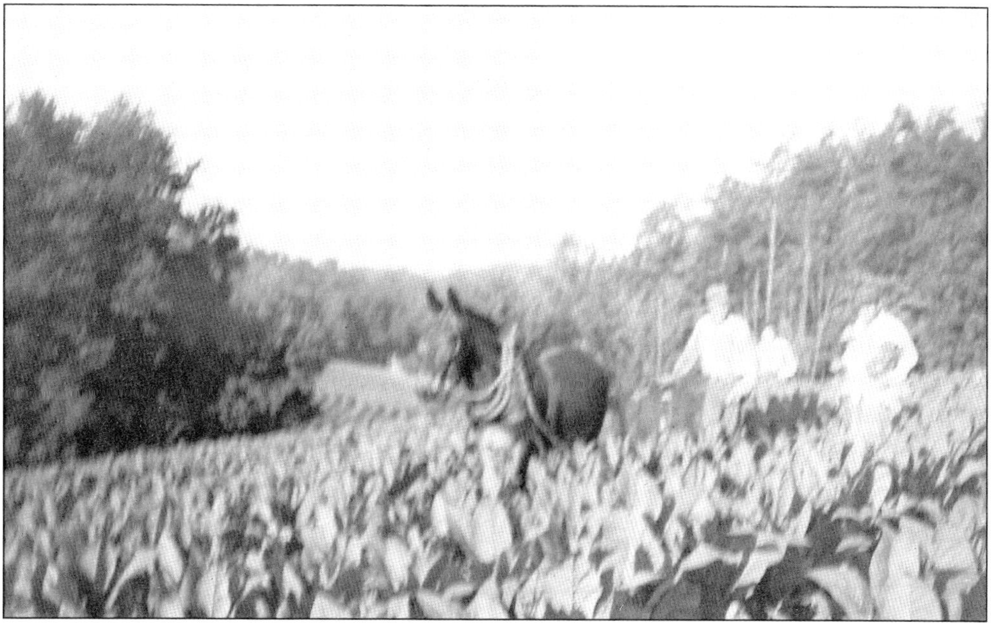

Mule Used When Priming Tobacco. With the mule's help, Coonie Rogers and Raymond Johnson are getting their day's work done. (Courtesy of Lenice Johnson.)

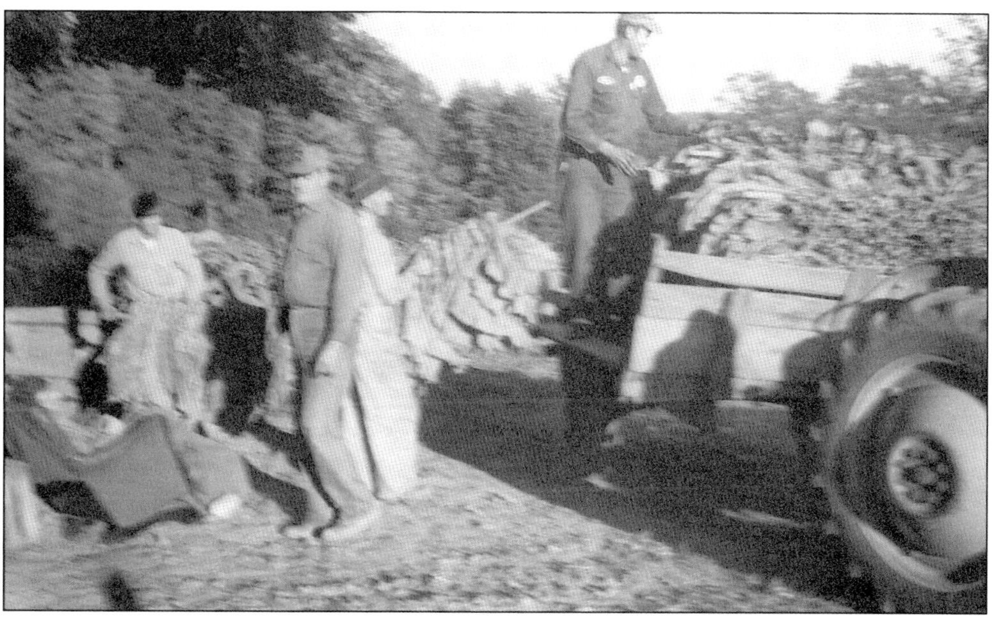

Loading Sticks of Tobacco on the Trailer. From left to right are Raymond Johnson, Coonie Rogers, Monroe Johnson, and Boyce Rogers. (Courtesy of Lenice Johnson.)

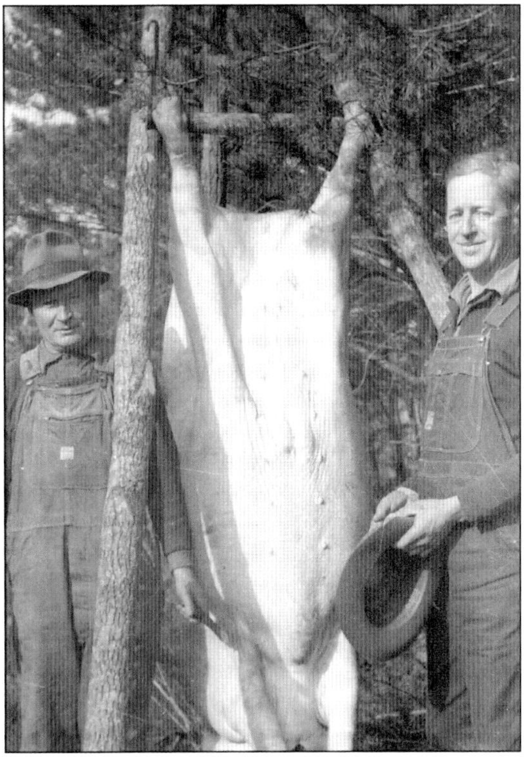

Hog Killing Time. The hog was the prime source of meat for families on the farm in early times. Usually late in November, when the weather would stay cold, the hogs were slaughtered. The meat was then cut up, cured, and smoked. The hams and shoulders were hung in the smokehouse while other parts of the hog were canned or shared with relatives and neighbors. Monroe Holt and Cricket Hill are pictured just after the hog was killed and scraped. (Courtesy of Lenice Johnson.)

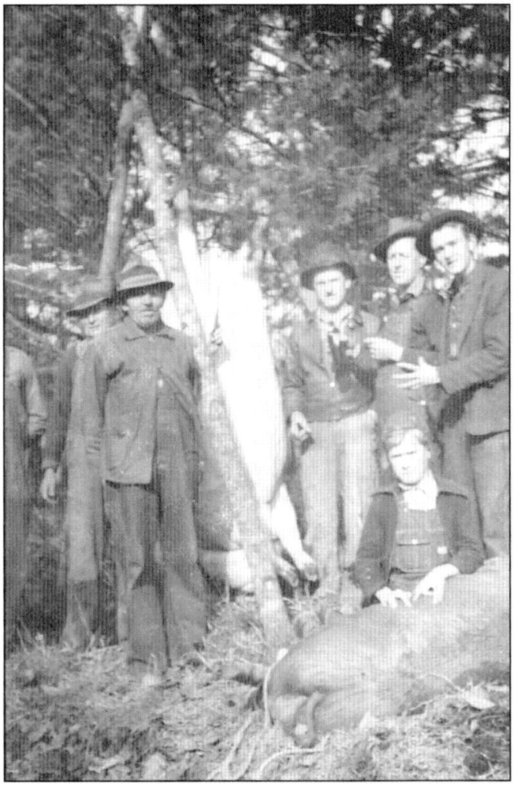

Families and Neighbors during Hog Killing Season. One hog appears to have been scraped clean and is ready to gut while another one is on the ground awaiting the same procedure. Plenty of hot water is needed when killing hogs. Pictured, from left to right, are Monroe Holt, George Johnson, Grover Inman, Cricket Hill, and Raymond Johnson. Hoover Holt is kneeling by the hog on the ground. (Courtesy of Lenice Johnson.)

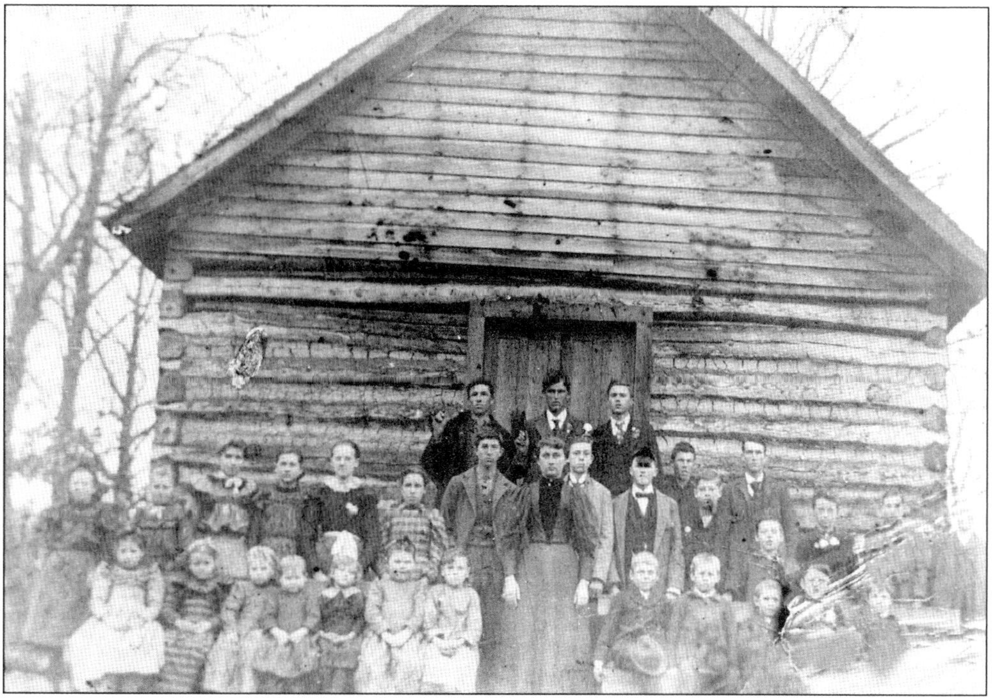

ALBION SCHOOL IN WESTFIELD, 1896. This school was located across the road from Albion Community Church. (Courtesy of C.W. Hill.)

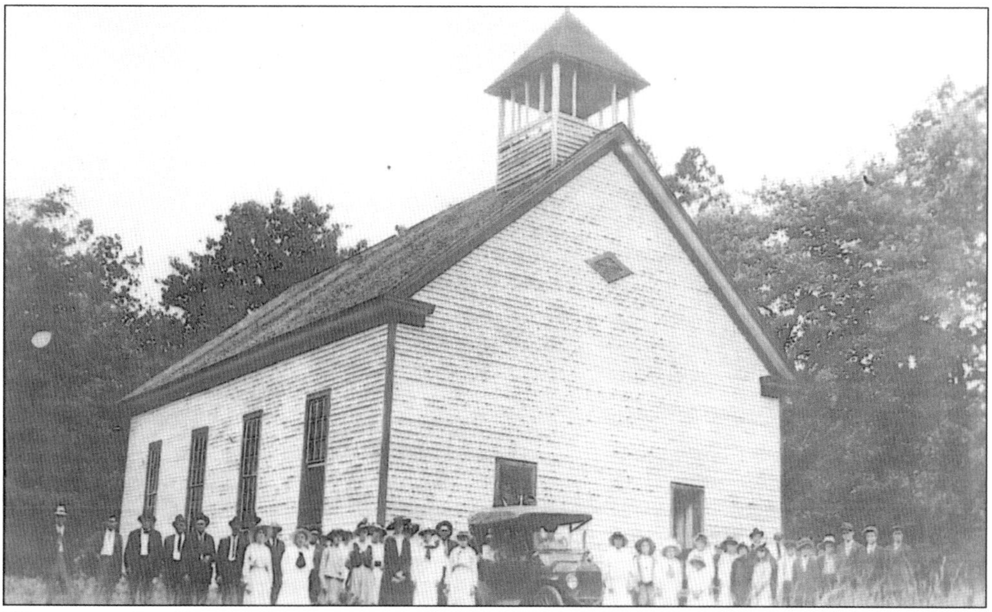

WESTFIELD FRIENDS MEETING HOUSE, c. 1910. Quaker worship services were held in Westfield as early as 1772 under the care of New Garden Quarterly Meeting. The area was referred to as "the western field" because it was west of New Garden Friends Meeting at Greensboro, North Carolina. Westfield Monthly Meeting of Friends was established November 13, 1786. (Courtesy of the Friends Historical Collection at Guilford College in Greensboro and Mildred Matthews.)

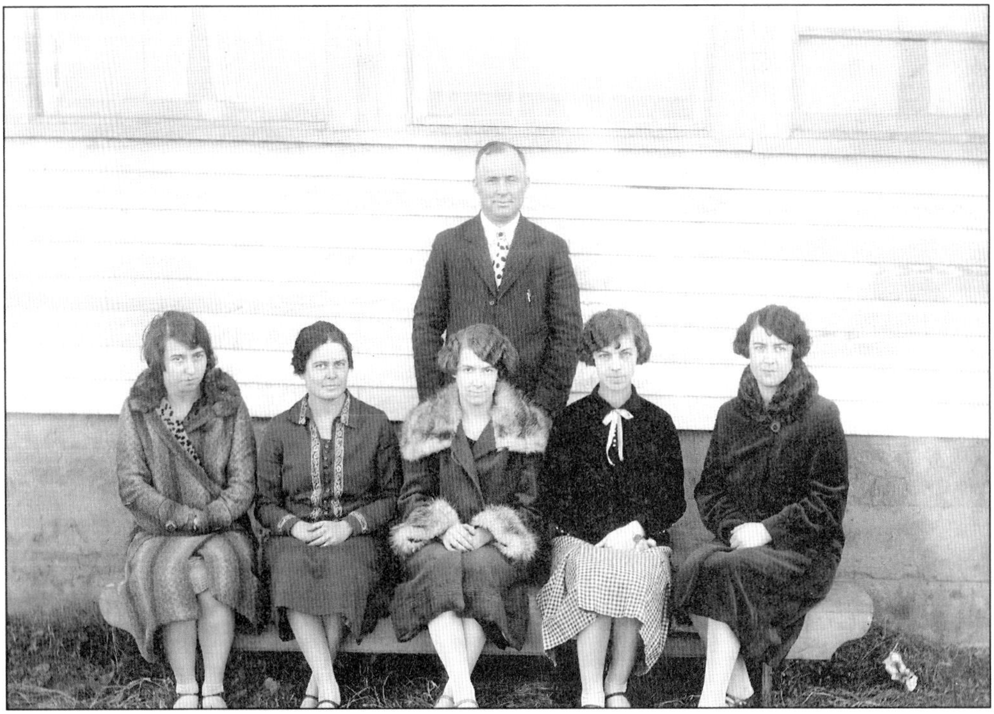

Westfield School Faculty, 1925–1926. Pictured, from left to right, are Ida Belle Clinard, Mollie Payne Tilley, Blanche Cook, Ethel Hauser, and Mycleta Hill. Principal O.H. Hauser is standing in the back. (Courtesy of Richard Hauser.)

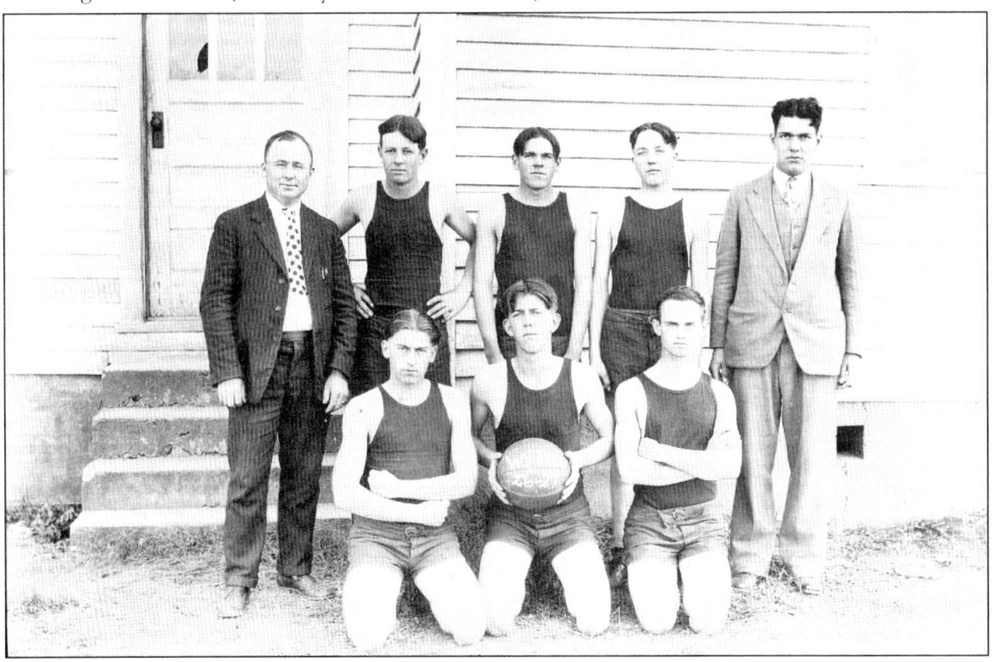

Westfield High School 1926–1927 Basketball Team. From left to right are the following: (first row) Tom Shelton, Walter Smith, and Raldolph Jessup; (second row) O.H. Hauser, Ty Inman, Jim Cook, Allen Jessup, and Frank Jessup. (Courtesy of Richard Hauser.)

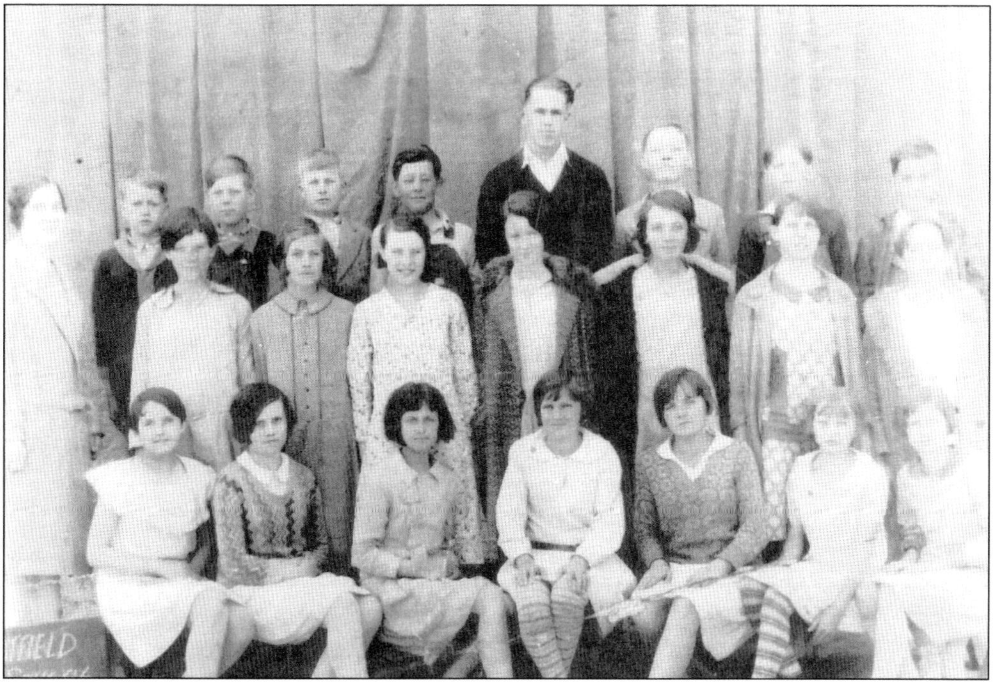

SIXTH GRADE CLASS AT WESTFIELD SCHOOL, C. 1927. Pictured, from left to right, are the following: (first row) Lavis Inman, Virginia Collins Love, Inez Hunter Love, Hallie Jackson Johnson, Ilene East Lytle, Lorene Love Hunter, and Erlene Love Vaden; (second row) Ima Mounce (teacher), Willie Norman Inman, Covie Bingman Brandt, Roberta Jessup, Ruth Owens Wright, Winnie Gibson Cook, Lavis Jackson Beamer, and Irene Cook Simmons; (third row) Reid Tilley, Walter Neal, Rufus Jessup, Robert Christian, Earlie Inman, Otis Arrington, Walter Beasley, and Randall East. (Courtesy of Lavis Inman.)

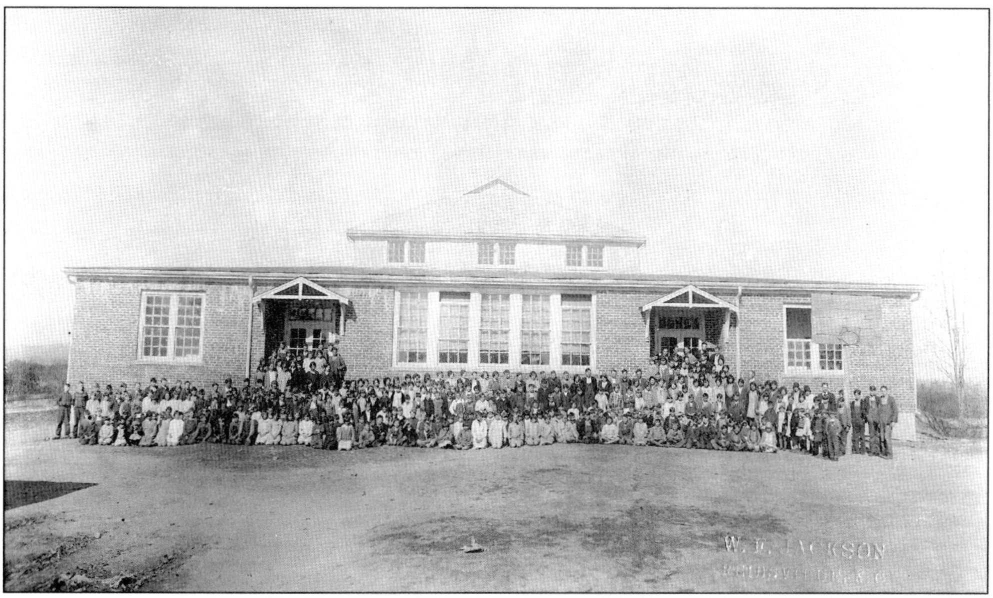

WESTFIELD SCHOOL, 1928. This photograph was made by W.F. Jackson of Reidsville, North Carolina. (Courtesy of C.W. Hill.)

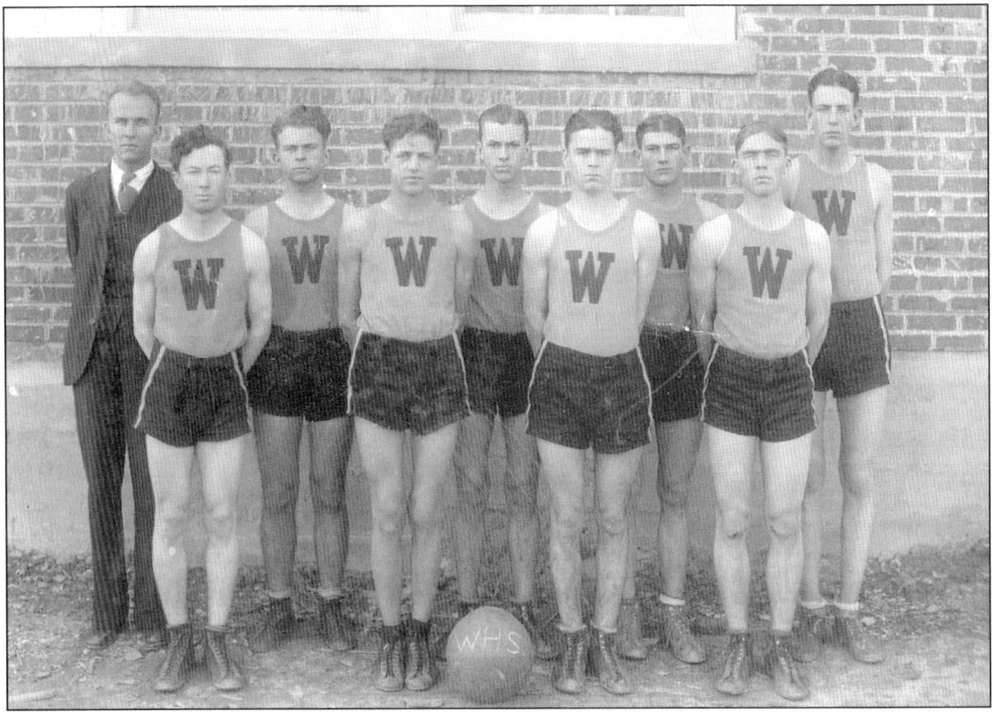

Westfield High School Boy's Basketball Team, c. 1930. Pictured, from left to right, are Luther Byrd (coach), Woodrow Owens, Glenn Hill, Boyce Cook, Harvey Hunter, Fred Owens, Hal Collins, Boyd Arrington, and Rex Taylor. (Courtesy of Richard Hauser.)

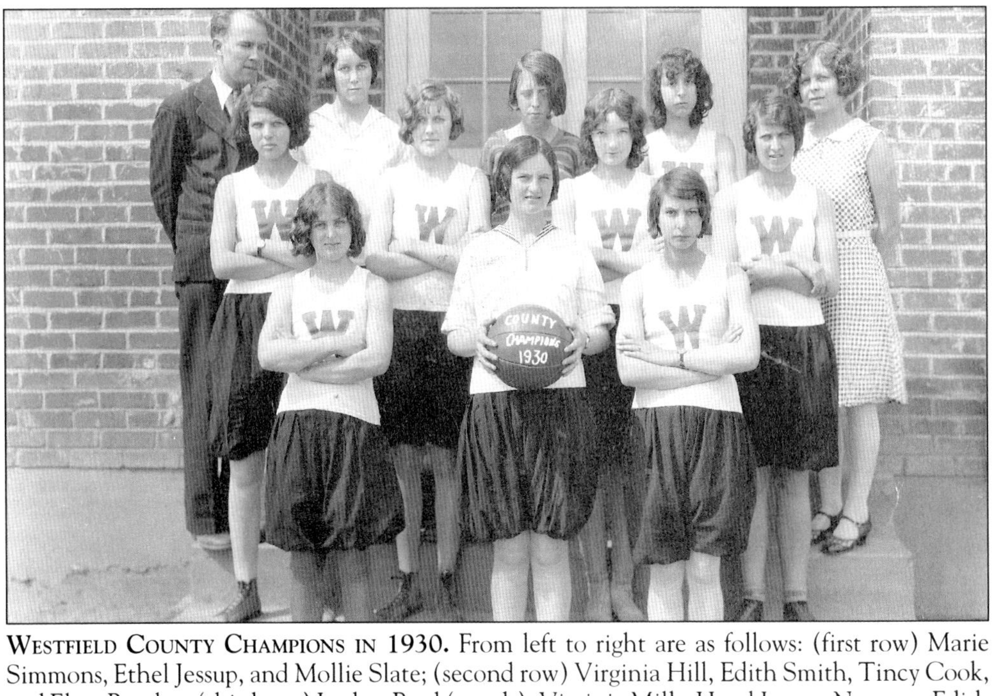

Westfield County Champions in 1930. From left to right are as follows: (first row) Marie Simmons, Ethel Jessup, and Mollie Slate; (second row) Virginia Hill, Edith Smith, Tincy Cook, and Elma Beasley; (third row) Luther Byrd (coach), Virginia Mills, Hazel Inman Norman, Edith Slate Bradley, and Ethel Hall (coach and teacher). (Courtesy of Richard Hauser.)

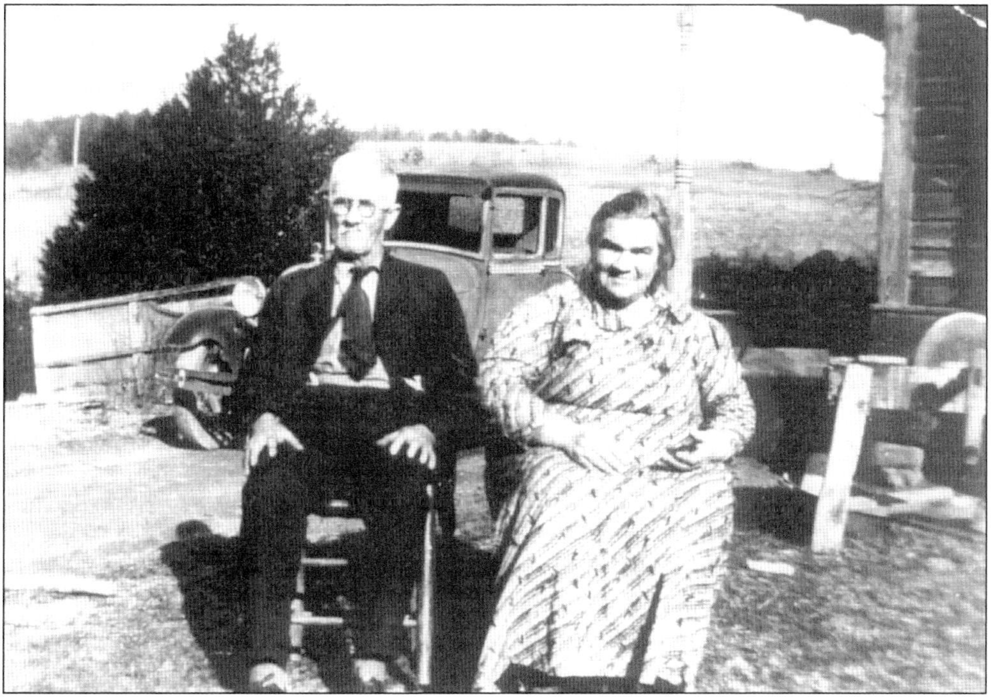

Relaxing in the Country before 1936. Edward Andrew and Caroline Cook Johnson are pictured at the old Haymore house, located at the intersection of Indian Grove and Holly Springs Roads. (Courtesy of Katie Hall.)

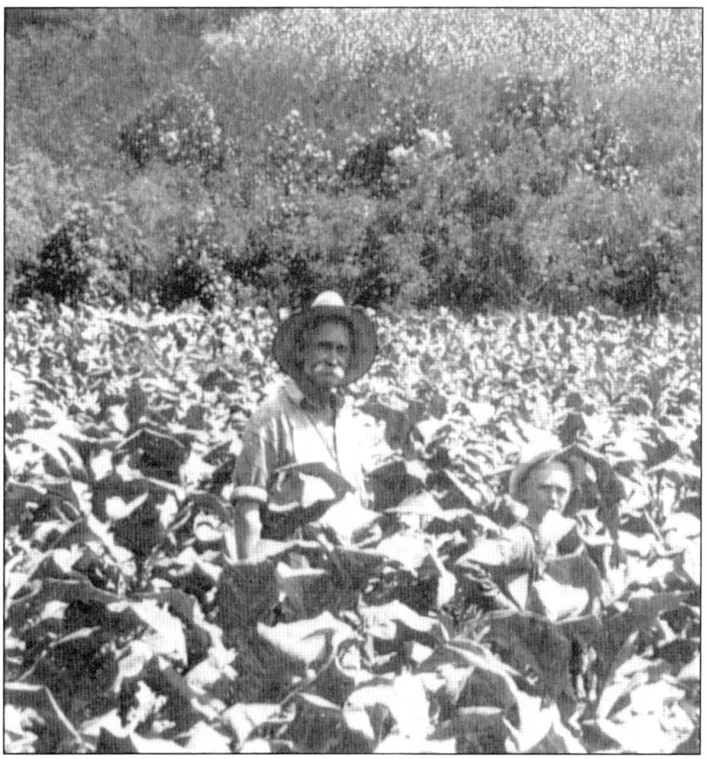

Field of Tobacco in the Holly Springs Area. Albert Franklin Haymore and his son Jack are seen here in the tobacco field, c. 1936. (Courtesy of Katie Hall.)

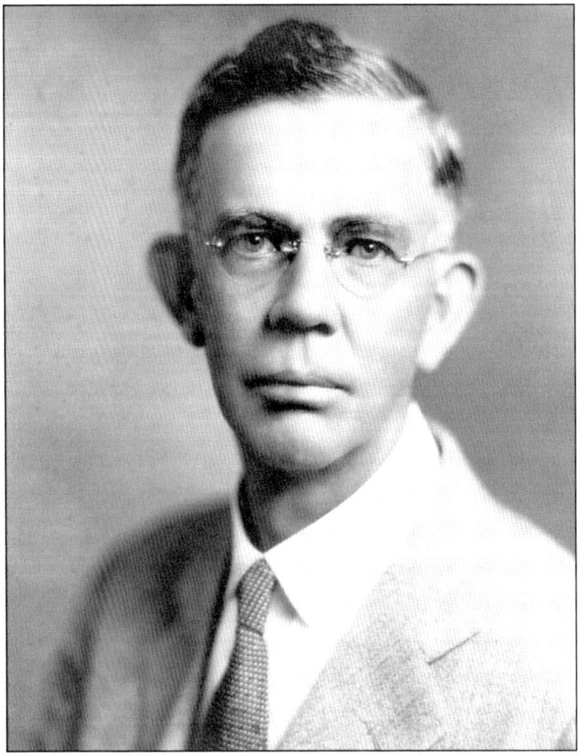

Dr. J. Thomas Smith. Dr. J. Thomas Smith (1877–1939) lived in the Westfield community his entire life, with the exception of the time that he spent securing his education. He not only served the medical needs of the community, but he also served as the pastor of several rural churches, including Westfield Baptist. In addition, he served as chairman of the Westfield School Board for a number of years. (Courtesy of Tim George.)

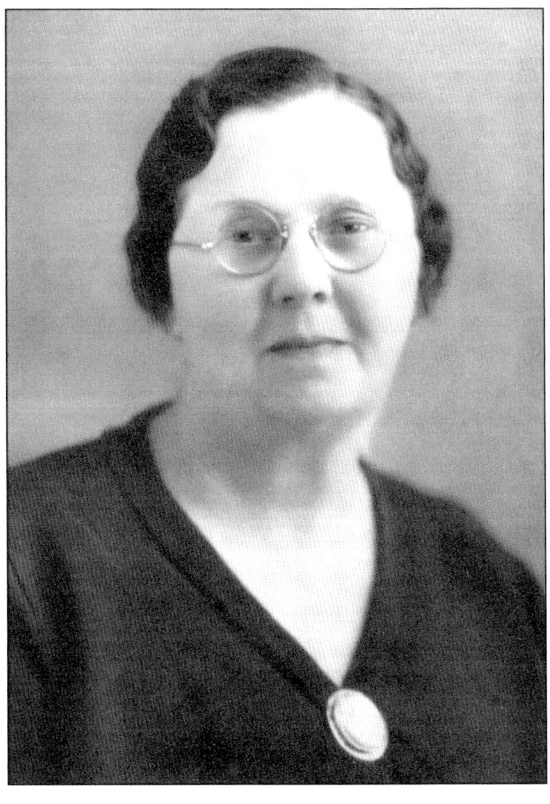

Mrs. Bettie George Smith. Bettie George Smith, the daughter of Bob George, married Dr. Tom Smith in July 1899. They were the parents of five children: Bernard DaCosta, Anslie Lester, John L., Walter, and Lavinia Nell. (Courtesy of Tim George.)

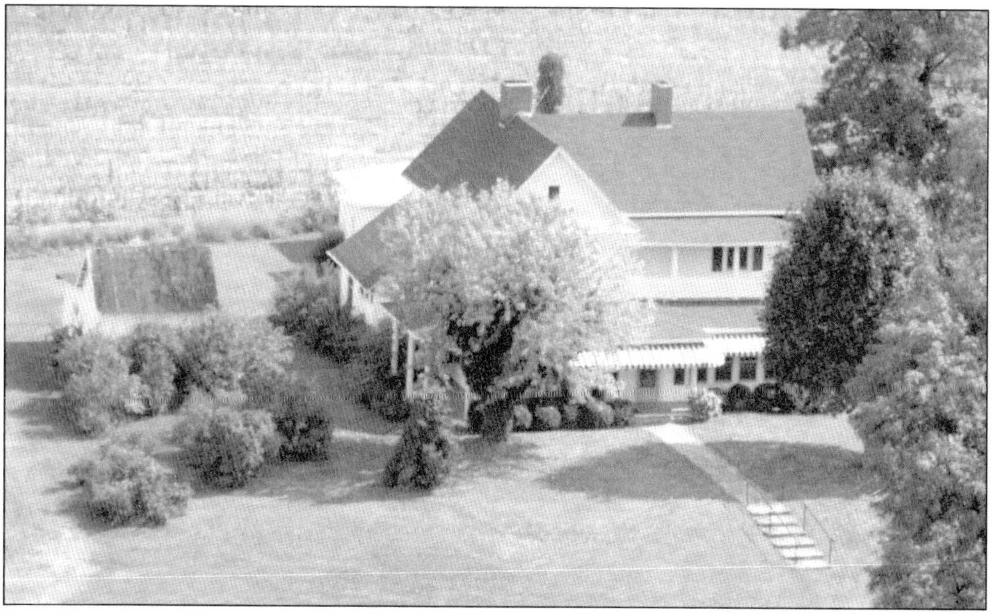

Dr. Tom Smith Homeplace. The Smith homeplace was built c. 1890. The family lived here, and Dr. Smith practiced medicine in a small building located on the north side of the house. (Courtesy of Tim George.)

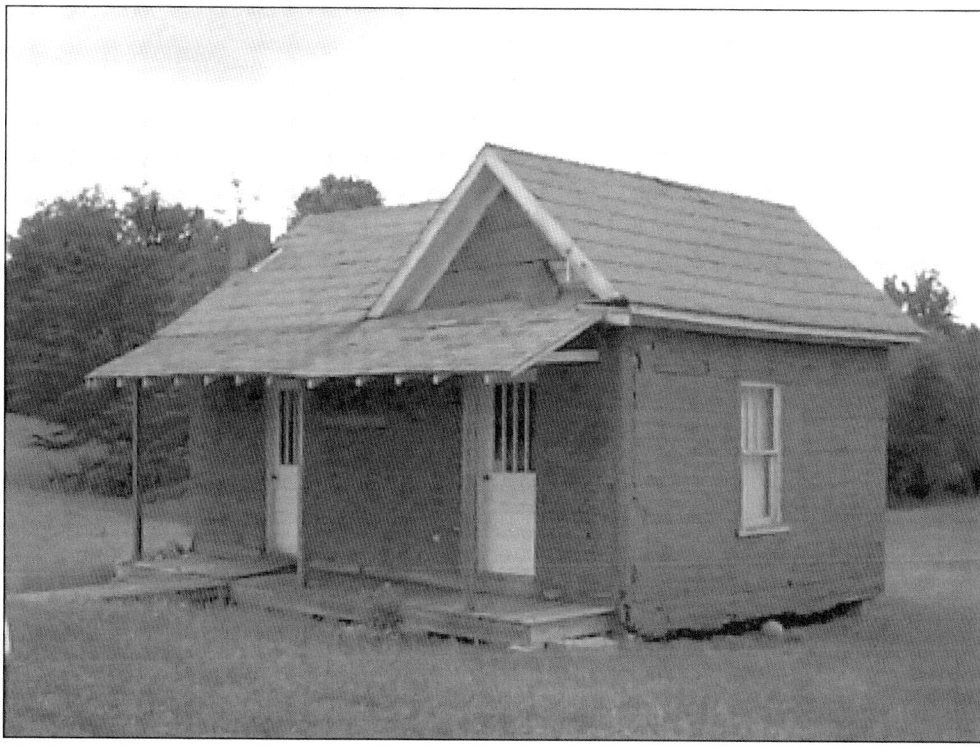

Dr. Tom Smith Office Building. Dr. Smith's office building sat in the yard of his home for many years. The building still stands today and is used as a polling location for voters. (Courtesy of Tim George.)

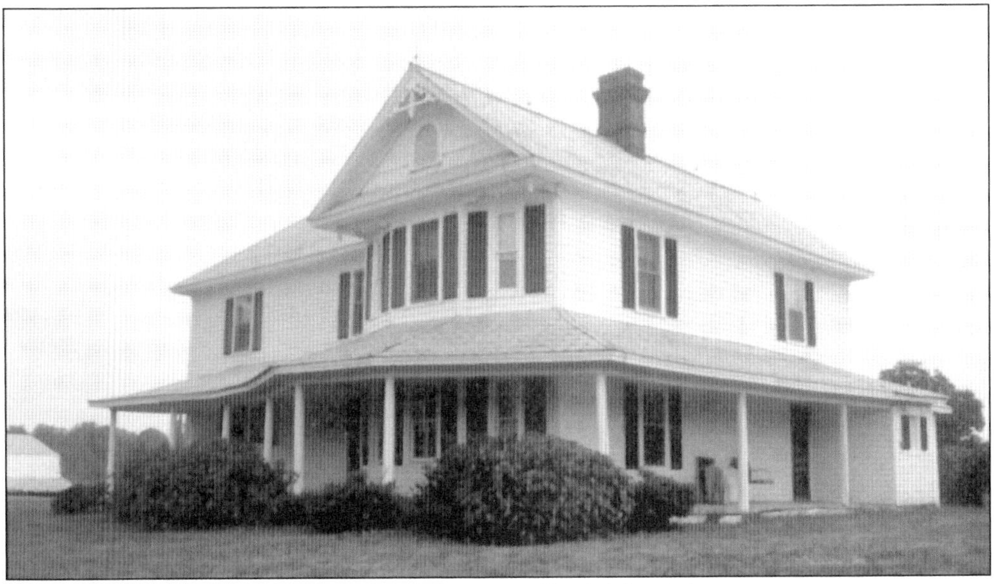

INMAN-SHELTON HOME IN WESTFIELD. (Courtesy of Ruth Minick.)

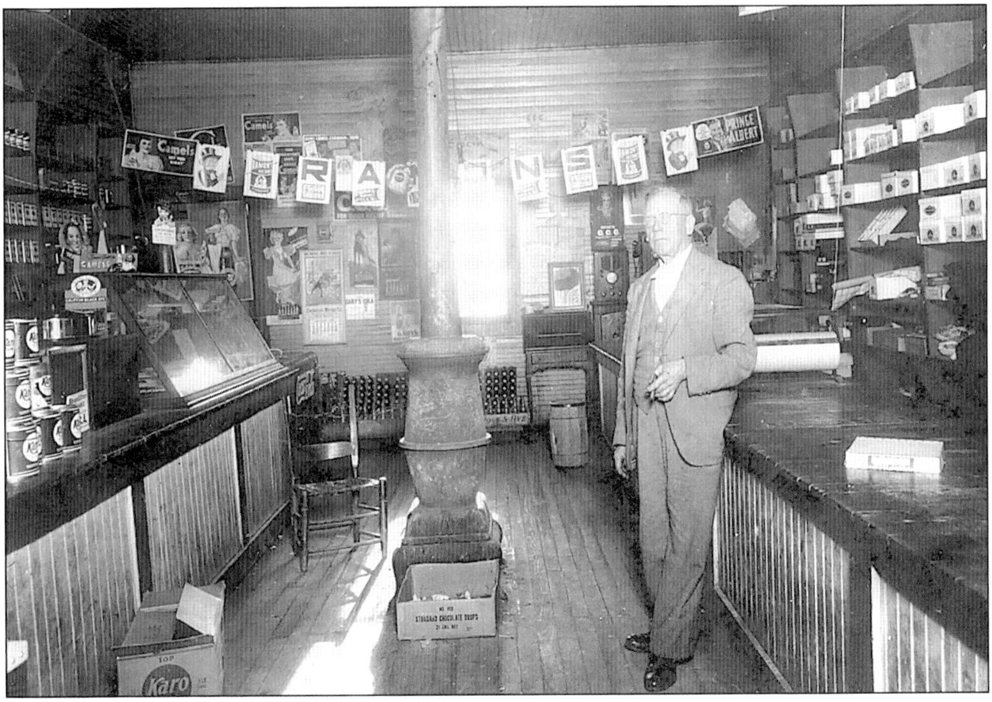

COUNTRY STORE IN THE 1930S. Eli Cephus Wood (1870–1951), the son of John and Nancy Lambert Wood, is pictured in his store in the Woodville community, located one-half mile below Woodville Church. He was a farmer and merchant for more than half a century, served on the Woodville School Committee for 25 years, and was one of the founders of the Woodville Baptist Church, where he was a deacon for 50 years. Note in the store the Covington Motor Company calendar; advertisements for Gary's Cola 5¢, Ramon's Herbs, and Slim Jim Daniels; and the box at the base of the stove that reads Standard Chocolate Drops. (Courtesy of Kaye Sisk.)

operator. $j=l-1,\ l,\ l+1$ follows from the general theory of angular momentum. For $l=0$, only one component $Y_l f(r)$ exists which corresponds to (3.2.5b) considered in §3.4.3. For $l>0$, (3.4.4b, 4c) and (3.2.2) can be separated into Y_{l+1}, Y_l and Y_{l-1} components associated, respectively, with the following radial equations

$$\left(-\frac{E_{j0}^2}{4}+M_m^2-\Phi_m\begin{pmatrix}\underline{x}\to 0\\ \underline{x}\to\infty\end{pmatrix}-\frac{1}{2l+1}\Delta_{l+1}\right)f(r)-\frac{2l}{2l+1}\Delta_{(l-1)-}g(r)-E_{j0}\frac{l}{2l+1}\left(\frac{\partial}{\partial r}-\frac{l}{r}\right)h(r)=0$$

$$\left(\frac{E_{j0}^2}{4}+M_m^2-\Phi_m\begin{pmatrix}\underline{x}\to 0\\ \underline{x}\to\infty\end{pmatrix}-\Delta_l\right)h(r)-E_{j0}\left(\frac{\partial}{\partial r}+\frac{l+2}{r}\right)f(r)+E_{j0}\left(\frac{\partial}{\partial r}-\frac{l-1}{r}\right)g(r)=0$$

$$\left(-\frac{E_{j0}^2}{4}+M_m^2-\Phi_m\begin{pmatrix}\underline{x}\to 0\\ \underline{x}\to\infty\end{pmatrix}+\frac{1}{2l+1}\Delta_{l-1}\right)g(r)-\frac{2l+2}{2l+1}\Delta_{(l+1)+}f(r)$$

$$+E_{j0}\frac{l+1}{2l+1}\left(\frac{\partial}{\partial r}+\frac{l+1}{r}\right)h(r)=0 \tag{3.4.5a}$$

$$\Delta_l=\frac{\partial^2}{\partial r^2}+\frac{2}{r}\frac{\partial}{\partial r}-\frac{l(l+1)}{r^2}=\left(\frac{\partial}{\partial r}+\frac{l+2}{r}\right)\left(\frac{\partial}{\partial r}-\frac{l}{r}\right)$$

$$\Delta_{l+}=\left(\frac{\partial}{\partial r}+\frac{l}{r}\right)\left(\frac{\partial}{\partial r}+\frac{l+1}{r}\right),\qquad \Delta_{l-}=\left(\frac{\partial}{\partial r}-\frac{l+1}{r}\right)\left(\frac{\partial}{\partial r}-\frac{l}{r}\right) \tag{3.4.5b}$$

In the $r\to 0,\ \infty$ regions, $\Phi_m(\underline{x})$ in (3.2.8a) depends only upon r and the separated wave functions (3.4.4) can be applied to (3.2.2).

These radial equations are sixfold degenerate, i.e., the six component equations of (3.2.2) yield the same (3.4.5). Near $r=0$, the radial wave functions are expanded as

$$f(r)=r^{\lambda}(f_0+f_1r+..),\ \ g(r)=r^{\lambda}(g_0+g_1r+..),\ \ h(r)=r^{\lambda}(h_0+h_1r+..) \tag{3.4.6}$$

where λ is determined by the indicial equation for (3.4.5) and takes on the values,

$$\lambda=l-1,\quad l,\quad l+1,\quad -l(f_0,g_0),\quad -l-1(h_0),\quad -l-2(f_0) \tag{3.4.7}$$

associated with the six solutions of (3.4.5). Solutions for the last three λ values, with the associated wave function components given in the parentheses, generally diverge at $r=0$ and are discarded. For the first three λ values in (3.4.7), one finds

λ	f_0	h_0	g_0	
$l-1$	0	0	g_0	(3.4.8a)

$$l \qquad 0 \qquad h_0 \qquad 0 \tag{3.4.8b}$$

$$l+1 \qquad f_0 \qquad 0 \qquad f_0(l+1)(2l+3) \tag{3.4.8c}$$

The three solutions associated with (3.4.8) provide the framework for the classification of the triplet, l>0 mesons in §5.6.2 below.

In the $r\to\infty$ limit, (4.3.4) below leads to

$$\begin{aligned} &\chi_r(\underline{x}\to\infty)=\psi_r(\underline{x}\to\infty)\propto \exp\left(-\tfrac{1}{2}d_h r^2\right)\to 0 \\ &\chi_\vartheta(\underline{x}\to\infty),\ \psi_\vartheta(\underline{x}\to\infty),\ \chi_\phi(\underline{x}\to\infty),\ \psi_\phi(\underline{x}\to\infty)\to 0 \end{aligned} \tag{3.4.9}$$

The indices r, ϑ and ϕ refer to the radial and angular components of $\underline{\psi}$ and $\underline{\chi}$. The asymptotic solutions (3.4.9) are independent of the angles.

Chapter 4

Normalization, Superposition Principle, Flavor-Independence, and Wave Functions

4.1. Remarks on Earlier Normalizations

Consider a Schrödinger wave function $\psi_{Sch}(X^{\mu})$. It is conventionally normalized according to

$$\int \left|\psi_{Sch}\left(X^{\mu}\right)\right| d^3\underline{X} = N_{Sch} = 1 \tag{4.1.1}$$

This normalization is based upon the probability density interpretation of the integrand. The existence of a positive definite norm $N_{Sch}=1$ is of great interpretational importance but there is no physical constraint underlying (4.1.1); N_{Sch} can be any positive constant. For a plane wave, (4.1.1) leads to

$$\psi_{Sch}\left(X^{\mu}\right) = \frac{1}{\sqrt{\Omega}} e^{-iEX^0 + i\underline{K}\,\underline{X}} \tag{4.1.2}$$

which becomes very small for large normalization volume Ω.

Consider next the normalization of the free particle Klein-Gordon (KG) wave function Ψ_{KG} satisfying (2.3.3) or

$$\left(\Box + m_{KG}^2\right)\Psi_{KG}\left(X^{\mu}\right) = 0 \tag{4.1.3}$$

which has the plane wave solution

$$\Psi_{KG} = A_{KG} e^{-iEX^0 + i\underline{K}\,\underline{X}}, \qquad E^2 = K^2 + m_{KG}^2 \tag{4.1.4}$$

Multiplying (4.1.3) by Ψ_{KG}^* and subtract it from its complex conjugate yields

$$\frac{\partial}{\partial X^{\mu}}\left(\Psi_{KG}^* \frac{\partial}{\partial X_{\mu}} \Psi_{KG} - c.c.\right) = 0 \tag{4.1.5}$$

Inserting (4.1.4) into (4.1.5) and integrating over X yields

$$\frac{\partial}{\partial X^0} N_{KG} = 0, \qquad N_{KG} = \Omega A_{KG}^2\, 2iE, \qquad \Omega = \int d^3\underline{X} \tag{4.1.6}$$

If the first of (4.1.6) is further integrated over X^0, it will have the same dimension as the action of the KG particle, a dimensionless Lorentz scalar. Integrating the Lorentz invariant (4.1.5) over X^μ will lead to the same conclusion. Therefore, N_{KG} is also a Lorentz scalar and can for instance not depend linearly upon E, which transforms as the time component of a four vector. Analogous to (4.1.1), N_{KG} is conventionally chosen as

$$N_{KG} = i \tag{4.1.7}$$

so that

$$A_{KG} = 1/\sqrt{2E\Omega} \tag{4.1.8}$$

which is the form used throughout the literature. Unlike the positive norm (4.1.1), N_{KG} in (4.1.6) can be a positive or negative imaginary number. The lack of a positive definite norm in the KG case has led to quite some debate during the early development of quantum mechanics and remains a basic, unsettled but ignored issue to the present time. There is also the question, why is the amplitude of the wave function of a KG particle energy-dependent, as in (4.1.8), while its Schrödinger counterpart (4.1.2) is not?

The answer to these two fundamental points is related to the following. The KG equation (4.1.3) describes a point particle of spin 0, which however does not exist. Now the scalar Ψ_{KG} in (4.1.3) can be replaced by a vector KG wave function $\Psi_{KG}{}^\mu$ in order to describe a spin 1 point particle. However, such a massive point particle of spin 1 transforming as a U(1) isosinglet also does not exist according to §6.2.2-3 below. These nonexsistences are consistent with the fact that the Schrödinger equation cannot be derived from these KG equations in some nonrelativistic limit.

The observed massless spin 1 point particle, the photon, cannot be described nonrelativistically. The observed massive point particles of spin 1 (gauge bosons) transforming according to SU(2)×U(1) in Sec. 7.4 below have as their source lepton wave functions so that their wave functions do not have the energy dependence of (4.1.8) (see (7.4.10, 7) below).

On the other hand, the Schrödinger equation is the nonrelativistic limit of the Dirac equation (A3) which describes an observable particle of spin ½, the lowest possible spin for a point particle.

On these grounds, application of the energy-dependent KG amplitude (4.1.8) in the literature hitherto may have led to erroneous conclusions.

4.2. Normalization of Meson Wave Functions

Following the method employed in the normalization of the KG amplitude, multiply (2.3.22a) by

$$\chi^*_{\grave{e}a} = (\chi_{\grave{a}e})^* \tag{4.2.1}$$

and the complete conjugate of (2.3.22b) by $\psi^{b\dot{d}}$. Subtraction of the resulting equations from each other, after some rearrangements using (B5, B7, B16), gives the analog of (4.1.5)

$$\begin{aligned} C_m &= \partial_{I\dot{b}a}\chi^{*a\dot{e}}\partial_{II\dot{e}f}\chi^{f\dot{b}} - \partial_{II}^{a\dot{b}}\psi_{\dot{b}f}\partial_{I}^{f\dot{e}}\psi^{*}_{\dot{e}a} \\ &= D_m = \left(\partial_{I\dot{b}a}\chi^{*a\dot{e}}\right)\left(\partial_{II\dot{e}f}\chi^{f\dot{b}}\right) - \left(\partial_{II}^{a\dot{b}}\psi_{\dot{b}f}\right)\left(\partial_{I}^{f\dot{e}}\psi^{*}_{\dot{e}a}\right) \end{aligned} \tag{4.2.2}$$

If the subtraction operation here is replaced by an addition operation, (4.2.2) would take a form similar to the first two terms in the Lagrangian density L_m of (6.1.2) below and has the same dimension. The associated action (6.1.1) is a real dimensionless Lorentz scalar. C_m and D_m, like L_m, are by virtue of their spinor form manifestly Lorentz invariants. Therefore,

$$\begin{aligned} &\int d^4x_I d^4x_{II}\left(C_m - C_m^*\right) = \int d^4x_I d^4x_{II}\left(D_m - D_m^*\right) \\ &= \text{imaginary, dimension less Lorentz scalar} \end{aligned} \tag{4.2.3}$$

We now specialize to the rest frame mesons characterized by the second of (3.2.10b) and of (3.2.11a) together with (3.2.5). With the aid of (3.1.1, 3, 4, 5, 9) and (5.7.1, 2) below, D_m can be simply shown to vanish. Noting that the meson wave functions must vanish at large r, (4.2.3) with (3.1.3c) becomes [H13 (3.6)]

$$\frac{1}{2}\int d^4x_I d^4x_{II}\left(C_m - C_m^*\right) = \int dX^0 \int \frac{\partial}{\partial X^0}\int dx^0 N_{mJ} = 0 \tag{4.2.4}$$

$$N_{mJ} = -i\frac{E_{J0}}{2}\Omega\int d^3\underline{x}\psi_J^2(r), \qquad \Omega = \int d^3\underline{X}, \qquad J = 1, 0 \tag{4.2.5}$$

Equations (4.2.3) and (4.2.4) require that N_{mJ} be a conserved quantity, at least in the limit of motionless mesons, of dimension energy. For a ground state meson at rest, the only observable quantity of this type is its mass E_{J0}. Therefore, the assignment [H13 (3.7a)]

$$N_{mJ} = -iE_{J0}\,\Omega/2\Omega_c \tag{4.2.6}$$

is made. Ω_c is interpreted as some finite volume in laboratory space $\underline{X}$ occupied by meson wave functions which acquire finite amplitudes due to possible interaction with other hadrons. Its size depends upon its application. Ω/Ω_c is taken to be a Lorentz scalar. A general, finite Ω_c however implies that it contains an $\underline{X}$ dependence so that separation of variables according to (3.1.5) no longer holds and the results from there and on become invalid. Therefore, Ω_c here is specified to be large enough so that these results and (4.2.6, 5) approximately hold. A criterion for such an Ω_c is given above (7.3.21) below and was found to be marginally satisfied for weak interaction in (7.522b) below.

The identification (4.2.6) corresponds to the unit probability assignment in (4.1.1) in quantum mechanics.

For mesons far away from other hadrons, i.e., free mesons, these amplitudes vanish as [H13 (3.7b)]

$$\Omega_c \to \Omega \to \infty \tag{4.2.7}$$

and the meson wave function is spread over the entire laboratory space.

The normalization assignment (4.2.6) is the consequence of the appearance of the *relative time* x^0 in the Lorentz invariant formulation, as is seen in (4.2.4). It largely resolves simultaneously the two seemingly unrelated questions raised by Wick [W4] on the Bethe-Salpeter amplitude [S3], namely, the lack of a positive definite norm and the unknown role of the relative time x^0.

From (4.2.5, 6), one finds the normalization condition

$$\int d^3\underline{x}\psi_J^2(r) = 1/\Omega_c, \qquad \psi_J \propto 1/\sqrt{\Omega_c} \tag{4.2.8}$$

which is independent of the meson energy E_{J0} and thus differs in this respect from the KG case of (4.1.4, 8). This fundamental difference stems from the presence of relative time x^0 here absent in the point particle Klein-Gordon case. On the other hand, (4.2.8) with (4.2.7) is in harmony with the amplitudes of the Schrödinger wave function in (4.1.2) and the Dirac wave function in (A13, A14).

The choice of i in (4.1.7) is not aesthetically appealing and is formally at odds with the normalization (4.1.1). On the other hand, the factor i in (4.2.6) is necessitated by (4.2.5) and is naturally associated with E_{J0} to form the time component of a four vector required by (4.2.3, 4).

4.3. Superposition Principle and Meson Wave Functions

4.3.1. Superposition Principle and Linear Meson Wave Equations

The linear superposition principle is a basic property of quantum mechanics. It is based upon the linearity of the Dirac equation. Different Fourier components of the wave functions can be added together to form wave packets, such as those present in a hydrogen atom. If such a wave packet is free, i.e., not affected by any external potential, and behaves like a Schrödinger particle in laboratory space, it will spread out in time accordance with the uncertainty principle [S5 §12].

The π^- meson can be captured by a proton to form a mesic atom. Comparison of this atom to the hydrogen atom above requires that this π^- meson must obey linear wave equations so that wave packets can be formed, at least when it is free or is captured by the Coulomb potential of the proton. In the latter case, the π^- meson is still very far away from the proton so that it is not in strong interaction with it and therefore can also be regarded as free. This linearity requirement is achieved by the free meson condition (4.2.7); whence the wave function amplitude (4.2.8) as well as the nonlinear confining potential Φ_{co} in (3.2.12) vanish and the meson wave equation (3.4.1) become linear. Although this linearity result has been obtained for rest frame π^- mesons, it obviously holds for the $\underline{K}\neq 0$ case as well except that (3.4.1) is to be replaced by the more general (3.1.8) with the integral in (3.2.8b) put to zero.

Such a state of the π^- meson is also obtainable by applying the energy minimization principle to (3.4.1). The meson energy E_0 there is minimized if the confining potential Φ_{co} vanishes. This is achieved by letting the π^- meson wave packet spread out over a large volume $\Omega\to\infty$, whereby the amplitude of its wave function vanishes according to (4.2.7, 8) and $\Phi_{co}\to 0$ follows from (3.2.12). In the more general $\underline{K}\neq 0$ case, (3.1.8) shows that the confining potential Φ_c of (3.2.8) enters only as $\Phi_c+M_m^2$, which may be regarded as an effective average quark mass squared. Since the total meson energy E_K must increase with the last mentioned quantity, it is minimized by $\Phi_c\to 0$, just as the $\underline{K}=0$ case above.

4.3.2. Solutions of Linear Meson Wave Equations [H25, H26]

The linearized (3.4.1) and (3.4.3) with $\Phi_{cJ}\to 0$ have a harmonic oscillator type of solution

$$\psi_{J0}(r)=\frac{1}{\sqrt{\Omega}}\exp\left(-\frac{d_h}{2}r^2\right)\sum_{v=0}^{n}a_v r^{s+v},\ d_h>0,\ a_0\neq 0,\ a_{odd}=0,\ n=2n_r \tag{4.3.1}$$

where n_r is the radial quantum number. An extra subscript 0 has been added to ψ_J in (3.4.1, 3) to indicate that they are of zeroth order in later perturbational calculations. The series terminates when

$$a_{n+2}=\frac{2d_h\left(s+n+\frac{3}{2}\right)-\frac{1}{4}\left(E_{00}^2-(m_p+m_r)^2\right)-d_{m0}}{(s+n+2)(s+n+3)-J(J+1)}a_n=0,\quad s=0\text{ or }-1,\quad J=0 \tag{4.3.2a}$$

$$a_{n+2}=\frac{2d_h\left(s+n-\frac{1}{2}\right)-\frac{1}{4}\left(E_{10}^2-(m_p+m_r)^2\right)-d_{m0}}{(s+n+2)(s+n-1)+2}a_n=0,\quad s=1\text{ or }2,\quad J=1 \tag{4.3.2b}$$

These gives the pseudoscalar and vector meson masses, E_{00} and E_{10}, respectively,

$$\frac{1}{4}E_{00}^2=\frac{1}{4}(m_p+m_r)^2-d_{m0}+3d_h,\quad s=0,\quad n=0,\quad J=0 \tag{4.3.3a}$$

$$\frac{1}{4}E_{10}^2=\frac{1}{4}(m_p+m_r)^2-d_{m0}+5d_h,\quad s=1,\quad n=2,\quad J=1 \tag{4.3.3b}$$

Here, the lowest allowed s and n values are chosen. For vector mesons, n = 0 would lead to a mass $E_{10}<E_{00}$ contrary to data. The next lowest value is n=2 used in (4.3.3b). For linearized (3.4.2b), (4.3.1) holds with $s=l$ and (4.3.3a) is replaced by

$$\frac{1}{4}E_{00}^2 = \frac{1}{4}(m_p + m_r)^2 - d_{m0} + (3+2l)d_h, \quad s = l, \quad n = 0, \quad J = 0 \tag{4.3.3c}$$

The normalized wave functions corresponding to (4.3.3a, 3b) are obtained from (4.3.1) and (4.2.8) and read

$$\psi_{00}(r) = \frac{1}{\sqrt{\Omega}}\alpha_{00}\exp\left(-\frac{d_h}{2}r^2\right), \quad \alpha_{00} = \left(\frac{d_h}{\pi}\right)^{3/4} = 0.0577\ \text{GeV}^{3/2}, \quad J = 0 \tag{4.3.4a}$$

$$\psi_{10}(r) = \frac{1}{\sqrt{\Omega}}\alpha_{10} r(1 - 2d_h r^2)\exp\left(-\frac{d_h}{2}r^2\right), \quad \alpha_{10} = 2.443\times10^{-3}\ \text{GeV}^{5/2}, \quad J = 1 \tag{4.3.4b}$$

where d_h=0.07 GeV^2 according to (5.2.2) below. Equation (4.3.4b) replaces [H25 (8b) with J=1]. By (3.4.2b), the wave function of orbitally excited singlets is known only in the r=0 and ∞ limits.

In (3.4.1) of [H18], the Coulomb potential d_m/r was used instead $-(d_h r)^2$ in (3.4.1) above and the solution (4.3.2) there

$$\psi_{00}(r) = \sqrt{\frac{d_m^3}{8\pi\Omega}}\exp\left(-\frac{d_m r}{2}\right) \tag{4.3.5a}$$

still holds with eigenvalues compatible with (4.3.3a), together with (5.2.2) and Table 5.2 below, if

$$\frac{d_m^2}{4} + d_{m0} = 0.4312\text{GeV}^2 \tag{4.3.5b}$$

However, a similar replacement of $-(d_h r)^2$ in (3.4.3) by d_m/r leads to no converging solution; (3.4.3) of [H18] contains sign errors and (4.3.3) there does not hold. Nevertheless, the quark masses and ground state meson spectra there and in [H6] remain unaltered here.

4.4. Flavor Independence of Ground State Mesons

Since (4.3.4) shows no dependence on mass or flavor, it holds for all rest frame two quark ground state mesons. This is in contrast to the KG wave function (4.1.4, 8) which depends upon the particle energy E and consequently the flavor content of the particle.

If a ground state pseudoscalar meson moves slowly, (4.3.4a) will be augmented by a "small component" triplet part determined from (3.1.8). In this case, $\Phi_{c0}(r)\to0$ of §4.3.1 is replaced by putting $\Phi_c(\underline{x})$ of (3.2.8b) to 0 so that (3.1.8) becomes linear and leads to (3.4.1, 3) with $\Phi_{cJ}\to0$ in the $\underline{K}$=0 limit. Put (4.3.3a, 3b) in the form

$$E_{J0}^2 - (m_p + m_r)^2 = -4d_{m0} - 8d_h\left(s + \frac{3}{2}\right), \qquad s = J \tag{4.4.1}$$

The first term has its origin in the laboratory space time X^μ and the second term, the quark mass term, in the internal space z of Sec. 2.3. The right side of (4.4.1) is associated with the relative space $\underline{x}$ and depends only upon the integration constants d_{m2} and d_{m0} in the quark-quark strong interaction potential (3.2.8a) and does not depend upon the flavor of the quarks. It corresponds to "potential energy" in conventional description. The flavor independence of (4.4.1), also of the wave functions (4.3.4) in relative space, can be considered as a symmetry under exchange of quark flavors, p,r=1,2,...6 in (4.4.1) and be called *flavor symmetry in relative space*. The corresponding conserved quantity is the left side of (4.4.1) with a value given by the integration constants in relative space on the right side of (4.4.1).

It is this flavor symmetry that renders the by itself badly broken SU(6) symmetry in internal space of §2.3.2 useful in classifying ground state mesons. That π^- consists of plane waves in §4.3.1 implies that all ground state pseudoscalar and vector mesons can also consist of plane waves, as was implied in §4.3.2.

4.5. Excited Meson Wave Functions

The ground state singlet and triplet l=0 mesons in §3.4.1 and §3.4.3 have been treated in §4.3.2 and Sec. 4.4. All other mesons in the classification scheme §3.4.1-4 are excited mesons. There are also both radially and orbitally excited singlet and triplet mesons but these will not be considered here.

Confinement of these mesons is similarly achieved by the quadratic confining potential $d_{m2}r^2$ in (3.2.8a) or $-d_h^2r^2$ in (3.4.1-3, 5a) which dominates over the nonlinear $\Phi_c(\underline{x})$ in (3.2.8c) when $r \to \infty$. In this limit, this potential leads to wave functions containing the confining exponential factor in (4.3.1).

For the excited mesons classified according to §3.4.1-3, the masses predicted from (4.3.3) with n greater than those given there and l>0, obtained by neglecting the nonlinear Φ_{cJ}, turn out to be appreciably lower than the measured ones (see Tables 5.6-8 below). Therefore, the confining potential Φ_c (3.2.8b) or rather Φ_m of (2.3.23) needs be included. This inclusion renders that the meson wave equations are no longer linear and the superposition principle of §4.3.1 breaks down. Thus, it is not possible to form wave packets for the excited mesons. Practically, this implies that they cannot be captured by a proton to form an atom, of the type of the mesic atom of §4.3.1, and that they cannot be observed as freely moving particles, as the pions or kaons can. Further, the wave functions are no longer spread out in a large volume, as in the free meson case (4.2.7), but are confined in some limited volume Ω_c smaller than that mentioned above (4.2.7). This in its turn leads via (2.3.23) to that Φ_m depends now upon both $\underline{X}$ and $\underline{x}$ so that the separable ansatz (3.1.5) no longer applies to the wave functions in (2.3.22).

The excited mesons therefore differ basically from the ground state mesons; they are more resonances than particles and have, with a few exceptions, all very large widths of the order of 100 MeV. By the uncertainty principle, this width corresponds to a time interval of 0.66×10^{-23} s. Even with the speed of light, such an excited meson can only travel 2 fm prior to its disintegration. In such short times and distances, there is no experimental technique to determine the wave packet nature of such mesons. A couple of excited $b\bar{b}$ states have width of tens of keV, but they have also not been seen as freely moving wave packets.

4.6. Confinement, Sizes of Mesons and Fundamental Length

The radial wave functions for the mesons in (4.3.1) are confined. This is achieved by the harmonic confining term $d_{m2}r^2$ in the potential Φ_m of (3.2.8a) which in its turn enters (3.4.1, 3), noting (3.2.21). This interquark potential Φ_m satisfies the fourth order (3.1.14); the higher order of derivatives in it allows r^2 to be a homogeneous solution. The higher order of (3.1.14) in its turn comes from (2.2.3) via (2.2.5) and (2 3 23).

The generalization of a product of two separable functions into one nonseparable function, due to introduction of interactions between them, is the second basic assumption mentioned in connection with (2.2.1-3). Confinement is a mathematical result of this assumption. This is analogous to that time dilation is a mathematical consequence of the assumption that the speed of light is the same in two coordinate systems in relative motion.

Physics comes out of mathematics, as was pointed out by V. Weisskopf (App G §5.5).

The size of free, rest frame pseudoscalar mesons in laboratory space extends to ∞ by (4.2.7). The corresponding size in relative spaces is seen from (4.3.4a),

$$r_0 = 1/\sqrt{d_h} = 3.78\,\text{GeV}^{-1} \approx 4.69\text{ fm}, \qquad \bar{r}_0 = 4.26\,\text{GeV}^{-1} \tag{4.6.1}$$

where (5.2.2) below has been consulted. $\bar{r}_0$ is obtained by averaging r over ψ_{00}^2 of (4.3.4a) in the relative space $\underline{x}$. The wave functions of excited mesons in relative space at large r are of the form (4.3.4) multiplied by some power of r. Therefore, the size (4.6.1) also approximately apply to them.

r_0 provides a reference length scale or a *fundamental length* for basic mesonic phenomena, analogous to that the charge and mass of the electron control the hydrogen atom radius, which provides a reference length scale for atomic phenomena.

In laboratory space, Sec. 4.5 shows that the excited mesons are limited to some finite, not large, volume Ω_c. The wave functions are no longer evenly distributed in the laboratory space $\underline{X}$ and separable in X and x. An adequate treatment of this nonseparable and nonlinear problem (2.3.22, 23) is beyond the scope of this book. To proceed, it will be *assumed* that the wave functions are independent of $\underline{X}$ inside a sphere of volume Ω_c and zero outside it,

$$\begin{aligned} &\psi_{exc}(X,x) = \psi_{exc}(x)\exp\left(-iE_{exc}X^0\right) && \text{for} \quad \left|\underline{X}\right|^3 < 3\Omega_c/4\pi \\ &\psi_{exc}(X,x) = 0 && \text{elsewhere} \end{aligned} \tag{4.6.2}$$

where the subscripts *exc* refers to excited mesons. The discontinuity in (4.6.2) invalidates the separability ansatz (3.1.5) so that its application leads at best to qualitative results or estimates in Sec. 5.5. below.

Chapter 5

Spectra, Classification and Motion of Mesons

In this chapter, the theoretical results of the last chapters will be applied to the mesons in the suggested quark model assignments for most of the low-lying mesons in the Particle Data Group data [P1]. The development follows largely that of [H6] but with d_m/r in the potential (3.2.8a) used there replaced by $d_{m2}r^2$ here.

5.1. Electromagnetic Masses of Mesons

Let the radial quantum number in (4.3.1) be included in (4.4.1), the l=0 meson masses are

$$E_{Jn} = \pm\sqrt{(m_p + m_r)^2 - 4d_{m0} + 8d_h\left(s + n' + \frac{3}{2}\right)}, \qquad s = J \tag{5.1.1}$$

where the upper sign is chosen. $n'=2n_r$=0, 2, 4... Note that $n'=0=n$ in (4.3.3a) but n'=0 refers to n=2 in (4.3.3b) assigned to the ground state vector meson. As was pointed out below (4.4.1), this meson mass is due to the quark masses of flavors p and r and their mutual strong interaction only. However, there is also a small electromagnetic contribution E_{emJ} due to the meson charge Q_m.

The electromagnetic radii r_{em0} of π^- and K^- are about 0.7 and 0.6 fm, respectively [D2, B3]. This magnitude will be assumed to hold for all ground state pseudoscalar mesons having the same absolute charge by virtue of the flavor independence of Sec. 4.4. Take r_{em0}=0.7 fm, the corresponding electromagnetic mass is

$$Q_m^2 E_{em0} = Q_m^2\, e^2/r_{em0} = Q_m^2 \times 2.1 \text{ MeV} \tag{5.1.2}$$

For vector mesons, such small corrections can be neglected and E_{em1}=0 can be set.next to the much larger E_{10}. The total meson mass to be compared to data is

$$E_{mJ} = E_{J0} + Q_m^2 E_{emJ} \tag{5.1.3}$$

5.2. Value of the Fundamental Length

Subtract (4.4.1) with J=0 and 1 from each other and make use of (5.1.3). One obtains the flavor independent relation

$$E_{m1}^2 - \left(E_{m0} - Q_m^2 E_{em0}\right)^2 = 8d_h \tag{5.2.1}$$

This prediction, that the difference of the squares of the masses of the vector and pseudoscalar mesons is nearly a constant agrees relatively well with data and has been observed long ago [F1, L3]. The masses of two quark ground state mesons [P1], (5.2.1) and the so-determined integration constant d_h are given in Table 5.1.

Table 5.1. Masses (GeV) of two quark ground state meson [P1], the differences of the squares of the vector and pseudoscalar meson masses and $2d_h$ (GeV^2) according to (5.2.1)

	$\pi^{\pm}$	$K^{\pm}$	K^0	$D^{\pm}$	D^0	D_s^{+}	$B^{\pm}$	B^0	B_s^0	η_c	η_b
E_{m0}	.13957	.49368	.49761	1.8696	1.8648	1.9683	5.279	5.274	5.367	2.983	9.399
	$\rho^{\pm}$	$K^{*\pm}$	K^{*0}	$D^{*\pm}$	D^{*0}	D_s^{*+}	B^*	B^*	B_s^{*0}	J/ψ	$Y(1S)$
E_{m1}	.7751	.89176	.8956	2.0103	2.0068	2.1121	5.325	5.325	5.415	3.097	9.46
(5.2.1)	.5813	.55152	.5544	.5458	.5499	.5868	.4807	.4774	.523	.6901	1.156
$2d_h$	.1453	.1379	.1386	.1364	.1375	.1467	1202	.1194	.1308	.1725	.289

One sees that the flavor independent (5.2.1) holds well despite the large mass differences between the π and the B_s mesons. The average value of $2d_h$, excluding the last two column, is 0.1348 GeV. A value closer to the light meson end, which is of greater basic importance, will be chosen to represent the average of the third and fourth rows in Table 5.1:

$$E_{m1}^2 - \left(E_{m0} - Q_m^2 E_{em0}\right)^2 \approx 0.56 \text{ GeV}^2, \qquad d_h \approx 0.07 \text{ GeV}^2 \tag{5.2.2}$$

This gives the fundamental length $r_0 \approx 4.69$ fm in (4.6.1). The $2d_h$ value for the η_c column starts to deviate from (5.2.2) appreciably which is marginally applicable. The last η_b column falls outside the validity region of (5.2.2) by a factor of 2.

The deviations of the values in the third row of Table 5.1 from the constant value (5.2.2) show that the flavor symmetry of (5.2.1) and Sec. 4.4 is slightly broken and also give the magnitude of this *flavor symmetry breaking*, which can be up to 10%. Here, it may be noted that D_s is the singlet member of a broken internal triplet, the pions and the ρ's belong to an isotriplet, while the remaining mesons belong to isodublets, except for B_s. However, η_c has been considered as a mixed meson containing $u\bar{u}$ and is therefore not a two quark meson; (2.3.27) and hence (5.1.1) does not strictly hold here (see (2.3.27) ff and Sec. 5.4 below). Also, such flavorless mesons may involve some conjectured coupling between the internal space (z_I, z_{II}) and relative space $\underline{x}$, both "hidden," mentioned in Sec. 5.4 of Appendix G. In this case, the total separable wave function in (2.3.19) using (3.1.5) is generalized;

$$\begin{aligned} &\chi_b^f(x_I, x_{II})\xi_r^p(z_I, z_{II}) \rightarrow \exp(-iK_\mu X^\mu) \\ &\times \left(\chi_b^f(\underline{x})\xi_r^p(z_I, z_{II}) + \chi_{1\xi b_r}^{f\ \ p}(\underline{x}, \text{real combinations of } z_I z_{II})\right) \end{aligned} \tag{5.2.3}$$

where the last term χ_l is small but not separable into $\underline{x}$ and z parts. This conjecture is aimed at a possible account for the fact that the last column in Table 5.1 yields a stronger breaking of the flavor independence symmetry. Such a scenario is also supported by deviations from flavor symmetry in the baryon case mentioned at the end of Sec. 11.1 below.

5.3. Quark Masses and Ground State Meson Spectra

Next, the five quark masses $m_1, \ldots m_5$ and the integration constant d_{m0} in (5.1.1) are determined. Inserting the masses of π^+, K^+, K^0, D^0 and B^0 in Table 5.1 into (5.1.1-3) and using (5.2.2), the five quark masses are expressed as functions of d_{m0}, which in its turn is fixed by the D_s^+ mass. The procedure is the same as that in [H6] and the result is given in Table 5.2.

Table 5.2. Quark masses and d_{m0} obtained from (5.1.1-3) using the masses π^+, K^+, K^0, D^0, D_s^+ and B^0 in Table 5.1 and quark contents of [P1]

m_1(GeV)	m_2-m_1	m_3	m_4	m_5	d_{m0}(GeV^2)
0.6592	0.00215	0.7431	1.6215	4.7786	0.64113

It may be noted that the u and d quark masses difference 2.15 MeV is about the same as the electromagnetic mass E_{emo} of (5.1.2).

The u, d and s quark masses, m_1, m_2 and m_3 respectively, are much higher than those given in the literature [L2]. The much lower pion masses in Table 5.1 are due to that the quark mass term in (5.1.1) is largely cancelled by the large d_{m0} value in Table 5.2. Equation (3.2.8a) states that there is a constant intreaction d_{m0} in the interquark potential between the quarks in meson even when both quarks coincide at r=0. However, there is no observable conflict as d_{m0}, like the quarks, refers to the same unobservable relative space x. The physical meaning of this constant interaction d_{m0} is unknown.

With these numbers, the remaining masses of two quark pseudoscalar and vector mesons are predicted from (5.1.1-3). The results are compared to data in Tables 5.3 and 5.4.

The predictions in Table 5.3 are fairly close to data. The predictions of Table 5.4 are also in relatively good agreement with data, in view of the very large width of ρ and K^* and that the effect of the flavor symmetry breaking mentioned below (5.2.2) has not been considered. Note that one of the predictions in Table 5.4 must be removed because it has been used to determine d_h in (5.2.2).

Table 5.3. Predicted and measured [P1] masses of flavored pseudoscalar mesons in MeV. The particle symbols stand for their masses

	Prediction	Data
B_s^0	5363.3	5366.89±0.19
B_c^+	6266	6274.9±0.8
D^+-D^0	4.73	4.822±0.015
B^0-B^+	0.11	0.31±0.06

Table 5.4. Predicted and measured [P1] masses of flavored vector mesons in MeV. The particle symbols stand for their masses

	Prediction	Data
ρ^+	760.9	775.11±0.34
K^{*+}	895.35	891.76±0.25
$K^{*0}-K^{*+}$	3.4	6.7±1.2
D^{*0}	2009.2	2006.85±0.05
$D^{*+}-D^{*0}$	2.4	3.3±0.8(old data)
D_s^{*+}	2104	2112.2±0.4
B^{*0}	5331.8	5324.65±0.25
$B^{*0}-B^{*+}$	2.2	-
B_s^{*0}	5415.2	5415.4±1.6
$B_s^{*}-B_s$	52	48.5±1.7
B_c^{*}	6308.4	-

For pions, the quark mass term in (4.4.1) nearly cancels the "potential well energy" terms on the right side of (4.4.1). This results in a very small mass E_{00} for pions. For heavy mesons, such as the B mesons, the quark mass term in (4.4.1) is much greater than the same "potential well energy" terms. The B meson mass is nearly the same as the sum of the both quark masses.

5.4. Ground State Mesons with Closed Flavor and GMO Formula

The mesons considered in the last section have open flavor and hence contains at most two quarks. Mesons with closed flavor can contain four or six flavors, as are exemplified by π^0 and η. The present results for two quark mesons is strictly not applicable (see §2.4.3) and additional approximations need to be introduced to obtain estimations of their masses. One such approximation a) is the replacement of (2.3.27) by the third of (2.4.13), (2.4.15) and (2.4.17) for π^0, η and η', respectively. As was pointed out in §2.4.3, this approximation is good for π^0 but not for η and η'. Another approximation b) is to regard the meson masses as some average of the masses E_{011}, E_{022} and E_{033} (see (2.4.11)) of the "fictitious" mesons consisting of $u\bar{u}$, $d\bar{d}$ and $s\bar{s}$, respectively, properly weighed by the internal wave functions in (2.4.8, 16).

In Sec. 6.2 below, it will be shown that pseudoscalar isosinglets with quark contents $u\bar{u}$+ $d\bar{d}$, $s\bar{s}$, $c\bar{c}$, $b\bar{b}$ or $t\bar{t}$, which include the "fictitious" states above, cannot exist on the grounds of U(1) gauge invariance and the zero mass of the photon. Therefore, a pseudoscalar meson with closed flavor does not have to have a counterpart in a vector meson with the same quark content. This differs from the open flavor cases in Table 5.1 where each pseudoscalar meson has a vector meson counterpart with the same quark content. The spectra of the closed flavor mesons are obtained from (5.1.1-3), using the approximations a) and b) above in the applicable cases, and are compared to data in Table 5.5.

Table 5.5. Estimated and measured [P1] masses in MeV for ground state mesons with closed flavor. I denotes the isospin of the multiplet the meson belongs to, J the spin and P the parity. The superscripts a) and b) refer to the approximations mentioned above in this section. Under b), the masses of the "fictitious" pseudoscalar mesons $u\bar{u}$, $d\bar{d}$ and $s\bar{s}$ are obtained from (5.1.1-3) and are in the notation of (2.4.11) E_{011}=115.018, E_{022}=156.767 and E_{033}=695.8, respectively. For vector mesons, they are E_{111}=757.1 for $u\bar{u}$ and E_{122}=764.6 for $d\bar{d}$

$IJ(P)$	Meson	Quark Content	Prediction	Data
$10(-)$	π^0	$u\bar{u}-d\bar{d}$	137.486[a)] 135.893[b)]	134.977
$00(-)$	η	$u\bar{u}+d\bar{d}-2s\bar{s}$	573.65[a)] 509.164[b)]	547.862
$00(-)$	η'	$u\bar{u}+d\bar{d}+s\bar{s}$	417.1[a)] 322.528[b)]	957.78
$00(-)$	η_c	$c\bar{c}+\ldots$	2965.2	2983.9
$01(-)$	ω	$u\bar{u}+d\bar{d}$	760.8[b)]	782.65
$01(-)$	ϕ	$s\bar{s}$	1021.84	1019.46
$01(-)$	J/ψ	$c\bar{c}+\ldots$	3058.2	3096.9
$01(-)$	$\Upsilon(1S)$	$b\bar{b}$	9496	9460.3

Differences between the predicted and measured masses in Table 5.5 are on the average much greater than the corresponding ones for mesons with open flavor in Tables 5.3 and 5.4. These are presently attributed to the approximations a) and b) mentioned above in this section and to the uncertain quark content due to mixing, in addition to the conjecture of coupling of space-time functions to internal functions indicated in (5.2.3).

The predicted π^0 mass using approximation b) is rather close to data. In fact, it can be adjusted to fit data exactly if the electromagnetic radius r_{em0} in Sec. 5.1 is taken to be 0.55 fm instead of 0.7 fm so that E_{em0} is 2.67 MeV instead of 2.1 MeV in (5.1.2). The η mass lies between the two approximatively predicted values.

The predicted η' masses are much too low. However, the conventional quark content of η' is an SU(3) singlet (2.4.16) and falls into the category of non-existent pseudoscalar isosinglets $u\bar{u}+d\bar{d}$, $s\bar{s}$, $c\bar{c}\ldots$ mentioned above in this section. Such an η' can therefore not exist from this point of view. It has been suggested [H7] that η' has also some $c\bar{c}$ content so that it is no longer an isosinglet. Such a $c\bar{c}$ content can enhance its mass to the observed mass level.

η_c is mixed, as was mentioned above (5.2.3). The predicted ϕ mass agrees rather well with data.

The mass squared operator and its eigenvalue in (2.3.21) are now compared to the Gell-Mann-Okubo(GMO) formula which also operates in the same kind of internal space. For mesons, (9.46) with the lower member of (9.49) in [L2] give the GMO squared mass

$$M_{GMO}^2 = a_{8m} + c_{8m}\left(I(I+1) - Y^2/4\right) \tag{5.4.1}$$

Here, I is the isospin, Y the hypercharge, a_{8m} and b_{8m} constants, and the small isospin symmetry breaking is neglected. M_{GMO} has been assigned to be the observed meson masses. It however does not include contributions from inter-quark interactions as is indicated by the d_{m0} and d_h constants in (5.1.1). It is more appropriate to compare M_{GMO} to the eigenvalue $2M_m$ in (2.4.1) representing the sum of the bare quark masses. Equating (5.4.1) to (2.4.1) with $m_1=m_2$ for pion and kaon gives

$$a_{8m} = \frac{4}{3}(2m_1 + m_3)m_3, \qquad c_{8m} = \frac{2}{3}(3m_1 + m_3)(m_1 - m_3) \tag{5.4.2}$$

Application of (5.4.1-2) and (2.4.15) to η leads to

$$M^2_{m\eta} - M^2_{GMO\eta} = \frac{4}{3}(m_3 - m_1)^2 \tag{5.4.3}$$

With Table 5.2, this discrepancy turns out to be very small, 0.45% only. Although the simplest assumption (2.3.25, 26) is compatible with the GMO formula in this case they differ basically in that the SU(3) generators (2.4.5) present in (5.4.1) are absent in (2.3.25, 26).

Furthermore, the quark masses in Table 5.2 obtained from meson spectra are also used for baryons in (9.3.19) below. The coefficients in the GMO formula for mesons (5.4.1) are different from those for baryons in (9.3.21) below. Thus, use of GMO formula instead of the simpler but not exact quark mass summation operator in (2.3.25, 26) and (9.3.13, 14) below will lead to three more parameters to be fixed by data. Apart from much reduced predictive power, such a use would greatly complicate the computer calculations in Sec. 11.1 below.

5.5. Radially Excited Mesons [H25]

The ground state meson spectra have been treated in the last two sections. They belong to the categories of singlet and triplet, l=0 mesons of §3.4.1 and §3.4.3, respectively. The remaining mesons in these categories are radially excited states of the same ground state mesons.

As a first approximation, (3.4.1, 3) are again linearized by neglecting nonlinear Φ_{cJ} in them and (5.1.1) applies. The results are shown in Tables 5.6 and 5.7.

The predicted masses E_{th} are 7-18% smaller than the measured ones E_{exp} in Table 5.6 and 4-18% in Table 5.7. These differences may tentatively be attributed to the above neglected nonlinear potential $\Phi_{cJ}(r)$ in (3.4.1, 3) in order to arrive at (5.1.1). Note that E_{th} from (5.1.1) using d_h=0.07 from (5.2.2) does not hold well for $\bar{b}b$ states. If $2d_h$=0.289 in Table 5.1 were used, the predicted masses shown in the braces in Tables 5.6-7 are somewhat but not much higher.

Actually, the full nonlinear (3.4.1, 3) have been solved numerically using an iterative procedure ([H5] Sec. 10, [H6] Sec. 7) for the first and second radially excited singlet and triplet mesons with d_h=0 and $d_m \neq 0$. The wave functions as well as the associated nonlinear potential $\Phi_{cJ}(r)$ are plotted in ([H5] Figures 1, 2, [H6] Figures 2, 3).

Table 5.6. Masses (MeV) of low-lying excited singlet l=0 mesons. Data E_{exp} [P1] are given in brackets [..]. Below these are the predicted masses E_{th} from (5.1.1) using Table 5.2 and (5.2.2). $N=n_r+1$. The differences $\Delta E^2/4= (E_{exp}{}^2- E_{th}{}^2)/4$ are shown in parentheses (..).The mass term for η in (4.3.3a) is given by (2.4.15). η_c is mostly a $\bar{c}c$ and η_b mostly a $\bar{b}b$ state

Isospin	$N^{2S+1}l_J=1^1S_0$	$=2^1S_0$	$=3^1S_0$
1	π	π(1300) [1200-1400] 1067.2 (0.1378)	π(1800) [1812±13] 1502 (0.2568)
1/2	K	K(1460) [1400, 1460] 1166.8 (0.1496, 0.1925)	K(1830) [≈1830] 1575.2 (0.2169)
0	η	η(1295) [1294±4] 1204 (0.0562)	η(1760) [1760±11] 1603 (0.132)
0	η_c	η_c(2S) [3638±1.2] 3148.4 (0.8313)	-
0	η_b	η_b(2S) [9999±3.5] 9.5256 (2.31) {9.634}	- -

Table 5.7. Masses (MeV) of low-lying radially excited triplet l=0 mesons. Data E_{exp} [P1] are given in brackets [..]. Below these are the predicted masses E_{th} from (5.1.1) using Table 5.2 and (5.2.2). $N=n_r+1$. The differences $\Delta E^2/4= (E_{exp}{}^2- E_{th}{}^2)/4$ are shown in parentheses (..)

Isospin	$N^{2S+1}l_J=1^3S_0$	$=2^3S_1$
1	ρ	ρ(1450) [1465±25] 1303.3 (0.1119)
0	ω	ω(1420) [1400-1450] 1303.3 (0.06535-0.101)
1/2	K^*(892)	K^*(1410) [1414±15] 1166.8 (0.1595)
0	ϕ	ϕ(1680) [1680±20] 1471 (0.1646)
0	J/ψ	ψ(2S) [3686.1±0.025] 3236 (0.7789)
0	$Y(1S)$	$Y(2S)$ [10023.26±0.31] 9555 (2.292) {9694.3}

These computations depend upon the choices of an unknown parameter, the amplitude of the wave function in Φ_c in (3.2.8b) or the finite sizes of the normalization box Ω_c of (4.2.8) or, equivalently, N_{CJn} of ([H6) (4d)) which is a volume integral over $\psi_J(r)^2$. Therefore, the contribution of $\Phi_{cJ}(r)$ to E_{th} can presently not be uniquely determined. More strictly, an $\underline{X}$ dependence is implicitly introduced in (4.6.2) so that the general wave function $\psi_J(X,x)$ of (3.1.5) is no longer separable in the laboratory coordinates (X_0, $\underline{X}$) and relative coordinates (x_0, $\underline{x}$), rendering the problem not manageable.

Qualitatively, assume (4.6.2) and let $\Phi_{cJ}(r)$ in (3.4.1, 3) be replaced by constants $\bar{\Phi}_{cJ}$. Correct predictions are achieved if $\bar{\Phi}_{cJ} = \Delta E^2/4 = (E_{exp}{}^2- E_{th}{}^2)/4$ shown in the parentheses ( ) in Tables 5.6, 7. If the nonlinear potential contribution is small relative to the quadratic confining potential, $\bar{\Phi}_{cJ}$<<the d_h terms in (4.3.3). Then (4.4.1) and $\Phi_{cJ}(r)$ of (3.2.17) still hold

approximately; $\bar{\Phi}_{cJ}$ becomes independent of flavor or quark masses and be a constant in each column of Tables 5.6, 7. The values $\Delta E^2/4$ in the parentheses are however not constant in each column. This due to that they are not small but comparable to the last terms in (4.3.3a, 3b)=$3d_h$, $5d_h$, $7d_h$... =0.21, 0.35, 0.49... for larger n values. Therefore, $\bar{\Phi}_{cJ}$ is flavor-dependent and this dependence, as well as that for ψ_J, increase with decreasing normalization volume $\Omega \to \Omega_c$, which generally decrease with increasing mass. These are seen from the numbers in the parentheses (..) in Tables 5.6, 7 in which $\Delta E^2/4$ become large for heavier mesons. Thus, the nonlinear potential Φ_{cJ} does contribute to the meson masses, in this case by 9-18% mentioned above.

5.6. Orbitally Excited Mesons [H25]

5.6.1. Orbitally Excited Singlet Mesons

The wave functions at $r \to 0, \infty$, is governed by (3.4.2) and is independent of the angles. The solutions at these limits are to be connected by an unknown solution dependent upon both r and ϑ in the intermediate r region. This nonseparable problem starting from (3.2.10b) is also beyond the reach of the present work.

Not being to treat this problem adequately, follow the procedures that led to Tables 5.6, 7 and linearize (3.4.2b) by putting Φ_{c0}=0, (4.3.3c) with $l \geq 1$ is obtained. It gives the masses in Table 5.8.

Table 5.8. Masses (MeV) of low-lying orbitally excited $l \geq 1$ singlet mesons. Data E_{exp} [P1] are given in brackets [..]. Below these are the predicted masses E_{th} from (4.3.3c) using Table 5.2 and (5.2.2). The differences $\Delta E^2/4 = (E_{exp}^2 - E_{th}^2)/4$ are shown in parentheses (..). * in front denotes a state not present in the quark model assignments in [P1]

Quark- content	$N_r{}^{2S+1}l_J = 1^1P_1$ $J^P = 1^+$	$= 1^1D_2$ $= 2^-$	$= 1^1F_3$ $= 3^+$	$= 1^1G_4$ $= 4^-$
$\bar{d}u$, $\bar{d}d$, $\bar{u}u$	$b_1(1235)$ [1229.5±3.2] 761 (0.2331)	$\pi_2(1670)$ [1672.4±3.2] 1067 (0.4143)		
$\bar{s}u$, $\bar{s}d$	$K_1(1270)$ [1273±7] 895.3 (0.2947)	$K_2(1770)$ [1773±8] 1166.8 (0.4455)	$*K_3(2320)$ [2324±24] 1386 (0.87)	$*K_4(2500)$ [2490±20] 1575.2 (0.9297)
$\bar{s}s$, $\bar{d}d$, $\bar{u}u$	$h_1(1170)$ [1170±20] $h_1(1380)$ [1386±19] 900.8 (0.1384) (0.2774)	$\eta_2(1645)$ [1617±5] $\eta_2(1870)$ [1842±8] 1204 (0.3109) (0.4858)		
$\bar{u}c$, $\bar{d}c$	$D_1(2420)$ [2422.2±1.8] 2009 (0.4603)			
$\bar{s}c$	$D_{s1}(2536)$ [2535.35±0.34] 2104 (0.593)			
$\bar{c}c$	$h_c(1P)$ [3526.21±0.25] 3058 (0.7707)			

These results are not surprisingly more coarse than those in Tables 5.6, 7 because the neglected nonlinear Φ_{c0} in (3.4.2b) actually contains angle dependence in the intermediate r region; more equations are required. The predicted masses E_{th} are now 14-38% smaller than the measured E_{exp}, as compared to 4-18% for the radially excited mesons. Again replace Φ_{c0} in (3.4.2b) by constant $\bar{\Phi}_{c0}$ and put it equal to $\Delta E^2/4 = (E_{exp}{}^2 - E_{th}{}^2)/4$ shown in the parentheses (..) in Table 5.8. The values in them are comparable or greater than the last term in (4.3.3c) $=5d_h, 7d_h... =0.35, 0.49...$, showing that the nonlinear potential Φ_{c0} contributes appreciably to the masses.

Like the behavior mentioned at the end of Sec.5.5, $\Delta E^2/4$ here also increase with the meson masses and, in addition, also with increasing orbital angular momentum l.

Note that the predicted values in the second columns in Tables 5.6 and 5.8 are the same for the same quark content. This is due to that (4.3.3a) and (4.3.3c) cannot distinguish between n=2, 4, 6... and $2l$=2, 4, 6... The differences are due to that the neglected Φ_{c0}´s are different in the intermediate r region. The approximately correct predictions in Tables 5.6-8 depend upon the quadratic confining potential $-d_h{}^2r^2$ in (3.4.1-3). On the other hand, potential models [L3, L4 §14.3.2] called for linear confinement potential, upon which $d_{m2}=0$ in the earlier edition of this book was based, as was mentioned below (3.2.19). There is however no conflict, only agreement in hind sight, if one notes that the squared mass $E_{J0}{}^2$ enters the same (3.4.1-3). For excited mesons, $E_{J0}{}^2$ is large and "sees" a quadratic confining potential $-d_h{}^2r^2$ at large r, equivalent to that E_{J0} "sees" a linear confining potential $-d_hr$.

5.6.2. Orbitally Excited Triplet Mesons

In the $r\to 0$ limit, the wave functions of these mesons are given by (3.4.6-8). For large r, the wave functions are of the form (4.3.4a) multiplied by some power of r, as was mentioned below (4.6.1). In the intermediate r region, $\Phi_c(\underline{x})$ in (3.2.8b), with ψ_0 and χ_0 there put to zero, again depend upon r and ϑ. This analogously causes that $\underline{\psi}(\underline{x})$ and $\underline{\chi}(\underline{x})$ cannot be put in the separable form (3.4.4). The wave function components are coupled to each other and we have to revert to (3.2.2). The unknown, nonseparable solutions in this region connects the known separable angle-independent solutions above for small and large r.

Equations (3.2.2) and (3.4.5) show that $E_0{}^2/4$ and $M_m{}^2$ no longer appear together as a difference, as in (3.4.1-3), so that flavor symmetry in relative space valid for the last mentioned equations no longer holds in §3.4.4 and here. This loss of flavor symmetry implies that we no longer have a simple mass formula of the type (5.1.1). Instead, (3.2.8b) with ψ_0, $\chi_0=0$ and (3.2.2) are to be solved. The complexities of these equations have however put their solutions beyond reach presently.

Not being able to provide even an approximate solution, as those leading to Tables 5.6-8 above, let (3.4.8) be used to approximately classify these triplet, l>0 mesons. For each l, there is a trio of solutions. Each solution generally involves all three spherical harmonics Y_{l+1}, Y_l and Y_{l-1} and is therefore not associated with any definite angular momentum. It however still possesses a definite parity; $\underline{\psi}(\underline{x}) \to \underline{\chi}(-\underline{x})$ under spatial inversion according to (3.3.2b).

Table 5.9. Orbitally excited triplet meson (§3.4.4) assignments. * on the left denotes states not present in [P1]. C denotes charge conjugation parity where applicable. +... means small admixtures of other $\bar{q}q$ pairs. § denotes possible radially excited mesons. The quantum numbers refer to the meson wave functions (3.4.4) in relative space. The wave functions associated with each λ is given by (3.4.6) and (3.4.8). For each orbital quantum number l, there are three meson states corresponding to $\lambda=l-1$, l and $l+1$ in (3.4.8). In the first two cases, $J=l-1$ and l respectively. For the last case, both $J=l-1$ and $J=l+1$ components are present, with the former dominating over the latter. $N_r = n_r + 1$

Quark content	$N_r{}^{2S+1}l_J=1^3P_0$ $\lambda(PC)=0(++)$	$=1^3P_1$ $=1(++)$	$=1^3P_2+1^3P_0$ $=2(++)$	$=1^3D_1$ $=1(--)$	$=1^3D_2$ $=2(--)$	$=1^3D_3+1^3D_1$ $=3(--)$
$\bar{d}u$, $\bar{d}d$, $\bar{u}u$	$a_0(980)$ $a_0(1450)$	$a_1(1260)$	$a_2(1320)$	$\rho(1700)$		$\rho_3(1690)$
$\bar{u}u$, $\bar{d}d$				$\omega(1600)$		$\omega_3(1670)$
$\bar{s}u$, $\bar{s}d$	$K^*_0(1430)$ $*§K^*_0(1950)$	$K_1(1400)$ $*§K_1(1650)$	$K^*_2(1430)$ $§K^*_2(1980)$	$K^*(1680)$	$K_2(1820)$ $*§K_2(2250)$	$K^*_3(1780)$
$\bar{s}s$, $\bar{d}d$, $\bar{u}u$	$*f_0(980)$ $f_0(1370)$ $*§f_0(1500)$ $f_0(1710)$	$f_1(1285)$ $f_1(1420)$	$f_2(1270)$ $f'_2(1525)$ $§f_2(1810)$ $§f_2(2010)$			
$\bar{s}s$						$\phi_3(1850)$
$\bar{u}c$, $\bar{d}c$			$D^*_2(2460)$			
$\bar{c}c+\ldots$	$\chi_{c0}(1P)$	$\chi_{c1}(1P)$	$\chi_{c2}(1P)$	$\psi(3770)$		
$\bar{b}b+\ldots$	$\chi_{b0}(1P)$ $*§\chi_{b0}(2P)$	$\chi_{b1}(1P)$ $*§\chi_{b1}(2P)$	$\chi_{b2}(1P)$ $*§\chi_{b2}(2P)$			
Quark content	$N_r{}^{2S+1}l_J=1^3F_2$ $\lambda(PC)=2(++)$	$=1^3F_3$ $=3(++)$	$=1^3F_4+1^3F_2$ $=4(++)$	$=1^3G_3$ $=3(--)$	$=1^3G_4$ $=4(--)$	$=1^3G_5+1^3G_3$ $=5(--)$
$\bar{d}u$, $\bar{d}d$, $\bar{u}u$			$a_4(2040)$		$*\rho_3(2250)$	$*\rho_5(2350)$
$\bar{s}u$, $\bar{s}d$			$K^*_4(2045)$			$*K^*_5(2380)$
$\bar{s}s$, $\bar{d}d$, $\bar{u}u$	$*f_2(1565)$ $*f_2(1640)$ $*§f_2(2150)$ $*f_2(2300)$ $*f_2(2340)$		$f_4(2050)$ $f_J(2220)$			
Quark content	$N_r{}^{2S+1}l_J=1^3H_4$ $\lambda(PC)=4(++)$	$=1^3H_5$ $=5(++)$	$=1^3H_6+1^3H_4$ $=6(++)$		$=2^3P_2+2^3P_0$ $=2(++)$	
$\bar{d}u$, $\bar{d}d$, $\bar{u}u$			$*a_6(2450)$			
$\bar{s}u$, $\bar{s}d$					$K^*_2(1980)$	
$\bar{s}s$, $\bar{d}d$, $\bar{u}u$	$*f_4(2300)$		$*f_6(2510)$		$f_2(1810)$ $f_2(2010)$	
$\bar{b}b+\ldots$					$\chi_{b2}(2P)$	

The approximate classification is further simplified if one considers only the leading terms in the expansion (3.4.6). To lowest order, (3.4.8a) shows that the wave function is $g_0r^{J-1}Y_{l-1}$ and angular momentum $J=l-1$ is assigned to the associated meson. The wave function associated with (3.4.8b) is $h_0r^JY_l$ and $J=l$ for this meson. The wave function associated with (3.4.8c) is $f_0(r^{J+1}Y_{l+1}+(l+1)(2l+3)r^{J-1}Y_{l-1})$ and involves both $J=l+1$ and $J=l-1$ components. The parity of these three states is $P=(-)^l$. The meson masses E_{j0} associated with each of these solutions are in general different for the same quark content and are eigenvalues of the sixth order equation system (3.2.2). Assignments of the corresponding mesons in [P1] according to the wave functions associated with (3.4.8) are given in Table 5.9.

Some of the f_2 mesons may also be reassigned to $1^3F_4+1^3F_2$ because the J=4 component is smaller than the J=2 component by a factor of 1/36, according to (3.4.8c), and may have eluded observation. For the same reason, the radially excited $2^3P_2+2^3P_0$ states may be modified $2^3F_4+2^3F_2$ states. It is also noted that states corresponding to the middle member of the trio $f(r)Y_{l+1}$, $h(r)Y_l$ and $g(r)Y_{l-1}$ tends to be underrepresented or absent. This may be related to that (3.4.4b), being symmetric in ψ and χ, contains both $f(r)Y_{l+1}$ and $g(r)Y_{l-1}$. While (3.4.4c), being antisymmetric in ψ and χ, contains only $h(r)Y_l$. Except for the last column, only n_r=0 states appear in Table 5.9. For n_r>0, the radial wave functions will extend themselves farther out from the origin. In this region, $\Phi_c(\underline{x})$ in (3.2.8a) becomes greater so that the separable solutions, which led to the classification of Table 5.9, have to be replaced by unknown, nonseparable solutions mentioned above. This leads to an n_r to l coupling which yields a more complicated and as yet unknown form of classification scheme.

5.7. Nonrelativistic Pseudoscalar Mesons

Up to now, mesons at rest have been treated. This is sufficient for meson spectra. The singlet and triplet parts of the meson wave functions in (3.1.8, 9) can then be decoupled to yield (3.2.1) and (3.2.2).

In the treatment of decays in the following chapters, however, mesons as decay products do move. As was mentioned at the end of Sec. 3.3, such a decoupling is not possible if the meson is moving with momentum $\underline{K}$ in the laboratory frame. In this case, the full (3.1.8) must be used which is however not amenable to analytical solutions. In this section, (3.1.8) will first be simplified by removing the unknown relative energy ω_K in (3.1.10a). The resulting equations are then considered approximately in the small and large $\underline{K}$ limits and in the limits of light and heavy pseudoscalar meson masses relative to the confining $(d_h r)^2$ in (3.4.1).

5.7.1. Meson Wave Equations with Null Relative Energy $\omega K = 0$

The null relative energy condition

$$\omega_K = 0 \tag{5.7.1}$$

will now be *assumed*. In this way, (3.1.8) with (3.1.10a) becomes real. If this not done, some wave functions in (3.1.8) become complex and cannot be determined definitely because ω_K is unknown. This in its turn will invalidate the classical energy-momentum relation (5.7.33) below for small K and jeopardize the solution (5.7.29) below for large K.

In addition to these practical considerations, the null relative energy assumption (5.7.1) may further be justified as follows. A meson consists of quark A with flavor p at x_I, associated with the total quark wave function $\psi_A{}^a(x_I)\xi_A{}^p(z_I)$, and antiquark B with antiflavor $\bar{r}$ at x_{II}, associated with $\psi_{B\dot{a}}(x_{II})\xi_{Br}(z_{II})$, as is implied in §2.3.4. Since the quarks are not observable, the relabelling achieved by interchanging x_I and x_{II} should not affect the observable laboratory coordinate X^μ of the meson. This condition yields a_m=1−a_m in (3.1.3a) and (5.71) follows from the choice (3.1.10a).

Further, M_m^2 in the basic meson wave equations (2.3.22) is symmetric in the both quark masses according to (2.3.27). It is an internal property not affected by manipulations in the relative space, such as $x_I \leftrightarrow x_{II}$. This is related to the flavor independence in relative space considered in Sec. 4.4. These results are independent of whether the meson in motion or not. Thus ω_0 vanishes, even if this is not necessary in (3.1.10a) to arrive at the rest frame meson equations (3.2.1-2). The physical role of ω_K is not understood presently, although the associated relative time x^0 is of central importance in the present theory, as can be seen in Sec. 4.2 and will be evident in the following chapters.

With (5.7.1), (3.1.10a) becomes

$$a_m = 1/2 \tag{5.7.2}$$

Separating (3.1.8) into singlet and triplet parts and using (3.1.9) and (5.7.2) leads to

$$\left\{\tfrac{1}{4}\left(E_K^2+\underline{K}^2\right)\chi_0-\tfrac{1}{2}E_K\underline{K}\underline{\chi}\right\}+\left[\Delta\chi_0-\left(\underline{K}\times\underline{\partial}\right)\underline{\chi}\right]=\left(d_{m0}-d_h^2r^2-M_m^2\right)\psi_0 \tag{5.7.3a}$$

$$\begin{aligned}&\left\{-\tfrac{1}{4}\left(E_K^2-\underline{K}^2\right)\underline{\chi}-\tfrac{1}{2}\underline{K}\left(\underline{K}\underline{\chi}\right)+\tfrac{1}{2}E_K\underline{K}\chi_0\right\}\\&-\left[2\underline{\partial}\left(\underline{\partial}\underline{\chi}\right)-\Delta\underline{\chi}+E_K\underline{\partial}\times\underline{\chi}+\underline{K}\times\underline{\partial}\chi_0\right]=\left(d_{m0}-d_h^2r^2-M_m^2\right)\underline{\psi}\end{aligned} \tag{5.7.3b}$$

$$\left\{\tfrac{1}{4}\left(E_K^2+\underline{K}^2\right)\psi_0-\tfrac{1}{2}E_K\underline{K}\underline{\psi}\right\}+\left[\Delta\psi_0+\left(\underline{K}\times\underline{\partial}\right)\underline{\psi}\right]=\left(d_{m0}-d_h^2r^2-M_m^2\right)\chi_0 \tag{5.7.3c}$$

$$\begin{aligned}&\left\{-\tfrac{1}{4}\left(E_K^2-\underline{K}^2\right)\underline{\psi}-\tfrac{1}{2}\underline{K}\left(\underline{K}\underline{\psi}\right)+\tfrac{1}{2}E_K\underline{K}\psi_0\right\}\\&-\left[2\underline{\partial}\left(\underline{\partial}\underline{\psi}\right)-\Delta\underline{\psi}-E_K\underline{\partial}\times\underline{\psi}-\underline{K}\times\underline{\partial}\psi_0\right]=\left(d_{m0}-d_h^2r^2-M_m^2\right)\underline{\chi}\end{aligned} \tag{5.7.3d}$$

ψ_0 and $\underline{\psi}$ in (5.7.3a, 3b) can be expressed as functions of χ_0 and $\underline{\chi}$ and their derivatives and inserted into (5.7.3c, 3d) to form 4 coupled fourth order differential equations for χ_0 and $\underline{\chi}$. If the ψ's were analytic for finite $\underline{x}$, then the χ's will have a singularity at $d_h^2r^2 = d_{m0} - M_m^2$ for kaon and pion but not for mesons with b or c quark according to Table 5.2. The roles of χ and ψ can be interchanged, as can be seen from (5.7.3).

5.7.2. Nonrelativistic Pseudoscalar Meson Wave Functions

The full (5.7.3) or the 4 coupled fourth order differential equations mentioned above are too complicated to tackle. Here, only slowly moving mesons with small $\underline{K}$ will be treated perturbatively. Because vector mesons have too short a lifetime to be seen in motion, only slowly moving, ground state pseudoscalar mesons are considered. Introduce the small expansion parameter

$$\varepsilon_0 = |\underline{K}|/E_0 << 1 \tag{5.7.4}$$

Expand E_K in (3.1.6) and the wave functions in (3.1.7a), suppressing the relative time factor in (3.1.9), in the form

$$\psi_0(\underline{x}) = \sum_i \psi_{0i}(\underline{x}), \quad \underline{\psi}(\underline{x}) = \sum_i \underline{\psi}_i(\underline{x}), \quad \underline{\psi}_0(\underline{x}) = \hat{r}\psi_1(r), \quad \psi \to \chi, \quad E_K = \sum_i E_{Ji} \tag{5.7.5}$$

where i denotes the *ith* order in ε_0 and (3.2.5b) has been generalized. Additional specifications may be added as superscript or subscript inside parentheses. Further, only freely moving mesons are considered so that Φ_c in (3.2.8a) drops out according to §4.3.1. Therefore, Φ_m of (3.2.8a) is independent of the meson wave functions (5.7.5).

To zeroth order in ε_0, (5.7.3) goes over to (3.2.10b) and

$$\chi_{00}(r) = -\psi_{00}(r), \qquad \underline{\chi}_0(r) = \underline{\psi}_0(r) = 0, \qquad E_K = E_0 = E_{00} \tag{5.7.6}$$

To first order in ε_0, (5.7.3) and (3.2.8) yield

$$\chi_{01} = 0, \qquad \psi_{01} = 0, \qquad E_{01} = 0 \tag{5.7.7a}$$

$$\begin{aligned}&\left(E_{00}^2/4 - \Delta\right)\underline{\chi}_1 + 2\underline{\partial}\left(\underline{\partial}\underline{\chi}_1\right) + E_{00}\underline{\partial}\times\underline{\chi}_1 + \left(d_{m0} - d_h^2 r^2 - M_m^2\right)\underline{\psi}_1 \\ &= \tfrac{1}{2}E_{00}\underline{K}\chi_{00} - \underline{K}\times\underline{\partial}\chi_{00}\end{aligned} \tag{5.7.7b}$$

$$\begin{aligned}&\left(E_{00}^2/4 - \Delta\right)\underline{\psi}_1 + 2\underline{\partial}\left(\underline{\partial}\underline{\psi}_1\right) - E_{00}\underline{\partial}\times\underline{\psi}_1 + \left(d_{m0} - d_h^2 r^2 - M_m^2\right)\underline{\chi}_1 \\ &= \tfrac{1}{2}E_{00}\underline{K}\psi_{00} + \underline{K}\times\underline{\partial}\psi_{00}\end{aligned} \tag{5.7.7c}$$

To second order in ε_0, the singlet part of (5.7.3) becomes

$$\begin{aligned}&\left(E_{00}^2/4 + \Delta\right)\chi_{02} - \left(d_{m0} - d_h^2 r^2 - M_m^2\right)\psi_{02} \\ &= -\underline{\partial}\left(\underline{K}\times\underline{\chi}_1\right) - \left(\tfrac{1}{2}E_{00}E_{02} + \tfrac{1}{4}\underline{K}^2\right)\chi_{00} + \tfrac{1}{2}E_{00}\underline{K}\underline{\chi}_1\end{aligned} \tag{5.7.8a}$$

$$\begin{aligned}&\left(E_{00}^2/4 + \Delta\right)\psi_{02} - \left(d_{m0} - d_h^2 r^2 - M_m^2\right)\chi_{02} \\ &= \underline{\partial}\left(\underline{K}\times\underline{\psi}_1\right) - \left(\tfrac{1}{2}E_{00}E_{02} + \tfrac{1}{4}\underline{K}^2\right)\psi_{00} + \tfrac{1}{2}E_{00}\underline{K}\underline{\psi}_1\end{aligned} \tag{5.7.8b}$$

The spherical symmetry present in the ε_0=0 limit is broken by the momentum $\underline{K}$ so that separation of variables in the relative space $\underline{x}$ cannot be carried out. This renders that each of (5.7.7, 8) consists of two coupled second order partial differential equations containing eight dependent variables and cannot be readily solved analytically. To obtain some estimates, (5.7.7, 8) will be treated by the following coarse approximations.

In the remainder of this chapter, the zeroth order wave function ψ_{00} of (5.7.6) for a free pseudoscalar meson at rest given by (4.3.4a) will be employed. Let

$$\underline{K} = (0,\ 0,\ K) \tag{5.7.9}$$

5.7.3. Approximative Heavy Meson Wave Functions

For heavy mesons, the the last term is small next to the first term on the right sides of (5.7.7b, 7c) when

$$E_{00} >> 2\sqrt{d_h} \approx 0.53\ \text{GeV} \tag{5.7.10}$$

Here, the magnitude of $\underline{\partial}$ in (5.7.7) is $d_h r$ according to (4.3.4a) where r has been replaced by r_0 of (4.6.1). This inequality holds roughly for mesons with b or c quark but not for kaon and pion.

The approximation consists of making the simplifying ansatz

$$\underline{\chi}_1(\underline{x}) = -\underline{\psi}_1(\underline{x}) \tag{5.7.11a}$$

in (5.7.7b, 7c). Addition and subtraction of thee two equations yields

$$\left(E_{00}^2/4 - \Delta + d_h^2 r^2 - d_{m0} + M_m^2\right)\underline{\psi}_1 = \tfrac{1}{2} E_{00}\underline{K}\psi_{00} - 2\underline{\partial}\left(\underline{\partial}\underline{\psi}_1\right) \tag{5.7.11b}$$

$$-E_{00}\underline{\partial} \times \underline{\psi}_1 = \underline{K} \times \underline{\partial}\psi_{00} \tag{5.7.11c}$$

The ansatz (5.7.11a) thus leads to that these two equations determine only one unknown $\underline{\psi}_1$; there has to be an inconsistency. Solving (5.7.11c) with (5.7.9) gives

$$\underline{\psi}_1(\underline{x}) = \frac{\underline{K}}{E_{00}}\psi_{00}(r) = (0,\ 0,\ \psi_{1z0}(\underline{x})) \tag{5.7.12}$$

which shows that $\underline{\psi}_1$ is of order ε_0. Inserting this expression into (5.7.11b) using (4.3.4a) gives

$$\frac{1}{2}E_{00}K\,\psi_{00}(r) = \frac{1}{2}E_{00}K\,\psi_{00}(r) + 2\frac{K}{E_{00}}d_h\left(1 - \widehat{z}\widehat{z}d_h r^2\right)\psi_{00}(r) \tag{5.7.13}$$

The last term comes from the last term in (5.7.11b) and causes that (5.7.13) cannot be satisfied and is inconsistent with (5.7.12).

However, the last term in (5.7.13) will be small for heavy mesons having large E_{00} so that (5.7.13) and the solution (5.7.12) both hold approximately. Replacing r by the effective value r_0 of (4.6.1) and putting $\hat{z}\hat{z} = 1/3$ via (3.1.7b), anticipating later angular integration, the criterion is that the ratio between the two terms on the right side of (5.7.13) be small. This gives another requirement for heavy meson approximation

$$\frac{8d_h}{3E_{00}^2} \approx \frac{0.187}{E_{00}^2} << 1 \tag{5.7.14}$$

This ration is 9.6 for pion, 0.762 for kaon and 0.054 for D meson. Thus, (5.7.14) is well satisfied by mesons with b or d quark but again not by kaons or pions. This inequality agrees roughly with that given by (5.7.10). There is however no great loss here; pions as decay products often move relativistically so that the first order (5.7.7) no longer holds in the first place.

The last terms in (5.7.11b) will also introduce a correction to (5.7.12). As an estimate, let the corrected (5.7.12) be an average of (5.7.12) and (5.7.13) multiplied by $2/E_{00}^2$ and generalized to include the x and y components of the last term in (5.7.11b);

$$\underline{\psi}_1(\underline{x}) = \left(\psi_{1x1}(\underline{x}),\ \psi_{1y1}(\underline{x}),\ \psi_{1z0}(\underline{x}) + \psi_{1z1}(\underline{x})\right) \tag{5.7.15}$$

$$\psi_{1x1}(\underline{x}) = -\frac{2K}{E_{00}^3}\hat{x}\hat{z}d_h^2 r^2 \psi_{00}(r), \qquad \psi_{1y1}(\underline{x}) = -\frac{2K}{E_{00}^3}\hat{y}\hat{z}d_h^2 r^2 \psi_{00}(r)$$
$$\psi_{1z1}(\underline{x}) = \frac{2K}{E_{00}^3} d_h\left(1 - \hat{z}\hat{z}d_h r^2\right)\psi_{00}(r) \tag{5.7.16}$$

If, instead of (5.7.11a),

$$\underline{\chi}_1(\underline{x}) = \underline{\psi}_1(\underline{x}) \tag{5.7.17}$$

then the both accompanying equations corresponding to (5.7.11b, 11c) cannot be made to be good approximations pf each other.

The second order equations (5.7.8) are treated analogously. Subtraction and addition of (5.7.8a) and (5.7.8b) leads to

$$\chi_{02}(\underline{x}) = -\psi_{02}(\underline{x}) \tag{5.7.18a}$$

$$\left(\frac{E_{00}^2}{4} + \Delta - d_h^2 r^2 + d_{m0} - M_m^2\right)\psi_{02} = -\left(\frac{E_{00}E_{02}}{2} + \frac{K^2}{4}\right)\psi_{00} + \frac{E_{00}\underline{K}\underline{\psi}_1}{2} \tag{5.7.18b}$$

$$\underline{\partial}\left(\underline{K} \times \underline{\psi}_1\right) = 0 \tag{5.7.18c}$$

The last equation is satisfied for $\underline{\psi}_1$ given by (5.7.12). It is slightly violated by (5.7.15, 16) but the violations contain odd powers of $\hat{r}$ and will vanish upon integration over the angles later. The left operator of (5.7.18b) is the same as the linearized ones in (3.4.1) and vanishes for $\psi_{02} \propto \psi_{00}$; ψ_{02} can be absorbed into the zeroth order ψ_{00} and put to 0. Thus,

$$\tfrac{1}{2} E_{00} \underline{K} \underline{\psi}_1 = -\left(\tfrac{1}{2} E_{00} E_{02} + \tfrac{1}{4} K^2\right)\psi_{00}, \qquad \psi_{02} = \chi_{02} = 0 \tag{5.7.19}$$

Inserting (5.7.12) into the first of (5.7.19) leads to

$$E_{02} = K^2 / 2E_{00} \tag{5.7.20}$$

5.7.4. Light Meson Wave Equations and "Decoupling" Approximation

In the limit opposite to (5.7.10),

$$E_{00} << 2\sqrt{d_h} \approx 0.53 \text{ GeV} \tag{5.7.21}$$

This inequality holds for pion but not for kaon and heavier mesons. In this limit, $E_{00} \to 0$ in (5.7.7b, 7c) which becomes

$$\underline{\chi}_1(\underline{x}) = \underline{\psi}_1(\underline{x}) \tag{5.7.22a}$$

$$\begin{aligned}\left(E_{00}^2/4 - \Delta\right)\underline{\psi}_1 + 2\underline{\partial}\left(\underline{\partial}\underline{\psi}_1\right) + \left(d_{m0} - d_h^2 r^2 - M_m^2\right)\underline{\psi}_1 &= \underline{K} \times \underline{\partial}\psi_{00} \\ = -\left(\hat{K} \times \hat{r}\right) K d_h r \psi_{00}(r), \qquad \hat{K} &= \underline{K}/K\end{aligned} \tag{5.7.22b}$$

where (5.7.6) and (4.3.4a) have been used and the small E_{00}^2 term has been retained for simpler identification with other results. The homogeneous part of (5.7.22b) consists of three second order differential equations coupled by the $\underline{\partial}(\underline{\partial}\underline{\psi}_1)$ term and has three solutions. The simplest one is to be found from the "decoupling" ansatz

$$\underline{\psi}_1(\underline{x}) = \left(\hat{K} \times \hat{r}\right)\psi_{10}(r), \qquad \left(\underline{\partial}\underline{\psi}_1\right) = 0 \tag{5.7.23}$$

$$\left(\frac{\partial^2}{\partial r^2} + \frac{2}{r}\frac{\partial}{\partial r} - \frac{2}{r^2} + d_h^2 r^2 - \frac{E_{00}^2}{4} - d_{m0} + M_m^2\right)\psi_{10}(r) = K d_h r \psi_{00}(r) \tag{5.7.24}$$

Note that ψ_{10} here is not the same as that in (4.3.4b). The homogeneous part of (5.7.24) is solved via the expansion

$$\psi_{10}(r) \to \psi_{10(s)}(r) = \sum_{\nu=0}^{\infty} a_{L\nu} r^{s+\nu} \tag{5.7.25}$$

Inserting this into (5.7.24) and putting its right side to 0 yields the recursion formula

$$a_{Ln+2}(s+n+1)(s+n+4) = \left(\frac{E_{00}^2}{4} + d_{m0} - M_m^2\right) a_{Ln} - d_h a_{Ln-2}, \quad a_{L0} \neq 0 \tag{5.7.26}$$

Putting $n = -2$, the indicial equation part yields

$$s = -2, \quad s = 1 \tag{5.7.27}$$

The solutions (5.7.25) have been obtained using a computer at Uppsala University, The first few terms of (5.7.25) are used as initial values. The solutions are proportional to sine and cosine functions with argument $d_h r^2/2$ so that they are oscillating. The amplitudes decrease slowly while the wave lengths also diminish with increasing r.

The particular integral of the "decoupled" (5.7.24) is

$$\psi_{10}(r) = K d_h \frac{\alpha_{00}}{\sqrt{\Omega}} p_{10}(r)$$

$$p_{10}(r) = \left[\psi_{10(-2)}(r)\int_0^r \psi_{10(1)}(t)\Delta(t)dt - \psi_{10(1)}(r)\int_0^r \psi_{10(-2)}(t)\Delta(t)dt\right]$$

$$\Delta(t) = t\exp\left(-\frac{1}{2}d_h t^2\right) \Big/ \left(\frac{\partial \psi_{10(-2)}(t)}{\partial t}\psi_{10(1)}(t) - \psi_{10(-2)}(t)\frac{\partial \psi_{10(1)}(t)}{\partial t}\right)$$

(5.7.28)

$p_{10}(r)$ is also oscillating; its amplitude also decrease slowly while the wave lengths diminish with increasing r.

There are in addition two "coupled" solutions involving $\underline{\partial}(\partial\psi_l)\neq 0$. These are more complicated and have not been found.

5.7.5. Extremely Relativistic Mesons

In limit of $\underline{K}=(0, 0, K\to\infty)$, the $\underline{K}^2$ terms given in the the braces of (5.7.3,) dominate. The singlet and triplet parts of (5.7.3) give a consistent solution

$$\psi_z = \psi_0, \qquad \chi_z = \chi_0, \qquad E_K^2 = K^2 \tag{5.7.29}$$

where z denotes the third component as was used in (5.7.15, 16). If the rest terms in these braces are of order K, they may balance off the terms in the brackets in (5.7.3) which are of order K

and lower. If however the rest terms in these braces are of order lower than K, then the terms in the brackets in (5.7.3) have to balance off among themselves. In this case, it is required that

$$|\underline{\partial}| \approx K \tag{5.7.30}$$

which in its turn implies that

$$\chi_0,\ \underline{\chi},\ \psi_0,\ \underline{\psi} = (\text{nondiverging power series in } \underline{x}) \times \exp(-Kr) \tag{5.7.31}$$

where Kr indicates a prototype dependence on $\underline{x}$ and can actually be more complicated.

Should solutions of the type (5.7.31) exist, they imply a decrease of the size of a meson at rest, r_0=4.69 fm in (4.6.1), to a size of the order of $1/K \ll 1/\sqrt{d_h}$ at high meson momenta. This reduction is in the relative space and parallels the corresponding Lorentz contraction in laboratory space $\underline{X}$. Thus, high energy mesons may be used to probe the hadronic structure of nucleons, similar to that the electrons are used to probe their electromagnetic structure.

5.7.6. Classical Energy-Momentum Relation

The classical relation

$$E_K^2 = E_{00}^2 + K^2 \tag{5.7.32}$$

is in agreement with the last of (5.7.29) in the $K\to\infty$ limit and holds for K=0 by definition for ground state pseudoscalar meson. To first order in ε_0, (5.7.32) also holds according to the last of (5.7.7a). To order ε_0^2 or K^2, (5.7.32) can be written as

$$E_K = \sqrt{E_{00}^2 + K^2} \approx E_{00} + E_{02}, \qquad E_{02} \approx K^2/2E_{00} \tag{5.7.33}$$

which has been shown for both heavy and light pseudoscalar mesons in (5.7.20). To higher orders in ε_0, (5.7.32) has not been established presently.

Chapter 6

Lagrangian Formalism and Electromagnetic Interactions

This chapter follows largely Sec. 2-5 of [H8], Sec. 2-4 of [H9] and [H10]. In the last two chapters, the unperturbed or zeroth order solutions to the equations of motion for free mesons at rest have been found. The energy eigenvalues associated with these solutions were applied to account for meson spectra. In this and the following two chapters, mainly first order perturbational problems pertaining to meson decay will be treated. For this purpose, the meson equations of motion need be cast in the form of actions.

6.1. Meson Action

6.1.1. Meson Action and Boundary Conditions

The equations of motion for two quark mesons (2.3.22) can be replaced by the meson action

$$S_m = \int d^4x_I d^4x_{II} L_m \tag{6.1.1}$$

$$2L_m = -\left(\partial_I^{a\dot{b}} \chi^*_{\dot{e}a}\right)\left(\partial_{II}^{f\dot{e}} \chi_{\dot{b}f}\right) - \left(\partial_{I\dot{c}a} \psi^{*d\dot{c}}\right)\left(\partial_{II\dot{e}d} \psi^{a\dot{e}}\right) - \left(M_m^2 - \Phi_m\right)\left(\chi^*_{\dot{e}a} \psi^{a\dot{e}} + \psi^{*d\dot{c}} \chi_{\dot{c}d}\right) + c.c. \tag{6.1.2}$$

where

$$\left(\partial_I^{a\dot{b}} \chi^*_{\dot{e}a}\right)\left(\partial_{II}^{f\dot{e}} \chi_{\dot{b}f}\right) = \partial_I^{a\dot{b}} \chi^*_{\dot{e}a} \partial_{II}^{f\dot{e}} \chi_{\dot{b}f} - \chi^*_{\dot{e}a} \partial_I^{a\dot{b}} \partial_{II}^{f\dot{e}} \chi_{\dot{b}f}, \qquad \chi \to \psi \tag{6.1.3}$$

has been consulted.

The meson wave functions χ and ψ in (6.1.2) must satisfy the following boundary conditions in the relative space x^μ and laboratory space X^μ via the transformation (3.1.3a). At large $|\underline{x}|$, χ and ψ must vanish if they are to be confined. They and their first derivatives also vanish for free mesons according to (4.3.4). At large X^μ, the conventional boundary conditions for a one particle wave function are taken over here; χ and ψ observe periodic boundary conditions at large $|\underline{X}|$ and are fixed in magnitude at large times $|X^0|$.

Shortly after the proposal of the Bethe-Salpeter equation, Wick [W4] pointed out that the boundary conditions for the associated wave functions have not been adequately formulated for a general two particle wave function. This status has remained the same to my knowledge. Here, the behavior of χ and ψ at large relative times $|x^0|$ are assumed to be same as those at large $|X^0|$. This is supported by the symmetric character of the dependence of χ and ψ on x_I^0 and x_{II}^0 in (3.1.10b). The linear transformation (3.1.3a) with (3.1.10a) does not alter this form of dependence. Therefore, if χ and ψ depend upon X^0 in a certain way, they are expected to depend upon x^0 in the same way, like their dependences on x_I^0 and x_{II}^0. This assumption is of fundamental importance because it allows us to formulate the present theory in the integral form (6.1.1). The relative time x^0 underlies the normalization condition (4.2.6) as well as the gauge boson mass (see §6.2.2 and (7.4.6) below).

6.1.2. Variational Problem

We now vary S_m with respect to χ^* and ψ^* and require it to be an extremum;

$$\delta S_m = 0 \tag{6.1.4}$$

The boundary conditions for χ and ψ above lead at large $|x^\mu|$ and $|X^\mu|$ to $\delta\chi=\delta\psi=0$ as well as that δ operated on the first derivatives of χ and ψ also vanish. With (3.1.3), the equation of motion for mesons (2.3.22) is recovered from (6.1.1, 2). Variation of S_m with respect to χ and ψ leads to the Hermitian conjugate of (2.3.22) describing the corresponding antimeson. It can be seen that (2.3.22) and its complex conjugate are the same except for $x_I \leftrightarrow x_{II}$. This reflects the fact that, apart from internal properties characterized by ξ, the meson is its own antimeson.

In recovering (2.3.22) from (6.1.1, 2), Φ_m has tacitly been assumed to be not affected by the variations of χ and ψ. Applications of the meson action S_m in this book reside in Chapters 6-8 and are limited to free, ground state mesons for which the nonlinear confining term Φ_c in (3.2.8) vanishes according to §4.3.1. The remaining terms in Φ_m are constant functions not affected by variations of χ and ψ. In Chapter 8, Φ_c is a first order perturbed quantity and $\delta\Phi_c$ is therefore a higher order perturbed quantity and can therefore be neglected.

S_m has not been applied to the excited mesons in Sec. 5.5-6. A possible application of S_m will require a restricted type of variation δ_r instead of δ in (6.1.4). This is due to that Φ_c is no longer small and depends upon variation of χ and ψ via (3.2.8b). δ_r is assumed to be a subset of the general and arbitrary variation δ such that

$$\int d^4x_I d^4x_{II} \delta_r \Phi_m \left(\chi^{*a\dot{e}} \psi_{\dot{e}a} + c.c.\right) = 0 \tag{6.1.5}$$

where

$$\Box_I \Box_{II} \delta_r \Phi_m = \frac{1}{4} g_s^4 \left(\psi^{e\dot{a}} \delta_r \chi^*_{\dot{a}e} + \chi^*_{\dot{a}e} \delta_r \psi^{e\dot{a}} + c.c.\right) \tag{6.1.6}$$

For the particular case (3.2.8b), $\Phi_m \to \Phi_c$ and

$$\delta_r \Phi_c(\underline{x}) = \frac{g_s^4}{8\pi} \int d^3\underline{x}' |\underline{x} - \underline{x}'| \mathrm{Re} \begin{pmatrix} \underline{\psi}(\underline{x}')\delta_r \underline{\chi}^*(\underline{x}') + \underline{\chi}^*(\underline{x}')\delta_r \underline{\psi}(\underline{x}') \\ -\psi_0(\underline{x}')\delta_r \chi_0^*(\underline{x}') - \chi_0^*(\underline{x}')\delta_r \psi_0(\underline{x}') \end{pmatrix} \tag{6.1.7}$$

With (6.1.5), the restricted form of (6.1.4)

$$\delta_r S_m = 0 \tag{6.1.8}$$

together with (6.1.1, 2) will reproduce (2.3.22) with Φ_m containing a confining term Φ_c that can be large.

6.1.3. Inclusion of Electromagnetic Fields at Quark and Hadron Levels

To include electromagnetic fields, (2.3.19) is generalized in the same way the quark wave equations are generalized to (2.3.11);

$$\begin{aligned}&\left(\partial_I^{a\dot{b}} + iq_{op}(z)A^{a\dot{b}}(x_I)\right)\left(\partial_{II}^{f\dot{e}} + iq_{op}(u)A^{f\dot{e}}(x_{II})\right)\chi_{\dot{b}f}(x_I, x_{II})\xi^p{}_r(z,u)\\&-\left(m_{2op}(z,u) - \Phi_m(x_I, x_{II})\right)\psi^{a\dot{e}}(x_I, x_{II})\xi^p{}_r(z,u) = 0\end{aligned} \tag{6.1.9a}$$

$$\begin{aligned}&\left(\partial_{I\dot{c}a} + iq_{op}(z)A_{\dot{c}a}(x_I)\right)\left(\partial_{II\dot{e}d} + iq_{op}(u)A_{\dot{e}d}(x_{II})\right)\psi^{a\dot{e}}(x_I, x_{II})\xi^p{}_r(z,u)\\&-\left(m_{2op}(z,u) - \Phi_m(x_I, x_{II})\right)\chi^*_{\dot{c}a}(x_I, x_{II})\xi^p{}_r(z,u) = 0\end{aligned} \tag{6.1.9b}$$

Multiplying these equations by $\xi^{r}{}_p(z,u)$, integrating over the z and u and employing (2.3.14, 24-27) yields the generalized (2.4.3)

$$\left(\partial_I^{a\dot{b}} + iq_p A^{a\dot{b}}(x_I)\right)\left(\partial_{II}^{f\dot{e}} - iq_r A^{f\dot{e}}(x_{II})\right)\chi_{(pr)\dot{b}f}(x_I, x_{II}) - \left(M_m^2 - \Phi_m(x_I, x_{II})\right)\psi^{a\dot{e}}_{(pr)}(x_I, x_{II}) = 0 \tag{6.1.10a}$$

$$\left(\partial_{I\dot{c}a} + iq_p A_{\dot{c}a}(x_I)\right)\left(\partial_{II\dot{e}d} - iq_r A_{\dot{e}d}(x_{II})\right)\psi^{a\dot{e}}_{(pr)}(x_I, x_{II}) - \left(M_m^2 - \Phi_m(x_I, x_{II})\right)\chi_{(pr)\dot{c}d}(x_I, x_{II}) = 0 \tag{6.1.10b}$$

The gauge fields A are introduced at the quark level because z=z_I and x_I in (6.1.9) are coordinates for the same quark I and u=z_{II} and x_{II} are those for quark II.

In (6.1.9), like (2.3.11), the gauge fields $A(x_I)$, $A(x_{II})$ at the quark level have been introduced. They are of interest in treating magnetic moments of mesons and baryons as an external magnetic field acts on the charged quarks. These are considered in Sec. 6.3 and 11.4. The source of these gauge fields is not quark current but externally applied magnetic field.

When two or more quarks are present, each has its own internal coordinate z_I and z_{II} (2.3.16), corresponding to two "colors" in QCD. At high energies, the associated $A(x_I)$, $A(x_{II})$ turn into colored gluons (Sec. 14.2-3).

In meson and baryon decay problems, there is no external magnetics field. The observable gauge fields, such as photon $A(X)$ or massive gauge bosons like $W^{\pm}(X)$, are introduced at the observable hadron level in laboratory frame X. These are seen in §6.2.1, §6.4.2 and §7.1.2. The sources of these observable gauge fields are the observable hadron currents (see e. g. §6.2.1, §7.4.2) similar to that in classical electrodynamics.

On the other hand, the source of the gauge field $A(x_I)$ introduced at the quark level is the unobservable quark current, compatible with that $A(x_I)$, hence also gluon, are not observable.

6.2. U(1) Gauge Invariance and Resolving the U(1) Problem

6.2.1. U(1) Gauge Invariance

The equations governing a quantum mechanical particle must be form invariant under Lorentz and appropriate gauge transformations. Lorentz invariance of the Lagrangian density (6.1.2) is manifest due to their spinor form. The simplest local gauge transformations are associated with the U(1) group. To consider such transformations, replace the decomposition (3.1.5) by the more general form

$$\chi^{a\dot{e}}(x_I, x_{II}) = \Psi(X)\chi^{a\dot{e}}(x), \qquad \chi \to \psi \tag{6.2.1}$$

The relative space coordinates x has been considered as "hidden variable" at the end of Sec. 3.1. Only the laboratory coordinates X are observables. The U(1) or Abelian transformation

$$\Psi(X) \to \Psi(X)\exp(ig_1'\varphi_{u1}(X)) \tag{6.2.2}$$

cannot change the physical results entailed by (6.1.2), because only $\Psi^*(X)\Psi(X)$, not $\Psi(X)$ itself, is measurable. Here g_I' is a coupling constant and φ_{uI} a real phase function. This necessitates the existence of a U(1) gauge field B in the minimal substitution on the meson level (see also §6.1.3);

$$\partial_I^{a\dot{b}} = \tfrac{1}{2}\partial_X^{a\dot{b}} - \partial^{a\dot{b}} \to \tfrac{1}{2}\left(\partial_X^{a\dot{b}} + ig_1'B^{a\dot{b}}(X)\right) - \partial^{a\dot{b}} \tag{6.2.3}$$

For $\partial_{II}^{a\dot{b}}$, the $\partial^{a\dot{b}}$ term changes sign. Here (3.1.4) and (5.7.2) have been employed. This gauge field $B(X)$ is introduced on the meson level because the coupling constant g_I' is not associated with any specific quark, as q_{op} in (6.1.9) does.

This U(1) gauge field transform like

$$B^{a\dot{b}}(X) \to B^{a\dot{b}}(X) - \partial_X^{a\dot{b}}\varphi_{u1}(X) \tag{6.2.4}$$

Substituting (6.2.3) into (6.1.2), (6.1.1) after switching the upper and lower indices yields

$$S_m \to S_{mu1} = \int dX^4 dx^4 \frac{1}{2}$$
$$\times \left\{ \begin{array}{l} -\left[\left(\tfrac{1}{2}\left(\partial_X^{a\dot{b}} + ig_1' B^{a\dot{b}}\right) - \partial^{a\dot{b}}\right)\Psi^*(X)\chi^*_{\dot{e}a}(\underline{x})\right]\left[\left(\tfrac{1}{2}\left(\partial_X^{f\dot{e}} + ig_1' B^{f\dot{e}}\right) + \partial^{f\dot{e}}\right)\Psi(X)\chi_{\dot{b}f}(\underline{x})\right] \\ -\left[\left(\tfrac{1}{2}\left(\partial_{X\dot{c}a} + ig_1' B_{\dot{c}a}\right) - \partial_{\dot{c}a}\right)\Psi^*(X)\psi^{*d\dot{c}}(\underline{x})\right]\left[\left(\tfrac{1}{2}\left(\partial_{X\dot{e}d} + ig_1' B_{\dot{e}d}\right) + \partial_{\dot{e}d}\right)\Psi(X)\psi^{a\dot{e}}(\underline{x})\right] \\ -\left(M_m^2 - \Phi_m(X,x)\right)\left(\Psi^*(X)\chi^*_{\dot{e}a}\Psi(X)\psi^{a\dot{e}} + c.c.\right) + c.c. \end{array} \right\} \tag{6.2.5}$$

where use has been made of (3.1.3c, 9) and (5.7.2). The U(1) gauge transformations (6.2.2, 4) leave the meson action (6.2.5) invariant.

The simplest and most common action employed for gauge fields is that for an electromagnetic field,

$$S_{u1} = -\int d^4X \tfrac{1}{4} F_B^{\mu\nu} F_{B\mu\nu} \tag{6.2.6a}$$

$$F_B^{\mu\nu} = \partial_X^{\mu} B^{\nu}(X) - \partial_X^{\nu} B^{\mu}(X) \tag{6.2.6b}$$

which is left invariant by the gauge transformation (6.2.4). The four vector B^{μ} is related to the mixed spinor $B^{a\dot{b}}$ by (C1a). The total action of a meson interacting with a U(1) gauge field is

$$S_{Tu1} = S_{mu1} + S_{u1} \tag{6.2.7}$$

6.2.2. Mass and Source of the U(1) Gauge Field

Variation of (6.2.5) with respect to $\overset{*}{\chi}_{\dot{e}a}(x_I, x_{II})$ and $\psi^{*d\dot{c}}(x_I, x_{II})$ reproduces (2.3.22) with substitutions of the form (6.2.3)

$$\left(\partial_I^{a\dot{b}} + \tfrac{i}{2} g_1' B^{a\dot{b}}(X)\right)\left(\partial_{II}^{f\dot{e}} + \tfrac{i}{2} g_1' B^{f\dot{e}}(X)\right)\chi_{\dot{b}f}(x_I, x_{II}) - \left(M_m^2 - \Phi_m(x_I, x_{II})\right)\psi^{a\dot{e}}(x_I, x_{II}) = 0 \tag{6.2.8a}$$

$$\left(\partial_{I\dot{b}c} + \tfrac{i}{2} g_1' B_{\dot{b}c}(X)\right)\left(\partial_{II\dot{e}d} + \tfrac{i}{2} g_1' B_{\dot{e}d}(X)\right)\psi^{c\dot{e}}(x_I, x_{II}) - \left(M_m^2 - \Phi_m(x_I, x_{II})\right)\chi_{\dot{b}d}(x_I, x_{II}) = 0 \tag{6.2.8b}$$

together with the subsidiary conditions

$$\frac{i}{2} g_1' \chi_{\dot{b}f}(x_I, x_{II})\left(\partial_X^{a\dot{b}} B^{f\dot{e}}(X) - \partial_X^{f\dot{e}} B^{a\dot{b}}(X)\right) = 0 \tag{6.2.9a}$$

$$\frac{i}{2} g_1' \psi^{c\dot{e}}(x_I, x_{II})\left(\partial_{X\dot{b}c} B_{\dot{e}d}(X) - \partial_{X\dot{e}d} B_{\dot{b}c}(X)\right) = 0 \tag{6.2.9b}$$

which comes from the last *c.c.* term in (6.2.5) needed to ensure the reality of S_{mu1}. For the pseudoscalar singlet (6.2.10) below, (6.2.9) specifies that, with (C1a), B^0 can be arbitrary but the plane wave $\underline{B}$ must be parallel to its momentum or that either one of them vanishes.

Consider at first a pseudoscalar meson at rest

$$\Psi(X) = \exp\left(-iE_0 X^0\right) \tag{6.2.10a}$$

$$\psi^{a\dot{e}}(\underline{x}) = \delta^{a\dot{e}}\psi_0(r) = -\chi^{a\dot{e}}(\underline{x}) \qquad \text{pseudoscalar} \tag{6.2.10b}$$

governed by (3.4.1). Substitute these into (6.2.5) and integrate it over x. The term quadratic in B determining the squared mass of the B field reads

$$\int d^4 X M_{u1}^2 \left(B_0(X)^2 - \underline{B}(X)^2\right) \tag{6.2.11}$$

$$M_{u1}^2 = 2g_1'^2 \int d^4 x \psi_0^2(r) = 2g_1'^2 \frac{\int dx^0}{\Omega} = 2g_1'^2 \frac{\tau_0}{\Omega} = 2g_1'^2 \frac{\infty}{\infty} = \text{finite} \tag{6.2.12}$$

where (C1a) as well as (4.3.4a) with $\psi_{00}=\psi_0$ have been used. The $B(X)$ field is thus massive. The origin of the gauge boson mass will be further discussed in §7.5.4 and §7.6.2 below.

6.2.3. Resolving the U(1) Problem

All the observed ground state pseudoscalar mesons belong to internal multiplets of rank two or higher. Thus, the π's belong to an SO(3) isomultiplet. The K's, D's and B's to SU(2) isodoublets and η to an approximative SU(3) isomultiplet. There is no pseudoscalar counterpart to the vector mesons $\omega(\bar{u}u+\bar{d}d)$, $\phi(\bar{s}s)$, $J/\psi(\bar{c}c)$, and $Y(\bar{b}b)$, which are U(1) isosinglets. Note that $\eta_c(2980)$ is not a pure $\bar{c}c$ state but mixed with lower mass $\bar{q}q$ pairs as was indicated above (5.2.3). This is known as the U(1) problem [W5, G4].

There have been many solutions to this problem [see e.g., A2, G4 and references therein]. All these solutions are to my knowledge relatively isolated and not connected to a sufficient number of other low energy phenomena, such as meson spectra, confinement, absence of Higgs bosons, etc.

The U(1) problem is resolved here as follows. If such a U(1) pseudoscalar isosinglet (6.2.10) exists, they must persist for a relatively long time because they cannot decay via strong or electromagnetic interactions. During their life time, they are accompanied by by a U(1) gauge boson field $B^\mu(X)$. Now, the only gauge boson field known is the massless electromagnetic field and the massive boson fields $W^\pm$ and Z^0 arising from the SU(2)×U(1) gauge transformations treated in the next chapter. Thus, the massive U(1) gauge boson $B^\mu(X)$ generated by any U(1) pseudoscalar isosinglet does not exist. It then follows the U(1) pseudoscalars themselves *cannot exist*; (6.2.10) drop out. This U(1) gauge field then becomes massless and can be identified as the electromagnetic field.

The nonexistence of pseudoscalar $u\bar{u}+d\bar{d}$, $s\bar{s}$, $c\bar{c}$, and $b\bar{b}$ forces them to form approximate isomultiplets of higher rank than one. Thus, $u\bar{u}+d\bar{d}$, and $s\bar{s}$ are combined to become η which is a member of an approximative SU(3) octet. As was mentioned above, $c\bar{c}$ is mixed to form $\eta_c(2980)$ and possibly also η' which are no longer isosinglets.

The U(1) isosinglet vector mesons ω, ϕ, J/ψ, and Y can exist; they can decay via strong or electromagnetic interactions fast.

6.3. Meson Magnetic Moment

6.3.1. Gauge Invariance and External Magnetic Field

The gauge transformations at quark level (see also §6.1.3)

$$\chi(X) \to \chi(X)\exp(iq_{op}(z)\varphi_{q1}(X)), \qquad \chi \to \psi \tag{6.3.1a}$$

$$A(X) \to A(X) - \partial\varphi_{q1}(X)/\partial X \tag{6.3.1b}$$

leave the quark wave equations (2.3.11) form invariant. Analogously, it is seen that (6.1.9) is invariant under the gauge transformations at quark level

$$\chi_{bf}(x_I, x_{II}) \to \chi_{bf}(x_I, x_{II})\exp(iq_{op}(z)\varphi_I(x_I) + iq_{op}(u)\varphi_{II}(x_{II})), \quad \chi \to \psi \tag{6.3.2a}$$

$$\chi^*_{\dot{b}f}(x_I, x_{II}) \to \chi^*_{\dot{b}f}(x_I, x_{II})\exp(-iq_{op}(z)\varphi_I(x_I) - iq_{op}(u)\varphi_{II}(x_{II})), \quad \chi \to \psi \tag{6.3.2b}$$

$$A^{a\dot{b}}(x_I) \to A^{a\dot{b}}(x_I) - \partial_I^{a\dot{b}}\varphi_I(x_I) \tag{6.3.2c}$$

$$A^{a\dot{b}}(x_{II}) \to A^{a\dot{b}}(x_{II}) - \partial_{II}^{a\dot{b}}\varphi_{II}(x_{II}) \tag{6.3.2d}$$

The φ's in (6.3.1, 2) are real phase functions. Since (6.1.10) follow from (2.3.11), they can be considered to incorporate these gauge invariance properties. While χ, ψ and Φ_m in (6.1.10) can be converted to be functions separable in X and x according to (3.1.5, 7a, 11), the gauge fields A in (6.1.10) cannot because they depend only upon x_I or x_{II}. With (3.1.3) and (5.7.2), one can write

$$\begin{aligned} A^{a\dot{b}}(x_I^\mu) &= A^{a\dot{b}}(X^\mu - \tfrac{1}{2}x^\mu) = A^{a\dot{b}}(X^\mu) - \tfrac{1}{2}x^\mu\partial_{X\mu}A^{a\dot{b}}(X^\mu) + \tfrac{1}{8}(x^\mu)^2\partial^2_{X\mu}A^{a\dot{b}}(X^\mu) + \dots \\ A_{\dot{e}d}(x_{II}^\mu) &= A_{\dot{e}d}(X^\mu + \tfrac{1}{2}x^\mu) = A_{\dot{e}d}(X^\mu) + \tfrac{1}{2}x^\mu\partial_{X\mu}A_{\dot{e}d}(X^\mu) + \tfrac{1}{8}(x^\mu)^2\partial^2_{X\mu}A_{\dot{e}d}(X^\mu) + \dots \end{aligned} \tag{6.3.3}$$

$A(X^\mu)$ is now identified as an external electromagnetic field in laboratory space. To treat the magnetic moment of a meson, $A(X^\mu)$ can without loss of generality be taken to give rise to a static and homogenous magnetic field

$$\underline{H}_{ex}\left(X^{\nu}\right)=\left(0,\ 0,\ H_{ex}\right)=\partial_{\underline{X}}\times\underline{A}\left(X^{\nu}\right) \tag{6.3.4a}$$

$$A^{\mu}\left(X^{\nu}\right)=\left(0,\ \underline{A}\left(X^{\nu}\right)\right),\ \underline{A}\left(X^{\nu}\right)=\left(0,\ H_{ex}X^{1},\ 0\right)+\text{functions independen t of } X^{1} \tag{6.3.4b}$$

Inserting (6.3.4b) into (6.3.3) leads to

$$A^{ab}\left(x_{I}\right)=-\underline{\sigma}^{ab}\left(0,\ H_{ex}X^{1},\ 0\right)+\tfrac{1}{2}x^{1}\underline{\sigma}^{ab}\left(0,\ H_{ex},\ 0\right)+\text{functions independen t of } x_{I} \tag{6.3.5a}$$

$$A_{\dot{e}d}\left(x_{II}\right)=\underline{\sigma}_{\dot{e}d}\left(0,\ H_{ex}X^{1},\ 0\right)+\tfrac{1}{2}x^{1}\underline{\sigma}_{\dot{e}d}\left(0,\ H_{ex},\ 0\right)+\text{functions independen t of } x_{II} \tag{6.3.5b}$$

6.3.2. Magnetic Moments of Mesons

Take the first operator in (6.1.10b) and operate on (6.1.10a) and re-apply (6.1.10b). After dropping the subscripts *pr*, one obtains

$$\begin{aligned}&\left(\partial_{I\dot{c}a}+iq_{p}A_{\dot{c}a}\left(x_{I}\right)\right)\left(\partial_{I}^{a\dot{b}}+iq_{p}A^{ab}\left(x_{I}\right)\right)\left(\partial_{II\dot{e}d}-iq_{r}A_{\dot{e}d}\left(x_{II}\right)\right)\left(\partial_{II}^{f\dot{e}}-iq_{r}A^{f\dot{e}}\left(x_{II}\right)\right)\chi_{\dot{b}f}\left(x_{I},x_{II}\right)\\&=\left(M_{m}^{2}-\Phi_{m}\left(x_{I},x_{II}\right)\right)^{2}\chi_{\dot{c}d}\left(x_{I},x_{II}\right)+R_{M}\end{aligned} \tag{6.3.6}$$

$$R_{M}=\left[\Phi_{m}\left(x_{I},x_{II}\right),\ \left(\partial_{I\dot{c}a}+iq_{p}A_{\dot{c}a}\left(x_{I}\right)\right)\left(\partial_{II\dot{e}d}-iq_{r}A_{\dot{e}d}\left(x_{II}\right)\right)\psi^{a\dot{e}}\left(x_{I},x_{II}\right)\right] \tag{6.3.7}$$

where $[A,B]=AB-BA$. Note that operators dependent upon x_I and those dependent upon x_{II} commute. Consider now the magnetic moments of ground state mesons at rest. The unperturbed wave functions in (6.1.10) or (6.3.6), obtained by dropping the qA terms, are according to (3.1.5) of the form

$$\psi^{a\dot{e}}\left(X,x\right)=\psi^{a\dot{e}}\left(x\right)\exp\left(-iE_{0}X^{0}\right),\qquad \psi\to\chi \tag{6.3.8}$$

The qA terms are considered as first order perturbations and will give rise to first order perturbations of the wave functions, denoted by the subscript 1. Make the ansatz,

$$\psi_{1}^{a\dot{e}}\left(X,x\right)=\left(\psi^{a\dot{e}}\left(x\right)+\psi_{1s}^{a\dot{e}}\left(\underline{X},\underline{x}\right)\right)\exp\left(-i\left(E_{0}+E_{1M}\right)X^{0}\right)-\psi^{a\dot{e}}\left(X,x\right),\ \psi\to\chi \tag{6.3.9}$$

where E_{1M} is a first order energy shift and ψ_{1s} a first order wave function perturbation in space caused by the qA terms.

The pseudoscalar meson has only one wave function component (4.3.4a) and has therefore *no magnetic moment.*

For vector mesons at rest, (6.3.6-9) with (3.1.4-7) and (5.7.2-3) leads to the first order equation

$$\begin{bmatrix} \left(i\tfrac{1}{2}\delta_{\dot{c}a}(E_0+E_{1M})-\partial_{\dot{c}a}+\tfrac{1}{2}\partial_{\underline{X}\dot{c}a}+iq_pA_{\dot{c}a}(x_I)\right) \\ \left(i\tfrac{1}{2}\delta^{a\dot{b}}(E_0+E_{1M})-\partial^{a\dot{b}}+\tfrac{1}{2}\partial^{a\dot{b}}_{\underline{X}}+iq_pA^{a\dot{b}}(x_I)\right) \\ \left(i\tfrac{1}{2}\delta_{\dot{e}d}(E_0+E_{1M})+\partial_{\dot{e}d}+\tfrac{1}{2}\partial_{\underline{X}\dot{e}d}-iq_rA_{\dot{e}d}(x_{II})\right) \\ \left(i\tfrac{1}{2}\delta^{f\dot{e}}(E_0+E_{1M})+\partial^{f\dot{e}}+\tfrac{1}{2}\partial_{\underline{X\dot{e}d}}-iq_rA^{f\dot{e}}(x_{II})\right) \\ -\left(i\tfrac{1}{2}\delta_{\dot{c}a}E_0-\partial_{\dot{c}a}\right)\left(i\tfrac{1}{2}\delta^{a\dot{b}}E_0-\partial^{a\dot{b}}\right)\left(i\tfrac{1}{2}\delta_{\dot{e}d}E_0+\partial_{\dot{e}d}\right)\left(i\tfrac{1}{2}\delta^{f\dot{e}}E_0+\partial^{f\dot{e}}\right) \end{bmatrix}\underline{\sigma}_{\dot{c}d}\,\underline{\chi}(\underline{x})-R_{M1}$$

$$=-\partial_{I\dot{c}a}\partial^{a\dot{b}}_{I}\partial_{II\dot{e}d}\partial^{f\dot{e}}_{II}\chi_{1s\dot{b}f}(X,x)+\left(M_m^2-\Phi_m(r)\right)^2\chi_{1s\dot{c}d}(X,x)+R_{M2}$$

$$\partial_{\underline{X}\dot{b}a}=\underline{\boldsymbol{\sigma}}_{\dot{b}a}\partial_{\underline{X}}, \qquad \partial^{b\dot{a}}_{\underline{X}}=-\underline{\boldsymbol{\sigma}}^{b\dot{a}}\partial_{\underline{X}} \tag{6.3.10a}$$

$$R_{M1}=\left[\Phi_m(r),\ \left(iq_pA_{\dot{c}a}(x_I)\right)\partial_{II\dot{e}d}-iq_rA_{\dot{e}d}(x_{II})\partial_{I\dot{c}a}\right)\psi^{a\dot{e}}(\underline{x})\right] \tag{6.3.10b}$$

$$R_{M2}=\left[\Phi_m(r),\ \partial_{I\dot{c}a}\partial_{II\dot{e}d}\psi^{a\dot{e}}_{1s}(\underline{X},\underline{x})\right] \tag{6.3.10c}$$

Here, (3.2.8, 12, 17) have been called upon. $R_{M1}+R_{M2}$ is linear in $\partial\Phi_m(r)/\partial r$ and $\partial^2\Phi_m(r)/\partial r^2$. Insert (6.3.5) and (3.2.5b) into (6.3.10), the first term on the left side of (6.3.10a) becomes after some algebra

$$\tfrac{1}{2}\left(\tfrac{1}{4}E_0^2+\Delta\right)\left[\tfrac{1}{2}E_{1M}E_0\underline{\sigma}_{\dot{c}d}\,\underline{\chi}(\underline{x})-2q_p\left(\underline{\sigma}_{\dot{c}}{}^{\dot{b}}\,\underline{H}_{ex}\right)\left(\underline{\sigma}_{\dot{b}d}\,\underline{\chi}(\underline{x})\right)-2q_r\left(\underline{\sigma}^{f}{}_{d}\,\underline{H}_{ex}\right)\left(\underline{\sigma}_{\dot{c}f}\,\underline{\chi}(\underline{x})\right)\right]+R_{MH} \tag{6.3.11a}$$

$$R_{MH}=i\left(q_p+q_r\right)H_{ex}x^1\frac{\partial}{\partial x^2}\left(\tfrac{1}{4}E_0^2+\Delta\right)\underline{\sigma}_{\dot{c}d}\,\underline{\chi}(\underline{x}) \tag{6.3.11b}$$

The both terms on the right side of (6.3.5a) contribute equally to the q_p term in (6.3.11a). The same obviously holds for (6.3.5b) in regard to the q_r term in (6.3.11a). The last terms in (6.3.5) are in addition the source of R_{MH}.

It is readily seen that certain linear combinations of the components of $\underline{\chi}(\underline{x})=(\chi^{(1)}, \chi^{(2)}, \chi^{(3)})=\hat{r}\,\chi_I(r)$ are eigen functions of the magnetic field operators $\underline{\sigma}_{\dot{c}}{}^{\dot{b}}\underline{H}_{ex}$ and $\underline{\sigma}^{f}{}_{d}\underline{H}_{ex}$ (see (6.3.15) below) with different eigenvalues that yield real energy splitting. The same components are however not eigenfunctions of the operator in R_{MH}, which gives no energy splitting. The operators in (6.3.10b) are imaginary and the operators in (6.3.10c) do not contain H_{ex}. From the energy splitting viewpoint, (6.3.10a) becomes

$$\tfrac{1}{2}\left(\tfrac{1}{4}E_0^2+\Delta\right)\left[\tfrac{1}{2}E_{1M}E_0\underline{\sigma}_{\dot{c}d}\,\underline{\chi}(\underline{x})-2q_p\left(\underline{\sigma}_{\dot{c}}{}^{\dot{b}}\,\underline{H}_{ex}\right)\left(\underline{\sigma}_{\dot{b}d}\,\underline{\chi}(\underline{x})\right)-2q_r\left(\underline{\sigma}^{f}{}_{d}\,\underline{H}_{ex}\right)\left(\underline{\sigma}_{\dot{c}f}\,\underline{\chi}(\underline{x})\right)\right]=0 \tag{6.3.12}$$

$$\partial_{I\dot{c}a}\partial^{a\dot{b}}_{I}\partial_{II\dot{e}d}\partial^{f\dot{e}}_{II}\chi_{1s\dot{b}f}(X,x)-\left(M_m^2-\Phi_m(r)\right)^2\chi_{1s\dot{c}d}(X,x)-R_{M2}=R_{M1}-R_{MH} \tag{6.3.13}$$

The right side of (6.3.13) provides a source for the perturbed functions χ_{1s} and ψ_{1s}. Another similar set of equations are obtained by interchanging (6.1.10a) and (6.1.10b) in arriving at equations that are essentially (6.3.6) and (6.3.7) with $\chi\leftrightarrow\psi$. These equations will analogously lead to basically (6.3.12) and (6.3.13) with $\chi \leftrightarrow \psi$. The former is the same as (6.3.12) because $\underline{\chi}(\underline{x})=\underline{\psi}(\underline{x})$ according to (3.2.5b) and (3.4.3). The latter together with (6.3.13) determine the two perturbed wave functions χ_{1s} and ψ_{1s}.

As was mentioned at the end of Sec. 3.1, $\underline{x}$ is considered as "hidden variable." Therefore, physical results in the laboratory space time X^{μ} can be obtained by multiplying (6.3.12) and (6.3.13) by $\left(\underline{\sigma}^{d\dot{c}}\ \underline{\chi}\right)$ and integrating over $\underline{x}$. After some algebra, it can be shown that the right side of (6.3.13) vanishes and a condition is imposed on its left side,

$$\int d^3\underline{x}\left(\underline{\sigma}^{d\dot{c}}\ \underline{\chi}(\underline{x})\right)\left(\partial_{I\dot{c}a}\partial_I^{a\dot{b}}\partial_{II\dot{e}d}\partial_{II}^{f\dot{e}}\chi_{1s\dot{b}f}(X,x)-\left(M_m^2-\Phi_m(r)\right)^2\chi_{1s\dot{c}d}(X,x)-R_{M2}\right)=0 \tag{6.3.14}$$

Such a multiplication and integration over $\underline{x}$ will however leave all terms in (6.3.12) finite. By writing out explicitly

$$\underline{\sigma}_{\dot{c}d}\,\underline{\chi}=\begin{pmatrix}\chi^{(3)} & \chi^{(1)}-i\chi^{(2)}\\ \chi^{(1)}+i\chi^{(2)} & -\chi^{(3)}\end{pmatrix},\qquad \underline{\sigma}_{\dot{c}}^{\ \dot{b}}\,\underline{H}_{ex}=\begin{pmatrix}H_{ex} & \\ & -H_{ex}\end{pmatrix} \tag{6.3.15}$$

Equation (6.3.12) yields

$$E_{1M}=0 \qquad \text{for} \qquad \chi_3$$
$$E_{1M}=\pm\mu_M H_{ex} \qquad \text{for} \qquad \chi_1\pm i\chi_2$$

where

$$\mu_M=\frac{1}{E_0}\left(q_p-q_r\right)=\frac{q_M}{E_0} \tag{6.3.16}$$

is the magnetic moment for the vector meson and q_M its charge. The magnetic moment is simply inversely proportional to the mass of the vector meson. Neutral vector meson has no magnetic moment.

With the mass data from [P1], the magnetic moments of ρ^+, K^{*+}, D^{*+}, D_s^{*+} and B^{*+} are 2.437, 2.105, 0.9336, 0.8883 and 0.3524 proton magnetons, respectively. No data is available to check these results.

6.4. Radiative Decay of Heavy Vector Meson V→Pγ [H10, 26]

In this section, the decay of a heavy ground state vector meson V into the corresponding pseudoscalar meson P and a photon γ, $V\rightarrow P\gamma$, is treated. The treatment is semi-classical; the electromagnetic field is not quantized. This is in accord with that the present theory is at quantum mechanical level and cannot be quantized, as will be discussed in Sec. 14.1 below.

Such decays have been treated earlier [H10] and also in the first edition of this book [H18]. The estimated $D^{*\pm}$ decay rate turned out to be too small compared to subsequent measurements. This section is the same as [H26] which follows basically the same development in [H10] with two main differences. Firstly, the assumption that the U(1) gauge field is limited to the two component photon field is removed. Secondly, the Coulomb form of wave functions of the ground state mesons adopted in [H10] and (4.3.2-3) of [H18] is replaced by harmonic oscillator form (4.3.4). The predicted ratio of J/ψ and $D^{*\pm}$ decay rates is within error limits. The magnitudes of these rates are also in order of magnitude agreement with data.

The methods developed here serve as prototypes for weak and strong decays considered in Chapters 7 and 8.

6.4.1. Wave Functions of Decaying Meson

For a free meson, the meson equations (2.3.22) with Φ_c=0 in (3.2.8a) hold. If an electromagnetic field A is introduced, (2.3.22) is replaced by (6.1.10) or (6.4.5) below. The magnitude of the difference between (2.3.22) and (6.4.5) is small, of the order of quark charges. Therefore, the associated decay $V \to P\gamma$ can be formulated as a first order perturbational problem. The wave functions of the decaying meson are taken to a modified form of (3.1.5, 6, 9) with (5.7.1),

$$\psi^{ab}(X,x) = \sum_K b_{JK}\left(\delta^{ab}\psi_{JK}(\underline{x}) - \underline{\sigma}^{ab}\underline{\psi}_{JK}(\underline{x})\right)\exp\left(-iE_{JK}X^0 + i\underline{K}_J\underline{X}\right) \tag{6.4.1}$$

$$\psi \to \chi \tag{6.4.2}$$

$$b_{JK} = a_{JK} + a_{JK}^{(1)}\left(X^0\right) \tag{6.4.3}$$

The subscript J=0,1 refers to pseudoscalar and vector mesons, respectively. a_{JK} is unity here but is in a quantized case in §6.4.4 below to be elevated to an annihilation operator annihilating an initial meson of spin J and momentum $\underline{K}$. $a^{(1)}{}_{JK}(X^0)$ is a first order amplitude that varies slowly with time and, in the quantized case in §6.4.4, becomes an operator that "slowly" transforms the initial vector meson to some intermediate state. It is zero at $X^0 = -\infty$. Similarly, $a^*{}_{JK}$ enters ψ^*, the complex conjugate of ψ, is also unity and is to be elevated to a creation operator creating a final state with the same J and $\underline{K}$. $a^{(1)*}{}_{JK}(X^0)$ is the complex conjugate of $a^{(1)}{}_{JK}(X^0)$ and, in the quantized case, becomes an operator that "slowly" creates the same final state as that created by $a^*{}_{JK}$. These quantization assignments are phenomenological and rudimentary.

In $V \to P\gamma$, $a^{(1)}{}_{JK}(X^0)$ is caused by the qA terms in (6.4.5) below and is hence of first order in quark charge. Pick out only one J value and one $\underline{K}$ value in the summations of (6.4.1). This leads to the simplified form

$$\chi^{ab}(X,x) = \chi_0^{ab} + \chi_1^{ab}, \qquad \chi_1^{ab} = \left(a_{JK}^{(1)}\left(X^0\right)/a_{JK}\right)\chi_0^{ab} \tag{6.4.4}$$

where the subscripts 0 and 1 denote orders in quark charge. $\chi_0^{a\dot b}$ is simply (6.4.1) with $a^{(1)}{}_{JK}(X^0)=0$.

6.4.2. Full U(1) Gauge Field

The photon is observable and the electromagnetic field is thus introduced on the meson level similar to the U(1) gauge field in (6.2.3-4) (see also §6.1.3)

$$\left(\partial_I^{a\dot b}+i\tfrac{1}{2}q_pA^{a\dot b}(X)\right)\left(\partial_{II}^{\dot f\dot e}-i\tfrac{1}{2}q_rA^{\dot f\dot e}(X)\right)\chi_{(pr)\dot bf}(X,x)-\left(M_m^2-\Phi_m(\underline{x})\right)\psi_{(pr)}^{a\dot e}(X,x)=0 \tag{6.4.5}$$

where (3.1.3a), (5.7.2) and the transition of (2.3.23) to (3.1.14) have been used. Here, ∂_I and ∂_{II} operate on χ only. Putting the time component A_0 to 0 and expand $\underline{A}(X)$ in plane waves, as in [H10 (3.3)],

$$\begin{gathered}\underline{A}(X)=\frac{1}{\sqrt{2E_\gamma\Omega}}\underline{e}\exp\left(-iE_\gamma X^0+i\underline{K}_\gamma\underline{X}\right),\qquad \underline{e}=\left(e_X,e_Y,e_Z\right)\\ \underline{A}(X)\rightarrow a_T\left(\underline{K}_\gamma\right)\underline{A}(X)\end{gathered} \tag{6.4.6}$$

where E_γ and $\underline{K}_\gamma$ are the energy and momentum of the photon and Ω a large normalization box. $a_T(\underline{K})$ is the analog of a_{JK} in (6.4.3) and is set to a unity here but is elevated to an operator annihilating a photon with polarization T in the quantized case below.

In [H10] and [H18], the unit vector $\underline{e}=(e_T,\ e_Z=0)=(e_X,\ e_Y,\ e_Z=0)$ for $\underline{K}_\gamma=(0,\ 0,\ K_\gamma)$ representing the photon field is associated with the both transverse modes T=1, 2. This assumption is removed here and $e_Z\neq 0$ is allowed here even if it is not part of the photon field.

6.4.3. First Order Relations

Inserting (6.4.4) into (6.4.5), multiplying it by $\chi^*_{\dot ea}$ and integrating over X and x, the first order part reads

$$\int d^4Xd^4x\chi^*_{0\dot ea}\begin{bmatrix}\partial_I^{a\dot b}\partial_{II}^{\dot f\dot e}\chi_{1\dot bf}-\left(M_m^2-\Phi_m\right)\psi_1^{a\dot e}\\ +i\tfrac{1}{2}q_pA^{a\dot b}(X)\partial_{II}^{\dot f\dot e}\chi_{0\dot bf}-i\tfrac{1}{2}q_r\partial_I^{a\dot b}A^{\dot f\dot e}(X)\chi_{0\dot bf}\end{bmatrix}=0 \tag{6.4.7}$$

Applying (6.1.3) and the second of (6.4.4) and noting that $a^{(1)}{}_{JK}(X^0)$ can with good approximation be moved to the left of ∂_I or ∂_{II} because it varies slowly over X^0, (6.4.7) becomes

$$\int d^4Xd^4x\begin{Bmatrix}\partial_I^{a\dot{b}}\left(a_{JK}^{(1)}\left(X^0\right)/a_{JK}\right)\chi_{0\dot{e}a}^{*}\partial_{II}^{f\dot{e}}\chi_{0\dot{b}f}+i\tfrac{1}{2}q_pA^{a\dot{b}}(X)\chi_{0\dot{e}a}^{*}\left(\partial_{II}^{f\dot{e}}\chi_{0\dot{b}f}\right)\\+i\tfrac{1}{2}q_r\left(\partial_I^{a\dot{b}}\chi_{0\dot{e}a}^{*}\right)A^{f\dot{e}}(X)\chi_{0\dot{b}f}-i\tfrac{1}{2}q_r\partial_I^{a\dot{b}}\chi_{0\dot{e}a}^{*}A^{f\dot{e}}(X)\chi_{0\dot{b}f}\\-\left(a_{JK}^{(1)}\left(X^0\right)/a_{JK}\right)\left[\left(\partial_I^{a\dot{b}}\chi_{0\dot{e}a}^{*}\right)\left(\partial_{II}^{f\dot{e}}\chi_{0\dot{b}f}\right)+\left(M_m^2-\Phi_m\right)\chi_{0\dot{e}a}^{*}\psi_0^{a\dot{e}}\right]\end{Bmatrix}=0 \tag{6.4.8}$$

The $a^{(1)}{}_{JK}(X^0)$ factor multiplying the brackets in (6.4.8) can with good approximation be moved outside the integral sign because it varies slowly with X^0. Substituting (6.1.3) once more into (6.4.8), it is seen that the surface term associated with the first term on the right of (6.1.3) vanishes upon integration. The remaining terms in the bracket also drop out by virtue of the equation of motion (2.3.22) for steady state mesons. The next to last terms in (6.4.7), the $-iq_r\partial_I$ term, is also a surface term and vanishes after integration, noting that $A(X)$ is real and satisfies periodic boundary conditions at large X^μ as in (6.4.6). Equation (6.4.8) can now be written as

$$S'_{mAd}=S'_{mAs} \tag{6.4.9}$$

$$S'_{mAd}=\int d^4Xd^4x\left[\partial_I^{a\dot{b}}\left(a_{JK}^{(1)}\left(X^0\right)/a_{JK}\right)\chi_{0\dot{e}a}^{*}\partial_{II}^{f\dot{e}}\chi_{0\dot{b}f}\right] \tag{6.4.10}$$

$$S'_{mAs}=i\int d^4Xd^4x\left\{\tfrac{1}{2}q_p\left[\chi_{0\dot{e}a}^{*}A^{a\dot{b}}(X)\left(\partial_{II}^{f\dot{e}}\chi_{0\dot{b}f}\right)\right]-\tfrac{1}{2}q_r\left[\chi_0^{*\dot{b}f}A_{\dot{f}e}(X)\left(\partial_{I\dot{a}b}\chi_0^{e\dot{a}}\right)\right]\right\} \tag{6.4.11}$$

The last relation has been extracted from (6.3.7) directly. The prime ´ attached to S_{mA} here serves to distinguish them from the real actions S_m of (6.1.1) and S´s in (7.1.1) below.

6.4.4. Rudimentary Quantization and Decay Amplitude

The semi-classical treatment mentioned in the beginning of this sections is analogous to the treatment of time-dependent problems in quantum mechanics [S5 Ch VIII, X] and in relativistic quantum mechanics [B4 Ch 7]. A justification is that the energies involved here are low so that typical field-theoretical effects such as vacuum polarization and self energy are small, just like that analogous effects are small in QED at low energies.

The following rudimentary quantization procedures are accordingly adopted. Let $|0\rangle$ and $\langle 0|$ denote vacuum states, one has conventionally,

$$\langle f|i\rangle=\langle 0|i\rangle=\langle f|0\rangle=0, \qquad \langle 0|0\rangle=\langle f|f\rangle=1 \tag{6.4.12a}$$

Let the initial and final states in $V\to P\gamma$ be

$$|i\rangle=\left|V\left(\underline{K}_1=0\right)\right\rangle, \qquad \langle f|=\left\langle P\left(\underline{K}_0\right),\gamma_T\left(\underline{K}_\gamma\right)\right| \tag{6.4.12b}$$

where V denotes a vector meson at rest which decays into a pseudoscalar meson P with momentum $\underline{K}_0$ and photon γ_T with momentum $\underline{K}_\gamma$.

Insert (6.4.4) into (6.4.10) and sandwich it between <f| and |i>. a_{10} in χ operated on the initial state |i> picks out the zeroth order initial vector meson at rest,

$$\chi_{0\dot{b}f}|i\rangle \rightarrow \underline{\sigma}_{\dot{b}f}\hat{r}\chi_{10}(r)\exp(-iE_{10}X^0)|0\rangle \tag{6.4.13}$$

where (6.4.1) and (3.2.4a, 5b) have been used and $\chi_{10}=\psi_{10}$ is given in (4.3.4b). Since (6.4.10) does not contain the final state photon $A(X)$, χ^* operating on the final state <f| becomes equivalent to the complex conjugate of the initial state (6.4.13). Using (3.1.4, 10a) and (5.7.1), letting the a's considered below (6.4.3) be elevated to operators according to the interpretations there and integrating over X^0 leads to

$$\langle f|S'_{mAd}|i\rangle = -i\frac{1}{4}E_{10}S_{fi}\int d^3\underline{X}\int d^4x\chi_{10}^2(r) \tag{6.4.14a}$$

$$S_{fi} = \langle f|a^*_{JK}a^{(1)}_{JK}(X^0\rightarrow\infty)|i\rangle \tag{6.4.14b}$$

S_{fi} corresponds to the conventional S-matrix element and is interpreted as the decay amplitude via the assignments of the a's below (6.4.3).

Next, place (6.4.11) between <f| and |i> of (6.4.12b) and elevate a_{JK} and a^*_{JK} to annihilation and creation operators, respectively. Similarly, $a_T(\underline{K}_\gamma)$ in (6.4.6) is also elevated to an operator mentioned below (6.4.6). Here, (6.4.13) is applicable. Operating (6.4.13) by the last of (6.4.6) leads to an expression

$$a_T(\underline{K}_\gamma)\underline{A}(X)|0\rangle \rightarrow a^*_T(\underline{K}_\gamma)\underline{A}(X)^*|0\rangle = \underline{A}(X)^*|\gamma_T\rangle \tag{6.4.15}$$

The left side is interpreted as annihilation of a photon of polarization T from the vacuum |0> which is equivalent to the creation of its antiparticle. The final state meson operator χ_0^* operating on <f| pick out a pseudoscalar meson having a momentum $\underline{K}$ with the wave function

$$\langle f|\chi^*_{0\dot{e}a} \rightarrow \left(\delta_{\dot{e}a}\chi^*_{0K}(\underline{x})+\underline{\sigma}_{\dot{e}a}\underline{\chi}^*_{0K}(\underline{x})\right)\exp\left(iE_{0K}X^0-i\underline{K}\underline{X}\right) \tag{6.4.16}$$

where $\underline{K}$ stands for $\underline{K}_J$ in (6.4.1) for J=0. Insert (6.4.13, 15, 6, 16), in that order, into <f|(6.4.11)|i>, apply (3.1.4, 10a) and (5.7.1) and integrate over X. The result reads

$$\langle f|S'_{mAs}|i\rangle = \frac{i}{\sqrt{2E_r\Omega}}(2\pi)^4\delta(E_{0K}+E_r-E_{10})\delta(\underline{K}+\underline{K}_\gamma)\int dx^0 I_q \tag{6.4.17}$$

$$I_q = \int d^3\underline{x}\begin{bmatrix}(q_p+q_r)\left(\underline{e}\underline{\chi}^*_{0K}(\underline{x})\right)\left(\partial\hat{r}\chi_{10}(r)\right)+\frac{1}{2}E_{10}\left(\underline{\chi}^*_{0K}(\underline{x})\times\underline{e}\right)\hat{r}\chi_{10}(r)\\ -(q_p-q_r)i\frac{1}{2}E_{10}\underline{e}\hat{r}\chi^*_{0K}(\underline{x})\chi_{10}(r)\end{bmatrix} \tag{6.4.18}$$

in which only one of T=1 or 2 in (6.4.6) has been included. The χ_0^* wave functions obey (5.7.3) which has not been solved, as was mentioned above (5.7.4).

For the heavy mesons containing b or c quark, Table 5.1 shows that the masses of the vector meson and the associated pseudoscalar meson are close to each other so that the latter moves slowly in a radiative decay of the former. For these mesons, the criteria (5.7.4, 10, 14) are satisfied and approximative solutions have been found. To zeroth order in ε_0, (5.7.6), holds. The first order solutions are given by (5.7.7a, 11a, 12, 15, 16) where χ_{00} stands for χ^*_{0K} and χ_1 for χ^*_{0K} in (6.4.18). Inserting these results together with (4.3.4) into (6.4.18) and carrying out the angular integrations, terms with odd powers of $\hat{r}$ vanish. We obtain

$$I_q = (q_p + q_r)\frac{K}{E_{0K}} e_Z I_{dh}$$
$$I_{dh} = 4\pi\alpha_{00}\alpha_{10}\int drr^2\left(1+\frac{2d_h}{E_{0K}^2}\left(1-\frac{1}{3}d_h r^2\right)\right)\left(1-7d_h r^2 + 2d_h^2 r^4\right)\exp\left(-d_h r^2\right) \tag{6.4.19}$$

Let the photon be directed along the Z axis consistent with (5.7.9) and put

$$\underline{K}_\gamma = (0,\ 0,\ K_\gamma) = -\underline{K} = (0, 0, -K) \tag{6.4.20}$$

the $i\underline{K}_\gamma\underline{X}$ term in (6.4.6) and the $-i\underline{KX}$ term in (6.4.16) cancel out in (6.4.11) and the last δ function in (6.4.17) drops out. Equating (6.4.14a) to (6.4.17) with (6.4.19, 20) according to (6.4.9), the decay amplitude is found to be

$$S_{fi} = -\frac{4}{E_{10}}\frac{1}{\sqrt{2E_r\Omega}}2\pi\,\delta(E_{0K} + E_r - E_{10})(q_p + q_r)e_Z I_{dh} \tag{6.4.21}$$

in which the integrals over the relative time x^0 and the laboratory space $\underline{X}$ have been cancelled out and (4.2.8) has been consulted.

6.4.5. Decay Rate

The decay rate is

$$\Gamma(V \to P\gamma) = \sum\nolimits_{\text{final states}} \left|S_{fi}\right|^2 / T_d = \sum\nolimits_T \sum\nolimits_K \left|S_{fi}\right|^2 / T_d \tag{6.4.22a}$$

where T_d is a long time during which decay takes place and Σ_T=2 for the both photon polarizations mentioned below (6.4.6). Further,

$$\sum\nolimits_K = \frac{\Omega}{(2\pi)^3}\int d^3\underline{K} \to \frac{\Omega}{(2\pi)^3}4\pi\int dKK^2 \tag{6.4.22b}$$

With (6.4.20) and $E_r = K_\gamma$, one finds

$$\delta(E_{0K} + E_r - E_{10}) = \delta\left(\sqrt{E_{00}^2 + K^2} + K - E_{10}\right) = \delta(K - K_0)(1 - K_0/E_{10})$$

(6.4.23a)

$$K_0 = \left(E_{10}^2 - E_{00}^2\right)/2E_{10} \tag{6.4.23b}$$

This δ function in (6.4.21) will be squared in (6.4.22a). Using (6.4.23a), this square becomes

$$[\delta(E_{0K} + E_r - E_{10})]^2 = \delta(K - K_0)\left(1 - \frac{K_0}{E_{10}}\right)^2 \frac{T_d}{2\pi} \tag{6.4.24}$$

(see for instance [B4 (7.9)]). Combining (6.4.21, 22, 24) leads to the decay rate

$$\Gamma(V \to P\gamma) = \frac{16}{\pi} \frac{K_0^3}{E_{10}^2\left(E_{00}^2 + K_0^2\right)}\left(1 - \frac{K_0}{E_{10}}\right)^2 (q_p + q_r)^2 e_Z^2 I_{dh}^2 \tag{6.4.25}$$

Here, e_Z is not fixed here but is a parameter <1. This is as far as the present semi-classical treatment can carry. Perhaps a quantized version of the present treatment, if possible to be devised, can fix this e_Z.

e_Z is the third, longitudinal, component of the unit verctor $\underline{e}$ in the photon field (6.4.6) and balances off the momentum $\underline{K_0}$ of the pseudoscalar meson. Its absence in the earlier treatment [H10] and the first edtion of this book led to the assumption that higher order effects were responsible for such radiative decays. This is now seen not to the case. e_Z, being separate from the photon associated with the transverse components e_X, e_Y in (6.4.6) is responsible for the decays.

The first order (6.4.11) can be complemented to include second order terms containing the square of the photon field $\underline{A}(X)$. The coefficient for this square representing the mass of the photon contains only odd powered $\hat{r}$ terms and vanishes after integration over the relative space $\underline{x}$. This verifies that the photon remains massless.

Finally, it is remarked that (6.4.25) remains unchanged if the employed equation for χ (6.4.5) were replaced by an equivalent equation for ψ analogous to (6.1.10b). This is due to that (6.1.10a, 10b) originate from (2.2.4a, 4b) which are invariant under the interchanges $\chi \leftrightarrow \psi$ and $I \leftrightarrow II$. The last one leads to a sign change of the relative coordinate $\underline{x}$ in (3.1.3a) but does not affect the decay amplitude (6.4.21).

6.4.6. Comparison with Data

Table 6.1 gives the $V \to P\gamma$ decay rate (6.4.25) for a number of heavy mesons most of them listed in Table 5.1.

Table 6.1. Decay rate $\Gamma(V \to P\gamma)$ for some heavy mesons. The meson momentum K_0 is given by (6.4.23b). The expansion parameter ε_0 is defined in (5.7.4). q_p and q_r are the quark charges. The predicted decay rate $\Gamma(V \to P\gamma)$ is given by (6.4.25) which holds only for nonrelativistic and heavy pseudoscalar mesons satisfying $\varepsilon_0 << 1$ of (5.7.4) and (5.7.10, 14). Only the mesons with b or c quark qualify. Equation (6.4.25) does not apply to K^*. This is indicated by the parentheses around the so-obtained decay rates. e_Z is the longitudinal polarization vector in the unit vector $\underline{e}$ in (6.4.6) and should be < 1 but is not fixed in the present nonquantized treatment. The underlined entries are the only ones available for direct comparison with predictions

	K_0(GeV)	$\varepsilon_0 = K_0/E_{00}$	$\lvert q_p + q_r \rvert$	$\Gamma(V \to P\gamma)/e_Z^2$ keV	Γ(data) [P1] keV
$\Upsilon(1S) \to \gamma\, \eta_b$	0.07	0.0075	2/3	7×10^{-4}	no data
$B_s^{*0} \to \gamma B_s^0$	0.0459	0.009	2/3	2.2×10^{-3}	dominant
$B^{*0} \to \gamma B^0$	0.0454	0.0086	2/3	1.2×10^{-4}	dominant
$B^{*\pm} \to \gamma B^\pm$	0.0451	0.0086	1/3	3×10^{-5}	dominant
$J/\psi \to \gamma\, \eta_c$	0.1114	0.037	4/3	$\underline{1.02}$	$\underline{1.58\pm0.37}$
$D_s^{*\pm} \to \gamma D_s^\pm$	0.139	0.0706	1/3	0.6	<1776
$D^{*0} \to \gamma D^0$	0.137	0.0735	4/3	11.65	<741
$D^{*\pm} \to \gamma D^\pm$	0.136	0.0726	1/3	$\underline{0.69}$	$\underline{1.33\pm0.33}$
$K^{*0} \to \gamma K^0$	0.31	0.623	2/3	(1707)	116
$K^{*+} \to \gamma K^\pm$	0.309	0.626	1/3	(436)	50.3

For mesons with b quark, there is no data available. The K^* decay rates are put inside parentheses to indicate that Γ of (6.4.25) is not applicable. This is due to that ε_0 is too large and does not satisfy the criteria (5.7.4) and the kaons are too light so that (5.7.10, 14) are violated. Further, the effect of the singularity associated with lighter mesons mentioned above §5.7.2 has not been investigated and may impact upon the validity of the approximations leading to (6.4.25). Still the predictions of (6.4.25) for kaons are included to indicate the trend that, as the mesons get lighter and move faster; the decay rates increase, Here, they are 10-15 times too high.

For mesons containing c quark, J/ψ and $D^{*\pm}$ rates from (6.4.25) can be compared to data. The ratio between these two measured rates is is 1.58/1.33=1.19 and can be 0.73 up to 1.95 within error limits. The predicted value 1.02/0.69=1.48 lies well within these limits. This agreement can hardly be any coincidence inasmuch as the ratio between their $(q_p + q_r)^2$ values is 16.

Putting $e_Z = 1$, the measured rates are greater than the predicted ones by a factor of 1.5-1.9. Since $e_Z < 1$ in the present semi-classical treatment, this factor is actually still greater. Nevertheless, the predicted values and data are of the same magnitude and may be regarded to be in basic agreement with each other. Consider that the mass ratios of K^*, D^* and B^* are 0.44 : 1: 2.86 while the ratios of predicted decay rates are 632 : 1 : 4.3×10^{-5}, the above discrepancy of a factor of 1.5-1.9 or greater is negligible. The approximations introduced in (5.7.15, 16) can however only lead to a correction of ±10% for D^* in (6.4.25).

These results show that the harmonic oscillator type of meson wave functions (4.3.4) yield not only meson spectra but also lead to useful decay predictions. Thus, they support the present normalization assignment (4.2.6). No other first principles' theory can make a prediction of this kind.

If the present semi-classical treatment can be quantized and $e_{Z.}$ be fixed, a wholly new problem, a more precise prediction can perhaps be found.

Chapter 7

Weak Decay of Kaon and Pion, Higgs and Ramifications

The basic ingredients providing the starting points of this chapter have been given in [H11], [H12], Sec. 6 and 7 of [H8], and §3.4 and §9.2 of [H13]. The Abelian gauge fields introduced in the last chapter are now extended to non-Abelian gauge fields to treat some basic semi-leptonic decays of kaons and pions. The gauge fields pertaining to the $SU(2)_I \times U(1)_Y$ group in the standard model [B8] turn out to be insufficient and are extended to those of the SU(3) group in Sec. 7.1. The Weinberg and the Cabibbo angles of SM are no longer free parameters but derivable from the quark, pion and kaon masses.

Presence of relative time between quarks in the present nonlocal theory can generate gauge boson mass without recourse to the Higgs boson in Sec. 7.4. This relative time also leads to the conjecture that the electromagnetic coupling in the conventional electro-weak model can be separated off, leaving behind a purely weak coupling constant $\approx 10^{-13}$ in Sec. 7.5. This is followed by the suggested assignment of the Higgs-like boson found in 2012 to a bound state of two charged gauge bosons W^+W^- in Sec. 7.6. The $K \to 3\pi$ problem is formulated in Sec. 7.7.

7.1. Actions for Semi-Leptonic Decay

7.1.1. Total and Gauge Boson Action

The weak decays considered here consist of two stages. In stage I, the pseudoscalar meson decays into an intermediate gauge boson alone or together with a lighter pseudoscalar meson. In stage II, the intermediate gauge boson can decay into a lepton-antilepton pair and this will be treated first below. It can also decay into a pair of pions and this will be considered in Sec. 7.7. The total action S_{T3} covering these processes contains actions for each of these particles,

$$S_{T3} = S_{GB} + S_{m3} + S_L + S_{Lm} + \kappa_\pi S_{m\pi} \tag{7.1.1}$$

where S_{m3} is the action for the decaying meson, S_L is the action for the leptons and S_{Lm} that for the finite lepton mass. $S_{m\pi}$ is the action for a pion-antipion pair regarded as decay products and will be given in §7.7.1 below. All these actions contain the gauge boson fields, whose action is given by S_{GB}. κ_π is a scale constant.

According to the present theory, the s quark is only slightly heavier than the d quark, as is seen in Table 5.2. Based upon this result, the equations of motion for mesons containing only the u, d and s quarks are approximately invariant under global SU(3) transformations, as was considered in §2.4.2. Therefore, these equations are also approximately invariant under local SU(3) transformations, achieved by replacing ϑ_l in (2.4.19b) by $\vartheta_l(X)$. As is well known, this transformation calls for the introduction of SU(3) gauge fields, analogous to the introduction of U(1) gauge field in §6.2.1.

In the remainder of this section, S_{GB} and S_{m3} are given and their approximate SU(3) gauge invariance shown. S_L is also given and its approximate SU(2)×U(1) gauge invariance considered. The fields in these three actions are coupled via the total action S_{T3} (7.1.1), which now appears to be inconsistent because there are eight SU(3) gauge fields in S_{GB} and S_{m3} but only four SU(2)×U(1) gauge fields in S_L. This inconsistency is removed by the degeneration mechanism given in §7.2.3 below.

The U(1) action (6.2.6) is now replaced by

$$S_{GB} = -\frac{1}{4}\int d^4X \sum_{l=1}^{8} G_l^{\mu\nu} G_{l\mu\nu} \tag{7.1.2a}$$

$$G_l^{\mu\nu}(X) = \partial_X^{\mu} W_l^{\nu} - \partial_X^{\nu} W_l^{\mu} - f_{jkl}\, g W_j^{\mu} W_k^{\nu} \tag{7.1.2b}$$

where f_{ijk} has appeared in (2.4.7). Using (C5), S_{GB} can be shown to be invariant under SU(3) gauge transformations (7.1.4) and (7.1.7b, 7d) below. Variation of S_{GB} with respect to the eight gauge boson fields W_l yields Yang-Mills type of equations of motions for these eight gauge bosons with zero mass (see (7.4.2) below).

7.1.2. Meson Action and Approximate SU(3) Gauge Invariance

The starting point is the single meson action (6.1.1), which is to be generalized to account for meson multiplets in the same way that led (2.3.22) to (2.4.3). Thus, the first term on the right side of (6.1.2) together with its complex conjugate is generalized according to

$$\left(\partial_I^{a\dot{b}} \chi^*_{\dot{e}a}\right)\left(\partial_{II}^{f\dot{e}} \chi_{\dot{b}f}\right) + c.c. \rightarrow \left(\partial_I^{a\dot{b}} \chi^+_{(rp)\dot{e}a}\right)\left(\partial_{II}^{f\dot{e}} \chi_{(pr)\dot{b}f}\right) + c.c. \tag{7.1.3a}$$

$$\chi^+_{(rp)\dot{e}a} = \chi^*_{(pr)\dot{e}a} = \left(\chi_{(pr)\dot{a}e}\right)^+ \qquad r, p = 1,2,3 \tag{7.1.3b}$$

where the superscript + denotes Hermitian adjoint and interchanges the flavor indices. Consistent with the convention given above (C3) for space time spinor indices, the first internal or flavor index r or p in (7.1.3b) refers to the row number in a matrix of the form (2.4.18) and the second index to the column number.

The minimal substitution with a U(1) gauge field (6.2.3) (see also §6.1.3), is generalized to one with gauge fields associated with the SU(3) group,

$$\begin{aligned}\partial_I^{a\dot{b}} &= \tfrac{1}{2}\partial_X^{a\dot{b}} - \partial^{a\dot{b}} \rightarrow D_{I\,ps}^{a\dot{b}} = \tfrac{1}{2}\left(\partial_X^{a\dot{b}}\delta_{ps} + i\tfrac{1}{2}g(\lambda_l)_{ps} W_l^{a\dot{b}}(X)\right) - \partial^{a\dot{b}}\delta_{ps} = \partial_I^{a\dot{b}}\delta_{ps} \\ &\quad + i\tfrac{1}{4}g(\lambda_l)_{ps} W_l^{a\dot{b}}(X) \\ \partial_{II}^{f\dot{e}} &= \tfrac{1}{2}\partial_X^{f\dot{e}} + \partial^{f\dot{e}} \rightarrow D_{II\,ps}^{f\dot{e}} = \partial_{II}^{f\dot{e}}\delta_{ps} + i\tfrac{1}{4}g(\lambda_l)_{ps} W_l^{f\dot{e}}(X)\end{aligned} \tag{7.1.4}$$

$$\frac{ig}{2}(\lambda_l)_{ps}W_l^{a\dot{b}}(X)=\frac{ig}{2}\begin{pmatrix} W_3+\frac{1}{\sqrt{3}}W_8 & \sqrt{2}W_I^+ & \sqrt{2}W_V^+ \\ \sqrt{2}W_I^- & -W_3+\frac{1}{\sqrt{3}}W_8 & \sqrt{2}W_U \\ \sqrt{2}W_V^- & \sqrt{2}\overline{W}_U & -\frac{2}{\sqrt{3}}W_8 \end{pmatrix}^{a\dot{b}} \tag{7.1.5a}$$

$$\begin{aligned} &\sqrt{2}W_I^{\pm}=W_1\mp iW_2, \qquad \sqrt{2}W_V^{\pm}=W_4\mp iW_5 \\ &\sqrt{2}W_U=W_6-iW_7 \qquad \sqrt{2}\overline{W}_U-W_6+iW_7 \end{aligned} \tag{7.1.5b}$$

where W_l are the wave functions of the eight gauge bosons and λ_l the eight Gell-Mann matrices.

Note that if internal function were attached to $\chi_{(pr)}$ in (7.1.3a) to become $\chi_{pr}z^P u_r$, as in (2.4.2), then the W's in (7.1.5) will also be accompanied by stepping operators [H12 (3.3)] exemplified by $W_V{}^+ \rightarrow W_V{}^+ z^1\partial/\partial z^3$, similar to (14.3.3) below. Notations in this case will be more cumbersome.

The expression (7.1.3a) now becomes

$$\left(D_{I\,ps}^{a\dot{b}+}\chi_{(rp)\dot{e}a}^{+}\right)\left(D_{II\,sq}^{f\dot{e}}\chi_{(qr)\dot{b}f}\right)+c.c. \tag{7.1.6}$$

The global SU(3) transformations (2.4.19) are now replaced by the local SU(3) transformations

$$\chi_{(qr)\dot{b}f}\rightarrow\chi'_{(qr)\dot{b}f}=U_{3qs}(X)\chi_{(sp)\dot{b}f}U_{3pr}^{-1}(X) \tag{7.1.7a}$$

$$U_{3qs}(X)=\exp\left(i\tfrac{1}{2}g(\lambda_l)_{qs}\vartheta_l(X)\right) \tag{7.1.7b}$$

This and (7.1.3b) give

$$\left(\chi'_{(qr)\dot{b}f}\right)^{+}=U_{3rp}(X)\chi_{(ps)f\dot{b}}^{+}U_{3sq}^{-1}(X)=\left(\chi_{(rq)f\dot{b}}^{+}\right)' \tag{7.1.7c}$$

where $\vartheta_l(X)$ are eight gauge functions.

The accompanying transformation of the gauge fields in (7.1.5) is [L4 §14.3.2]

$$\begin{aligned}(\lambda_l)_{qr}W_l^{a\dot{b}}(X)\rightarrow(\lambda_l)_{qr}W_l'^{a\dot{b}}(X)=U_{3qs}(X)(\lambda_l)_{sp}W_l^{a\dot{b}}(X)U_{3pr}^{-1}(X)\\ +\frac{2i}{g}\left(\partial_X^{a\dot{b}}U_{3qs}(X)\right)U_{3sr}^{-1}(X)\end{aligned} \tag{7.1.7d}$$

The expression (7.1.6) is invariant under the SU(3) gauge transformations (7.1.7).

The second term on the right side of (6.1.2) is similarly generalized to a form analogous to (7.1.6). The resulting meson action is

$$S_{m3} = \int d^4 X d^4 x L_{m3} \tag{7.1.8a}$$

$$\begin{aligned} 2L_{m3} &= -\left(D^{ab+}_{I\,ps}\chi^{+}_{(rp)\dot{e}a}\right)\left(D^{f\dot{e}}_{II\,sq}\chi_{(qr)\dot{b}f}\right) - \left(D^{+}_{I\,ps\,\dot{a}b}\psi^{+e\dot{a}}_{(rp)}\right)\left(D_{II\,sq\,\dot{f}e}\psi^{b\dot{f}}_{(qr)}\right) \\ &- \chi^{+}_{(rp)\dot{e}a}\left(M^{2}_{mpr} - \Phi_m\right)\psi^{a\dot{e}}_{(pr)} - \psi^{+a\dot{e}}_{(rp)}\left(M^{2}_{mpr} - \Phi_m\right)\chi_{(pr)\dot{e}a} + c.c. \end{aligned} \tag{7.1.8b}$$

In the SU(3) symmetry limit, the small quark mass differences are neglected so that $M_{mpr}=M_m$ according to §2.4.2. The M_m^2 terms in (7.1.8b) are also invariant under the SU(3) transformations (7.1.7a, 7b). Therefore, S_{m3} is invariant under the transformations (7.1.7) in this limit. During stage I, the last three actions in (7.1.1) drop out and the total action S_{T3} is approximately SU(3) gauge invariant.

Generalizing (2.4.3) to include gauge fields according to (7.1.4) yields

$$D^{a\dot{b}}_{I\,ps} D^{f\dot{e}}_{II\,sq}\chi_{(qr)\dot{b}f} - \left(M^{2}_{mpr} - \Phi_m\right)\psi^{a\dot{e}}_{(pr)} = 0 \tag{7.1.9a}$$

$$D_{I\,ps\dot{c}a} D_{II\,sq\dot{e}d}\psi^{a\dot{e}}_{(qr)} - \left(M^{2}_{mpr} - \Phi_m\right)\chi_{(pr)\dot{c}d} = 0 \tag{7.1.9b}$$

These equations of motion are also recovered by varying (7.1.8) with respect to χ^{+} and ψ^{+} together with the subsidiary conditions, analogous to (6.2.9),

$$\begin{aligned} &(i/4) g \chi_{\dot{b}f}(x_I, x_{II})\left(\partial^{a\dot{b}}_{X} W_l^{f\dot{e}}(X) - \partial^{f\dot{e}}_{X} W_l^{a\dot{b}}(X)\right) = 0 \\ &(i/4) g \psi^{c\dot{e}}(x_I, x_{II})\left(\partial_{X\dot{c}a} W_{l\dot{e}d}(X) - \partial_{X\dot{e}d} W_{l\dot{c}a}(X)\right) = 0 \end{aligned} \tag{7.1.10}$$

for a given member of the SU(3) multiplet for χ, ψ and for W_l. These conditions stem from the *c.c.* term in (7.1.8b). For the singlet (7.3.14) below, (7.1.10) specifies that, with (C1a), W_l^0 can be arbitrary but $\underline{W_l}$ must be parallel to its momentum or that either one of them vanishes.

7.1.3. Lepton Action and Approximate SU(2)×U(1) Gauge Invariance

The internal indices appearing in the lepton action are limited to *1* and *2*, because the leptons appear in doublets. In the standard model [B8, L5 §22.2], the lepton wave functions are left handed doublets and right handed singlets and the action in spinor form noting (C13) reads

$$S_{L,SM} = S_{Lr,SM} + S_{Ll,SM} \tag{7.1.11}$$

$$S_{Lr,SM} = -i\tfrac{1}{4}\int d^4 X \chi_{La}\left(\partial^{a\dot{b}}_{X} + i\tfrac{1}{2} g' Y_r C^{a\dot{b}}\right)\chi_{L\dot{b}} + c.c.$$

$$S_{Ll,SM} = -i\frac{1}{4}\int d^4 X \left(\psi^{\dot{a}}_{\nu L}, \psi^{\dot{a}}_{L}\right) D_{\dot{a}b} \begin{pmatrix} \psi^{b}_{\nu L} \\ \psi^{b}_{L} \end{pmatrix} + c.c. \tag{7.1.12a}$$

$$D_{\dot{a}b} = \partial_{X\dot{a}b} + \frac{i}{2}g\begin{pmatrix} W_3 + \frac{g'}{g}Y_lC & \sqrt{2}W_l^+ \\ \sqrt{2}W_l^- & -W_3 + \frac{g'}{g}Y_lC \end{pmatrix}_{\dot{a}b} \tag{7.1.12b}$$

The accompanying action for lepton mass, which is different from that of the standard model (see §7.6.1 below), is

$$S_{Lm} = -\tfrac{1}{2}\int d^4Xm_L\left(\psi_L^{\dot{a}}\chi_{L\dot{a}} + c.c.\right) \tag{7.1.13}$$

Here L denotes the leptons, electron and muon, r and l right and left handedness, respectively, ν_L the associated neutrino, ψ^b the left handed spinor and $\chi_{\dot{b}}$ the corresponding right handed spinor according to (C13), g' the charge associated with the U(1) gauge field like g_l' in (6.2.3), $C^{a\dot{b}}$ the U(1) gauge field analogous to $B^{a\dot{b}}(X)$ in (6.2.3), and Y the weak hypercharge. Using the Gell-Mann-Nishijima relation $Q=I_3+Y/2$, where Q is the charge and I_3 the third component of the weak isospin, one finds

$$Y_l = -1, \qquad Y_r = -2 \tag{7.1.14}$$

$S_{L,SM}$ is invariant under the $SU(2)_l\times U(1)_Y$ group of local gauge transformations. Variation of (7.1.11-13) with respect to the lepton wave functions produces the corresponding equations of motion for the leptons.

The gauge fields in the lepton action S_L must be compatible with those in the other actions in (7.1.1). Therefore, S_L cannot contain quantities like g' and $C_{\dot{a}b}(X)$ absent in the other actions. The quantity corresponding to hypercharge Y in (7.1.5a) is 1 because it can couple to the SU(3) specific doublet $\psi_{(13)}$ and $\psi_{(23)}$ in (2.4.18) associated with K^+ and K^0. Comparison of the parentheses in (7.1.12b) containing the gauge fields to (7.1.5a), with its third row and column removed according to the above compatibility, suggests the identification

$$\frac{g'}{g}C_{\dot{a}b}(X) \rightarrow \frac{1}{\sqrt{3}}W_{8\dot{a}b}(X) \tag{7.1.15}$$

Thus,

$$S_L = S_{Ll} + S_{Lr} \tag{7.1.16}$$

$$S_{Lr} = -i\frac{1}{4}\int d^4X\chi_{La}\left(\partial_X^{a\dot{b}} - ig\frac{1}{\sqrt{3}}W_8^{a\dot{b}}\right)\chi_{L\dot{b}} + c.c. \tag{7.1.17a}$$

$$S_{Ll}=-\frac{i}{4}\int d^4X\left(\psi^{\dot a}_{\nu L},\psi^{\dot a}_{L}\right)\left[\partial_{X\dot ab}+\frac{i}{2}g\begin{pmatrix}W_3-\frac{1}{\sqrt3}W_8 & \sqrt2 W_l^+\\ \sqrt2 W_l^- & -W_3-\frac{1}{\sqrt3}W_8\end{pmatrix}_{\dot ab}\right]\begin{pmatrix}\psi^b_{\nu L}\\ \psi^b_L\end{pmatrix}+cc. \quad (7.1.17b)$$

S_L is invariant under the $SU(2)_I\times U(1)_Y$ group of transformations,

$$\chi_{L\dot a}\rightarrow\chi_{L\dot a}\exp\left(-i\tfrac{1}{\sqrt3}g\vartheta_8(X)\right) \quad (7.1.18)$$

$$\begin{pmatrix}\psi^b_{\nu L}\\ \psi^b_L\end{pmatrix}\rightarrow U_{21-}(X)\begin{pmatrix}\psi^b_{\nu L}\\ \psi^b_L\end{pmatrix} \quad (7.1.19)$$

$$(\sigma_l)_{qs}W_{l\dot ab}\rightarrow U_{21+qs}(X)(\sigma_l)_{sp}W_{l\dot ab}U^{-1}_{21+pr}(X)+\frac{2i}{g}\left(\partial_{X\dot ab}U_{21+qs}(X)\right)U^{-1}_{21+sr}(X) \quad (7.1.20a)$$

$$W_{8\dot ab}\rightarrow W_{8\dot ab}-\partial_{X\dot ab}\vartheta_8(X) \quad (7.1.20b)$$

$$U_{21\pm qs}(X)=\exp\left\{i\tfrac{1}{2}g\left[(\sigma_l)_{qs}\vartheta_l(X)\pm\delta_{qs}\tfrac{1}{\sqrt3}\vartheta_8(X)\right]\right\} \quad (7.1.21)$$

Here, l runs from 1 to 3 and δ is the usual delta function, as is in (A11). This group of transformations is a subset of the SU(3) transformations (7.1.7) with the meson wave functions χ replaced by the lepton wave functions (7.1.17b).

In S_{Lm} of (7.1.13), the difference between the muon and electron masses on the one hand and the vanishing mass of the neutrinos on the other breaks the SU(2) symmetry, much like that differences between different quark masses break the SU(3) symmetry considered in §2.4.2. In the so-called Glashow model [H11 Sec. 2] adopted here, this noninvariance of S_{Lm} is disregarded.

The SU(2)×U(1) gauge fields in (7.1.17) manifest themselves as the $W^\pm$, Z and A bosons in (7.2.2) below. Their masses M_W and M_Z, hence energies, according to (7.4.9) and (7.4.18c) below are very large and these energies are transferred to the decay products, electron or muon and their neutrinos indicated in (7.1.17b). Contributions from the derivative terms there are therefore much greater than S_{Lm} due to the relative smallness of the lepton masses therein. In this high energy limit, S_{Lm} can be neglected and SU(2)×U(1) gauge invariance holds.

At energies much lower than the M_W and M_Z, S_{Lm} is no longer small and the SU(2)×U(1) gauge invariance breaks down. But then, the $W^\pm$ and Z bosons cannot be present and enter as virtual states in the decays treated here; there is no contradiction. In this manner, the Glashow model is justified.

An analogous procedure will be consistently applied to the SU(3) gauge symmetry, which is an extension of the SU(2)×U(1) symmetry here, for the light mesons in regard to the quark mass differences. This has been mentioned above (2.4.5) and will be considered at the end of Sec. 7.2.

7.2. The Weinberg Angle and Degeneracy of Su(3) Gauge Fields

7.2.1. Origin of the Weinberg Angle

Before proceeding to the decay problems, a prediction of the Weinberg angle is made.

In the standard model, there are two independent electro-weak coupling constants g and g'. It is customary to introduce the unitary Weinberg transformation

$$Z_{\dot{a}b} = W_{3\dot{a}b}\cos\vartheta_W - C_{\dot{a}b}\sin\vartheta_W, \qquad A_{\dot{a}b} = W_{3\dot{a}b}\sin\vartheta_W + C_{\dot{a}b}\cos\vartheta_W \tag{7.2.1a}$$

$$\tan\vartheta_W = g'/g, \qquad e = g\sin\vartheta_W \tag{7.2.1b}$$

into (7.1.12). The Weinberg angle ϑ_W and g are the two unknown constants to be determined by data. The matrix operator in (7.1.12b) now becomes

$$\frac{i}{2}g\begin{pmatrix} Z/\cos\vartheta_W & \sqrt{2}W_I^+ \\ \sqrt{2}W_I^- & -2A\sin\vartheta_W - Z(\cos 2\vartheta_W/\cos\vartheta_W) \end{pmatrix}_{\dot{a}b} \tag{7.2.2}$$

In the total action S_{T3} (7.1.1), which includes the lepton action (7.1.16), however, there is only one weak coupling constant g; there is no need to fix an extra constant $\sin\vartheta_W$. Conversely, the origin of the Weinberg angle may be inferred by identifying

$$C_{\dot{a}b}(X) \rightarrow W_{8\dot{a}b}(X) \tag{7.2.3a}$$

in (7.1.15). Assuming this, (7.1.15) yields

$$\tan\vartheta_W = 1/\sqrt{3}, \qquad \vartheta_W = 30^\circ, \qquad \sin^2\vartheta_W = 0.25 \tag{7.2.3b}$$

$$e = g/2 \tag{7.2.3c}$$

which is close to the measured value of $\sin^2\vartheta_W \approx 0.23$ [L4 §14.5.1].

In the limit of SU(3) symmetry limit, (7.2.3) suggests that the Weinberg angle in the scalar strong interaction hadron theory is just another form of $1/\sqrt{3}$ arising from normalization of the eighth Gell-Mann matrix λ_8. In other words, g' just stands for $g/\sqrt{3}$. Deviation from (7.2.3) is attributed to that the SU(3) symmetry is broken to first order, mentioned in §2.4.2 and treated in the following §7.2.2.

Nature is economical in dealing out fundamental constants. To hand out two natural constants g' and g or e within a factor of $\sqrt{3}$ appears to be wasteful. This aesthetical and practical defect is removed in the present theory by means of (7.2.3).

7.2.2. Broken Local SU(3) Symmetry and Weinberg's Angle

As was mentioned above (2.4.5), the SU(3) symmetry is broken slightly by the somewhat higher mass m_3 of the s quark relative to m_1 and m_2, the masses of the u and d quarks. This symmetry breaking is reflected in the $M_{mpr}{}^2\,\psi_{(pr)}$ type of expressions in (2.4.3) and in the meson action (7.1.8). Neglecting the small differences between m_1 and m_2, (2.4.1, 13, 15) show that there are only three pseudoscalar meson masses which are put in the form,

$$M_{m\pi}^2 = M_{m\pi 0}^2 = m_{1-2}^2, \quad M_{mK}^2 = m_{1-2}^2(1+\Delta_3)^2, \quad \Delta_3 = \frac{\Delta m_3}{2m_{1-2}}$$

$$M_{m\eta}^2 = m_{1-2}^2(1+\Delta_8), \quad \Delta_8 = \frac{4}{3}\frac{\Delta m_3}{m_{1-2}} + \frac{2}{3}\left(\frac{\Delta m_3}{m_{1-2}}\right)^2 \qquad (7.2.4a)$$

$$m_1,\, m_2 \to m_{1-2} = (m_1 + m_2)/2 = 0.6603 \text{ MeV}$$
$$\Delta m_3 = m_3 - m_{1-2} = 0.08283 \text{ MeV} \qquad (7.2.4b)$$

$$\Delta_3 = 0.06272, \quad \Delta_8 = 0.1777 \qquad (7.2.4c)$$

where Table 5.2 has been consulted. Similarly,

$$\psi_{(12)} = \psi_{(21)} = \psi_{(\pi 0)} = \psi_{(\pi)}, \quad \psi_{(13)} = \psi_{(31)} = \psi_{(23)} = \psi_{(32)} = \psi_{(K)}, \quad \psi \to \chi \qquad (7.2.5)$$

in (2.4.18). These wave functions in rest frame have been obtained via Chapter 3 and §4.3.2 and differ only by three phases containing the meson masses $E_{0\pi}$, E_{0K} and $E_{0\eta}$ according to (2.4.10). Thus, the SU(3) symmetry breaking expression $M_{mpr}{}^2\,\psi_{(pr)}$ can be put in the form,

$$M_{mpr}^2\psi_{(pr)} = \begin{pmatrix} M_{m\pi}^2\psi_{(\pi)} + M_{m\eta}^2\psi_{(\eta)} & M_{m\pi}^2\psi_{(\pi)} & M_{mK}^2\psi_{(K)} \\ M_{m\pi}^2\psi_{(\pi)} & -M_{m\pi}^2\psi_{(\pi)} + M_{m\eta}^2\psi_{(\eta)} & M_{mK}^2\psi_{(K)} \\ M_{mK}^2\psi_{(K)} & M_{mK}^2\psi_{(K)} & -2M_{m\eta}^2\psi_{(\eta)} \end{pmatrix}$$

$$= \begin{pmatrix} 1+(1+\Delta_8)P_{\eta-\pi} & 1 & (1+\Delta_3)^2 P_{K-\pi} \\ 1 & -1+(1+\Delta_8)P_{\eta-\pi} & (1+\Delta_3)^2 P_{K-\pi} \\ (1+\Delta_3)^2 P_{K-\pi} & (1+\Delta_3)^2 P_{K-\pi} & -2(1+\Delta_8)P_{\eta-\pi} \end{pmatrix} m_{1-2}^2\psi_{(\pi)} \qquad (7.2.6a)$$

$$P_{K-\pi} = \exp\left(-i(E_{0K} - E_{0\pi})X^0\right), \qquad P_{\eta-\pi} = \exp\left(-i(E_{0\eta} - E_{0\pi})X^0\right) \qquad (7.2.6b)$$

This mass term is of zeroth order in g. It is expected to affect the originally SU(3) symmetry preserving terms of first order in g, $g(\lambda_l)_{pr}W_l\psi$ in (7.1.8b) via (7.1.4) such that they too loose this symmetry. How these terms are modified to break the symmetry is unknown, except that the degree of symmetry breaking should be of the same magnitude as $\Delta m_3/m_{1-2}$ in (7.2.6). There are infinitely many ways to break the SU(3) symmetry of the g and g^2 terms in (7.1.8). In general, this symmetry breaking will involve i) new unknown functions or ii) new unknown constants. In these cases, the results to be obtained will contain these unknowns and can hence not be evaluated.

Therefore, the criterion "*no new unknown is allowed in the symmetry breaking*" will be adopted in the following. If i) is not allowed, then the only possibility is to modify g to g_l, i.e., the weak charge associated with the different gauge fields W_l are different. In view of (7.2.4-6) and (7.1.5a), the generalization takes the form

$$g(\lambda_l)_{ps}W_l\psi_{(sr)} \to g_l(\lambda_l)_{ps}W_l\psi_{(sr)}$$
$$= \begin{pmatrix} gW_3+g_8W_8/\sqrt{3} & g\sqrt{2}W_I^+ & g_{4-7}\sqrt{2}W_V^+ \\ g\sqrt{2}W_I^- & -gW_3+g_8W_8/\sqrt{3} & g_{4-7}\sqrt{2}W_U \\ g_{4-7}\sqrt{2}W_V^- & g_{4-7}\sqrt{2}\overline{W}_U & -2g_8W_8/\sqrt{3} \end{pmatrix} \begin{pmatrix} 1+P_{\eta-\pi} & 1 & P_{K-\pi} \\ 1 & -1+P_{\eta-\pi} & P_{K-\pi} \\ P_{K-\pi} & P_{K-\pi} & -2P_{\eta-\pi} \end{pmatrix} \psi_{(\pi)}$$
$$g=g_1=g_2=g_3, \qquad g_{4-7}=g_4=g_5=g_6=g_7 \tag{7.2.7}$$

If ii) above is not allowed, Δg_{4-7} and Δg_8 can only depend upon the known SU(3) symmetry breaking parameter Δm_3 in a way not containing any new constant. Such a dependence, apart from a sign, can be determined from a comparison of (7.2.6) and (7.2.7). The phases P_{K}-π and P_η-π are of magnitude unity. The dimension of gW in (7.2.7) is (length)$^{-1}$ while the dimension of M_m^2 in (7.2.6) is (length)$^{-2}$. Therefore, such a comparison gives the identification

$$\frac{g_{4-7}}{g}=1+\Delta_3, \qquad \frac{g_8}{\sqrt{3}g}=\sqrt{1+\Delta_8} \tag{7.2.8}$$

which together with (7.2.4) yields

$$\frac{g_{4-7}}{g}=1\pm\frac{\Delta m_3}{2m_{1-2}}=1\pm0.0627, \quad \frac{g_8}{\sqrt{3}g}=\sqrt{1\pm\frac{4\Delta m_3}{3m_{1-2}}+\frac{2}{3}\left(\frac{\Delta m_3}{m_{1-2}}\right)^2}=\begin{pmatrix}1+0.0852\\1-0.0817\end{pmatrix} \tag{7.2.9}$$

The lower minus sign is introduced because one does not know at this stage whether Δm_3 will give rise to higher or lower weak charges g_{4-7} and g_8. The forms (7.2.8-9) appear to satisfy the above criterion uniquely and are also the simplest possible. It is noted that (7.2.6a) and (7.2.7) still preserves SU(2)$_I$ symmetry and, in the limit of $\Delta m_3\to 0$, the original SU(3) symmetry is restored.

With the SU(3) symmetry preserving (7.1.5a) replaced by the SU(3) symmetry breaking parentheses containing gW in (7.2.7), it is seen that the identification (7.1.15) is replaced by

$$\frac{g'}{g}C_{\dot{a}b}(X)\to\frac{1}{\sqrt{3}}\frac{g_8}{g}W_{8\dot{a}b}(X) \tag{7.2.10}$$

Consequently, the first of (7.2.1b) with the first of (7.2.3b) now becomes

$$\tan\vartheta_W = \frac{g_8}{\sqrt{3}g} = \frac{1}{\sqrt{3}}\begin{pmatrix} 1+0.08124 \\ 1-0.08172 \end{pmatrix} \tag{7.2.11}$$

The lower case is chosen because it gives

$$\sin^2\vartheta_W = 0.2194, \qquad \vartheta_W = 27.93^0 \tag{7.2.12}$$

in good agreement with data 0.2223 [P1]. This value will also later lead to a lower mass of the Z gauge boson in (7.4.18c) and is therefore preferred. It replaces the SU(3) symmetry preserving value 0.25 given in (7.2.3b). The lower case in the first of (7.2.9) also shows that the weak charge $g_{4\text{-}7}$ of (7.2.7) associated with $W_4, \ldots W_7$ is about 6% lower than g associated with pions.

With (7.2.10), the lepton action (7.1.17) together with (7.2.1a, 2, 3a) becomes

$$S_{Lr} = -i\tfrac{1}{4}\int d^4X\chi_{La}\left(\partial_X^{a\dot{b}} + ie\left(-A^{a\dot{b}} + \tan\vartheta_W Z^{a\dot{b}}\right)\right)\chi_{L\dot{b}} + c.c. \tag{7.2.13a}$$

$$S_{Ll} = -\frac{i}{4}\int d^4X\left(\psi_{\nu L}^{\dot{a}}, \psi_L^{\dot{a}}\right)\left[\partial_{X\dot{a}b} + i\frac{g}{2}\begin{pmatrix} Z/\cos\vartheta_W & \sqrt{2}W_I^+ \\ \sqrt{2}W_I^- & -2A\sin\vartheta_W - Z\left(\cos 2\vartheta_W/\cos\vartheta_W\right) \end{pmatrix}_{\dot{a}b}\right]\begin{pmatrix} \psi_{\nu L}^b \\ \psi_L^b \end{pmatrix}$$
$$+c.c. \tag{7.2.13b}$$

The charge of the charged lepton spinors $\psi_L{}^b$ and $\chi_{L\dot{b}}$ is correctly represented in the electromagnetic field terms.

Similarly, the SU(3) symmetry preserving (7.1.5a) now becomes

$$i\frac{g}{2}(\lambda_l)_{ps}W_{l\dot{a}b}(X) \to i\frac{g_l}{2}(\lambda_l)_{ps}W_{l\dot{a}b}(X)$$
$$= i\frac{g}{2}\begin{pmatrix} 2A\sin\vartheta_W + Z\cos 2\vartheta_W/\cos\vartheta_W & \sqrt{2}W_I^+ & (g_{4-7}/g)\sqrt{2}W_V^+ \\ \sqrt{2}W_I^- & -Z/\cos\vartheta_W & (g_{4-7}/g)\sqrt{2}W_U \\ (g_{4-7}/g)\sqrt{2}W_V^- & (g_{4-7}/g)\sqrt{2}\overline{W}_U & -2A\sin\vartheta_W + 2Z\sin^2\vartheta_W/\cos\vartheta_W \end{pmatrix}_{\dot{a}b} \tag{7.2.14}$$

In the limit of SU(3) symmetry $\Delta m_3 \to 0$ and (7.2.14) becomes

$$i\frac{g}{2}(\lambda_l)_{ps}W_{l\dot{a}b}(X) = i\frac{g}{2}\begin{pmatrix} A+\frac{1}{\sqrt{3}}Z & \sqrt{2}W_I^+ & \sqrt{2}W_V^+ \\ \sqrt{2}W_I^- & -\frac{2}{\sqrt{3}}Z & \sqrt{2}W_U \\ \sqrt{2}W_V^- & \sqrt{2}\overline{W}_U & -A+\frac{1}{\sqrt{3}}Z \end{pmatrix}_{\dot{a}b} \tag{7.2.15}$$

7.2.3. Degeneracy of SU(3) Gauge Fields and Extended Glashow Model

Lorentz invariance of the total action (7.1.1) is guaranteed by the tensor or spinor forms of the member actions. Approximative gauge invariances for each of these actions have been demonstrated in Sec. 7.1 ($S_{m\pi}$ will be given by (7.7.3) below). Gauge invariance is a requirement of quantum mechanics saying that the local phases of the lepton and meson wave functions do not affect the physical results. This necessitates the introduction of four gauge fields in (7.1.17) and eight gauge fields in (7.1.8, 9) via (7.1.4-5).

Having served these purposes, gauge symmetries place no further constraint on the development and specialization of these actions but may still be helpful in some cases. This is analogous to that one no longer needs to consider Lorentz invariance when specializing Dirac's equation for application to the hydrogen atom. As Wigner remarked: "Once the equation of motion is known, we do not need symmetry anymore." The equations of motion of the meson, lepton and gauge boson fields have been obtained by varying the individual actions in the total action S_{T3} (7.1.1) in Sec. 7.1.

All the fields interact with the gauge boson fields in S_{T3}, which serves the purpose of coupling of these fields in stage II of §7.1.1. Variations of S_{T3} with respect to the gauge fields in §7.4.2 below put these couplings in form of decay of these bosons into lepton pairs. As was mentioned above, there are four known gauge fields $W_I^{\pm}$, Z and A in (7.2.2) or $W_I^{\pm}$, W_3 and W_8 in the lepton action (7.1.17) but eight $W_I^{\pm}$, W_3, W_8, $W_V^{\pm}$, W_U, and $\overline{W}_U$ in the meson action S_{m3} (7.1.8) and gauge boson action S_{GB} (7.1.2) via (7.2.14-15). The last four gauge fields are new, have not been observed and are converted into the four known ones as follows.

Grossly speaking, W_I^- converts a d quark to a u quark and W_V^- converts an s quark to a u quark. Because the s and d quarks have the same charge, so do $W_I^{\pm}$ and $W_V^{\pm}$. In the limit of SU(3) symmetry, the s and d quarks have the same mass and are hence indistinguishable. Therefore, the degeneracy

$$\sqrt{2}\,W^{\pm}_{V\dot{a}b}(X)\to\sqrt{2}W^{\pm}_{I\dot{a}b}(X) \qquad \text{SU(3) symmetry} \qquad (7.2.16)$$

holds in (7.2.15). Analogously, W_U converts an s quark into a d quark and Z can be viewed as converting a d or $\bar{d}$ quark into itself. In the limit of SU(3) symmetry, both conversions become the same. The formal degeneration analogous to (7.2.16) is seen in (7.2.15):

$$\sqrt{2}W_{U\dot{a}b}(X)=W_{6\dot{a}b}(X)-iW_{7\dot{a}b}(X), \quad W_{6\dot{a}b}(X)\to-2Z_{\dot{a}b}(X)/\sqrt{3}, \quad W_{7\dot{a}b}(X)=0 \qquad (7.2.17)$$

W_7 can removed by a suitable "degeneration" gauge transformation using (7.1.7) which reduces the complex gauge fields W_U and $\overline{W}_U$ in (7.1.5) to one real neutral gauge field Z.

The neutral kaon wave functions K^0 and $\bar{K}^0$ entering (7.1.8-9) couple to $\overline{W}_U$ and W_U, respectively. However, they do not represent physical kaons in weak decay and are conventionally decomposed according to [K3 (16.32)]

$$\psi_{(23)} = \left(\psi_{(KL)} + \psi_{(KS)}\right)/\sqrt{2} \quad \text{or symbolically} \quad K^0 = \left(K_L^0 + K_S^0\right)/\sqrt{2}$$
$$\psi_{(32)} = \left(\psi_{(KL)} - \psi_{(KS)}\right)/\sqrt{2} \quad \text{or symbolically} \quad \overline{K}^0 = \left(K_L^0 - K_S^0\right)/\sqrt{2} \qquad (7.2.18)$$
$$\psi \to \chi$$

where $\psi_{(KS)}$ and $\psi_{(KL)}$ are eigenstates of the discrete CP operator with eigenvalues 1 and –1, respectively. The internal functions are

$$K^0 = z^2 z_3, \quad \overline{K}^0 = (K^0)^* = z_2 z^3 \qquad (7.2.19)$$

according to the assignments of (2.3.12, 4).

In the SU(3) symmetry breaking case, the masses of the *s* and *d* quarks differ by a small amount. This difference affects the strong interaction part of S_{m3} but not directly the weak interaction part, which is related to charges. The charges of the quarks and gauge bosons are not affected. The direct effect of this symmetry breaking can only take place via the associated weak charges in (7.2.7). Accordingly, the degenerations (7.2.16-17) for (7.2.15) are replaced by the corresponding ones in the more general (7.2.14);

$$\frac{g_{4-7}}{g}\sqrt{2}W^{\pm}_{V\dot{a}b}(X) \to \sqrt{2}W^{\pm}_{I\dot{a}b}(X) \qquad (7.2.20)$$

$$\frac{g_{4-7}}{g}\sqrt{2}\begin{pmatrix}\overline{W}_{U\dot{a}b}\\ W_{U\dot{a}b}\end{pmatrix} = \frac{g_{4-7}}{g}\left(W_{6\dot{a}b} \pm iW_{7\dot{a}b}\right) \to -\frac{Z_{\dot{a}b}}{\cos\vartheta_W} \qquad (7.2.21)$$

With these degenerations, S_{m3} and S_{GB} only contain the four known gauge boson present in the lepton action S_L (7.1.17) and the total action S_{T3} (7.1.1) is now self consistent in this regard. Thus, in spite of the SU(3) internal symmetry called for to represent kaons, there are no new, unobserved gauge bosons.

The approximation to be adopted in the rest of this chapter is to put $\Delta_{m3}=0$ at first so that the meson action (7.1.8) is invariant under SU(3) transformations (7.1.7). After having obtained results of first and second order in g utilizing this symmetry, Δ_{m3} of (7.2.4c) is restored as if it had that value all along. This procedure may therefore be called the "extended Glashow model" because it is entirely analogous to the Glashow model for lepton action in which the mass difference between the electron or muon and neutrino has been neglected when establishing SU(2)×U(1) gauge invariance. Δ_{m3} plays the role of the lepton masses in S_{Lm} and the mesons in (7.1.8) play the roles of the leptons in (7.1.17b). Justification of this "extended Glashow model" is analogously based upon the large masses M_W and M_Z and energies associated with the $W^{\pm}$ and Z bosons and follow the same reasoning as that given at the end of Sec. 7.1.

7.3. Decay of Pion and Kaon to Gauge Bosons

7.3.1. Ordering of Wave Functions

Turn now to stage I in §7.1.1 and derive expressions for the decay amplitudes. The methods developed for $V \to P\gamma$ in Sec. 6.4 will be followed. Analogous to (6.4.1-3), where the index J can be dropped here, the meson wave functions in S_{m3} (7.1.8) are written in the form

$$\psi^{a\dot{b}}_{(pr)}(X,x) = \left(a_{pr} + a^{(1)}_{pr}(X^0)\right)\left(\delta^{a\dot{b}}\psi_{0(pr)K}(\underline{x}) - \underline{\sigma}^{a\dot{b}}\underline{\psi}_{(pr)K}(\underline{x})\right)\exp\left(-iE_{prK}X^0 + i\underline{K}_{pr}\underline{X}\right)$$
$$= \psi^{a\dot{b}}_{0(pr)}(X,x) + \psi^{a\dot{b}}_{1(pr)}(X,x) = \left(1 + \frac{a^{(1)}_{pr}(X^0)}{a_{pr}}\right)\psi^{a\dot{b}}_{0(pr)}(X,x)$$
$$\psi \to \chi \tag{7.3.1}$$

Analogous to the assignments below (6.4.3), $a_{pr}=1$ here but is elevated into an annihilation operator in the quantized cases below. $a_{pr}^{(1)}(X^0)$ is a first order quantity varying slowly with the time X^0. The subscripts pr have also been attached to E_K and $\underline{K}$ analogous to M_m^2 in (2.4.1).

The terms in the actions that make up S_{T3} of (7.1.1), i.e., (7.1.2, 8, 16, 17), can now be grouped in powers of the small parameter g or e. Only the lowest order and independent quantities are listed in the two alternatives below:

$$\text{First order:} \quad g, \quad a^{(1)}_{pr}(X^0), \quad \partial_X \text{ in } S_{GB}, \quad \psi^{\dot{a}}_L\psi^{b}_L, \quad \chi_{La}\chi_{L\dot{b}} \tag{7.3.2a}$$

$$\begin{aligned}&\text{First order:} \quad g, \quad W, \quad \partial_X \text{ in } S_{GB}, \quad \psi_L, \quad \chi_L \\ &\text{Second order:} \quad a^{(1)}_{pr}(X^0)\end{aligned} \tag{7.3.2b}$$

These both alternatives are equivalent except that the nonlinear gWW term in (7.1.2b) is of the same order as the other ones there for the first alternative (7.3.2a) but is of one order higher in the second alternative (7.3.2b). The latter is more consistent with the standard model considered in §7.6.1 below and will be adopted. However, the former alternative will be formally used in the exposition below, bearing the difference on the gWW term in mind.

7.3.2. First Order Relations

Insert (7.3.1) into (7.1.9), multiply (7.1.9a) by $\chi^*_{0\dot{e}a(rp)}$ and (7.1.9b) by $\psi^{*d\dot{c}}_{0(rp)}$, add them together, and integrate over X and x. The first order quantities can be put in the form (6.4.9)

$$S'_{m3d} = S'_{m3s} \tag{7.3.3}$$

S'_{m3d} is a surface term analogous to (6.4.10)

$$S'_{m3d} = \int d^4Xdx^4 \left[\partial_I^{a\dot{b}}\left(a_{pr}^{(1)}\left(X^0\right)/a_{pr}\right)\chi^{+}_{0(rp)\dot{e}a}\partial_{II}^{f\dot{e}}\chi_{0(pr)\dot{b}f} + \partial_{I\dot{c}a}\left(a_{pr}^{(1)}\left(X^0\right)/a_{pr}\right)\psi^{+d\dot{c}}_{0(rp)}\partial_{II\dot{e}d}\psi^{a\dot{e}}_{0(pr)}\right] \tag{7.3.4}$$

The source part S'_{m3s} of the first order terms contains the gW terms in (7.1.8), ignoring the *c.c.* term there. It together with (7.1.4) and the left of (7.2.7) reads

$$S'_{m3s} = -\int d^4Xdx^4 \frac{ig_l}{4}\left\{\begin{matrix}\chi^{+}_{0(rp)\dot{e}a}\left(\lambda_l\right)_{ps}W_l^{a\dot{b}}\left(\partial_{II}^{f\dot{e}}\chi_{0(sr)\dot{b}f}\right) - \left(\partial_I^{a\dot{b}}\chi^{+}_{0(rp)\dot{e}a}\right)\left(\lambda_l\right)_{ps}W_l^{f\dot{e}}\chi_{0(sr)\dot{b}f} \\ +\psi^{+d\dot{c}}_{0(rp)}\left(\lambda_l\right)_{ps}W_{l\dot{c}a}\left(\partial_{II\dot{e}d}\psi^{a\dot{e}}_{0(sr)}\right) - \left(\partial_{I\dot{c}a}\psi^{+d\dot{c}}_{0(rp)}\right)\left(\lambda_l\right)_{ps}W_{l\dot{e}d}\psi^{a\dot{e}}_{0(sr)} + R_s\end{matrix}\right\} \tag{7.3.5a}$$

$$\frac{ig_l}{4}R_s = \partial_I^{a\dot{b}}\chi^{+}_{0(rp)\dot{e}a}\left(\lambda_l\right)_{ps}W_l^{f\dot{e}}\chi_{0(sr)\dot{b}f} + \partial_{I\dot{c}a}\psi^{+d\dot{c}}_{0(rp)}\left(\lambda_l\right)_{ps}W_{l\dot{e}d}\psi^{a\dot{e}}_{0(sr)} \tag{7.3.5b}$$

The surface term R_s corresponds to the $iq_r\partial_l$ terms in (6.4.8).

7.3.3. Rudimentary Quantization

In stage I of the present decay mentioned in §7.1.1, an initial pseudoscalar meson P_i decays into an intermediate gauge boson W alone or together with a lighter pseudoscalar meson P_f; $P_i \to WP_f$. This has the same form as the radiative decay $V \to \gamma P$ considered in Sec. 6.4 above. The formalism of §6.4.4 can largely be taken over here.

However, there is a physical difference; the initial V and final P have the same quark content because γ is is neutral and flavorless while P_f and P_i have different quark contents since W can carry off flavor. Therefore, flavor indices $r, p, q\ldots$ will be attached to P_i, W and P_f here as in (7.3.1). .

Let the initial and final states of stage I of §7.1.1 be

$$|i\rangle = \left|P_{i(pr)}\left(E_{pr}\right)\right\rangle, \qquad p \neq r \tag{7.3.6}$$

$$\langle f| = \left\langle P_{f(rp)}\left(K^{\mu}_{f1rp}\right), W_{(ps)}\right| \tag{7.3.7a}$$

The subscript K in (7.3.1) is zero for the initial state and is suppressed. The initial state is a kaon or a charged pion characterized by sr with $s \neq r$ and the final states pion by one of

$$(rp) = (12) \text{ for } \pi^+ = \pi+,\ (rp) = (21) \text{ for } \pi^- = \pi-,\ (rp) = (11-22) \text{ for } \pi^0 = \pi 0 \tag{7.3.8}$$

where the corresponding pion symbols given after the parentheses will be used synonymously. When rp=11 or 22, it represents a $u\bar{u}$ or a $d\bar{d}$ state which does not exist. These final states are interpreted as that the quark and antiquark annihilate each other leaving behind a *vacuum pseudoscalar meson state* to be discussed further below (7.3.19). In this case, (7.3.7a) becomes

$$\langle f| = \left\langle P_{f(rr)}(0), W_{ps}\right| = \left\langle 0, W_{ps}\right| \tag{7.3.7b}$$

W_{ps} is the intermediary gauge bosom field representing the other final state of stage I and is related to (7.2.7) by

$$g_l(\lambda_l)_{ps} W_{l\dot{a}b} = g_l \sqrt{2} W_{ps\,\dot{a}b}, \qquad p \neq s \tag{7.3.9a}$$

which can be written as

$$\begin{aligned} &g W_{12} = g W_I^+, \quad g_{4-7} W_{13} = g_{4-7} W_-^+, \quad g_{4-7} W_{23} = g_{4-7} W_U, \\ &g W_{21} = g W_I^-, \quad g_{4-7} W_{31} = g_{4-7} W_V^+, \quad g_{4-7} W_{32} = g_{4-7} \overline{W}_U \end{aligned} \tag{7.3.9b}$$

a_{pr} in (7.3.1) is now elevated to become an annihilation operator according to the assignment below (6.4.3) so that

$$a_{pr} \left| P_{i(pr)}(E_{pr}) \right\rangle = |0\rangle \tag{7.3.10a}$$

Similarly, a^*_{rp} is interpreted as an equivalent creation operator acting on |0> or an annihilation operator acting on <f| and

$$a^*_{rp}|0\rangle = \left| P_{f1(rp)}(K^\mu_{f1rp}) \right\rangle, \qquad \left\langle P_{f1(rp)}(K^\mu_{f1rp}) \right| a^*_{rp} = \langle 0| \tag{7.3.10b}$$

Obviously,

$$a_{rp}|i\rangle = a_{rp}\left| P_{i(sr)}(E_{sr}) \right\rangle = 0, \qquad rp \neq sq \tag{7.3.11}$$

The gauge boson W_{ps} plays the role of the photon $\underline{A}(X)$ in (6.4.6, 15) which corresponds here to

$$\begin{aligned} &W_{ps}(X) \to a_W W_{ps}(X) \\ &a_W W_{ps}(X) = |0\rangle \to a^*_W W^*_{ps}(X)|0\rangle = W^*_{ps}(X)|W_{ps}\rangle \end{aligned} \tag{7.3.12}$$

where a_W is an operator annihilating a gauge boson W_{ps} and $a^*{}_W$ is the corresponding creation operator. Similar to (6.4.15), the annihilation of a gauge boson W_{ps} from the vacuum |0> is equivalent to the creation of its antiparticle $W^*{}_{ps}$.

Consistent with (6.4.14b), one writes the decay amplitude

$$S_{fi} = \langle f | a^+_{rp} a^{(1)}_{pr}(X^0 \to \infty) | i \rangle \tag{7.3.13}$$

Following §6.4.4, the first order part S_{T31} of S_{T3} in (7.1.1) is placed between <f| and |i>. Consider at first the contribution stemming from S_{m3d} in (7.3.4). The zeroth order wave functions for a pseudoscalar meson at rest are according to (7.3.1) and (3.4.1)

$$\psi^{a\dot{b}}_{0(pr)}(X,x)=\delta^{a\dot{b}}\psi_{o(pr)}(r)\exp\left(-iE_{pr}X^0\right), \qquad \psi\to\chi \tag{7.3.14a}$$

$$\psi_{o(pr)}(r)=-\chi_{o(pr)}(r)=\psi_o(r) \tag{7.3.14b}$$

The last quantity is given by (4.3.4a). With (7.3.13-14), (7.3.4) yields

$$\left\langle f\left|S^{'}_{m3d}\right|i\right\rangle=-iE_{pr}S_{fi}\int d^3\underline{X}dx^0d^3\underline{x}\,\psi_0^2(r)=-iE_{pr}S_{fi}\tau_0 \tag{7.3.15}$$

analogous to (6.4.14a). The second of (4.2.5) $\int d^3\underline{X}=\Omega\to\infty$ by (4.2.7-8) and

$$\tau_o=\int dx^0\to\infty \tag{7.3.16}$$

is a relative time. Combining (7.3.15) with (7.3.3) leads to

$$S_{fi}=i\frac{1}{E_{pr}\tau_0}\left\langle f\left|S^{'}_{m3s}\right|i\right\rangle \tag{7.3.17}$$

where E_{pr} is the mass of the initial state pseudoscalar meson present in (7.3.6, 14a).

7.3.4. Amplitude for Decay to Gauge Boson, Vacuum Meson State

In the source matrix element $\langle f|S'_{m3s}|i\rangle$, the surface term R_s in (7.3.5) turns out not to contribute similar to that the surface term $iq_r\partial$ in (6.4.8) does not contribute. After elevating the amplitudes of the wave functions entering S'_{m3s} to annihilation and creation operators according to the assignments below (6.4.3), the quantities operated by ∂ in (7.3.5b) do not depend upon X^μ. This is due to that the initial and final state four momenta must cancel each other. Further, the meson wave functions vanish at large r due to confinement (4.3.4). With (3.1.4), it is readily seen that the R_s term of (7.3.5) vanishes in the source matrix element after integration over $\underline{x}$. With (7.3.5, 6, 7, 9-12, 14), one obtains, corresponding to (6.4.17-18), for positive energy solutions denoted by the superscript (+),

$$\left\langle f\left|S^{'}_{m3s}\right|i\right\rangle^{(+)}=-\frac{ig_I}{4}\sqrt{2}\int d^4Xdx^4\times$$
$$\begin{Bmatrix}\chi^{+}_{f1(rp)\dot{e}a}W^{*a\dot{b}}_{ps}\left(\partial_{II\dot{b}}{}^{\dot{e}}\chi_{0(sr)}(r)\exp\left(-iE_{sr}X^0\right)\right)-\left(\partial^{a\dot{b}}_{I}\chi^{+}_{f1(rp)\dot{e}a}\right)W^{*\;\dot{e}}_{ps\dot{b}}\chi_{0(sr)}(r)\exp\left(-iE_{sr}X^0\right)\\+\psi^{+d\dot{c}}_{f1(rp)}W^{*}_{ps\dot{c}a}\left(\partial^{a}_{II\,d}\psi_{0(sr)}(r)\exp\left(-iE_{sr}X^0\right)\right)-\left(\partial_{I\dot{c}a}\psi^{+d\dot{c}}_{f1(rp)}\right)W^{*a}_{ps\,d}\psi_{0(sr)}(r)\exp\left(-iE_{sr}X^0\right)\end{Bmatrix} \tag{7.3.18}$$

where raising and lowering of spinor indices follow those in (C9). The internal subscript (sr) attached to χ_0 and ψ_0 in (7.3.5) has been dropped. For negative energy meson wave functions corresponding to the lower sign in (5.1.1), (7.3.5a) together with (7.3.12) similarly leads to

$$\langle f|S'_{m3s}|i\rangle^{(-)} = \frac{ig_l}{4}\sqrt{2}\int d^4Xdx^4 \times$$
$$\begin{Bmatrix} \chi^{(-)e\dot{a}}_{f1(rp)}W_{sp\dot{a}b}\partial_{Ile}{}^{b}\chi_{0(sr)}(r)\exp\left(-i|E_{rs}|X^0\right)-\left(\partial_{I\dot{a}b}\chi^{(-)e\dot{a}}_{f1(rp)}\right)W_{spe}{}^{b}\chi_{0(sr)}(r)\exp\left(-i|E_{rs}|X^0\right) \\ \psi^{(-)}_{f1(rp)\dot{d}c}W^{c\dot{a}}_{sp}\partial_{I\dot{l}\dot{a}}{}^{\dot{d}}\psi_{0(sr)}(r)\exp\left(-i|E_{rs}|X^0\right)-\left(\partial^{c\dot{a}}_{I}\psi^{(-)}_{f1(rp)\dot{d}c}\right)W_{sp\dot{a}}{}^{\dot{d}}\psi_{0(sr)}(r)\exp\left(-i|E_{rs}|X^0\right) \end{Bmatrix} \tag{7.3.19}$$

The superscript (–) denotes negative energy meson wave functions.

Consider at first the final states (7.3.7b). The initial state pseudoscalar meson at rest is a singlet having mass E_{sr}, as has been represented in (7.3.18). The meson final state denoted by the subscript $f1$ is a vacuum meson state which will be taken here as the neutral pion π^0 that has lost its four momentum to the intermediate gauge boson $W(X)$. The relative space part of the meson wave functions is unchanged, inasmuch as this part depends only upon the "hidden variable" $\underline{x}$ and is not directly observable [H12 Sec. 1]. One of the open flavors s or r of the initial meson state is thus converted by this $W(X)$ to the other in the final meson state, in which the quark and antiquark have the same flavor and are regarded to annihilate each other virtually;

$$\psi^{*\dot{d}c}_{f1(pr)}(X,x) = \psi^{*}_{0wvac(pr)}(r)\delta^{\dot{d}c} \tag{7.3.20a}$$

in (7.3.18). Here, the subscript w refers to weak decay and vac to vacuum meson state. Accordingly, (4.3.4a) with the normalization (4.2.8) becomes

$$\psi_{0wvac}(r) = \frac{1}{\sqrt{\Omega}}\alpha_{00}\exp\left(-\frac{d_h}{2}r^2\right) = \sqrt{\frac{\Omega}{\Omega_{wvac}}}\psi_{00}(r),\quad \Omega_c = \Omega_{wvac} = \text{finite} \tag{7.3.20b}$$

Departure from (4.3.4a) where $\Omega_c \to \Omega \to \infty$ is due to the following. In (4.3.4a), which describes a real meson, $\Omega \to \infty$ is needed to accommodate the different de Broglie wave lengths so that wave packets representing the real meson can be built and observed. In the vacuum meson state, no meson is observed and there is no need for $\Omega_c \to \Omega \to \infty$; $\Omega_c \to \Omega_{wvac}$ in (7.3.20b) suffices. The interpretation is that the vacuum meson state is not spread out widely and thinly but is limited to some finite and large volume Ω_{wvac} akin to the large Ω_c mentioned above (4.2.7). In this way, separation of variables in (3.1.5) still approximately hold.

$\Omega_c = \Omega_{wvac}$ here can be estimated as follows. The derivative term in (7.3.18) is (3.1.4) operating on (3.1.5) with $\underline{K}=0$ using (4.3.4). $\Omega_c = \Omega_{wvac}$=finite in (7.3.20b) implies that it has an $\underline{X}$ dependence so that the $\partial_{\underline{X}}$ term in (3.1.4) no longer vanishes but has a magnitude of $(\Omega_c)^{-1/3}$, which must be << the ∂_{X0} term $= -iE_{J0}$ and the $\underline{\partial}$ term $\approx 2d_h r_0$ according to (4.3.4) putting $r = r_0$. Thus, the criterion is $(\Omega_c)^{1/3} >> 7$ GeV^{-1} for pion and 2 GeV^{-1} for kaon and also 2 GeV^{-1} observing (4.6.1). It is marginally satisfied by (7.5.22b) for weak interactions below.

With (7.1.3b), (7.3.7b, 8, 14, 20), (7.3.23) below, (3.1.4), and (5.7.2), (7.3.18) is evaluated to be

$$\langle f|S'_{m3s}|i\rangle = g_l E_{pr}\sqrt{\frac{\Omega}{\Omega_{wvac}}}\int d^4Xd^4xW^{0*}_{rp}(X)\psi^2_0(r)\exp\left(-iE_{pr}X^0\right) \tag{7.3.21}$$

The same result is also obtained using (7.3.19) instead. In obtaining this result, it is noted that in (7.3.18) $\underline{W}_{rp}$ only couples to $\underline{\partial}$ which operates on $\psi_0^2(r)$. Such terms vanish upon integration over $\underline{x}$ because $\psi_0(r)$ vanishes at large $\underline{x}$. The decay amplitude (7.3.17) becomes

$$S_{fi} = i\frac{g_l}{\tau_0}\sqrt{\frac{\Omega}{\Omega_{wvac}}}\int d^4Xd^4xW_{rp}^{0*}(X)\psi_0^2(r)\exp\left(-iE_{pr}X^0\right) \tag{7.3.22}$$

Owing to (7.3.6) and (2.4.18), this relation holds for $\pi^{\pm}$ and kaons only. This result can also be obtained starting from either (7.1.9a) or (7.1.9b), without the addition operation mentioned above (7.3.3).

7.3.5. Amplitude for Decay to Pion and Gauge Boson

Turning to (7.3.7a), rs=11 and 22 each contains a π^0 according to (2.4.18) and (7.3.8). Consider at first $\pi^+ \to \pi^0 W_l^+$, which is the only possibility. The π^0 and W_l^+ can now move in opposite directions and both the singlet and triplet components of the wave functions of the π^0 enter. With (7.3.8), (3.1.1), and (3.1.5) adapted to the present case, the final states in (7.3.18) can be written as

$$\begin{aligned}\chi^{+}_{f1(11)\dot{e}a} &= -\chi^{+}_{f1(22)\dot{e}a} = \frac{1}{\sqrt{2}}\chi^{+}_{f1(\pi 0)\dot{e}a} = \frac{1}{\sqrt{2}}\left(\chi^{*}_{0f1\pi 0}\delta_{\dot{e}a} + \underline{\sigma}_{\dot{e}a}\underline{\chi}^{*}_{f1\pi 0}\right) \\ &= \frac{1}{\sqrt{2}}\left(\chi^{*}_{0\pi 0x}(\underline{x})\delta_{\dot{e}a} + \underline{\sigma}_{\dot{e}a}\underline{\chi}^{*}_{\pi 0x}(\underline{x})\right)\exp\left(iE_{f1\pi 0}X^0 - i\underline{K}_{f1\pi 0}\underline{X}\right), \quad \chi \to \psi\end{aligned} \tag{7.3.23}$$

Inserting these expressions with (7.3.8) into (7.3.18) and make use of (3.1.4) and (5.7.2), (7.3.17) for $\pi^+ \to \pi^0 W_l^+$ becomes after some calculation

$$\begin{aligned}S_{fi} &= \frac{i}{E_{\pi+}\tau_0}\left\langle \pi^0, W_l^- \middle| S'_{m3s} \middle| \pi^+ \right\rangle = \frac{-ig}{4E_{\pi+}\tau_0}\int d^4Xd^4x\exp\left(i\left(E_{f1\pi 0} - E_{\pi+}\right)X^0 - i\underline{K}_{f1\pi 0}\underline{X}\right) \\ &\times\left\{\begin{array}{l}\psi_0(r)W_l^{0+}\left[\left(E_{\pi+} + E_{f1\pi 0}\right)\left(\chi^{*}_{0\pi 0x} - \psi^{*}_{0\pi 0x}\right) - \underline{K}_{f1\pi 0}\left(\underline{\chi}^{*}_{\pi 0x} - \underline{\psi}^{*}_{\pi 0x}\right) + i2\underline{\partial}\left(\underline{\chi}^{*}_{\pi 0x} - \underline{\psi}^{*}_{\pi 0x}\right)\right] \\ -\psi_0(r)\underline{W}_l^{+}\left[\begin{array}{l}\left(E_{\pi+} + E_{f1\pi 0}\right)\left(\underline{\chi}^{*}_{\pi 0x} - \underline{\psi}^{*}_{\pi 0x}\right) - \underline{K}_{f1\pi 0}\left(\chi^{*}_{0\pi 0x} - \psi^{*}_{0\pi 0x}\right) + i2\underline{\partial}\left(\chi^{*}_{0\pi 0x} - \psi^{*}_{0\pi 0x}\right) \\ + 2\underline{\partial}\times\left(\underline{\chi}^{*}_{\pi 0x} + \underline{\psi}^{*}_{\pi 0x}\right) - i\left(\underline{\chi}^{*}_{\pi 0x} + \underline{\psi}^{*}_{\pi 0x}\right)\times\underline{K}_{f1\pi 0}\end{array}\right] \\ -2\left(\underline{\partial}\psi_0(r)\right)\left[\underline{W}_l^{+}\times\left(\underline{\chi}^{*}_{\pi 0x} + \underline{\psi}^{*}_{\pi 0x}\right) + i\underline{W}_l^{+}\left(\chi^{*}_{0\pi 0x} - \psi^{*}_{0\pi 0x}\right) - iW_l^{0+}\left(\underline{\chi}^{*}_{\pi 0x} - \underline{\psi}^{*}_{\pi 0x}\right)\right]\end{array}\right\}\end{aligned} \tag{7.3.24}$$

where the subscript x denotes the hidden relative space part of the wave functions, such as those in (5.7.6, 22a). The same result is obtained using (7.3.19) instead. Because the mass difference of π^+ and π^0 is small compared to the π^0 mass, π^0 will move very slowly so that $\underline{K}_{f1\pi 0}$ is of first order in ε_0 of (5.7.4). To zeroth order in ε_0, (5.7.6) holds for π^0. Further, (5.7.21) holds for π^0 so that the first order (5.7.22) applies. These renders that many terms in (7.3.24) drop out. The zeroth order $\chi_{0\pi 0}$ in (7.3.24) is given by (4.3.4a). The first order $\underline{\chi}_{\pi 0}$ has been considered in §5.7.4 where only one of the three possible solutions, the "decoupled" (5.7.28), has been found and will be adopted here. Now terms containing odd powers of $\hat{r}$ in (3.1.7b) also vanish upon integration over the angles. Equation (7.3.24) can now be simplified to

$$S_{fi} = \frac{ig}{2\Omega E_{\pi+}} \int d^4X \exp\left(i\left(E_{f1\pi 0} - E_{\pi+}\right)X^0 - i\underline{K}_{f1\pi 0}\underline{X}\right)$$
$$\times\left[\left(E_{\pi+} + E_{f1\pi 0}\right)W_I^{0+}(X) + \underline{K}_{f1\pi 0}\underline{W}_I^{+}(X)C_k\right] \tag{7.3.25a}$$

$$C_k = 1 - \frac{16\pi}{3}\alpha_{00}^2 d_h c_{k0} \approx -1.55$$

$$c_{k0} = \int_0^\infty dt t^2 \exp\left(-\frac{1}{2}d_h t^2\right)\left(\frac{\partial p_{10}(t)}{\partial t} - \frac{p_{10}(t)}{t} + d_h t p_{10}(t)\right) = 652.8 \text{ GeV}^{-5}$$

(7.3.25b)

where p_{10} is given by (5.7.28) and high accuracy in the computing was required. The first order term $\underline{K}\underline{W}_I^+$ will have different forms if the "coupled" solutions mentioned beneath (5.7.28) were used instead.

There are four kaon decays in (7.3.18), which together with (7.3.17) yields the following decay amplitudes analogous to (7.3.24);

$$K^- \to \pi^0 W_V^- : \quad S_{fi} = -\frac{ig_{4-7}}{4E_{K-}} \int d^4X d^3\underline{x} \exp\left(i\left(E_{f1\pi 0} - E_{K-}\right)X^0 - i\underline{K}_{f1\pi 0}\underline{X}\right)$$
$$\times\left\{\begin{array}{l} \psi_0(r)W_V^{0-}\left[\left(E_{K-} + E_{f1\pi 0}\right)\left(\chi^*_{0\pi 0x} - \psi^*_{0\pi 0x}\right) - \underline{K}_{f1\pi 0}\left(\underline{\chi}^*_{\pi 0x} - \underline{\psi}^*_{\pi 0x}\right) + i2\underline{\partial}\left(\underline{\chi}^*_{\pi 0x} - \underline{\psi}^*_{\pi 0x}\right)\right] \\ -\psi_0(r)\underline{W}_V^- \left[\begin{array}{l} \left(E_{K-} + E_{f1\pi 0}\right)\left(\underline{\chi}^*_{\pi 0x} - \underline{\psi}^*_{\pi 0x}\right) - \underline{K}_{f1\pi 0}\left(\chi^*_{0\pi 0x} - \psi^*_{0\pi 0x}\right) + i2\underline{\partial}\left(\chi^*_{0\pi 0x} - \psi^*_{0\pi 0x}\right) \\ + 2\underline{\partial} \times \left(\underline{\chi}^*_{\pi 0x} + \underline{\psi}^*_{\pi 0x}\right) - i\left(\underline{\chi}^*_{\pi 0x} + \underline{\psi}^*_{\pi 0x}\right) \times \underline{K}_{f1\pi 0} \end{array}\right] \\ -2\left(\underline{\partial}\psi_0(r)\right)\left[\underline{W}_V^- \times \left(\underline{\chi}^*_{\pi 0x} + \underline{\psi}^*_{\pi 0x}\right) + i\underline{W}_V^-\left(\chi^*_{0\pi 0x} - \psi^*_{0\pi 0x}\right) - iW_V^{0-}\left(\underline{\chi}^*_{\pi 0x} - \underline{\psi}^*_{\pi 0x}\right)\right] \end{array}\right\}$$

(7.3.26a)

$K^- \to \pi^- \overline{W}_U$: $S_{fi} = \sqrt{2} \times$ right of (7.3.26a) with $W_V^- \to \overline{W}_U$ and subscript ${}_{\pi 0} \to {}_{\pi -}$ (7.3.26b)

$\overline{K}^0 \to \pi^+ W_V^-$: $S_{fi} = \sqrt{2} \times$ right of (7.3.26a) with subscripts ${}_{K-} \to {}_{\overline{K}0}$ and ${}_{\pi 0} \to {}_{\pi +}$ (7.3.27a)

$\overline{K}^0 \to \pi^0 \overline{W}_U$: $S_{fi} = (-) \times$ right of (7.3.26a) with $W_V^- \to \overline{W}_U$ and subscript ${}_{K-} \to {}_{\overline{K}0}$ (7.3.27b)

The amplitudes of the conjugate decays are analogously obtained from the complex conjugate of (7.3.18) in (7.3.26, 27) and read

$K^+ \to \pi^0 W_V^+$, $\pi^+ W_U$:

$S_{fi} = -(7.3.26)$ with ${}_{K-} \to {}_{K+}$ and $W_V^- \to W_V^+$ (26a), $\overline{W}_U \to W_U$, ${}_{\pi -} \to {}_{\pi +}$ (26b)

(7.3.28)

$$K^0 \rightarrow \pi^- W_V^+ ,\ \pi^0 W_U :$$
$$S_{fi} = -(7.3.27) \text{ with } {}_{\bar{K}0} \rightarrow {}_{K0} \text{ and } W_V^- \rightarrow W_V^+ ,\ {}_{\pi+} \rightarrow {}_{\pi-} \text{ (27a)},\ \overline{W}_U \rightarrow W_U \text{ (27b)} \tag{7.3.29}$$

By (7.2.18), K^0 and $\bar{K}^0$ are decomposed to the physical $K^0{}_S$ and $K^0{}_L$. Since $K^0{}_S$ decays very fast and does not participate in the decays (7.3.27, 29) [P1], it is dropped here. The remaining $K^0{}_L$ couples to different intermediate gauge bosons to form three pion final states. Analogously, the W_U's degenerate into the physical Z boson. With (7.2.18, 21), (7.3.17, 29) go over to

$$K_L^0 \rightarrow \pi^0 Z :\quad S_{fi} = \pm \frac{1}{2\cos\vartheta_W} \text{right of (7.3.26a) with } W_V^- \rightarrow Z \text{ and subscript } {}_{K-} \rightarrow {}_{KL} \tag{7.3.30}$$

where the upper and lower signs come from (7.3.27b) and the second of (7.3.29), respectively. The subscript $_{KL}$ refers to $K^0{}_L$. Thus, (7.3.27a) and the first of (7.3.29) leads to

$$K_L^0 \rightarrow \pi^\pm W_V^\mp :\ S_{fi} = \pm \text{right of (7.3.26a) with subscripts } {}_{K-} \rightarrow {}_{KL},\ {}_{\pi 0} \rightarrow {}_{\pi\pm} \tag{7.3.31}$$

where the upper and lower indices refer to (7.3.27a) and the first of (7.3.29), respectively.

7.3.6. Amplitude for Decay to Two Gauge Bosons, Second Order Relations

The amplitudes obtained in §7.3.4-5 are of first order in g according to (7.3.2a) and contain one gauge boson. The treatment there can be modified to yield second order amplitudes containing two gauge bosons. First let

$$a_{pr}^{(1)}\left(X^0\right) \rightarrow a_{pr}^{(1)}\left(X^0\right) + a_{pr}^{(2)}\left(X^0\right) \tag{7.3.32}$$

in (7.3.1), where the superscript (2) denotes second order perturbation. Next, (7.3.3) is replaced by

$$S'_{m3d2} = S'_{m3s2} \tag{7.3.33}$$

where the subscript *2* denotes second order contributions. The left side is (7.3.4) with the superscripts (*1*)→(*2*). The right side of (7.3.33) is obtained from (7.3.5) in which

$$\partial_{II}, \partial_I \rightarrow i\tfrac{1}{4} g\left(\lambda_{l'}\right)_{ps} W_{l'}(X) \tag{7.3.34}$$

according to (7.1.4), supressing the internal indices. The results is

$$S'_{m3s2} = \int d^4 X dx^4 \frac{g_l g_{l'}}{16} \begin{Bmatrix} \chi^{+}_{0(rp)\dot{e}a}(\lambda_l)_{ps} W_l^{a\dot{b}}(\lambda_{l'})_{sq} W_{l'}^{f\dot{e}} \chi_{0(qr)\dot{b}f} \\ +\psi^{+d\dot{c}}_{0(rp)}(\lambda_l)_{ps} W_{l\dot{c}a}(\lambda_{l'})_{sq} W_{l'\dot{e}d} \psi^{a\dot{e}}_{0(qr)} \end{Bmatrix} \tag{7.3.35}$$

In general, there is also a second order source term of the form

$$i\tfrac{1}{4} g(\lambda_l) W_l(X) a^{(1)}(X^0) \tag{7.3.36}$$

that contributes to (7.3.35). For reasons given below, this term is dropped because it will not contribute to π^+, $K^+ \to \mu^+ \nu_\mu \gamma$ to be considered here.

The initial state (7.3.6) is the same. The final state (7.3.7b) is modified to

$$\langle f| = \langle P_{f(rr)}(0), W_{rq}, W_{qp}| = \langle 0, W_{rq}, W_{qp}| \tag{7.3.37}$$

The treatments of §7.3.3-4 and §7.2.3 can be taken over and (7.3.17) and (7.3.22) are modified to

$$\begin{aligned} S_{fi} &= i\frac{1}{E_{pr}\tau_0}\langle f|S'_{m3s2}|i\rangle \\ &= -\frac{ge}{2E_{pr}\tau_0}\sqrt{\frac{\Omega}{\Omega_{wvac}}}\int d^4 X d^4 x \psi_0^2(r) \underline{A}_{rq}(X) \underline{W}_{qp}(X) \exp(-iE_{pr}X^0) \end{aligned} \tag{7.3.38}$$

where (7.1.4), (7.2.14) and (7.2.1b) have been employed.

By (7.3.13) and (7.3.22), $a^{(1)}(X)$ in (7.3.36) is proportional to $W^0_{qp}(X)$. $(\lambda_l)W_l(X)$ in (7.3.36) becomes $\underline{A}_{rq}(X)$ in (7.3.38) which does not couple to the singlet $W^0_{qp}(X)$. Therefore, (7.3.36) does not contribute here.

7.4. Decay Amplitude for Gauge Bosons → Lepton Pair and Photon

7.4.1. General Considerations

Turn now to stage II of the decay mentioned in §7.1.1, i.e., the decay of the gauge bosons present in the decay amplitudes S_{fi} in the last two paragraphs. The gauge bosons can also decay into two types of end products, namely, a pair of leptons contained in S_L of (7.2.13) and a pair of pions contained in $S_{m\pi}$ in (7.1.1).

Further, (7.1.2) can by means of (7.1.5b), (7.2.1a, 3a) and (C4-5) be transformed to

$$S_{GB}=-\frac{1}{4}\int d^4X\left\{\begin{array}{l}\partial_{X\dot{a}b}W_I^{+c\dot{d}}\left(\partial_X^{b\dot{a}}W^-_{I\dot{d}c}-\partial_{X\dot{d}c}W_I^{-b\dot{a}}\right)+\partial_{X\dot{a}b}W_V^{+c\dot{d}}\left(\partial_X^{b\dot{a}}W^-_{V\dot{d}c}-\partial_{X\dot{d}c}W_V^{-b\dot{a}}\right)\\ +\partial_{X\dot{a}b}\overline{W}_U^{c\dot{d}}\left(\partial_X^{b\dot{a}}W_{U\dot{d}c}-\partial_{X\dot{d}c}W_U^{b\dot{a}}\right)\\ +\frac{1}{2}\partial_{X\dot{a}b}Z^{c\dot{d}}\left(\partial_X^{b\dot{a}}Z_{\dot{d}c}-\partial_{X\dot{d}c}Z^{b\dot{a}}\right)+\frac{1}{2}\partial_{X\dot{a}b}A^{c\dot{d}}\left(\partial_X^{b\dot{a}}A_{\dot{d}c}-\partial_{X\dot{d}c}A^{b\dot{a}}\right)\end{array}\right\}$$
$$+g(.....) \tag{7.4.1}$$

The last term denotes terms containing g, which by (7.2.7) should actually be generalized to g_I. A term containing g_I will break the SU(3) symmetry of (7.4.1). Such a generalization will complicate the calculations but will have no effect on the results below because these g terms will contribute to order g^2(see (7.4.2) below) and can be neglected.

The gauge boson wave functions are obtained by varying the second order part of the total action S_{T3} with respect to W, Z or A.

7.4.2. Generation of Mass of Charged Gauge Boson

There are four charged bosons, $W_I^{\pm}$ and $W_V^{\pm}$. The W_V^+ case will be worked out below. The results obtained also hold for the W_V^- case by appropriate complex conjugation. The $W_I^{\pm}$ cases are the same as the $W_V^{\pm}$ cases by virtue of (7.2.7, 20).

Variations of (7.4.1) with respect to $W_I^{-a\dot{b}}$ defined in (7.1.5b) yields

$$\delta S_{GB}/\delta W_I^{-a\dot{b}}=\frac{1}{2}\Box W^+_{I\dot{b}a}-\frac{1}{4}\partial_{X\dot{b}a}\left(\partial_X^{c\dot{d}}W^+_{I\dot{d}c}\right)+\frac{1}{2}g^2V_{C\dot{b}a}\left(W_I^+\right) \tag{7.4.2a}$$

$$g^2V_{C\dot{b}a}\left(W_I^+\right)=g^2\left(\delta_{\dot{b}a}V_C^0\left(W_I^+\right)+\underline{\sigma}_{\dot{b}a}\underline{V}_C\left(W_I^+\right)\right) \tag{7.4.2b}$$

$$\begin{array}{l}V_C^0\left(W_I^+\right)=W_I^{0+}\left(\underline{W}_I^+\underline{W}_I^-\right)-W_I^{0-}\left(\underline{W}_I^+\right)^2\\ \underline{V}_C\left(W_I^+\right)=-\underline{W}_I^+\left(W_I^{0+}W_I^{0-}-\left(\underline{W}_I^+\underline{W}_I^-\right)\right)+\underline{W}_I^-\left(\left(W_I^{0+}\right)^2-\left(\underline{W}_I^+\right)^2\right)\end{array} \tag{7.4.2c}$$

With (7.1.4) and (7.2.7), the second order part of S_{m3} of (7.1.8) containing W_V^+ and W_V^- are coupled to a rest frame $K^+(K^-)$ characterized by the flavor indices 13(31) in the next equation. Applying (7.2.20) and vary this part with respect to $W_I^-(W_I^+)$ yields

$$\delta S_{m3}/\delta W_I^{\pm a\dot{b}}\rightarrow-\frac{g^2}{16}\int d^4xW_I^{\mp f\dot{e}}\left[\begin{array}{l}\left(\chi^*_{0(13)\dot{e}a}\chi_{0(31)\dot{b}f}+\chi^*_{0(31)\dot{b}f}\chi_{0(13)\dot{e}a}+\chi^*_0\leftrightarrow\chi_0\right)\\ +\left(\psi_{0(13)\dot{e}a}\psi^*_{0(31)\dot{b}f}+\psi_{0(31)\dot{b}f}\psi^*_{0(13)\dot{e}a}+\psi^*_0\leftrightarrow\psi_0\right)\end{array}\right] \tag{7.4.3a}$$

If $K^+(K^-)$ is replaced by $\pi^+(\pi^-)$, this relation becomes

$$\delta S_{m3}/\delta W_I^{\pm a\dot{b}}=(7.4.3a)\ \text{with index } 3\rightarrow 2 \tag{7.4.3b}$$

Inserting (7.3.14) and (4.3.4a) into (7.4.3) yields

$$\delta S_{m3} / \delta W_I^{\pm a\dot{b}} \to -\frac{g^2}{2}\frac{\tau_0}{\Omega} W_I^{\mp b\dot{a}} \tag{7.4.4}$$

Note that this relation is not in the Lorentz covariant form because only the time components of the χ's in (7.4.3a) are used. The same variation of (7.2.13) yields

$$\delta S_L / \delta W_I^{-a\dot{b}} \to \frac{g}{2\sqrt{2}} \psi_{\nu L\dot{b}} \psi_{La} \tag{7.4.5}$$

In (7.4.3-5), source terms not containing $W_I^{\pm}$ have been dropped.

Variation of (7.1.1) with respect to $W_I^{-a\dot{b}}$ gives the equation of motion for $W_{I\dot{b}a}^{+}$. With (7.4.2, 4, 5), this variation yields,

$$\Box W_{I\dot{b}a}^{+} - \tfrac{1}{2}\partial_{X\dot{b}a}\left(\partial_X^{c\dot{d}} W_{I\dot{d}c}^{+}\right) + g^2 V_{C\dot{b}a}\left(W_I^{+}\right) - M_W^2 W_I^{+b\dot{a}} = -\frac{g}{\sqrt{2}} \psi_{\nu L\dot{b}} \psi_{La} \tag{7.4.6a}$$

where

$$M_W^2 = g^2 \frac{\tau_0}{\Omega} = \frac{\infty}{\infty} \tag{7.4.6b}$$

is the square of the mass of the charged gauge boson [H13 §3.4] and is by (7.3.16) a ratio ∞/∞=finite similar to M_{uI}^2 in (6.2.12). It is seen that the origin of the gauge boson mass lies in the presence of the relative time x^0 in a Lorentz covariant formulation. This relative time is absent in conventional, local theories, which call for the unseen Higgs bosons for mass generation. This will be discussed further in §7.5.4 and §7.6.2 below. That Higgs boson is not needed to generate M_W was first shown in [H8 Sec. 6].

The real meson wave function (7.3.14) used in (7.4.4) to get (7.4.6b) can be replaced by the vacuum state meson wave function (7.3.20), which can be regarded as providing a background condensate for generation of M_W playing the role of the Higgs condensate in the standard model. Since this vacuum state meson (7.3.20) is massless, it avoids the problem encountered by the massive Higgs condensate in e. g. cosmology [W6 p247].

An analog to (7.4.6b) is

$$\frac{\sqrt[3]{\Omega} \to \infty}{X^0 \to \infty} \to 1 = \text{light speed } c \text{ in natural unit} \tag{7.4.6c}$$

where Ω is the normalization volume of the electromagnetic field in (6.4.6) and X^0 is the laboratory time.

Contracting (7.4.6a) by $\delta^{a\dot{b}}$ and $\underline{\sigma}^{a\dot{b}}$ yields

$$-\frac{\partial}{\partial X^0}\left(\frac{\partial}{\partial \underline{X}}\underline{W}_I^+\right)+g^2V_C^0\left(W_I^+\right)-M_W^2W_I^{0+}=-\frac{g}{2\sqrt{2}}\psi_{\nu L\dot{a}}\Psi_{La} \tag{7.4.7a}$$

$$\Box\underline{W}_I^+ +\frac{\partial}{\partial \underline{X}}\left(\frac{\partial}{\partial X^0}W_I^{0+}+\frac{\partial}{\partial \underline{X}}\underline{W}_I^+\right)+g^2\underline{V}_C\left(W_I^+\right)+M_W^2\underline{W}_I^+=-\frac{g}{2\sqrt{2}}\underline{\sigma}^{a\dot{b}}\psi_{\nu L\dot{b}}\Psi_{La} \tag{7.4.7b}$$

Choose $\vartheta_4(X)-i\,\vartheta_5(X)$ in (7.1.7b) such that (7.1.7d) via (7.2.20) leads to the Coulomb gauge

$$\left(\partial/\partial\underline{X}\right)\underline{W}_I^+=0$$

Further, the ordering (7.3.2b) adopted relegates the nonlinear g^2V_C terms in (7.4.6-7) to higher order, by two, relative to the rest of the terms there. In the absence of the lepton source terms on the right of (7.4.7), it yields to lowest order

$$W_I^{0+}=0 \tag{7.4.8a}$$

$$\Box\underline{W}_I^+ +M_W^2\underline{W}_I^+=0 \tag{7.4.8b}$$

$\underline{W}_I^-$ is identified with the observed charged gauge boson $\underline{W}$ [P1] with the mass

$$M_W=80.379\ \text{GeV} \tag{7.4.9}$$

which, like the light velocity c in (7.4.6c), may be considered as a fundamental constant instead of the Fermi constant in (7.4.29) below. The time component W_I^{0+} associated with $\underline{W}_I^+$ in (7.4.8) vanishes in agreement with the nonobservation of such a singlet charged gauge boson W^0 accompanying the observed triplet $\underline{W}$. If Higgs boson were used to generate the gauge boson mass, such a singlet W^0 with same mass (7.4.9) should also be seen, contrary to observation, as will be discussed in §7.6.2 below.

If the Lorentz gauge

$$\partial_X^{c\dot{d}}W_{I\dot{d}c}^+=0$$

were employed, (7.4.8b) remains unchanged and (7.4.8a) becomes

$$\Box W_I^{0+}-M_W^2W_I^{0+}=0$$

This implies that W_I^{0+} has an imaginary mass of (7.4.9) and therefore must vanish and (7.4.8a) remains in effect valid.

The energy and momentum of the virtual gauge bosons in (7.4.7) are determined by those of the lepton pair and are generally much smaller than the mass (7.4.9) and can therefore be dropped. Hence, (7.4.7) reduces to

$$M_W^2 W_I^{0+} = \frac{g}{2\sqrt{2}} \psi_{La}^{(-)} \psi_{\nu L\dot{a}}^{(+)} \tag{7.4.10a}$$

$$M_W^2 \underline{W}_I^{+} = -\frac{g}{2\sqrt{2}} \underline{\sigma}^{b\dot{a}} \psi_{\nu L\dot{a}}^{(+)} \psi_{Lb}^{(-)} \tag{7.4.10b}$$

While the triplet $\underline{W}_I^+$ can exist freely and hence be seen, as is shown in (7.4.8b), it can also be a virtual intermediate state as is seen in (7.4.10b). On the other hand, the singlet W_I^{0+} cannot be observed as is shown in (7.4.8a), but can only be a charged, virtual intermediate singlet as is seen in (7.4.10a).

As was pointed out in the beginning of §7.4.2, the above results for the charged kaons also holds for the charged pions which enter (7.4.3b). One can see that (7.4.10) is not obtainable with the ordering (7.3.2a) for which the g^2V_C terms are of the same order as the other terms in (7.4.7) and cannot be neglected. Retaining this nonlinear term practically excludes any explicit and simple solution of the form (7.4.10).

Note that (7.4.4, 6a) are no longer Lorentz covariant because the triplet part of the meson wave functions vanish for rest frame mesons (7.3.14). This has led to that the signs in front of M_W^2 in (7.4.7a) and (7.4.7b) are different. Thus, M_W^2 there may be considered as a 4×4 diagonal matrix with the element $-M_W^2$ for the time component and $+M_W^2$ for the spatial components. For a meson in motion, both the singlet and triplet wave functions in (5.7.3) would be present in (7.4.3) and the simple forms of (7.4.4, 6a) are lost. The 4×4 matrix for M_W^2 above is no longer diagonal and mixes the four W_I^- components, leading to higher order equations for them. Further, the elements of this nondiagonal matrix cannot be evaluated presently because wave functions for mesons in motion are unknown, except approximately for slowly moving mesons, as was considered in Sec. 5.7.

The present situation therefore differs basically from that in which the massive gauge bosons are generated by Higgs boson. The so-generated M_{WH}^2 is a scalar given by (7.6.6b) below and is independent of an eventual motion of the Higgs boson.

7.4.3. Decay of Charged Gauge Boson into Lepton Pair

The plane wave solutions of freely moving leptons satisfy (A3) with I_B=0 and the first of (A15). The solutions (A13, A14) can be put in terms of the spinors of (C11),

$$\psi_{\nu L\dot{b}}^{(+)} = \frac{1}{\sqrt{\Omega_L}} u_{\nu L\dot{b}}^{(+)} \exp\left(iE_{\nu L} X^0 - i\underline{K}_{\nu L}\underline{X}\right)$$

$$\begin{pmatrix} u_{\nu L\dot{1}}^{(+)} \\ u_{\nu L\dot{2}}^{(+)} \end{pmatrix} = \frac{1}{\sqrt{2E_{\nu L}}}\left[\begin{pmatrix} K_{\nu L1} - iK_{\nu L2} \\ E_{\nu L} - K_{\nu L3} \end{pmatrix}, \begin{pmatrix} -E_{\nu L} - K_{\nu L3} \\ -K_{\nu L1} - iK_{\nu L2} \end{pmatrix}\right] \tag{7.4.11a}$$

$$\psi_{Lb}^{(-)} = \frac{1}{\sqrt{\Omega_L}} u_{Lb}^{(-)} \exp\left(iE_L X^0 + i\underline{K}_L\underline{X}\right)$$

$$\begin{pmatrix} u_{L1}^{(-)} \\ u_{L2}^{(-)} \end{pmatrix} = \frac{1}{\sqrt{2E_L(E_L + M_L)}}\left[\begin{pmatrix} E_L + M_L - K_{L3} \\ -K_{L1} + iK_{L2} \end{pmatrix}, \begin{pmatrix} -K_{L1} - iK_{L2} \\ E_L + M_L + K_{L3} \end{pmatrix}\right] \tag{7.4.11b}$$

where the superscripts (+) and (–) denote positive and negative energy, respectively. Negative energy solutions are chosen for the lepton with mass M_L. Ω_L is a large normalization volume for the leptons. The comma in the brackets separates the spin up and spin down solutions.

Inserting (7.4.6b, 11) into (7.4.10a) yields

$$gW_l^{0+} = \frac{1}{2\sqrt{2}}\frac{\Omega}{\tau_0}\frac{1}{\Omega_L} u_{La}^{(-)} u_{\nu L\dot{a}}^{(+)} \exp\left(i\left(E_{\nu L} + E_L\right)X^0 - i\left(\underline{K}_{\nu L} - \underline{K}_L\right)\underline{X}\right) \tag{7.4.11c}$$

Noting (7.3.9b), (7.4.11c) is inserted into (7.3.22). Carrying out the integration over X^0, it leads to

$$\langle f| = \langle 0, W| = \langle 0, L^{(-)}\nu_L^{(+)}|, \qquad |i\rangle = |\pi^+ \text{ or } K^+\rangle \tag{7.4.12}$$

$$S_{fi} = i\frac{\pi}{2\sqrt{2}}\frac{\Omega}{\tau_0}\frac{1}{\tau_0\Omega_L}\delta\left(E_L + E_{\nu L} - E_{pr}\right)u_{La}^{(-)}u_{\nu L\dot{a}}^{(+)}I_{L\nu} \tag{7.4.13a}$$

$$I_{L\nu} = \int d^3\underline{X}d^4x\sqrt{\frac{\Omega}{\Omega_{wvac}}}\,\psi_0^2(r)\exp\left(i\left(\underline{K}_L - \underline{K}_{\nu L}\right)\underline{X}\right) \tag{7.4.13b}$$

These results stem from the *c.c.* term in (7.1.8b). Here, $L^{(-)}$ and $\nu_L^{(+)}$ refer to the indices in (7.4.11) characterizing the final lepton states. Further, the ψ's of (7.4.11) have been tacitly quantized so that the final state of (7.4.12) picks out the appropriate lepton wave functions in (7.4.10, 13). This is analogous to that the meson wave function (7.3.1) has been quantized in connection with (7.3.10a).

7.4.4. Neutral Gauge Boson Mass and Decay into Lepton Pair

Consider next the decay of the W_U and $\bar{W}_U$ bosons via the degeneracy (7.2.21) to the Z boson. By means of (7.4.1) and (7.2.13), the equivalent of (7.4.2) and (7.4.5) become

$$\frac{\delta S_{GB}}{\delta Z^{a\dot{b}}} \to \frac{1}{4}\Box Z_{\dot{b}a} - \frac{1}{8}\partial_{X\dot{b}a}\left(\partial_X^{c\dot{d}} Z_{\dot{d}c}\right) - g^2(\ldots) \tag{7.4.14}$$

$$\frac{\delta S_L}{\delta Z^{a\dot{b}}} \to \frac{g}{8\cos\vartheta_W}\left(2\psi_{\nu La}\psi_{\nu L\dot{b}} - 2\cos 2\vartheta_W \psi_{La}\psi_{L\dot{b}} + 4\sin^2\vartheta_W \chi_{La}\chi_{L\dot{b}}\right) \tag{7.4.15}$$

where the last term in (7.4.14) denotes terms of order g^2.

Contribution from S_{m3} is similar to that of (7.4.3a). With (7.1.4) and (7.2.7), the second order part of S_{m3} of (7.1.8) containing W_U and $\bar{W}_U$ are coupled to K^0 or $\bar{K}^0$ characterized by the subscripts (23) and (32) to χ and ψ there. Apply the degeneration (7.2.21) to this part and vary it with respect to $Z^{a\dot{b}}$ yields the analog of (7.4.3a)

$$\begin{aligned}\frac{\delta S_{m3}}{\delta Z^{a\dot{b}}} &\to -\frac{g^2}{32\cos^2\vartheta_W}\int d^4x Z^{f\dot{e}}\begin{bmatrix}\left(\chi^*_{0(23)\dot{e}a}\chi_{0(23)\dot{b}f} + \chi^*_{0(32)\dot{b}f}\chi_{0(32)\dot{e}a} + \chi_0^* \leftrightarrow \chi_0\right)\\ +\left(\psi_{0(32)\dot{e}a}\psi^*_{0(32)\dot{b}f} + \psi_{0(23)\dot{b}f}\psi^*_{0(23)\dot{e}a} + \psi_0^* \leftrightarrow \psi_0\right)\end{bmatrix}\\ &= -\frac{g^2}{4\cos^2\vartheta_W}\frac{\tau_0}{\Omega}Z^{b\dot{a}}\end{aligned} \tag{7.4.16}$$

where the procedure intervening (7.4.3b) and (7.4.4) has been applied. Similarly, source terms in (7.4.14-15) not containing Z have been dropped. Inserting (7.4.14-16) into the variation of (7.1.1) with respect to $Z^{a\dot{b}}$ yields the analog of (7.4.6),

$$\begin{aligned}&\Box Z_{\dot{b}a} - \tfrac{1}{2}\partial_{X\dot{b}a}\left(\partial_X^{c\dot{d}} Z_{\dot{d}c}\right) + g^2 V_{Z\dot{b}a}(Z) - M_Z^2 Z^{b\dot{a}}\\ &= -\frac{g}{2\cos\vartheta_W}\left(2\psi^{(+)}_{\nu L\dot{b}}\psi^{(-)}_{\nu La} - 2\cos 2\vartheta_W \psi^{(+)}_{L\dot{b}}\psi^{(-)}_{La} + 4\sin^2\vartheta_W \chi^{(-)}_{L\dot{b}}\chi^{(+)}_{La}\right)\end{aligned} \tag{7.4.17a}$$

$$M_Z^2 = \frac{1}{\cos^2\vartheta_W}g^2\frac{\tau_0}{\Omega} = \frac{M_W^2}{\cos^2\vartheta_W} \tag{7.4.17b}$$

where g^2V_Z corresponds to (7.4.2b, 2c) and is a modified form of it.

Following the steps intervening (7.4.7) and (7.4.10), (7.4.17a) leads to the analog of (7.4.8),

$$Z^0 = 0 \tag{7.4.18a}$$

$$\Box \underline{Z} + M_Z^2 \underline{Z} = 0 \tag{7.4.18b}$$

Here, $\underline{Z}$ is identified with the neutral gauge boson Z [P1] with the mass

$$M_Z = \frac{M_W}{\cos\vartheta_W} = 91.02\ \text{GeV} \tag{7.4.18c}$$

This mass is close to the measured 91.1876 GeV [P1], differing from it by only −0.18%. If the SU(3) symmetry breaking is removed, (7.2.3b) replaces (7.2.12) and $M_Z=2M_W/\sqrt{3}=92.81$ GeV which is +1.8% off.

The time component Z^0 is also neutral and has the same mass M_Z. Analogous to W_I^{0+} in (7.4.8a) and (7.4.10a), it cannot exist freely in agreement with the nonobservation of such a singlet neutral gauge boson Z^0. Just like W_I^{0+} in (7.4.10a), however, Z^0 can be present as a virtual intermediary neutral gauge boson.

In passing, it is noted that variation of S_{m3} (7.1.8) using (7.2.14) with respect to the electromagnetic field A, analogous to (7.4.16), will give rise to a mass M_A to the A field of the same magnitude as M_Z, M_W, contrary to experience. This apparent difficulty is removed if we note that only the fields entering the decay amplitudes S_{fi} of (7.3.17-19) are of interest. Since A does not enter these S_{fi}, it may be dropped in S_T (7.1.1) and variation of it with respect to A gives zero; there is no contradiction to data.

In (7.4.17a), $\psi_{La}^{(-)}$ and $\psi_{\nu L\dot{b}}^{(+)}$ have been given in (7.4.11). The remaining wave functions in (7.4.17a) are obtained from (A13), (A14) and (C11) in the same way as (7.4.11) was. They read

$$\psi_{\nu La}^{(-)} = \frac{1}{\sqrt{\Omega_L}} u_{\nu La}^{(-)} \exp\left(iE_{\nu L}X^0 + i\underline{K}_{\nu L}\underline{X}\right)$$

$$\begin{pmatrix} u_{\nu L1}^{(-)} \\ u_{\nu L2}^{(-)} \end{pmatrix} = \frac{1}{\sqrt{2E_{\nu L}}}\left[\begin{pmatrix} E_{\nu L} - K_{\nu L3} \\ -K_{\nu L1} + iK_{\nu L2} \end{pmatrix}, \begin{pmatrix} -K_{\nu L1} - iK_{\nu L2} \\ E_{\nu L} + K_{\nu L3} \end{pmatrix}\right] \tag{7.4.19a}$$

$$\psi_{L\dot{b}}^{(+)} = \frac{1}{\sqrt{\Omega_L}} u_{L\dot{b}}^{(+)} \exp\left(iE_L^{(+)}X^0 - i\underline{K}_L^{(+)}\underline{X}\right)$$

$$\begin{pmatrix} u_{L\dot{1}}^{(+)} \\ u_{L\dot{2}}^{(+)} \end{pmatrix} = \frac{1}{\sqrt{2E_L^{(+)}\left(E_L^{(+)} + M_L\right)}}\left[\begin{pmatrix} K_{L1}^{(+)} - iK_{L2}^{(+)} \\ E_L^{(+)} + M_L - K_{L3}^{(+)} \end{pmatrix}, \begin{pmatrix} -E_L^{(+)} - M_L - K_{L3}^{(+)} \\ -K_{L1}^{(+)} - iK_{L2}^{(+)} \end{pmatrix}\right] \tag{7.4.19b}$$

$$\chi_{L\dot{b}}^{(-)} = \frac{1}{\sqrt{\Omega_L}} v_{L\dot{b}}^{(-)} \exp\left(iE_L X^0 + i\underline{K}_L\underline{X}\right)$$

$$\begin{pmatrix} v_{L\dot{1}}^{(-)} \\ v_{L\dot{2}}^{(-)} \end{pmatrix} = \frac{1}{\sqrt{2E_L\left(E_L + M_L\right)}}\left[\begin{pmatrix} -K_{L1} + iK_{L2} \\ E_L + M_L + K_{L3} \end{pmatrix}, \begin{pmatrix} -E_L - M_L + K_{L3} \\ K_{L1} + iK_{L2} \end{pmatrix}\right] \tag{7.4.20a}$$

$$\chi_{La}^{(+)} = \frac{1}{\sqrt{\Omega_L}} v_{La}^{(+)} \exp\left(iE_L^{(+)} X^0 - i\underline{K}_L^{(+)} \underline{X}\right)$$

$$\begin{pmatrix} v_{L1}^{(+)} \\ v_{L2}^{(+)} \end{pmatrix} = \frac{1}{\sqrt{2E_L^{(+)}\left(E_L^{(+)} + M_L\right)}} \left[\begin{pmatrix} E_L^{(+)} + M_L + K_{L3}^{(+)} \\ K_{L1}^{(+)} - iK_{L2}^{(+)} \end{pmatrix}, \begin{pmatrix} K_{L1}^{(+)} + iK_{L2}^{(+)} \\ E_L^{(+)} + M_L - K_{L3}^{(+)} \end{pmatrix} \right] \tag{7.4.20b}$$

A superscript (+) has been introduced into the right sides of (7.4.19b) and (7.4.20b) in order to distinguish these E and K from the corresponding quantities in (7.4.11b) and (7.4.20a), respectively. It is also tacitly attached to $E_{\nu L}$ and $\underline{K}_{\nu L}$ in (7.4.11a) for applications here.

Following the steps of the last paragraph and dropping the first three terms in (7.4.17a), contracting it by $\delta^{a\dot{b}}$ and making use of (7.4.19-20) yields the equivalent of (7.4.11c),

$$gZ^0 = \frac{\cos\vartheta_W}{2} \frac{\Omega}{\tau_0} \frac{1}{\Omega_L} \begin{pmatrix} 2u_{\nu L\dot{a}}^{(+)} u_{\nu La}^{(-)} \exp\left(i\left(E_{\nu L}^{(+)} + E_{\nu L}\right)X^0 - i\left(\underline{K}_{\nu L}^{(+)} - \underline{K}_{\nu L}\right)\underline{X}\right) \\ +\left(4\sin^2\vartheta_W v_{L\dot{a}}^{(-)} v_{La}^{(+)} - 2\cos 2\vartheta_W u_{La}^{(-)} u_{L\dot{a}}^{(+)}\right) \\ \times \exp\left(i\left(E_L^{(+)} + E_L\right)X^0 - i\left(\underline{K}_L^{(+)} - \underline{K}_L\right)\underline{X}\right) \end{pmatrix} \tag{7.4.21}$$

where the choices of positive and negative energy solutions are the same as those given in (7.4.11c). Note that the superscript *0* here refers to the time component of a four vector and not charge.

For *pr=23* and *32*, (7.3.22) refers to the amplitudes for K^0 coupled to $\bar{W}_U{}^0$ and $\bar{K}^0$ to $W_U{}^0$, respectively. With (7.2.21-22) and (7.4.21), it is found to be

$$S_{fi}\left(K^0, \overline{K}^0 \to Z^0 \to L^+L^-\right)$$
$$= i\frac{\pi}{2\sqrt{2}} \frac{\Omega}{\tau_0} \frac{1}{\tau_0 \Omega_L} \delta\left(E_L^{(+)} + E_L - E_{Ks}\right)\left(4\sin^2\vartheta_W v_{La}^{(+)} v_{L\dot{a}}^{(-)} - 2\cos 2\vartheta_W u_{La}^{(-)} u_{L\dot{a}}^{(+)}\right) I_{LL} \tag{7.4.22}$$

$$I_{LL} = \int d^3\underline{X} d^4x \sqrt{\frac{\Omega}{\Omega_{wvac}}} \psi_0^2(r) \exp\left(i\left(\underline{K}_L - \underline{K}_L^{(+)}\right)\underline{X}\right) \tag{7.4.23}$$

which is the analog of (7.4.13).

For Z^0 decaying into a pair of neutrinos, simplification can already be achieved here if one anticipates

$$\underline{K}_{\nu L}^{(+)} = \underline{K}_{\nu L} \tag{7.4.24}$$

which is obvious for this two body final state but is formally obtained first in the next section after integrations over $\underline{K}_{\nu L}^{(+)}$ and $\underline{K}_{\nu L}$. It then follows that $E_{\nu L}^{(+)}=E_{\nu L}=|\underline{K}_{\nu L}|$. With these results, it is easily seen that $u_{\nu L\dot{a}}^{(+)}u_{\nu La}^{(-)}$ in (7.4.21) vanishes for any spin combination. Therefore,

$$S_{fi}\left(K^0, \overline{K}^0 \to Z^0 \to \nu_L\overline{\nu}_L\right)=0 \qquad (7.4.25)$$

7.4.5. Decay Amplitude for $\pi^+ \to \pi^0 e+\nu_e$

This decay, also called pion beta decay, has been treated long ago in the literature based upon the so-called conserved vector current (CVC) hypothesis. Källén [K3 (14.94)] gives the phenomenological decay amplitude

$$\begin{aligned} S_{fi(K)}\left(\pi^+ \to \pi^0 e^+ \nu_e\right) &= -i\int dX^0 \left\langle \pi^0, e^+, \nu_e \left|\delta H_1\right| \pi^+\right\rangle = i\frac{G}{2\Omega\Omega_L}\frac{1}{\sqrt{E_{\pi+}E_{f1\pi0}}} \\ &\times \left\{\left(k_{\mu\pi+}+k_{\mu f1\pi0}\right)\overline{u}_{\nu e}^{(+)}\left(\underline{K}_{\nu e}\right)\left(1-\gamma_5\right)\gamma_\mu u_e^{(-)}\left(-\underline{K}_e\right)\right\} \\ &\times \int d^4X \exp\left(i\left(K_{f1\pi0}^\mu + K_e^\mu + K_{\nu e}^\mu - K_{\pi+}^\mu\right)X_\mu\right) \end{aligned} \qquad (7.4.26)$$

where $k_\mu=(\underline{K}, iE)$, u and γ are given in the notation of [K3 p514-18] and G is the Fermi constant.

In the present theory, no additional assumption like the CVC hypothesis above is required. For $L=e$, (7.4.10) become

$$W_I^{0+} = \frac{g}{2\sqrt{2}}\frac{1}{M_W^2}\psi_{ea}^{(-)}\psi_{\nu e\dot{a}}^{(+)} \qquad (7.4.27a)$$

$$\underline{W}_I^{+} = -\frac{g}{2\sqrt{2}}\frac{1}{M_W^2}\underline{\sigma}^{b\dot{a}}\psi_{eb}^{(-)}\psi_{\nu e\dot{a}}^{(+)} \qquad (7.4.27b)$$

Noting (7.4.7), let

$$\begin{aligned} \psi_{\nu e\dot{a}}^{(+)} &= \frac{1}{\sqrt{\Omega_L}}u_{\nu e\dot{a}}^{(+)}\left(\underline{K}_{\nu e}\right)\exp\left(iE_{\nu e}X^0 - i\underline{K}_{\nu e}\underline{X}\right) \\ \psi_{eb}^{(-)} &= \frac{1}{\sqrt{\Omega_L}}u_{eb}^{(-)}\left(-\underline{K}_e\right)\exp\left(iE_eX^0 - i\underline{K}_e\underline{X}\right) \end{aligned} \qquad (7.4.28)$$

where the sign of $\underline{K}_e$ has been chosen to be opposite to that of $\underline{K}_L$ in (7.4.13) for the final state <f1|=<0, W|. The Fermi constant is related to M_W^2 by [L5 (22.83), P1]

$$G = \frac{1}{4\sqrt{2}}\frac{g^2}{M_W^2} = 1.1664 \times 10^{-5}\ \text{GeV}^{-2} \tag{7.4.29a}$$

in the present theory; this expression can be combined with (7.4.6b) to give

$$G = \frac{1}{4\sqrt{2}}\frac{\Omega}{\tau_0} \tag{7.4.29b}$$

Thus, the Fermi constant is a ratio ∞/∞ = finite and is a fundamental constant. Alternatively, M_W of (7.4.6b, 9) can be taken as a fundamental constant instead. Inserting (7.4.28, 29a) into (7.4.27) and the resulting expressions into (7.3.25), one gets

$$\begin{aligned} S_{fi}\left(\pi^+ \to \pi^0 e^+ \nu_e\right) &= i\frac{G}{2\Omega\Omega_L}\frac{1}{E_{\pi+}}\left\{\begin{matrix}\left(E_{\pi+} + E_{f1\pi 0}\right)u_{\nu e\dot{a}}^{(+)}\left(\underline{K}_{\nu e}\right)u_{ea}^{(-)}\left(-\underline{K}_e\right) \\ -C_k \underline{K}_{f1\pi 0}\underline{\sigma}^{a\dot{b}}u_{ea}^{(-)}\left(-\underline{K}_e\right)u_{\nu e\dot{b}}^{(+)}\left(\underline{K}_{\nu e}\right)\end{matrix}\right\} \\ &\times \int d^4X \exp\left(i\left(E_{\nu e} + E_e + E_{f1\pi 0} - E_{\pi+}\right)X^0 - i\left(\underline{K}_{\nu e} + \underline{K}_e + \underline{K}_{f1\pi 0}\right)\underline{X}\right) \end{aligned} \tag{7.4.30}$$

where the correction factor $\propto c_{k0}$ in (7.3.25) has been dropped. By working out the braced expression in (7.4.30) by means of (7.4.11) and compared it to the braced expression in (7.4.26) evaluated by means of (A2-5, A2-6, A2-24, A2-25) of [K3], it turns out that the both results are equal. With this result, (7.4.30) and (7.4.26) are related by

$$S_{fi}\left(\pi^+ \to \pi^0 e^+ \nu_e\right) \cong \sqrt{\frac{E_{f1\pi 0}}{E_{\pi+}}}\, S_{fi(K)}\left(\pi^+ \to \pi^0 e^+ \nu_e\right) \tag{7.4.31}$$

to zeroth order in ε_0 in (5.7.4); apart from the small difference between the π^0 energy and the π^+ mass, the classical phenomenological result $S_{fi(K)}$ of (7.4.26) is *derived* from the first principles' theory here. The first order corrections are different because $C_k \neq 1$ in (7.3.25b) but they are small. This also holds if the "decoupled" (5.7.28) used above were replaced by an eventual "coupled" solution mentioned beneath (5.7.28).

7.4.6. Decay Amplitudes for $K \to \pi$ + Lepton Pair

These amplitudes have been given by (7.3.26-29) in terms of the W's. Consider at first the kaon decay via $W_V^{\pm}$ in (7.3.26a) and the first of (7.3.28). The conversion of W_V^+ into an equivalent positron and an electron neutrino via (7.2.16, 20) has been given by (7.4.27). Conversion into a muon and a muon neutrino is obtained by

$$(7.4.27)\ \text{with}\ e \to \mu \tag{7.4.32}$$

From (7.3.26-29), one sees that

$$S_{fi}\left(K^{+}\to\pi^{0}L^{+}\nu_{L}\right)=S_{fi}\left(K^{-}\to\pi^{0}L^{-}\overline{\nu}_{L}\right)$$
$$\approx\frac{1}{\sqrt{2}}S_{fi}\left(\overline{K}^{0}\to\pi^{-}L^{+}\nu_{L}\right)=\frac{1}{\sqrt{2}}S_{fi}\left(K^{0}\to\pi^{+}L^{-}\overline{\nu}_{L}\right) \tag{7.4.33}$$

where the ≈ sign becomes = in the limit of $SU(2)_I$ symmetry in which the masses of $K^{\pm}$, K^0 and $\overline{K}^0$ are the same, as do the masses of $\pi^{\pm}$ and π^0.

Unlike π^0 in $\pi^+\to\pi^0e^+\nu_e$, which is nearly stationary, the pions in the kaon decays are generally relativistic. Thus, ε_0 of (5.7.4) is not a small quantity and the estimate meson wave functions of §5.7.4 derived for slow mesons cannot be used in S_{fi} of (7.3.26-29). Therefore, the absolute magnitudes of the decay amplitudes in (7.4.33), as well as those associated with the W_U and $\overline{W}_U$ decays, using (7.2.21-22), cannot be evaluated presently.

7.4.7. Decay Amplitudes for K^+, $\pi^+\to\gamma+$ Lepton Pair

Analogous to (7.4.6a), the total action (7.1.1) is now varied with respect to the electromagnetic field $A^{a\dot{b}}$. The last two terms in (7.1.1) do not contain $A^{a\dot{b}}$ and do not contribute. For the present decay, variation of S_{m3} (7.1.8) using (7.1.4) and (7.2.14) also vanishes. Variation of S_L (7.2.13) leads to a constant source representing a static magnetic field generated by the charged lepton moving with a constant speed and decoupled from the photon. Finally, variation of S_{GB} (7.4.1) takes the form (7.4.14) with Z replaced by A. Choosing the Lorentz gauge, one find to order g the usual

$$\Box A_{\dot{b}a}=0 \tag{7.4.34}$$

Its vector part has the solution (6.4.6).

Inserting this solution and (7.4.10b) into (7.3.38) and carrying out the X^0 integration give the second order equivalent of (7.4.13),

$$S_{fi2}=\frac{\pi}{8}\frac{g^{2}e}{E_{pr}\sqrt{E_{r}\tau_{0}M_{W}^{2}}}\frac{1}{\sqrt{\Omega_{r}\Omega_{L}}}\delta\left(E_{r}+E_{L}+E_{\nu L}-E_{pr}\right)\underline{e}_{T}\underline{\sigma}^{\dot{b}a}u_{\nu L\dot{a}}^{(+)}u_{Lb}^{(-)}I_{Lr} \tag{7.4.35a}$$

$$I_{Lr}=\int d^{3}\underline{X}d^{4}x\sqrt{\frac{\Omega}{\Omega_{wvac}}}\psi_{0}^{2}(r)\exp\left(i\left(\underline{K}_{r}+\underline{K}_{L}-\underline{K}_{\nu L}\right)\underline{X}\right) \tag{7.4.35b}$$

7.5. Decay Rates and Detachment of Weak and Electromagnetic Couplings

The total decay rate is related to the decay amplitude by

$$\Gamma = \sum_{\text{final spins}} \sum_{\text{final momenta}} \left| S_{fi} \right|^2 / T_d \tag{7.5.1}$$

analogous to (6.4.22a). Similar to (6.4.22b), summation over the final momenta $\underline{K}_f$ for each of the decay products is replaced by a integral of the form

$$\sum_{Kf} = \frac{\Omega_f}{(2\pi)^3} \int d^3 \underline{K}_f \tag{7.5.2}$$

where Ω_f is a large normalization volume for the wave function of this final state particle denoted by f.

7.5.1. $\pi+ \rightarrow \pi^0 e+\nu_e$

For the amplitude (7.4.30), (7.5.1) with (7.5.2) becomes

$$\Gamma\left(\pi^+ \rightarrow \pi^0 e^+ \nu_e\right) = \frac{\Omega\Omega_L^2}{(2\pi)^9} \sum_{\text{final spins}} \frac{1}{T_d} \int d^3 \underline{K}_{\pi 0} d^3 \underline{K}_{e+} d^3 \underline{K}_\nu \left| S_{fi}\left(\pi^+ \rightarrow \pi^0 e^+ \nu_e\right)\right|^2 \tag{7.5.3}$$

This decay rate has been obtained and evaluated long ago and has been given by [K3 (14.95)], using $S_{fi(K)}$ of (7.4.26) instead of S_{fi} of (7.4.30). The calculation has been outlined in [K3 §14.7]. Let

$$\Delta_\pi = E_{\pi+} - E_{\pi 0} \quad \text{and} \quad \varepsilon_\pi = \mathrm{M}_e^2 / \Delta_\pi^2$$

and neglect Δ_π^2 next to $4E_\pi^2$, [K3 (14.109)] gives

$$\frac{1}{\tau_{\beta(K)}} = \Gamma\left(\pi^+ \rightarrow \pi^0 e^+ \nu_e\right) = \frac{G^2}{192\pi}\left(1 + \frac{E_{\pi 0}}{E_{\pi+}}\right)^3 \Delta_\pi^5$$
$$\times \left[\frac{2}{5}\sqrt{1-\varepsilon_\pi}\left(2 - 9\varepsilon_\pi - 8\varepsilon_\pi^2\right) + 6\varepsilon_\pi^2 \ln \frac{1+\sqrt{1-\varepsilon_\pi}}{\sqrt{\varepsilon_\pi}}\right] = \frac{1}{2.457 \text{ sec.}} \tag{7.5.4}$$

where the E's stand for the masses. $\tau_{\beta(K)}$ is just outside the error limit of the measured 2.54 sec.±3.3% [P1]. If (7.5.3) with (7.4.31) is used, the predicted decay time is 4 times too short. This not accounted for presently; perhaps a factor of 2 is missing somewhere.

7.5.2. $\pi^+, K^+ \rightarrow L^+\nu_L$

The decay rate is obtained by inserting (7.4.13) into (7.5.1) and making use of (7.5.2). This procedure is well known [K3 §15.2] but will be modified for the present application. One obtains

$$\Gamma\left(\pi^+, K^+ \rightarrow L^+\nu_L\right) = \frac{\pi^2}{8}\frac{\Omega^2}{\tau_0^2}\frac{1}{\tau_0^2}\frac{1}{(2\pi)^7}\int d^3\underline{K}_L I_{uu} \tag{7.5.5a}$$

$$I_{uu} = \sum_{\text{spins}}\int d^3\underline{K}_{\nu L}\frac{\Omega}{\Omega_{wvac}} I_{L\nu 1} I^*_{L\nu 1}\left|u^{(+)}_{\nu L\dot{a}} u^{(-)}_{La}\right|^2 \delta\left(E_L + E_{\nu L} - E_{pr}\right) \tag{7.5.5b}$$

where

$$\left|\delta\left(E_L + E_{\nu L} - E_{pr}\right)\right|^2 = \frac{T_d}{2\pi}\delta\left(E_L + E_{\nu L} - E_{pr}\right) \tag{7.5.6}$$

[B4 (7.9)]. Performing the integration over $\underline{X}$ in (7.4.13b) yields

$$I_{L\nu 1} = (2\pi)^3 \delta\left(\underline{K}_L - \underline{K}_{\nu L}\right)\int d^4x \psi_0^2(r) = I^*_{L\nu 1} \tag{7.5.7}$$

Substituting this expression for one of the two $I_{L\nu 1}$'s in (7.5.5b) and carrying out the integration over $\underline{K}_{\nu L}$ leads to

$$I_{uu} = (2\pi)^3\left(\int d^4x \psi_0^2(r)\right)\frac{\Omega}{\Omega_{wvac}} I_{Nd}\Sigma_{uu}\delta\left(E_L + E_{\nu L} - E_{pr}\right), \quad \underline{K}_L = \underline{K}_{\nu L} \tag{7.5.8}$$

$$\Sigma_{uu} = \sum_{\text{spins}}\left|u^{(+)}_{\nu L\dot{a}} u^{(-)}_{La}\right|^2_{\underline{K}_L = \underline{K}_{\nu L}} \tag{7.5.9a}$$

$$I_{Nd} = \int d^3\underline{X} d^4x \psi_0^2(r) \tag{7.5.9b}$$

Insert (7.4.11a, 11b) into (7.5.9a) and carry out the sum over all possible spin combinations. The result is

$$\Sigma_{uu} = \left(1 + \frac{M_L}{E_L}\right)\left(1 - \frac{\left|\underline{K}_L\right|}{E_L + M_L}\right)^2 \tag{7.5.10}$$

Digress for a moment to the normalization of meson wave functions and let

$$-iN_d = 2\int dx^0 N_{mJ} \tag{7.5.11}$$

in (4.2.4). The imaginary sign comes obviously from the left side of (4.2.4). Since N_{mJ} is a conserved quantity of dimension energy, N_d must be a scalar quantity and expected to transform as a dimensionless Lorentz scalar, which can however be large. One finds from (7.5.9b) and (4.2.5)

$$N_d = E_{00}\int d^3\underline{X}d^4x\psi_0^2(r) = F_{pr}I_{Nd} \text{ – large dimensionless Lorentz scalar} \tag{7.5.12}$$

Here, the meson mass E_{00} has been identified as the mass E_{pr} of the initial state meson in (7.3.1).

Return now to (7.5.8) and apply the formula

$$\delta(f(x)) = \frac{\delta(x-x_0)}{\left|\partial f(x)/\partial x\right|_{x=x_0}}, \qquad f(x_0)=0 \tag{7.5.13}$$

to the δ function therein. We obtain

$$\delta(E_L + E_{\nu L} - E_{pr})_{\underline{K}_L=\underline{K}_{\nu L}} = \delta\left(\sqrt{K_L^2 + M_L^2} + K_L - E_{pr}\right) = \frac{E_L}{E_{pr}}\delta(K_L - K_{L0}) \tag{7.5.14a}$$

$$K_{L0} = \frac{1}{2E_{pr}}\left(E_{pr}^2 - M_L^2\right) \tag{7.5.14b}$$

Insert (7.5.10, 12, 14) into (7.5.8), which in its turn is substituted into (7.5.5a). After performing the integration over $\underline{K}_L$, the decay rate takes the form

$$\Gamma(\pi^+, K^+ \to L^+\nu_L) = \frac{1}{64\pi}\frac{1}{E_{pr}}\frac{N_d}{\tau_0^4}\frac{\Omega^3}{\Omega_{wvac}}\int d^4x\psi_0^2(r)M_L^2\left(1-\frac{M_L^2}{E_{pr}^2}\right)^2 \tag{7.5.15}$$

Employing (4.2.8) and (7.4.6b), (7.5.15) becomes

$$\Gamma(\pi^+, K^+ \to L^+\nu_L) = \frac{F_W^2}{16\pi}\frac{1}{E_{pr}}M_L^2\left(1-\frac{M_L^2}{E_{pr}^2}\right)^2 \tag{7.5.16a}$$

$$F_W^2 = \frac{N_d}{4\tau_0^3}\frac{\Omega^2}{\Omega_{wvac}} = \frac{1}{4}\frac{g^4}{M_W^4}\frac{N_d}{\Omega_{wvac}\tau_0} \tag{7.5.16b}$$

$$M_W^2 = \frac{g^2\tau_0}{\Omega} \tag{7.4.6b)=(7.5.16c}$$

Here, *pr=12* and *13* and $E_{12}=E_{\pi+}$ and $E_{13}=E_{K+}$. For $L=\mu$ and e, (7.5.16) yields the ratio

$$\frac{\Gamma(\pi^+ \to e^+\nu_\mu)}{\Gamma(\pi^+ \to \mu^+\nu_e)} = \frac{M_e^2}{M_\mu^2}\left(\frac{E_{\pi+}^2 - M_e^2}{E_{\pi+}^2 - M_\mu^2}\right)^2 \tag{7.5.17}$$

in agreement with that of the literature [L5 (21.22)], apart from radiative corrections. Further, (7.5.16) yields

$$\frac{\Gamma(K^+ \to \mu^+\nu_\mu)}{\Gamma(\pi^+ \to \mu^+\nu_\mu)} = \left(\frac{E_{\pi+}}{E_{K+}}\right)^5\left(\frac{E_{K+}^2 - E_\mu^2}{E_{\pi+}^2 - E_\mu^2}\right)^2 \approx 1.41 \tag{7.5.18}$$

which is not too far from 1.34 obtained from data [P1]. F_W is related to the conventional charged pion decay constant F_π which enter the decay rates according to [L5 (21.20) and p606],

$$\Gamma(\pi^+ \to \mu^+\nu_\mu) = (F_\pi \cos\vartheta_C)^2 \frac{G^2M_\mu^2}{8\pi E_{\pi+}^3}\left(E_{\pi+}^2 - M_\mu^2\right)^2 \tag{7.5.19a}$$

$$\Gamma(K^+ \to \mu^+\nu_\mu) = (F_\pi \sin\vartheta_C)^2 \frac{G^2M_\mu^2}{8\pi E_{K+}^3}\left(E_{K+}^2 - M_\mu^2\right)^2 \tag{7.5.19b}$$

where ϑ_C is the Cabibbo angle to be determined by data. Such an angle is however absent in (7.5.16), which therefore has a greater predictive power. Comparison of (7.5.18) to the ratio of (7.5.19a) and (7.5.19b) leads to the prediction

$$\tan\vartheta_C = \frac{E_{\pi+}}{E_{K+}} = 0.2827 \tag{7.5.20}$$

which is not too far from the measured 0.2312 [P1]. From (7.5.16, 19, 20), one finds

$$F_W^2 = 2F_\pi^2 \frac{G^2}{\left(E_{\pi+}^{-2} + E_{K+}^{-2}\right)} \tag{7.5.21}$$

Using the value $F_\pi cos\,\vartheta_C$=0.128 GeV [L5 (21.21)] and (7.4.29), (7.5.21, 20) give the redefined dimensionless weak coupling constant

$$F_W^2 = 8.0314\times 10^{-14} \tag{7.5.22a}$$

Inserting this value into (7.5.16b) and making use of (7.4.29a), (7.5.12) and (4.2.7, 8) gives

$$\frac{N_d}{\Omega_{wvac}\tau_0}=\frac{E_{00}}{\Omega_{wvac}}=7.6975\times10^{-5}\ \text{GeV}^4,\ \Omega_{wvac}^{1/3}=\begin{pmatrix}12.2\\18.6\end{pmatrix}\text{GeV}^{-1}\ \text{for}\ \begin{pmatrix}\pi^{\pm}\\ \text{K}^0\end{pmatrix}\qquad(7.5.22\text{b})$$

Ω_{wva} is indeed large and marginally satisfies the criterion above (7.3.21). The magnitude of the rates π, $K\rightarrow$lepton pair is not predicted but has to be fixed by data (7.5.22). The ratios of the rates are correctly predicted. This is due to the presence of the vacuum meson state here. When the vacuum meson state is replaced by a real meson state, as in $\pi^+\rightarrow\pi^0 e^+\nu_e$, $\Omega_{wvac}\rightarrow\Omega\rightarrow\infty$ and the magnitude of the rate itself (7.5.4) is correctly predicted.

7.5.3. Detachment of Weak and Electromagnetic Couplings Conjecture

In the standard electro-weak model, the strength of weak interactions is given by the square of the Fermi constant G, as exemplified by (7.5.19). In its turn, G is proportional to the conventional weak coupling constant g^2 according to (7.4.29a), where M_W^2 is regarded as a constant given in (7.4.9). The strength of electromagnetic interactions is determined by the fine structure constant $\alpha=e^2/4\pi$. These both types of charges, g and e, are coupled by a new parameter, the Weinberg angle ϑ_W, according to (7.2.1).

This parameter is predicted in (7.2.12). The rate of the same decay as that of (7.5.19), given by (7.5.16), contains however no g. Consistently, the Fermi constant G itself is also independent of g according to (7.4.29b) because M_W is proportional to g according to (7.4.6b). In fact, the weak charge g can be eliminated altogether and be replaced by $e/\sin\vartheta_W$ according to the last of (7.2.1b), where ϑ_W has been predicted to be 27.93° in (7.2.12) and is not an independent parameter or universal constant to be fixed by data.

Here, the strength of weak interactions given by the *weak coupling constant* F_W^2 of (7.5.16b) or G of (7.4.29b) is thus *detached* from the corresponding strength of electromagnetic interactions given by the *fine structure constant* $\alpha=e^2/4\pi$. Using (7.5.22a), F_W^2 is about 1.1×10^{-11} times weaker than $e^2/4\pi=1/137$. Note however that the formation of the weak gauge boson field Z and the electromagnetic field A according to the SU(2)xU(1) formalism remains intact.

Such a detachment is a conjecture presently because it has not been investigated generally involving other weak decays and that the calculated (7.5.20) is somewhat too large. But it is supported by such a detachment also in neutron decay considered in §12.6.4 below.

7.5.4. Gauge Boson Mass, ∞/∞ and Cabibbo Angle

As has been mentioned below (7.4.6), the squared mass the gauge boson, M_W^2 in (7.5.16c) or (7.4.6b), is a ratio of a large relative time τ_0 and a large volume Ω associated with the pseudoscalar meson wave functions that generate it. The physics underlying their finite ratio is not understood presently, because they are ostensibly independent of each other. A finite, universal τ_0/Ω indicates that there may be some connection between a possible weak relative time dependence and a weak laboratory space dependence of the rest frame meson wave function. Let

$$\Omega = l_X l_Y l_Z \tag{7.5.23}$$

where l stands for length and X, Y and Z the Cartesian axes in laboratory space. There are infinitely many ways to form a finite ratio between τ_0 and Ω, each approaching infinity. The three prototypes are

$$\tau_0 \to \infty, \qquad l_Z = c_\tau \tau_0, \qquad l_X l_Y = \text{finite}, \qquad l_Z \propto \tau_0 \tag{7.5.24a}$$

$$\tau_0 = \frac{a_\tau}{l_a}, \qquad a_\tau \to \infty, \qquad l_X l_Y = c_a a_\tau, \qquad l_Z = \text{finite}, \qquad l_X,\ l_Y \propto \sqrt{\tau_0} \tag{7.5.24b}$$

$$\tau_0 = \frac{\Omega}{l_\Omega^2}, \qquad \Omega = l_X l_Y l_Z \to \infty, \qquad l_X,\ l_Y,\ l_Z \propto (\tau_0)^{1/3} \tag{7.5.24c}$$

where l_a and l_Ω are finite length constants, a_τ an area, the c's finite dimensionless constants, and (7.5.16c) has been used. In (7.5.24a), the volume Ω is limited to an infinite long tube of cross section $c_\tau l_X l_Y$. In (7.5.24b), Ω is limited to an infinitely extended slab of thickness l_X. In (7.5.25c), Ω is allowed to go to infinity in all three directions. Only this case gives that correct dimension for M_W^2.

The weak coupling constant F_W^2 is also a ∞/∞ ratio according to (7.5.16b), where $N_d \to \infty$ according to (7.5.11, 12). Corresponding to (7.5.24a, 24b), F_W^2 turns out to depend asymmetrically upon one or two of l_X, l_Y, l_Z. This asymmetry is removed in the case of (7.5.24c).

It can also be seen that the most straight forward choice l_X, l_Y, $l_Z \propto \tau_0 \to \infty$ would lead to difficulties. Inserting this into (7.5.16b, 16c, 23) yields

$$\tau_0 \to \infty, \qquad \Omega \propto \tau_0^3, \qquad M_W^2 \propto \tau_0^{-2} \to 0 \tag{7.5.25}$$

which contradicts (7.4.9).

Finally, prediction of the Cabibbo angle ϑ_C in (7.5.20) depends upon the presence of the $1/E_{pr}$ factor in (7.5.16a), which in its turn depends upon the application of the large normalization constant N_d in (7.5.12). If this normalization condition is not utilized and I_{Nd} of (7.5.9b) is computed using the meson wave functions (7.3.14b) and (4.3.4a), one finds simply

$$I_{Nd} = \tau_0 \tag{7.5.26}$$

Inserting this relation into (7.5.12) and substituting the result into (7.5.15) converts (7.5.16b) to

$$\frac{F_W^2}{E_{pr}} = \frac{g^4}{4M_W^4}\frac{1}{\Omega_{wvac}} \tag{7.5.27}$$

This causes that the $1/E_{pr}$ factor in (7.5.16a) drops out so that the correct Cabibbo angle cannot be predicted and, in addition, the relatively good agreement between the second order predictions of the ratio $\Gamma(K^+)/\Gamma(\pi^+)$ with data in (7.5.49) below will be ruined.

7.5.5. K^0, $\overline{K}^0 \rightarrow$ Lepton Pairs

From (7.4.25), it follows that

$$\Gamma\left(K^0, \overline{K}^0 \succ K_S^0, K_L^0 \rightarrow \nu_\mu \overline{\nu}_\mu, \nu_e \overline{\nu}_e\right) = 0 \tag{7.5.28}$$

in agreement with data [P1]. The data however are given only for $K_S{}^0$ and $K_L{}^0$[P1]. By (7.2.18), the decays of $K_S{}^0$ and $K_L{}^0$ are composed of K^0 and $\overline{K}^0$ decays in equal amount. Since the form of the amplitudes (7.4.22) and (7.4.13) are the same, the derivation of the decay rate for the latter in §7.5.2 can be mostly taken over for the former. The main difference is that (7.5.9a) is to be replaced by

$$\Sigma_{uu} = \sum\nolimits_{spins} \left|4\sin^2\vartheta_W v_{L\dot{a}}^{(-)} v_{La}^{(+)} - 2\cos 2\vartheta_W u_{L\dot{a}}^{(+)} u_{La}^{(-)}\right|^2_{\underline{K}_L^{(+)} = \underline{K}_L} \tag{7.5.29}$$

Insert (7.4.11b, 19b, 20) into (7.5.29) and note that $\underline{K}_L{}^{(+)} = \underline{K}_L$, hence $E_L{}^{(+)} = E_L$, are anticipated analogous to (7.4.24). The four spin combinations cancel out so that

$$\Sigma_{uu} = 0 \tag{7.5.30}$$

Analogous to (7.5.5, 8, 9a), (7.5.30) leads to that the equivalent of (7.5.16a) becomes

$$\Gamma\left(K^0, \overline{K}^0 \rightarrow L^+L^-\right) = \Gamma\left(K^0, \overline{K}^0 \rightarrow K_S^0, K_L^0 \rightarrow \mu^+\mu^-, e^+e^-\right) = 0 \tag{7.5.31}$$

in near agreement with the very small branching ratios $\approx 10^{-12}$ - 10^{-9} found [P1].

These results show that the virtual time component of the neutral gauge boson Z^0 described by (7.4.21) does not decay into any lepton pair. Finally, it is remarked that π^0 cannot decay weakly via Z to for example e^+e^-. This is due to that, unlike $\pi^\pm$ and kaons, which have open flavors and must decay via weak interaction, π^0 has closed flavor.

7.5.6. $K \to \pi$ + Lepton Pairs

The decay rates for (7.4.33) are

$$2\Gamma\left(K^{+} \to \pi^{0} L^{+} \nu_{L}\right) = 2\Gamma\left(K^{-} \to \pi^{0} L^{-} \overline{\nu}_{L}\right)$$
$$\approx \Gamma\left(\overline{K}^{0} \to \pi^{+} L^{-} \vec{\nu}_{L}\right) = \Gamma\left(K^{0} \to \pi^{-} L^{\nu +}{}_{L}\right) \tag{7.5.32}$$

In accordance with (7.2.18),

$$\Gamma\left(K_{S}^{0} \to \pi^{\pm} L^{\mp}, \overline{\nu}_{L}, \nu_{L}\right) = \Gamma\left(K_{L}^{0} \to \pi^{\pm} L^{\mp}, \overline{\nu}_{L}, \nu_{L}\right)$$
$$= \Gamma\left(\overline{K}^{0} \to \pi^{+} L^{-} \vec{\nu}_{L}\right) = \Gamma\left(K^{0} \to \pi^{-} L^{+} \nu_{L}\right) \tag{7.5.33}$$

The left of this relation agrees with data [P1] to 0.11% for $L=\mu$ and 0.02% for $L=e$. These numbers are less than the experimental errors for these decays.

Comparison of the measured decay rates for charged and neutral kaons shows that the predicted factor 2 [L5 (11.119)] in (7.5.32) is to be replaced by 2.05 for $L=\mu$ and 1.93 for $L=e$. These discrepancies are presently attributed to the neglect of the u and d quark mass differences mentioned below (7.4.33).

Finally, (7.4.25) and (7.5.29, 30) also leads to

$$\Gamma\left(K^{\pm} \to \pi^{\pm} L^{+} L^{-}, \pi^{\pm} \overline{\nu}_{L} \nu_{L}\right) = \Gamma\left(K^{0}, \overline{K}^{0} \to \pi^{0} L^{\pm} L^{\mp}, \pi^{0} \overline{\nu}_{L} \nu_{L}\right) = 0 \tag{7.5.34}$$

This also agrees with data [P1], which show no such decays. For the right part of (7.5.34), agreement with data is inferred from that neither K_S^0 nor K_L^0 decays into such final states.

7.5.7. $K^{+}, \pi^{+} \to \mu^{+} \nu_{\mu} \gamma$

Analogous to §7.5.2, the rate of this second order decay is found by inserting (7.4.35) into (7.5.1) using (7.5.2) and (7.5.6-7) type of expression,

$$\Gamma\left(\pi^{+}, K^{+} \to L^{+} \nu_{L} \gamma\right) = \frac{1}{256(2\pi)^{5}} \frac{g^{4} e^{2}}{\tau_{0}^{2} M_{W}^{4}} \frac{1}{E_{pr}^{2} E_{r}} \frac{\Omega}{\Omega_{wvac}} \int d^{3} \underline{K}_{r} \int d^{3} \underline{K}_{L}$$
$$\int d^{3} \underline{K}_{\nu L} \delta\left(E_{r} + E_{L} + E_{\nu L} - E_{pr}\right) \delta\left(\underline{K}_{r} + \underline{K}_{L} - \underline{K}_{\nu L}\right) \left(\int d^{4} x \psi_{0}^{2}(r)\right) \Sigma_{uu\gamma}$$
$$\int d^{3} \underline{X} \int d^{4} x \psi_{0}^{2}(r) \exp\left(i\left(\underline{K}_{r} + \underline{K}_{L} - \underline{K}_{\nu L}\right) \underline{X}\right)$$

(7.5.35a)

$$\Sigma_{uu\gamma} = \sum\nolimits_{spins} \underline{e}_{T} \underline{\sigma}^{b\dot{a}} \left| u_{\nu L \dot{a}}^{(+)} u_{Lb}^{(-)} \right|^{2} \tag{7.5.35b}$$

Carrying out the $\underline{K}_{\nu L}$ integration leads to

$$\Gamma\left(\pi^+, K^+ \to L^+ \nu_L \gamma\right) = \frac{F_W^2}{64(2\pi)^5} \frac{e^2}{E_{pr}^3} \int d^3 \underline{K}_r I_K \tag{7.5.36a}$$

$$I_K = \int d^3 \underline{K}_L \frac{1}{E_r} \delta(f(\cos \vartheta_{Lr}))(\Sigma_{uu\gamma})_{(\underline{K}_{\nu L} = \underline{K}_L + \underline{K}_r)} \tag{7.5.36b}$$

$$\delta(f(\cos \vartheta_{Lr})) = \delta\left(K_r + \sqrt{K_L^2 + M_L^2} + \sqrt{K_r^2 + K_L^2 - 2\cos \vartheta_{Lr}} - E_{pr}\right) \tag{7.5.36c}$$

where (7.5.16b) and (4.2.8) have been employed. ϑ_{Lr} is the angle between $\underline{K}_L$ and $\underline{K}_r$ which has been put to (0, 0, K_r) in (7.5.36b). This δ function vanishes except for

$$\cos \vartheta_{Lr} = \cos \vartheta_{Lr0} = \pm \frac{1}{2K_r K_L}\left(E_{pr}^2 + M_L^2 - 2E_{pr} K_r - 2(E_{pr} - K_r)\sqrt{K_L^2 + M_L^2}\right) \tag{7.5.37}$$

Thence,

$$\int d^3 \underline{K}_L \delta(f(\cos \vartheta_{Lr})) = 2\pi \int dK_L \frac{K_L}{K_r}\left(E_{pr} - K_r - \sqrt{K_L^2 + M_L^2}\right) \tag{7.5.38}$$

Making use of (7.4.11), summing over the spins, as in (7.5.10), and over the photon polarizations T=1, 2, the equivalent of (7.5.10) becomes

$$(\Sigma_{uu\gamma})_{(\underline{K}_{\nu L} = \underline{K}_L + \underline{K}_r)} = 4\left[1 + \frac{K_r K_L \cos \vartheta_{Lr0} + K_L^2 \cos^2 \vartheta_{Lr0}}{(E_{pr} - K_r)\sqrt{K_L^2 + M_L^2} - K_L^2 - M_L^2}\right] \tag{7.5.39}$$

Inserting (7.5.38-39) into (7.5.36b) leads to

$$I_K = \frac{2\pi}{K_r^2} \int dK_L K_L \left(E_{pr} - K_r - \sqrt{K_L^2 + M_L^2}\right)(\Sigma_{uu\gamma})_{(\underline{K}_{\nu L} = \underline{K}_L + \underline{K}_r)} \tag{7.5.40}$$

Insert (7.5.37) into (7.5.39) which in its turn is inserted into (7.5.40). Changing the integration variable to

$$E_L = \sqrt{K_L^2 + M_L^2} \tag{7.5.41}$$

(7.5.40) can be integrated to yield

$$I_K = \frac{8\pi}{K_r^2} \Big|_{E_{L-}}^{E_{L+}} \left\{ \frac{B_0}{2}\left(\pm 1 + \frac{B_0}{K_r^2} \right) E_L + \left(\begin{pmatrix} 0 \\ B_1/2 \end{pmatrix} - \frac{B_0 B_1}{4K_r^2} \right) E_L^2 + \left(\frac{B_1^2}{12K_r^2} - \frac{1}{3} \right) E_L^3 \right\} \tag{7.5.42a}$$

$$B_0 = E_{pr}^2 + M_L^2 - 2E_{pr}K_r, \qquad B_1 = 2(E_{pr} - K_r) \tag{7.5.42b}$$

Here, the integration limits $E_{L\pm}$ are obtained from (7.5.41) together with the boundary condition

$$\cos^2 \vartheta_{Lr} = 1 \tag{7.5.43}$$

With (7.5.37) and (7.5.41, 42b, 43), one finds

$$E_{L\pm} = \frac{B_0 B_1 \pm \sqrt{B_0^2 B_1^2 - 4(B_0^2 + 4K_r^2 M_L^2) E_{pr}(E_{pr} - 2K_r)}}{4E_{pr}(E_{pr} - 2K_r)} \tag{7.5.44}$$

The upper and lower signs in (7.5.42a) refer to $\cos \vartheta_{Lr} = +1$ and -1, respectively.

Inserting (7.5.42a) into (7.5.36a) gives

$$\Gamma(\pi^+, K^+ \to L^+ \nu_L \gamma) = \frac{F_W^2}{8(2\pi)^3} \frac{e^2}{E_{pr}^3} \int dK_r \left\{ \frac{B_0}{2}\left(\pm 1 + \frac{B_0}{K_r^2} \right)(E_{L+} - E_{L-}) \right.$$
$$\left. + \left(\begin{pmatrix} 0 \\ B_1/2 \end{pmatrix} - \frac{B_0 B_1}{4K_r^2} \right)(E_{L+}^2 - E_{L-}^2) + \left(\frac{B_1^2}{12K_r^2} - \frac{1}{3} \right)(E_{L+}^3 - E_{L-}^3) \right\} \tag{7.5.45}$$

The boundaries limiting the allowed K_r and K_L values in (7.5.45) are determined by putting the argument in (7.5.36c) to 0 together with (7.5.43),

$$E_{pr} = K_r + \sqrt{K_L^2 + M_L^2} + |K_r \pm K_L| \tag{7.5.46}$$

which is illustrated in Figure 7.1.

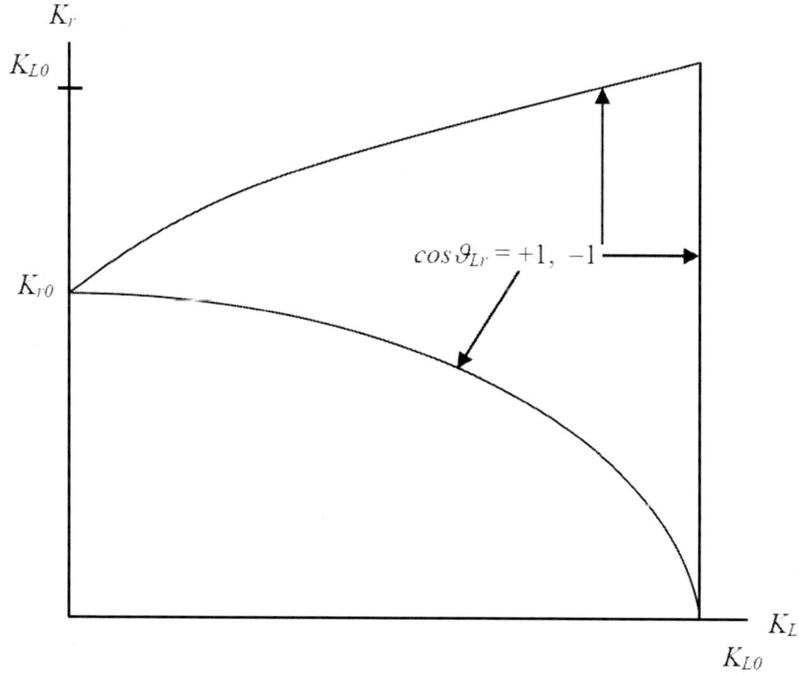

Figure 7.1. The allowed Kr and KL values in the integral of (7.5.45) are limited to the triangle-like area.

In this figure,

$$K_{L0} = \left(E_{pr}^2 - M_L^2\right)/2E_{pr}, \qquad K_{r0} = \left(E_{pr} - M_L\right)/2 \tag{7.5.47}$$

For the boundaries in Figure 7.1, (7.5.45) becomes

$$\begin{aligned}
\Gamma\left(\pi^+, K^+ \to L^+\nu_L\gamma\right) = {} & \frac{F_W^2}{8(2\pi)^3}\frac{e^2}{E_{pr}^3}\left[\int_0^{K_{r0}} dK_r\left\{\left(\frac{B_0}{2} + \frac{B_0^2}{4K_r^2}\right)\left(E_{L+0} - E_{L-}\right)\right.\right. \\
& -\frac{B_0 B_1}{4K_r^2}\left(E_{L+0}^2 - E_{L-}^2\right) + \left(\frac{B_1^2}{12K_r^2} - \frac{1}{3}\right)\left(E_{L+0}^3 - E_{L-}^3\right)\Big\} \\
& + \int_{K_{r0}}^{K_{L0}} dK_r\left\{\left(\frac{B_0^2}{4K_r^2} - \frac{B_0}{2}\right)\left(E_{L+0} - E_{L-}\right) + \frac{B_1}{2}\left(1 - \frac{B_0}{2K_r^2}\right)\left(E_{L+0}^2 - E_{L-}^2\right)\right. \\
& \left.\left. + \left(\frac{B_1^2}{12K_r^2} - \frac{1}{3}\right)\left(E_{L+0}^3 - E_{L-}^3\right)\right\}\right], \qquad E_{L+0} = \sqrt{K_{L0}^2 + M_L^2}
\end{aligned} \tag{7.5.48}$$

The integrand is a measure of the photon spectrum which shows discontinuous jump at $K_r = K_{r0}$. The ratio R_{disc} of these two amplitudes is the ratio between the two braces evaluated at $K_r = K_{r0}$ and $E_{L-} = M_L$ according to Figure 7.1.

With $E_{pr} = 0.4937$ GeV for K^+ and 0.1396 for π^+ and $M_L = 0.10566$ for μ^+ [P1], (7.5.22a) and $e^2/4\pi = 1/137$, (7.5.48) has been integrated on a computer to yield

$$\Gamma(K^+ \to \mu^+ \nu_\mu \gamma) = 1.22 \times 10^{-10} \text{ eV} \qquad \text{data[P1]} = 3.3 \times 10^{-10} \text{ eV}$$
$$\Gamma(\pi^+, \to \mu^+ \nu_\mu \gamma) = 0.98 \times 10^{-12} \text{ eV} \qquad \text{data[P1]} = 5.06 \times 10^{-12} \text{ eV}$$
$$\Gamma(K^+)/\Gamma(\pi^+) = 125 \qquad \text{data[P1]} = 65 \tag{7.5.49}$$

The agreements in magnitude with data may be accepted presently at the quantum mechanical level. The computer results also show that the photon intensity rises from $K_r = 0$ to a maximum before reaching $K_r = K_{r0}$, where it jumps up by a factor R_{disc} and then decreases to 0 at $K_r = K_{L0}$. The predictions

$$R_{disc} = 5.26 \text{ for } K^+ \to \mu^+ \nu_\mu \gamma \text{ and } 1.31 \text{ for } \pi^+ \to \mu^+ \nu_\mu \gamma \tag{7.5.50}$$

can be tested.

When μ^+ is replaced by e^+ with $M_L = 0.00511$ GeV [P1], (7.5.49) is turned into

$$\Gamma(K^+ \to e^+ \nu_\mu \gamma) = 1.03 \times 10^{-10} \text{ eV} \qquad \text{data[P1]} = 5 \times 10^{-13} \text{ eV}$$
$$\Gamma(\pi^+ \to e^+ \nu_\mu \gamma) = 0.296 \times 10^{-10} \text{eV} \qquad \text{data[P1]} = 1.87 \times 10^{-14} \text{ eV} \tag{7.5.51}$$

The huge disagreements with data are not understood presently. The small ratio $\Gamma(\pi^+ \to e^+ \nu_e)/\Gamma(\pi^+ \to \mu^+ \nu_\mu)$ in (7.5.17) stems from the M_L^2 factor in (7.5.16a) which in its turns comes from W^0 in (7.3.22) via (7.5.10). This W^0 is here replaced by $\underline{W}$ in (7.3.38) which led to (7.5.39) and the suppressing factor M_L^2 factor in (7.5.16a) is lost in (7.5.48). However, a qualitative argument may be mentioned. When a photon is introduced into K^+, $\pi^+ \to L^+ \nu_L$ of §7.5.2, it may interact dynamically with L^+. This interaction, apart from the static interaction mentioned in §7.4.7, has not been included here. Viewing the photon as a virtual $e^+ – e^-$ pair, it will hardly change the motion of the heavy μ^+ but will do so for the light e^+. This may lead to reduced phase space and hence the decay rate.

If there is also a dynamic interaction between the photon and the meson, it is expected to affect the lighter π^+ more than K^+. This trend agrees with (7.5.49) where the decay rate of π^+ is farther from data the that of K^+.

7.6. Purely Leptonic Interactions, Standard Model, Higgs as Bound State *W+W–*, and Muon Decay

Purely leptonic interactions have been treated rather successfully in the standard model. In this case, it will be shown that the total action (7.1.1) reduces to a form close to that of the standard model so that some of the results obtained from this model can be taken over here.

7.6.1. Standard Model and Purely Leptonic Interactions

In the standard model [P1 Higgs Bosons Mini Reviews, P2 p713-716, L5 §22.2-3], S_{m3} of (7.1.1) is replaced by two actions, S_H for Higgs and S_q for quarks. The equivalent of (7.1.1) is

$$S_{SM} = S_{GB,SM} + \sum_{\mu,e} S_{L,SM} + S_{LmH} + S_H + S_q \tag{7.6.1}$$

Here, $S_{L,SM}$ has been given by (7.1.11). S_{LmH} is the lepton mass term and is an integral over trilinear products of the left- and right-handed lepton fields and the Higgs field. The action for the Higgs field is

$$S_H = \int d^4X \frac{1}{4}\left[\left(\sigma_{\mu}^{ab} D_{\dot{b}a}\Phi_H\right)^{+}\left(\sigma^{\mu ab} D_{\dot{b}a}\Phi_H\right) - \frac{M_H^2}{\rho_H^2}\left(\Phi_H^{+}\Phi_H - \rho_H^2\right)^2\right] \tag{7.6.2a}$$

$$\Phi_H = \begin{pmatrix} \Phi_{H+} \\ \Phi_{H0} \end{pmatrix} \tag{7.6.2b}$$

where $\rho_H=(\sqrt{2}G)^{-1/2}\approx 246$ GeV, M_H the mass of the Higgs boson and $D_{\dot{b}a}$ has been given in (7.1.12b) with $Y_l=1$. Φ_{H+} and Φ_{H0} transform in the same way as the ψ members in (7.1.19) do;

$$\Phi_H \to U_{21-}(X)\Phi_H \tag{7.6.3}$$

$S_{GB,SM}$ is essentially a subset of S_{GB} (7.1.2),

$$S_{GB,SM} = -\frac{1}{4}\int d^4X\left(\sum_{l=1}^{3} G_l^{\mu\nu}G_{l\mu\nu} + F_C^{\mu\nu}F_{C\mu\nu}\right)$$
$$G_l^{\mu\nu}(X) = \partial_X^{\mu}W_l^{\nu} - \partial_X^{\nu}W_l^{\mu} - \varepsilon_{jkl}gW_j^{\mu}W_k^{\nu}, \quad F_C^{\mu\nu}(X) = \partial_X^{\mu}C^{\nu} - \partial_X^{\nu}C^{\mu} \tag{7.6.4}$$

S_{SM} is a invariant under $SU(2)_l\times U(1)_Y$ gauge transformations (7.1.19-21) with W_8 reverted back to C according to the reverse of (7.1.15). In passing, it is noted that the invariance of S_{LmH} is achieved by its construction. This is in contrast to S_{Lm} of (7.1.13) which is not invariant under

SU(2) gauge transformations. This noninvariance has been disregarded according to the approximation below (7.1.21).

In the SU(2) part of the transformations, there are three phase functions, ϑ_1, ϑ_2 and ϑ_3 in (7.1.21) that can arbitrarily chosen. Using two of them, (7.6.2b) can be transformed to

$$\Phi_H = \begin{pmatrix} 0 \\ \rho_H + \chi_H(X) \end{pmatrix} \tag{7.6.5}$$

where $\chi_H(X)$ is a Higgs field with mass M_H.

For the purpose of mass generation or for purely leptonic interactions, S_q does not enter and can be dropped. Following §7.4.2 and varying (7.6.1) with respect to $W_I^{-a\dot{b}}$ yields the analog of (7.4.6),

$$\Box W^+_{I\dot{b}a} - \tfrac{1}{2}\partial_{X\dot{b}a}\left(\partial^{c\dot{d}}_X W^+_{I\dot{d}c}\right) + g^2 V_{C\dot{b}a}\left(W_I^+\right) + M^2_{WH} W^+_{I\dot{b}a} = -\frac{g}{\sqrt{2}}\psi_{\nu L\dot{b}}\psi_{La} \tag{7.6.6a}$$

$$M_{WH} = \frac{g\rho_H}{\sqrt{2}} \tag{7.6.6b}$$

where the g^2 term is the same as (7.4.2b).

Choosing the Lorentz gauge below (7.4.9) and dropping the g^2V_C term according to the ordering above (7.4.8), (7.6.6a) in component form becomes

$$\Box W_I^{0+} + M^2_{WH} W_I^{0+} = -\frac{g}{2\sqrt{2}}\psi_{\nu L\dot{a}}\psi_{La} \tag{7.6.7a}$$

$$\Box \underline{W}_I^+ + M^2_{WH}\underline{W}_I^+ = -\frac{g}{2\sqrt{2}}\underline{\sigma}^{a\dot{b}}\psi_{\nu L\dot{b}}\psi_{La} \tag{7.6.7b}$$

Follow the consideration above (7.4.10a), neglect the gauge boson energy and momentum relative to its mass. These steps turn (7.6.7) to the equivalent of (7.4.10),

$$M^2_{WH} W_I^{0+} = -\frac{g}{2\sqrt{2}}\psi_{\nu L\dot{a}}\psi_{La} \tag{7.6.8a}$$

$$M^2_{WH}\underline{W}_I^+ = -\frac{g}{2\sqrt{2}}\underline{\sigma}^{b\dot{a}}\psi_{\nu L\dot{a}}\psi_{Lb} \tag{7.6.8b}$$

In (7.6.2a), the Higgs boson mass $M_H = \rho_H(\lambda/2)^{1/2}$ and the nonlinear self-coupling constant λ are unknown. A Higgs-like boson with $M_H \approx 125.09$ GeV and spin$\neq$1 has been found recently [A1]. This H(125) can presently not be identified as the above Standard Model Higgs. Its isospin, 1/2 in (7.6.2b), has not been established; the accompanying charged Higgs in (7.6.2b) has not been found years after publication of [A1].

ρ_H in (7.6.6b) not only generates the W_I mass M_{WH} but can also generate the fermion masses $M_f = f_f \rho_H$ where f_f are proportionality constants in S_{LmH} [L5 (22.58), (22.70)] but cannot account for $M_f << M_W$ [P4 p713-4]. Further, as M_{WH} is "blurred" by its large width of about 2.5% of M_{WH} [P1], ρ_H is also "blurred" to the same degree via (7.6.6b). This will be incompatible with $f = e$, the electron, whose mass is known to an accuracy of 10^{-7}.

7.6.2. Comparison to Standard Model and Replacement of Higgs Bosons by Kaons

Comparison of (7.6.6) to (7.4.6) shows that both are basically same apart from for the origin of the gauge boson mass and the transformation properties of the mass term. In (7.6.6a), this term transforms like the other terms do; so this equation is Lorentz covariant. In (7.4.6a), the mass term transforms as a covariant vector while the others as contravariant vectors. This is due to that the Higgs field (7.6.2b) generating M_{WH} transforms like a Lorentz scalar while M_W of (7.4.6) is generated by the decaying pseudoscalar meson whose wave function $\psi_{0(pr)}$ of (7.3.14) is the time component of a Lorentz four vector so that (7.4.6a) is not Lorentz covariant. This has been considered in §7.4.2.

In the absence of the source terms on the right of (7.6.7), (7.6.7b) becomes the same as (7.4.8b) and can account for the observed vector gauge boson $\underline{W}$. However, the singlet W_I^{0+} in (7.6.7a) also obeys a similar equation and has the same mass M_{WH}, contrary to (7.4.8a). But such a singlet has not been observed; yet it is needed as an intermediary in the decay of the pseudoscalar mesons in §7.4.3. Such a conceptual difficulty is absent in §7.4.2 according to the interpretation below (7.4.10).

Even if a real Higgs boson, not the Higgs-like H(125) mentioned near the end of §7.6.1, will be found, it does not affect the present theory which is supposedly still at its infancy far from being capable of accounting for complex proton-proton collisions such as those in the LHC.

Comparison of the actions (7.6.1) and (7.1.1) shows that the first two terms on the right sides correspond to each other. The third terms both refer to lepton masses and have been briefly considered below (7.6.4). The basic difference between these two total actions is that the Higg's action S_H and the quark action S_q of the standard model are replaced by the meson action S_{m3} (7.1.8). As has been shown in this chapter, S_{m3} alone gives rise to the decay amplitude for the mesons in terms of massive gauge fields. In the standard model, however, S_H is introduced solely for the purpose of generating masses for the gauge bosons. Still, one has not been able to obtain such a decay amplitude from S_q. This is one of many examples showing that the incapability of the standard model are removed in the present scalar strong interaction hadron theory.

The action S_{m3} involves the whole pseudoscalar octet mesons so that it can account for decays such as $K \rightarrow \pi +$ lepton pairs. For purely leptonic interactions, $S_q=0$ and the role of S_{m3} becomes simply that of S_H, i.e., generation of gauge boson masses. For this purpose, we do not need to include all eight mesons represented by $\psi_{(pr)}$ in (7.1.8) or (2.4.18); an isodoublet or the isotriplet inside the octet would suffice. These are provided by the kaon doublets and the pion triplet, which is preferred because it has lower mass. But the simplest choice, which also directly correspond to the Higgs doublet (7.6.2b) is the kaon doublet

$$\psi_{(pr)} \to \psi_{(p3)} = \begin{pmatrix} \psi_{(13)} \\ \psi_{(23)} \end{pmatrix} = \begin{pmatrix} \psi_{K+} \\ \psi_{K0} \end{pmatrix}, \qquad \psi \to \chi \tag{7.6.9}$$

Inserting this expression into (7.1.8) leads to that the D operators there are to be modified by removing the third row and column in the gW matrix in (7.2.7). In this matrix, W_8 is further reverted back to C by the reverse of (7.1.15), similar to that done for the standard model below (7.6.4). Thus, (7.1.4) is modified to

$$D_{I\,ps}^{a\dot{b}} \to D_{I\,ps}^{\prime a\dot{b}} = \partial_I^{a\dot{b}}\delta_{ps} + i\tfrac{1}{4}g(\sigma_I)_{ps}W_I^{a\dot{b}}(X) + i\tfrac{1}{4}g'\delta_{ps}C^{a\dot{b}}(X) \tag{7.6.10}$$

where the gauge field part is the same as that in (7.1.12b). Consistent with this change, S_{GB} and S_L on (7.1.1) also turns to $S_{GB,SM}$ and $S_{L,SM}$, respectively. For purely leptonic interaction, therefore, (7.1.1) becomes

$$S_{T3} \to S_{T21} = \kappa_{u3}S_{GB,SM} + S_{L,SM} + S_{Lm} + S_{m21} \tag{7.6.11}$$

$$S_{m3} \to S_{m21} = \int d^4X d^4x \frac{1}{2}\left\{ \begin{matrix} \chi^{+}_{(3p)\dot{e}a} D_{I\,ps}^{\prime a\dot{b}} D_{II\,sq}^{\prime f\dot{e}} \chi_{(q3)\dot{b}f} + \psi^{+e\dot{a}}_{(3p)} D'_{I\,ps\dot{a}b} D'_{II\,sq\dot{f}e} \psi^{b\dot{f}}_{(q3)} - \\ - \chi^{+}_{(3p)\dot{e}a}\left(M^2_{mp3} - \Phi_m\right)\psi^{a\dot{e}}_{(p3)} - \psi^{+e\dot{a}}_{(3p)}\left(M^2_{mp3} - \Phi_m\right)\chi_{(p3)\dot{e}a} + c.c. \end{matrix} \right\} \tag{7.6.12}$$

Noting the remarks about S_{Lm} made below (7.6.4), S_{T21} is invariant under the same $SU(2)_I \times U(1)_Y$ gauge transformations as S_{SM} is. Analogous to (7.6.5), two of the three phase functions can be used to convert (7.6.9) to

$$\psi_{(p3)} \leftarrow \begin{pmatrix} 0 \\ \psi_{(23)} \end{pmatrix} = \begin{pmatrix} 0 \\ \psi_{K0} \end{pmatrix} \tag{7.6.13}$$

Comparison of the (7.6.1) with S_q=0 and (7.6.11) shows that the both actions are basically the same apart from the mechanism of the mass generation in S_H and S_{m21}. The role of the wave function $\rho_H+\chi_H(X)$ in (7.6.5) is taken over by an integral over relative space time x involving the wave functions for the neutral kaon (7.6.13). From the viewpoint of W_I^+ mass generation via K^0, (7.6.12) and (7.1.8) with $W_V^+ \to W_I^+$ are the same. Variation of (7.6.11) with respect to $W_I^{+a\dot{b}}$ gives (7.4.6) with $W_V \to W_I$. Consequently, (7.4.10) goes over to

$$M_W^2 \kappa W_I^{0+} = \frac{g}{2\sqrt{2}}\psi^{(+)}_{\nu L\dot{a}}\psi^{(-)}_{La} \tag{7.6.14a}$$

$$M_W^2 \underline{W}_I^+ = -\frac{g}{2\sqrt{2}}\underline{\sigma}^{b\dot{a}}\psi^{(+)}_{\nu L\dot{a}}\psi^{(-)}_{Lb} \tag{7.6.14b}$$

A comparison with the standard model result (7.6.8) can now be made among the following three points.

1) *Intermediate* $W_I^{\pm}$. Comparison of (7.6.8b) with (7.6.14b), noting (7.4.32), leads to the identification

$$M_{WH}^2 = M_W^2 \tag{7.6.15a}$$

which by (7.6.6b) and (7.4.6b) becomes

$$\rho_H^2 = 2\tau_0/\Omega \tag{7.6.15b}$$

The constant $\rho_H=(\sqrt{2}G)^{-1/2}\approx 246$ GeV in the Higgs wave function corresponds to the ratio of two large quantities each approaching infinity. Comparison of (7.6.8a) and (7.6.14a) gives rise to minus signs on the right of (7.6.15a, 15b). This however does not affect the observable quantities which depend upon the square of the quantities in (7.6.15), as is shown in (7.5.1).

These comparisons show that *standard model results for purely leptonic interactions mediated by* the charged gauge boson fields *can in essence be derived here*. This is demonstrated by muon decay in the next paragraph. It is understood that the right sides of (7.6.8) or (7.6.14) are interpreted to include higher order effects and the associated consequences of application of QED.

2) *Intermediate Z*. Here, (7.4.17) replaces (7.4.6). The equations corresponding to (7.6.8) is the same equations with

$$W_I^{0-} \to Z^0, \qquad \underline{W}_I^- \to \underline{Z}, \qquad M_Z \to M_{ZH} = M_{WH}/\cos\vartheta_W \tag{7.6.16}$$

where (7.4.18c) has been consulted. Comparison of the so-obtained standard model equation with (7.4.17) follows the same steps given in 1) above. This is possible because (7.4.17a) and (7.4.6a) differ essentially in the source terms on their right sides. The results is therefore entirely analogous to that of 1) with the same provisions. Thus, standard model results for purely leptonic interaction mediated by the neutral gauge boson fields can in essence be derived here in the limit of SU(3) symmetry.

3) Virtual K^0 and π^0. So far, K^0 in S_{m21} has been regarded as a motionless real meson. However, its mass E_{K0} does not appear in the mass generation process. This is due to that the gauge boson mass terms in (7.6.12) are of the form $\psi^* W^+ W^- \psi$ and the energy dependence of ψ in (7.3.14a) is cancelled by that of ψ^*. Therefore, E_{K0} can be less than the meson mass in (7.6.12) without affecting mass generation. This virtual meson state differs from the vacuum meson state of (7.3.7b, 20) for which the energy momentum of the meson vanishes. Replacement of a Higgs condensate by a vacuum meson state condensate has been mentioned beneath (7.4.6b).

The same result can also be obtained if K^0 is replaced by π^0. This can be achieved by using an isotriplet action given in [H8 §7, H11 §9, H14 §2], analogous to the kaon doublet action of (7.6.12).

7.6.3. Bound State of W^+W^- and Higgs-like Boson [H23, H24]

The mass of the Higgs-like H(125) mentioned near the end of §7.6.1 is not too far from that of two charged gauge bosons W^+ and W^- or $2M_W = 160.8$ GeV; a bound state of W^+W^- will be considered. The spin and isospin of this state are both zero and no charged bound state is involved. Such composite type of approaches have been considered [P1 Status of Higgs Boson Physics] from models but not starting from any first principles' theory.

In high energy p-p collisions, many $W^\pm$ bosons are produced close to each other. Consider a possible bound state of a positively charged gauge boson A at x_I and a negatively charged gauge boson B at space time x_{II}. In (7.4.8b), the nonlinear g^2 term in (7.4.7b) has been neglected. This term will now be restored because in the absence of the small lepton source term on the right of (7.4.7b), the amplitude if the gauge boson field $\underline{W}_I^+$ can be large so that the trilinear g^2 term given by (7.4.2c) can be appreciable in spite of the small g^2. When applied to gauge boson A, (7.4.8b) becomes

$$\Box_I \underline{W}_A^+(x_I) - g^2\left[\left(\underline{W}_A^+(x_I)\right)^2 \underline{W}_A^-(x_I) - \left(\underline{W}_A^-(x_I)\underline{W}_A^+(x_I)\right)\underline{W}_A^+(x_I)\right] = -M_W^2 \underline{W}_A^+(x_I) \tag{7.6.17a}$$

$$\Box_{II} \underline{W}_B^-(x_{II}) - g^2\left[\left(\underline{W}_B^-(x_{II})\right)^2 \underline{W}_B^+(x_{II}) - \left(\underline{W}_B^+(x_{II})\underline{W}_B^-(x_{II})\right)\underline{W}_B^-(x_{II})\right] = -M_W^2 \underline{W}_B^-(x_{II}) \tag{7.6.17b}$$

where (7.4.8a) has been noted and the isospin index I has been dropped. Equation (7.6.17a) can also be derived from SM but this runs into the difficulty that M_W there has to be generated by an SM Higgs which has not been established.

The nonlinear g^2 terms couple W^+ and W^- and provide a weak confinement of them below.

To form a bound state, multiply together both sides of (7.6.17a) and (7.6.17b). This is entirely analogous to the formation of meson wave equations by multiplying together the left and right sides of the quark wave equations (2.1.1) and the antiquark wave equations (2.1.3).

In both case, the dynamic and interaction terms are on the left sides while the constant mass terms are on the right sides. Follow (2.2.1) and generalize the product wave functions to a nonseparable bound state wave function

$$\underline{W}_A^+(x_I)\underline{W}_B^-(x_{II}) = W_{Am}^+(x_I)W_{Bm}^-(x_{II}) \rightarrow Y(x_I, x_{II}) \tag{7.6.18}$$

where $m = 1, 2, 3$ denotes the spatial axes. The product equation reads

$$\Box_I \Box_{II} Y(x_I, x_{II}) + g^4\left[Y^2(x_I, x_{II}) + \left|Y(x_I, x_{II})\right|^2\right] Y(x_I, x_{II}) = M_W^4 Y(x_I, x_{II}) \tag{7.6.19}$$

Here, generalizations of off diagonal tensor elements $W_{Am}^+(x_I)W_{Bn}^-(x_{II})$ with $m \neq n$ have been dropped. This is analogous to leaving out the unseen "nonlocal" diquarks of (2.2.2) in the product of the quark wave equations (2.1.1) and the antiquark wave equations (2.1.3) to arrive at the meson wave equations (2.2.4). Also, generalizations of doubly charged elements $W_A^\pm(x_I)W_B^\pm(x_{II})$ are left out. Further, the g^2 terms have also been dropped because they contain $W_{Am}^\pm(x_I)$ type of factors not paired off to $W_{Bn}^\pm(x_{II})$ type of expressions and the final state contain no such unpaired gauge bosons. The corresponds to putting the unpaired off quark wave functions in the above product to arrive at (2.2.4).

Note that the equivalent of (7.6.19) for a bound state of two neutral gauge bosons $\overline{Z}Z$ cannot be formed due the forms of (7.1.2), (7.2.1) and (7.4.17).

Apply (3.1.3a) with (5.7.2) and let

$$Y(x_I, x_{II}) \to Y(X, x) \tag{7.6.20a}$$

where X is the coordinate of the bound state Y and x the relative coordinate between the both gauge bosons. Here, x is an observable contrary to x in (3.1.3a, 5a) which is a hidden variable because quarks are not observable.

The left-most 4th order derivative operator in (7.6.19) is however not separable in X and x. Hence, the right of (7.6.20a) is also not separable. The general solutions of (7.6.19-20a) is beyond the scope of this book. Here, a solution, possibly the simplest one, will be presented by limiting (7.6.20a) to be independent of $\underline{X}$, i.e.,

$$Y(X, x) \to Y_B(X^0)y(x) \tag{7.6.20b}$$

Following (3.1.9), let $y(x)=y(\underline{x})\exp(i\omega_0 x^0)$ where ω_0 is now the relative energy between the both gauge bosons and is put to 0, analogous to the null relative energy condition §5.7.1. Thus, $y(x)=y(\underline{x})$. Further, consider only the lowest energy state with zero angular momentum so that $y(\underline{x})=y(|\underline{x}|)=y(r)$ where r is the distance between the both gauge bosons. Under such conditions, it can be shown that Y in (7.6.20) is real so that the both Y^2 expressions inside the brackets of (7.6.19) are equal. Analogous to (3.1.10b), let $Y_B(X^0) = \exp(-iE_BX^0)$ where E_B is the energy of the bound state. Now (7.6.19) can be reduced to

$$\left\{\left(\frac{1}{4}E_B^2 + \Delta\right)^2 + 2g^4 y^2(r) - M_W^4\right\}y(r) = 0, \qquad \Delta = \frac{1}{r^2}\frac{\partial}{\partial r}r^2\frac{\partial}{\partial r} \tag{7.6.21}$$

The dimension of $y(r)$ is (energy)^2. The nonlinear self-interaction g^4 term is of the same order as that in the action for Higgs boson (7.6.2a) and in some soliton equations. Although this coupling is small, the resulting amplitude of $y(r)$ may not be [see e.g., L5 Ch 7]. The second order derivatives in these examples differs however from the fourth order derivatives in (7.6.21), which has to be treated numerically. If a solution exists, an upper limit of the bound state energy E_B can be found as follows.

Putting g=0, (7.6.21) is linearized and can be written in the form

$$(\Delta + \alpha_+)(\Delta + \alpha_-)y(r) = 0, \qquad \alpha_\pm = \frac{1}{4}\left(E_B^2 \pm 4M_W^2\right) \tag{7.6.22}$$

which reminds one of a particle moving in a three dimensional square well potential [S5 §15]. Equation (7.6.21) can be separated into

$$\left(\frac{\partial^2}{\partial r^2}+\alpha_+\right)\chi_+(r)=0, \qquad \left(\frac{\partial^2}{\partial r^2}+\alpha_-\right)\chi_-(r)=0, \qquad \chi(r)=ry(r) \tag{7.6.23}$$

Assume at first $\alpha_- < 0$. Since $\alpha_+ > 0$,

$$\chi_+(r)=B_B\sin(\sqrt{\alpha_+}\,r), \qquad \chi_-(r)=C_B\exp(-\sqrt{|\alpha_-|}\,r) \tag{7.6.24}$$

where B_B and C_B are constants of dimension energy. The first of (7.6.24) satisfies the boundary condition $y(r\to 0)$=finite but not $y(r\to\infty)=0$. The second of (7.6.24) satisfies the boundary condition $y(r\to\infty)=0$ but not $y(r\to 0)$=finite. Analogous to the square well potential problem [S5 §15], χ_+ and χ_- in (7.6.24) are joined at some radius $r=r_i$ by requiring $(\partial\chi_+(r)/\partial r)/\chi_+(r)=(\partial\chi_-(r)/\partial r)/\chi_-(r)$ which leads to

$$\sqrt{\alpha_+}\,/\tan(\sqrt{\alpha_+}\,r_i)=-\sqrt{|\alpha_-|} \tag{7.6.25}$$

which fixes r_i. Inserting (7.6.24) into (7.6.22) leads to $E_B=2M_W$. Inserting this value into the second of (7.6.22) does not lead to the assumed $\alpha_-<0$ but to $\alpha_-=0$. Although this α_- does give $y(r\to\infty)\propto 1/r\to 0$, this form of $y(r)$ is not normalizable. Therefore, there is no meaningful solution to (7.6.21) without the nonlinear g^4 term. Coulomb attraction is negligible here.

The nonlinear term in (7.6.21) is real and positive and when combined with the $-M_W^4$ term forms dimensionally an effective mass term $-M_{Weff}^4$ with $M_{Weff}<M_W$. $E_B=2M_W$ now becomes $E_B=2M_{Weff}$ and the second of (7.6.23) leads to the required $\alpha_-<0$. If a solution to (7.6.21) exists, the inequality, bound state W^+W^- energy $E_B<2M_W=160.8$ GeV, is obtained.

Noting that the dimension of $W^\pm$ is energy and the only energy scale associated with free $W^\pm$ is its mass M_W. By (7.6.18, 20), $y(r)$ in (7.6.21) may be put to M_W^2 in a dimensional approximation. Further, the Δ term in (7.6.21) will be neglected because the first of (7.6.24) holds for a small region $r < r_i$ and the second of (7.6.24) is not far from a constant because α_- is not far from 0 according to the lines following (7.6.25). For $g^2=0.4175$ from (7.2.1b, 7.2.12), close to $g^2=(0.652)^2=0.425$ [B8 p484], (7.6.21) leads to an estimate not far from the Higgs-like boson with $M_H\approx 125.09$ GeV [A1];

$$E_B\approx 2M_{Weff}=2M_W\sqrt[4]{(1-2g^4)}=144.4\,\text{GeV} \tag{7.6.26}$$

To get a more precise value of E_B, the soliton-like (7.6.21) has to be solved on a computer. Using the last of (7.6.23), (7.6.21) becomes

$$\frac{\partial^4\chi(r)}{\partial r^4}+\frac{1}{2}E_B^2\frac{\partial^2\chi(r)}{\partial r^2}+2g^4\frac{\chi^2(r)}{r^2}\chi(r)+\left(\frac{1}{16}E_B^4-M_W^4\right)\chi(r)=0 \tag{7.6.27}$$

which can be converted into a first order system like that in Sec 10.4,

$$w_1 = \frac{\chi(r)}{B_B\beta_+}, \qquad \frac{\partial w_1}{\partial r} = w_2, \qquad \frac{\partial w_2}{\partial r} = w_3, \qquad \frac{\partial w_3}{\partial r} = w_4$$

$$\frac{\partial w_4}{\partial r} = -\frac{1}{2}E_B^2 w_3 - 2g^4\left(\frac{B_B\beta_+ w_1(r)}{r}\right)^2 w_1(r) - \left(\frac{1}{16}E_B^4 - M_W^4\right)w_1(r) = 0$$

(7.6.28)

When $r \to 0$, (7.6.27) and the first of (7.6.24) leads to

$$w_{10} = r - \beta_+^2 r^3/3, \qquad w_{20} = 1 - \beta_+^2 r^2/2, \qquad w_{30} = -\beta_+^2 r, \qquad w_{40} = -\beta_+^2$$

$$\beta_+^2 = \frac{1}{2}E_B^2 - g^4 B_B^2 + \sqrt{\left(\frac{1}{2}E_B^2 - g^4 B_B^2\right)^2 - \frac{1}{16}E_B^4 + M_W^4}$$

(7.6.29)

As $r \to \infty$, the second of (7.6.24) satisfies (7.6.27) and the asymptotic solution is

$$w_{1\infty} = \frac{\chi_-(r)}{C_B} = \exp(-\beta_- r), \qquad w_{2\infty} = -\beta_- w_{1\infty}$$

$$w_{3\infty} = \beta_-^2 w_{1\infty}, \qquad w_{4\infty} = -\beta_-^3 w_{1\infty}, \qquad \beta_- = \sqrt{|\alpha_-|}$$

(7.6.30)

Numerical integration of (7.6.28) starts from r=0 with (7.6.29) forward (w_+) and from $r\cong\infty$ with (7.6.30) backward (w_-). Both solutions meet at r_i and are joined continuously there. Corresponding to (7.6.25) are

$$\frac{w_{2+}(r_i)}{w_{1+}(r_i)} = \frac{w_{2-}(r_i)}{w_{1-}(r_i)}, \qquad \frac{w_{3+}(r_i)}{w_{1+}(r_i)} = \frac{w_{3-}(r_i)}{w_{1-}(r_i)}, \qquad \frac{w_{4+}(r_i)}{w_{1+}(r_i)} = \frac{w_{4-}(r_i)}{w_{1-}(r_i)}$$

(7.6.31)

These three conditions fix the three unknown parameters, the bound state energy E_B, the bound state amplitude B_B and the junction radius r_i for a given g^2.

Dividing the left sides in (7.6.31) by their respective right sides gives 1 for each of the three conditions. The computed results will deviate from these three 1's. Denote the greatest of these three deviations by Δ_{max}. Let the amplitude $B=b_0M_W=b_0 80.385$ GeV.

A Fortran 77 computer program has been written for (7.6.28-31) employing the same Runge-Kutta integration subroutine "dverk" to be used for the baryon wave functions in Figure 11.1 below. The calculations are run on computers of the Department of Information Technology at Uppsala University.

The forward integration mostly starts at $r=10^{-6}$ GeV^{-1} but other powers have also been used to check consistency. Because of (7.6.30), the backward integration must start from rather large r, here 0.5 GeV^{-1}, but other values < 1 have also been employed to check consistency.

In the "dverk" subroutine, denote the integration step length by d_s. The inter-gauge boson distance r that enter the computations is $r_c=k_d d_s$, where k_d is the number of steps needed to reach r_c. Only at these discrete r_c values can the solutions be printed out. This subroutine only allows $k_d \leq 2^{10}=1024$. For backward integrations starting from $r\approx 0.5$ GeV^{-1}, d_s has a minimum $d_{sm}=0.5/1024\approx 0.000488$ GeV^{-1}. Let r_{ci} be the r_c closest to r_i and $r_{ci}=k_{di}d_s$. Three step lengths, $d_s = d_{sm}$, $2d_{sm}$ and $4d_{sm}$, corresponding to k_{di}, $k_{di}/2$ and $k_{di}/4$, respectively, for a given r_{ci} will be used.

A bound state solution exists when the three conditions of (7.6.31) is exactly satisfied. This requires that $\Delta_{max}=0$. Among the three parameters that fix (7.6.31), E_b and b_0 are continuous and can be specified to any degree of accuracy. But the third parameter r_i is according to the last paragraph limited to the discrete r_{ci} which can differ from r_i by $<d_{sm}\neq 0$. Therefore, $\Delta_{max}\neq 0$ and minima of Δ_{max} are sought. For such minima encountered here, it is sufficient to specify Δ_{max} up to 0.01%. This error margin leads to that E_B needs be accurate up to 0.001 GeV and b_0 up to 0.0001.

A criterion for the existence of a bound state solution will be taken to be $\Delta_{max}<\Delta_{err}$, an error due to the finite integration step length; $\Delta_{err}=d_s/r_{ci}=2d_{sm}/r_{ci}$. Table 7.1 below shows that only $r_i\approx 0.032$-0.033 are of interest so that $\Delta_{err}=2d_{sm}/r_i\approx 3\%$ and the criterion becomes $\Delta_{max}<3\%$. This criterion is not absolute or derivable but is regarded as a plausible first approximation.

The parameter space $0<r_i<0.5$ GeV^{-1}, $0<b_0<10$ for $g^2=0.4175$ and $100<E_B<156$ GeV has been scanned with rather fine meshes near the approximate solutions where Δ_{max} reach minima. The results are

$$E_B = 155.81\,\text{GeV},\quad g^2 b_0 = 0.812,\quad r_i = 0.03418\text{GeV}^{-1},\quad \Delta_{\max} = 2.69\% \qquad (7.6.32)$$

satisfying the criterion $\Delta_{max}<3\%$. The wave function $\chi(r)$ is given by the full curve in Figure 1 of [H23]

The existence of solution (7.6.32) shows that the gWW term in (7.1.2b) which gives rise to the g^4 term in (7.6.27) is responsible for a *new nonlinear, intrinsic confinement mechanism* at the quantum mechanical level. Because g^4 is small, the confinement is weak, as is signified by that $E_b\approx 155.81$ GeV in (7.6.32) is just slightly smaller than $2M_W=160.77$ GeV. This confinement mechanism is implicit in the numerical treatment but not transparent and hence not understood presently.

The corresponding gWW term in the QCD Lagrangian density [L5 (18.3)] also gives rise to confinement of colored quarks which is a quantum field theory effect [G6, P3]. These both confinement mechanisms are basically different. The present bound state is a counterpart to the QCD glueball.

The predicted E_B of $\approx$ 156 GeV in (7.6.32) is too high to account for the H(125). However, the mean distances between the both gauge bosons $r_i\approx 0.032$-0.033 are very small, far smaller than those at which the bare g and M_W are determined. At such distances, quantum field effects like vacuum polarization can no longer be neglected. Such effects are estimated below.

Return to the gauge boson action (7.1.2) and the meson action (7.1.8). These correspond to the QCD action formed from the QCD Lagrangian density [L5 (18.3)]. The gluon part in this action is the same as (7.1.2) if the gluons are replaced by the gauge bosons $W_{i'}$. Therefore, quantization of this gluon part in [L5 Ch 18] can be taken over to apply to (7.1.2). The remaining quark related part in the QCD action differ from the meson action (7.1.8); the former has been quantized in [L5 Ch 18] while the latter is nonlocal and cannot be quantized according to Table 14.1 below. These parts provide the charges that generate the gluons and gauge bosons W_l, respectively, but do not affect their actions.

The running coupling constant [L5 (18.155)] with no massless quarks is

$$\frac{g_L^2}{g_l^2}=\left[1+\frac{11g_l^2}{8\pi^2}\log\left(\frac{l}{L}\right)\right]^{-1} \tag{7.6.33}$$

where L^3 and l^3 are two different normalization volumes corresponding to the both infrared cutoffs L and l in the logarithmically divergent integral [L5 (18.121)] leading to (7.6.33). Let $L=L_R$ and $g=g_R$, where R stands for "renormalized." Choose l^3 to be a large normalization box L_f^3 in which the bare coupling constant g has been determined so that g_l can be approximated by the bare g used above. In this case, (7.6.33) can be approximated to

$$g_R^2=g^2\left[1+\frac{11g^2}{8\pi^2}\log\left(\frac{L_f}{L_R}\right)\right]^{-1}, \qquad L_R\to r, \qquad L_f>r \tag{7.6.34}$$

In the bound state, the both gauge bosons are so close to each other that the normalization volume for their wave functions are greatly reduced. The effect is roughly taken into account by the approximation $L_R \to r$, the distance between the both gauge bosons, in (7.6.34).

The distances $r_i \approx 0.032$-0.033 are not extremely small and the Fermi constant (7.4.29a) $\propto g^2/M_W^2$ may be assumed to remain valid there so that the renormalized gauge boson mass M_{WR} becomes

$$M_{WR}=M_W g_R/g \tag{7.6.35}$$

Here, $\Delta_{err}=d_{sm}/r_i \approx 1.5\%$ and $\Delta_{err}=4d_{sm}/r_i \approx 6\%$ are also considered. The corresponding criteria are $\Delta_{max}<\Delta_{err}\approx 1.5\%$ and $\Delta_{max}<\Delta_{err}\approx 6\%$, respectively. The computations that led to (7.6.32) using the step length $d_s=2d_{sm}$ are repeated using $d_s=d_{sm}$ instead. The result (7.6.32) remains unchanged but now the criterion becomes $\Delta_{max}<1.5\%$ and is not satisfied by the solution (7.6.31) with bare g and M_W values and such a bound state no longer exists.

With M_W=80.385 GeV, (7.4.29a) gives g^2=0.426356. For this case, the calculations leading to (7.6.32) is repeated with the bare g and M_W replaced by the renormalized $g_R(r)$ of (7.6.34) and $M_{WR}(r)$ of (7.6.35). Because r can be larger than L_f in the integration, the replacements are limited to $L_f>r$ in (7.6.34). The results corresponding to (7.6.32) are shown in Table 7.1.

Table 7.1. Results of numerical solution of (7.6.28)-(7.6.31) with the bare g and M_W replaced by the renormalized $g_R(r)$ of (7.6.34) and $M_{WR}(r)$ of (7.6.35) for g^2=0.426356. E_B , b_0, and r_i for each L_f are varied such that Δ_{max}, the greatest deviation from the exact (7.6.31), reaches a minimum.
Only the underlined two cases satisfy the extrapolated criterion $\Delta_{max}<\Delta_{err}\approx 0.75\%$ below and can be solutions. k_{di} is the number of integration steps needed to reach r_{ci}, the printout r_c value nearest to the joint distance r_i in (7.6.31), for three different integration step lengths, $4d_{sm}$, $2d_{sm}$ and d_{sm}. * denotes that k_{di}=60 was excluded due the above $k_d \leq 2^{10}$=1024 limitation in the backward integration

L_f GeV^{-1}	0.20	0.20	0.30	0.30	0.34	0.35	0.36	0.40	0.50
k_{di}	16	33,66	17	33,66	17,34,68	17,34,68	17,34,68	17,34,68	15,30*
Δ_{max} %	33.57	30.18	6.20	1.71	<u>0.50</u>	<u>0.35</u>	1.04	2.42	32.73
b_0	1.2753	1.3466	1.5277	1.4108	1.6792	1.7143	1.7486	1.8760	1.9161
E_b GeV	104.635	105.337	112.708	113.179	115.951	116.845	117.773	121.825	131.227

For L_f=0.20 and 0.30, k_{di}=33 and 66 refer to the same r_{ci}. Since 33/2=16.5 is not an integer, k_{di}=17 and 16 refer to this r_{ci} + and – $2d_{sm}$ respectively. It is seen that Δ_{max} is lower for the smallest step length d_{sm} accompanying k_{di}=66, as expected. The four cases with k_{di}=17, 34 and 68 are accompanied by the step lengths d_s=$4d_{sm}$, $2d_{sm}$ and d_{sm}, respectively, correspond to the same r_{ci} and yield the same integration results. This shows that the computer accuracy is independent of these step lengths; only printouts do. Extrapolating these cases by reducing d_s one more step down to $d_{sm}/2$, $\Delta_{err}\rightarrow d_{sm}/2r_i$. The so-extrapolated criterion becomes $\Delta_{max}<0.75\%$ which is satisfied only by the two underlined cases in Table 7.1. A further reduction leads to $\Delta_{max}<0.375\%$ which is only satisfied by the L_f=0.35 case. If the step length is reduced by half once more, $\Delta_{max}<0.1875\%$ and there is no solution for any case in Table 7.1.

The L_f=0.35 case with Δ_{max}=0.35% in Table 7.1 is rather close to 0 and may be regarded as a solution to the bound state and is tentatively assigned to H(125). The so-estimated mass $E_b\approx$117 GeV is also rather close to the observed 125.09 GeV [A1]. Coulomb attraction is negligible. The wave functions for this case is shown in Figure 7.2.

Equation (7.6.34) shows that L_f is an infrared cutoff and represents the size of the normalization box for a $W^{\pm}$ boson. Its mass M_W=80.385 GeV is interpreted to have been determined when this boson is separated from other interacting particles by $>L_f$. L_f=0.35 GeV^{-1} in Table 7.1 appears to be compatible to some of the experimental conditions determining M_W. Also, E_b gets closer to the measured 125 GeV with increasing L_f. But why Δ_{max} is small enough for the present bound state to exist only when $L_f\approx$0.35 GeV^{-1} is not understood.

Existence of the solution Figure 7.2 justifies the approximation to neglect $\underline{X}$ dependence in $Y_B(X^0)$ in (7.6.20b). An effect of weak such dependence may qualitatively be included by letting $E_B^2\rightarrow E_{BX}^2-K_B^2$ in (7.6.21), where E_{BX} is the new total energy of the bound state and K_B plays the role of its momentum. $E_{BX}>E_B\approx$117 GeV in Table 7.1 and is moved closer to the measured 125.09 GeV.

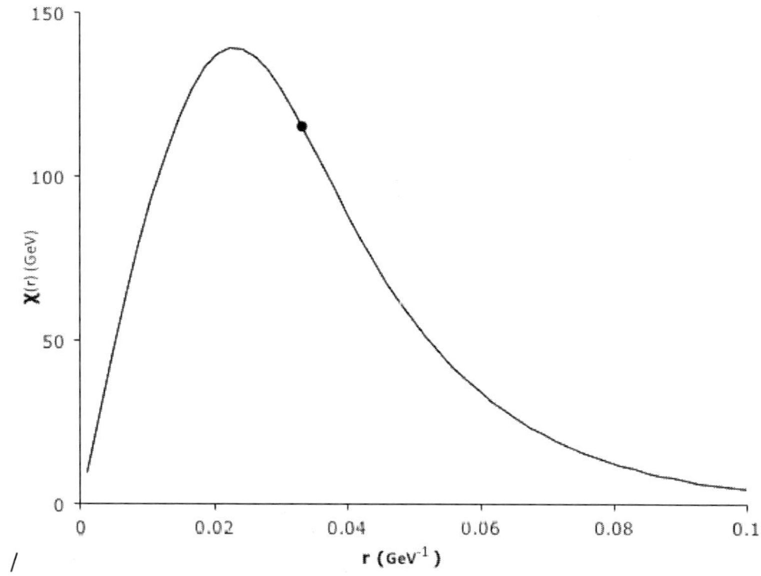

Figure 7.2. The bound state wave function $\chi(r)$ for the L_f=0.35 GeV^{-1} case in Table 7.1. The forward and backward integrations are joined at the dot marked point.

Attempts have been made to replace (7.6.34), based upon spherical symmetry [H23 (22), L5 (18.121)], by models including deviations from this symmetry when W^+ and W^- are close to each other. No solution was found.

This bound state decays to leptons, pseudoscalar mesons and nucleons principally via the actions (7.1.13), (7.1.8) and (12.2.7-8) below. These decays differ from those of the Higgs boson in the standard model [B8 p146].

7.6.4. Muon Decay

The successful standard model results for $\mu\to\ \bar{\nu}_e\nu_\mu e$ are in essence derived below from the present theory.

1) *Standard Model Results.* The decay amplitude of [K3 14.22, 8] is

$$S_{fi(K)}\left(\mu\to e\bar{\nu}_e\nu_\mu\right)=-i\int dX^0\left\langle e,\bar{\nu}_e,\nu_\mu\left|H_1\right|\mu\right\rangle=-\frac{i}{\Omega_e\Omega_\mu}\sum_i\sum_{\lambda=1}^{4}J_{(e\mu)i\lambda}J_{(\nu\mu\nu e)i\lambda}$$

$$\times\int d^4X\exp\left(i\left(K_e^\sigma+K_{\nu e}^\sigma+K_{\nu\mu}^\sigma-K_\mu^\sigma\right)X_\sigma\right) \tag{7.6.36a}$$

$$J_{(e\mu)i\lambda}=\bar{u}_e^{(+)}\left(\underline{K}_e\right)O_{i\lambda}u_\mu^{(+)}\left(\underline{K}_\mu\right) \tag{7.6.36b}$$

$$J_{(\nu\mu\nu e)i\lambda}=\bar{u}_{\nu\mu}^{(+)}\left(\underline{K}_{\nu\mu}\right)O_{i\lambda}\frac{1}{\sqrt{2}}\left(g_i+ig_i'\gamma_5\right)u_{\nu e}^{(-)}\left(-\underline{K}_{\nu e}\right) \tag{7.6.36c}$$

where the left of (7.6.36a) and $O_{i\lambda}$ are in the notation of [K3] and i denotes the five interaction types S, V, T, A, and P given in Table 13-1 of [K3]. This decay amplitude leads to correct predictions.

2) *Muon Decay Actions.* In the present theory, the starting point is a modified form of (7.1.1),

$$S_{T2} = S_{GB3} + S_{m2} + S_{\mu} + S_{\mu m} + S_{e} + S_{em} \tag{7.6.37}$$

where S_{GB3} is S_{GB} of (7.1.2) with l=1,2,3 and S_{m2} is the SU(2) part of S_{m3} in (7.1.8). The remaining lepton actions are shown in (7.1.13, 16, 17). The amplitude for muon decay will now be derived from (7.6.37) and shown to be essentially the same as the standard model amplitude (7.6.36). The procedure is analogous to that employed for $\pi^{+}\to \pi^{0}e^{+}\nu_e$ in §7.4.5.

Treatment of (7.6.37) that follows is basically the same as that for kaon decay in Sec. 7.3 and 7.4. The role of the meson action S_{m3} in (7.1.1, 8) is taken over by S_μ+$S_{\mu m}$ in § 7.1.3 for the decay of a muon into a ν_μ and a gauge boson W_I^- together with S_{m2} for the generation of the mass of this W_I^-. The roles of the remaining actions S_e+S_{em} for the electron and $\bar{\nu}_e$ and S_{GB3} for the gauge boson are the same as in (7.1.1).

3) *Muon Decay into a Gauge Boson.* The ordering of the quantities contained in (7.6.37) is the same as that of (7.3.2b) with L limited to e. The muon now takes place of the kaon or pion in Sec. 7.3 and the equivalent of (7.3.1) becomes

$$\psi_{\mu}^{b}(X) = \left(1 + \frac{a_{\mu}^{(1)}(X^0)}{a_{\mu}}\right)\psi_{\mu 0}^{b}(X), \quad \psi_{\mu 0}^{b}(X) = \frac{1}{\sqrt{\Omega_\mu}} u_{\mu}^{b(+)} \exp\left(-iE_{\mu}X^0 + i\underline{K}_{\mu}\underline{X}\right) \tag{7.6.38a}$$

$$u_{\mu}^{b(+)} = \begin{pmatrix} u_{\mu}^{1(+)} \\ u_{\mu}^{2(+)} \end{pmatrix} = \frac{1}{\sqrt{2E_{\mu}(E_{\mu}+M_{\mu})}} \left[\begin{pmatrix} E_{\mu}+M_{\mu}-K_{\mu 3} \\ -K_{\mu 1}-iK_{\mu 2} \end{pmatrix}, \begin{pmatrix} -K_{\mu 1}+iK_{\mu 2} \\ E_{\mu}+M_{\mu}+K_{\mu 3} \end{pmatrix} \right] \tag{7.6.38b}$$

$$\psi \to \chi \tag{7.6.38c}$$

analogous to (7.4.19b).

The initial and final states of (7.3.6, 7) become here

$$\left|i\right\rangle = \left|\mu\left(E_{\mu} = M_{\mu}, \underline{K}_{\mu} = 0\right)\right\rangle, \qquad \left\langle f\right| = \left\langle \nu_{\mu}, W_{I}^{-}\right| \to \left\langle \nu_{\mu}, e, \bar{\nu}_{e}\right| \tag{7.6.39}$$

Putting the first order part of S_{m2} to 0, which is equivalent to (7.3.3), and sandwiching it between <f| and |i>, one obtains the analog of (7.3.13, 22),

$$S_{fi} = \langle f | a_{\mu}^{+} a_{\mu}^{(1)} (X^0 \to \infty) | i \rangle$$
$$= i \frac{g}{16} \frac{\sqrt{2}}{\Omega_{\mu}} \langle f | \int d^4 X u_{\nu\mu}^{(+)\dot{a}} W_{I\dot{a}b}^{-} (X) u_{\mu}^{(+)b} \exp \left(i \left(K_{\nu\mu\sigma} - K_{\mu\sigma} \right) X^{\sigma} \right) | i \rangle$$

(7.6.40)

4) *Decay of W_I^+ into e and $\bar{\nu}_e$ and Decay Amplitude.* This decay has been treated in §7.4.1-3, except for the interchange of W_I^+ and W_I^- and for the replacement of kaon by π^0 for mass generation. The last point has been considered at the end of §7.6.2. S_{m2} in (7.6.37) refers to the triplet of pions.

Variation of the fourth order part of (7.6.37) with respect to W_I^- leads to the analog of (7.4.11c),

$$W_{I\dot{a}b}^{-} = \frac{g}{\sqrt{2} M_W^2} \frac{1}{\Omega_e} u_e^{(+)\dot{b}} (\underline{K}_e) u_{\nu e}^{(-)a} (\underline{K}_{\nu e}) \exp \left(i \left(E_e + |E_{\nu e}| \right) X^0 - i \left(\underline{K}_e + \underline{K}_{\nu e} \right) \underline{X} \right) \quad (7.6.41)$$

Inserting this result into (7.6.40) leads to the decay amplitude

$$S_{fi} \left(\mu \to e \bar{\nu}_e \nu_{\mu} \right) = i \frac{g^2}{8 M_W^2} \frac{1}{\Omega_{\mu} \Omega_e} u_{\mu}^{(+)b} u_e^{(+)\dot{b}} u_{\nu\mu}^{(+)\dot{a}} u_{\nu e}^{(-)a}$$
$$\times \int d^4 X \exp \left(i \left(E_{\nu\mu} + |E_{\nu e}| + E_e - M_{\mu} \right) X^0 + i \left(\underline{K}_{\nu\mu} + \underline{K}_e + \underline{K}_{\nu e} \right) \underline{X} \right)$$

(7.6.42)

5) *Comparison with Standard Model.* Return to (7.6.36) and keep only the V and A interactions. Table 13-1 of [K3] defines

$$O_V^{\lambda} = \gamma^{\lambda}, \qquad O_A^{\lambda} = -\gamma^{\lambda} \gamma_5 \quad (7.6.43)$$

Because there is only one coupling constant, the Fermi constant G, put

$$|g_V| = |g_V'| = |g_A| = |g_A'| = G \quad (7.6.44)$$

in (14.51a) of [K3]. Since the interactions affect only the left handed parts of the lepton wave functions,

$$g_V = g_V' = -g_A = -g_A' = G \quad (7.6.45)$$

is set. With the muon at rest in (7.6.36), one finds

$$S_{fi} \left(\mu \to e \bar{\nu}_e \nu_{\mu} \right) = S_{fi(K)} \left(\mu \to e \bar{\nu}_e \nu_{\mu} \text{ with } i = V,\ A \text{ and } \lambda = 4 \right) \quad (7.6.46)$$

analogous to (7.4.31) for $\pi^+ \to \pi^0 e^+ \nu_e$. The decay amplitude S_{fi} derived from the actions (7.6.37) agrees with that of the standard model $S_{fi(K)}$ limited to the time components λ =4 of the currents in (7.6.36b, 36c) and to V-A interactions. The absence of contributions from the spatial components λ =1,2,3 in (7.6.42) is due that only the time component of the meson wave function (7.3.14) generates the gauge boson mass. This is reflected in that (7.4.4) and (7.6.41) are no longer covariant under the SL(2,C) group of transformations.

The general case in which the decaying kaon is moving, corresponding to that the virtual π^0 has a momentum in 4) above, should involve more terms that correspond to the λ =1,2,3 contributions in (7.6.36). The simple form (7.4.4) is lost and will involve integrals over the vector parts of the meson wave functions $\underline{\psi}$ and $\underline{\chi}$ in (3.1.7a) leading to very complicated forms of $W_I^{(\pm)}$ in (7.4.10). Further, (3.1.8) determining these $\underline{\psi}$ and $\underline{\chi}$ has not been solved, except for some dimensional analyses in some limits in Sec. 5.7. This general case has not been treated.

On the other hand, it may in principle be possible to transform away the spatial part of the material current in (7.6.36b) so that $S_{fi}=S_{fi}(K)$ here.

6) *On the Concept of Purely Leptonic Interactions.* In the standard model, muon decay is a purely leptonic process independent of the existence of hadrons. However, this model requires the unseen Higgs boson.

In the present approach, the role of the Higgs is played by the virtual π^0 in 4) above. Muon decay, hence weak interactions in general, therefore necessitates the existence of mesons, here the virtual π^0, hence quarks. *Leptons cannot exist alone but must coexist with quarks.* The usual conception of purely leptonic processes therefore no longer holds.

7.7. Formulation of the *K→3π* Problem

Pions in kaon decays are generally relativistic, such as that in the semi-leptonic decay in §7.4.6. The wave functions of such pions in relative space differ considerably from that for a pseudoscalar meson at rest and are unknown, as was mentioned below (7.4.33). Analogous to the case of §7.4.6, the associated decay amplitudes can likewise not be calculated generally.

In $K \to 3\pi$, however, the pions move relatively slowly so that expansion in the small parameter $\varepsilon_0=K/E_0$ of (5.7.4) can be applied. The wave functions of such pions have been considered in §5.7.4 and are determined by (5.7.22b) which however can presently not be solved. Therefore, no prediction can be given here.

7.7.1. Variation of Pion Action

In the beginning of §7.1.1, it was mentioned that $K \to \pi L \nu_L$ consists of two stages. In stage I, the K decays into a π and an intermediate gauge boson. In stage II, the intermediate gauge boson decays into a lepton-antilepton pair treated in Sec. 7.4 and 7.5. Here, this boson decays instead to a pair of π's. In (7.1.1), $\kappa_\pi S_{m\pi}$ takes over the role of S_L+S_{Lm}. This transition is accomplished by modifying (7.4.5, 6) and (7.4.15, 17) according to

$$M_W^2 W_I^{\mp e\dot{f}} = M_W^2 (W_I^{\mp 0}\delta^{e\dot{f}} - \underline{\sigma}^{e\dot{f}}\,\underline{W}_I^{\mp}) \to 2\delta S_L/\delta W_I^{\pm f\dot{e}} \to 2\kappa_\pi\,\delta S_{m\pi}/\delta W_I^{\pm f\dot{e}} \tag{7.7.1}$$

$$M_Z^2 Z^{e\dot{f}} = M_Z^2 (Z^0 \delta^{e\dot{f}} - \underline{\sigma}^{e\dot{f}} \underline{Z}) \to 4\delta S_L / \delta Z^{\dot{f}\dot{e}} \to 4\kappa_\pi \, \delta S_{m\pi} / \delta Z^{\dot{f}\dot{e}} \tag{7.7.2}$$

where terms next to the gauge boson mass terms have been neglected.

$S_{m\pi}$ is taken to be the SU(2) part of S_{m3}. The kaon and η wave functions drop out because they are not the decay products of $W^{\pm}$ and Z. In stage II of §7.1.1, this action replaces the lepton action in (7.1.1). Making use of (7.1.4, 8) and (7.2.14, 20), the pion action is written out as

$$\begin{aligned} S_{m\pi} = \frac{1}{2}\int d^4X \int d^4y \Bigg\{ & \begin{pmatrix} \frac{1}{\sqrt{2}}\chi^*_{f3(\pi 0)} & \chi^*_{f3(\pi +)} \\ \chi^*_{f3(\pi -)} & -\frac{1}{\sqrt{2}}\chi^*_{f3(\pi 0)} \end{pmatrix}_{\dot{e}a} \left[\partial^{a\dot{b}}_{III} - i\frac{g}{4} \begin{pmatrix} Z\frac{\cos 2\vartheta_W}{\cos\vartheta_W} & \sqrt{2}W_I^+ \\ \sqrt{2}W_I^- & -\frac{Z}{\cos\vartheta_W} \end{pmatrix}^{a\dot{b}} \right] \\ \times & \left[\partial^{\dot{f}\dot{e}}_{IV} + i\frac{g}{4} \begin{pmatrix} Z\frac{\cos 2\vartheta_W}{\cos\vartheta_W} & \sqrt{2}W_I^+ \\ \sqrt{2}W_I^- & -\frac{Z}{\cos\vartheta_W} \end{pmatrix}^{\dot{f}\dot{e}} \right] \begin{pmatrix} \frac{1}{\sqrt{2}}\chi^{(-)}_{f2(\pi 0)} & \chi^{(-)}_{f2(\pi +)} \\ \chi^{(-)}_{f2(\pi -)} & -\frac{1}{\sqrt{2}}\chi^{(-)}_{f2(\pi 0)} \end{pmatrix}_{\dot{b}f} \\ & + \left(M^2_{mpr} - \Phi_m\right) \text{term} + c.c. + \text{corresponding } \psi \text{ terms} \Bigg\} \end{aligned} \tag{7.7.3}$$

Here, ∂_{III} operates on χ^* on its left side. The ψ terms are obtained from the χ terms by $\chi \to \psi$ and the interchanges upper $\leftrightarrow$ lower indices and dotted $\leftrightarrow$ undotted indices, according to (7.1.8b). The *c.c.* terms are found by the same interchange dotted $\leftrightarrow$ undotted indices and $i \leftrightarrow -i$. Summation over the flavor indices *r, p, s*... in (7.1.8b) has been written out in matrix multiplication form here and the flavor contents of the fields therein given by these indices have been replaced by particle symbols according to (7.1.5b) and (7.2.1a, 3a) together with (2.4.18).

The pion wave functions χ and ψ in (7.7.3), associated with the decay of the gauge bosons, are functions of the quark coordinates x_{III} and x_{IV}. These differ from the quark coordinates x_I and x_{II} for the initial kaon in S_{m3}, much like the strong interaction case of the decay of a vector meson into two pseudoscalar mesons, such as $D^* \to D\pi$, considered in (8.1.1-2) below. In S_{m3}, the transformation

$$x^\mu = x^\mu_{II} - x^\mu_I, \qquad X^\mu = \tfrac{1}{2}(x^\mu_I + x^\mu_{II}) \tag{7.7.4}$$

has been made according to (3.1.3a, 10a) and the null energy condition [H10 Sec. 4.1] or (5.7.1). In (7.7.3), (7.7.4) is replaced by

$$y^\mu = x^\mu_{IV} - x^\mu_{III}, \qquad X^\mu = \tfrac{1}{2}(x^\mu_{III} + x^\mu_{IV}) \tag{7.7.5}$$

The relative coordinates x^μ and y^μ are hidden variables [H12 Sec. 1] and are integrated over in S_{m3} and (7.7.3).

The subscripts *f2* and *f3* in (7.7.3) actually refer to the same meson therein and are anticipated here and will, upon quantization of the χ's and ψ's, refer to final state *2* meson and final state *3* meson, respectively. These mesons will then be different and also differ from the final state *1* meson which is not a decay product of the gauge boson and is denoted by the subscripts *f1* in (7.3.26a). Similarly, the superscript (–) is to be ignored in (7.7.3) but will upon quantization later refer to meson with negative energy.

The action (7.7.3) is now to be varied with respect to $W_I^{\pm}(X)$ and $Z(X)$ as required by (7.7.1, 2). For simplicity of notation, only expressions for $W_I^{+}(X)$ will be written down. The $W_I^{-}(X)$ results are obtained by letting the superscript $+ \rightarrow -$ and vice versa in the $W_I^{+}(X)$ results. Thus,

$$\kappa_\pi \frac{\delta S_{m\pi}}{\delta W_I^{+f\dot{e}}} \rightarrow \frac{g}{8}\kappa_\pi \int d^4y \left\{ \begin{array}{l} i\left[\begin{array}{l} \chi^*_{f3(\pi-)\dot{b}f}\,\partial^{a\dot{b}}_{IV}\chi^{(-)}_{f2(\pi0)\dot{e}a} - \left(\partial^{a\dot{b}}_{III}\chi^*_{f3(\pi-)\dot{e}a}\right)\chi^{(-)}_{f2(\pi0)\dot{b}f} \\ -\chi^*_{f3(\pi0)\dot{b}f}\,\partial^{a\dot{b}}_{IV}\chi^{(-)}_{f2(\pi-)\dot{e}a} + \left(\partial^{a\dot{b}}_{III}\chi^*_{f3(\pi0)\dot{e}a}\right)\chi^{(-)}_{f2(\pi-)\dot{b}f} \\ +\psi \text{ terms} \end{array} \right] \\ + c.c. \text{ terms} \end{array} \right\} \tag{7.7.6}$$

Similarly, variation of (7.7.3) with respect to $Z(X)$ yields

$$\kappa_\pi \frac{\delta S_{m\pi}}{\delta Z^{f\dot{e}}} \rightarrow \frac{-\kappa_\pi g}{8\cos\vartheta_W} \int d^4y \left\{ \begin{array}{l} i\left[\begin{array}{l} (\cos 2\vartheta_W - 1)\frac{1}{2}\left(\chi^*_{f3(\pi0)\dot{b}f}\,\partial^{a\dot{b}}_{IV}\chi^{(-)}_{f2(\pi0)\dot{e}a} - \left(\partial^{a\dot{b}}_{III}\chi^*_{f3(\pi0)\dot{e}a}\right)\chi^{(-)}_{f2(\pi0)\dot{b}f}\right) \\ + \cos 2\vartheta_W \left(\chi^*_{f3(\pi-)\dot{b}f}\,\partial^{a\dot{b}}_{IV}\chi^{(-)}_{f2(\pi+)\dot{e}a} - \left(\partial^{a\dot{b}}_{III}\chi^*_{f3(\pi-)\dot{e}a}\right)\chi^{(-)}_{f2(\pi+)\dot{b}f}\right) \\ -\left(\chi^*_{f3(\pi+)\dot{b}f}\,\partial^{a\dot{b}}_{IV}\chi^{(-)}_{f2(\pi-)\dot{e}a} - \left(\partial^{a\dot{b}}_{III}\chi^*_{f3(\pi+)\dot{e}a}\right)\chi^{(-)}_{f2(\pi-)\dot{b}f}\right) + \psi \text{ terms} \end{array} \right] \\ + c.c. \text{ terms} \end{array} \right\} \tag{7.7.7}$$

The ψ and *c.c.* terms in (7.7.6, 7) are found by the same prescription given below (7.7.3).

7.7.2. Pion Wave Functions and Ordering of the Pion Action

The pion wave functions in (7.7.6, 7) are decomposed analogous to [H10 (3.1)] or (7.3.1) complemented by a relative time factor. For instance,

$$\begin{aligned} &\chi^{(-)}_{f2(\pi-)\dot{e}a}(x_{III}, x_{IV}) = \chi^{(-)}_{f2(\pi-)\dot{e}a}(X, y) = a^{(-)}_{f2(\pi-)}\left(\delta_{\dot{e}a}\chi_{02-}(\underline{y}) + \underline{\sigma}_{\dot{e}a}\underline{\chi}_{2-}(\underline{y})\right) \\ &\times \exp\left(i\omega^{(-)}_{2-}y^0 - iE^{(-)}_{2-}X^0 + i\underline{K}_{2-}\underline{X}\right), \qquad \chi \rightarrow \psi \end{aligned} \tag{7.7.8}$$

where $a_{f2(\pi-)}^{(-)}$ is unity here but can later be elevated to an operator annihilating a π^- with negative energy $E_{2-}^{(-)} < 0$ and momentum $\underline{K}_{2-}$ which is equivalent to the creation of a π^- with positive energy

$$-E^{(-)}_{2-} = \left|E^{(-)}_{2-}\right| = E_{2-} \tag{7.7.9}$$

This quantization procedure is anticipated here. y^0 is the relative time between the quarks constituting the π^- and $\omega_{2-}^{(-)}$ the associated relative energy. To be consistent with (7.7.5, 4), the null energy condition (5.7.1) also holds so that

$$\omega_{2-}^{(-)} = 0 \tag{7.7.10}$$

At rest, $\underline{K}_{2-}$=0 and $\chi_{02-}(\underline{y})$=0 by (5.7.6). The normalized meson wave function is given by (4.3.4a),

$$\chi_{02-}(\underline{y}) = \chi_0(\underline{y}) = -\psi_0(\underline{y}) = \frac{1}{\sqrt{\Omega_\pi}}\alpha_{00}\exp\left(-\frac{d_h}{2}r_y^2\right) \tag{7.7.11}$$

where reference has been made to

$$\underline{y} = (y^1, y^2, y^3) = r_y(\sin\vartheta_y\cos\varphi_y, \sin\vartheta_y\sin\varphi_y, \cos\vartheta_y) = \hat{y}r_y \tag{7.7.12}$$

Ω_π is a large normalization volume for the pions decayed from the gauge boson.

To first order in K, (5.7.22) applies. Among the three possible solutions to (5.7.22b), only one of them, the "decoupled" solution (5.7.23, 28) has been found. In terms of the quantities in (7.7.8), this solution reads

$$\underline{\chi}_{2-}(\underline{y}) \to \underline{\chi}(\underline{y}) = \underline{\psi}(\underline{y}) \to \underline{\psi}_1(\underline{y}) = (\hat{K}\times\hat{r}_y)\psi_{10}(r_y) = (\underline{K}\times\hat{r}_y)d_h\frac{\alpha_{00}}{\sqrt{\Omega_\pi}}p_{10}(r) \tag{7.7.13}$$

where the subscript y refers to the $\underline{y}$ space. χ_{f3}^*, ψ_{f3}^*, $\psi_{f2}^{(-)}$ etc in (7.7.6, 7) are decomposable in entirely the same fashion as was done in (7.7.8-13).

The operators ∂_{III} and ∂_{IV} in (7.7.6, 7) have similar forms as those in (3.1.4). Noting (7.7.4, 5), these read

$$\begin{aligned}\partial_{III}^{a\dot{b}} &= -\delta^{a\dot{b}}\frac{1}{2}\frac{\partial}{\partial X^0} - \underline{\sigma}^{a\dot{b}}\frac{1}{2}\frac{\partial}{\partial \underline{X}} + \delta^{a\dot{b}}\frac{\partial}{\partial y^0} + \underline{\sigma}^{a\dot{b}}\frac{\partial}{\partial \underline{y}} \\ \partial_{IV}^{a\dot{b}} &= -\delta^{a\dot{b}}\frac{1}{2}\frac{\partial}{\partial X^0} - \underline{\sigma}^{a\dot{b}}\frac{1}{2}\frac{\partial}{\partial \underline{X}} - \delta^{a\dot{b}}\frac{\partial}{\partial y^0} - \underline{\sigma}^{a\dot{b}}\frac{\partial}{\partial \underline{y}}\end{aligned} \tag{7.7.14}$$

The expressions (7.7.8-13) can now be inserted into (7.7.6, 7). By (7.7.10) type of conditions, terms containing $\partial/\partial y_0$ in (7.7.14) drop out. The same conditions however lead to that the other terms in (7.7.6, 7) become proportional to $\int dy_0 = \tau_0 \to \infty$ as in (7.3.16). By (7.4.6b), the left of (7.7.1, 2) is of second order, i.e., of order g^2. The right sides are by (7.7.17) below of order $\kappa_\pi g$. Thus κ_π should be a first order quantity of order g, which $\to 0$ in the zeroth order limit. κ_π must $\to 0$ here such that $\kappa_\pi \int dy_0$ is finite. The magnitude of this quantity is unknown but will here be fixed by a *dimensional estimate* requiring that in (7.7.1, 2) variations of S_L and of $\kappa_\pi S_{m\pi}$ are of the same magnitude. From (7.4.5, 15, 19, 20),

$$\left|\frac{\delta S_L}{\delta W_I^{\pm}}\right| \approx \frac{g}{4\sqrt{2}}\frac{1}{\Omega_L}, \qquad \left|\frac{\delta S_L}{\delta Z}\right| \approx \frac{g}{8\cos\vartheta_W}\frac{1}{\Omega_L} \tag{7.7.15}$$

where Ω_L is the normalization volume of the leptons. Using (7.7.14) in (7.7.6, 7), the dominating term is seen to be the $\partial/\partial \underline{y}$ term which by (7.7.8, 11, 12) produces a factor of $d_h r \approx d_h r_0$. Further, χ_{f3}^* in (7.7.6, 7) has a similar form as (7.7.8), differing from it mainly in the phase factor. Thus, (7.7.11) also holds for $\chi_{f3}(\underline{y})$ so that

$$\int d^3\underline{y}\,\chi_{f3}^*(\underline{y})\chi_{02}(\underline{y}) = \frac{1}{\Omega_\pi} \tag{7.7.16}$$

which is simply the normalization condition (4.2.8). Neglecting the small vector function (7.7.13), a typical term in the brackets of (7.7.6, 7) leads to

$$\kappa_\pi\left|\frac{\delta S_{m\pi}}{\delta W_I^{\pm}}\right| \approx \kappa_\pi\frac{g}{8}d_h r_0\frac{1}{\Omega_\pi}\int dy^0, \quad \kappa_\pi\left|\frac{\delta S_{m\pi}}{\delta Z}\right| \approx \kappa_\pi\frac{g}{8\cos\vartheta_W}d_h r_0\frac{1}{\Omega_\pi}\int dy^0 \tag{7.7.17}$$

Equating these to (7.7.15), putting $\Omega_\pi = \Omega_L$ and observing (4.6.1) leads to the *dimensional estimate*

$$\kappa_\pi\int dy^0 \approx \frac{\sqrt{2}}{d_h r_0}, \frac{1}{d_h r_0} \to c_\pi\frac{1}{d_h r_0}, \qquad r_0 = 1/\sqrt{d_h} = 3.78\,\text{GeV}^{-1} \tag{7.7.18}$$

From this viewpoint, there is only one scale constant in the relative space time y for an integrand in (7.7.6, 7), namely $d_h r_0$ in (7.7.11). c_π is a constant dependent upon the assignments (7.7.15, 17) but should not deviate very much from the magnitude unity;

$$c_\pi \approx 1 \tag{7.7.19}$$

7.7.3. Evaluation of the Gauge Boson Fields and Further Development

The expressions (7.7.8-14) and their modification hold for ψ and for final state 3 meson wave function and are inserted into (7.7.6, 7) in order to obtain expressions of $W_I^{\pm}$ and Z in (7.7.1, 2). A typical term in (7.7.6, 7), exemplified by the first term in the brackets of (7.7.6), becomes

$$\chi_{f3(\pi-)\dot{b}f}^*(X,y)\partial_{IV}^{a\dot{b}}\chi_{f2(\pi0)\dot{e}a}^{(-)}(X,y) = \frac{\alpha_{00}^2}{\Omega_\pi}\exp\left(i(E_{3-}+\left|E_{20}^{(-)}\right|)X^0 + i(\underline{K}_{20}-\underline{K}_{3-})\underline{X}\right)$$
$$\times\left(-\delta_{\dot{e}f}\frac{i}{2}\left|E_{20}^{(-)}\right|\left(\exp\left(-d_h r_y^2\right)+\left(\underline{K}_{3-}\times\hat{y}\right)\left(\underline{K}_{20}\times\hat{y}\right)d_h^2 p_{10}^2(r_y)\right)+\underline{\sigma}_{\dot{e}f}\underline{G}_3\right)$$

(7.7.20a)

$$\underline{G}_3 = +\frac{1}{2}\left|E_{20}^{(-)}\right|\left(\underline{K}_{20} \times \hat{y}\right) \times \left(\underline{K}_{3-} \times \hat{y}\right) d_h^2 p_{10}^2\left(r_y\right)$$
$$-\frac{i}{2}\underline{K}_{20} \exp\left(-d_h r_y^2\right) - \frac{i}{2}\left[\underline{K}_{20} \times \left(\underline{K}_{20} \times \hat{y}\right)\right] \times \left(\underline{K}_{3-} \times \hat{y}\right) d_h^2 p_{10}^2\left(r_y\right)$$
$$-id_h \exp\left(-\frac{1}{2}d_h r_y^2\right)\left[\underline{\partial}_y \times \left(\underline{K}_{20} \times \hat{y} p_{10}\left(r_y\right)\right) + d_h \underline{y} \times \left(\underline{K}_{3-} \times \hat{y}\right) p_{10}\left(r_y\right)\right]$$

(7.7.20b)

where $p_{10}(r_y)$ is given by (5.7.28). The odd powered $\hat{y}$ terms in (7.7.20) have been omitted in anticipation that they vanish when (7.7.20) is operated by

$$\int d^3\underline{y} = \int_0^\infty r_y^2 dr_y \int_0^\pi \sin\vartheta_y d\vartheta_y \int_0^{2\pi} d\varphi_y \tag{7.7.21}$$

in (7.7.6) below where (7.7.12) is used. The remaining terms in the brackets of (7.7.6, 7) have analogously be evaluated.

Further developments follow the same steps as those given from (7.7.22) to the end of Sec. 7.7 of [H18]. But there is a main difference; the coarse dimensional approximation of (3.5.23, 24) underlying (7.7.13) in [H18] have been replaced by the formal perturbational result (5.7.28) used here.

Inserting the so-evaluated (7.7.6, 7) into (7.7.1, 2) to obtain expressions for the gauge fields $W^{\pm}$ and Z, which in their turn are inserted into (7.3.26), using (7.2.20), to yield decay amplitudes S_{fi} analogous to that for pion beta decay of (7.3.25). From such S_{fi}, the decay matrix element $M_{\alpha\beta\gamma}$ as functions of the pion energies and momenta can be extracted, as in (7.7.34-42) of [H18]. Here, α is the number of charges pions and β and γ the charges of the final state pions, *f2* and *f3*, respectively.

7.7.4. Failure of the "Decoupled" Solution (5.7.23, 28)

The so-obtained $M_{\alpha\beta\gamma}$ are compared to the corresponding decay matrix element M_{PDG} given by [P1] or (7.8.47) of [H18] and parametrized in terms of the Dalitz slope parameters g, h, j k... and the pion energies. Equating $|M_{100}|^2$ for $K^- \rightarrow \pi^- \pi^0 \pi^0$ to the corresponding one in ----$|M_{PDG}|^2$ leads to the prediction g=–0.185 and h=0.0172 which disagree with data g_{exp}=0.626 and h_{exp}=0.052 [P1]. Furthermore, the predicted g and h turned out to be constants depending only upon the masses of the pions and the kaon and independent of the value of C_k of (7.3.25b) containing the "decoupled" perturbed wave function $p_{10}(r)$ of (5.7.28), as may be expected. The small k slope parameter however depends upon $p_{10}(r)$.

A tentative conclusion is that the "decoupled" solution (5.7.28) does not hold for the pions in $K \rightarrow 3\pi$ and the "coupled" solution to (5.7.22b) mentioned beneath (5.7.28) should be used. But this complicated (5.7.22b) has not been solved and hence no prediction can be obtained here.

Chapter 8

On Strong Decay of Mesons

In the last chapter, weak interactions are mediated by SU(3) gauge fields in laboratory space. Their strength is determined by the Fermi constant G (7.4.29a) and F_W^2 (7.5.22a). In Chapter 6, electromagnetic interactions are based upon U(1) gauge field in laboratory space. The associated strength is given by the fine structure constant $\alpha=e^2/4\pi$. In this chapter, strong decays will take place via perturbations of the nonlinear intrameson interaction potential $\Phi_m(x_I,x_{II})$ in for instance (2.3.22). Their strength turns out to be given by g_s^8 below, where g_s^2 is the quark-antiquark scalar strong coupling constant in (2.1.2, 4).

In the gauge fields of Chapters 6 and 7, there is only one strongly interacting particle, the meson, at a time. This meson is free and does not interact strongly with another meson so that the free meson wave functions of (4.3.4) hold. In the strong decays here, however, two mesons are created from one and hence are close to and interact with each other strongly to start with. The volume Ω in (4.3.4) no longer $\to\infty$ but becomes some finite, not large Ω_c during this early stage. As was mentioned below (4.2.6), the invalidates the separability ansatz of (3.1.5) so that such strong decays can presently not be treated to arrive at decay rates similar to those obtained in Chapters 6 and 7.

The problem of 0ZI rule obeying decays of a vector meson into two slow pseudoscalar mesons $V\to PP$ is formulated together with the sister processes $V\to VV$, $P\to PP$ and $P\to VV$. The problem of $\pi^0\to\gamma\gamma$ via intermediary virtual $\pi^+\pi^-$ and $\rho^+\rho^-$ is similarly formulated. None of these problems could be resolved presently; there is no prediction to confront data.

Data show that the decay rates of $V\to PP$ and the associated $V\to P\gamma$ of Chapter 6 are of the same magnitude. This and the presence of relative time among quarks in hadrons leads to the conjecture that the strong coupling $\alpha_s\approx0.12$ related to g_s^2 and the fine structure constant $\alpha=1/137$ are related to each other. This suggests the hypothesis that the strong and electromagnetic interactions ar unified by a common electro-strong coupling constant and fits well with the detachment of weak and electromagnetic couplings of §7.5.3.

8.1. Meson Equations Involving Four Quarks

8.1.1. Coupled Four Quark Equations

In the simplest OZI rule obeying $V\to PP$ or $P\to VV$, four quarks are involved. Quark A located at x_I having flavor p in z_I space and antiquark B located at x_{II} with antiflavor $\bar{r}$ in z_{II} space form the initial V or P. The space time equations assigned to them have been given by (2.1.1-4). When internal functions are included, (2.1.1, 3) are replaced by the form (2.3.11) with q_{op} and V_{PB} put to zero. The wave functions of these quarks are then

$$\chi_{A\dot{b}}(x_I)\xi_A^{\xi p}(z_I),\quad \psi_A^a(x_I)\xi_A^{\xi p}(z_I),\quad \chi_B^f(x_{II})\xi_{Br}^{\xi}(z_{II}),\quad \psi_{B\dot{e}}(x_{II})\xi_{Br}(z_{II}) \tag{8.1.1}$$

In addition, a quark-antiquark pair comprising quark C of flavor q and antiquark D of antiflavor $\bar{q}$ is created from the vacuum. The initial meson V or P, denoted by AB, decays into two mesons PP or VV, denoted by AD and CB or AB and CD. Quasi-classically, one may try to give this created pair CD the same status as the quarks AB in the initial meson. In this case, their wave functions corresponding to (8.1.1) would be

$$\chi_{C\dot{b}}(x_{III})\xi_C^{\xi q}(z_{III}),\quad \psi_C^a(x_{III})\xi_C^{\xi q}(z_{III}),\quad \chi_D^f(x_{IV})\xi_{Dq}^{\xi}(z_{IV}),\quad \psi_{D\dot{e}}(x_{IV})\xi_{Dq}(z_{IV}) \tag{8.1.2}$$

which satisfy (2.3.11) type of equations and (2.1.1, 3) with $A \to C$, $B \to D$, $I \to III$, and $II \to IV$. In addition, (2.1.2, 4) needs be further modified to include contributions from the C and D quarks. For instance, (2.1.2) would be replaced by

$$\Box_I V_{SBCD}(x_I) = \tfrac{1}{2} g_s^2 \left(\psi_B^b(x_I)\chi_{Bb}(x_I) + \psi_C^b(x_I)\chi_{Cb}(x_I) + \psi_D^b(x_I)\chi_{Db}(x_I) + c.c.\right) \tag{8.1.3}$$

Internal functions are not included on the right side of (8.1.3) for the same reasons given below (2.3.19). Here, quarks interact only pair-wise; genuine three quark or four quark interactions have been neglected.

Even with these simplified interactions, the four quark problem posed by four sets of equations of the form (2.1.1, 2) which are coupled by nonlinear terms like those on the right side of (8.1.3) would be very complicated even before generalizations of the form (2.2.1-3). The complications are mainly due to the increase of the number of independent variables, from x_I and x_{II} to x_I, x_{II}, x_{III}, and x_{IV}.

It will however turn out that such a doubling of the number of independent variables, hence also the ensuing complications, may be side-stepped if one recalls the basic steps in $K^+ \to \mu^+ \nu_\mu$ in the last chapter and tries to taken them over for applications in this chapter.

8.1.2. Intermediary Scalar Potential Perturbation

Ostensibly, $K^+ \to \mu^+ \nu_\mu$ involves four fermions, the u and $\bar{s}$ quarks, μ^+ and ν_μ and would require four set of coordinates to describe them, similar to the $V \to PP$ case in the previous paragraph. Nevertheless, only two sets, X and x obtained from x_I and x_{II} according to (3.1.3a), appear in the calculations. This is due to the division of a semi-leptonic decay into two stages in §7.1.1. In stage I, K^+, described in terms of X and x, decays into a gauge boson $W^-(X)$ and a vacuum pseudoscalar meson state explained below (7.3.8, 19). In stage II, $W^-(X)$ in its turn decays into μ^+ and ν_μ. In this last stage, K^+ has already "disappeared" in X space so that this X can now be "reused" by the μ^+ and ν_μ wave functions. This is possible because μ^+ and ν_μ have been treated as different states of the same particle related to each other by SU(2) gauge transformations, as can be seen from (7.1.12, 19). Here, the Glashow model mentioned below (7.1.21) has been assumed. Therefore, only X, the "reused" X, is needed in the wave functions describing them. In this way, extra and independent coordinates for μ^+ and ν_μ do not enter the decay formalism.

This procedure to describe semi-leptonic decay will be analogously taken over here. The difference is largely the replacement of the intermediate gauge boson $W(X)$ by $\Phi_{Im4}(x_I,x_{II})$, a perturbation of the strong scalar intrameson potential $\Phi_m(x_I,x_{II})$ mentioned in the beginning of this chapter. In stage I, V or P decays into a virtual intermediate state Φ_{Im4J}, to be defined in (8.2.4) ff below, and a *vacuum meson state*, analogous to the vacuum pseudoscalar meson state defined below (7.3.19). In stage II, the perturbational Φ_{Im4J} decays into PP or VV whose wave functions depend upon the "reused" x_I and x_{II}. Again PP or VV considered as different states of the same meson so they share the same x_I and x_{II}.

In this manner, the extra independent coordinates x_{III} and x_{IV} in (8.1.2) no longer need to enter the formalism below. Since the internal coordinates z_{III} and z_{IV} are on equal footing with x_{III} and x_{IV} as is implied in §2.3.1 (see also (2.3.15, 18)), they also do not appear in the following formalism.

8.1.3. Mixed Quark Wave Functions and Equations

In accordance with the approach put forth in the last paragraph, introduce wave functions of the type (8.1.2, 1) for the $\bar{q}q$ pair DC created from vacuum by the following generalization of (8.1.1),

$$\begin{aligned}\chi_{A\dot{b}}(x_I)\xi^p_A(z_I) &\rightarrow \chi_{A\dot{b}}(x_I)\xi^p_A(z_I)+\chi_{C\dot{b}}(x_I)\xi^q_C(z_I)\\ \psi^a_A(x_I)\xi^p_A(z_I) &\rightarrow \psi^a_A(x_I)\xi^p_A(z_I)+\psi^a_C(x_I)\xi^q_C(z_I)\end{aligned} \tag{8.1.4a}$$

$$\begin{aligned}\chi^f_B(x_{II})\xi_{Br}(z_{II}) &\rightarrow \chi^f_B(x_{II})\xi_{Br}(z_{II})+\chi^f_D(x_{II})\xi_{Dq}(z_{II})\\ \psi_{B\dot{e}}(x_{II})\xi_{Br}(z_{II}) &\rightarrow \psi_{B\dot{e}}(x_{II})\xi_{Br}(z_{II})+\psi_{D\dot{e}}(x_{II})\xi_{Dq}(z_{II})\end{aligned} \tag{8.1.4b}$$

In this ansatz, χ_C, ψ_C, χ_D, and ψ_D are considered to be small during stage I of the decay so that they can be regarded as small perturbations of the quark wave functions for A and B generating the initial meson V or P. Later, in stage II, their amplitudes have grown to be of the same magnitude as those for A and B so that the right sides of (8.1.4a) become mixed quark states and the right sides of (8.1.4b) represent mixed antiquark states.

With (8.1.4), the quark wave equations (2.1.1-4) including internal functions as in (2.3.11) are generalized to

$$\begin{aligned}&\partial_I^{a\dot{b}}\left(\chi_{A\dot{b}}(x_I)\xi^p_A(z_I)+\chi_{C\dot{b}}(x_I)\xi^q_C(z_I)\right)-iV_{BD}(x_I)\left(\psi^b_A(x_I)\xi^p_A(z_I)+\psi^b_C(x_I)\xi^q_C(z_I)\right)\\ &=im_{Aop}(z_I)\left(\psi^b_A(x_I)\xi^p_A(z_I)+\psi^b_C(x_I)\xi^q_C(z_I)\right)\end{aligned} \tag{8.1.5a}$$

$$\begin{aligned}&\partial_{I\dot{c}b}\left(\psi^b_A(x_I)\xi^p_A(z_I)+\psi^b_C(x_I)\xi^q_C(z_I)\right)-iV_{BD}(x_I)\left(\chi_{A\dot{c}}(x_I)\xi^p_A(z_I)+\chi_{C\dot{c}}(x_I)\xi^q_C(z_I)\right)\\ &=im_{Aop}(z_I)\left(\chi_{A\dot{c}}(x_I)\xi^p_A(z_I)+\chi_{C\dot{c}}(x_I)\xi^q_C(z_I)\right)\end{aligned} \tag{8.1.5b}$$

$$\partial_{II\dot{e}f}\left(\chi_B^f(x_{II})\xi_{Br}(z_{II})+\chi_D^f(x_{II})\xi_{Dq}(z_{II})\right)-iV_{AC}(x_{II})\left(\psi_{B\dot{e}}(x_{II})\xi_{Br}(z_{II})+\psi_{D\dot{e}}(x_{II})\xi_{Dq}(z_{II})\right)$$
$$=im_{Bop}(z_{II})\left(\psi_{B\dot{e}}(x_{II})\xi_{Br}(z_{II})+\psi_{D\dot{e}}(x_{II})\xi_{Dq}(z_{II})\right) \quad (8.1.6a)$$

$$\partial_{II}^{d\dot{e}}\left(\psi_{B\dot{e}}(x_{II})\xi_{Br}(z_{II})+\psi_{D\dot{e}}(x_{II})\xi_{Dq}(z_{II})\right)-iV_{AC}(x_{II})\left(\chi_B^d(x_{II})\xi_{Br}(z_{II})+\chi_D^d(x_{II})\xi_{Dq}(z_{II})\right)$$
$$=im_{Bop}(z_{II})\left(\chi_B^d(x_{II})\xi_{Br}(z_{II})+\chi_D^d(x_{II})\xi_{Dq}(z_{II})\right) \quad (8.1.6b)$$

$$\Box_I V_{BD}(x_I)=\frac{1}{2}g_s^2\left[\left(\psi_B^b(x_I)+\psi_D^b(x_I)\right)\left(\chi_{Bb}(x_I)+\chi_{Db}(x_I)\right)+c.c.\right] \quad (8.1.7)$$

$$\Box_{II} V_{AC}(x_{II})=\frac{1}{2}g_s^2\left[\left(\psi_A^b(x_{II})+\psi_C^b(x_{II})\right)\left(\chi_{Aa}(x_{II})+\chi_{Ca}(x_{II})\right)+c.c.\right] \quad (8.1.8)$$

Consistent with (2.1.2, 4), the internal functions in (8.1.4) have been dropped in (8.1.7, 8). This is due to that the V's are scalar potential in space time and are independent of internal functions which characterize the mass and charge of the quarks. This point has been discussed below (2.3.19).

8.1.4. Construction of Coupled Meson Equations

In Chapter 2, wave equations for a single isolated meson (2.3.19, 23) were constructed by first multiplying the wave equations (2.1.1, 2) for quark A with (2.1.3, 4) for antiquark B. The same procedure will now be repeated using (8.1.5, 7) and (8.1.6, 8) instead. The initial meson AB can decay into either i) AD and CB or ii) AB and CD. In each case, only three of the four mesons AB, AD, CB and CD enter; the fourth can be dropped. In the following, only case i) will be treated explicitly. The interchange $B\leftrightarrow D$ among the decay products turn case i) results into those for case ii). Repeating the three steps in Chapter 2 leads to the following equations replacing (2.3.19, 23):

$$\partial_I^{a\dot{b}}\partial_{II\dot{e}f}\begin{pmatrix}\chi_{AB\dot{b}}^f(x_I,x_{II})\xi_r^p(z_I,z_{II})+\chi_{AD\dot{b}}^f(x_I,x_{II}) \\ \times\xi_q^p(z_I,z_{II})+\chi_{CB\dot{b}}^f(x_I,x_{II})\xi_r^q(z_I,z_{II})\end{pmatrix}=\left(\Phi_{m4}(x_I,x_{II})-m_{2op}(z_I,z_{II})\right)$$
$$\times\left(\psi_{AB\dot{e}}^a(x_I,x_{II})\xi_r^p(z_I,z_{II})+\psi_{AD\dot{e}}^a(x_I,x_{II})\xi_q^p(z_I,z_{II})+\psi_{CB\dot{e}}^a(x_I,x_{II})\xi_r^q(z_I,z_{II})\right) \quad (8.1.9a)$$

$$\partial_{I\dot{b}c}\partial_{II}^{d\dot{e}}\begin{pmatrix}\psi_{AB\dot{e}}^b(x_I,x_{II})\xi_r^p(z_I,z_{II})+\psi_{AD\dot{e}}^b(x_I,x_{II}) \\ \times\xi_q^p(z_I,z_{II})+\psi_{CB\dot{e}}^b(x_I,x_{II})\xi_r^q(z_I,z_{II})\end{pmatrix}=\left(\Phi_{m4}(x_I,x_{II})-m_{2op}(z_I,z_{II})\right)$$
$$\times\left(\chi_{AB\dot{c}}^d(x_I,x_{II})\xi_r^p(z_I,z_{II})+\chi_{AD\dot{c}}^d(x_I,x_{II})\xi_q^p(z_I,z_{II})+\chi_{CB\dot{c}}^d(x_I,x_{II})\xi_r^q(z_I,z_{II})\right) \quad (8.1.9b)$$

$$V_{BD}(x_I)V_{AC}(x_{II}) \to \Phi_{m4}(x_I, x_{II}) = \Phi_{mAB}(x_I, x_{II}) + \Phi_{1m4}(x_I, x_{II}) \tag{8.1.10a}$$

$$\Box_I \Box_{II} \Phi_{mAB}(x_I, x_{II}) = -\tfrac{1}{2} g_s^4 \operatorname{Re} \psi_{AB}^{a\dot{b}}(x_I, x_{II}) \chi_{AB\dot{b}a}^*(x_I, x_{II}) \tag{8.1.10b}$$

$$\Box_I \Box_{II} \Phi_{1m4}(x_I, x_{II})$$
$$= -\frac{1}{4} g_s^4 \begin{bmatrix} \psi_{AD}^{a\dot{b}}(x_I, x_{II}) \chi_{CB\dot{b}a}^*(x_I, x_{II}) + \psi_{CB}^{a\dot{b}}(x_I, x_{II}) \chi_{AD\dot{b}a}^*(x_I, x_{II}) \\ + \psi_{CB}^{a\dot{b}}(x_I, x_{II}) \chi_{CB\dot{b}a}^*(x_I, x_{II}) + \psi_{AD}^{a\dot{b}}(x_I, x_{II}) \chi_{AD\dot{b}a}^*(x_I, x_{II}) \\ + \psi_{AB}^{a\dot{b}}(x_I, x_{II}) \chi_{CB\dot{b}a}^*(x_I, x_{II}) + \psi_{CB}^{a\dot{b}}(x_I, x_{II}) \chi_{AB\dot{b}a}^*(x_I, x_{II}) \\ + \psi_{AB}^{a\dot{b}}(x_I, x_{II}) \chi_{AD\dot{b}a}^*(x_I, x_{II}) + \psi_{AD}^{a\dot{b}}(x_I, x_{II}) \chi_{AB\dot{b}a}^*(x_I, x_{II}) \end{bmatrix} + c.c. \tag{8.1.10c}$$

Because $\xi^p{}_r$, $\xi^p{}_q$ and $\xi^q{}_r$ are independent of each other, (8.1.9) splits up into three equations, one for each ξ. Upon application of (2.3.21), one obtains

$$\partial_I^{a\dot{b}} \partial_{II}^{f\dot{e}} \chi_{AB\dot{b}f}(x_I, x_{II}) = \left(M_{AB}^2 - \Phi_{m4}(x_I, x_{II})\right) \psi_{AB}^{a\dot{e}}(x_I, x_{II}) \tag{8.1.11a}$$

$$\partial_{I\dot{c}b} \partial_{II\dot{e}d} \psi_{AB}^{b\dot{e}}(x_I, x_{II}) = \left(M_{AB}^2 - \Phi_{m4}(x_I, x_{II})\right) \chi_{AB\dot{c}d}(x_I, x_{II}) \tag{8.1.11b}$$

$$(8.1.11) \text{ with } AB \to AD \tag{8.1.12}$$

$$(8.1.11) \text{ with } AB \to CB \tag{8.1.13}$$

For the simplest mass operator form (2.3.25, 26), $M_{AB}{}^2$ takes on the form (2.4.1). All other product equations drop out in the same manner as the corresponding ones considered in Sec. 2.2.

Equations (8.1.10-13) form a set of seven equations for the seven variables ψ_{AB}, χ_{AB}, $AB \to AD$, $AB \to CB$ and Φ_{m4}. The various meson wave functions for AB, AD and CB are coupled via the Φ's of (8.1.10). Equations (8.1.10b, 11) include the zeroth order terms which account for the initial meson AB. Evidently, only the first two terms in the bracket of (8.1.10c) will contribute to Φ_{1m4}; the remaining terms drop out because the associated mesons do not appear among the decay products.

8.2. Formulation of Strong Decay $V \to PP$ and Impasse

8.2.1. First Order Relations

The development of $V \to P\gamma$ of Sec. 6.4 and $K^+ \to L^+ \nu_L$ of Sec. 7.3 can be largely taken over here. The confinement potential in (8.1.10a) is given by the last two terms in (3.2.8a) together with (3.2.21),

$$\Phi_{mAB} \approx d_{m0} - d_h^2 r^2 \tag{8.2.1}$$

Further, (3.2.8c) drops out via (3.2.5b) and (4.2.7, 8). ψ_{AB} and χ_{AB} are expanded in the form (6.4.1-3) modified by the extra subscripts AB attached to the wave functions. Insert the so-modified (6.4.1-3) into (8.1.11), multiply (8.1.11a) by $\overset{*}{\chi}_{0AB\dot{e}a}$ and (8.1.11b) by $\psi^{*d\dot{c}}_{0AB}$, add them together, and integrate over X and x. Noting (8.1.10a), the first order terms can by analogy to (6.4.9) and (7.3.3-5) be written as

$$S'_{mABd} = S'_{mABs} \tag{8.2.2}$$

$$S'_{mABd} = \int d^4Xdx^4 \left[\partial_I^{a\dot{b}}\left(a_{J0}^{(1)}\left(X^0\right)/a_{J0}\right)\overset{*}{\chi}_{0AB\dot{e}a}\partial_{II}^{f\dot{e}}\chi_{0AB\dot{b}f} + \partial_{I\dot{c}a}\left(a_{J0}^{(1)}\left(X^0\right)/a_{J0}\right)\psi^{*d\dot{c}}_{0AB}\partial_{II\dot{e}d}\psi^{a\dot{e}}_{0AB}\right] \tag{8.2.3a}$$

$$S'_{mABs} = -\int dX^4dx^4\Phi_{1m4}\left(\overset{*}{\chi}_{0AB\dot{e}a}\psi^{a\dot{e}}_{0AB} + c.c.\right) \tag{8.2.3b}$$

8.2.2. Impasse of $V \rightarrow PP$ and Its Verification

Analogous to (7.3.6, 7b), the initial and final states in stage I are taken to be

$$|i\rangle = \left|AB_J\left(E_{J0}, K_J = 0\right)\right\rangle, \qquad \langle f| = \langle 0, \Phi_{1m4J}| \tag{8.2.4}$$

where AB stands for the initial meson and J its spin. Φ_{1m4J} stands for the virtual intermediate state consisting of $\Phi_{1m4}(x_I,x_{II})$ together with the observable properties, i.e., spin, four momentum and flavors of the initial meson. It plays the same role as the intermediate gauge boson W_{rp} does in (7.3.7b). While W_{rp} decays into a pair of leptons, Φ_{1m4J} decays into a pair of mesons. Analogous to the implication below (7.3.9), Φ_{1m4J} is also implicitly understood to pick out the wave functions of the final pair.

The initial meson AB_J decays into a *vacuum meson state*, represented by $\langle 0|$ in (8.2.4), similar to that described below (7.3.19). The wave function of this state described by (7.3.20) holds for J=0 or an initial pseudoscalar meson. For J=1 or an initial vector meson, this form is to be replaced by that of (4.3.4b). A major difference is introduced here by the replacement

$$\Omega_{wvac} \rightarrow \Omega_{svac} \tag{8.2.5}$$

in (7.3.20) representing the volume occupied by the vacuum meson state associated with strong interaction, denoted by the subscript s.

The discussion of Ω_{wvac} below (7.3.20) can be taken over here. However, as was pointed out in the beginning of this chapter, Ω_{svac} is no longer large, as Ω_{swvac} is below (7.3.20). This invalidates the separability ansatz of (3.1.5), as was mentioned above §8.1.1 and below (4.2.6) so that the wave function of this vacuum meson state cannot be found. Thus, an *impasse* is reached for $V \to PP$; *no decay rate can be derived here.*

In this and the next section, this impasse will be verified. The unknown, limited Ω_{svac} will be treated like the large Ω_{wvac} is §7.3.4 ff so that the decay rate treatment there can largely be taken over. The so-predicted $D^{*+} \to D^+\pi^0$ decay rate was found to be much smaller than data in Table 8.1 below. Also, Ω_{svac} obtained from $\phi \to K^+K^-$ in (8.3.12) below turned out to be much smaller than the required large Ω_{wvac} verified in (7.5.22b). These results verify this impasse.

Another reason for carrying out this verification is to introduces expressions entering the unified strong and electromagnetic coupling hypothesis of §8.3.4.

Return from this digression on impasse to (8.2.5). Sandwiching (8.2.3a) between <f| and |i> of (8.2.4) and follow the same steps that led to (6.4.14) and (7.3.15) yields

$$\langle f|S'_{mABd}|i\rangle = -iE_{J0}S_{fiJ}\Omega\int d^4x\psi^2_{J0}(r) \tag{8.2.6a}$$

$$S_{fi} = \langle f|a^*_{J0}a^{(1)}_{J0}(X^0 \to \infty)|i\rangle \tag{8.2.6b}$$

where ψ_{J0} are those of (4.3.1). Insert now (8.2.3b) between <f| and |i> of (8.2.4). One obtains the analog of (7.3.21),

$$\langle f|S'_{mABs}|i\rangle = 4\int d^4X\,d^4x\sqrt{\frac{\Omega}{\Omega_{svac}}}\psi^2_{J0}(r)\Phi_{1m4}(X,x)\exp\left(-iE_{J0}X^0\right) \tag{8.2.7}$$

where (6.4.1) modified according to §8.2.1, (3.2.5b) and the second of (3.4.2b) and of (3.4.3) have been noted. Combining (8.2.2, 3a, 6, 7) leads to the decay amplitude for the initial meson with spin J,

$$S_{fiJ} = i\frac{4}{E_{J0}}\frac{1}{\Omega}\int d^4X\,d^3\underline{x}\sqrt{\frac{\Omega}{\Omega_{svac}}}\psi^2_{J0}(r)\Phi_{1m4}(X,x)\exp\left(-iE_{J0}X^0\right)\Big/\int d^3\underline{x}\psi^2_{J0}(r) \tag{8.2.8}$$

This result can also be obtained starting from either (8.1.11a) or (8.1.11b).

8.2.3. Perturbed Scalar Potential Equation

The perturbed potential Φ_{lm4} in the virtual intermediate state Φ_{lm4J} must satisfy the condition

$$\Phi_{1m4} << \Phi_{mAB} \tag{8.2.9}$$

in (8.1.10a) to allow for a perturbational calculation. The magnitudes of (8.2.1) are

$$\Phi_{mAB} \approx d_{m0} - d_h^2 \bar{r}_J^{-2} \approx \begin{Bmatrix} 0.55 & J=0 \\ 0.32 & J=1 \end{Bmatrix} \tag{8.2.10}$$

where $\bar{r}_0$ is that of (4.6.1). $\bar{r}_1 \approx 8.1$ GeV^{-1} is the counterpart of $\bar{r}_0$ for J=1 obtained by averaging r over ψ_{10}^2 of (4.3.4b) in the relative space $\underline{x}$. d_{m0} is given in Table 5.2. ψ_{AB} and χ_{AB} are expanded in the form (6.4.1-3) modified by the extra subscripts AB attached to the wave functions.

During early stage I, (8.2.9) is satisfied by virtue of the perturbational character of χ_C, ψ_C, χ_D, and ψ_D in (8.1.4) because these wave functions take part in the generalizations of the type (2.2.1) to arrive at terms on the right of (8.1.10c) but not (8.1.10b). During late stage II, the pseudoscalar mesons in V decay are sufficiently far apart thet they can be regarded as free mesons having amplitude $1/\sqrt{\Omega} \to 0$ according to (4.3.4a) together with (5.7.12, 19, 23, 28). Here, we are limited to slowly moving mesons, as in the cases treated below. With the last-mentioned expressions, (8.1.10c) becomes small and (8.2.9) holds. Similarly, the final decay products, the twin photons in $\pi^0 \to \rho^+\rho^- \to \gamma\gamma$ mentioned above §8.1.1, are described by wave functions $\propto 1/\sqrt{\Omega_r} \to 0$. Therefore, (8.2.9) is analogously satisfied during the late stage II in this case.

In the intermediary stage, i.e., during late stage I and early stage II, the amplitudes of perturbational χ_C, ψ_C, χ_D, and ψ_D may no longer be small. Further, the newly formed PP in V decay are still close to each other so that they interact strongly and the $1/\sqrt{\Omega} \to 0$ dependence of (4.3.4a) is replaced by $1/\sqrt{\Omega_c}$=finite of (4.2.8). In this intermediary stage, the bracket of (8.1.10c) may therefore not be small. To conform to (8.2.9), use is made of the hypothesis of unified strong and electromagnetic coupling $g_s^4 \propto e$ of (8.3.11) below and is thus a small parameter.

According to the end of Sec. 8.1, (8.1.10c) becomes

$$\Box_I \Box_{II} \Phi_{1m4} = -\frac{1}{4} g_s^4 \left(\psi_{AD}^{a\dot{b}} \chi^*_{CB\dot{b}a} + \psi_{CB}^{a\dot{b}} \chi^*_{AD\dot{b}a} + \psi_{AD}^{*b\dot{a}} \chi_{CB\dot{a}b} + \psi_{CB}^{*b\dot{a}} \chi_{AD\dot{a}b} \right) \tag{8.2.11}$$

At large times indicated by (8.2.6b), the pseudoscalar mesons AD and CB in V decay are sufficiently apart so that they may be regarded as free meson having wave function of the form (3.1.5, 9). Any other more general form than these would complicate the calculations greatly and practically prohibit any analytical solution.

Analogous to the choice of negative energy for the massive lepton in $K^+ \to L^+ \nu_L$, shown in (7.4.11b), negative energy solutions will be chosen for AD. In this case, (8.2.11) becomes

$$\Box_I \Box_{II} \Phi_{1m4} = -\frac{1}{2} g_s^4 \left(\psi_{0jKAD}(\underline{x}) \chi^*_{0jKCB}(\underline{x}) - \underline{\psi}_{jKAD}(\underline{x}) \underline{\chi}^*_{jKCB}(\underline{x}) + \psi \leftrightarrow \chi \right)$$
$$\times \exp\left(i\left(E_{jKAD} + E_{jKCB}\right) X^0 + i\left(\underline{K}_{jAD} - \underline{K}_{jCB}\right) \underline{X} \right) \tag{8.2.12}$$

where j denotes the spin of the decay product mesons. Further, only the first and last terms in the parentheses of (8.2.11) contribute because we anticipate

$$E_{J0} = E_{jKAD} + E_{jKCB} \tag{8.2.13a}$$

from (8.2.8) after integration over X^0. The middle two terms there will produce zero after such an integration. The roles of these two groups of terms in (8.2.8) are reversed if negative energy solutions are chosen for *CB* instead.

Since the right side of (8.2.12) is separated in *X* and $\underline{x}$, the left side must be so also;

$$\Phi_{1m4}(X,\underline{x}) = \Phi_{1jK}(\underline{x})\exp\left(i\left(E_{jKAD} + E_{jKCB}\right)X^0 + i\left(\underline{K}_{jAD} - \underline{K}_{jCB}\right)\underline{X}\right) \tag{8.2.14}$$

We further anticipate

$$\underline{K}_{jAD} = \underline{K}_{jCB} = \underline{K}_j \tag{8.2.13b}$$

from the integral over $\underline{X}$ in (8.2.8). Inserting (8.2.13, 14) into (8.2.12) and making use of (3.1.3) and (5.7.2), one finds

$$\left(\Delta + \frac{1}{4}E_{J0}^2\right)^2 \Phi_{1jK}(\underline{x}) = \frac{1}{2} g_s^4 \Xi_{jK}(\underline{x}) \tag{8.2.15a}$$

$$\begin{aligned}\Xi_{jK}(\underline{x}) &= -\psi_{0jKAD}(\underline{x})\chi_{0jKCB}^*(\underline{x}) + \underline{\psi}_{jKAD}(\underline{x})\underline{\chi}_{jKCB}^*(\underline{x}) \\ &- \chi_{0jKAD}(\underline{x})\psi_{0jKCB}^*(\underline{x}) + \underline{\chi}_{jKAD}(\underline{x})\underline{\psi}_{jKCB}^*(\underline{x})\end{aligned} \tag{8.2.15b}$$

8.2.4. Green's Function and Decay Amplitude

Green's function for (8.1.15) satisfies

$$\left(\Delta + \frac{1}{4}E_{J0}^2\right)^2 G(\underline{x},\underline{x}') = \delta(\underline{x} - \underline{x}') \tag{8.2.16a}$$

$$G(\underline{x},\underline{x}') = -\frac{1}{4\pi E_{J0}} \sin\left(\frac{1}{2}E_{J0}|\underline{x} - \underline{x}'|\right) \tag{8.2.16b}$$

In the $E_{J0} \to 0$ limit, (8.2.16b) reduces to

$$G(\underline{x},\underline{x}') = -\frac{|\underline{x} - \underline{x}'|}{8\pi} \tag{8.2.17}$$

which is the confining Green's function (3.2.6b) for the initial meson AB. Note that homogeneous solutions of the type

$$d_m/\left|\underline{x}-\underline{x}'\right|,\quad d_{m0}\quad \text{or}\quad d_{m2}\left|\underline{x}-\underline{x}'\right|^2$$

in (3.2.8a) cannot be added to the right side of (8.2.16b) due to the presence of E_{J0} in (8.2.16a). Application of (8.2.16) to (8.2.15) yields

$$\Phi_{1jK}(\underline{x}) = -\frac{g_s^4}{8\pi E_{J0}} \int d^3\underline{x}' \Xi_{jK}(\underline{x}') \sin\left(\frac{1}{2}E_{J0}\left|\underline{x}-\underline{x}'\right|\right) \tag{8.2.18}$$

For j=0, we limit ourselves to nonrelativistic pseudoscalar mesons. The products of the triplet wave functions in (8.2.15b) are of order $\varepsilon_0^2 << 1$ according (5.7.4, 12, 23) and can be dropped. The remaining terms in (8.2.15b) depend only upon r and are flavor independent according to (5.7.6) and Sec. 4.4,

$$\Xi_{0K}(\underline{x}) \approx \Xi_{0K}(r) \approx \Xi_{00}(r) = 2\psi_0^2(r) \tag{8.2.19}$$

For j=1, it has been shown in [H18 §8.4.5] that only the vector part of the virtual intermediate $\rho^+\rho^-$ in $\pi^0\to\gamma\gamma$ will couple to $\gamma\gamma$. Therefore, products of the singlet wave functions in (8.2.15b) can be dropped so that

$$\Xi_{1K}(\underline{x}) = \underline{\psi}_{1KAD}(\underline{x})\underline{\chi}^*_{1KCB}(\underline{x}) + \underline{\chi}_{1KAD}(\underline{x})\underline{\psi}^*_{1KCB}(\underline{x}) \tag{8.2.20}$$

The angular integrations in (8.2.18) can be carried out to yield

$$\Phi_{10K}(r) = -\frac{4g_s^4}{E_{J0}^4}\left\{\begin{matrix} \dfrac{\cos R}{R}\displaystyle\int_0^R dR'R'(\sin R' - R'\cos R')\Xi_{0K}(r') + \sin R\int_0^R dR'R'\sin R'\Xi_{0K}(r') \\ -\cos R\displaystyle\int_R^\infty dR'R'\cos R'\Xi_{0K}(r') + \dfrac{\sin R}{R}\int_R^\infty dR'R'(\cos R' + R'\sin R')\Xi_{0K}(r') \end{matrix}\right\} \tag{8.2.21a}$$

$$R = E_{J0}r/2 \tag{8.2.21b}$$

In the limit of $E_{J0}\to 0$ in (8.2.15, 16),

$$\sin\left(\frac{1}{2}E_{J0}\left|\underline{x}-\underline{x}'\right|\right) \to \frac{1}{2}E_{J0}\left|\underline{x}-\underline{x}'\right| \tag{8.2.22}$$

and (8.2.18) and (8.2.21) reduce to the forms (3.2.12) and (3.2.17), respectively.

Inserting (8.2.14) into (8.2.8), carrying out the X^0 integration and noting (8.2.21) leads to the decay amplitude

$$S_{fiJ} = i\frac{8\pi}{E_{J0}}\frac{1}{\Omega}\delta\left(E_{jKAD} + E_{jKCB} - E_{J0}\right)I_{Kj}\overline{\Phi}_{10K}(r) \tag{8.2.23a}$$

$$I_{Kj} = \int d^3\underline{X}\exp\left[i\left(\underline{K}_{jCB} - \underline{K}_{jAD}\right)\underline{X}\right] \tag{8.2.23b}$$

$$\overline{\Phi}_{10K}(r) = \int d^3\underline{x}\sqrt{\frac{\Omega}{\Omega_{svac}}}\psi_J^2(r)\Phi_{10K}(r) \Big/ \int d^3\underline{x}\psi_J^2(r) \tag{8.2.23c}$$

8.3. Unified Strong and Electromagnetic Coupling Hypothesis

8.3.1. Decay Rate for Slow Pseudoscalar Mesons

For $V \to PP$, the decay rate is given by the form (6.4.22) or (7.5.1, 2);

$$\Gamma(V \to PP) = \sum_{\text{finalstates}}\left|S_{fi}\right|^2 / T_d = \frac{\Omega_f^2}{(2\pi)^6}\int d^3\underline{K}_{0AD}d^3\underline{K}_{0CB}\left|S_{fi}\right|^2 / T_d \tag{8.3.1}$$

Inserting (8.2.23) into (8.3.1) leads to the analog of (7.5.5),

$$\Gamma(V \to PP) = \frac{1}{2\pi^5}\frac{1}{E_{10}^2}\frac{1}{\Omega^2}C_{CG}^2\int d^3\underline{K}_{0CB}I_{PP} \tag{8.3.2a}$$

$$I_{PP} = \int d^3\underline{K}_{0AD}I_{K0}I_{K0}^*\left|\Omega_f\overline{\Phi}_{10K}\right|^2\delta\left(E_{0KAD} + E_{0KCB} - E_{10}\right) \tag{8.3.2b}$$

where the equivalent of (7.5.6) has been used. Because such decays are of strong interaction nature, the branching ratio determined by the isospin Clebsch-Gordan coefficient C_{CG} has been inserted. Carrying out the integration in (8.2.23b) yields

$$I_{K0} = (2\pi)^3\delta\left(\underline{K}_{0CB} - \underline{K}_{0AD}\right) = I_{K0}^* \tag{8.3.3}$$

Substituting this expression into one of the two I_K's in (8.3.2b) and carrying out the integration yields

$$I_{PP} = (2\pi)^3\Omega\left|\Omega_f\overline{\Phi}_{10K}\right|^2\delta\left(E_{0KAD} + E_{0KCB} - E_{10}\right) \tag{8.3.4}$$

together with (8.2.13b). Ω is the same as I_{Kj} of (8.2.23b) observing (8.2.13b) or

$$\Omega = \int d^3\underline{X}\exp\left(i(\underline{0})\underline{X}\right) = \left(2\pi\delta(0)\right)^3 \tag{8.3.5}$$

which is a large volume.

In [H18], (8.2.21) using (8.2.19) with (4.3.5a) could be integrated to yield an algebraic expression (8.3.5) there. Here, however, (4.3.5a) is to be replaced by (4.3.4a) and this integral can now not be carried out analytically but has to be worked out numerically. For $J=1$, $j=0$ and $\Omega=\Omega_f$ in (4.3.4a), the results are denoted by the same $\Phi_{1000}(r)$. Inserting (4.3.4b) and this $\Phi_{1000}(r)$ into (8.2.23c) with $J=1$, $j=0$ and carrying out the integration yields

$$\Omega_f \overline{\Phi}_{100} = \frac{g_s^4}{8\pi E_{10}} \sqrt{\frac{\Omega}{\Omega_{svac}}} I_{100} \tag{8.3.6}$$

The relevant I_{100} values are given in Table 8.1 below.

Substituting (5.7.32) together with (8.2.13b) into the δ function in (8.3.4) and making use of (7.5.13) leads to

$$\delta(E_{0KAD} + E_{0KCB} - E_{10}) = \delta(K_0 - K_{00}) \frac{1}{E_{10} K_0} \sqrt{E_{00AD}^2 + K_0^2} \sqrt{E_{00CB}^2 + K_0^2} \tag{8.3.7a}$$

$$K_{00} = \frac{1}{2E_{10}} \sqrt{\lambda_3}, \qquad \lambda_3 = E_{10}^4 + E_{00AD}^4 + E_{00CB}^4 - 2E_{10}^2 (E_{00AD}^2 + E_{00CB}^2) - 2E_{00AD}^2 - 2E_{00CB}^2 \tag{8.3.7b}$$

where E_{00AD} and E_{00CB} are the masses of the mesons AD and CB, respectively.

Insert now (8.3.6, 7a) into (8.3.4), which in its turn is substituted into (8.3.2a). After performing the integration using (8.2.13b), one obtains

$$\Gamma(V \to PP) = f_s^2 C_{CG}^2 I_{100}^2 \frac{K_{00}}{E_{10}^5} \sqrt{E_{00AD}^2 + K_{00}^2} \sqrt{E_{00CB}^2 + K_{00}^2} \tag{8.3.8a}$$

$$f_s^2 = \frac{g_s^8}{4\pi^3} \frac{1}{\Omega_{svac}} \tag{8.3.8b}$$

for slowly moving pseudoscalar mesons AD and CB.

8.3.2. Decay Rate and Application to Data

The decay rate (8.3.8) together with I_{100} in (8.3.6), (8.3.7b) and the meson masses E_{10}, E_{00AD} and E_{00CB} can be applied to data [P1]. As was mentioned in the beginning of §8.1.4, the type ii) decay $AB \to AB+CD$, where CD represents π^0 here, becomes the same as the type i) decay $AB \to AD+CB$ treated above if $B \leftrightarrow D$ in the decay products.

Further, (8.3.8) holds only for very slowly moving decay products, as was pointed out below (8.2.18). For such mesons, data [P1] exist only for $D^{*+} \to D^+\pi^0$ and $\phi(1020) \to K^+K^-$

(K^0K^9). The last decay is used to fix the unknown f_s^2 of (8.3.8b). The results are given in Table 8.1 together with

$$f_s^2 = 5.6 \text{ GeV}^3 \tag{8.3.9}$$

The so predicted $\Gamma(D^{*+} \to D^+\pi^0)$ is ~ 3×10^{-4} times smaller than data so that the *impasse* mentioned below (8.2.5) is verified.

The number 25.6 keV in Table 8.1 was <40.2 keV in [H18 Table 8.1] so that there was no contradiction to data in [H18 Table 8.1] for $D^{*+} \to D^+\pi^0$. Years later, the new data 25.6 keV now contradicts the predictions of both (8.3.8) and [H18 (8.3.8)] confirming this *impasse*.

Table 8.1. Decay rates and parameters for $V \to PP$. ε_0^2 here denotes the product of the ε_0's in column 2 for the both decay products and is a measure of departure from the assumption (8.2.19) in which the motion of the decay products is neglected. C_{CG} is the isospin Clebsch-Gordon coefficient. I_{100} is defined in (8.3.6) and holds strictly for $\varepsilon_0=0$ and will be modified by a factor $1\pm\varepsilon_0^2$ for small ε_0^2. $\Gamma(\phi \to K^+K^-)$ is used as input to fix the unknown f_s^2 of (8.3.8b) to become (8.3.9). The predicted D^{*+} decay rate is obtained from (8.3.8, 7b, 9) together with the masses from [P1]

	$\varepsilon_0=K_0/E_{00}$	ε_0^2	C_{CG}^2	I_{100}	Γ(8.3.8) keV	Γ(data) [P1] keV
$D^{*+} \to D^+\pi^0$	0.021(D) 0.284(π)	0.00596	1/3	−0.01365	0.0074	25.6
$\phi \to K^+K^-$	0.257	0.066	1/2	0.6113	Input	2190

8.3.3. Ratio of $V \to P\gamma$ and $V \to P\pi$ Decay Rates

Although many other decay rates have not been measured, except for upper limits, branching raio data [P1] exist so that ratios

$$R_{\gamma\pi} = \frac{\Gamma(V \to P\gamma)}{\Gamma(V \to P\pi^0)}, \qquad R_{\gamma\pi A} = R_{\gamma\pi}\frac{C_{CG}^2}{(q_p + q_r)^2} \tag{8.3.10}$$

can be formed. Here, $R_{\gamma\pi A}$ is a adjusted form of $R_{\gamma\pi}$ that removes the $(q_p + q_r)^2$ dependence in (6.4.25) and the C_{CG}^2 dependence in (8.3.8a) putting the mesons on equal footing for mutual comparison. The results are shown Table 8.2.

Table 8.2. Ratios of $V \to P\gamma$ and $V \to P\pi^0$ decay rates from (8.3.10) and [P1]. E_{10} is the V mass and E_{00} the P mass

V	D_s^{*+}	D^{*+}	D^{*0}	|	K^{*+}	K^{*0}	ρ^{+}
$(q_p+q_r)^2$	1/9	1/9	16/9		1/9	4/9	1/9
C_{CG}^2	1/3	1/3	1/3		1/3	2/3	1
$E_{10}-E_{00}$ GeV	0.144	0.141	0.142	|	0.3985	0.3981	0.6355
$R_{\gamma\pi}$ [P1]	16.12	0.0521	0.5456	|	0.00247	0.001	0.00046
$R_{\gamma\pi A}$	46.36	0.1563	0.1023	|	0.0074	0.0015	0.00414

8.3.4. Unified Strong and Electromagnetic Coupling Hypothesis

The driving force of $V\to P\gamma$ and $V\to PP$ lies in the greater radius $\bar{r}_1\approx 8.1$ GeV^{-1} of the vector meson wave function mentioned below (8.2.10) relative to that for the pseudoscalar meson $\bar{r}_0\approx 4.26$ GeV^{-1} in (4.6.1). The squared energy of V is abou 0.56 GeV^2 greater than that for P according to (5.2.2). This difference in energy is released when $V\to P$. For $V\to P\gamma$, it is used to create a photon and impart it and P with momenta. For $V\to PP$, it is used to create a virtual quark-antiquark pair CD, separate them from each so that each of them becomes part of a P, and impart both P's with momenta.

The driving force is thus the same for $V\to P\gamma$ and $V\to PP$. For $D^*\to D\gamma$ and $D^*\to D\pi^0$, the π^0 mass is small relative to the D mass and may to some extent be regarded as a massless particle like the γ. Further, the phase space available for these decays are rather small due to the small differences between the D^* and D masses, barely covering the π^0 mass, as are seen to the left of | on the 4th line of Table 8.2. From these qualitative reasonings, one may expect that these both decay rates should be of similar order of magnitude. Indeed, the adjusted ratios $R_{\gamma\pi A}$=0.102, 0,156 in Table 8.2 are not too far from order of magnitude 1.

For $K^*(\rho)$ decays, the π^0 mass is not negligible next to the $K(\pi)$ mass. Further, the available phase space is much greater due to the large difference between $K^*(\rho)$ and $K(\pi)$ masses, as is seen to the right of | on the 4th line of Table 8.2. Therefore, the reasonings applied to D^* decay above do not apply here. The is also verified in Table 8.2; the adjusted ratios $R_{\gamma\pi A}$=0.0015 to 0.0074 deviate from order of magnitude 1 by large factors. The D_s^* case is complicated by the s quark does not present in π^0.

Each type of decay or interaction is characterized by its characteristic coupling strength. The coupling strength in the electromagnetic decay rate (6.4.25) is the fine structure constant α=1/137. The weak coupling strength is F_W^2 in the two-particle final state decay rate (7.5.16) dependent upon Ω_{wvac} and is G^2 in the three particle final state decay rate (7.5.4, 7.4.29b,). These both coupling strengths are independent of α but are ratios of ∞/∞ dependent upon the relative time scale τ_0, as was discussed in §7.5.4.

The coupling strength for strong decay $V\to PP$ is f_s^2 of (8.3.8b) and consists of a combination of two types of coupling strength; a dimensionless coupling constant g_s^8 analogous to α in the electromagnetic decays and $1/\Omega_{svac}$, analogous to $1/\Omega_{wvac}$ in the weak decay case in (7.5.16b). Thus, there appears to be a redundancy in the specification of the strong coupling strength; only one of the two coupling strength is needed and the other one may be removed. Now $1/\Omega_{svac}$ does not contain the relative time scale τ_0 and can therefore not be identified with any combination of ∞/∞ associated with F_W^2 of (7.5.16b) and G^2 of (7.4.29b) which depend upon τ_0. Hence the removal can only be achieved by identifying g_s^8 with α.

That the $D^{*0}\to D^0\gamma$ and $D^0\pi$ decay rates are of the same magnitude supports the identification of g_s^8 with α. This is further aided by noting that the $\eta\to\gamma\gamma$ and 3π decay rates are also of the same magnitude.

On these grounds, the following *hypothesis unifying the strong and electromagnetic couplings* is advanced,

$$\left(g_s^2/4\pi\right)^4 \equiv \alpha_s^4 = \alpha = e^2/4\pi \approx 1/137 \tag{8.3.11a}$$

$$\alpha_s \approx (\pm 1, \pm i)\times 0.2923 \tag{8.3.11b}$$

The factor 1/4π has been attached to g_s^2 for analogy with α. The value of the strong coupling constant $\alpha_s \approx 0.29$ among the quarks in (2.1.2, 4) is of the same magnitude as ≈0.12 cited in the literature [P1].

This hypothesis is also in harmony with "*Nature is economical in dealing out fundamental constants*" mentioned at the end of §7.2.1. To hand out two natural constants α and α_s within the relatively small factor of 0.12×137≈16.5 likewise appears to be wasteful. This aesthetical defect is removed by (8.3.11).

The hypothesis (8.3.11) eliminates another "fundamental parameter" α_s in the literature, in addition to the removal of the weak charge g and the Weinberg angle ϑ_W in §7.2.1 and the Cabibbo angle ϑ_C in (7.5.20). The three charges g, e and $\sqrt{\alpha_s}$ associated with the three basic types of interactions, the weak, electromagnetic and strong interactions, are thus reduced to one, the electron charge $-e$. This unification further implies that the *existence of electrons requires that quarks or hadrons must also exist*. The current concept of *electro-weak* interactions which unifies electromagnetic and weak interactions is, in view of §7.5.3 and (8.3.11), here replaced by what may be called *electro-strong* interactions.

The purely strong interaction coupling strength for meson decay here resides in Ω_{svac} of (8.3.8b). Combining (8.3.8b, 9, 11a) yields

$$\Omega_{svac}^{1/3} = 0.64\,\mathrm{GeV}^{-1} \tag{8.3.12}$$

which is << $(\Omega_{wvac})^{1/3}$= 12.2, 18.6 of (7.5.22b) and is contrary to the assumption that Ω_{svac} should be large made below (8.2.5). The *impasse* there is verified here.

8.4. Formulation of $\pi^0\to\gamma\gamma$

Steinberger [S6] first predicted the rate to be 13.8 eV. The virtual intermediate state was assumed to be a proton-antiproton pair. Then came the vector meson dominance (VMD) models [G5, R3, S7, B5] in which the virtual intermediate state was assumed to be dominated by vector mesons. A third type of treatment took place in the frame work of current algebra [A3] and the virtual intermediate state consists of quarks. There are variations of these three types of "models."

This decay was treated from the first principles in [H14] and [H18 Sec. 8.4]. The result however depended upon that of $V \rightarrow PP$ in [H18 Secs. 8.1-3]. The new data in Table 8.1, considered at the end §8.3.2 however show that such $V \rightarrow PP$ predictions are incorrect and an *impasse* was reached. This invalidates the results of [H18 §8.4.4-8]. Therefore, only the formulation of [H18 §8.4.1-3] will be reproduced here up to the point of an *impasse* corresponding to that of §8.3.2 and mentioned earlier below (8.2.5). No decay rate can be given here. Eventual further development is left to the future.

8.4.1. Isotriplet Meson Wave Equations

In the absence of s and heavier quarks, it is sufficient to consider the $SU(2)_I$ part of the approximately SU(3) gauge invariant action S_{m3} of (7.1.8). Under some circumstances, it can be more convenient to work with meson equations transforming according to the regular representation of SU(2), i.e., SO(3) (Special Orthogonal group of rank 3) which is also the group for three dimensional rotations. Here, the basis vector generating the representations of this group is the π or ρ triplet, which is usually written either in Cartesian basis denoted by the subscripts $C=1$, 2 and 3 or in spherical basis by $s= +, 0$ and $-$ (for π^+, π^0, π^-, $\pi \rightarrow \rho$).

The relationship between meson wave functions in (7.1.8b) and those in the isotriplet formalism χ_t has been indicated in (7.3.8) above. In component form,

$$\chi_{ts} = \begin{pmatrix} \chi_{t+} \\ \chi_{t0} \\ \chi_{t-} \end{pmatrix} = \begin{pmatrix} \chi_{(12)} \\ \left(\chi_{(11)} - \chi_{(22)}\right)/\sqrt{2} \\ \chi_{(21)} \end{pmatrix}, \qquad \chi \rightarrow \psi \tag{8.4.1a}$$

where (2.4.18) has been consulted. Alternatively,

$$\chi_{tC} = \begin{pmatrix} \chi_{t1} \\ \chi_{t2} \\ \chi_{t3} \end{pmatrix} = \begin{pmatrix} \left(\chi_{t+} + \chi_{t-}\right)/\sqrt{2} \\ i\left(\chi_{t+} - \chi_{t-}\right)/\sqrt{2} \\ \chi_{t0} \end{pmatrix}, \qquad \chi \rightarrow \psi \tag{8.4.1b}$$

The Gell-Mann matrices λ_l in (7.1.5a), which are generators of the SU(3) group, are now replaced by the generators of the SO(3) group S_{Cl} or S_{sl};

$$S_{s1} = \frac{1}{\sqrt{2}}\begin{pmatrix} 0 & 1 & 0 \\ 1 & 0 & 1 \\ 0 & 1 & 0 \end{pmatrix}, \qquad S_{s2} = \frac{1}{\sqrt{2}}\begin{pmatrix} 0 & -i & 0 \\ i & 0 & -i \\ 0 & i & 0 \end{pmatrix}, \qquad S_{s3} = \begin{pmatrix} 1 & 0 & 0 \\ 0 & 0 & 0 \\ 0 & 0 & -1 \end{pmatrix}$$

(8.4.2a)

$$S_{C1} = \begin{pmatrix} 0 & 0 & 0 \\ 0 & 0 & -i \\ 0 & i & 0 \end{pmatrix}, \qquad S_{C2} = \begin{pmatrix} 0 & 0 & i \\ 0 & 0 & 0 \\ -i & 0 & 0 \end{pmatrix}, \qquad S_{C3} = \begin{pmatrix} 0 & -i & 0 \\ i & 0 & 0 \\ 0 & 0 & 0 \end{pmatrix} \tag{8.4.2b}$$

S_{Cl} can be turned into S_{sl} and vice versa by a well-known similarity transformation. Both satisfy the same commutation rules as do λ_l, i.e., (2.4.7), but with the index l limited to *1*, *2* and *3*.

The derivative (7.1.4) now takes the form

$$\partial_I^{a\dot{b}} = \tfrac{1}{2}\partial_X^{a\dot{b}} - \partial^{a\dot{b}} \rightarrow D_{Is}^{a\dot{b}} = \tfrac{1}{2}\left(\partial_X^{a\dot{b}} + i\tfrac{1}{2}gS_{sl}W_l^{a\dot{b}}(X)\right) - \partial^{a\dot{b}}$$

$$= \partial_I^{a\dot{b}} + i\frac{g}{4}\begin{pmatrix} W_3 & W_l^- & 0 \\ W_l^+ & 0 & W_l^- \\ 0 & W_l^+ & -W_3 \end{pmatrix}^{a\dot{b}} \tag{8.4.3a}$$

$$\partial_I^{a\dot{b}} = \tfrac{1}{2}\partial_X^{a\dot{b}} - \partial^{a\dot{b}} \rightarrow D_{IC}^{a\dot{b}} = \tfrac{1}{2}\left(\partial_X^{a\dot{b}} + i\tfrac{1}{2}gS_{Cl}W_l^{a\dot{b}}(X)\right) - \partial^{a\dot{b}}$$

$$= \partial_I^{a\dot{b}} + i\frac{g}{4}\begin{pmatrix} 0 & -iW_3 & -iW_2 \\ iW_3 & 0 & -iW_1 \\ iW_2 & iW_1 & 0 \end{pmatrix}^{a\dot{b}} \tag{8.4.3b}$$

where (3.1.4), (5.7.2) and (7.1.5b) have been consulted. The meson wave equations (2.4.3) are now generalized to

$$\begin{aligned} D_{Is}^{a\dot{b}} D_{II\,s}^{f\dot{e}} \chi_{ts\dot{b}f} - \left(M_{ms}^2 - \Phi_m\right)\psi_{ts}^{a\dot{e}} &= 0 \\ D_{I\,s\dot{b}c} D_{II\,s\dot{e}d} \psi_{ts}^{c\dot{e}} - \left(M_{ms}^2 - \Phi_m\right)\chi_{ts\dot{b}d} &= 0 \end{aligned} \tag{8.4.4a}$$

$$M_{ms}^2 = \begin{pmatrix} M_{m+}^2 & 0 & 0 \\ 0 & M_{m0}^2 & 0 \\ 0 & 0 & M_{m-}^2 \end{pmatrix} \tag{8.4.4b}$$

In the limit of SO(3) symmetry, the M_m's in (8.4.4) are the same. In this limit, (8.4.4a) is covariant under the SO(3) gauge transformations

$$\chi_{ts}^{a\dot{e}} \rightarrow \chi_{ts}'^{a\dot{e}} = O_3(X)\chi_{ts}^{a\dot{e}}, \qquad \chi \rightarrow \psi \tag{8.4.5a}$$

$$S_{sl}W_l^{a\dot{b}} \to S_{sl}W_l'^{a\dot{b}} = O_3(X)S_{sl}W_l^{a\dot{b}}O_3^{-1}(X) + \frac{2i}{g}\left(\partial_X^{a\dot{b}}O_3(X)\right)O_3^{-1}(X) \tag{8.4.5b}$$

$$O_3(X) = \exp\left[i\tfrac{1}{2}gS_{sl}\vartheta_l(X)\right] \tag{8.4.5c}$$

Obviously, the spherical basis in (8.4.4, 5) can be replaced by the Cartesian basis using (8.4.1b, 2b, 3b) instead together with an obvious modification of (8.4.4b).

Since $\pi^0 \to \gamma\gamma$ is not a weak decay, the charged gauge bosons $W^{\pm}$ in (8.4.3a) can be dropped. In component form, (8.4.4a) becomes

$$\begin{aligned} &\partial_I^{a\dot{b}}\partial_{II}^{f\dot{e}}\chi_{t0\dot{b}f} - \left(M_{m0}^2 - \Phi_m\right)\psi_{t0}^{a\dot{e}} = 0 \\ &\partial_{I\dot{b}c}\partial_{II\dot{e}d}\psi_{t0}^{c\dot{e}} - \left(M_{m0}^2 - \Phi_m\right)\chi_{t0\dot{b}d} = 0 \end{aligned} \tag{8.4.6a}$$

$$\begin{aligned} &\left(\partial_I^{a\dot{b}} \pm ig\tfrac{1}{4}W_3^{a\dot{b}}\right)\left(\partial_{II}^{f\dot{e}} \pm ig\tfrac{1}{4}W_3^{f\dot{e}}\right)\chi_{t\pm\dot{b}f} - \left(M_{m\pm}^2 - \Phi_m\right)\psi_{t\pm}^{a\dot{e}} = 0 \\ &\left(\partial_{I\dot{b}c} \pm ig\tfrac{1}{4}W_{3\dot{b}c}\right)\left(\partial_{II\dot{e}d} \pm ig\tfrac{1}{4}W_{3\dot{e}d}\right)\psi_{t\pm}^{c\dot{e}} - \left(M_{m\pm}^2 - \Phi_m\right)\chi_{t\pm\dot{b}d} = 0 \end{aligned} \tag{8.4.6b}$$

8.4.2. Prototype Mechanism for $\pi^0 \to \gamma\gamma$

W_3 has been identified in the literature [L5 p670] to be the electromagnetic field,

$$A^{a\dot{b}}(X) = W_3^{a\dot{b}}(X) \tag{8.4.7}$$

This can be seen here as follows. Choose two of the three ϑ_l's in (8.4.5c) such that $\chi_{t\pm}$, hence also $\psi_{t\pm}$, are gauged away. Equation (8.4.6b) then drops out. Further, (8.4.6a) does not contain W_3. Variation of an action constructed from (8.4.6) in conjunction with the gauge boson action (7.6.4) with respect to W_3 shows that W_3 is massless [H8 §7]. Therefore, the identification of (8.4.7) is possible. If the SU(3) symmetry result $g=2e$ of (7.2.3c) is employed, the correct charges of the $t\pm(\pi^{\pm}, \rho^{\pm})$ wave functions in (8.4.6b) are obtained.

Since g is small, the gW_3 terms in (8.4.6b) are considered as perturbations. In the absence of W_3, (8.4.6) is considered to be of zeroth order in g. Since π^0 is a pseudoscalar meson, let the zeroth order wave functions in (8.4.6) be singlets. The presence of W_3 in (8.4.6) must be balanced by perturbations superimposed upon the zeroth order wave functions. With (3.1.1), write

$$\chi_{ts}^{a\dot{e}} = \chi_{0ts}\delta^{a\dot{e}} - \underline{\chi}_{1ts}\underline{\sigma}^{a\dot{e}}, \qquad \chi \to \psi \tag{8.4.8}$$

where χ_{0ts} denotes the zeroth order wave functions for the π's and the subscript 1 denotes perturbation of first order in g. The first order singlet wave functions have been absorbed into the zeroth order ones. Higher order terms are not included here.

Inserting (8.4.8) into (8.4.6) leads to the zeroth order meson wave equations

$$\begin{aligned}
&\partial_I^{a\dot b}\partial_{II}^{f\dot e}\chi_{0ts}\delta_{\dot b f} - \left(M_{ms}^2 - \Phi_m\right)\psi_{0ts}\delta^{a\dot e} = 0 \\
&\partial_{I\dot b c}\partial_{II\dot e d}\psi_{0ts}\delta^{c\dot e} - \left(M_{ms}^2 - \Phi_m\right)\chi_{0ts}\delta_{\dot b d} = 0
\end{aligned} \tag{8.4.9}$$

and the first order equations

$$\partial_I^{a\dot b}\partial_{II}^{f\dot e}\underline{\chi}_{1t\pm}\underline{\sigma}_{\dot b f} + \left(M_{m\pm}^2 - \Phi_m\right)\underline{\psi}_{1t\pm}\underline{\sigma}^{a\dot e} = \pm ie\tfrac{1}{2}\left(\underline{A\sigma}^{a\dot b}\partial_{II}^{f\dot e} + \partial_I^{a\dot b}\underline{A\sigma}^{f\dot e}\right)\delta_{\dot b f}\chi_{0t\pm} \tag{8.4.10a}$$

$$\partial_{I\dot b c}\partial_{II\dot e d}\underline{\psi}_{1t\pm}\underline{\sigma}^{c\dot e} + \left(M_{m\pm}^2 - \Phi_m\right)\underline{\chi}_{1t\pm}\underline{\sigma}_{\dot b d} = \mp ie\tfrac{1}{2}\left(\underline{A\sigma}_{\dot b c}\partial_{II\dot e d} + \partial_{I\dot b c}\underline{A\sigma}_{\dot e d}\right)\delta^{ce}\psi_{0t\pm} \tag{8.4.10b}$$

Here, (8.4.7) have been introduced. Further, the time component A^0 of the electromagnetic field has been removed by a suitable gauge transformation (8.4.5).

Putting s=0 in (8.4.9), it is seen that π^0 cannot decay to any gauge boson but must decay strongly through some perturbation Φ_{1m} of the confining potential Φ_m, whose source is a product of two meson wave functions according to (2.3.23). On the other hand, the electromagnetic field is only coupled to the charged triplet mesons in (8.4.10). These considerations together with (8.4.9, 10) suggest the prototype of the decay mechanism depicted by the quark line diagram of Figure 8.1.

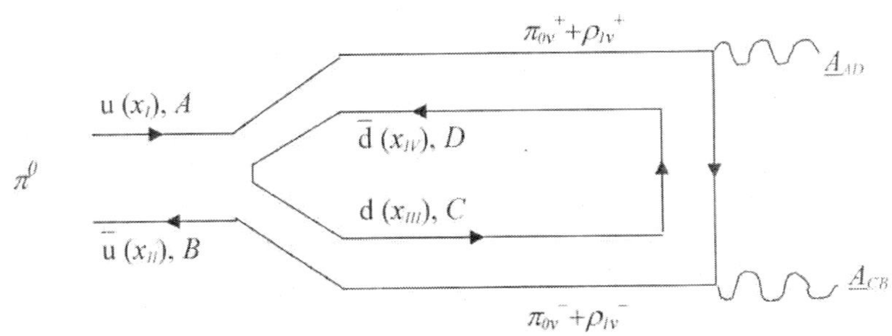

Figure 8.1. Mechanism of π0→γγ. This diagram is to be complemented by a similar diagram with u→d and subscript + ↔ − so that $\pi 0 = (\bar{u}u - \bar{d}d)/\sqrt{2}$ is adequately represented. xI, xII, xIII, and xIV are the coordinates of the four quarks A, C, B and D, respectively, mentioned in §8.1.1. The subscript v denotes virtuality, 0 zeroth order in e and 1 first order in e. A virtual $\bar{d}d$ pair is created from the vacuum. This pair together with $\bar{u}u$ from π0 form two charged intermediary mesons π0v±+ρ1v±. The first order virtual charged vector mesons ρ1v± decay into two real photons AAD and ACB together with a pair of zeroth order virtual charged pseudoscalar mesons π0v±, which in their turn annihilate each other.

This mechanism makes use of the four quarks considered in §8.1.1 and cannot be fully represented by the two quark equations (8.4.9, 10). However, (8.4.9, 10) have their correspondences in Figure 8.1. Thus, π^0 is described by (8.4.9) with s=0 and $\pi_{0v}^{\pm}$ are associated with $s=\pm$ in (8.4.9). $\rho_{Iv}{}^{\pm}$ are associated with the left sides of (8.4.10). Their decay products $\pi_{0v}{}^{\pm}$ and $\underline{A}_{AD}$ and $\underline{A}_{CB}$ are associated to the right sides of (8.4.10).

8.4.3. Virtual Intermediate Meson Wave Equations and Impasse

A full four quark treatment is presently not feasible, as was mentioned in §8.1.1. On the other hand, the two quark equations (8.4.9, 10) are inadequate for the four-quark problem posed by Figure 8.1. Therefore, the coupled meson equations of §8.1.4, based upon the mixed quark wave equations of §8.1.3, used for strong decay in Sec. 8.2 will be used as a compromise to treat $\pi^0 \to \gamma\gamma$ approximately.

To zeroth order in e. the left part of Figure 8.1 represents a form of $P \to PP$ mentioned in §8.1.2 and has been worked out in Sec. 8.1 and 8.2. In addition, there is a first order part VV which arises due to the introduction of the electromagnetic gauge fields, as is indicated by (8.4.10). The mesons AD and CB described by (8.1.12, 13) are now associated with the middle part of Figure 8.1. The treatment of Sec. 8.1 and 8.2 does not include gauge fields and hence does not cover the right half of Figure 8.1. To represent the final state $\gamma\gamma$, electromagnetic field A_{AD} and A_{CB} associated with the U(1) group are introduced into (8.1.12, 13) via the usual minimal substitution

$$\partial_X^{a\dot{b}} \to \partial_X^{a\dot{b}} + ieA_{AD}^{a\dot{b}}(X) = \partial_X^{a\dot{b}} + ie\left(\delta^{a\dot{b}} A_{0AD}(X) - \underline{\sigma}^{a\dot{b}}\, \underline{A}_{AD}(X)\right)$$
$$AD \to CB, \qquad\qquad e \to -e$$

analogous to (6.2.3). Substituting these expressions into (8.1.12, 13) and consulting (3.1.4) and (5.7.2) leads to

$$\left(\partial_I^{a\dot{b}} + ie\tfrac{1}{2}A_{AD}^{a\dot{b}}\right)\left(\partial_{II}^{f\dot{e}} + ie\tfrac{1}{2}A_{AD}^{f\dot{e}}\right)\overset{+}{\chi}_{AD\dot{b}f} - \left(M_{AD}^2 - \Phi_m\right)\psi_{AD}^{+a\dot{e}} = 0 \tag{8.4.11a}$$

$$\left(\partial_{I\dot{b}c} + ie\tfrac{1}{2}A_{AD\dot{b}c}\right)\left(\partial_{II\,\dot{e}d} + ie\tfrac{1}{2}A_{AD\dot{e}d}\right)\psi_{AD}^{c\dot{e}} - \left(M_{AD}^2 - \Phi_m\right)\overset{+}{\chi}_{AD\dot{b}D} = 0 \tag{8.4.11b}$$

$$(8.4.11) \text{ with } e \to -e,\ AD \to CB, \text{ and } {}^{+} \to {}^{-} \tag{8.4.12}$$

The superscripts + and – here indicate the signs of the charges associated with these wave functions; + here does not denote Hermitian conjugation, as in (7.1.3b). These equations take over the roles of (8.4.6b). Analogous to (8.4.8), let

$$\overset{+}{\chi}_{AD\dot{b}f} = \overset{+}{\chi}_{0AD}(X,x)\delta_{\dot{b}f} + \overset{+}{\underline{\chi}}_{1AD}(X,x)\underline{\sigma}_{\dot{b}f}, \qquad \chi \to \psi \tag{8.4.13a}$$

$$\psi_{CB}^{-a\dot{e}} = \overset{-}{\psi}_{0CB}(X,x)\delta^{a\dot{e}} - \overset{-}{\underline{\psi}}_{1CB}(X,x)\underline{\sigma}^{a\dot{e}}, \qquad \psi \to \chi \tag{8.4.13b}$$

Substituting these expressions into (8.4.11, 12) leads to the zeroth order analog of (8.4.9)

$$\partial_I^{a\dot{b}}\partial_{II}^{b\dot{a}}\chi_{0AD}^{+}(X,x)-2\left(M_{AD}^{2}-\Phi_{mAB}-\Phi_{1m4}\right)\psi_{0AD}^{+}(X,x)=0$$
$$\partial_{I\dot{b}c}\partial_{II\dot{c}b}\psi_{0AD}^{+}(X,x)-2\left(M_{AD}^{2}-\Phi_{mAB}-\Phi_{1m4}\right)\chi_{0AD}^{+}(X,x)=0 \qquad (8.4.14)$$

$$(8.4.14) \text{ with } AD\to CB \text{ and } {}^{+}\to{}^{-} \qquad (8.4.15)$$

where (8.1.10a) has been consulted. The first order equations corresponding to (8.4.10) are

$$\partial_I^{a\dot{b}}\partial_{II}^{f\dot{e}}\underline{\chi}_{1AD}^{+}(X,x)\underline{\sigma}_{\dot{b}f}+\left(M_{AD}^{2}-\Phi_{mAB}-\Phi_{1m4}\right)\underline{\psi}_{1AD}^{+}(X,x)\underline{\sigma}^{a\dot{e}}$$
$$=i\tfrac{1}{2}e\left(\underline{A}_{AD}(X)\underline{\sigma}^{a\dot{b}}\partial_{II}^{f\dot{e}}+\partial_I^{a\dot{b}}\underline{A}_{AD}(X)\underline{\sigma}^{f\dot{e}}\right)\delta_{\dot{b}f}\chi_{0AD}^{+}(X,x) \qquad (8.4.16a)$$

$$\partial_{I\dot{b}c}\partial_{II\dot{e}d}\underline{\psi}_{1AD}^{+}(X,x)\underline{\sigma}^{c\dot{e}}+\left(M_{AD}^{2}-\Phi_{mAB}-\Phi_{1m4}\right)\underline{\chi}_{1AD}^{+}(X,x)\underline{\sigma}_{\dot{b}d}$$
$$=i\tfrac{1}{2}e\left(\underline{A}_{AD}(X)\underline{\sigma}_{\dot{b}c}\partial_{II\dot{e}d}+\partial_{I\dot{b}c}\underline{A}_{AD}(X)\underline{\sigma}_{\dot{e}d}\right)\delta^{c\dot{e}}\psi_{0AD}^{+}(X,x) \qquad (8.4.16b)$$

$$(8.4.16a,16b) \text{ with } e\to -e,\ AD\to CB \text{ and } {}^{+}\to{}^{-} \qquad (8.4.17a,17b)$$

The final state of $V\to PP$ in Sec. 8.3 is a pair of real pseudoscalar mesons that move away from each other and no longer interact with each other after a short time. In Figure 8.1, however, $\pi_{0v}^{\pm}$ are not final states but virtual intermediate pseudoscalar mesons. They are at rest because the initial meson AB is at rest and the created pair CD is likewise so. Therefore, π_{0v}^{+} and π_{0v}^{-} are close to each other, as is seen in Figure 8 1, and interact with each strongly prior to their mutual annihilation in the final state.

As was pointed out in the beginning of this chapter, the volume Ω in (4.3.4) for these mesons no longer $\to\infty$ but becomes limited in laboratory space to some finite volume Ω_c. In weak interactions, $\Omega_c\to\Omega_{wvac}$ below (7.3.20b) is relatively large. For strong interactions, the relation turns to (8.2.5) where Ω_{svac} is no longer large. As was mentioned below (8.2.5), this invalidates the separability ansatz of (3.1.5) so that an analogous *impasse* is similarly reached here; *no decay rate can be derived here*. Eventual further development is left to the future.

Chapter 9

Construction of Equations of Motion for Baryon

The construction of a set of equations of motion for baryons is likewise guided by the principles of Sec. 1.5 and follows the related steps of [H15]. It is entirely analogous to the construction of the meson wave equations of Chapter 2.

9.1. Quark Wave and Potential Equations

A baryon consists of three quarks. In a unified theory, the quark-quark interaction must be the same in both baryons and mesons. Following Sec. 2.1, the *first step* is to assume that the quarks in a baryon act on each other pairwise via the same massless scalar interaction between the quarks in a meson. Any genuine three body interaction will drop out later in Sec. 9.2 below and are therefore not included here.

Let x_I, x_{II} and x_{III} denote the coordinates of the quarks A, B, and C, respectively. For simplicity, x_I, x_{II} and x_{III} as arguments are replaced by I, II and III, respectively. The starting quark equations corresponding to (2.1.1-4) are

$$\partial_I^{a\dot{b}}\chi_{A\dot{b}}(I)-i\left(V_{AB}(I)+V_{AC}(I)\right)\psi_A^a(I)=im_A\psi_A^a(I) \tag{9.1.1a}$$

$$\partial_{I\dot{b}c}\psi_A^c(I)-i\left(V_{AB}(I)+V_{AC}(I)\right)\chi_{A\dot{b}}(I)=im_A\chi_{A\dot{b}}(I) \tag{9.1.1b}$$

$$\partial_{II}^{d\dot{e}}\chi_{B\dot{e}}(II)-i\left(V_{BC}(II)+V_{BA}(II)\right)\psi_B^d(II)=im_B\psi_B^d(II) \tag{9.1.2a}$$

$$\partial_{II\,\dot{e}f}\psi_B^f(II)-i\left(V_{BC}(II)+V_{BA}(II)\right)\chi_{B\dot{e}}(II)=im_B\chi_{B\dot{e}}(II) \tag{9.1.2b}$$

$$\partial_{III}^{g\dot{h}}\chi_{C\dot{h}}(III)-i\left(V_{CA}(III)+V_{CB}(III)\right)\psi_C^g(III)=im_C\psi_C^g(III) \tag{9.1.3a}$$

$$\partial_{III\,\dot{h}k}\psi_C^k(III)-i\left(V_{CA}(III)+V_{CB}(III)\right)\chi_{C\dot{h}}(III)=im_C\chi_{C\dot{h}}(III) \tag{9.1.3b}$$

$$\Box_I\left(V_{AB}(I)+V_{AC}(I)\right)=\frac{1}{2}g_s^2\begin{pmatrix}\psi_B^e(I)\chi_{Be}(I)+\psi_B^{\dot{e}}(I)\chi_{B\dot{e}}(I)+\\+\psi_C^g(I)\chi_{Cg}(I)+\psi_C^{\dot{g}}(I)\chi_{C\dot{g}}(I)\end{pmatrix} \tag{9.1.4a}$$

$$\Box_{II}\left(V_{BC}(II)+V_{BA}(II)\right)=\frac{1}{2}g_s^2\begin{pmatrix}\psi_C^g(II)\chi_{Cg}(II)+\psi_C^{\dot{g}}(II)\chi_{C\dot{g}}(II)+\\+\psi_A^a(II)\chi_{Aa}(II)+\psi_A^{\dot{a}}(II)\chi_{A\dot{a}}(II)\end{pmatrix} \tag{9.1.4b}$$

$$\Box_{III}\left(V_{CA}(III)+V_{CB}(III)\right)=\frac{1}{2}g_s^2\begin{pmatrix}\psi_A^a(III)\chi_{Aa}(III)+\psi_A^{\dot{a}}(III)\chi_{A\dot{a}}(III)+\\+\psi_B^e(III)\chi_{Be}(III)+\psi_B^{\dot{e}}(III)\chi_{B\dot{e}}(III)\end{pmatrix} \tag{9.1.4c}$$

9.2. Baryon Wave Equations in Space Time

Following the procedure of Sec. 2.2, the left sides of (9.1.1-3) are multiplied together to form triple products containing all three quark wave functions. The corresponding right sides are analogously multiplied together with the operators placed to the left of the wave functions. Consider at first the right side terms, We can form two types of such products. Type a) consists of products with three dotted or three undotted indices, such as $\psi_A{}^a(I)\,\psi_B{}^d(II)\,\psi_C{}^{ag}(III)$. Type b) products contain mixed dotted and undotted indices, such as $\chi_{A\dot{b}}(I)\chi_{C\dot{h}}(III)\psi_B^f(II)$.

Fierz and Pauli [F2] have shown that rank three spinors transforming as type b) can represent spin 3/2 particles. Such a spinor can also include representation of spin 1/2 particles [B6]. These particles can obviously be associated respectively with quartet baryons, such as the Δ baryons, and doublet baryons, such as the nucleons. The *first part* of the *second step* is the generalization to nonseparable baryons wave functions akin to (2.2.1),

$$\chi_{A\dot{b}}(I)\chi_{C\dot{h}}(III)\psi_B^f(II)\to\chi_{\dot{b}\dot{h}}^{\ f}(I,III,II) \tag{9.2.1a}$$

$$\psi_A^c(I)\psi_C^k(III)\chi_{B\dot{e}}(II)\to\psi^{ck}_{\ \ \dot{e}}(I,III,II) \tag{9.2.1b}$$

The subscripts *A*, *B* and *C* are dropped via the interpretation that it is not possible to distinguish the quarks from each other inside a baryon.

Turning to the left side terms of the product equations mentioned in the beginning of this section. The *second part* of the *second step* by analogy to (2.2.3) consists of the generalization of *VVV* term to the nonseparable intrabaryon potential

$$\left(V_{AB}(I)+V_{AC}(I)\right)\left(V_{CA}(III)+V_{CB}(III)\right)\left(V_{BC}(II)+V_{BA}(II)\right)\to\Phi_b(I,III,II) \tag{9.2.2}$$

Product terms containing one *V* drop out on the same ground given above (2.2.4), i.e., there are no free quarks in the baryon system so that the right sides, hence also the left sides, of (9.1.4) vanish. Product terms containing *V*(*I*)*V*(*II*) type of expressions also drop out for the same reason. If *V*(*I*)*V*(*II*) is generalized to $\Phi_m(I,II)$ type of form similar to (2.2.3), the products on the right sides of (9.1.4a, 4b) will be analogously generalized as in (2.2.1, 2). The result is the creation of objects transforming like mesons or "nonlocal" diquarks. Since such objects are not observed in ground state baryons at least, they are dropped. Therefore, the generalized form of $V(I)V(II)$ on the left side likewise vanish.

The result of the multiplications and generalizations started at the beginning of this section with these two parts of the second step is

$$\begin{aligned} &\partial_I^{a\dot{b}}\partial_{III}^{g\dot{h}}\partial_{II\,\dot{e}f}\chi_{\dot{b}\dot{h}}^{\;\;f}(I,III,II) = -i\left(m_A m_B m_C + \Phi_b(I,III,II)\right)\psi^{ag}_{\;\;\dot{e}}(I,III,II) \\ &\partial_{I\,\dot{b}c}\partial_{III\,\dot{h}k}\partial_{II}^{d\dot{e}}\psi^{ck}_{\;\;\dot{e}}(I,III,II) = -i\left(m_A m_B m_C + \Phi_b(I,III,II)\right)\chi_{\dot{b}\dot{h}}^{\;\;d}(I,III,II) \end{aligned} \tag{9.2.3}$$

This set of baryon wave equations in space time contains 2×8=16 wave function components of (9.2.1), far less than 4×4×4=64, the number of wave function components in the Bethe-Salpeter formalism for baryons. This reduction is number great simplifies mathematical handling.

The rank three spinors (9.2.1) have eight components each and can be decomposed according the Clebsch-Gordan series [L2 p225]

$$\underline{2}\otimes\underline{2}\otimes\underline{2} = \underline{4}\oplus\underline{2}_s\oplus\underline{2}_a \tag{9.2.4}$$

By means of the invariant antisymmetric tensors ε^{ab} (B4) and (B15), each member of (9.2.1) can be decomposed into a doublet antisymmetric in the first two indices and a sextet symmetric in these indices;

$$\begin{aligned} &\chi_{\dot{b}\dot{h}}^{\;\;f} = \chi_{[\dot{b}\dot{h}]}^{\;\;f} + \chi_{\{\dot{b}\dot{h}\}}^{\;\;f}, \quad \chi_{[\dot{b}\dot{h}]}^{\;\;f} = \tfrac{1}{2}\left(\chi_{\dot{b}\dot{h}}^{\;\;f} - \chi_{\dot{h}\dot{b}}^{\;\;f}\right), \quad \chi_{\{\dot{b}\dot{h}\}}^{\;\;f} = \tfrac{1}{2}\left(\chi_{\dot{b}\dot{h}}^{\;\;f} + \chi_{\dot{h}\dot{b}}^{\;\;f}\right), \quad \varepsilon^{\dot{b}\dot{h}}\chi_{\{\dot{b}\dot{h}\}}^{\;\;f} = 0 \\ &\psi^{ck}_{\;\;\dot{e}} = \psi^{[ck]}_{\;\;\dot{e}} + \psi^{\{ck\}}_{\;\;\dot{e}}, \quad \psi^{[ck]}_{\;\;\dot{e}} = \tfrac{1}{2}\left(\psi^{ck}_{\;\;\dot{e}} - \psi^{kc}_{\;\;\dot{e}}\right), \quad \psi^{\{ck\}}_{\;\;\dot{e}} = \tfrac{1}{2}\left(\psi^{ck}_{\;\;\dot{e}} + \psi^{kc}_{\;\;\dot{e}}\right), \quad \varepsilon_{ck}\psi^{\{ck\}}_{\;\;\dot{e}} = 0 \end{aligned} \tag{9.2.5}$$

These functions are the same as those in (9.2.3) omitting the arguments $(I,III,II)=(x_I,x_{III},x_{II})$ for clarity. The antisymmetric doublet corresponding to $\underline{2}_a$ in (9.2.4) reads

$$\begin{aligned} &\chi^f = \varepsilon^{\dot{b}\dot{h}}\chi_{\dot{b}\dot{h}}^{\;\;f} = \chi_{\dot{1}\dot{2}}^{\;\;f} - \chi_{\dot{2}\dot{1}}^{\;\;f} = \varepsilon^{\dot{b}\dot{h}}\chi_{[\dot{b}\dot{h}]}^{\;\;f} \\ &\psi_{\dot{e}} = \varepsilon_{ck}\psi^{ck}_{\;\;\dot{e}} = \psi^{21}_{\;\;\dot{e}} - \psi^{12}_{\;\;\dot{e}} = \varepsilon_{ck}\psi^{[ck]}_{\;\;\dot{e}} \end{aligned} \tag{9.2.6}$$

The sextet can be decomposed into a doublet $\underline{2}_s$ in (9.2.4) of mixed symmetry, being symmetric in the indices inside the braces, but antisymmetric when an upper index and a lower index are interchanged,

$$\begin{aligned} &\chi_{0\dot{a}} = \tfrac{1}{2}\chi_{\{\dot{a}\dot{c}\}c}, \qquad \chi_{0\dot{1}} = \tfrac{1}{2}\left(\chi_{\{\dot{1}\dot{2}\}}^{\;\;1} - \chi_{\{\dot{1}\dot{1}\}}^{\;\;2}\right), \qquad \chi_{0\dot{2}} = \tfrac{1}{2}\left(\chi_{\{\dot{2}\dot{2}\}}^{\;\;1} - \chi_{\{\dot{1}\dot{2}\}}^{\;\;2}\right) \\ &\psi_0^a = -\tfrac{1}{2}\psi^{\{ac\}\dot{c}}, \qquad \psi_0^1 = \tfrac{1}{2}\left(\psi^{\{12\}}_{\;\;\dot{1}} - \psi^{\{11\}}_{\;\;\dot{2}}\right), \qquad \psi_0^2 = \tfrac{1}{2}\left(\psi^{\{22\}}_{\;\;\dot{1}} - \psi^{\{12\}}_{\;\;\dot{2}}\right) \end{aligned} \tag{9.2.7}$$

and a quartet $\underline{4}$ in (9.2.4) totally symmetric under the interchange of any pair of indices,

$$\chi_{3/2} = \chi^{1}_{\{\dot{1}\dot{1}\}}, \qquad \chi_{-3/2} = -\chi^{2}_{\{\dot{2}\dot{2}\}},$$
$$\chi_{1/2} = -\tfrac{1}{\sqrt{3}}\left(\chi^{1}_{\{\dot{2}\dot{1}\}} + \chi^{1}_{\{\dot{1}\dot{2}\}} + \chi^{2}_{\{\dot{1}\dot{1}\}}\right), \qquad \chi_{-1/2} = \tfrac{1}{\sqrt{3}}\left(\chi^{2}_{\{\dot{1}\dot{2}\}} + \chi^{2}_{\{\dot{2}\dot{1}\}} + \chi^{1}_{\{\dot{2}\dot{2}\}}\right)$$

$$\chi \to \psi, \quad \text{lower dotted indices} \leftrightarrow \text{upper undotted indices} \tag{9.2.8}$$

Turning to the potential equations (9.1.4). The left and right sides of (9.1.4a), (9.1.4b) and (9.1.4c) are multiplied together observing (9.2.2). We obtain

$$\Box_I \Box_{III} \Box_{II}\, \Phi_b(I,III,II) = \frac{1}{8} g_s^6$$
$$\times \left(\left\{ \left[\begin{cases} \chi_{B\dot b}(I)\chi_{B\dot h}(III)\psi^a_A(II)\psi^{\dot b}_B(I)\psi^{\dot h}_B(III)\chi_{Aa}(II) + \chi_{B\dot b}(I)\chi_{B\dot h}(III)\chi_{A\dot a}(II)\psi^{\dot b}_B(I)\psi^{\dot h}_B(III)\psi^{\dot a}_A(II) \\ + \chi_{B\dot b}(I)\psi^a_B(III)\psi^h_A(II)\psi^{\dot b}_B(I)\chi_{Ba}(III)\chi_{Ah}(II) \\ + \chi_{B\dot b}(I)\psi^h_B(III)\chi_{A\dot a}(II)\psi^{\dot b}_B(I)\chi_{Bh}(III)\psi^{\dot a}_A(II) + c.c. \end{cases} \right. \right. \right.$$
$$\left. + \text{same terms with the second B index} \to A \right]$$
$$\left. + \text{same terms with A} \to \text{C} \right\}$$
$$\left. + \text{same terms with the first B index} \to \text{C} \right) \tag{9.2.9}$$

The first term in the inner braces can be generalized via (9.2.1), dropping the A, C, B indices as was mentioned there. The next three terms are similarly generalized into

$$\chi_{B\dot b}(I)\chi_{B\dot h}(III)\chi_{A\dot a}(II)\psi^{\dot b}_B(I)\psi^{\dot h}_B(III)\psi^{\dot a}_A(II) \to \chi_{\dot b\dot h\dot a}(I,III,II)\psi^{\dot b\dot h\dot a}(I,III,II)$$
$$\chi_{B\dot b}(I)\psi^a_B(III)\psi^h_A(II)\psi^{\dot b}_B(I)\chi_{Ba}(III)\chi_{Ah}(II) \to \psi_{\dot b}{}^{ah}(I,III,II)\chi^{\dot b}{}_{ah}(I,III,II)$$
$$\chi_{B\dot b}(I)\psi^h_B(III)\chi_{A\dot a}(II)\psi^{\dot b}_B(I)\chi_{Bh}(III)\psi^{\dot a}_A(II) \to \chi_{\dot b}{}^{h}{}_{\dot a}(I,III,II)\psi^{\dot b}{}_{h}{}^{\dot a}(I,III,II) \tag{9.2.10}$$

None of the spinors on the right side transforms like those in (9.2.1); they differ in form with respect to the first two indices. They do not enter the equations of motion (9.2.3) and are therefore put to zero. The *c.c.* term and the remaining terms in (9.2.9) are treated entirely analogously and lead to terms composed of those in (9.2.1) and their *c.c.* In this way, (9.2.9) is simplified to

$$\Box_I \Box_{III} \Box_{II}\, \Phi_b(I,III,II) = \frac{1}{4} g_s^6 \left\{ \chi_{\dot b\dot h}{}^{f}(I,III,II)\psi^{\dot b\dot h}{}_{f}(I,III,II) + c.c. \right\} \tag{9.2.11}$$

which together with (9.2.3) are the baryon wave equations in space time. Note that the ψ term in (9.2.11) is the *c.c.* of ψ on the right of (9.2.1b).

Consider at first the above exposition from the viewpoint of baryon spectra. Classification of known baryon multiplets has shown that a free baryon consists of a quark-diquark pair rather than three separate quarks [L2 (12.79) ff]. To form such a diquark, the form of (9.2.1) calls for that x_{III} merges into x_I so that (9.2.1) becomes

$$\chi_{A\dot{b}}(I)\chi_{C\dot{h}}(III)\psi_B^f(II) \to \chi_{A\dot{b}}(I)\chi_{C\dot{h}}(I)\psi_B^f(II) \to \chi_{\dot{b}\dot{h}}^{\ f}(I,II) \tag{9.2.12a}$$

$$\psi_A^c(I)\psi_C^k(III)\chi_{B\dot{e}}(II) \to \psi_A^c(I)\psi_C^k(I)\chi_{B\dot{e}}(II) \to \psi^{ck}_{\ \ \dot{e}}(I,II) \tag{9.2.12b}$$

The decomposition (9.2.5-8) also holds for (9.2.12).

The *third part* of the *second step* consists of the merge of x_{III} with x_I (9.2.12). In this step, the original three body problem is reduced to a more tractable two body problem. With the merging of quarks A and C into a diquark, the interaction between them vanishes; V_{AC}, V_{CA} in (9.2.2) and the corresponding terms on the right sides of (9.1.4) and (9.2.9) drop out. Noting these and applying (9.2.12), (9.2.11) becomes

$$\Box_I \Box_I \Box_{II} \Phi_b(I,II) = \frac{1}{4} g_s^6 \left\{ \chi_{\dot{b}\dot{h}}^{\ f}(I,II)\psi^{\dot{b}\dot{h}}_{\ \ f}(I,II) + c.c. \right\} \tag{9.2.13a}$$

A specialization of this expression is

$$\Box_I \Box_I \Box_{II} \Phi_b(I,II) = \frac{1}{4} g_s^6 \left\{ \chi_{\{\dot{b}\dot{h}\}}^{\ \ f}(I,II)\psi^{\{\dot{b}\dot{h}\}}_{\ \ \ f}(I,II) + c.c. \right\} \tag{9.2.13b}$$

where the braced indices are interchangeable. Correspondingly, (9.2.3) becomes

$$\begin{aligned} \partial_I^{a\dot{b}} \partial_I^{g\dot{h}} \partial_{II\,\dot{e}f} \chi_{\dot{b}\dot{h}}^{\ f}(I,II) &= -i\left(m_A m_B m_C + \Phi_b(I,II)\right)\psi^{ag}_{\ \ \dot{e}}(I,II) \\ \partial_{I\,\dot{b}c} \partial_{I\,\dot{h}k} \partial_{II}^{d\dot{e}} \psi^{ck}_{\ \ \dot{e}}(I,II) &= -i\left(m_A m_B m_C + \Phi_b(I,II)\right)\chi_{\dot{b}\dot{h}}^{\ d}(I,II) \end{aligned} \tag{9.2.14}$$

These are the baryon counterpart of (2.2.4, 5). Since there are only two independent coordinates, x_I for the diquark and x_{II} for the quark, in these equations, the neglect of genuine three quark interaction above (9.1.1) is justified.

As to the triple products containing at least one of (9.1.1, 2, 3) and one of (9.1.4a, 4b, 4c), these likewise drop out. The reasons are the same as those given beneath (9.2.2) which led to that the V and VV terms there drop out. This is analogous to the corresponding discussion for the meson case beneath (2.2.5).

9.3. Baryon Internal Functions and Total Wave Equations

To include flavor dependence, the quark equations (9.1.1-3) are generalized to the form (2.3.11). Analogously, (9.1.1-3) are multiplied by $\xi_A{}^p(z_I)$, $\xi_B{}^q(z_{II})$ and $\xi_C{}^s(z_{III})$, respectively. m_A, m_B and m_C are replaced by mass operators of the form of (2.3.13). Following a procedure similar to that in Sec. 2.3, the so-modified (9.1.1-3) are multiplied together and the generalizations of second step in Sec. 9.2 are analogously repeated.

9.3.1. Baryon Internal or Flavor Functions

The *first part* of the *third step* is the analog of (2.3.18a) for mesons. Using (2.3.12), the baryon internal function is written as

$$\xi_A^p(z_I)\xi_B^q(z_{II})\xi_C^s(z_{III}) = z_I^p z_{II}^q z_{III}^s \leftrightarrow \xi^{psq}(z_I, z_{III}, z_{II}) \tag{9.3.1}$$

Consider the SU(3) case, (9.3.1) is decomposed into irreducible multiplets analogous to those in (2.4.8). The corresponding Clebsch-Gordan series reads [C3 (3.32)]

$$\underline{3}\otimes\underline{3}\otimes\underline{3} = (\underline{6}\oplus\underline{3}^*)\otimes\underline{3} = (\underline{6}\otimes\underline{3}) + (\underline{3}^*\otimes\underline{3}) = (\underline{10}\oplus\underline{8}_s) + (\underline{8}_a\oplus\underline{1}) \tag{9.3.2}$$

The corresponding decomposition of (9.3.1) can be achieved by means of the totally antisymmetric operator ε_{sqr}, ε_{123}=1, analogous to (9.2.4, 6-8),

$$\underline{10}: \qquad \xi^{\{psq\}}(z_I, z_{III}, z_{II,}) \qquad \text{totally symmetric in } p, s, q \tag{9.3.3a}$$

$$\underline{8}_s: \qquad \eta_r^p(z_I, z_{III}, z_{II,}) = \xi^{\{ps\}q}(z_I, z_{III}, z_{II,})\varepsilon_{sqr} \tag{9.3.3b}$$

$$\underline{8}_a: \qquad \eta_{(a)r}^{\ p}(z_I, z_{III}, z_{II,}) = \xi^{[ps]q}(z_I, z_{III}, z_{II,})\varepsilon_{sqr} \tag{9.3.3c}$$

$$\underline{1}: \qquad \eta_{(1)}(z_I, z_{III}, z_{II,}) = \xi^{psq}(z_I, z_{III}, z_{II,})\varepsilon_{psq} \tag{9.3.3d}$$

As in (9.2.5), $\{ps\}$ denotes symmetry and $[ps]$ antisymmetry under interchange of p and s.

To be consistent with the diquark-quark description of a free baryon, z_{III} is similarly merged into z_I by analogy to (9.2.12) and (9.3.1) becomes

$$\xi_A^p(z_I)\xi_B^q(z_{II})\xi_C^s(z_{III}) \to \xi_A^p(z_I)\xi_B^q(z_{II})\xi_C^s(z_I) = z_I^p z_{II}^q z_I^s \leftrightarrow \xi^{psq}(z_I, z_{II}) \tag{9.3.4}$$

Application to (9.3.3) leads to

$$\underline{10}: \qquad \xi^{\{psq\}}(z_I, z_{II}) \qquad \text{totally symmetric in } p, s, q \tag{9.3.5a}$$

$$\underline{8}_s: \qquad \eta_r^p(z_I, z_{II}) = \xi^{\{ps\}q}(z_I, z_{II})\varepsilon_{sqr} \tag{9.3.5b}$$

$$\underline{8}_a: \qquad \eta_{(a)r}^{\ p}(z_I, z_{II}) = \xi^{[ps]q}(z_I, z_{II})\varepsilon_{sqr} = 0 \tag{9.3.5c}$$

$$\underline{1}: \qquad \eta_{(1)}(z_I, z_{II}) = \xi^{psq}(z_I, z_{II})\varepsilon_{psq} = 0 \tag{9.3.5d}$$

9.3.2. Total Baryon Wave Functions

The total wave functions of the ground state baryons in the SU(3) scheme are obtained by combining (9.2.1) and (9.3.1),

$$\chi_{\dot{b}\dot{h}}^{\;\;f}(I,III,II)\xi^{psq}(z_I,z_{III},z_{II}), \qquad \psi^{ck}_{\;\;\dot{e}}(I,III,II)\xi^{psq}(z_I,z_{III},z_{II}) \tag{9.3.6}$$

These can be decomposed into baryon multiplets according to (9.2.6-8) combined with (9.3.3),

$$\underline{4}\otimes\underline{10},\ \text{totally symmetric spin } 3/2 \text{ decuplet: } \left(\chi_{3/2},\chi_{1/2},\chi_{-1/2},\chi_{-3/2},\psi_{3/2},\psi_{1/2},\psi_{-1/2},\psi_{-3/2},\right)\xi^{\{psq\}} \tag{9.3.7a}$$

$$\underline{2}_s\otimes\underline{8}_s,\ \text{mixed symmetric spin } 1/2 \text{ octet}: \qquad \chi_{0\dot{a}}\,\eta_r^{\;p}, \qquad \psi_0^{\;a}\,\eta_r^{\;p} \tag{9.3.7b}$$

$$\underline{2}_a\otimes\underline{8}_a,\ \text{mixed antisymmetric spin } 1/2 \text{ octet}: \quad \chi^f\,\eta_{(a)r}^{\quad p}, \qquad \psi_{\dot{e}}\,\eta_{(a)r}^{\quad p} \tag{9.3.7c}$$

$$0\otimes\underline{1},\quad 0 \text{ singlet}: \qquad 0 \tag{9.3.7d}$$

where the arguments (I,III,II) and (z_I,z_{III},z_{II}) have been omitted.

The assignments (9.3.7) are dictated by the following *symmetric quark postulate: "The total baryon wave functions must be totally symmetric under the simultaneous interchange of the space-time index and the internal index associated with one quark with those associated with another quark."* This constitutes the *second part* of the *third step*. The essence of this postulate is supported by the approximately correct calculations of the baryon magnetic moments [L2 p238]. This postulate plays a role akin to that of Pauli's theorem in conventional quantum mechanics in eliminating extraneous solutions. The role of identical particles in Pauli's theorem is taken over here by quarks which, being not observable, are indistinguishable, hence appear as identical inside hadrons.

For free baryons, (9.2.12) and (9.3.4) apply and (9.3.5c, d) leads to that the singlet $\underline{1}$ and mixed antisymmetric octet $\underline{8}_a$ drops out, in agreement with data. In addition, it will be shown in connection with (10.2.1b) and the conclusion beneath (10.2.5) below that (9.2.14) does not have any solution for the $\underline{2}_a$ of (9.2.6) associated with $\underline{8}_a$ in (9.3.7c).

The simplified notations $z_I=z$ and $z_{II}=u$ of (2.3.16, 17) are now introduced and generalized to include $z_{III}=v$. The mass term $m_A m_B m_C$ in (9.2.3) is generalized by analogy to (2.3.18b):

$$m_{1op}(z_I)m_{1op}(z_{III})m_{1op}(z_{II}) = m_{1op}(z)m_{1op}(v)m_{1op}(u) \to m_{3op}(z,v,u) \tag{9.3.8}$$

This is the *third part* of the *third step* and is the internal counterpart of the space time generalization (9.2.2). This third step generalizes (9.2.3) to the total baryons wave equations

$$\begin{aligned}
\partial_I^{a\dot{b}}\partial_I^{g\dot{h}}\partial_{II\,\dot{e}f}\,\chi_{\dot{b}\dot{h}}^{\;\;f}(I,III,II)\xi^{psq}(z,v,u) &= -i\left(m_{3op}(z,v,u)+\Phi_b(I,III,II)\right)\psi^{ag}_{\;\;\dot{e}}(I,III,II)\xi^{psq}(z,v,u)\\
\partial_{I\,\dot{b}c}\partial_{I\,\dot{h}k}\partial_{II}^{d\dot{e}}\psi^{ck}_{\;\;\dot{e}}(I,III,II)\xi^{psq}(z,v,u) &= -i\left(m_{3op}(z,v,u)+\Phi_b(I,III,II)\right)\chi_{\dot{b}\dot{h}}^{\;\;d}(I,III,II)\xi^{psq}(z,v,u)
\end{aligned} \tag{9.3.9}$$

The equation for Φ_b (9.2.11) is not affected by the inclusion of internal functions for the same reason given beneath (2.3.19). Equations (9.3.9) and (9.2.11) are the set of total baryon wave equations and may themselves be regarded as a *basic postulate*, instead of the three steps of assumptions given in this chapter, of the scalar strong interaction hadron theory for baryons. Note that ξ^{psq} is not limited to the SU(3) case (9.3.3); *c* and *b* quarks may be present.

Invariance of (9.3.9) and (9.2.11) under proper Lorentz transformations and space inversion are manifest due to their spinor form, on similar grounds as those mentioned above (2.3.20). Application of (B31) to (9.2.1) leads to

$$\chi_{\dot{b}\dot{h}}^{f}\left(x_I^0, \underline{x}_I, x_{III}^0, \underline{x}_{III}, x_{II}^0, \underline{x}_{II}\right) \leftrightarrow \psi^{bh}{}_{\dot{f}}\left(x_I^0, -\underline{x}_I, x_{III}^0, -\underline{x}_{III}, x_{II}^0, -\underline{x}_{II}\right)$$

under space inversion.

For a free baryon, (9.2.12) and (9.3.4) apply and (9.3.8, 9) become

$$m_{1op}(z_I) m_{1op}(z_{III}) m_{1op}(z_{II}) \to m_{1op}(z) m_{1op}(z) m_{1op}(u) \to m_{3op}(z, u) \tag{9.3.10}$$

$$\partial_I^{a\dot{b}} \partial_I^{g\dot{h}} \partial_{II\dot{e}f} \chi_{\{\dot{b}\dot{h}\}}^{f}(I, II) \xi^{\{ps\}q}(z, u) = -i\left(m_{3op}(z, u) + \Phi_b(I, II)\right) \psi^{\{ag\}}{}_{\dot{e}}(I, II) \xi^{\{ps\}q}(z, u)$$

$$\partial_{I\dot{b}c} \partial_{I\dot{h}k} \partial_{II}^{d\dot{e}} \psi^{\{ck\}}{}_{\dot{e}}(I, II) \xi^{\{ps\}q}(z, u) = -i\left(m_{3op}(z, u) + \Phi_b(I, II)\right) \chi_{\{\dot{b}\dot{h}\}}^{d}(I, II) \xi^{\{ps\}q}(z, u) \tag{9.3.11}$$

Observing (9.3.5c, d), only the symmetric (9.3.7a, b) survive here. This and (9.2.13b), giving $\Phi_b(I,II)$, are the total *equations of motion for free, ground state baryons* in diquark-quark configuration.

9.3.3. Internal or Flavor Functions and Mass Operator

Analogous to (2.3.25), (9.3.8) is put to

$$m_{3op}(z, v, u) = m_{1op}^3(z, v, u) \tag{9.3.12}$$

Similarly, (2.3.26) is generalized to

$$m_{1op}(z, v, u) = \frac{1}{2} m_q \left(z^q \partial_{zq} + v^q \partial_{vq} + u^q \partial_{uq}\right) \tag{9.3.13}$$

where the flavor index q is summed over. For a free baryon, (9.2.12) and (9.3.4) apply and (9.3.12) becomes

$$m_{3op}(z,u) = m_{1op}^3(z,u) \tag{9.3.14}$$

and the v term drops out in (9.3.13).

The total equations of motion for baryons are now specified by (9.2.11), (9.3.9), (9.3.12), and (9.3.13). For baryon spectra considerations, the simpler equations of motion for free baryon or diquark-quark, (9.3.11, 14) and (9.2.13) can be used. Equation (9.3.11) is separable in x and z if the baryon internal function $\xi^{\{ps\}q}$ is an eigenfunction of $m_{3op}(z,u)$. With (9.3.14), we can write

$$m_{3op}(z,u)\xi^{\{ps\}q}(z,u) = M_b^3 \xi^{\{ps\}q}(z,u) \tag{9.3.15}$$

$$\partial_I^{a\dot{b}} \partial_I^{g\dot{h}} \partial_{II\,\dot{e}f} \chi_{\{\dot{b}\dot{h}\}}^{f}(I,II) = -i\left(M_b^3 + \Phi_b(I,II)\right)\psi^{\{ag\}}_{\dot{e}}(I,II) \tag{9.3.16a}$$

$$\partial_{I\,\dot{b}c} \partial_{I\,\dot{h}k} \partial_{II}^{d\dot{e}} \psi^{\{ck\}}_{\dot{e}}(I,II) = -i\left(M_b^3 + \Phi_b(I,II)\right)\chi_{\{\dot{b}\dot{h}\}}^{d}(I,II) \tag{9.3.16b}$$

where the eigenvalue M_b^3 is the separation constant between functions in space time and in internal space and corresponds to M_m^2 for mesons in (2.3.21, 22). If there exists no eigenvalue, (9.3.16) can still be obtained. Multiplying (9.3.16) by the complex conjugate of the baryon internal function and integrating over the internal space leads to

$$M_b^3 = \frac{\int dv_{zq} dv_{uq} \xi_{\{ps\}q}(z,u) m_{3op}(z,u) \xi^{\{ps\}q}(z,u)}{\int dv_{zq} dv_{uq} \xi_{\{ps\}q}(z,u) \xi^{\{ps\}q}(z,u)} \tag{9.3.17}$$

which corresponds to (2.3.24) for mesons. This M_b^3 is not the strict separation constant like M_b^3 in (9.3.15) but both represent the quark mass contribution to the baryon mass.

The baryon internal functions are analogous to the corresponding meson internal functions (2.4.8). With (9.3.4) and (9.3.5a, b), they are

$$\eta_r^p(z,u) = z^p z^s u^q \varepsilon_{rsq} \tag{9.3.18a}$$

$$\xi^{\{psq\}}(z,u) = z^p z^s u^q + z^p u^s z^q + u^p z^s z^q \tag{9.3.18b}$$

Inserting (9.3.18) into (9.3.15) yields

$$M_b^3 = \frac{1}{8}\left(m_p + m_s + m_q\right)^3 \tag{9.3.19}$$

which is the counterpart of (2.3.27). This form will however not distinguish between Σ^0 and Λ, which according to (9.3.18a) have the internal functions

$$\eta_1^1 - \eta_2^2 = 2z^1z^2u^3 - \left(z^2u^1 + z^1u^2\right)z^3 \qquad \text{for } \Sigma^0 \tag{9.3.20a}$$

$$\eta_1^1 + \eta_2^2 - 2\eta_3^3 = 3\left(z^2u^1 - z^1u^2\right)z^3 \qquad \text{for } \Lambda \tag{9.3.20b}$$

The situation is analogous to that for the η meson at the end of Sec. 5.4. For baryons, (5.4.1) becomes (9.46) of [L2],

$$M_{GMOb} = a_{8b} + b_{8b}Y + c_{8b}\left(I(I+1) - Y^2/4\right) \tag{9.3.21}$$

For the same reason as that mentioned beneath (5.4.1), M_{GMOb} is equated to $2M_b$ of (9.3.19) with $m_1 = m_2$ for the neutron, Σ^0 and Ξ^0. This fixed the three constants

$$a_{8b} = 2m_1 + m_3, \qquad b_{8b} = m_1 - m_3, \qquad c_{8b} = 0 \tag{9.3.22}$$

The last relation shows that terms containing eigenvalues of operators containing the SU(3) generators (2.4.5) present in (9.3.21) as well as in (5.4.1) are absent in the quark mass summation operator m_{Iop} in (9.3.13, 14) and (2.3.25, 26). It is the quadratic I^2 that differentiates Σ^0 from Λ in (9.3.20) and this accounts for that (9.3.19) is the same for Σ^0 and Λ. Thus, the simple form (9.3.14) needs be modified to include such generators. The pros and cons of (9.3.14, 19) versus (9.3.21) are the same as those mentioned at the end of Sec. 5.4.

Chapter 10

Reduction of Baryon Wave Equations

The basic set of equations of motion for free baryon in diquark-quark configuration is given by (9.3.16) and (9.2.13b). Reduction of these equations is analogous to that of the meson equations of Sec. 3.1 and follows [H15] closely.

Equations determining the doublet wave functions (9.2.7) can be formally obtained as follows. The e, f and d indices in (9.3.16) are raised and lowered. Multiply the so modified (9.3.16a) and (9.3.16b) by $\delta_{\dot{e}g}$ /2 and $\delta^{d\dot{h}}$ /2, respectively, and apply (9.2.7). Equation (9.3.16) is now reduced to

$$\partial_{I}^{a\dot{b}}\partial_{II}^{f\dot{e}}\partial_{I}^{e\dot{h}}\,\tfrac{1}{2}\chi_{\{\dot{b}\dot{h}\}f}(I,II)=-i\left(M_{b}^{3}+\Phi_{b}(I,II)\right)\psi_{0}^{a}(I,II) \tag{10.0.1a}$$

$$\partial_{I\dot{b}c}\partial_{II\dot{e}h}\partial_{I\dot{h}k}\,\tfrac{1}{2}\psi^{\{ck\}\dot{e}}(I,II)=i\left(M_{b}^{3}+\Phi_{b}(I,II)\right)\chi_{0\dot{b}}(I,II) \tag{10.0.1b}$$

The doublet wave functions on the right sides of (10.0.1) are expressed in terms of the left side ones which in general contains both the doublet and quartet wave functions (9.2.7, 8).

Analogously, (9.2.14) can be contracted by the ε^{ab} tensor in (9.2.6) and becomes

$$\begin{aligned}
&\partial_{I}^{a\dot{b}}\varepsilon_{ag}\partial_{I}^{g\dot{h}}\partial_{II\dot{e}f}\chi_{\dot{b}\dot{h}}^{\;f}(I,II)=-i\left(m_{A}m_{B}m_{C}+\Phi_{b}(I,II)\right)\psi_{\dot{e}}(I,II)\\
&\partial_{I\dot{b}c}\varepsilon^{\dot{b}\dot{h}}\partial_{I\dot{h}k}\partial_{II}^{d\dot{e}}\psi^{ck}_{\;\;\dot{e}}(I,II)=-i\left(m_{A}m_{B}m_{C}+\Phi_{b}(I,II)\right)\chi^{d}(I,II)
\end{aligned} \tag{10.0.2}$$

If the symmetric quark postulate [H15] beneath (9.3.7) is employed, (10.0.1) takes a simpler form. After raising and lowering the d, e and f indices and dropping the arguments, the baryon wave functions in (9.3.11) can be decomposed into the form

$$\chi_{\{\dot{b}\dot{h}\}f}\xi^{\{ps\}q}\rightarrow\chi_{0\dot{b}}\delta_{\dot{h}f}\left(\xi^{\{ps\}q}-\xi^{\{psq\}}\right)+\chi_{\{\dot{b}\dot{h}f\}}\xi^{\{psq\}} \tag{10.0.3a}$$

$$\psi^{\{ck\}\dot{e}}\xi^{\{ps\}q}\rightarrow\psi_{0}^{c}\delta^{k\dot{e}}\left(\xi^{\{ps\}q}-\xi^{\{psq\}}\right)+\psi^{\{ck\dot{e}\}}\xi^{\{psq\}} \tag{10.0.3b}$$

Observing (9.2.8), the last terms in (10.0.3) correspond to $\underline{4}\times\underline{10}$ of (9.3.7a). The internal functions in the parentheses have 6×3−10=8 components so that the first terms on the right of (10.0.3) correspond to $\underline{2}_s\times\underline{8}_s$ of (9.3.7b). This is seen more directly by contracting (10.0.3) by ε_{rsq} via (9.3.5b, 5c),

$$\varepsilon_{rsq}\left(\chi_{\{\dot{b}\dot{h}\}f},\ \psi^{\{ck\}\dot{e}}\right)\xi^{\{ps\}q}=\left(\chi_{0\dot{b}}\delta_{\dot{h}f},\ \psi_{0}^{c}\delta^{k\dot{e}}\right)\eta_{r}^{p} \tag{10.0.4}$$

The operations (10.0.3a, 4) reduce the first of (9.3.11) to the doublet wave equation

$$\partial_I^{a\dot{b}}\partial_I^{g\dot{f}}\partial_{II}^{f\dot{e}}\chi_{0\dot{b}}(I,II)\eta_r^p(z,u)=-i\left(m_{3op}(z,u)+\Phi_b(I,II)\right)\psi_0^a(I,II)\delta^{g\dot{e}}\eta_r^p(z,u) \tag{10.0.5}$$

Contracting by $\delta_{\dot{e}g}$ and noting (9.3.15), (10.0.5) can be turned into

$$\partial_I^{a\dot{b}}\partial_{II}^{f\dot{e}}\partial_I^{e\dot{f}}\tfrac{1}{2}\chi_{0\dot{b}}(I,II)=-i\left(M_b^3+\Phi_b(I,II)\right)\psi_0^a(I,II) \tag{10.0.6a}$$

Analogously, the second of (9.3.11) reduces to

$$\partial_{I\dot{b}c}\partial_{II\dot{e}h}\partial_{I\dot{h}e}\tfrac{1}{2}\psi_0^c(I,II)=-i\left(M_b^3+\Phi_b(I,II)\right)\chi_{0\dot{b}}(I,II) \tag{10.0.6b}$$

These two equations are the same as (10.0.1) with

$$\chi_{\{\dot{b}\dot{h}\}f}=\chi_{0\dot{b}}\delta_{\dot{h}f},\qquad \psi^{\{ck\}\dot{e}}=-\psi_0^c\delta^{k\dot{e}} \tag{10.0.7}$$

10.1. Baryon Equations in Relative Space

The coordinate transformations (3.1.3, 4), (3.1.9) with $\varphi(\underline{x})$ representing the baryon relative wave functions, and (3.1.10a) are taken over here. But x_I is now the coordinate of the diquark and x_{II} that of the quark. Equation (3.1.5) is replaced by

$$\begin{aligned}\chi_{\{\dot{a}\dot{c}\}}{}^{e}(x_I,x_{II})&=\chi_{\{\dot{a}\dot{c}\}}{}^{e}(\underline{x})\exp\left(-iK_\mu X^\mu+i\omega_K x^0\right)\\ \psi^{\{ac\}}{}_{\dot{e}}(x_I,x_{II})&=\psi^{\{ac\}}{}_{\dot{e}}(\underline{x})\exp\left(-iK_\mu X^\mu+i\omega_K x^0\right)\end{aligned} \tag{10.1.1}$$

where $K_\mu=(E_0,-\underline{K})$, as in (3.1.6). Normalization will be considered in Sec. !0.3. As in Sec. 3.2, we consider only the rest frame baryons and put $\underline{K}=0$. The modified relations mentioned above (10.1.1) will remove the unknown relative energy ω_K and allow for a decoupling of the doublet wave functions in (10.2.1a) from the quartet wave functions in (10.5.1) in the general six component wave functions in (10.1.2) below. This is entirely analogous to the decoupling of the singlet and triplet mentioned below (3.1.10a).

The basic set (9.3.16) and (9.2.13b) now reduce to

$$\begin{aligned}&\left(i\delta^{a\dot{b}}E_0/2+\underline{\sigma}^{a\dot{b}}\underline{\partial}\right)\left(i\delta^{g\dot{h}}E_0/2+\underline{\sigma}^{g\dot{h}}\underline{\partial}\right)\left(i\delta_{\dot{e}f}E_0/2+\underline{\sigma}_{\dot{e}f}\underline{\partial}\right)\chi_{\{\dot{b}\dot{h}\}}{}^{f}(\underline{x})\\ &=-i\left(M_b^3+\Phi_b(\underline{x})\right)\psi^{\{ag\}}{}_{\dot{e}}(\underline{x})\\ &\left(i\delta_{\dot{b}c}E_0/2-\underline{\sigma}_{\dot{b}c}\underline{\partial}\right)\left(i\delta_{\dot{h}k}E_0/2-\underline{\sigma}_{\dot{h}k}\underline{\partial}\right)\left(i\delta^{d\dot{e}}E_0/2-\underline{\sigma}^{d\dot{e}}\underline{\partial}\right)\psi^{\{ck\}}{}_{\dot{e}}(\underline{x})\\ &=-i\left(M_b^3+\Phi_b(\underline{x})\right)\chi_{\{\dot{b}\dot{h}\}}{}^{d}(\underline{x})\end{aligned} \tag{10.1.2}$$

$$\Delta\Delta\Delta\Phi_b(\underline{x}) = \frac{1}{4} g_s^6 \left\{ \chi_{\{\dot{b}\dot{h}\}}^{f}(\underline{x}) \psi^{*\{\dot{b}\dot{h}\}}_{f}(\underline{x}) + c.c. \right\} \tag{10.1.3a}$$

$$\psi^{*\{\dot{b}\dot{h}\}}_{f}(\underline{x}) = \left(\psi^{\{bh\}}_{\dot{f}}\right)^*, \qquad \chi^{*\,\dot{f}}_{\{bh\}} = \left(\chi^{f}_{\{\dot{b}\dot{h}\}}\right)^* \tag{10.1.3b}$$

Here, it is seen that the requirement mentioned below (3.1.10a) is analogously fulfilled here. In the absence of the interaction potential Φ_b and quark motion represented by ∂, (10.1.2) leads to that the baryon mass E_0 reduces to the sum of the quark masses via (9.3.19).

Green's function of (10.1.3) satisfies

$$\Delta\Delta\Delta G_b(\underline{x}, \underline{x}') = \delta(\underline{x} - \underline{x}') \tag{10.1.4a}$$

$$G_b(\underline{x}, \underline{x}') = -\frac{1}{96\pi} |\underline{x} - \underline{x}'|^3 \tag{10.1.4b}$$

Operating (10.1.4b), which is regular everywhere, by Δ yields

$$\Delta G_b(\underline{x}, \underline{x}') = -\frac{1}{8\pi} |\underline{x} - \underline{x}'| \tag{10.1.5}$$

which together with (3.2.6) reproduces (10.1.4a). Analogous to (3.2.8), there are also homogenous solutions to (10.1.4) and these are the corresponding ones in (3.2.8a) together with $|\underline{x}| = r$ from (3.2.6b) and an $|\underline{x}|^4$ term. The solution to (10.1.3) is

$$\Phi_b(\underline{x}) = \Phi_{bc}(\underline{x}) + \frac{d_b}{r} + d_{b0} + d_{b1} r + d_{b2} r^2 + d_{b4} r^4 \tag{10.1.6a}$$

$$\Phi_{bc}(\underline{x}) = \frac{g_s^6}{192\pi} \int d^3\underline{x}' |\underline{x} - \underline{x}'|^3 \operatorname{Re}\left(\chi_{\{\dot{b}\dot{h}\}}^{f}(\underline{x}') \psi^{*\{\dot{b}\dot{h}\}}_{f}(\underline{x}')\right) \tag{10.1.6b}$$

Here, the d_b's are 5 integration constants to the sixth order potential equation (10.1.3a) without the source term on its right side. This is the case for free baryons, for which the right side of (10.1.3a) and (10.1.6b) drop out via (10.3.12) below. These constants do not depend upon the relative space $\underline{x}$ but can depend upon quantities outside the relative space such as baryon flavor which are characterized by the internal function $\eta^p{}_r$ in the internal space z_I, z_{II} as in (9.3.5b). They are analogous to the integration constants d_m, d_{m0} and d_{m2} for the meson case in (3.2.8) which however turned out to be independent of meson flavor, as was mentioned below (4.4.1). Thus, there can be a difference in this respect between the three d_m constants for mesons and the five d_b constants for baryons.

In the $|\underline{x}| \to 0$ limit, we have

$$\Phi_b(|\underline{x}| \to 0) = d_b / r \tag{10.1.7a}$$

Asymptotically,

$$\Phi_{bc}\left(|\underline{x}|\to\infty\right)=\alpha_c^3 r^3,\qquad \alpha_c^3=\frac{g_s^6}{192\pi}\int d^3\underline{x}\,\mathrm{Re}\left(\chi_{\{\dot{b}\dot{h}\}}{}^{f}(\underline{x})\psi^{*\{\dot{b}\dot{h}\}}{}_{f}(\underline{x})\right)$$

(10.1.7b)

Both of these potentials are independent of the angles in the relative space. In the first edition of this book, d_{b4}=0 [H18 (10.1.8)] obtained by mimicking [H18 (3.2.20)], which was however revoked in (3.2.21). Therefore, d_{b4}=0 is also revoked here to become

$$d_{b4}\neq 0 \tag{10.1.8}$$

so that the leading confining term at large r is now in general $d_{b4}r^4$ in (10.1.6a), analogous to $d_{m2}r^2$ in (3.2.8a).

10.2. Doublet Wave Equations and Confinement

10.2.1. Doublet Wave Equations in Relative Space

Insert (10.1.1) into (10.0.1) and put $\underline{K}$=0. The quartet wave functions of (9.2.8) drop out and we obtain the rest frame doublet baryon wave equations for $\underline{2}_s$ in (9.2.7) and (9.3.7b),

$$\begin{aligned}&\left(i\delta^{a\dot{b}}E_{0d}/2+\underline{\sigma}^{a\dot{b}}\underline{\partial}\right)\left(E_{0d}^2/4+\Delta\right)\chi_{0\dot{b}}(\underline{x})=i\left(M_b^3+\Phi_{bd}(\underline{x})\right)\psi_0^a(\underline{x})\\&\left(i\delta_{\dot{b}c}E_{0d}/2-\underline{\sigma}_{\dot{b}c}\underline{\partial}\right)\left(E_{0d}^2/4+\Delta\right)\psi_0^c(\underline{x})=i\left(M_b^3+\Phi_{bd}(\underline{x})\right)\chi_{0\dot{b}}(\underline{x})\end{aligned}$$

(10.2.1a)

A similar set of equations is obtained from (10.0.2) for $\underline{2}_a$ in (9.2.6) and (9.3.7c) using the same exponential ansatz as in (10.1.1),

$$\begin{aligned}&\left(i\delta^{a\dot{b}}E_{0d}/2-\underline{\sigma}^{a\dot{b}}\underline{\partial}\right)\left(E_{0d}^2/4+\Delta\right)\psi_{\dot{b}}(\underline{x})=-i\left(M_b^3+\Phi_{bd}(\underline{x})\right)\chi^a(\underline{x})\\&\left(i\delta_{\dot{b}c}E_{0d}/2-\underline{\sigma}_{\dot{b}c}\underline{\partial}\right)\left(E_{0d}^2/4+\Delta\right)\chi^c(\underline{x})=i\left(M_b^3+\Phi_{bd}(\underline{x})\right)\psi_{\dot{b}}(\underline{x})\end{aligned}$$

(10.2.1b)

By limiting the baryon wave functions on the right of (10.1.6b) to doublet wave functions, (10.1.6) becomes

$$\Phi_{bd}(\underline{x})=\Phi_{cd}(\underline{x})+\frac{d_b}{r}+d_{b0}+d_{b1}r+d_{b2}r^2+d_{b4}r^4 \tag{10.2.2a}$$

$$\Phi_{cd}(\underline{x}) = -\frac{g_s^6}{72\pi}\int d^3\underline{x}'|\underline{x}-\underline{x}'|^3 \,\mathrm{Re}\left(\chi_{0a}^*(\underline{x}')\psi_0^a(\underline{x}')\right), \qquad \chi_{0a}^* = (\chi_{0\dot{a}})^* \tag{10.2.2b}$$

Here, the subscript d refers to specialization to doublets. Note that if $\underline{K}\neq 0$, the doublet and quartet wave function components couple and the full (10.1.2) and (10.1.6b) must be used. analogous to the meson case mentioned at the end of Sec. 3.3. Separation of r, ϑ and ϕ variables will then no longer be possible. The doublet wave functions (9.2.7) will remain as "large components" and the quartet wave functions (9.2.8) will enter as "small components" of the order of $|\underline{K}|$ in (10.1.2) and (10.1.6b).

10.2.2. Doublet Radial Wave Equations and Asymptotic Solutions

If $\Phi_{bd}(\underline{x})$ depends only upon r, which according to (10.1.7) is the case at least in the $|\underline{x}|\to 0$ and ∞ limits, (10.2.1) can be separated. One can recognize that (10.2.1a) has a form similar to that of the Dirac equation (C10) with a central potential and $A, V_{PB}\to 0$. The forms of the solutions [B7] to such a Dirac equation can therefore take over here. For each total angular momentum value j, there are two possible orbital angular momentum values, namely, $l= j-½$ and $l= j+½$. In terms of the spinors (C11), the corresponding wave functions are

$$\psi_0^a(\underline{x}) = \pm g_l(r)\sqrt{\frac{(l\pm m+\tfrac{1}{2})}{2l+1}}\,Y_{l\, m\mp\frac{1}{2}}(\vartheta,\phi) + i f_l(r)\sqrt{\frac{(l\mp m+\tfrac{3}{2})}{2l+3}}\,Y_{l+1\, m\mp\frac{1}{2}}(\vartheta,\phi)$$
$$\text{for} \quad j = l+\tfrac{1}{2} \tag{10.2.3a}$$

$$\psi_0^a(\underline{x}) = g_l(r)\sqrt{\frac{(l\mp m+\tfrac{1}{2})}{2l+1}}\,Y_{l\, m\mp\frac{1}{2}}(\vartheta,\phi) \pm i f_l(r)\sqrt{\frac{(l\pm m-\tfrac{1}{2})}{2l-1}}\,Y_{l-1\, m\mp\frac{1}{2}}(\vartheta,\phi)$$
$$\text{for} \quad j = l-\tfrac{1}{2} \tag{10.2.3b}$$

where the upper signs hold for $a=1$ and the lower ones for $a=2$. $\chi_{0\dot{a}}$ is found by changing the signs of $f_l(r)$ in (10.2.3). With (10.2.3a, 3b), (10.2.1a) yields eight radial equations which degenerate into two such

$$\left[\frac{E_{0d}}{2}\left(\frac{E_{0d}^2}{4}+\Delta_l\right)+M_b^3+\Phi_{bd}(|\underline{x}|\to 0,\infty)\right]g_l(r)+\left(\frac{E_{0d}^2}{4}+\Delta_l\right)\left(\frac{\partial}{\partial r}+\frac{1+\kappa}{r}\right)f_l(r)=0 \tag{10.2.4a}$$

$$\left[-\frac{E_{0d}}{2}\left(\frac{E_{0d}^2}{4}+\Delta_{l\pm 1}\right)+M_b^3+\Phi_{bd}(|\underline{x}|\to 0,\infty)\right]f_l(r)+\left(\frac{E_{0d}^2}{4}+\Delta_{l\pm 1}\right)\left(\frac{\partial}{\partial r}+\frac{1-\kappa}{r}\right)g_l(r)=0 \tag{10.2.4b}$$

$$\text{for } j = l\pm\tfrac{1}{2}, \begin{pmatrix}\text{upper}\\ \text{lower}\end{pmatrix} \text{ sign and } \kappa = \begin{pmatrix} l+1 \\ -l \end{pmatrix} \tag{10.2.4c}$$

where Δ_l has been given in (3.4.5b) and

$$\Phi_{bd}\left(\left|\underline{x}\right| \to 0\right) = \frac{d_b}{r} \tag{10.2.5a}$$

$$\Phi_{cd}\left(\left|\underline{x}\right| \to \infty\right) = -\frac{g_s^6}{72\pi} r^3 \int d^3\underline{x}\,\mathrm{Re}\left(\chi_{0a}^*(\underline{x})\psi_0^a(\underline{x})\right) = \alpha_d^3 r^3 \tag{10.2.5b}$$

according to (10.2.2).

Applying the same expansion (10.2.3) to the first of (10.2.1b), one obtains (10.2.4) with the sign of E_{0d} changed. For the second of (10.2.1b), however, (10.2.4) with the sign of g or f changed is found. These two sets of radial equations are incompatible with each other and (10.2.1b) has therefore no solution. This shows that in addition to that $\underline{8}_a$ vanishes in (9.3.5c, 7c), $\underline{2}_a$ in (9.3.7c) also drops out consistently.

Note that (10.2.4) holds for all r for free baryons for which the nonlinear confining potential Φ_{cd} of (10.2.2b) vanishes (see discussion below (10.3.14)). The assignments of signs of f and g in (10.2.3a) differ from the corresponding ones in [H15 (6.3)] which reads

$$(10.2.3a)\ \text{with}\ g_l \to g_l, \quad \chi_{0\dot{a}} = \psi_0^a\ \text{with}\ f_l \to -f_l \tag{10.2.3c}$$

As a consequence, (10.2.4) differs from the corresponding [H15 (6.4)] in the sign of f.

The both $j=\pm½$ cases are convertible into each other. Putting $l\to l-1$ and $g\leftrightarrow if$ in (10.2.3a) converts it into (10.2.3b). Putting $l\to l-1$, $E_{0d}\to -E_{0d}$ and $g\leftrightarrow f$ in the upper case of (10.2.4) converts it into the lower case. If j is required to be the same, $l\to l-1$ is removed. In this way, only one set of radial equations needs be treated.

Of the six asymptotic solutions to (10.2.4, 5b), four are complex and one diverges at large r. For the case of [H18 (10.1.8)], d_{b4}=0, the remaining solution reads

$$g_l(r\to\infty) = f_l(r\to\infty) = \text{constant} \times \exp\left(-\alpha_d r^2/2\right), \quad \alpha_d > 0 \tag{10.2.6}$$

For free, rest frame baryon doublets, the right side of (10.2.2b) vanishes by $\Omega\to\infty$ in (10.3.8, 12, 14) below. Thus, for d_{b4}<0 and d_{b4}=0, d_{b2}<0, (10.2.6) is replaced, respectively, by

$$g_l(r\to\infty) = f_l(r\to\infty) \propto \exp\left(\frac{3}{7} p_v \left|d_{b4}\right|^{1/3} r^{7/3}\right), \quad p_v = -1,\ \exp(\pm i\frac{\pi}{3}) \tag{10.2.7a}$$

$$g_l(r\to\infty) = -f_l(r\to\infty) \propto \exp\left(\frac{3}{5} p_v \left|d_{b2}\right|^{1/3} r^{5/3}\right) \tag{10.2.7b}$$

The d_{b4}=0, d_{b2}<0 case of (10.2.7b) is supported by data to be mentioned beneath Figure 11.1b and Table 11.2 below. The nonlinear potential (10.2.5b) is not too different from the linearized confining potential $d_{b2}r^2$ in (10.1.6a) so that the asymptotic solutions (10.2.6) and

(10.2.7b) with $p_1=-1$ are also not too different. These solutions would correspond to the wave functions associated with the harmonic oscillator confinement model [F3], which has been rather successful in organizing the wealth of low energy baryon data.

Near the origin, the six independent solutions of (10.2.4) are

$$j=l+\tfrac{1}{2}: \qquad f_l(r\to 0)=0, \quad g_l(r\to 0)=c_{g+}(\lambda_+)r^{\lambda_+}, \quad \lambda_+=l+2,\ l,\ -l-1$$
$$g_l(r\to 0)=0, \quad f_l(r\to 0)=c_{f+}(\lambda_+)r^{\lambda_+}, \quad \lambda_+=l+1,\ -l,\ -l-2 \tag{10.2.8a}$$

$$j=l-\tfrac{1}{2}: \qquad f_l(r\to 0)=0, \quad g_l(r\to 0)=c_{g-}(\lambda_-)r^{\lambda_-}, \quad \lambda_-=l,\ -l+1,\ -l-1$$
$$g_l(r\to 0)=0, \quad f_l(r\to 0)=c_{f-}(\lambda_-)r^{\lambda_-}, \quad \lambda_-=l+1,\ l-1,\ -l \tag{10.2.8b}$$

where the c's are constant amplitudes.

Inserting (10.2.3) into (10.2.2b) leads to that Φ_{cd} depends upon the angles for $l>0$ and (10.2.1a) with (10.2.3) is no longer separable, except at the $r\to 0$ and $r\to\infty$ limits governed by (10.2.4). The separable solutions (10.2.3) with (10.2.8) and (10.2.6) at $r\to 0$ and $r\to\infty$ are to be connected by the unknown nonseparable solutions to (10.2.1a, 2). This situation is analogous to the $l>0$ case for mesons in §3.4.2 discussed in the beginning of §5.6.1.

In the absence of orbital excitations, $l=0$ and only $j=l+\tfrac{1}{2}$ of (10.2.3a) applies. Φ_{cd} of (10.2.2b) turns out to be independent of the angles for all r, just like the case for the $l=0$ mesons treated in §3.4.1. Equations (10.2.1a) can now be separated. Inserting (10.2.3a) with $l=0$ into (10.2.2b) and making use of the procedure intervening (3.2.14) and (3.2.17), we obtain analogously

$$\Phi_{cd}(r)=-\frac{g_s^6}{360\pi}\left[\begin{array}{l}\int_0^r dr'r'^2\left(f_0^2(r')-g_0^2(r')\right)\left(5r^4+10r^2r'^2+r'^4\right)/r+\\ +\int_r^\infty dr'r'\left(f_0^2(r')-g_0^2(r')\right)\left(5r'^4+10r^2r'^2+r^4\right)\end{array}\right] \tag{10.2.9}$$

In the $r=0$ and ∞ limits, (10.2.9) yields

$$\Phi_{cd}(r\to 0)=-\frac{g_s^6}{72\pi}\int_0^\infty dr r^5\left(f_0^2(r)-g_0^2(r)\right) \tag{10.2.10}$$

$$\Phi_{cd}(r\to\infty)=-\frac{g_s^6}{72\pi}r^3\int_0^\infty dr'r'^2\left(f_0^2(r')-g_0^2(r')\right)=\alpha_{d0}^3 r^3 \tag{10.2.11}$$

Equation (10.2.4) now goes over to

$$\left[\frac{E_{0d}^3}{8}+M_b^3+\Phi_{bd}(r)+\frac{E_{0d}}{2}\Delta_0\right]g_0(r)+\left(\frac{E_{0d}^2}{4}+\Delta_0\right)\left(\frac{\partial}{\partial r}+\frac{2}{r}\right)f_0(r)=0 \qquad (10.2.12a)$$

$$\left[\frac{E_{0d}^3}{8}-M_b^3-\Phi_{bd}(r)+\frac{E_{0d}}{2}\Delta_1\right]f_0(r)-\left(\frac{E_{0d}^2}{4}+\Delta_1\right)\frac{\partial}{\partial r}g_0(r)=0 \qquad (10.2.12b)$$

which holds for all r. Here, $\Phi_{bd}(r)$ is given by (10.2.2a) with $\underline{x}\rightarrow r$ together with (10.2.9). Equation (10.2.12) determines the properties of $J^P=½^+$ baryons, including their radially excited states.

10.2.3. Ground State Doublet Wave Functions at Origin

The six negative λ values in (10.2.8) will in general lead to wave functions diverging at the origin and hence are discarded. In the absence of orbital excitations, $l=0$, only (10.2.8a) applies and $\lambda_+=0$, 1 and 2. It is natural to associate the first one, i.e., $\lambda_+=l$, $l=0$, with the ground state $J^P=½^+$ baryons, such as the nucleons. For this state, (10.2.3a, 8a) yields

$$m=\frac{1}{2} \qquad \psi_0^1(r\rightarrow 0)=\frac{1}{\sqrt{4\pi}}c_{g+}(0), \qquad \psi_0^2(r\rightarrow 0)=0$$
$$\chi_{0\dot{a}}(r\rightarrow 0)=\psi_0^a(r\rightarrow 0) \qquad (10.2.13a)$$

$$m=-\frac{1}{2} \qquad \psi_0^1(r\rightarrow 0)=0, \qquad \psi_0^2(r\rightarrow 0)=-\frac{1}{\sqrt{4\pi}}c_{g+}(0)$$
$$\chi_{0\dot{a}}(r\rightarrow 0)=\psi_0^a(r\rightarrow 0) \qquad (10.2.13b)$$

For the other two states, (10.2.3a, 8a) with $m=½$ leads to

$$\lambda_+=l+1,\ l=0; \qquad \psi_0^1(r\rightarrow 0)=i\frac{1}{\sqrt{4\pi}}c_{f+}(1)r\cos\vartheta$$
$$\psi_0^2(r\rightarrow 0)=i\frac{1}{\sqrt{4\pi}}c_{f+}(1)r\sin\vartheta\exp(i\phi), \quad \chi_{0\dot{a}}(r\rightarrow 0)=\psi_0^a(r\rightarrow 0) \qquad (10.2.14)$$

$$\lambda_+=l+2,\ l=0; \qquad \psi_0^1(r\rightarrow 0)=-\frac{1}{\sqrt{4\pi}}c_{g+}(2)r^2$$
$$\psi_0^2(r\rightarrow 0)=0, \qquad \chi_{0\dot{a}}(r\rightarrow 0)=-\psi_0^a(r\rightarrow 0) \qquad (10.2.15)$$

10.2.4. Relations to Dirac's Equation

The wave equations in relative space (10.2.1a) for a doublet baryon at rest can be related to Dirac's equation in two-spinor form (B23) with V_{SB}=0. Multiplying (10.2.1a) by the exponential factor on the right of (10.1.1) with $\underline{K}$=0 leads to wave functions of the form

$$\begin{pmatrix} \psi_0^1(\underline{x}) \\ \psi_0^2(\underline{x}) \end{pmatrix} \exp\left(-iE_0 X^0 + i\omega_0 x^0\right) = \begin{pmatrix} \psi_0^1\left(X^0, x\right) \\ \psi_0^2\left(X^0, x\right) \end{pmatrix}$$
$$\begin{pmatrix} \chi_{0\dot{1}}(\underline{x}) \\ \chi_{0\dot{2}}(\underline{x}) \end{pmatrix} \exp\left(-iE_0 X^0 + i\omega_0 x^0\right) = \begin{pmatrix} \chi_{0\dot{1}}\left(X^0, x\right) \\ \chi_{0\dot{2}}\left(X^0, x\right) \end{pmatrix} \qquad (10.2.16)$$

which are basically (10.1.1) with $\underline{K}$=0. Let now the quark at x_{II} merge into the diquark at x_I so that the relative coordinates $x = x_{II} - x_I = 0$ in (3.1.3a). In this way, the originally doublet baryon having finite extension becomes a point particle, such as a electron. Replace the wave functions in (10.2.1a) by $\chi_{0\dot{b}}\left(X^0, x \to 0\right)$ and $\psi_0^a(X^0, x\to 0)$, it is seen that the operators $\underline{\partial}$ and $\underline{\Delta}$ operating in the relative space $\underline{x}$ drop out and (10.2.2a) leads in the absence of $\underline{x}$ to

$$\Phi_b(\underline{x}) = d_{b0} = \text{constant} \qquad (10.2.17)$$

Equation (10.2.1a), dropping the subscript d, now becomes

$$i\delta^{a\dot{b}} E_0 \chi_{0\dot{b}}\left(X^0, x \to 0\right) = i\left(8\left(M_b^3 + d_{b0}\right)/E_0^2\right)\psi_0^a\left(X^0, x \to 0\right)$$
$$i\delta_{\dot{b}c} E_0 \psi_0^c\left(X^0, x \to 0\right) = i\left(8\left(M_b^3 + d_{b0}\right)/E_0^2\right)\chi_{0\dot{b}}\left(X^0, x \to 0\right) \qquad (10.2.18)$$

Since the baryon is at rest, its energy can be read from (10.2.1a) with (10.2.17),

$$E_0 = 2\left(M_b^3 + d_{b0}\right)^{1/3} = m_{eff} \qquad (10.2.19)$$

where M_b has been given in (9.3.19). Making use of (C3a) and noting (10.2.16) and (10.2.19), (10.2.18) becomes

$$\partial_X^{a\dot{b}} \chi_{0\dot{b}}\left(X^0, 0\right) = i m_{eff} \psi_0^a\left(X^0, 0\right)$$
$$\partial_{X\dot{b}c} \psi_0^c\left(X^0, 0\right) = i m_{eff} \chi_{0\dot{b}}\left(X^0, 0\right) \qquad (10.2.20)$$

The wave functions are obtainable from (10.1.1) with $\underline{x}$=0 and $\underline{K}$=0 together with (10.2.13),

$$\begin{pmatrix} \psi_0^1\left(X^0, 0\right) \\ \psi_0^2\left(X^0, 0\right) \end{pmatrix} = \exp\left(-iE_0 X^0\right) \frac{1}{\sqrt{4\pi}} c_{g+}(0) \begin{pmatrix} 1, & 0 \\ 0, & -1 \end{pmatrix}, \quad \chi_{0\dot{a}}\left(X^0, 0\right) = \psi_0^a\left(X^0, 0\right)$$
$$(10.2.21)$$

where the commas separate the m=½ from the m=−½ solutions. With (C11), (10.2.21) can be expressed in the conventional four component Dirac wave functions for a positive energy point baryon with $\underline{K}$=0,

$$(\psi_1,\psi_2,\psi_3,\psi_4)=\exp(-iE_0X^0)\frac{1}{\sqrt{4\pi}}c_{g+}(0)\begin{pmatrix}1, & 0, & 0, & 0\\ 0, & -1, & 0, & 0\end{pmatrix} \quad \text{for } m=\pm\tfrac{1}{2} \tag{10.2.22}$$

which apart from a phase factor agrees with (A13) and (A14) with $N_D=c_{g+}(0)/\sqrt{4}\pi$. Therefore, m=½ and −½ in (10.2.3a) correspond to the spin up and down, respectively.

As was mentioned at the end of §10.2.1, a doublet baryon in motion ($\underline{K}\neq0$) can no longer be described by the doublet wave functions (9.2.7) alone but require also the quartet wave functions (9.2.8). For small K, however, the quartet wave functions are small and of order K, just like that the vector meson wave functions are small and of order K in §5.7.2-4. If one ignores terms of order K^2, (10.0.1) with (10.1.1) reduces to (10.2.1a) with a K term in the first parentheses and a $\underline{K}\partial$term in the second. In the $\underline{x}\to0$ limit, this modified (10.2.1a) reduces to a modified form of of (10.2.18) with (10.2.19),

$$\begin{aligned}&\left(i\delta^{a\dot{b}}E_0-i\underline{K\sigma}^{a\dot{b}}\right)\chi_{0\dot{b}}(X,0)=im_{eff}\psi_0^a(X,0)\\ &\left(i\delta_{\dot{b}c}E_0+i\underline{K\sigma}_{\dot{b}c}\right)\psi_0^c(X,0)=im_{eff}\chi_{0\dot{b}}(X,0)\end{aligned} \tag{10.2.23}$$

where (3.1.4) has been used. Equation (10.2.23) can be written as

$$\begin{aligned}&\partial_X^{a\dot{b}}\chi_{0\dot{b}}(X,0)=im_{eff}\psi_0^a(X,0)\\ &\partial_{X\dot{b}c}\psi_0^c(X,0)=im_{eff}\chi_{0\dot{b}}(X,0)\end{aligned} \tag{10.2.24}$$

which has the same form as the Dirac equation for a free particle (B23) with V_{SB}=0. Equation (10.2.24) replaces (10.2.20) and holds for small K. With this equation, the classical energy momentum relation (5.7.32) is established to order K for the doublet baryons.

By reducing a baryon with extension to a point particle, much of the underlying physics determining the baryon properties are irretrievably lost. Nevertheless, the point particle description (10.2.24) of a slow baryon can be a good approximation if the baryon behaves like a point particle when interacting with another particle. For instance, in low energy pion-nucleon scattering, the short-range strong potential of the nucleon may be considered to originate from a point source. Similarly, in low energy Mott scattering, the proton charge may be approximated by a point charge. In these cases, the quark structure of the nucleon does not enter the problem.

The point particle approximation does however not apply to weak interactions in which the different quarks, broadly speaking, interact differently with the gauge boson and the $\underline{x}\to0$ limit leading to (10.2.24) cannot be taken. At large K, the Dirac description (10.2.24) breaks down; the full (9.3.16) needs be resorted to.

10.3. Normalization of Doublet Wave Functions

The amplitudes of the doublet baryon wave functions in (10.2.3), hence also the amplitude constants in (10.2.6-8), are not free but, as it turns out, are approximately fixed by a normalization procedure analogous to that of Sec. 4.2 for mesons. Analogous to (10.1.3b), we define

$$\psi_0^{*\dot{a}} = \left(\psi_0^a\right)^*, \qquad \chi_{0a}^* = \left(\chi_{0\dot{a}}\right)^* \tag{10.3.1}$$

Take the complex conjugate of (9.3.16b) and multiply it by $\psi_d^{\{bh\}}(I,II)$. Add the resulting equation to (9.3.16a) multiplied by $\chi_{\{ag\}}^{*\dot{e}}(I,II)$ and rearrange the indices to obtain

$$\chi_{\{ag\}\dot{e}}^* \partial_I^{a\dot{b}} \partial_{II}^{f\dot{e}} \partial_I^{g\dot{h}} \chi_{\{\dot{b}\dot{h}\}f} + \psi^{\{bh\}\dot{d}} \partial_{I\dot{c}b} \partial_{II\dot{d}e} \partial_{I\dot{k}h} \psi^{*\{\dot{c}\dot{k}\}e} = 0 \tag{10.3.2a}$$

Take the complex conjugate of (9.3.16a) and multiply it by $\chi_{\{\dot{a}\dot{g}\}}^{e}(I,II)$. Add the resulting equation to (9.3.16b) multiplied by $\psi_d^{*\{\dot{b}\dot{h}\}}(I,II)$ and rearrange the indices to obtain

$$\chi_{\{\dot{a}\dot{g}\}e} \partial_I^{b\dot{a}} \partial_{II}^{e\dot{f}} \partial_I^{h\dot{g}} \chi_{\{bh\}\dot{f}}^* + \psi^{*\{\dot{b}\dot{h}\}d} \partial_{I\dot{b}c} \partial_{II\dot{e}d} \partial_{I\dot{h}k} \psi^{\{ck\}\dot{e}} = 0 \tag{10.3.2b}$$

which is the complex conjugate of (10.3.2a).

If (9.3.16) is replaced by a Dirac equation in analogous spinor form, the corresponding sum of (10.3.2a) and (10.3.2.b) becomes the continuity equation for the probability current density associated with the Dirac particle and leads to a conserved total probability. This total probability is conventionally set to 1 and this fixes the amplitude of the Dirac wave function. However, the probability interpretation is not unique; the conserved total probability can for instance be any constant without affecting the predictive power of the Dirac equation. The situation is entirely analogous to that for a Schrödinger and Klein- Gordon particle considered in Sec. 4.1. This arbitrariness in wave function amplitude is largely removed for doublet baryons below.

Analogous to (4.2.2), (10.3.2a) is put in the form

$$C_b = \partial_I^{a\dot{b}} \chi_{\{ag\}\dot{e}}^* \partial_{II}^{f\dot{e}} \partial_I^{g\dot{h}} \chi_{\{\dot{b}\dot{h}\}f} + \partial_{I\dot{c}b} \psi^{\{bh\}\dot{d}} \partial_{II\dot{d}e} \partial_{I\dot{k}h} \psi^{*\{\dot{c}\dot{k}\}e} = \tag{10.3.3a}$$

$$= D_b = \left(\partial_I^{a\dot{b}} \chi_{\{ag\}\dot{e}}^*\right)\left(\partial_{II}^{f\dot{e}} \partial_I^{g\dot{h}} \chi_{\{\dot{b}\dot{h}\}f}\right) + \left(\partial_{I\dot{c}b} \psi^{\{bh\}\dot{d}}\right)\left(\partial_{II\dot{d}e} \partial_{I\dot{k}h} \psi^{*\{\dot{c}\dot{k}\}e}\right) \tag{10.3.3b}$$

which is Lorentz invariant by virtue of its spinor form. Therefore,

$$\frac{1}{2}\int d^4x_I d^4x_{II}\left(C_b + C_b^*\right) = \frac{1}{2}\int d^4x_I d^4x_{II}\left(D_b + D_b^*\right)$$
$$= \text{real Lorentz invariant with dimension of inverse of four volume} \tag{10.3.4}$$

Unlike the corresponding (4.2.3) for mesons, (10.3.4) is not dimensionless. This is due to the merging of two quark coordinates $x_{III} \to x_I$ in (9.2.12) so that the four volume $\int d^4x_{III}$, which would have been applied to (10.3.4), drops out. This choice is an extension of the point particle consideration that led to (4.1.2) and the two quark treatment that led to (4.2.8); both amplitudes are independent of the particle energy.

Analogous to Sec. 4.2 for mesons, we specialize (10.3.4) to the doublets (9.2.7) at rest ($\underline{K}$=0). In this case, the quartet wave functions (9.2.8) can be omitted. Formally, this can be accomplished by letting $g \to e$ and $h \to d$ in (10.3.3). Noting (9.2.7), (10.3.3) turns into

$$\frac{1}{2}C_b \to C_{bd} = \partial_I^{a\dot{b}}\chi^*_{0a}\partial_{II}^{f\dot{e}}\partial_I^{e\dot{h}}\chi_{\{\dot{b}\dot{h}\}f} + \partial_{I\dot{c}b}\psi_0^b\partial_{II\dot{d}e}\partial_{I\dot{k}d}\psi^{*\{\dot{c}\dot{k}\}e}$$
$$= D_{bd} = \left(\partial_I^{a\dot{b}}\chi^*_{0a}\right)\left[\partial_{II}^{f\dot{e}}\partial_I^{e\dot{h}}\chi_{\{\dot{b}\dot{h}\}f}\right] + \left(\partial_{I\dot{c}b}\psi_0^b\right)\left[\partial_{II\dot{d}e}\partial_{I\dot{k}d}\psi^{*\{\dot{c}\dot{k}\}e}\right] \leftarrow \frac{1}{2}D_b \tag{10.3.5}$$

This expression can also be obtained by multiplying (10.0.1a) by χ^*_{0a} and adding the resulting equation to the complex conjugate of (10.0.1b) multiplied by ψ^b_0.

Inserting (9.2.7) with the dependence of (10.1.1) into the brackets of (10.3.5) yields

$$\partial_{II}^{f\dot{e}}\partial_I^{e\dot{h}}\chi_{\{\dot{b}\dot{h}\}f}(I,II) = -2\left(E_{0d}^2/4+\Delta\right)\chi_{0\dot{b}}(X,x) \tag{10.3.6a}$$

$$\partial_{I\dot{k}d}\partial_{II\dot{d}e}\psi^{*\{\dot{c}\dot{k}\}e}(I,II) = -2\left(E_{0d}^2/4+\Delta\right)\psi_0^{*\dot{c}}(X,x) \tag{10.3.6b}$$

Inserting (10.3.6) into (10.3.5) and applying (3.1.4, 10a) leads to

$$C_{bd} = \left(\frac{1}{2}-\frac{\omega_0}{E_{0d}}\right)\frac{\partial}{\partial X^0}\left[\chi^*_{0b}(\underline{x})\left(\frac{E_{0d}^2}{4}+\Delta\right)\chi_{0\dot{b}}(\underline{x}) + \psi_0^b(\underline{x})\left(\frac{E_{0d}^2}{4}+\Delta\right)\psi_0^{*\dot{b}}(\underline{x})\right]$$
$$+\underline{\sigma}_{\dot{b}a}\underline{\partial}\left[\psi_0^a(\underline{x})\left(\frac{E_{0d}^2}{4}+\Delta\right)\psi_0^{*\dot{b}}(\underline{x})\right] - \underline{\sigma}^{a\dot{b}}\underline{\partial}\left[\chi^*_{0a}(\underline{x})\left(\frac{E_{0d}^2}{4}+\Delta\right)\chi_{0\dot{b}}(\underline{x})\right]$$
$$= D_{bd} = -\left[\left(\frac{i}{2}E_{0d}\delta^{a\dot{b}} + \underline{\sigma}^{a\dot{b}}\underline{\partial}\right)\chi^*_{0a}(\underline{x})\right]\left[\left(\frac{E_{0d}^2}{4}+\Delta\right)\chi_{0\dot{b}}(\underline{x})\right]$$
$$-\left[\left(\frac{i}{2}E_{0d}\delta_{\dot{b}a} - \underline{\sigma}_{\dot{b}a}\underline{\partial}\right)\psi_0^a(\underline{x})\right]\left[\left(\frac{E_{0d}^2}{4}+\Delta\right)\psi_0^{*\dot{b}}(\underline{x})\right] \tag{10.3.7}$$

We further limit ourselves to doublet baryons without orbital excitation, l=0. Equation (10.2.3a) ff with l=0 yields

$$m=\frac{1}{2},\quad \psi_0^1(\underline{x})=\frac{1}{\sqrt{4\pi}}\left(g_0(r)+if_0(r)\cos\vartheta\right),\qquad \chi_{0\dot{1}}(\underline{x})=\left(\psi_0^1(\underline{x})\right)^*$$
$$\psi_0^2(\underline{x})=\frac{1}{\sqrt{4\pi}}if_0(r)\sin\vartheta\exp(i\phi),\qquad \chi_{0\dot{2}}(\underline{x})=-\psi_0^2(\underline{x})$$
(10.3.8a)

$$m=-\frac{1}{2},\quad \psi_0^1(\underline{x})=\frac{1}{\sqrt{4\pi}}if_0(r)\sin\vartheta\exp(-i\phi),\qquad \chi_{0\dot{1}}(\underline{x})=-\psi_0^1(\underline{x})$$
$$\psi_0^2(\underline{x})=\frac{1}{\sqrt{4\pi}}\left(-g_0(r)+if_0(r)\cos\vartheta\right),\quad \chi_{0\dot{2}}(\underline{x})=\left(\psi_0^2(\underline{x})\right)^*$$
(10.3.8b)

Similarly, (10.2.3c) ff with l=0 yields

$$m=\frac{1}{2},\quad \psi_0^1(\underline{x})=\frac{1}{\sqrt{4\pi}}\left(-g_0(r)+if_0(r)\cos\vartheta\right),\quad \chi_{0\dot{1}}(\underline{x})=-\left(\psi_0^1(\underline{x})\right)^*$$
$$\psi_0^2(\underline{x})=\frac{1}{\sqrt{4\pi}}if_0(r)\sin\vartheta\exp(i\phi),\qquad \chi_{0\dot{2}}(\underline{x})=\psi_0^2(\underline{x})$$
(10.3.8c)

$$m=-\frac{1}{2},\quad \psi_0^1(\underline{x})=\frac{1}{\sqrt{4\pi}}if_0(r)\sin\vartheta\exp(-i\phi),\quad \chi_{0\dot{1}}(\underline{x})=\psi_0^1(\underline{x})$$
$$\psi_0^2(\underline{x})=\frac{1}{\sqrt{4\pi}}\left(g_0(r)+if_0(r)\cos\vartheta\right),\quad \chi_{0\dot{2}}(\underline{x})=-\left(\psi_0^2(\underline{x})\right)^*$$
(10.3.8d)

The analog of (4.2.4, 5) is obtained by inserting (10.3.8) into (10.3.7) and integrating over $\underline{x}$;

$$\int d^3\underline{x}\left(C_{bd}+C_{bd}^*\right)=\frac{\partial}{\partial X^0}N_{dr}=\int d^3\underline{x}\left(D_{bd}+D_{bd}^*\right)=0 \qquad (10.3.9a)$$

$$N_{dr}=2\int drr^2\left[\frac{E_{0d}^2}{4}\left(g_0^2(r)+f_0^2(r)\right)-\left(\partial g_0(r)\right)^2-\left(\partial f_0(r)\right)^2-\frac{2}{r^2}f_0^2(r)\right] \qquad (10.3.9b)$$

In arriving at these relations f_0 and g_0 must vanish at large r, as in (10.2.6) or the first line of (10.2.7). With (10.3.9a, 5) and (3.1.3c), (10.3.4) becomes

$$\int dX^0\frac{\partial}{\partial X^0}\int dx^0\Omega N_{dr}=0,\qquad \Omega=\int d^3\underline{X}$$
(10.3.10)

which is of dimension $1/l_x^4$ for (10.3.4); l_x is a unit length associated with the space-time components of a position four vector.

For (10.3.4), ΩN_{dr} here is regarded as a conserved quantity of dimension $1/l_x^5$. $1/l_x$ is of dimension energy and the only observable energy available for the rest frame doublet baryon under consideration is its mass E_{0d}. ΩN_{dr} is the baryon equivalent to N_{mJ} of (4.2.4). Thus, analogous to (4.2.6) for mesons, the identification

$$\Omega|N_{dr}| = E_{0d}^5 \frac{\Omega}{\Omega_{cb}} \tag{10.3.11}$$

is made. Ω_{cb} is similarly interpreted as the finite volume in laboratory space $\underline{X}$ occupied by the doublet baryon wave functions which acquire finite amplitudes due to interaction with other hadrons by a similar mechanism mentioned below (4.2.6). For a free doublet baryon, i.e., a baryon far away from other particles, the analog of (4.2.7) is

$$\Omega_{cb} \to \Omega \to \infty \tag{10.3.12}$$

Combining (10.3.11) and (10.3.9b) leads to the normalization condition corresponding to (4.2.8),

$$\frac{|N_{dr}|2}{E_{0d}^2} = \int drr^2 \left| g_0^2(r) + f_0^2(r) - \frac{4}{E_{0d}^2}\left[(\partial g_0(r))^2 + (\partial f_0(r))^2 + \frac{2}{r^2} f_0^2(r)\right]\right| = \frac{2E_{0d}^3}{\Omega_{cb}} \tag{10.3.13}$$

which leads to

$$\begin{gathered}(f_0(r),\ g_0(r)) = \frac{a_g}{\sqrt{\Omega_{cb}}}(f_{00}(r),\ g_{00}(r)), \qquad a_g^2 = \frac{E_{0d}^5}{|N_{dr0}|} \\ N_{dr0} = N_{dr} \text{ in } (10.3.9\text{b}) \text{ with } f_0(r), g_0(r) \text{ replaced by } f_{00}(r), g_{00}(r)\end{gathered} \tag{10.3.14}$$

Here, $f_{00}(r)$ and $g_{00}(r)$ are dimensionless. This normalization has a more complicated form than the corresponding one (4.2.8) for mesons. This has no consequence for the linearized forms of (10.2.1a, 12) with the nonlinear potential $\Phi_{cd}(r)$ of (10.2.2b) put to 0 which is achieved by (10.3.12).

If Ω_{cb} in (10.3.12) is finite, then $f_0(r)$ and $g_0(r)$ and the nonlinear potential $\Phi_{cd}(\underline{x})$ in (10.2.2b) do not vanish. In this case, the value of a_g in (10.3.4) is of interest. This potential is analogous to the corresponding nonlinear potential $\Phi_c(\underline{x})$ (3.2.8b) which contributes to the mass of excited mesons in Sec. 5.5 above. Thus, the more complicated normalization (10.3.14) may be of importance for excited baryon spectra.

For freely moving baryons, the reasoning of §4.3.1 analogously holds and the baryon wave equation (9.3.16) must be linear so that the superposition principle holds and baryon wave packets can be constructed. This requires that Φ_b in (9.3.16) or (10.1.6) is independent of the baryon wave functions or that their amplitudes in (10.1.6b), hence also (10.1.7b), vanish. By

(10.3.14), (10.3.12) is recovered and the baryon wave functions now spread over the entire laboratory space $\underline{X}$. However, these baryon wave functions are still confined in relative space $\underline{x}$ by the linearized confining potential in (10.2.2a).

10.4. Linear Baryon Radial Equations and First Order System

For ground state doublet baryons, such as the nucleons, Λ, etc. the wave equations must be linear to accommodate the superposition principle and building of wave packets, just like the case for pseudoscalar and vector mesons of Sec. 4.3. This implies that the nonlinear confining potential (10.2.2b) vanishes and (10.3.12) applies. Like the confined mesons in Sec. 4.3, these baryon wave functions are analogously confined by the $d_{b2}r^2$ term in (10.2.2a) according to the results mentioned below (10.2.7b). Therefore, separation of variables according to (10.2.3) is possible and the linearized doublet radial equations (10.2.4) with Φ_{bd} given by (10.2.2a) and Φ_{cd}=0 hold. The radially excited states are described by the same equations and are therefore similarly confined, analogous to the radially excited mesons of Sec. 5.5. Thus, (10.2.4) and (10.2.2a) with Φ_{cd}=0 hold for both the ground state and radially excited doublet baryons.

The linearized (10.2.4) and (10.2.2a) with Φ_{cd}=0 are a special case of the analogously linearized (9.3.16) and (9.2.13b), to which we have to turn if the doublet baryon is in motion, discussed at the end of §10.5.1 below. From the linearized (9.3.16), the quartet radial equations (10.5.10) below are derived and are hence also linear. This circumstance is analogous to that for pseudoscalar and vector mesons discussed in the beginning of Sec. 4.4.

Even these linearized radial equations, (10.2.4) and (10.2.2a) with Φ_{cd}=0 are not easily handled. This can be seen that the integer power series (10.2.8) near r=0 are not easily connected to the fractional power series solutions of the form of the first line of (10.2.7) for large r. To facilitate practical solutions, these linearized equations are transformed into a first order system of equations below.

According to the last section, Φ_{bc} is dropped in (10.1.6a), which together with (10.1.8) is inserted into (10.2.4) to yield

$$\left(\left(\frac{\partial}{\partial r}+\frac{L+2}{r}\right)\left(\frac{\partial}{\partial r}-\frac{L}{r}\right)+\frac{E_{bL}^2}{4}\right)\left(\frac{\partial}{\partial r}+\frac{L+2}{r}\right)f_{bL}(r)$$
$$+\left(\frac{E_{bL}}{2}\left(\frac{\partial}{\partial r}+\frac{L+2}{r}\right)\left(\frac{\partial}{\partial r}-\frac{L}{r}\right)+\frac{E_{bL}^3}{8}+M_b^3+d_{b0}+\frac{d_b}{r}+d_{b1}r+d_{b2}r^2+d_{b4}r^4\right)g_{bL}(r)=0$$
$$\left(-\frac{E_{bL}}{2}\left(\frac{\partial}{\partial r}+\frac{L+3}{r}\right)\left(\frac{\partial}{\partial r}-\frac{L+1}{r}\right)-\frac{E_{bL}^3}{8}+M_b^3+d_{b0}+\frac{d_b}{r}+d_{b1}r+d_{b2}r^2+d_{b4}r^4\right)f_{bL}(r)$$
$$+\left(\left(\frac{\partial}{\partial r}+\frac{L+3}{r}\right)\left(\frac{\partial}{\partial r}-\frac{L+1}{r}\right)+\frac{E_{bL}^2}{4}\right)\left(\frac{\partial}{\partial r}-\frac{L}{r}\right)g_{bL}(r)=0 \qquad (10.4.1)$$

where $L=l$ in (10.2.4) for $j=l+1/2$. $f_{bL}(r)$ and $g_{bL}(r)$ are eigenfunctions regular at r=0 and vanishing at $r=\infty$ together with the corresponding discrete, real and positive eigenvalues E_{bL}, if they exist, are sought. For $L=l=0$, $f_{b0}(r)$ and $g_{b0}(r)$ are the same as $f_0(r)$ and $g_0(r)$ in (10.2.12).

Equation (10.4.1) is now converted to a standard form of a first order equation system for which formal solutions near the singularities are known [C4 Ch 4, 5]. Introducing

$$w_1(r)=-f_{bL}(r),\quad w_2(r)=\left(\frac{\partial}{\partial r}+\frac{L+2}{r}\right)w_1(r),\quad w_3(r)=\left(\frac{\partial}{\partial r}-\frac{L}{r}\right)w_2(r)$$

$$w_4(r)=g_{bL}(r),\quad w_5(r)=\left(\frac{\partial}{\partial r}-\frac{L}{r}\right)w_4(r),\qquad w_6(r)=\left(\frac{\partial}{\partial r}-\frac{L+1}{r}\right)w_5(r) \tag{10.4.2}$$

we obtain

$$w_k{}'(r)=\left(\frac{A_{kn}}{r}+B_{kn}+C_{kn}\left(r,r^2.r^4\right)\right)w_n(r) \tag{10.4.3a}$$

$$A_{kn}=\begin{pmatrix} -L-2 & & & & & \\ & L & & & & \\ & & -L-2 & d_b & \frac{E_{bL}(2L+3)}{2} & \\ & & & L & & \\ & & & & L+1 & \\ d_b & & & & & -L-3 \end{pmatrix} \tag{10.4.3b}$$

$$B_{kn}=\begin{pmatrix} & 1 & & & & \\ & & 1 & & & \\ & -\frac{E_{bL}^2}{4} & & \frac{E_{bL}^3}{8}+M_b^3+d_{b0} & & \frac{E_{bL}}{2} \\ & & & & 1 & \\ & & & & & 1 \\ -\frac{E_{bL}^3}{8}+M_b^3+d_{b0} & & -\frac{E_{bL}}{2} & & -\frac{E_{bL}^2}{4} & \end{pmatrix} \tag{10.4.3c}$$

$$C_{kn}=\begin{pmatrix} 0 & 0 & 0 & 0 & 0 & 0 \\ 0 & & & & & \\ 0 & & & d_{b1}r+d_{b2}r^2+d_{b4}r^4 & & \\ 0 & & & & & \\ 0 & & & & & \\ d_{b1}r+d_{b2}r^2+d_{b4}r^4 & & & & & \end{pmatrix} \tag{10.4.3d}$$

The conversion (10.4.2) is similarly chosen such that the singularities at r=0 and ∞ do not get stronger in (10.4.3). The indicial equation of (10.4.3) is

$$\det\left|\lambda\delta_{kn} - A_{kn}\right| = (\lambda + L + 3)(\lambda + L + 2)^2(\lambda - L)^2(\lambda - L - 1) = 0 \tag{10.4.4}$$

λ is related to λ_+ in (10.2.8a) and to λ_q in (10.5.18) below, L=0 refers to l=0 in (10.2.8a) and L=1 to l=1 in (10.2.8a) but applied to (10.5.18) below. By means of (10.4.3b) and (10.4.2), the roots of (10.4.4) reproduce those given by (10.2.8a) and for L=1, also those of (10.5.18) below.

More conventionally [C4 §4.5], (10.4.2, 3) are replaced by

$$w_1(r) = -f_{bL}(r), \qquad w_4(r) = g_{bL}(r)$$

$$\frac{\partial w_1}{\partial r} = \frac{w_2}{r}, \qquad \frac{\partial w_2}{\partial r} = \frac{w_3}{r}, \qquad \frac{\partial w_4}{\partial r} = \frac{w_5}{r}, \qquad \frac{\partial w_5}{\partial r} = \frac{w_6}{r}$$

$$\frac{\partial w_3}{\partial r} = w_1\left[L(L+1)(L+2)\frac{1}{r} - \frac{E_{bL}^2}{4}(L+2)r\right] + w_2\left[\left(L^2 + 2L + 2\right)\frac{1}{r} - \frac{E_{bL}^2}{4}r\right] - w_3\frac{L+1}{r}$$

$$+ w_4\left[d_b r + \left(\frac{E_{bL}^3}{8} + M_b^3 + d_{b0}\right)r^2 + d_{b1}r^3 + d_{b2}r^4 + d_{b4}r^6 - \frac{E_{bL}}{2}L(L+1)\right]$$

$$+ (w_5 + w_6)\frac{E_{bL}}{2}$$

$$\frac{\partial w_6}{\partial r} = w_1\left[d_b r + \left(-\frac{E_{bL}^3}{8} + M_b^3 + d_{b0}\right)r^2 + d_{b1}r^3 + d_{b2}r^4 + d_{b4}r^6 + \frac{E_{bL}}{2}(L+1)(L+2)\right]$$

$$+ w_6\frac{L+1}{r} \tag{10.4.5}$$

which yields an indicial equation equivalent to (10.2.8).

A more direct approach is to start from (10.4.1) and write

$$f_{bL}(r) = -\sum_{\nu=0}^{\infty} a_\nu r^{\lambda+\nu}, \qquad g_{bL}(r) = \sum_{\nu=0}^{\infty} b_\nu r^{\lambda+\nu} \tag{10.4.6}$$

Insertion into (!0.4.1) leads to the recursion formula

$$a_\nu = -\frac{1}{(\lambda+\nu+L+2)(\lambda+\nu-L-1)}\frac{E_{bL}^2}{4}a_{\nu-2} + \frac{1}{\lambda+\nu+L+2}\frac{E_{bL}}{2}b_{\nu-1}$$

$$+ \frac{1}{(\lambda+\nu+L+2)(\lambda+\nu+L)(\lambda+\nu-L-1)}$$

$$\times\left[d_b b_{\nu-2} + \left(M_b^3 + d_{b0} + \frac{E_{bL}^3}{8}\right)b_{\nu-3} + d_{b1}b_{\nu-4} + d_{b2}b_{\nu-5} + d_{b4}b_{\nu-7}\right] \tag{10.4.7a}$$

$$b_\nu = -\frac{1}{(\lambda+\nu+L+1)(\lambda+\nu-L)}\frac{E_{bL}^2}{4}b_{\nu-2} - \frac{1}{\lambda+\nu-L}\frac{E_{bL}}{2}a_{\nu-1}$$

$$+\frac{1}{(\lambda+\nu+L+1)(\lambda+\nu-L)(\lambda+\nu-L-2)}$$
$$\times\left[d_b a_{\nu-2}+\left(M_b^3+d_{b0}-\frac{E_{bL}^3}{8}\right)a_{\nu-3}+d_{b1}a_{\nu-4}+d_{b2}a_{\nu-5}+d_{b5}a_{\nu-7}\right] \tag{10.4.7b}$$

10.5. Quartet Wave Equations and Confinement

10.5.1. Quartet Wave Equations in Relative Space

Remove the doublet components described by (10.2.1a) from the rest frame baryons equations (10.1.2, 6). We are left with the quartet baryon wave equations

$$\begin{aligned}&\left(i\delta^{a\dot{b}}E_{0q}/2+\underline{\sigma}^{a\dot{b}}\underline{\partial}\right)\left(i\delta^{g\dot{h}}E_{0q}/2+\underline{\sigma}^{g\dot{h}}\underline{\partial}\right)\left(i\delta_{\dot{e}f}E_{0q}/2+\underline{\sigma}_{\dot{e}f}\underline{\partial}\right)\chi_{\{\dot{b}\dot{h}}{}^{f\}}(\underline{x})\\&=-i\left(M_b^3+\Phi_{bq}(\underline{x})\right)\psi^{\{ag}{}_{\dot{e}\}}(\underline{x})\\&\left(i\delta_{\dot{b}c}E_{0q}/2-\underline{\sigma}_{\dot{b}c}\underline{\partial}\right)\left(i\delta_{\dot{h}k}E_{0q}/2-\underline{\sigma}_{\dot{h}k}\underline{\partial}\right)\left(i\delta^{d\dot{e}}E_{0q}/2-\underline{\sigma}^{d\dot{e}}\underline{\partial}\right)\psi^{\{ck}{}_{\dot{e}\}}(\underline{x})\\&=-i\left(M_b^3+\Phi_{bq}(\underline{x})\right)\chi_{\{\dot{b}\dot{h}}{}^{d\}}(\underline{x})\end{aligned} \tag{10.5.1}$$

$$\Phi_{bq}(\underline{x})=\Phi_{cq}(\underline{x})+\frac{d_b}{r}+d_{b0}+d_{b1}r+d_{b2}r^2+d_{b4}r^4 \tag{10.5.2a}$$

$$\Phi_{cq}(\underline{x})=\frac{g_s^6}{192\pi}\int d^3\underline{x}'\left|\underline{x}-\underline{x}'\right|^3\operatorname{Re}\left(\chi_{\{\dot{b}\dot{h}}{}^{f\}}(\underline{x}')\psi^{*\{\dot{b}\dot{h}}{}_{f\}}(\underline{x}')\right) \tag{10.5.2b}$$

Here, the χ's and ψ's are totally symmetric in their indices, the subscript q refers to specialization to quartets and (10.1.8) has been consulted. In terms of (9.2.8), (10.5.2b) becomes

$$\Phi_{cq}(\underline{x})=\frac{g_s^6}{192\pi}\int d^3\underline{x}'\left|\underline{x}-\underline{x}'\right|^3\sum_{\mu=-3/2}^{\mu=3/2}\operatorname{Re}\left(\chi_\mu(\underline{x}')\psi_\mu^*(\underline{x}')\right) \tag{10.5.3}$$

Note that if $\underline{K}\neq 0$, the quartet and doublet wave function components in (9.2.7, 8) couple and the full (9.3.16) with (10.1.1, 6b) must be used. Analogous to the doublet case at the end of §10.2.1, the quartet wave functions (9.2.8) will remain as "large components" and the doublet wave function (9.2.7) will enter as "small components" of the order $|\underline{K}|$ in (10.1.2, 6b).

10.5.2. Quartet Radial Wave Equations for j ≥ 3/2

The totally symmetric wave functions in (10.5.1, 2) have been grouped into two quartets according to (9.2.8). There are four values of the orbital angular momentum l that can combine with the spin angular momentum s=3/2 to produce a total angular momentum j, namely,

$$j = l+\frac{3}{2},\ l+\frac{1}{2},\ l-\frac{1}{2},\ \text{and}\ l-\frac{3}{2} \tag{10.5.4}$$

This result as well as $j=\pm\frac{1}{2}$ in (10.2.3) are special cases of a more general theorem on the eigenvalues $j(j+1)$ of the sum of the squares of two commuting angular momentum operators, here the orbital angular momentum operator $\underline{L}=\underline{r}\times\underline{\partial}$ and the spin operators $\underline{S}=(S^1, S^2, S^3)$ [B6]

$$S^1 = \begin{pmatrix} 0 & \frac{1}{2\sqrt{3}} & 0 & 0 \\ \frac{1}{2\sqrt{3}} & 0 & 1 & 0 \\ 0 & 1 & 0 & \frac{1}{2\sqrt{3}} \\ 0 & 0 & \frac{1}{2\sqrt{3}} & 0 \end{pmatrix},\quad S^2 = i\begin{pmatrix} 0 & \frac{-1}{2\sqrt{3}} & 0 & 0 \\ \frac{1}{2\sqrt{3}} & 0 & -1 & 0 \\ 0 & 1 & 0 & \frac{-1}{2\sqrt{3}} \\ 0 & 0 & \frac{1}{2\sqrt{3}} & 0 \end{pmatrix},\quad S^3 = \begin{pmatrix} \frac{3}{2} & 0 & 0 & 0 \\ 0 & \frac{1}{2} & 0 & 0 \\ 0 & 0 & \frac{-1}{2} & 0 \\ 0 & 0 & 0 & \frac{-3}{2} \end{pmatrix} \tag{10.5.5a}$$

$$\underline{S}^2 = s(s+1), \qquad s = 3/2 \tag{10.5.5b}$$

$$\underline{J} = \underline{L} + \underline{S}, \qquad \underline{J}^2 = j(j+1) \tag{10.5.5c}$$

For the doublet case, $\underline{S}$ are simply the Pauli matrices.

Analogous to the expansion of the doublet wave functions in (10.2.3), each of the four combinations in (10.5.4) can be expanded into spherical harmonics. Consider at first $j=l+3/2$ and let m be the eigenvalue of the third component of $\underline{J}$. The expansion is

$$j = l+\frac{3}{2},\quad \chi_\mu(\underline{x}) = \sum_{\nu=-3/2}^{\nu=3/2} C\left(j+\nu, \frac{3}{2}, j; m-\mu, \mu\right) Y_{j+\nu, m-\mu}(\vartheta,\phi)\, g_{j+\nu}(r) \tag{10.5.6a}$$

$$\psi_\mu(\underline{x}) = \sum_{\nu=-3/2}^{\nu=3/2} (-)^{\nu+1/2} C\left(j+\nu, \frac{3}{2}, j; m-\mu, \mu\right) Y_{j+\nu, m-\mu}(\vartheta,\phi)\, g_{j+\nu}(r) \tag{10.5.6b}$$

where μ=±3/2 and ±1/2. The C's are Clebsch-Gordan coefficients and have for instance been tabulated by Condon and Shortly [C2]. In the notation of Rose [R4], these are

$$g_{j+3/2} = if_j,\quad C\left(j+\frac{3}{2},\frac{3}{2},j;m\mp\frac{3}{2},\pm\frac{3}{2}\right) = \mp\sqrt{\frac{(j\mp m+1)(j\mp m+2)(j\mp m+3)}{(2j+3)(2j+2)(2j+4)}}$$

$$C\left(j+\frac{3}{2},\frac{3}{2},j;m\mp\frac{1}{2},\pm\frac{1}{2}\right) = \pm\sqrt{\frac{3(j+m+1)(j-m+1)(j\mp m+2)}{(2j+3)(2j+2)(2j+4)}}$$

$$g_{j+1/2} = g_j,\quad C\left(j+\frac{1}{2},\frac{3}{2},j;m\mp\frac{3}{2},\pm\frac{3}{2}\right) = \sqrt{\frac{3(j\pm m)(j\mp m+1)(j\mp m+2)}{2j(2j+2)(2j+3)}}$$

$$C\left(j+\frac{1}{2},\frac{3}{2},j;m\mp\frac{1}{2},\pm\frac{1}{2}\right) = -(j\pm 3m)\sqrt{\frac{j\mp m+1}{2j(2j+2)(2j+3)}}$$

$$g_{j-1/2} = ih_j,\quad C\left(j-\frac{1}{2},\frac{3}{2},j;m\mp\frac{3}{2},\pm\frac{3}{2}\right) = \mp\sqrt{\frac{3(j\pm m-1)(j\pm m)(j\mp m+1)}{(2j-1)2j(2j+2)}}$$

$$C\left(j-\frac{1}{2},\frac{3}{2},j;m\mp\frac{1}{2},\pm\frac{1}{2}\right) = \mp(j\mp 3m+1)\sqrt{\frac{j\pm m}{(2j-1)2j(2j+2)}}$$

$$g_{j-3/2} = k_j,\quad C\left(j-\frac{3}{2},\frac{3}{2},j;m\mp\frac{3}{2},\pm\frac{3}{2}\right) = \sqrt{\frac{(j\pm m-2)(j\pm m-1)(j\pm m)}{(2j-2)(2j-1)2j}}$$

$$C\left(j-\frac{3}{2},\frac{3}{2},j;m\mp\frac{1}{2},\pm\frac{1}{2}\right) = \sqrt{\frac{3(j+m)(j-m)(j\pm m-1)}{(2j-2)(2j-1)2j}}$$

(10.5.7)

Here, $g_{j+\nu}$ has been renamed. The spherical harmonics and radial wave functions contained in (10.5.6) are

$$j = l+\frac{3}{2},\qquad Y_l k_j,\qquad Y_{l+1}h_j,\qquad Y_{l+2}g_j,\quad \text{and}\quad Y_{l+3}f_j \tag{10.5.8}$$

Inserting (10.5.6) into (10.5.3) leads to that Φ_{cq} depends upon the angles, including the l=0 case, so that (10.5.1) is not separable. In the $|\underline{x}|\to 0$ and ∞ limits, (10.5.2) becomes independent of the angles;

$$\Phi_{bq}(|\underline{x}|\to 0) = \frac{d_b}{r}$$

$$\Phi_{cq}(|\underline{x}|\to\infty) = \frac{g_s^6}{192\pi}r^3\int d^3\underline{x}\sum_{\mu=-3/2}^{\mu=3/2}\mathrm{Re}\left(\chi_\mu(\underline{x})\psi_\mu^*(\underline{x})\right) = \alpha_q^3 r^3$$

(10.5.9)

In these limits, (10.5.1) is separable. Insert (9.2.8) and (10.5.3) into each of the eight component equations of (10.5.1) and make use of (10.5.7). Each of the four spherical harmonics in (10.5.6) is associated with a radial equation. After considerable algebra, it is shown that all the eight component equations in (10.5.1) yield the same set of radial equations

$$\left[\frac{E_{0q}^3}{8} - M_b^3 - \Phi_{bq}\left(\left|\underline{x}\right| \to 0 \text{ or } \infty\right) + \frac{E_{0q}}{2}\frac{3}{2j+2}\Delta_{j+3/2}\right]f_j(r)$$
$$-\frac{E_{0q}}{2}\frac{\sqrt{3(2j-1)(2j+3)}}{2j+2}\Delta_{(j-1/2)-}h_j(r) - \sqrt{\frac{(2j-1)(2j+3)}{4j(j+1)}}\Delta_{(j-1/2)-}\left(\frac{\partial}{\partial r} - \frac{j-3/2}{r}\right)k_j(r)$$
$$+\left[\frac{E_{0q}^2}{4}\sqrt{\frac{3j}{j+1}} + \sqrt{\frac{3}{4j(j+1)}}\Delta_{j+3/2}\right]\left(\frac{\partial}{\partial r} - \frac{j+1/2}{r}\right)g_j(r) = 0 \tag{10.510a}$$

$$\left[-\frac{E_{0q}^3}{8} - M_b^3 - \Phi_{bq}\left(\left|\underline{x}\right| \to 0 \text{ or } \infty\right) + \frac{E_{0q}}{2}\frac{4j-3}{2j}\Delta_{j+1/2}\right]g_j(r)$$
$$+\frac{E_{0q}}{2}\frac{\sqrt{3(2j-1)(2j+3)}}{2j}\Delta_{(j-3/2)-}k_j(r) + \left[\frac{E_{0q}^2}{4}\sqrt{\frac{3j}{j+1}} + \sqrt{\frac{3}{4j(j+1)}}\Delta_{j+1/2}\right]\left(\frac{\partial}{\partial r} + \frac{j+5/2}{r}\right)f_j(r)$$
$$+\sqrt{\frac{(2j-1)(2j+3)}{j(j+1)}}\left[\frac{E_{0q}^2}{4} - \frac{1}{2}\Delta_{j+1/2}\right]\left(\frac{\partial}{\partial r} - \frac{j-1/2}{r}\right)h_j(r) = 0 \tag{10.5.10b}$$

$$\left[\frac{E_{0q}^3}{8} - M_b^3 - \Phi_{bq}\left(\left|\underline{x}\right| \to 0 \text{ or } \infty\right) - \frac{E_{0q}}{2}\frac{4j+7}{2j+2}\Delta_{j-1/2}\right]h_j(r)$$
$$-\frac{E_{0q}}{2}\frac{\sqrt{3(2j-1)(2j+3)}}{2j+2}\Delta_{(j+3/2)+}f_j(r) + \left[\frac{E_{0q}^2}{4}\sqrt{\frac{3(j+1)}{j}} - \sqrt{\frac{3}{4j(j+1)}}\Delta_{j-1/2}\right]\left(\frac{\partial}{\partial r} - \frac{j-3/2}{r}\right)k_j(r)$$
$$+\sqrt{\frac{(2j-1)(2j+3)}{j(j+1)}}\left[\frac{E_{0q}^2}{4} - \frac{1}{2}\Delta_{j-1/2}\right]\left(\frac{\partial}{\partial r} + \frac{j+3/2}{r}\right)g_j(r) = 0 \tag{10.5.10c}$$

$$\left[-\frac{E_{0q}^3}{8} - M_b^3 - \Phi_{bq}\left(\left|\underline{x}\right| \to 0 \text{ or } \infty\right) + \frac{E_{0q}}{2}\frac{3}{2j}\Delta_{j-3/2}\right]k_j(r)$$
$$+\frac{E_{0q}}{2}\frac{\sqrt{3(2j-1)(2j+3)}}{2j}\Delta_{(j+1/2)+}g_j(r) - \sqrt{\frac{(2j-1)(2j+3)}{4j(j+1)}}\Delta_{(j+1/2)+}\left(\frac{\partial}{\partial r} + \frac{j+5/2}{r}\right)f_j(r)$$
$$+\left[\frac{E_{0q}^2}{4}\sqrt{\frac{3(j+1)}{j}} - \sqrt{\frac{3}{4j(j+1)}}\Delta_{j-3/2}\right]\left(\frac{\partial}{\partial r} + \frac{j+1/2}{r}\right)h_j(r) = 0 \tag{10.5.10d}$$

where the Δ operators have been defined in (3.4.5b). For free quartet baryons, the nonlinear confinement potential Φ_{cq} (10.5.3) must vanish according to the reasoning given near the end of Sec. 10.3. $\Phi_{bq}(\underline{x})$ in (10.5.2a) now depends only upon r and (10.5.10) holds for all r.

Equation (10.5.10) is a system of four third order equations and has 12 solutions and holds generally for $j=l+3/2$, $l\geq 0$. The asymptotic solutions are of the form of (10.2.6) with $\alpha_d \to \alpha_q$ or the first line of (10.2.7). This can be verified by putting f_j, g_j, h_j, and k_j to such asymptotic forms and inserting them into (10.5.10).

Near the origin, we make the expansion

$$\begin{pmatrix} f \\ g \\ h \\ k \end{pmatrix} = r^{\lambda} \begin{pmatrix} f_0 + f_1 r + \ldots \\ g_0 + g_1 r + \ldots \\ h_0 + h_1 r + \ldots \\ k_0 + k_1 r + \ldots \end{pmatrix} \tag{10.5.11}$$

Inserting (10.5.11) into (10.5.10) leads to the following 12 roots of the indicial equation;

$$\begin{aligned} f_0 = h_0 = 0, \qquad & \lambda = j+\frac{5}{2},\ j+\frac{1}{2},\ j+\frac{1}{2},\ j-\frac{3}{2},\ -j+\frac{1}{2},\ -j-\frac{3}{2} \\ g_0 = k_0 = 0, \qquad & \lambda = j+\frac{3}{2},\ j-\frac{1}{2},\ -j+\frac{3}{2},\ -j-\frac{1}{2},\ -j-\frac{1}{2},\ -j-\frac{5}{2} \end{aligned} \tag{10.5.12}$$

Analogous to (3.4.7), the six λ values with $-j$ will in general lead to diverging solutions at $r=0$ and are discarded. Among the remaining ones, the $\lambda=j+1/2$ and $j+3/2$ cases turn out to yield indeterminate k_0/g_0 ratios and are left out for eventual future investigation. Therefore, only the following three solutions remain;

$$\lambda = j-\frac{3}{2}, \qquad f_0 = h_0 = g_0 = 0, \qquad \chi_\mu, \psi_\mu \propto k_0 r^{j-3/2} Y_{j-3/2} \tag{10.5.13a}$$

$$\lambda = j-\frac{1}{2}, \qquad f_0 = k_0 = g_0 = 0, \qquad \chi_\mu, \psi_\mu \propto h_0 r^{j-1/2} Y_{j-1/2} \tag{10.5.13b}$$

$$\begin{aligned} \lambda = j+\frac{5}{2}, \qquad f_0 = h_0 = 0, \qquad & k_0 = -\left(\frac{j}{2}+1\right)\sqrt{\frac{(2j-1)(2j+3)}{3}}\, g_0 \\ & \chi_\mu, \psi_\mu \propto r^{j+5/2}\left(g_0 Y_{j+1/2} + k_0 Y_{j-3/2} \right) \end{aligned} \tag{10.5.13c}$$

$$j = l + \frac{3}{2} \geq \frac{3}{2} \tag{10.5.13d}$$

The form of (10.5.13) is similar to that of the corresponding solutions (3.4.8, 6, 4) for triplet, $l>0$ mesons.

10.5.3. Quartet Radial Wave Equations for j = 1/2

Equation (10.5.10) holds for $j>½$ and contains four radial wave functions. It corresponds to (3.4.5) for the triplet, $l>0$ meson case, which contains three radial wave functions. Two of these three functions drop out for the l=0 case in §3.4.3. Similarly, the number of radial functions in (10.5.10) will also be reduced for the j=½ case.

As is seen in (10.5.4), the j=½ case can only be obtained from the last three combinations there but not from the j=l+3/2 case treated in §10.5.2. This situation is reminiscent of the doublet case discussed below (10.2.5) where j=l–½ wave functions (10.2.3b) can be obtained from the j=l+½ wave functions (10.2.3a) by some symbol changes. In an analogous manner, the quartet wave functions for the last three combinations in (10.5.4) can be obtained from (10.5.6) with $j\to j-1$, $j-2$ and $j-3$. The spherical harmonics and radial wave functions associated with these cases are by analogy to (10.5.8),

$$j=l+\frac{1}{2},\qquad Y_{l-1}k_{j-1},\quad Y_l h_{j-1},\quad Y_{l+1}g_{j-1},\ \text{and}\ \ Y_{l+2}f_{j-1}\tag{10.5.14a}$$

$$j=l-\frac{1}{2},\qquad Y_{l-2}k_{j-2},\quad Y_{l-1}h_{j-2},\quad Y_l g_{j-2},\ \text{and}\ \ Y_{l+1}f_{j-2}\tag{10.5.14b}$$

$$j=l-\frac{3}{2},\qquad Y_{l-3}k_{j-3},\quad Y_{l-2}h_{j-3},\quad Y_{l-1}g_{j-3},\ \text{and}\ \ Y_l f_{j-3}\tag{10.5.14c}$$

It is obvious that the radial wave equations associated with these cases are of the same form as (10.5.10) with $j\to j-1$, $j-2$ and $j-3$, respectively.

Consider the l=0 case for (10.5.10) which now holds for j=3/2. Conversion of this case to the l=0 case for (10.5.14a) starts by letting $j=3/2\to j=1/2$. According to (10.5.6, 7), (10.5.10d) is associated with Y_{l-1}, which however does not exist for l=0. Therefore, (10.5.10d) drops out. The associated radial function $k_{1/2}$ in (10.5.10) and $k_{-1/2}$ in (10.5.14a) become meaningless and can thus be put to zero. Making use of this result and inserting j=½ into (10.5.10c) further leads to $h_{1/2}=0$. In the remaining two equations, (10.5.10a, 10b), therefore, only the $f_{1/2}$ and $g_{1/2}$ terms remain. This is further ensured by observing that the coefficients of the $h_{1/2}$ and $k_{1/2}$ terms in (10.5.10a, 10b) vanish for j=½.

For this case, the sum in (10.5.3) turns out to be independent of the angles and proportional to $f_{1/2}^2(r)-g_{1/2}^2(r)$. The angular integrations in (10.5.3) can now be carried out, as in (10.2.9), to yield

$$\Phi_{cq}(r)=\frac{g_s^6}{1920\pi}\left[\begin{array}{l}\int_0^r dr'r'^2\left(f_{1/2}^2(r')-g_{1/2}^2(r')\right)\left(5r^4+10r^2r'^2+r'^4\right)/r\\ +\int_r^\infty dr'r'\left(f_{1/2}^2(r')-g_{1/2}^2(r')\right)\left(5r'^4+10r^2r'^2+r^4\right)\end{array}\right]\tag{10.5.15}$$

Equation (10.5.10) now reduces to

$$j=\frac{1}{2},\qquad \left[\frac{E_{0q}^3}{8}+M_b^3+\Phi_{bq}(r)+\frac{E_{0q}}{2}\Delta_1\right]g_{1/2}(r)-\left(\frac{E_{0q}^2}{4}+\Delta_1\right)\left(\frac{\partial}{\partial r}+\frac{3}{r}\right)f_{1/2}(r)=0$$

$$\left[\frac{E_{0q}^3}{8}-M_b^3-\Phi_{bq}(r)+\frac{E_{0q}}{2}\Delta_2\right]f_{1/2}(r)+\left(\frac{E_{0q}^2}{4}+\Delta_2\right)\left(\frac{\partial}{\partial r}-\frac{1}{r}\right)g_{1/2}(r)=0 \qquad (10.5.16)$$

which holds for all r because (10.5.15), hence (10.5.2a), depends only upon r and separation according to (10.5.6) is possible. Equations (10.5.15) and (10.5.16) are nearly the same as the corresponding doublet equations (10.2.9) and (10.2.12). In fact, (10.5.15) is formally –3/16 times (10.2.9). Equations (10.5.16) and (10.2.12) are formally obtained from (10.2.4) with upper sign by putting l=1 and 0, respectively. The relations between these quartet and doublet cases are entirely analogous to those between the singlet, l=0 and triplet, l=0 cases of §3.4.1 and §3.4.3, respectively.

The closeness of (10.5.16) to the doublet, l=0 case (10.2.12) enables us to take over the results worked out for the latter case. In the $r\to 0$ and ∞ limits, (10.5.15) yields

$$\Phi_{cq}(r\to 0)=\frac{g_s^6}{384\pi}\int_0^\infty dr\, r^5\left(f_{1/2}^2(r)-g_{1/2}^2(r)\right) \qquad (10.5.17a)$$

$$\Phi_{cq}(r\to\infty)=\frac{g_s^6}{384\pi}r^3\int_0^\infty dr' r'^2\left(f_{1/2}^2(r')-g_{1/2}^2(r')\right)=\alpha_q^3 r^3 \qquad (10.5.17b)$$

analogous to (10.2.10, 11). Near the origin, (10.5.13) no longer holds but the solution is given by (10.2.8a) with l=1,

$$g_{1/2}(r\to 0)=c_{gq}(\lambda_q)r^{\lambda_q},\qquad f_{1/2}(r\to 0)=0,\qquad \lambda_q=3,\,1,\,-2 \qquad (10.5.18a)$$

$$f_{1/2}(r\to 0)=c_{fq}(\lambda_q)r^{\lambda_q},\qquad g_{1/2}(r\to 0)=0,\qquad \lambda_q=2,\,-1,\,-3 \qquad (10.5.18b)$$

Radial wave functions converging at r=0 are associated with λ_q=3 and 1 in (10.5.18a) and λ_q=2 in (10.5.18b).

Chapter 11

Baryon Wave Functions, Classification and Magnetic Moment

Although the equations of motion for mesons [H5] and for baryons [H15] were both published in the early 1990's, subsequent work took almost wholly in the meson sector. This is due to that the two coupled second order meson wave equations (2.3.22) can via (3.1.8) be decomposed into two separated second order differential equations (3.2.3-4) for meson at rest. These last equations have analytical solutions, providing the zeroth order background upon which higher order perturbational problems could be built and treated in Chapters 6-8.

On the other hand, the two coupled third order equations for baryon doublets (10.2.1a) cannot be decoupled and reduced to lower order equations. The are eventually reduced to the six first order equations (10.4.5).

Due to the large number of unknown potential constants in (10.2.2a), (10.4.5) cannot be solved. Instead, a *less ambitious approach with curtailed predictive power* will be adopted. The masses of the neutron, Σ^0 and Ξ^0 and of the quarks involved will be used as input and convergent wave functions $w_1 \ldots w_6$ in (10.4.5) will be sought in Sec.11.1 using computers.

In Sec.11.2-3, baryons are classified and in Sec. 11.4, magnetic moments of ground state baryons are approximately predicted.

11.1. Confined Doublet Baryon Wave Functions

11.1.1. Numerical Treatment of the Radial Wave Equations

For the doublet baryons of Sec.10.2, L=0 in (10.4.5), the radial wave functions can be expanded in power series in r according to (10.4.6-7). At large r, (10.2.7) shows that the solutions can be approximated by power series in $r^{1/3}$. Therefore, the series of (10.4.6-7) becomes infinite and (10.4.5) has to be solved numerically. Expand the w's around the regular singular point r=0,

$$w_\alpha(r) \rightarrow \sum_{\lambda+} w_{(\lambda+)\alpha}(r) = \sum_{\lambda+} \sum_{\beta=0}^{\infty} r^{\lambda+} w_{(\lambda+)\alpha\beta} r^\beta, \quad \alpha = 1,2,....6 \qquad (11.1.1)$$

where λ_+ can take on six values given by (10.2.8a). The three cases with possible $\lambda_+ < 0$ are excluded because they lead to diverging $w_\alpha(r$=0). The remaining cases, apart from the normalization considerations of (10.3.13, 14), yield for orbital quantum number l=0

$$\lambda_+ = 0, \qquad w_{(0)40} = 1, \qquad w_{(0)10} = 0 \qquad (11.1.2a)$$

$$\lambda_+ = 1, \qquad w_{(1)40} = 0, \qquad w_{(1)10} = w_{(1)} \qquad (11.1.2b)$$

$$\lambda_+ = 2, \qquad w_{(2)40} = w_{(2)}, \qquad w_{(2)10} = 0 \tag{11.1.2c}$$

where the amplitude in (11.1.2a) has been normalized to unity. $w_{(1)}$ and $w_{(2)}$ are amplitudes for the remaining two solutions. Write out the left of (11.1.1),

$$w_\alpha(r) = w_{(0)\alpha}(r) + w_{(1)\alpha}(r) + w_{(2)\alpha}(r) \tag{11.1.3}$$

Substituting this with the right of (11.1.1) into (10.4.5), which is then numerically solved as an initial value problem using (11.1.2) and $\beta = 0$ - 4 for small r initially.

In (10.4.5), M_b is given by (9.3.19) in which the quark masses m_ν are consistently taken to be the same as those for the mesons obtained in Table 5.2. E_{b0} is the baryon mass. There are also five unknown d_b constants. If they were independent of baryon flavor, i.e., baryon species, as is the case for mesons pointed out below (10.1.6) and (4.4.1), they have to be obtained from data, i.e., baryon masses.

Noting that the present internal model leading to (9.3.19, 20) cannot distinguish M_b for Λ from that for Σ^0 and, neglecting the small electromagnetic splittings, there are only seven baryon masses, those of the neutron, Σ^0, Ξ^0, Σ_c^0, Ξ_c^0, Ω_c^0, and Λ_b^0, available. In principle, these seven masses fix the five d_b's and the two parameters $w_{(1)}$ and $w_{(2)}$ in (11.1.2), totaling seven constants, in the eigenvalue problem (10.4.5), leaving no further predictive power at least on the ground state baryon level. Furthermore, such an approach leads to a huge computational task and it is uncertain that these five d_b's and $w_{(1)}$ and $w_{(2)}$ can be uniquely fixed in this way.

11.1.2. Sets of Wave Functions and Potential Constants, d_{b4}=0

For the last-mentioned reasons, no attempt to predict the baryon spectra in the conventional way from (10.4.5) will not made here. Instead, a *less ambitious approach* will be adopted to extract *partial predictive power* from (10.4.5). The procedure is to insert the known E_{b0} and M_b of the neutron, Σ^0 and Ξ^0 and use the quark masses in Table 5.2 as input and adjust the above seven constants over suitable ranges such that the solutions of (10.4.5) satisfy boundary condition of the form (10.2.7b) at $r \to \infty$ or converge there.

This procedure has been carried out in the first edition of this book [H18 Ch 11], which has been simplified by the assumption d_{b4}=0 [H18 (10.1.8)], reducing the above seven constants to six such. To find the convergent radial wave functions $g_{b0}(r)$ and $f_{b0}(r)$ in (10.4.5) via $g_{00}(r)$ and $f_{00}(r)$ in (10.3.14) practically, (10.4.5) was solved as an initial value problem on computers of the Department of Information Technology at Uppsala University. A Fortran 77 Runge-Kutta integration subroutine "dverk" was employed.

The search criterion is that the radial wave functions $g_{00}(r)$ and $f_{00}(r)$ with $g_{00}(0)$=1 are required to be less than a small amplitude Δ_g when the quark-diquark distance r is large, typically r=r_{mn}>6-8 GeV^{-1}, to conform to the p_ν=−1 boundary condition (10.2.7b). When r is too large, typically r=r_{mx}>9-10 GeV^{-1}, the complex p_ν and diverging boundary solutions in (10.2.7b) take over due to accumulated small computing errors. Therefore, Δ_g is required to be very small, practically $\Delta_g < \Delta_{gm} \approx 0.001$-0.004, inside a range of $r_{mx} - r_{mx} \approx 3$ GeV^{-1}.

Once the leading potential term's continuous coefficient $d_{b2}<0$ in (10.2.2a) with $d_{b4}=0$ is chosen, the remaining five constants are scanned through a suitable five-dimensional space in searching for a point with minimum Δ_g. At this point, the five constants as well as $g_{OO}(r)$ and $f_{OO}(r)$ are fixed. $\Delta_g>\Delta_{gm}$ mostly and are not associated with converging solution. Another d_{b2} value is then chosen and the five-dimensional space is scanned through again. This process is repeated until $\Delta_g<\Delta_{gm}$ or a converging solution with a specific $d_{b2}=d_{b2c}$ value is found. A confirmation is that when d_{b2} moves across d_{b2c}, $g_{OO}(r)$ and $f_{OO}(r)$ change sign at large r.

The result is that there is a large number of d_{b2c} values leading to confined wave functions, each of which associated with its unique set of these six constants. Some of these sets are shown in Table 11.1.

Table 11.1. Values of the five d_b constants in (10.4.5) and $w_{(1)}$ and $w_{(2)}$ in (11.1.2) for some converging solutions of (10.4.5). Only the d_{b2}=–0.3202 case for the neutron has been shown to exist according to §12.6.3 below

	$d_{b4}=0$ GeV^7	$d_{b2}\approx$ GeV^5	d_{b1} GeV^4	d_{b0} GeV^3	d_b GeV^2	$w_{(1)}$ GeV	$-w_{(2)}$ GeV^2
neutron		–0.140	1.0439	–3.0	0.695	0.016	0.0288
Σ^0		–0.1411	1.336	–4.06	1.085	0.0415	0.0691
Ξ^0		–0.141	1.111	–3.568	0.924	0.0019	0.0851
neutron		–0.1641	1.334	–3.719	1.013	0.0668	0.045
Σ^0		–0.1641	1.279	–3.706	0.990	0.0353	0.0756
Ξ^0		–0.1641	1.220	–3.691	0.9177	0.0523	0.0721
neutron		–0.3202	2.272	–4.922	1.024	0.1827	0.0674
Σ^0		–0.3202	2.167	–4.783	1.032	0.0586	0.0662
Ξ^0		–0.3202	2.142	–4.899	1.083	0.1191	0.1061
neutron		–0.4462	2.968	–5.749	1.035	0.247	0.0859
Σ^0		–0. 4462	2.831	–5.541	1.066	0.1624	0.090
Ξ^0		–0. 4462	2.768	–5.516	1.033	0.121	0.0974
neutron		–0.575	3.658	–6.55	1.064	0.2943	0.102
Σ^0		–0.575	3.471	–6.224	1.073	0.203	0.0997
Ξ^0		–0. 575	3.383	–6.147	1.029	0.195	0.1164
neutron		–0.975	5.572	–8.328	0.8173	0.4278	0.1576
Σ^0		–0.975	5.319	–7.895	0.9048	0.316	0.1298
Ξ^0		–0.975	5.090	–7.441	0.6859	0.2902	0.1391

These results show that the four d_b's and $w_{(1)}$ and $w_{(2)}$ differ among the three baryons and hence depend upon baryon flavor, contrary to that in the meson case mentioned below (10.1.6) and (4.4.1).

This table can obviously be extended to include the above-mentioned Σ_c^0, Ξ_c^0, Ω_c^0, and Λ_b^0 baryons as well. For illustration, the three wave functions for d_{b2}=–0.4462 and the neutron wave functions for d_{b2}=–0.3202 are plotted in Figure 11.1.

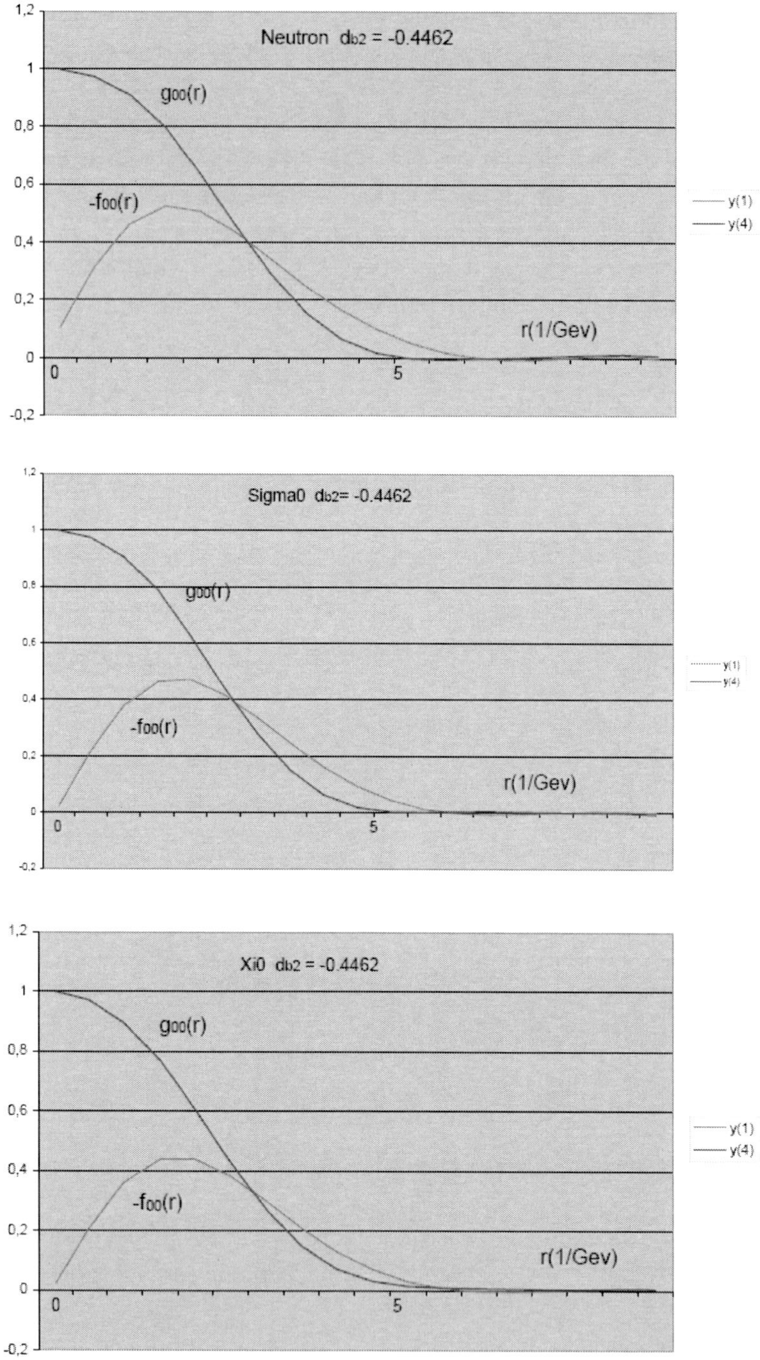

Figure 11.1a. Baryon radial wave functions fb0(r) and gb0(r) in (10.4.5-7) normalized according to (10.3.14) for the db2 =–0.4462 case in Table 11.1. r is the quark-diquark distance. These solutions have no experimental support.

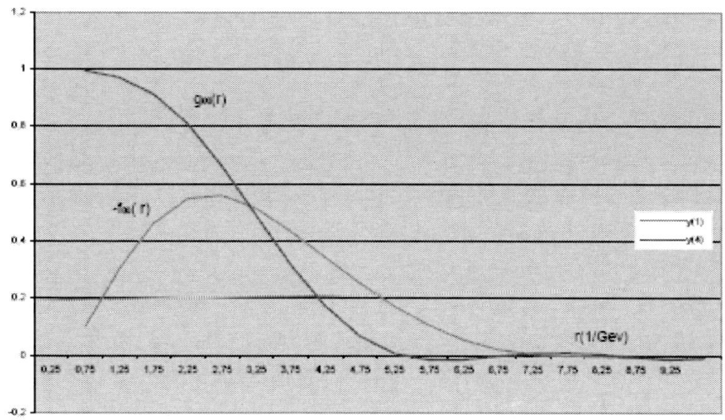

Figure 11.1b. Neutron radial wave functions $f_{b0}(r)$ and $g_{b0}(r)$ in (10.4.5-7) normalized according to (10.3.14) for the d_{b2}=–0.3202 case in Table 11.1. r is the quark-diquark distance. This wave function has been used to evaluate neutron decay parameters in §12.6.3 below.

The predicted results of Table 11.1 together with the wave functions $f_{O0}(r)$ and $g_{O0}(r)$ illustrated in Figure 11.1a has not confronted data. Further, they leads to too many solutions; there can only be at most one set in Table 11.1 that corresponds to the observed baryons. Since the baryon masses E_{b0} has already be used as input, there are no further zeroth order prediction. The predicted wave functions of the form of Figure 11.1 can however enter as zeroth order background for prediction of some first order perturbational phenomenon. These both problems are treated for neutron decay in §12.6.3 below, which shows that only the d_{b2} =–0.3202 GeV^5 case for neutron in Table 11.1 leads to agreement to data. The remaining convergent solution for neutron leads to results in disagreement with data. Predictions for Σ^0 and Ξ^0 in Table 11.1 have not confronted data.

The quark-diquark potential $d_{b2}r^2$ in (10.2.2a) used to obtain Table 12.1 below is thus of the same form as the quark-antiquark potential $d_{m2}r^2$ in (3.2.8a, 21) used to account for meson data. Both confinement potentials are of harmonic oscillator type (see Sec. 4.6).

11.1.3. Unique Sets of Wave Functions and Potential Constants, $d_{b4}\neq 0$

Turning to (10.1.8) and generalize §11.1.2 above to include the d_{b4}<0 case. The treatment is the same but leads to that the numerous sets of solutions conforming to the boundary condition (10.2.7b) reduce to one single set for each baryon satisfying the boundary condition (10.2.7a). The results corresponding to Table 11.1 are shown in Table 11.2.

Here, Δ_g has been confined inside a range of $r_{mx}-r_{mx}\approx 2.5$ GeV^{-1}. The four decimal accuracy in Table 11.1 is increased to eight here because the calculations are more sensitive to the new leading potential $d_{b4}r^4$. The Fortran 77 computer program itself works with an accuracy of 12 decimals. The constants in Table 11.2 are accurate up to ~ 0.05%. Plots of $f_{O0}(r)$ and $g_{O0}(r)$ are like those in Figure 11.1 except that $f_{O0}(r)$ is of opposite sign. For the neutron, such plots will yield results disagreeing with data in §12.6.3 below. Therefore, the convergent solution associated with the neutron in Table 11.2 is dropped. Again, results for Σ^0 and Ξ^0 are not tested.

Table 11.2. Values of the five d_b constants in (10.4.5) and $w_{(1)}$ and $w_{(2)}$ in (11.1.2) for the neutron, Σ^0 and Ξ^0 determined from (10.4.5)

	neutron	Σ^0	Ξ^0
d_{b4} GeV^7	−0.00321779	−0.00439883	−0.00555589
d_{b2} GeV^5	0.09311960	0.09860858	0.11791396
d_{b1} GeV^4	0.10797097	0.13697715	0.12029265
d_{b0} GeV^3	−1.82031026	−1.90573205	−2.05818547
d_b GeV^2	0.15865445	0.06040028	0.04931174
$w_{(1)}$	0.13257103	0.09293369	0.08834692
$w_{(2)}$	0.05155696	0.07102012	0.08847678
Δ_g	0.00115	0.00115	0.00125

11.1.4. On Functions Nonseparable in Relative Space x and Internal Space z

Consider a two electron system. When the both electrons are far apart, it is described by two independent Dirac wave functions $\psi_\alpha(x_I)$ and $\psi_\beta(x_{II})$ totaling eight wave function components. When they are closer to each other the product wave functions $\psi_\alpha(x_I)\,\psi_\beta(x_{II})$ must be generalized to the nonseparable $\psi_{\alpha\beta}(x_I,x_{II})$ having 16 components governed by the Bethe-Salpeter equation which includes the interaction between the both electrons. The eight extra wave function components are associated with this interaction and are small perturbations when both electrons are not too close to each other. This example illustrates the conjecture below.

The approximate solutions in §11.1.1 are based upon the construction that the total baryon wave functions are separable in x and z in (9.3.6) or, more specifically, in relative space wave function $\psi_0^a(\underline{x})$ and internal space functions $\eta_r^p(z_I,z_{II})$ in (9.3.7b). According to the epistemological considerations in Sec. 5.4 of [H16 or Appendix G], these both spaces are "hidden," on par with each other, and at the so-called "level logic2" and can be combined to form a larger manifold (x,z_I,z_{II}). In this case the product form $\psi_0^a(\underline{x})\,\eta_r^p(z_I,z_{II})$ in (9.3.7b) needs be generalized to the nonseparable form $\Psi_0{}^a{}_r{}^p(x,z_I,z_{II})$. A conjecture is now made that the mass operator $m_{3op}(z_I,z_{II})$ of (9.3.14), which contains $\partial/\partial z$ via (2.3.13), is also generalized to a nonseparable, as yet unknown form $m_{3op}(z_I,z_{II},x)$, which may also contain $\partial/\partial x$, analogous to the generalization of the masses operator $m_{2op}(z_I,z_{II})$ to $m_{2op}(z_I,z_{II},x)$ in Sec.5.4 of [Appendix G]. This generalization may for instance be such that when $r=|\underline{x}|$ falls outside some region of values, $m_{3op}(z_I,z_{II},x)$ degenerates back to $m_{3op}(z_I,z_{II})$.

The product wave function $\psi_0^a(\underline{x})\,\eta_r^p(z_I,z_{II})$ in (9.3.7b) has 10 components, two from a=1, 2 and eight from p=r=1, 2, 3(less the singlet). The generalized, nonseparable $\Psi_0{}^a{}_r{}^p(x,z_I,z_{II})$ has 2×8=16 wave function components, six more than 10 components. These six extra components are associated with this presently unknown dependence of $m_{3op}(z_I,z_{II},x)$ upon x. They may be the cause of the approximative nature of the results in Table 11.1.

Actually, the generalization from separable to nonseparable forms can already be formally introduced at the quark level, because the quark space-time x and internal space z are also "hidden" variables at "level logic2" in Sec. 5.4 of [H16 or Appendix G]. In this case, the following generalization is to be introduced into (2.3.11),

$$\chi_{\dot{b}}(X)\xi^{p}(z) \to \Xi_{\dot{b}}^{\ p}(X,z), \qquad \psi^{a}(X)\xi^{p}(z) \to \Psi^{ap}(X,z)$$
$$m_{1op}(z) \to m_{1op}(z,X) \qquad (11.1.4)$$

Again, the form of $m_{1op}(z_I,X)$ is unknown.

11.2. Classification Scheme for Doublet Baryons

An attempt is made to classify most of the known doublet baryons according to (10.2.8), much like the classification of the triplet, $l>0$ mesons in §5.6.2. The starting point is [P1] with its quark model assignments in terms of flavor-spin SU(6) basis and "bands" referring to unspecified excitations. These assignments are replaced by those in (10.2.8) containing the six linearly independent solutions of (10.2.1-4) near the origin and are shown in Table 11.3. The angular momenta and parity assignments of [P1] have also been changed due to considerations mentioned in relation to Table 11.4 below.

Table 11.3. Classification of doublet baryons given in [P1] according to (10.2.8) with parity $P=(-)^{l+1}$. The subscripts to $\lambda_\pm$ refer to the multiplet $l_{2I,\,2j}$ and a, b or c refers to a specific $\lambda_\pm$ value in (10.2.8) or to a linear combination of solutions associated with different $\lambda_\pm$ values. To avoid divergence at $r=0$, $\lambda_\pm \geq 0$. Assignments given in [P1] are shown in parentheses and correspond to (10.2.8b) or $j=l-1/2$. They are replaced by the neighbouring ones corresponding to (10.2.8a) or $j=l+1/2$

$l_{2I,\,2j}$	j^P	Octet members	Singlets	$j=l\pm½$	$\lambda_\pm$ (10.2.8)
$(P_{11})S_{11}$	$(1/2^+)1/2^-$	$N(939)$, $\Lambda(1116)$, $\Sigma(1193)$, $\Xi(1318)$		$1/2=(1-1/2)0+1/2$	λ_{+S11a}
$(P_{11})S_{11}$	$(1/2^+)1/2^-$	$N(1440)$, $\Lambda(1600)$, $\Sigma(1660)$, $\Xi(?)$		$1/2=(1-1/2)0+1/2$	λ_{+S11b}
$(P_{11})S_{11}$	$(1/2^+)1/2^-$	$N(1710)$, $\Lambda(1810)$, $\Sigma(1880)$, $\Xi(?)$	$\Lambda(?)$	$1/2=(1-1/2)0+1/2$	λ_{+S11c}
$(S_{11})P_{11}$	$(1/2^-)1/2^+$	$N(1535)$, $\Lambda(1670)$, $\Sigma(1620)$, $\Xi(?)$	$\Lambda(1405)$	$1/2=(0+1/2)1-1/2$	λ_{-P11a}
$(S_{11})P_{11}$	$(1/2^-)1/2^+$	$N(1650)$, $\Lambda(1800)$, $\Sigma(1750)$, $\Xi(?)$		$1/2=(0+1/2)1-1/2$	λ_{-P11b}
$(P_{13})D_{13}$	$(3/2^+)3/2^-$	$N(1720)$, $\Lambda(1890)$, $\Sigma(?)$, $\Xi(?)$		$3/2=(1+1/2)2-1/2$	λ_{-D13a}
$(D_{13})P_{13}$	$(3/2^-)3/2^+$	$N(1520)$, $\Lambda(1690)$, $\Sigma(1670)$, $\Xi(1820)$	$\Lambda(1520)$	$3/2=(2-1/2)1+1/2$	λ_{+P13a}
$(D_{13})P_{13}$	$(3/2^-)3/2^+$	$N(1700)$, $\Lambda(?)$, $\Sigma(?)$, $\Xi(?)$		$3/2=(2-1/2)1+1/2$	λ_{+P13b}
$(F_{15})D_{15}$	$(5/2^+)5/2^-$	$N(1680)$, $\Lambda(1820)$, $\Sigma(1915)$, $\Xi(2030)$		$5/2=(3-1/2)2+1/2$	λ_{+D15a}
$(D_{15})F_{15}$	$(5/2^-)5/2^+$	$N(1675)$, $\Lambda(1830)$, $\Sigma(1775)$, $\Xi(?)$		$5/2=(2+1/2)3-1/2$	λ_{+F15a}
$(G_{17})F_{17}$	$(7/2^-)7/2^+$	$N(2190)$, $\Lambda(?)$, $\Sigma(?)$, $\Xi(?)$	$\Lambda(2100)$	$7/2=(4-1/2)3+1/2$	λ_{+F17a}
$(H_{19})G_{19}$	$(9/2^+)9/2^-$	$N(2220)$, $\Lambda(2350)$, $\Sigma(?)$, $\Xi(?)$		$9/2=(5-1/2)4+1/2$	λ_{+G19a}
$(G_{19})H_{19}$	$(9/2^-)9/2^+$	$N(2250)$, $\Lambda(?)$, $\Sigma(?)$, $\Xi(?)$		$9/2=(4+1/2)5-1/2$	λ_{-H19a}

11.3. Classification Scheme for Quartet Baryons

For the quartet baryons, there are four possible values for each j in (10.5.4), rather than two in the doublet case (10.2.3). For each j and l pair, there are three radial modes (10.5.13), analogous to the radial modes associated with the $\lambda_{\pm}=l+\ldots$ roots in (10.2.8) for doublets. These three radial modes are characterized by the power λ in (10.5.11) which has the values

$$\lambda = \lambda_l,\ \lambda_{l+1},\ \lambda_{l+4} \tag{11.3.1}$$

For j=3/2, (10.5.13d, 13a) yields

$$j = l + \frac{3}{2}, \qquad \lambda_l = j - \frac{3}{2} = l \tag{11.3.2a}$$

By analogy to (10.5.14), one obtains

$$j = l + \frac{1}{2}, \qquad \lambda_l = l - 1 \tag{11.3.2b}$$

$$j = l - \frac{1}{2}, \qquad \lambda_l = l - 2 \tag{11.3.2c}$$

$$j = l - \frac{3}{2}, \qquad \lambda_l = l - 3 \tag{11.3.2d}$$

An attempt to classify the decuplet baryons proceeds along the same line applied to doublet baryons in Sec. 11.2. The results are given in Table 11.4.

Table 11.4. Tentative classification of the decuplet baryons including those given in [P1] according to (11.3.1, 2). Notations, restrictions as well as the assignments of the λ values are analogous to those in Sec. 11.2

$l_{2I,\,2j}$	j^P	Decuplet members	j in (11.3.1, 2)		λ in (11.3.1)
P_{31}	$1/2^+$	$\Delta(1910)$, $\Sigma(?)$, $\Xi(?)$, $\Omega(?)$	$j=l-½$	$l=1$	λ_{P31a}
S_{31}	$1/2^-$	$\Delta(1620)$, $\Sigma(?)$, $\Xi(?)$, $\Omega(?)$	$j=l+½$	$l=0$	λ_{S31a}
P_{33}	$3/2^+$	$\Delta(1232)$, $\Sigma(1385)$, $\Xi(1530)$, $\Omega(1672)$	$j=l+½$	$l=1$	λ_{P33a}
P_{33}	$3/2^+$	$\Delta(1600)$, $\Sigma(?)$, $\Xi(?)$, $\Omega(?)$	$j=l+½$	$l=1$	λ_{P33b}
D_{33}	$3/2^-$	$\Delta(1700)$, $\Sigma(?)$, $\Xi(?)$, $\Omega(?)$	$j=l-½$	$l=2$	λ_{D33a}
F_{35}	$5/2^+$	$\Delta(1905)$, $\Sigma(?)$, $\Xi(?)$, $\Omega(?)$	$j=l-½$	$l=3$	λ_{F35a}
D_{35}	$5/2^-$	$\Delta(1930)$, $\Sigma(?)$, $\Xi(?)$, $\Omega(?)$	$j=l+½$	$l=2$	λ_{D35a}
F_{37}	$7/2^+$	$\Delta(1950)$, $\Sigma(2030)$, $\Xi(?)$, $\Omega(?)$	$j=l+½$	$l=3$	λ_{F37a}
$H_{3,11}$	$11/2^+$	$\Delta(2420)$, $\Sigma(?)$, $\Xi(?)$, $\Omega(?)$	$j=l+½$	$l=5$	$\lambda_{H3,11a}$

Any assignment of the λ's are far more uncertain than those in the doublet case. A numerical, confined solution of the effectively 12th order radial equations (10.5.10) is far more complex to obtain than that for the effectively 6th order equations (10.2.4) for the doublet baryons.

11.4. Baryon Magnetic Moment [H22]

Treatment of baryon magnetic moment is analogous to that for vector meson in Sec. 6.3. It has been done in [H9], in which two approximations had been made and the predicted values were about 1/3 of data. These two approximations are removed here and the factor 1/3 drops out; the results are now in approximate agreement with data.

11.4.1. Baryon Wave Equations and Electromagnetic Field

The ground state diquark-quark baryon wave equations (9.3.11) no longer applies if electromagnetic field is present. The interaction of electromagnetic field with the quarks depends upon the charges of the quarks; it is flavor dependent. Therefore, the merge of quarks III and I in (9.2.12) to form a diquark cannot be done if electromagnetic effect is to be accounted for. However, (9.2.1) has to be retained. Since the internal coordinates are on equal footing with the space time coordinates, z_{III} can also not be merged into z_I in (9.3.4). But (9.3.1) must be retained.

Incorporation of the electromagnetic field acting on the quarks is shown on the left of (2.3.11) or (6.1.9) (see also §6.1.3). The total baryon wave equations (9.3.9) are now generalized to become [H9 (5.1)],

$$\begin{aligned}&\left(\partial_I^{a\dot{b}}+iq_{op}(z)A^{a\dot{b}}(x_I)\right)\left(\partial_{III}^{g\dot{h}}+iq_{op}(v)A^{g\dot{h}}(x_{III})\right)\left(\partial_{II\dot{e}f}+iq_{op}(u)A_{\dot{e}f}(x_{II})\right)\times\\&\chi^{f}_{\{\dot{b}\dot{h}\}}(x_I,x_{III},x_{II})\xi^{psq}(z,v,u)\\&=-i\left(m_{3op}(z,v,u)+\Phi_b(x_I,x_{III},x_{II})\right)\psi_{\dot{e}}^{\{ag\}}(x_I,x_{III},x_{II})\xi^{psq}(z,v,u)\end{aligned} \tag{11.4.1a}$$

$$\begin{aligned}&\left(\partial_{I\dot{b}c}+iq_{op}(z)A_{\dot{b}c}(x_I)\right)\left(\partial_{III\dot{h}k}+iq_{op}(v)A_{\dot{h}k}(x_{III})\right)\left(\partial_{II}^{d\dot{e}}+iq_{op}(u)A^{d\dot{e}}(x_{II})\right)\times\\&\psi_{\dot{e}}^{\{ck\}}(x_I,x_{III},x_{II})\xi^{psq}(z,v,u)\\&=-i\left(m_{3op}(z,v,u)+\Phi_b(x_I,x_{III},x_{II})\right)\chi^{d}_{\{\dot{b}\dot{h}\}}(x_I,x_{III},x_{II})\xi^{psq}(z,v,u)\end{aligned} \tag{11.4.1b}$$

where q_{op} is the quarks charge operator (2.3.14).

Gauge invariance of (11.4.1) is shown in the same way as that for mesons in (6.3.1, 2) extended to include a third quark. For magnetic moment purposes, the external electromagnetic potential is static and has only spatial components. The time components of the three A fields in (11.4.1) can be gauged away by suitably choosing the phase functions $\varphi_I(x_I)$ and $\varphi_{II}(x_{II})$ in (6.3.2) together with an analogously defined $\varphi_{III}(x_{III})$. Thus,

$$A^{a\dot{b}}(x_I) = -\underline{\sigma}^{a\dot{b}}\,\underline{A}(\underline{x}_I),\quad A^{g\dot{h}}(x_{III}) = -\underline{\sigma}^{g\dot{h}}\,\underline{A}(\underline{x}_{III}),\quad A_{\dot{e}f}(x_{II}) = \underline{\sigma}_{\dot{e}f}\,\underline{A}(\underline{x}_{II}) \qquad (11.4.2)$$

11.4.2. Internal Baryon Wave Functions

The internal wave function (9.3.1) for the baryon octet is $\underline{8}_s$ of (9.3.3b) and can for instance be obtained by completing the construction of [C3 p71]. When normalized, these are [H9 (8.1)],

$$\xi(p) = \xi^{112} = \frac{1}{\sqrt{6}}\left(2z^1v^1u^2 - z^1v^2u^1 - z^2v^1u^1\right), \qquad \xi(n) = \xi^{221}$$
$$\xi(\Sigma^+) = \xi^{113},\quad \xi(\Sigma^-) = \xi^{223}, \qquad \xi(\Xi^0) = \xi^{331},\quad \xi(\Xi^-) = \xi^{332}$$
$$\xi(\Sigma^0) = \xi^{123} = \frac{1}{\sqrt{12}}\left(2z^1v^2u^3 + 2z^2v^1u^3 - z^2v^3u^1 - z^3v^2u^1 - z^1v^3u^2 - z^3v^1u^2\right)$$
$$\xi(\Lambda) = \xi_\Lambda^{123} = \frac{1}{2}\left(z^2v^3u^1 + z^3v^2u^1 - z^1v^3u^2 - z^3v^1u^2\right)$$
$$(11.4.3)$$

In the ground state, z_I=z and z_{III}=v merge according to (9.3.4) and (11.4.3) reduces to (9.3.18a, 20). The internal functions and operators in (11.4.1) can now be removed by multiplying it by ξ_{psq} and integrate over v_{zq}, v_{uq} and an analogously defined v_{vq}, as in (2.3.24), making use of (2.3.10). For the q_{op}'s, let

$$q_I = \int dv_{zq}dv_{uq}dv_{vq}\xi_{psq}(z,v,u)q_{op}(z)\xi^{psq}(z,v,u)$$
$$q_{III} = q_I \text{ with } q_{op}(z)\to q_{op}(v), \qquad q_{II} = q_I \text{ with } q_{op}(z)\to q_{op}(u)$$
$$(11.4.4)$$

using (2.3.14). For the octet in (11.4.3), (11.4.4) has been evaluated and tabulated in Table 11.5 below in which q_I+q_{II}+q_{III} is also the baryon charge.

11.4.3. Transformation into Laboratory and Relative Coordinates

Taking the left operator of (11.4.1b) and operating it on (11.4.1a) and using (11.4.1b, 2, 4) leads to

$$\begin{aligned}&\left\{\left(\partial_{I\dot{c}a}+iq_I\underline{\sigma}_{\dot{c}a}\underline{A}(\underline{x}_I)\right)\left(\partial_I^{a\dot{b}}-iq_I\underline{\sigma}^{a\dot{b}}\underline{A}(\underline{x}_I)\right)\right\}\left\{\begin{array}{l}\left(\partial_{III\dot{d}g}+iq_{III}\underline{\sigma}_{\dot{d}g}\underline{A}(\underline{x}_{III})\right)\\ \times\left(\partial_{III}^{g\dot{h}}-iq_{III}\underline{\sigma}^{g\dot{h}}\underline{A}(\underline{x}_{III})\right)\end{array}\right\}\\ &\times\left\{\left(\partial_{II}^{k\dot{e}}-iq_{II}\underline{\sigma}^{k\dot{e}}\underline{A}(\underline{x}_{II})\right)\left(\partial_{II\dot{e}f}+iq_{II}\underline{\sigma}_{\dot{e}f}\underline{A}(\underline{x}_{II})\right)\right\}\chi^{f}_{\{\dot{b}\dot{h}\}}(x_I,x_{III},x_{II})=\\ &=-\left(M_b^3+\Phi_b(r)\right)^2\chi^{k}_{\{\dot{c}\dot{d}\}}(x_I,x_{III},x_{II})+R_{B\{\dot{c}\dot{d}\}}^{\;\;k}(\psi,q)\end{aligned}\tag{11.4.5a}$$

$$R_{B\{\dot{c}\dot{d}\}}^{\;\;k}(\psi,q)=i\left[\begin{array}{l}\Phi_b(r),\ \left(\partial_{I\dot{c}a}+iq_I\underline{\sigma}_{\dot{c}a}\underline{A}(\underline{x}_I)\right)\\ \times\left(\partial_{III\dot{d}g}+iq_{III}\underline{\sigma}_{\dot{d}g}\underline{A}(\underline{x}_{III})\right)\left(\partial_{II}^{k\dot{e}}-iq_{II}\underline{\sigma}^{k\dot{e}}\underline{A}(\underline{x}_{II})\right)\end{array}\right]\psi_{\dot{e}}^{\{ag\}}(x_I,x_{III},x_{II})\tag{11.4.5b}$$

where $[A,B]=AB-BA$. Note that Φ_b for a free baryon and m_{3op} are not affected by the perturbative A fields and operate only on zeroth order wave functions in which the merges (9.2.12) and (9.3.4) have taken place. A sister pair of equations are obtained for ψ and $R_B(\chi,q)$ by reversing the roles of (11.4.1a) and (11.4.1b) in the process leading to (11.4.5), which is also the counterpart of (6.3.6, 7) for vector meson. In (11.4.5a), the three braced operators refer to different coordinates and therefore commute with each other.

The zeroth order part of (11.4.5) depends only upon the diquark coordinate x_I and the quark coordinate x_{II}. These have been transformed into a laboratory coordinate X and a quark-diquark relative coordinate x in (10.1.1) according to (3.1.3a). Here, all three coordinates enter; (3.1.3a) must be enlarged to include a third coordinate. Following [H9 (6.1, 4)], let

$$\begin{aligned}x^\mu&=x^\mu_{II}-x^\mu_{I,III}, & X^\mu&=(1-a_b)x^\mu_{I,III}+a_b x^\mu_{II}\\ y^\mu&=x^\mu_{III}-x^\mu_{I}, & x^\mu_{I,III}&=(1-c_b)x^\mu_{I}+c_b x^\mu_{III}\end{aligned}\tag{11.4.6}$$

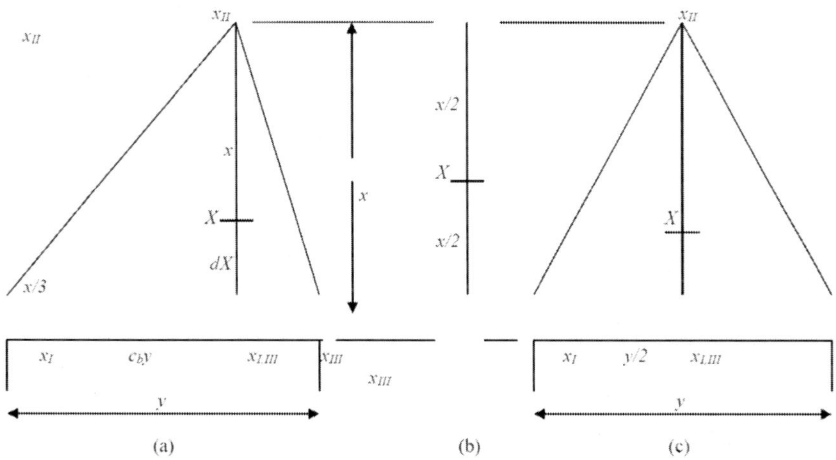

Figure 11.2. (a) illustrates the general (11.4.6), (b) the zeroth order quark-diquark configuration with x_I=x_{III}=$x_{I,III}$, a_b=1/2 used in (10.1.1) and (c) a special case of (a) with c_b=1/2 and a_b=1/3 giving a maximally allowed E_{Ib} in (11.4.14) below.

The relative energies in [H9 (6.4)] has been put to 0 in accordance with (5.7.1). Alternatively, (3.1.10a) type of relations can be used to remove them to arrive at (10.1.2). Further, a_b and c_b are constants like a_m in (3.1.3a), X is the laboratory coordinate of the baryon and x and y are the relative coordinates of the quarks shown in Figure 11.2a.

Instead of (3.1.4), (11.4.6) leads to

$$\begin{aligned}
\partial_I^{a\dot{b}} &= (1-a_b)(1-c_b)\left(-\delta^{a\dot{b}}\frac{\partial}{\partial X^0}-\underline{\sigma}^{a\dot{b}}\frac{\partial}{\partial \underline{X}}\right)+(1-c_b)\left(\delta^{a\dot{b}}\frac{\partial}{\partial x^0}+\underline{\sigma}^{a\dot{b}}\frac{\partial}{\partial \underline{x}}\right)\\
&\quad+\delta^{a\dot{b}}\frac{\partial}{\partial y^0}+\underline{\sigma}^{a\dot{b}}\frac{\partial}{\partial \underline{y}}\\
\partial_{III}^{g\dot{h}} &= (1-a_b)c_b\left(-\delta^{g\dot{h}}\frac{\partial}{\partial X^0}-\underline{\sigma}^{g\dot{h}}\frac{\partial}{\partial \underline{X}}\right)+c_b\left(\delta^{g\dot{h}}\frac{\partial}{\partial x^0}+\underline{\sigma}^{g\dot{h}}\frac{\partial}{\partial \underline{x}}\right)-\delta^{g\dot{h}}\frac{\partial}{\partial y^0}-\underline{\sigma}^{g\dot{h}}\frac{\partial}{\partial \underline{y}}\\
\partial_{II\dot{e}f} &= a_b\left(-\delta_{\dot{e}f}\frac{\partial}{\partial X^0}+\underline{\sigma}_{\dot{e}f}\frac{\partial}{\partial \underline{X}}\right)-\delta_{\dot{e}f}\frac{\partial}{\partial x^0}+\underline{\sigma}_{\dot{e}f}\frac{\partial}{\partial \underline{x}}
\end{aligned} \tag{11.4.7}$$

Let the external magnetic field $\underline{H}_{ex}$ be directed along the third axis, as in (6.3.4), and expand (11.4.2) around X, as in (6.3.5), we find

$$\begin{aligned}
&\underline{H}_{ex} = (0, 0, H_{ex}) = \frac{\partial}{\partial \underline{X}}\times \underline{A}(\underline{X}), \quad \underline{A}(\underline{X}) = H_{ex}\frac{1}{2}(-X^2, X^1, 0)+\frac{\partial}{\partial \underline{X}}\varphi_g(\underline{X})\\
&\underline{A}(\underline{x}_I) = \underline{A}(\underline{X})-a_b\underline{A}(\underline{x})-c_b\underline{A}(\underline{y}), \qquad \underline{A}(\underline{x}_{II}) = \underline{A}(\underline{X})+(1-a_b)\underline{A}(\underline{x})\\
&\underline{A}(\underline{x}_{III}) = \underline{A}(\underline{X})-a_b\underline{A}(\underline{x})+(1-c_b)\underline{A}(\underline{y})
\end{aligned} \tag{11.4.8}$$

where $\varphi_g(\underline{X})$ is a gauge function which is taken to be a constant below

11.4.4. First Order Relations and Magnetic Moment

Introduction of the external field $\underline{H}_{ex}$ will produce a perturbation of χ and ψ in (11.4.5) so that in terms of (11.4.6),

$$\begin{aligned}
&\chi^k_{\{\dot{c}\dot{d}\}}(X, x, y) \to \chi^k_{\{\dot{c}\dot{d}\}}(x, y)\exp(-iEX^0)\\
&\to \left(\chi^k_{0\{\dot{c}\dot{d}\}}(\underline{x})+\chi^k_{1\{\dot{c}\dot{d}\}}(\underline{x}, \underline{y})\right)\exp\left(-i(E_{1b}+E_0)X^0\right), \qquad \chi^k_{\{\dot{c}\dot{d}\}} \to \psi^{\{ag\}}_{\dot{e}}
\end{aligned} \tag{11.4.9}$$

where the subscripts 0 and 1 denote zeroth order and first order perturbation, respectively. x_0 and y_0 drop out owing to (11.4.8). X^0 and x associated with χ_0 and ψ_0 refer to Figure 11.2b; the latter enters the zeroth order (10.1.2). Insert (11.4.9) into (11.4.5) and employ (11.4.6-8). We wish to obtain the perturbed baryon energy E_{1b} as a function of the first order q´s there. With (11.4.6-9) and Figure 11.2a, the first order part of the first braces in (11.4.5a) reads

$$-2E_{1b}E_0(1-a_b)^2(1-c_b)^2\delta_{\dot c}^{\dot b}+q_I\sigma_{3\dot c}^{\dot b}H_{ex}+2i\delta_{\dot c}^{\dot b}q_I\underline{A}(\underline{x}_I)\frac{\partial}{\partial\underline{x}} \tag{11.4.10}$$

The zeroth order part of the remaining two braces in (11.4.5a) is found from (11.4.6) and Figure 11.2b and is

$$\delta_{\dot d}^{\dot h}\,\delta_f^k\,O_b,\qquad O_b=\left(\frac{E_0^2}{4}+\Delta\right)^2,\qquad \Delta=\left(\frac{\partial}{\partial\underline{x}}\right)^2 \tag{11.4.11}$$

The first order parts of the second and third braces in (11.4.5a) are analogously found; the associated zeroth order parts are of the same form as the last of (11.4.11). The first order part of (11.4.5) now reads

$$\begin{aligned}&\begin{bmatrix}-2E_{1b}E_0\left\{(1-a_b)^2(1-c_b)^2+(1-a_b)^2c_b^2+a_b^2\right\}O_b\chi_{0\{\dot c\dot d\}}^{k}(\underline{x})\\ +q_I\sigma_{3\dot c}{}^{\dot b}H_{ex}O_b\chi_{0\{\dot b\dot d\}}^{k}(\underline{x})+q_{III}\sigma_{3\dot d}{}^{\dot h}H_{ex}O_b\chi_{0\{\dot c\dot h\}}^{k}(\underline{x})+q_{II}\sigma_3{}^k{}_fH_{ex}O_b\chi_{0\{\dot c\dot d\}}^{f}(\underline{x})\end{bmatrix}\\ &\times\exp\left(-iEX^0\right)=-\begin{pmatrix}\partial_{I\dot ca}\partial_I^{a\dot b}\partial_{III\dot dg}\partial_{III}^{g\dot h}\partial_{II}^{k\dot e}\partial_{II\dot ef}\chi_{1\{\dot b\dot h\}}^{f}(\underline{x},\underline{y})\\ +\left(M_b^3+\Phi_b(r)\right)^2\chi_{1\{\dot c\dot d\}}^{k}(\underline{x},\underline{y})\end{pmatrix}\exp\left(-iEX^0\right)+R_{B1\{\dot c\dot d\}}^{\;k}(\psi_1,0)\\ &+R_{B1\{\dot c\dot d\}}^{\;k}(\psi_0,q)-2i\left[q_I\underline{A}(\underline{x}_I)+q_{III}\underline{A}(\underline{x}_{III})-q_{II}\underline{A}(\underline{x}_{II})\right]\frac{\partial}{\partial\underline{x}}O_b\chi_{0\{\dot c\dot d\}}^{k}(\underline{x})\exp\left(-iEX^0\right)\end{aligned} \tag{11.4.12}$$

where R_{BI} is the first order part of (11.4.5b). Some second order terms also enter here but can be dropped later.

Divide (11.4.12) by

$$O_b\chi_{\{\dot c\dot d\}}^{k}(\underline{x})\exp\left(-iEX^0\right) \tag{11.4.13}$$

its left side turns into constants for the c_b and a_b values to be employed in 11.4.14) below while its right side depends upon the relative coordinates x and y. Both sides must therefore be equal to the separation constants C_{s1} for the first case in (11.4.14) and C_{s2} for the second. An equivalent way is to move the Δ and $\Delta\Delta$ terms in O_b of (11.4.11) on the left side of (11.4.12) to its right side, keeping $(E_0/2)^4$ on the left side. As a first approximation, C_{s1} and C_{s2} are set to 0 to arrive at a unique solution.

Putting the right side of (11.4.12) to 0 leads to an equation for the first order $\chi_1(x,y)$ and $\psi_1(x,y)$ with the last two terms in (11.4.12) as source. A sister equation can be similarly found by taking the left operator of (11.4.1a) and operating it on (11.4.1b) instead of that used to obtain (11.4.5).

Putting the left side of (11.4.12) to 0 and choosing the spinor indices as follows leads to the equivalent of [H9 (7.3)],

$$O_b\left[-2E_{1b}E_0\left\{(1-a_b)^2(1-c_b)^2+(1-a_b)^2c_b^2+a_b^2\right\}\begin{pmatrix}\chi_{0\mathrm{i}}\\ \chi_{0\dot{2}}\end{pmatrix}+(q_I+q_{III}-q_{II})H_{ex}\begin{pmatrix}\chi_{0\mathrm{i}}\\ -\chi_{0\dot{2}}\end{pmatrix}\right]$$
$$=0,\qquad \chi_{0\mathrm{i}}=-\frac{3}{4}\chi^{2}_{0\{\mathrm{ii}\}}(\underline{x}),\qquad \chi_{0\dot{2}}=\frac{3}{4}\chi^{1}_{0\{\dot{2}\dot{2}\}}(\underline{x})$$
(11.4.14)

The χ_0´s are eigenfunctions of the $q\sigma_3$ operators in (11.4.12) and are splitted by them. Either the spin up wave functions (10.3.8a) or the spin up wave functions (10.3.8c) can be used. The space dependent part associated with O_b in (11.4.14) drops out, just like that in [H9 (4.5b)] or (6.3.12) for vector meson. The maximally allowed stationary energy shift E_{1b} is found for c_b=1/2 and a_b=1/3, same as [H9 (7.9)]. Let E_p be the proton mass, the baryon magnetic moment reads

$$\mu_b=\frac{E_{1b}}{H_{ex}}=\frac{E_p}{E_0}\frac{3}{e}(q_I+q_{III}-q_{II})\ \text{proton magneton} \qquad (11.4.15)$$

which is 3 times the 1994 result [H9 (7.10)] without neglect of quark motion beneath [H9 (8.3)]. The results are shown in Table 11.5 and are in approximate agreement with data.

Table 11.5. Octet baryon magnetic moments from (11.4.15) using the q's from (11.4.4). There is no data for Σ^0, only the transition magnetic moment $\Sigma^0\to\Lambda$

	proton	neutron	Λ	Σ^+	Σ^0	Σ^-	Ξ^0	Ξ^-
$q_I/e=q_{III}/e$	1/2	−1/6	−1/12	1/2	1/12	−1/3	−1/6	−1/3
q_{II}/e (11.4.3)	0	1/3	1/6	0	−1/6	−1/3	1/3	−1/3
μ_b (11.4.15)	3	−1.997	−0.841	2.367	0.787	−0.783	−1.427	−0.71
μ_b data	2.793	−1.913	−0.613	2.458	1.61($\Sigma^0\to\Lambda$)	−1.16	−1.25	−0.6507

It is conjectured that the differences between prediction and data on lines 4 and 5 are due to that the separation constants C_{s1} and C_{s2} are not 0 and depend upon Q_i and q_{II}.

Chapter 12

Neutron Decay and Possible Nonconservation of Angular Momentum

This chapter has been largely adapted from [H19]. The neutron life and the A(or B) asymmetry parameter are largely correctly predicted in §12.6.3 below starting from the equations of motion for baryons (9.3.16) via the first order radial wave equations (10.4.5) and their solutions in Table 11.1 and Figure 11.1b. These two predictions are the only measurable ones so far obtained from (9.3.16). Nevertheless, since they hardly can be any accidental coincidence, they support the validity of (9.3.16) and hence SSI.

12.1. Background

The present theory of nuclear β-decay is based upon the electro-weak part of the standard model [P1, B8]. The starting point is the four fermion point interaction Lagrangian density

$$L_F = -C_V\left(\overline{\psi}_p \gamma_\mu \psi_n\right)\left(\overline{\psi}_e \gamma_\mu \psi_\nu\right) \tag{12.1.1}$$

for neutron decay

$$n \to p + e^- + \overline{\nu} \tag{12.1.2}$$

first proposed by Fermi in 1934. Here C_ν is a constant. Subsequently, (12.1.1) has been generalized to the β-interaction Hamiltonian currently in use [K3 (13.9)],

$$H_W = \frac{1}{\sqrt{2}}\sum_i \int d^3\underline{X}\left(\psi_p O_i \psi_n\right)\left(C_i \overline{\psi}_e O_i \psi_\nu + C_i' \overline{\psi}_e O_i \gamma_5 \psi_\nu\right) + h.c. \tag{12.1.3}$$

Here, i refers to the scalar, vector, tensor, axial vector, and pseudoscalar interactions between the nucleon and lepton currents. The O_i's contain γ_μ and γ_5 and the C's are generally complex.

Based upon (12.1.3), lepton kinematics and conventional conservation laws, including angular momentum conservation, Jackson et al. [J3] derived in 1957 a number of decay rate formulae. The most frequently used one is

$$dW = \text{constant} \times d^3\underline{K}_e d^3\underline{K}_\nu \delta\left(E_e + E_\nu + E_p - E_n\right)$$
$$\times \xi\left[1 + a\frac{\underline{K}_e \underline{K}_\nu}{E_e E_\nu} + \frac{\langle \underline{J}_n \rangle}{J_n}\left(A\frac{\underline{K}_e}{E_e} + B\frac{\underline{K}_\nu}{E_\nu} + D\frac{\underline{K}_e \times \underline{K}_\nu}{E_e E_\nu} + R\frac{\underline{K}_e \times \underline{\sigma}_e}{E_e}\right) + \ldots\right] \tag{12.1.4}$$

in which the final spins have been summed over for a given initial neutron polarization $\langle \underline{J}_n \rangle$. Here, the K's denote momenta, E energy and $\underline{\sigma}_e$ the electron polarization. The constants a, A, B, D, R, and ξ depend upon the C's and the nucleon current consisting of a vector and an axial vector part in the so-called V-A theory. Experiments on neutron decay have since then largely been devoted to determine these constants in this 60 year old (12.1.4) and related formulae [L6, S8-S11 and references therein]. These have, however, yielded little physical insight into the decay mechanism.

The standard Hamiltonian (12.1.3) is a phenomenological model, not derivable from any first principles' theory. It treats nucleon as a point particle and hence ignores its quark structure. There are in principle 20 real C constants in (12.1.3), leaving the theory with little predictive power. This hints at a superfluousness of (12.1.3), which is not invariant under SU(2) gauge transformations. Such an invariance would give rise to an intermediate vector boson W which couples to a left-handed $\bar{\nu} e$ pair.

Therefore, despite its noble origin and general acceptance, this model (12.1.3) does not differ in principle from the large number of phenomenological models, constructed for different and narrow application angles, present in a vast body of literature.

Angular momentum conservation has not been established experimentally in free neutron decay. Most of the experiments make use of nuclei and the conclusion is that angular momentum is conserved. But a nucleus poses a highly complex, unsolved many body problem and experiments with it cannot lead to any firm conclusion on angular momentum conservation in free neutron decay.

In this chapter, free neutron decay will be treated using the equations of motion for doublet baryon and its development in Chapters 9-11, incorporating vector gauge fields of §7.1.2 and new tensor gauge fields. The results obtained, not reachable from (12.1.4), include a prediction of the life of the neutron in approximate agreement with data and a rather accurate prediction of the A or B asymmetry parameter.

The scalar strong interaction hadron theory SSI has been anchored on many data points in the meson sector in Chapters 5-8. The two contact points with data just mentioned together with Sec. 11.4 for the baryon magnetic moment lend further credibility of this theory also in the baryon sector, hence to this theory as a whole.

12.2. Introduction of Vector and Tensor Gauge Fields

12.2.1. Action-Like Integrals for Doublet Baryons

The starting point is the equation of motion for doublet baryons (10.0.1). Multiply (10.0.1a) from the left by $\chi_{0a}{}^*$ and (10.0.1b) by $-\psi_0^{\dot{b}*}$, subtract the resulting expressions from their complex conjugates and integrate over x_I and x_{II}, one obtains

$$S_\chi^{'} = \frac{1}{2i}\int dx_I^4 dx_{II}^4 \left(\chi_{0a}^{*}\partial_{II}^{f\dot{e}}\partial_I^{e\dot{h}}\partial_I^{a\dot{b}}\,\tfrac{1}{2}\chi_{\{\dot{b}\dot{h}\}f} + i\left(M_b^3 + \Phi_b\right)\chi_{0a}^{*}\psi_0^{a} - c.c.\right) \qquad (12.2.1)$$

$$S'_{\psi} = \frac{1}{2i} \int dx_I^4 dx_{II}^4 \left(-\psi_0^{*\dot{b}} \partial_{II\dot{e}h} \partial_{I\dot{h}k} \partial_{I\dot{b}c} \tfrac{1}{2} \psi^{\{ck\}\dot{e}} + i\left(M_b^3 + \Phi_b\right) \psi_0^{*\dot{b}} \chi_{0\dot{b}} - c.c. \right) \tag{12.2.2}$$

where * is an extra sign denoting complex conjugate. The positions of ∂_I and ∂_{II} have been changed so that the summations over the *e* and *h* indices conform to matrix multiplication convention and that the both ∂_I's appear next to each other to reflect that they operate on the diquark part indicated by the braces.

These integrals will not be varied with respect to χ_{0u}* and $\psi_0^{\dot{b}*}$ in an attempt to reproduce (10.0.1); handling of the last *c.c.* term and the necessary boundary conditions will require efforts beyond the scope of this chapter. Nor is such a variation necessary for the present purposes. If the solutions to (10.0.1) is inserted into (12.2.1-2), we obtain

$$S'_{\chi} \to S'_{\chi 0} = 0, \qquad S'_{\psi} \to S'_{\psi 0} = 0 \tag{12.2.3}$$

12.2.2. Nonminimal Substitution and Tensor Gauge Field

The minimal substitution of (7.1.4) led to the introduction of the vector gauge boson field W_I which is naturally associated with the vector part *V* of the V-A theory mentioned beneath (12.1.4). The axial vector part *A* is an asymmetrical part of a tensor *T*(*X*) which can be introduced by the following nonminimal substitution,

$$\begin{aligned} \partial_I^{e\dot{h}} \partial_I^{a\dot{b}} \chi_{\{\dot{h}\dot{b}\}f} &\to \partial_I^{e\dot{h}} \partial_I^{a\dot{b}} \chi_{\{\dot{h}\dot{b}\}f} \\ &+ \frac{i}{4} g \left[W^{e\dot{h}}(X) \partial_I^{a\dot{b}} + W^{a\dot{b}}(X) \partial_I^{e\dot{h}} + \frac{1}{2} T^{e\dot{h}a\dot{b}}(X) + \frac{i}{4} g W^{e\dot{h}}(X) W^{a\dot{b}}(X) \right] \chi_{\{\dot{b}\dot{h}\}f} \end{aligned} \tag{12.2.4}$$

$$\begin{aligned} \partial_{I\dot{h}k} \partial_{I\dot{b}c} \psi^{\{kc\}\dot{e}} &\to \partial_{I\dot{h}k} \partial_{I\dot{b}c} \psi^{\{kc\}\dot{e}} \\ &+ \frac{i}{4} g \left[W_{\dot{h}k}(X) \partial_{I\dot{b}c} + W_{\dot{b}c}(X) \partial_{I\dot{h}k} + \frac{1}{2} T_{\dot{h}k\dot{b}c}(X) + \frac{i}{4} g W_{\dot{h}k}(X) W_{\dot{b}c}(X) \right] \psi^{\{ck\}\dot{e}} \end{aligned} \tag{12.2.5}$$

Here, the subscript *I* in W_I of (7.1.5) has been dropped. The right side of (12.2.4) can readily be shown to be invariant under the U(1) gauge transformations

$$\begin{aligned} &W^{a\dot{b}}(X) \to W^{a\dot{b}}(X) - \partial_X^{a\dot{b}} \phi_s(X), \quad T^{e\dot{h}a\dot{b}}(X) \to T^{e\dot{h}a\dot{b}}(X) - \partial_X^{e\dot{h}} \partial_X^{a\dot{b}} \phi_s(X) \\ &\chi_{\{\dot{h}\dot{b}\}f} \to \chi_{\{\dot{h}\dot{b}\}f} \exp\left(\tfrac{i}{2} g \phi_s(X)\right) \end{aligned} \tag{12.2.6}$$

where $\phi_s(X)$ is a local phase and (7.1.4) has been consulted. The right side of (12.2.5) transforms analogously.

12.2.3. SU(3) Tensor Gauge Fields and Gauge Invariance

These expressions are now generalized to include SU(3) gauge fields analogous to (2.4.2, 3) and (7.1.4). Limiting ourselves to baryon doublets in (9.3.7b), (12.2.1-2) with (12.2.4-5) are generalized, with the sign of the tensor term changed in (12.2.5), to

$$S_\chi = \frac{1}{2i}\int dx_I^4 dx_{II}^4 \chi^*_{tp\,0a} \times$$
$$\left[\begin{array}{l} \left\{\partial_{II}^{f\dot e}\delta_{ps} + \frac{i}{4}g(\lambda_l)_{ps}W_l^{f\dot e}\right\} \\ \times\left\{\partial_I^{e\dot h}\partial_I^{a\dot b}\delta_{sq}\delta_{qr} + \frac{i}{4}g\left[\begin{array}{l}\delta_{sq}(\lambda_l)_{qr}W_l^{e\dot h}\partial_I^{a\dot b} + (\lambda_l)_{sq}W_l^{a\dot b}\delta_{qr}\partial_I^{e\dot h} + \frac{1}{2}(\lambda_l)_{sq}(\lambda_{l'})_{qr}T_{ll'}^{e\dot h a\dot b} \\ + \frac{i}{4}g\left\{(\lambda_l)_{sq}W_l^{e\dot h}\right\}\left\{(\lambda_{l'})_{qr}W_{l'}^{a\dot b}\right\}\end{array}\right]\right\}\chi_{rt\{\dot b\dot h\}f} \\ + i\left(M_b^3 + \Phi_b\right)(-2)\psi^a_{pt} - c.c. \end{array}\right]$$

(12.2.7)

$$S_\psi = \frac{1}{2i}\int dx_I^4 dx_{II}^4 (-)\psi^{*\dot b}_{tp\,0} \times$$
$$\left[\begin{array}{l} \left\{\partial_{II\,\dot e h}\delta_{ps} + \frac{i}{4}g(\lambda_l)_{ps}W_{l\,\dot e h}\right\} \\ \times\left\{\partial_{I\,\dot h k}\partial_{I\,\dot b c}\delta_{sq}\delta_{qr} + \frac{i}{4}g\left[\begin{array}{l}\delta_{sq}(\lambda_l)_{qr}W_{l\,\dot h k}\partial_{I\,\dot b c} + (\lambda_l)_{sq}W_{l\,\dot b c}\delta_{qr}\partial_{I\,\dot h k} - \frac{1}{2}(\lambda_l)_{sq}(\lambda_{l'})_{qr}T_{ll'\,\dot h k\dot b c} \\ + \frac{i}{4}g\left\{(\lambda_l)_{sq}W_{l\,\dot h k}\right\}\left\{(\lambda_{l'})_{qr}W_{l'\,\dot b c}\right\}\end{array}\right]\right\}\psi_{rt}^{\{\dot c k\}\dot e} \\ + i\left(M_b^3 + \Phi_b\right)2\chi_{pt\,0\dot b} - c.c. \end{array}\right]$$

(12.2.8)

Equation (12.2.7) is invariant with respect to the SU(3) gauge transformations (7.1.7), with the obvious replacement of the two meson indices by the three baryon indices associated with χ in (12.2.7), together with a generalization of the second of (12.2.6),

$$(\lambda_l)_{sq}(\lambda_{l'})_{qr}T_{ll'}^{e\dot h a\dot b}(X)\chi_{rt\{\dot b\dot h\}f} \to \left((\lambda_l)_{sq}(\lambda_{l'})_{qr}T_{ll'}^{e\dot h a\dot b}(X) + \frac{2i}{g}\left(\partial_X^{e\dot h}\partial_X^{a\dot b}U_{3sq}(X)\right)U_{3qr}^{-1}(X)\right)\chi_{rt\{\dot b\dot h\}f} \tag{12.2.9}$$

Analogously, the same invariance also holds for (12.2.8) with (12.2.9) replaced by

$$(\lambda_l)_{sq}(\lambda_{l'})_{qr}T_{ll'\dot h k\dot b c}(X)\psi_{rt}^{\{\dot c k\}\dot e} \to \left((\lambda_l)_{sq}(\lambda_{l'})_{qr}T_{ll'\dot h k\dot b c}(X) - \frac{2i}{g}\left(\partial_{X\dot h k}\partial_{X\dot b c}U_{3sq}(X)\right)U_{3qr}^{-1}(X)\right)\psi_{rt}^{\{\dot c k\}\dot e} \tag{12.2.10}$$

For application to neutron decay, only the SU(2) part of (7.1.4-5) is needed and l and l' run from 1 to 3. Apart from the flavor indices l and l', the tensor $T_{ll'}^{e\dot h a\dot b}$ has 16 components, 10 symmetrical and 6 asymmetrical, which in its turn is grouped into a vector E (electric field in electromagnetism) and an axial vector H (magnetic field), which is assigned to the axial vector A mentioned above (12.2.4). Identification of the tensor components corresponding to H has been given in [L1 §4-5] which are found by means of the invariant aymmetrical operator ε_{kl} of (B15). These are

$$T_{ll'}^{\dot{h}\dot{b}} = T_{ll'}^{e\dot{h}a\dot{b}} \varepsilon_{ea} = \frac{1}{2}\left(T_{ll'}^{\dot{h}\dot{b}21} - T_{ll'}^{\dot{h}\dot{b}12}\right)$$

$$T_{ll'}^{\{1\dot{2}\}} = T_{ll'}^{\{\dot{2}1\}} = 2iH_3, \qquad T_{ll'}^{\dot{1}\dot{1}} = -2i(H_1 + iH_2), \qquad T_{ll'}^{\dot{2}\dot{2}} = 2i(H_1 - iH_2) \tag{12.2.11}$$

The remaining 13 components of $T_{ll'}^{e\dot{h}a\dot{b}}$ do not enter here and are put to zero.

12.3. First Order Relations

The gauge boson and tensor field in (12.2.7-8) are decay products of the neutron whose wave functions now acquire a weak time dependence. Following (6.4.1) or (7.3.1), let the nucleon wave functions in (12.2.7-8) take the form

$$\chi_{\{\dot{b}\dot{h}\}f}(X,x) = \left(a_{op} + a_{op}^{(1)}(X^0)\right)\chi_{\{\dot{b}\dot{h}\}f}(\underline{x})\exp\left(-iEX^0 + i\underline{K}\,\underline{X}\right)$$

$$= \left(1 + \frac{a_{op}^{(1)}(X^0)}{a_{op}}\right)\chi_{0\{\dot{b}\dot{h}\}f}(X,x) = \chi_{0\{\dot{b}\dot{h}\}f}(\underline{x})\exp\left(-iEX^0 + i\underline{K}\,\underline{X}\right) + \chi_{1\{\dot{b}\dot{h}\}f}(X,x)$$

$$\chi \rightarrow \psi \tag{12.3.1}$$

where E is the energy, $\underline{K}$ the momentum, $a_{op}=1$, and $a_{op}^{(1)}(X^0)$ is a first order quantity varying slowly with time. Both can be elevated to operators in quantized case, as are described beneath (6.4.2). Ordering of these small quantities $a_{op}^{(1)}(X^0)$, g, W_l etc is the same as that in (7.3.2). The subscripts 0, 1 denote zeroth order and first order quantities, respectively.

Following the rudimentary quantization procedure of (6.4.12-15), let the initial and final states be denoted by

$$|i\rangle = |n(\underline{K}_n = 0)\rangle, \qquad \langle f| = \langle p(\underline{K}_p), W(E_W, \underline{K}_W), T(E_W, \underline{K}_W)| \tag{12.3.2}$$

respectively. n, p, W, T denote the neutron, proton, gauge boson, and tensor gauge field, respectively. Further,

$$\langle 0|i\rangle = \langle f|0\rangle = \langle f|i\rangle = 0, \qquad \langle 0|0\rangle = \langle i|i\rangle = \langle f|f\rangle = 1 \tag{12.3.3}$$

Let a_{op} in (12.3.1) and its Hermitian conjugate a_{op}^+ be elevated to annihilation and creation operators analogous to that mentioned below (6.4.2). Insert (12.3.1) into (12.2.7) and sandwich the resulting expression between <f| and |i>. There are two types of first order terms: i) those containing $a_{op}^{(1)}(X^0 \rightarrow \infty)$ and ii) those linear in gW and gT.

Carrying out integration over the time X^0 and employing (3.1.4) and (5.7.2), the type i) terms read

$$S_{fi}\int d^3\underline{X}\int d^4x\left\{-i\chi^*_{0a}(\underline{x})\left(\frac{E_n^2}{4}+\Delta\right)\chi_{0\dot{a}}(\underline{x})\right\},\quad S_{fi}=\left\langle f\left|a^+_{op}a^{(1)}_{op}\left(X^0\to\infty\right)\right|i\right\rangle \tag{12.3.4}$$

in which the *c.c.* term in (12.2.7) contributes equally. S_{fi} is the decay amplitude. Here, (9.2.7) has been used putting the quartet functions in (9.2.8) to zero. This leads to

$$\begin{aligned}&\chi_{\{1\dot{1}\}1}=\tfrac{4}{3}\chi_1,\quad \chi_{\{1\dot{2}\}2}=\tfrac{2}{3}\chi_1,\quad \chi_{\{2\dot{1}\}1}=\tfrac{2}{3}\chi_{\dot{2}},\quad \chi_{\{2\dot{2}\}2}=\tfrac{4}{3}\chi_{\dot{2}},\quad \chi_{\{1\dot{1}\}2}=\chi_{\{2\dot{2}\}1}=0\\ &\psi^{\{11\}\dot{1}}=-\tfrac{4}{3}\psi^1,\quad \psi^{\{12\}\dot{2}}=-\tfrac{2}{3}\psi^1,\quad \psi^{\{21\}\dot{1}}=-\tfrac{2}{3}\psi^2,\quad \psi^{\{22\}\dot{2}}=-\tfrac{4}{3}\psi^2,\quad \psi^{\{11\}\dot{2}}=\psi^{\{22\}\dot{1}}=0\end{aligned} \tag{12.3.5}$$

For the evaluation of the type ii) terms, the final state <f| in (12.3.2) will contain the gauge fields,

$$\begin{aligned}&\left(W_1^{a\dot{b}}(X)-iW_2^{a\dot{b}}(X)\right)/\sqrt{2}=W^{-a\dot{b}}(X)=W^{-0}\delta^{a\dot{b}}-\underline{\sigma}^{a\dot{b}}\underline{W}^-=w^{a\dot{b}}\exp\left(iE_WX^0-i\underline{K}_W\underline{X}\right)\\ &=\left(w_0\delta^{a\dot{b}}-\underline{\sigma}^{a\dot{b}}\underline{w}\right)\exp\left(iE_WX^0-i\underline{K}_W\underline{X}\right)\end{aligned} \tag{12.3.6}$$

$$\left(T_{13}^{eha\dot{b}}-T_{31}^{eha\dot{b}}+iT_{32}^{eha\dot{b}}-iT_{23}^{eha\dot{b}}\right)/\sqrt{2}=T^{eha\dot{b}}(X)=t^{eha\dot{b}}\exp\left(iE_WX^0-i\underline{K}_W\underline{X}\right) \tag{12.3.7}$$

where (7.1.4-5) limited to its SU(2) part has been consulted. The initial and final nucleon states in (12.3.2) will have a laboratory space time dependence of the form given in (12.3.1) with subscripts p for proton and n for neutron attached to the variables there. Here, use has been made of (9.3.7b) and of (9.3.18a) which gives tp=31 for proton and rt=23 for neutron in place for l, l' in T of (12.2.7). After summing over the flavor indices t, p, s, q, and r and carrying out the integration over X, the type ii) terms become

$$\begin{aligned}&\frac{g}{4\sqrt{2}}(2\pi)^4\delta\left(\underline{K}_p+\underline{K}_W\right)\delta\left(E_p+E_W-E_n\right)\times\\ &\int d^4x\left\{w_0\left[\chi^*_{p0a}(\underline{x})\left(-2\left(\frac{E_n^2}{4}+\Delta\right)-E_n^2\right)\chi_{n0\dot{a}}(\underline{x})+c.c.\right]-i\left[\chi^*_{p0a}(\underline{x})\partial^{f\dot{e}}_{II}t^{\dot{h}\dot{b}ea}\chi_{n0\{\dot{b}\dot{h}\}f}(\underline{x})+c.c.\right]\right\}\end{aligned} \tag{12.3.8}$$

where (12.3.5) has been used and E_W and K_W terms have been neglected because they are small relative to $|\partial_{,II}\chi|/|\chi|$. With (12.2.11), (12.3.7) and (B5), the 16 t's in (12.3.8) reduce similarly to three for an axial vector:

$$t^{\dot{h}\dot{b}} = t^{e\dot{h}a\dot{b}}\varepsilon_{ea} = \frac{1}{2}\left(t^{\dot{h}\dot{b}21} - t^{\dot{h}\dot{b}12}\right), \qquad t^{ea} = t^{e\dot{h}a\dot{b}}\varepsilon_{\dot{h}\dot{b}} = \frac{1}{2}\left(t^{ea\dot{2}\dot{1}} - t^{ea\dot{1}\dot{2}}\right)$$
$$t^{\dot{1}\dot{1}} = t^{22} = t_{\dot{2}\dot{2}} = t_{11}, \qquad t^{\dot{2}\dot{2}} = t^{11} = t_{\dot{1}\dot{1}} = t_{22}, \qquad t^{12} = t^{21} = -t^{\{\dot{1}\dot{2}\}} = t_{\{\dot{1}\dot{2}\}} = -t_{\{12\}}$$
$$T^{\dot{h}\dot{b}}(X) = t^{\dot{h}\dot{b}}\exp\left(iE_W X^0 - i\underline{K}_W \underline{X}\right), \qquad T^{ea}(X) = t^{ea}\exp\left(iE_W X^0 - i\underline{K}_W \underline{X}\right)$$

(12.3.9)

12.4. Decay Amplitude

The decay amplitude $S_{fi\chi}$ for the χ function is found by putting (12.3.4) to the negative of (12.3.8). Letting $\Omega = \int d^3\underline{X}$, the result is

$$S_{fi\chi} = -\frac{ig}{4\sqrt{2}}(2\pi)^4\delta\left(\underline{K}_p + \underline{K}_W\right)\delta\left(E_p + E_W - E_n\right)\times$$
$$\frac{\int d^3\underline{x}\left\{w_0\left[\chi^*_{p0a}(\underline{x})\left(-2\left(\frac{E_n^2}{4} + \Delta\right) - E_n^2\right)\chi_{n0\dot{a}}(\underline{x}) + c.c.\right] - i\left[\chi^*_{p0a}(\underline{x})\partial^{f\dot{e}}_{II}t^{\dot{h}bea}\chi_{n0\{\dot{b}\dot{h}\}f}(\underline{x}) + c.c.\right]\right\}}{\Omega\int d^3\underline{x}\left\{\chi^*_{0a}(\underline{x})\left(\frac{E_n^2}{4} + \Delta\right)\chi_{0\dot{a}}(\underline{x})\right\}}$$

(12.4.1)

In an analogous fashion, the decay amplitude $S_{fi\psi}$ for the ψ function is obtained from (12.2.8) and reads

$$S_{fi\psi} = -\frac{ig}{4\sqrt{2}}(2\pi)^4\delta\left(\underline{K}_p + \underline{K}_W\right)\delta\left(E_p + E_W - E_n\right)\times$$
$$\frac{\int d^3\underline{x}\left\{w_0\left[\psi^{*\dot{a}}_{p0}(\underline{x})\left(-2\left(\frac{E_n^2}{4} + \Delta\right) - E_n^2\right)\psi^a_{n0}(\underline{x}) + c.c.\right] + i\left[\psi^{*\dot{a}}_{p0}(\underline{x})\partial_{II\dot{e}d}t_{\dot{d}\dot{a}hb}\psi^{\{bh\}\dot{e}}_{n0}(\underline{x}) + c.c.\right]\right\}}{\Omega\int d^3\underline{x}\left\{\psi^{*\dot{a}}_0(\underline{x})\left(\frac{E_n^2}{4} + \Delta\right)\psi^a_0(\underline{x})\right\}}$$

(12.4.2)

The starred wave functions in nominators of (12.4.1-2) represent final states or proton, irrespective the nucleon labels; the *c.c.* terms will turn out to contribute equally and can be dropped together with an overall factor 2 multiplying the right of (12.4.1-2). The wave functions in denominators of (12.4.1-2) are those of the initial neutron, as <f| has been included in S_{fi} of (12.3.4).

The proton may have a different *m* or spin value in (10.3.8) relative to that pertaining to the initial neutron in (12.4.1-2). There are four combinations which are denoted by

$$\begin{array}{lcccc} \text{neutron} & m=\frac{1}{2} & \frac{1}{2} & -\frac{1}{2} & -\frac{1}{2} \\ \text{proton} & m=\frac{1}{2} & -\frac{1}{2} & \frac{1}{2} & -\frac{1}{2} \\ \text{notation} & F+ & GT+ & GT- & F- \end{array} \tag{12.4.3}$$

As there are two equally correct solutions (10.3.8a-8b) and (10.3.8c-8d), (12.3.4) and (12.3.8) are to be averaged over these two equally probable solutions. The averaging will turn out to not affect (12.3.4) so that it can be carried out for $S_{fi\chi}$ and $S_{fi\psi}$ of (12.4.1-2) directly to obtain $S_{fi\chi av}$ and $S_{fi\psi av}$. It removes terms containing $f_0(r)g_0(r)$ or their derivatives that will appear in (12.4.1-2) after application of (10.3.8a-8b) or (10.3.8c-8d) and (12.4.3). Such terms will for instance differentiate between neutron spin up and spin down decay rates contrary to the measured A asymmetry coefficient [P1]. Inserting (10.3.8a-8b) and (10.3.8c-8d) into (12.4.1) and (12.4.2) for the four combinations of (12.4.3), making use of (3.1.4) and (5.7.2) for ∂_{II}, summing over the spinor indices, employing (12.3.9), and integrating over the angles ϑ and ϕ in the relative space, one finds that the both averaged decay amplitudes $S_{fi\chi av}$ and $S_{fi\psi av}$ are the same, as may be expected from the symmetry between the χ part (12.2.7) and the ψ part (12.2.8);

$$S_{fi\chi av}=S_{fi\psi av}=\begin{pmatrix} S_{fiF+} \\ S_{fiGT+} \\ S_{fiGT-} \\ S_{fiF-} \end{pmatrix}=-i\frac{g}{2\sqrt{2}}\frac{(2\pi)^4}{\Omega}\delta(E_p+E_W-E_n)\delta(\underline{K}_p+\underline{K}_W)\frac{1}{N_{dr}}$$

$$\times\left[-2w_0\left(N_{dr}+E_n^2\left(I_{g0}+I_{f0}\right)\right)\begin{pmatrix}1\\0\\0\\1\end{pmatrix}-i\frac{2}{3}E_n\left(I_{g0}-\frac{I_{f0}}{3}\right)\begin{pmatrix}t^{\{12\}}\\-t^{22}\\t^{11}\\-t^{\{12\}}\end{pmatrix}\right] \tag{12.4.4}$$

$$I_{g0}=\int_0^\infty drr^2g_0^2(r),\quad I_{f0}=\int_0^\infty drr^2f_0^2(r),\quad I_{g00}=\int_0^\infty drr^2g_{00}^2(r),\quad I_{f00}=\int_0^\infty drr^2f_{00}^2(r) \tag{12.4.5}$$

where N_{dr} is given by (10.3.9b) and g_{00} and f_{00}. are defined (10.3.14).

12.5. Expressions for Vector and Tensor Gauge Fields

12.5.1. Mass Generation of *W* Boson via Virtual *π0*

In the analogous meson case, the pion beta decay $\pi^+\to\pi^0e^+\nu_e$ of §7.4.5, the gauge boson W_I decays into a pair of leptons, as is seen in (7.4.27). The mass of the W_I boson comes from the $(gW_I)^2$ terms in the meson action integral S_{m3} (7.1.8) via (7.4.4) and (7.4.6b) and is generated by the integral of the |pion wave functions|^2 over the relative space x. It can be seen from (7.4.3a, 4) that the energy of pion does not enter and can be zero. In this case, the pion is virtual.

In the corresponding action-like integrals S_χ and S_ψ of (12.2.7-8), there is no such $(gW_I)^2$ mass term, only terms of the form $(gW_I)(g\partial_{,II}W_I)$. Therefore, the gauge boson W_I from neutron decay cannot decay into a pair of leptons via the integrals (12.2.7-8) for neutrons.

The interpretation of this situation is that gauge boson W_I in the neutron case here decays into a pair of leptons via a virtual π^0 action as has been considered at the end of §7.6.2 and employed earlier for muon decay in §7.6.4 4). In the pion beta decay, the W_I is positively charged and decays into a lepton pair via (7.4.10). In neutron decay, the W_I or W is negatively charged and W_I^- in (7.4.5) is replaced by W_I^+ so that (7.4.5) and (7.4.6a), neglecting the first three terms there and noting (7.4.10), are modified to

$$\frac{M_W^2}{2}W_I^{-b\dot{a}}=\frac{M_W^2}{2}\begin{pmatrix}W_0-W_3 & -W_1+iW_2\\ -W_1-iW_2 & W_0+W_3\end{pmatrix}=\delta S_L/\delta W_I^{+a\dot{b}}$$
$$=\frac{g}{2\sqrt{2}}\psi_{L\dot{b}}^{(+)}\psi_{\nu La}^{(-)}=\frac{g}{2\sqrt{2}}\begin{pmatrix}\psi_{L\dot{1}}^{(+)}\psi_{\nu L1}^{(-)} & \psi_{L\dot{1}}^{(+)}\psi_{\nu L2}^{(-)}\\ \psi_{L\dot{2}}^{(+)}\psi_{\nu L1}^{(-)} & \psi_{L\dot{2}}^{(+)}\psi_{\nu L2}^{(-)}\end{pmatrix} \tag{12.5.1}$$

where the gauge boson mass is given by (7.4.6b) and (7.4.9).

12.5.2. Variation of the Total Action for Neutron Decay

Having found an expression for w_0 in (12.4.4) from (12.5.1) via (12.3.6), expressions for the other unknowns t^{ab} there will be obtained in this and the next paragraph. The vector gauge boson fields (12.5.1) was found by varying the total action (7.1.1), after removing its last term, with respect to W^- in §7.4.2. For neutron decay, the meson action S_{m3} in (7.1.1) is to be replaced by the corresponding baryons actions (12.2.7-8), $S_\chi \pm S_\psi$, and the vector gauge boson action S_{GB} be replaced by a gauge boson-tensor field action S_{GBT}. Equation (7.1.1) is here replaced by

$$S_{Tn}=S_{GBT}+\kappa_b\left(S_{\chi av}-S_{\psi av}\right)+S_L+S_{Lm} \tag{12.5.2}$$

Here, the lepton actions S_L+S_{Lm} are the same as those in (7.1.13,16). κ_b is a dimensionless coupling constant that, for instance, signifies that the action-like baryon integrals S_χ and S_ψ differ basically from the meson action S_{m3} in (7.1.1) in that the normalization of the wave function amplitudes are different. $S_{\chi av}(S_{\psi av})$ denotes that $S_\chi(S_\psi)$ has been averaged over the both equally probable solutions (10.3.8a-8b) and (10.3.8c-8d) for the baryon wave functions that enter it, just like that $S_{fi\chi}$ and $S_{fi\psi}$ of (12.4.1-2) have been averaged to $S_{fi\chi av}$ and $S_{fi\psi av}$ in (12.4.4).

The – sign in (12.5.2) is chosen because (12.5.2) will lead to an expression for t^{ab} in (12.4.4); if this sign is replaced by +, the needed (12.5.3) below will vanish. Further, this – sign will remove terms linear in gW, as is implied by $S_{fi\chi av}-S_{fi\psi av}=0$ from (12.4.4). This will cause $S_{\chi av}-S_{\psi av}$ in (12.5.2) to possess $(gW)^2$ terms, apart from the t^{ab} terms, to that order and render it to have an extremum when solutions near the correct ones are inserted into $S_{\chi av}-S_{\psi av}$.

Unlike S_{GB} in (7.1.2) given by (7.1.2), S_{GBT} in (12.5.2) is unknown. If the tensor gauge field is to have an equation of motion like that for the gauge boson (7.4.6), S_{GBT} is expected to contain terms of the form $(\partial_X W)(\partial_X T)$. Physical existence and interpretation of the tensor gauge field are not known and will be left to eventual future work. For the present purpose, it is sufficient to obtain an expression for t^{ab} from (12.5.2) for use in (12.4.4).

Follow the steps of §7.4.2 and vary (12.5.2) with respect to $W_I^{+a\dot{b}}$. The unknown S_{GBT} is expected to give rise to energy-momentum terms of the form $(\partial_X^2 T)$ corresponding to the first terms on the left of (7.4.6a), which have been neglected because they are much smaller than the gauge boson mass term that follows them in (7.4.6a). Similarly, the obtained $(\partial_X^2 T)$ terms can also be dropped on the same ground so the exact but unknown form of S_{GBT} is of no concern here. Variation of the S_L+S_{Lm} terms in (12.5.2) with respect to $W_I^{+a\dot{b}}$ is analogous to that given by (7.4.5) and leads to (12.5.1).

12.5.3. Expressions for Tensor and Vector Gauge Fields

Variation of $S_{\chi av}-S_{\psi av}$ in (12.5.2) with respect to $W_I^{+a\dot{b}}$ is limited to terms of order g^2. When evaluating the average $S_{\chi av}(S_{\psi av})$ using (10.3.8a-8b) and (10.3.8c-8d), it is practically sufficient to use one of them, for instance (10.3.8a-8b) for $S_\chi(S_\psi)$ of (12.2.7-8), and drop the $f_0(r)g_0(r)$ terms, as was mentioned beneath (12.4.3).

In the evaluation of (12.2.7-8), use is made of (12.3.1), (12.3.5), (3.1.4), (5.7.2). When summing over the flavor indices t, p, s, q, and r, tp=32 and rt=23 for neutron and (12.3.6-7) ff are employed. Carrying out the angular integrations, one finds

$$\frac{\delta\kappa_b\left(S_{\chi av}-S_{\psi av}\right)}{\delta W^{+a\dot{b}}}\rightarrow U_{\dot{b}a}=\begin{pmatrix} U_0+U_3 & U_1-iU_2 \\ U_1+iU_2 & U_0-U_3 \end{pmatrix} \tag{12.5.3}$$

$$U_0=\frac{\kappa_b g^2}{96}E_n\tau_0\left(I_{g0}-\frac{1}{3}I_{f0}\right)7W_3^-(X)\begin{pmatrix} 1 \\ -1 \end{pmatrix}=-\frac{g}{4\sqrt{2}}\left(\psi_{L\dot{1}}^{(+)}\psi_{\nu L1}^{(-)}+\psi_{L\dot{2}}^{(+)}\psi_{\nu L2}^{(-)}\right) \tag{12.5.4}$$

$$U_3=-\frac{\kappa_b g^2}{96}E_n\tau_0\left(I_{g0}-\frac{1}{3}I_{f0}\right)3W_0^-\begin{pmatrix} 1 \\ -1 \end{pmatrix}-i\frac{\kappa_b g^2}{24}\tau_0\left(I_{g0}+I_{f0}\right)T^{12}(X)\begin{pmatrix} 1 \\ 1 \end{pmatrix}=-\frac{g}{4\sqrt{2}}\left(\psi_{L\dot{1}}^{(+)}\psi_{\nu L1}^{(-)}-\psi_{L\dot{2}}^{(+)}\psi_{\nu L2}^{(-)}\right) \tag{12.5.5}$$

$$U_1-iU_2=-i\frac{\kappa_b g^2}{24}\tau_0\left(-T^{11}\right)(X)\begin{pmatrix} 2I_{f0}/3 \\ I_{g0}+I_{f0}/3 \end{pmatrix}=-\frac{g}{4\sqrt{2}}\psi_{L\dot{1}}^{(+)}\psi_{\nu L2}^{(-)} \tag{12.5.6}$$

$$U_1+iU_2=-i\frac{\kappa_b g^2}{24}\tau_0 T^{22}(X)\begin{pmatrix} I_{g0}+I_{f0}/3 \\ 2I_{f0}/3 \end{pmatrix}=-\frac{g}{4\sqrt{2}}\psi_{L\dot{2}}^{(+)}\psi_{\nu L1}^{(-)},\quad \tau_0=\int dx^0 \tag{12.5.7}$$

where the upper and lower rows in the U's refer to neutron spin up m=1/2 and spin down m=–1/2, respectively, in (10.3.8). Further, (12.5.3) has been equated to the negative of (12.5.1) as is prescribed in (12.5.2). Note that U_0 in (12.5.4) does not contain W_0, which however enters (12.5.1) and stems from the virtual π^0 action in (7.4.4).

Comparing the X dependence of W's, T's and the ψ's in (12.5.4-7) via (12.3.6, 9) and (7.4.19) and replacing L and νL there by e and ν, respectively, we find

$$E_W = E_\nu + E_e^{(+)}, \qquad \underline{K}_W = \underline{K}_e^{(+)} - \underline{K}_\nu \tag{12.5.8}$$

Removing the X dependence in (12.5.4-7) and observing (7.4.6b) and (12.3.6, 9), we obtain

$$0 = \frac{1}{M_W^2 \Omega}\frac{g}{4\sqrt{2\Omega_\nu \Omega_e}}\left(u_{L1}^{(+)}u_{\nu L1}^{(-)} + u_{L2}^{(+)}u_{\nu L2}^{(-)}\right) + \frac{7}{96}E_n\left(I_{g0} - I_{f0}/3\right)\kappa_b w_3\begin{pmatrix}1\\-1\end{pmatrix} \tag{12.5.9}$$

$$t^{\{12\}} = -i\frac{24}{M_W^2\Omega\left(I_{g0}+I_{f0}\right)}\frac{g}{4\sqrt{2\Omega_\nu\Omega_e}}\left(u_{L1}^{(+)}u_{\nu L1}^{(-)} - u_{L2}^{(+)}u_{\nu L2}^{(-)}\right) + i\frac{3}{4}E_n\frac{\left(I_{g0}-I_{f0}/3\right)}{\left(I_{g0}+I_{f0}\right)}\kappa_b w_0\begin{pmatrix}1\\-1\end{pmatrix} \tag{12.5.10a}$$

$$-t^{11}\kappa_b\begin{pmatrix}2I_{f0}/3\\ I_{g0}+I_{f0}/3\end{pmatrix} = -i\frac{24}{M_W^2\Omega}\frac{g}{4\sqrt{2\Omega_\nu\Omega_e}}u_{L1}^{(+)}u_{\nu L2}^{(-)}$$

$$t^{22}\kappa_b\begin{pmatrix}I_{g0}+I_{f0}/3\\ 2I_{f0}/3\end{pmatrix} = -i\frac{24}{M_W^2\Omega}\frac{g}{4\sqrt{2\Omega_\nu\Omega_e}}u_{L2}^{(+)}u_{\nu L1}^{(-)} \tag{12.5.10b}$$

The w's in (12.3.6) are similarly found from (12.5.1) and read

$$w_0 = \frac{1}{M_W^2}\frac{g}{2\sqrt{2\Omega_\nu\Omega_e}}\left(u_{L1}^{(+)}u_{\nu L1}^{(-)} + u_{L2}^{(+)}u_{\nu L2}^{(-)}\right), \quad w_3 = \frac{1}{M_W^2}\frac{g}{2\sqrt{2\Omega_\nu\Omega_e}}\left(u_{L1}^{(+)}u_{\nu L1}^{(-)} - u_{L2}^{(+)}u_{\nu L2}^{(-)}\right) \tag{12.5.11}$$

12.5.4. Decay Amplitude as Function of Lepton Wave Functions

Equations (12.5.9-11) can now be inserted into (12.4.4). Here, it is noted that the neutron spin is up or m=1/2 for the upper two amplitudes corresponding to the upper case in (12.5.9-10) and down or m=–1/2 for the lower two amplitudes corresponding to the lower case in (12.5.9-10). Thus, the w_0 in the third component of a triplet (12.5.5, 10a) become a singlet to be combined to the w_0 in (12.5.11). Analogously, the singlet (12.5.9), when inserted into (12.4.4) becomes the third component of a triplet to be combined with (12.5.10a). Effectively, the $7W_3$ in (12.5.4) and $3W_0$ in (12.5.5) switch place after insertion into (12.4.4). These two terms are not the dominating ones but will lead to corrections given by the two c's(< 0.4 or so) in (12.5.16) below. The resulting decay amplitude, noting (12.5.8) and (12.4.5), reads

$$S_{fi} = \begin{pmatrix} S_{fiF+} \\ S_{fiGT+} \\ S_{fiGT-} \\ S_{fiF-} \end{pmatrix} = i\frac{g^2}{8}\frac{1}{M_W^2}\frac{(2\pi)^4}{\Omega\sqrt{\Omega_v\Omega_e}}\delta\left(E_p + E_v + E_e^{(+)} - E_n\right)\delta\left(\underline{K}_p + \underline{K}_e^{(+)} - \underline{K}_v\right)\frac{1}{N_{dr}}$$

$$\times \begin{bmatrix} b_{F+0} & 0 & 0 & b_{F+3} \\ 0 & b_{GT+p} & 0 & 0 \\ 0 & 0 & b_{GT-m} & 0 \\ b_{F-0} & 0 & 0 & b_{F-3} \end{bmatrix} \begin{pmatrix} \left(u_{L\dot{1}}^{(+)}u_{vL1}^{(-)} + u_{L\dot{2}}^{(+)}u_{vL2}^{(-)}\right) \\ u_{L\dot{2}}^{(+)}u_{vL1}^{(-)} \\ u_{L\dot{1}}^{(+)}u_{vL2}^{(-)} \\ \left(u_{L\dot{1}}^{(+)}u_{vL1}^{(-)} - u_{L\dot{2}}^{(+)}u_{vL2}^{(-)}\right) \end{pmatrix} \tag{12.5.12}$$

$$b_{F+0} = b_{F-0} = -2\left(N_{dr} + E_n^2\left(I_{g0} + I_{f0}\right)\right)\frac{1}{1 + c_{F0}} \tag{12.5.13}$$

$$b_{F+3} = -b_{F-3} = -\frac{8E_n}{\kappa_b}\frac{\left(I_{g0} - I_{f0}/3\right)}{a_g^2\left(I_{g00} + I_{f00}\right)}\left(1 + c_{F3}\right) \tag{12.5.14}$$

$$b_{GT+p} = b_{GT-m} = b_{GT} = \frac{16E_n}{\kappa_b}\frac{\left(I_{g0} - I_{f0}/3\right)}{a_g^2\left(I_{g0} + I_{f0}/3\right)} \tag{12.5.15}$$

$$c_{F0} = \frac{1}{16}E_n\kappa_b a_g^2\left(I_{g00} - I_{f00}/3\right), \qquad c_{F3} = \frac{7}{48}E_n a_g^2\left(I_{g00} - I_{f00}/3\right) \tag{12.5.16}$$

Because κ_b in (12.5.2) can be incorporated into the wave functions χ and ψ, it can be absorbed into the normalization condition (10.3.13) by choosing a different normalization constant or equivalently a different normalized amplitude a_g given in (10.3.14).

12.6. Decay Rate, *A* and *B* Parameters and Mean Interquark Distance

12.6.1. Decay Rate

As in (7.5.1), the decay rate is

$$\Gamma = \sum\nolimits_{\text{finalstates}}\left|S_{fi}\right|^2 / T_d \tag{12.6.1}$$

where T_d is a long decay time. The subscript "final states" refers to the four final lepton spin states and all possible momenta of the proton, electron and antineutrino, like that in (7.5.2). The decay rates are

$$\begin{pmatrix}\Gamma_{F\pm}\\ \Gamma_{GT\pm}\end{pmatrix}=\frac{\Omega\Omega_e\Omega_\nu}{(2\pi)^9}\int d^3\underline{K}_p\int d^3\underline{K}_e\int d^3\underline{K}_\nu\frac{1}{T_d}\sum\nolimits_{\text{espins}}\sum\nolimits_{\nu\text{spins}}\begin{pmatrix}\left|S_{fiF\pm}\right|^2\\ \left|S_{fiGT\pm}\right|^2\end{pmatrix} \tag{12.6.2}$$

The square of S_{fi} contains squares of the δ functions in (12.5.12), which are "linearized" by (7.5.6) type of formula. Following the common approach, integration over the recoil momenta $\underline{K}_p$ in (12.6.2) is carried out first. By (12.5.8), this gives $\underline{K}_p=\underline{K}_\nu-\underline{K}_e$, where the superscript (+) has been dropped. Introduce

$$\underline{K}_\nu=K_\nu(k_{\nu1},\,k_{\nu2},\,k_{\nu3}),\qquad k_{\nu\pm}=k_{\nu1}\pm ik_{\nu2}=\sin\vartheta_n\exp(\pm i\phi_\nu),\qquad k_{\nu3}=\cos\vartheta_\nu$$
$$K_{e\pm}=K_{e1}\pm iK_{e2}=K_e\sin\vartheta_e\exp(\pm i\phi_e),\qquad K_{e3}=K_e\cos\vartheta_e \tag{12.6.3}$$

These and (12.5.12) are inserted into the decay rate expression (12.6.2) to produce

$$\begin{pmatrix}\Gamma_{F\pm}\\ \Gamma_{GT\pm}\end{pmatrix}=\frac{g^4}{8192\pi^5M_W^4N_{dr}^2}\int dK_eK_e^2\int dK_\nu K_\nu^2\delta(E_p+E_e+E_\nu-E_n)\left(1+\frac{m_e}{E_e}\right)\begin{pmatrix}I_{F\pm}\\ I_{GT\pm}\end{pmatrix} \tag{12.6.4}$$

$$\begin{pmatrix}I_{F\pm}\\ I_{GT\pm}\end{pmatrix}=\int d\vartheta_e\sin\vartheta_e d\phi_e\int d\vartheta_\nu\sin\vartheta_\nu d\phi_\nu\sum\nolimits_{\text{espins}}\sum\nolimits_{\nu\text{spins}}\begin{pmatrix}i_{F\pm}\\ i_{GT\pm}\end{pmatrix} \tag{12.6.5}$$

$$\sum\nolimits_{\text{espins}}\sum\nolimits_{\nu\text{spins}}(i_{F\pm})=i_{F\pm\uparrow\uparrow}+i_{F\pm\uparrow\downarrow}+i_{F\pm\downarrow\uparrow}+i_{F\pm\downarrow\downarrow} \tag{12.6.6}$$

$$\sum\nolimits_{\text{espins}}\sum\nolimits_{\nu\text{spins}}(i_{GT\pm})=i_{GT\pm\uparrow\uparrow}+i_{GT\pm\uparrow\downarrow}+i_{GT\pm\downarrow\uparrow}+i_{GT\pm\downarrow\downarrow} \tag{12.6.7}$$

where both arrows denote the spin directions, separated by the commas in (7.4.19), of the electron and the antineutrino and

$$i_{F\pm\uparrow\uparrow}=\left|(-b_{F\pm0}+b_{F\pm3})\left(1-\frac{K_{e3}}{E_e+m_e}\right)k_{\nu-}+(b_{F\pm0}+b_{F\pm3})\frac{K_{e-}}{E_e+m_e}(1-k_{\nu3})\right|^2 \tag{12.6.8a}$$

$$i_{F\pm\uparrow\downarrow}=\left|(b_{F\pm0}-b_{F\pm3})\left(1-\frac{K_{e3}}{E_e+m_e}\right)(1+k_{\nu3})+(-b_{F\pm0}-b_{F\pm3})\frac{K_{e-}}{E_e+m_e}k_{\nu+}\right|^2 \tag{12.6.8b}$$

$$i_{F\pm\downarrow\uparrow}=\left|(-b_{F\pm0}-b_{F\pm3})\left(1+\frac{K_{e3}}{E_e+m_e}\right)(1-k_{\nu3})+(b_{F\pm0}-b_{F\pm3})\frac{K_{e+}}{E_e+m_e}k_{\nu-}\right|^2 \tag{12.6.8c}$$

$$i_{F\pm\downarrow\downarrow}=\left|(b_{F\pm0}+b_{F\pm3})\left(1+\frac{K_{e3}}{E_e+m_e}\right)k_{v+}+(-b_{F\pm0}+b_{F\pm3})\frac{K_{e+}}{E_e+m_e}(1+k_{v3})\right|^2 \tag{12.6.8d}$$

$$i_{GT+\uparrow\uparrow}=\left|(b_{GT+p})\left(1-\frac{K_{e3}}{E_e+m_e}\right)(1-k_{v3})\right|^2,\quad i_{GT-\uparrow\uparrow}=\left|(-b_{GT-m})\frac{K_{e-}}{E_e+m_e}k_{v-}\right|^2 \tag{12.6.9a}$$

$$i_{GT+\uparrow\downarrow}=\left|(-b_{GT+p})\left(1-\frac{K_{e3}}{E_e+m_e}\right)k_{v+}\right|^2,\quad i_{GT-\uparrow\downarrow}=\left|(b_{GT-m})\frac{K_{e-}}{E_e+m_e}(1+k_{v3})\right|^2 \tag{12.6.9b}$$

$$i_{GT+\downarrow\uparrow}=\left|(-b_{GT+p})\frac{K_{e+}}{E_e+m_e}(1-k_{v3})\right|^2,\quad i_{GT-\downarrow\uparrow}=\left|(b_{GT-m})\left(1+\frac{K_{e3}}{E_e+m_e}\right)k_{v-}\right|^2 \tag{12.6.9c}$$

$$i_{GT+\downarrow\downarrow}=\left|(b_{GT+p})\frac{K_{e+}}{E_e+m_e}k_{v+}\right|^2,\quad i_{GT-\downarrow\downarrow}=\left|(-b_{GT-m})\left(1+\frac{K_{e3}}{E_e+m_e}\right)(1+k_{v3})\right|^2 \tag{12.6.9d}$$

Let

$$\Delta_m=E_n-E_p\approx m_n-m_p=1.2933\text{ Mev} \tag{12.6.10}$$

Equation (12.6.5) can now be evaluated using (12.6.8-9), and (12.6.3). Carrying out the angular integrations, it is found that the cross terms in (12.6.8) drop out and one finds

$$\begin{pmatrix}I_{F\pm}\\ I_{GT\pm}\end{pmatrix}=4\pi^2\begin{pmatrix}2b_{F\pm0}^2+2b_{F\pm3}^2\\ b_{GT}^2\end{pmatrix}\frac{16E_e}{E_e+m_e} \tag{12.6.11}$$

which is independent of the antineutrino energy $E_\nu=K_\nu$. Carrying out the K_ν integration in (12.6.4) using (12.6.10), one gets

$$\int dK_\nu K_\nu^2\delta(E_p+E_e+E_\nu-E_n)\begin{pmatrix}I_{F\pm}\\ I_{GT\pm}\end{pmatrix}=(\Delta-E_e)^2\begin{pmatrix}I_{F\pm}\\ I_{GT\pm}\end{pmatrix} \tag{12.6.12}$$

where $0\le K_\nu\le\Delta-E_e$. Inserting (12.6.11-12) into (12.6.4), changing the variable dK_eK_e to dE_eE_e and noting (12.5.13-15) leads to

$$\begin{pmatrix}\Gamma_{F\pm}\\ \Gamma_{GT\pm}\end{pmatrix}=\begin{pmatrix}\Gamma_F\\ \Gamma_{GT}\end{pmatrix}=\frac{1}{128\pi^3}\frac{g^4}{M_W^4}\frac{1}{N_{dr}^2}\int dE_eP_F(E_e)\begin{pmatrix}2b_{F\pm0}^2+2b_{F\pm3}^2\\ b_{GT}^2\end{pmatrix} \tag{12.6.13}$$

$$P_F(E_e) = \sqrt{E_e^2 - m_e^2}\, E_e (\Delta - E_e)^2 \tag{12.6.14}$$

where $m_e \le E_e \le \Delta + m_e$ and $P_F(E_e)$ is the conventional Fermi electron energy spectrum.

The life of the neutron is

$$\tau_{th} = \frac{h}{2\pi} \frac{1}{(\Gamma_F + \Gamma_{GT})} \tag{12.6.15}$$

where h is the Planck constant.

12.6.2. Asymmetry Parameters *A* and *B*

The asymmetry coefficients A and B are obtained from (12.6.5), just like (12.6.11), but without carrying out integration over ϑ_ν and ϑ_e, respectively. One finds,

$$\begin{pmatrix} I_{F+} + I_{GT+} \\ I_{F-} + I_{GT-} \end{pmatrix} = \int d\vartheta_e \sin\vartheta_e 4\pi^2 \begin{pmatrix} b_{FGT+} \\ b_{FGT-} \end{pmatrix} \frac{8E_e}{E_e + m_e} \left(1 + A_\pm \frac{K_e}{E_e} \cos\vartheta_e \right)$$

$$b_{FGT} = b_{FGT+} = 2b_{F+0}^2 + 2b_{F+3}^2 + b_{GT+p}^2 = b_{FGT-} = 2b_{F-0}^2 + 2b_{F-3}^2 + b_{GT-m}^2$$

$$A_+ = \left(4b_{F+0}b_{F+3} - b_{GT+p}^2\right)/b_{FGT+} = -A_- = -\left(4b_{F-0}b_{F-3} + b_{GT-m}^2\right)/b_{FGT-} \tag{12.6.16}$$

The antineutrino moves in the opposite direction relative to that of the neutrino so that $\underline{K}_\nu$ is to be replaced by $-\underline{K}_\nu$ in (12.5.8), hence also (12.5.12). With this replacement, both $\underline{K}_e$ and $\underline{K}_\nu$ are now on equal footing in these both expressions and (12.6.5) can be written in the form

$$\begin{pmatrix} I_{F+} + I_{GT+} \\ I_{F-} + I_{GT-} \end{pmatrix} = \int d\vartheta_\nu \sin\vartheta_\nu 4\pi^2 \begin{pmatrix} b_{FGT+} \\ b_{FGT-} \end{pmatrix} \frac{8E_e}{E_e + m_e} \left(1 + B_\pm \cos\vartheta_\nu \right)$$

$$B_+ = \left(4b_{F+0}b_{F+3} + b_{GT}^2\right)/b_{FGT} = -B_- = -\left(4b_{F-0}b_{F-3} - b_{GT}^2\right)/b_{FGT} \tag{12.6.17}$$

12.6.3. Comparison with Data

The expressions in (12.6.15-17) have been evaluated using (12.5.13-16), (12.4.5) and the normalized radial wave functions $g_{00}(r)$ and $f_{00}(r)$ for the neutron associated with the solutions in Table 11.1. This has been carried out and the results have been shown in [H18 Table 12.1(log2 should be log$2^{5/3}$)]. This table shows that only wave functions associated with $d_{b2}=-0.3202$ yield approximately correct values of the decay parameters; the other five d_{b2}

leads to decays times τ_{th} that disagree with data. Further, convergent wave function for the neutron associated with the $d_{b4}\neq0$ case in Table 11.2 also leads to disagreement with data. The d_{b2}=–0.3202 results using the wave functions in Figure 11.1b are compared to data in Table 12.1.

Table 12.1. Values of the calculated decay rate τ_{th} and A and B asymmetry coefficients given by (12.6.15-17) and Γ_{GT}/Γ_F by (12.6.13) are presented for the d_{b2}=–0.3202 case for the neutron given in Table 11.1. The coupling constant κ_b in (12.5.2,13-16) is chosen such that in the second line, the A coefficient agrees with data [P1], in the third line, the B coefficient agrees with data, and in the fourth line, $\tau_{th}=\tau_{exp}$. The integrals appearing in (12.5.13-16), given by (12.4.5), depend upon the approximate, normalized radial wave functions for the neutron $g_{00}(r)$ and $f_{00}(r)$ shown in Figure 11.1b for the d_{b2}=–0.3202 case.

$$\Gamma_A/\Gamma_V = \left(2b_{F+3}^2 + b_{GT+p}^2\right)/2b_{F+0}^2 \approx 4.8\text{–}5.5$$

for all these cases

	κ_b	A	B	Γ_{GT}/Γ_F	τ_{th} sec
	9.5488	–0.1184	0.9784	1.215	891.01
	9.3699	–0.1262	0.9807	1.24	865.77
	9.4719	–0.1218	0.9794	1.107	880.16
PDG data [P1]		–0.1184±0.001	0.9807±0.003		880.2±1(τ_{exp})

When the coupling constant κ_b in (12.5.2,13-16) is chosen such that A agrees with data, B is within error limits and τ_{th} differ from τ_{exp} by 1.2%. When the choice leads to that B agrees with data, A differ from data by 5.7% and τ_{th} differ from τ_{exp} by 1.55%. Taking the average of these both cases, τ_{th}=878.4 sec which is 0.2% smaller than τ_{exp}. This small difference can easily be absorbed into the error margins of A and B. Finally, if $\tau_{th}=\tau_{exp}$, A is off by 2% and B is within error limits.

Thus, two of the three measured neutron decay parameters A, B and τ_{exp} are approximately predicted. These results are sufficiently close to data and can hardly be any coincidence, inasmuch as they are directly derived from a first principles' formulation. This justifies the identification of the d_{b2}=–0.3202 GeV^5 case for the neutron in Table.11.1 and Figure 11.1b as describing the neutron in the quark-diquark relative space. Note also that the numerical treatment of §11.1.1 may introduce some errors and possible source of approximations conjectured in §11.1.4 may enter.

12.6.4. Diquark-Quark Potential and Mean Distance

1) *Diquark-Quark Interaction.* For the neutron case in Table 12.1, the interquark potential $\Phi_b(r)=\Phi_{bd}(|\underline{x}|)-\Phi_{cd}(|\underline{x}|)$ in (10.2.2), using the d_b values in Table 11.1, is plotted in Figure 12.1.

$\Phi_{bd}(|\underline{x}|)$ is a specialization of the general three quark potential $\Phi_b(I,III,II)$ of (9.2.2) which contains six interquark strong potentials denoted by six V's. When applied to ground state baryons, two of the quarks having the same flavor merge into a diquark which is separated from the remaining quark having different flavor by $\underline{x}$. The six V's now reduce to four which are all the same and are denoted by $V_s(r)$; the scalar strong interaction between two quarks depend only upon the distance between them. Equation (9.2.2) turns into [H30 A22]

$$\Phi_b(r) = 2V_s^3(r),\ V_s(r) = V_{AB}(x_I) = V_{BA}(x_{II}),\ V_s(r) = \left|\frac{\Phi_b(r)}{2}\right|^{1/3} \exp\left(\mp\left(1, \pm\frac{2/3}{1/3}\right)i\pi\right) \quad (12.6.18)$$

$V_s(r)$ is the real scalar strong quark-quark interaction in (9.1.1-4) representing the u and d interaction here. In general, it can be complex when the right sides in (9.1.4) or (9.2.9) drop out. The quasi-classical force $-\partial V_s(r)/\partial r$ is repulsive, $\to +\infty$ as $r \to 0$ and prevents u-d merger. This is contrary to the merger of the quarks at x_{III} and x_I in (9.2.12) to form a diquark corresponding to uu here. These may be of interest in internucleon interactions in nuclei. $\Phi_b(r)$ does not have any classical analog.

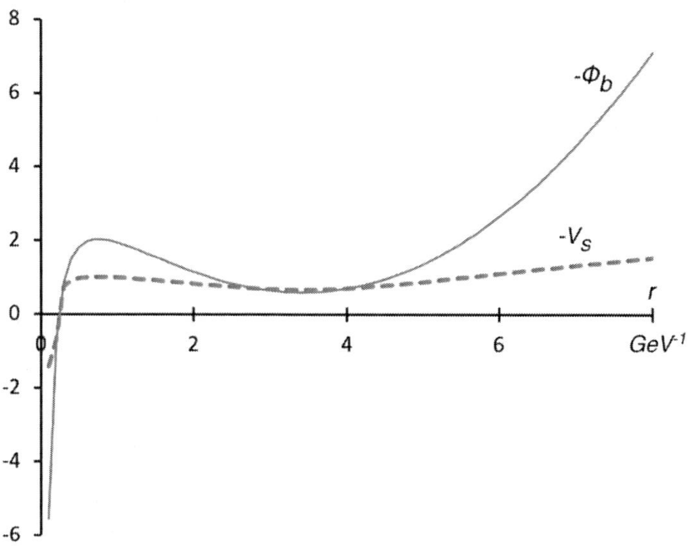

Figure 12.1. Strong interaction potential $\Phi_b(r) = \Phi_{bd}(r) = \Phi_{bd}(|\underline{x}|) - \Phi_{cd}(|\underline{x}|)$ in (10.2.2) in units of GeV^3 for the neutron case in Table 12.1. The corresponding u-d strong interaction potential $V_s(r)$ in (12.6.18), in units of GeV, is also shown.

2) *Quark-Antiquark Interaction.* It is of interest to compare $V_s(r)$ to the corresponding u quark and antiquark $\bar{d}$ interaction $V_{sm}(r)$ in π^+ meson. $V_s(r)$ in (12.6.18) is the same as $V_{SB}(x_I)$ and $V_{SA}(x_{II})$ in (2.1.1-4), inasmuch as these are real and independent of complex conjugation. The intrameson strong interaction potential corresponding to Φ_b in (12.6.18) is Φ_m in (2.2.3) which by analogy reads

$$V_{SA}(x_{II})V_{SB}(x_I) \to \Phi_m(x_I, x_{II}) \to \Phi_m(r) \quad (12.6.19)$$

The analogue of (10.2.2) in mesons is (3.2.8), which by (3.2.21), Table 5.2 and (5.2.2) yields [H30 (A27), (A28)]

$$\Phi_m(r)=\Phi_m(\underline{x})+\Phi_c(x)=d_{m0}+d_m/r+d_{m2}r^2 \to 0.64113-0.0049r^2 \text{ GeV}^2 \quad (12.6.20)$$

$$V_{sm}(r)=\mp\sqrt{\Phi_m(r)}=\mp\sqrt{0.64113-0.0049r^2} \approx \mp\left(0.8-0.0038r^2-7.3\times10^{-6}.r^4...\right) \text{ GeV} \quad (12.6.21)$$

This u and $\bar{d}$ interaction $V_{sm}(r)$ in meson corresponds to $V_s(r)$ for u-d strong interaction in nucleon shown in Figure 12.1. A comparison shows that both have the same magnitude of 0.67-0.9 GeV for $r\approx1.6$ - 5.1 GeV^{-1} or 2 - 6 fm where the bulk of the wave functions are concentrated, as can be seen from Figure 11.1b and (4.3.4a). The strengths of the strong interquark potentials in nucleon and meson are about the same and they support each other.

Here, it is noted that $V_{sm}(r)$ in (12.6.21) has been determined from meson spectra in Chapter 5 and holds for any combination of a quark and an antiquark; the quark-quark strong interaction takes place in the hidden relative space and is flavor independent.

3) *Mean Diquark-Quark Distance.* The baryon doublet wave functions $\chi_{0\dot{b}}(\underline{x})$ and $\psi_0^a(\underline{x})$ are determined by (10.2.1). These have been separated into angular and radial parts in (10.2.3). In ground state, these radial wave functions are denoted by $f_0(r)$ and $g_0(r)$ satisfying (10.2.12) and have been plotted in Figure 11.1b for the neutron in Table 12.1. An average value of the diquark-quark separation r, denoted by r_a, is [H32 (2.5), H30 below A29]

$$r_a=\frac{\int d\underline{x}^3 r\left(\left(\chi_{0\dot{b}}(\underline{x})\right)^*\chi_{0\dot{b}}(\underline{x})+\left(\psi_0^a(\underline{x})\right)^*\psi_0^a(\underline{x})\right)}{\int d\underline{x}^3\left(\left(\chi_{0\dot{b}}(\underline{x})\right)^*\chi_{0\dot{b}}(\underline{x})+\left(\psi_0^a(\underline{x})\right)^*\psi_0^a(\underline{x})\right)}=\frac{\int drr^3\left(g_0^2(r)+f_0^2(r)\right)}{\int drr^2\left(g_0^2(r)+f_0^2(r)\right)}=3.05 \text{ fm} \quad (12.6.22)$$

12.6.5. Detachment of Weak and Electromagnetic Couplings

Γ_{GT}/Γ_F and Γ_A/Γ_V in Table 12.1 have not been measured. Γ_A/Γ_V is the ratio between the decay rates stemming from the axial vector or tensor part and the vector part in the decay amplitude (12.4.4). Both these ratios are > 1 and shows that the axial vector or tensor part of the amplitude is greater than that of the vector part. They behave qualitatively in a similar way as does the conventional $(g_A/g_V)^2=1.611$ [P1], which lies between Γ_{GT}/Γ_F and Γ_A/Γ_V but cannot be related to them.

In the present theory, there is only one weak coupling constant g in (12.2.4-6) identified or associated with g_V in the literature [P1]. The gauge transformations (12.2.4-6) does not allow that the axial vector or tensor field is associated with a different coupling constant g_A. That $\Gamma_A>\Gamma_V$ is due to that the normalization type of constant κ_b in (12.5.2), the only free parameter in these calculations, is connected to Γ_A but not to Γ_V and that κ_b is rather large in Table 12.1.

Even this g or g_V will drop out in the decay rate. Equation (12.6.13) shows that the magnitude of neutron decay rate is proportional to $(g/M_W)^4$. Now, M_W^2 itself is proportional to g^2 according to (7.4.6b) so that

$$\frac{g^4}{M_W^4} = 32G_F^2 = \left(\frac{\Omega}{\int dx^0}\right)^2 \tag{12.6.23}$$

is independent of g. Here, G_F is the Fermi constant of (7.4.29). Since $g=e/\sin\vartheta_W$, where ϑ_W is the Weinberg angle and $-e$ the electron charge, (12.6.23) is independent of e.

Because ϑ_W is not a basic constant in the present theory but can be derived as in (7.2.3, 12), the more genuine weak coupling (12.6.23) is detached from the much stronger electromagnetic coupling characterized by e, just like such a detachment found in the meson case in §7.5.3. *Nature is too economical* to deal out two fundamental constants g and e that are so close to each other. Instead, the strength of weak interactions is characterized by the dimensionless constant $F_W^2=8.031\times10^{-14}$ in (7.5.22a) which is much smaller than the corresponding strength of electromagnetic interactions $\alpha=1/137$.

On the contrary, based upon an analysis of some vector meson decay rates, the strong coupling α_s and electromagnetic coupling $\alpha=1/137$ are unified into one single "electro-strong" coupling via the hypothesis [H13 (9.2)] or (8.3.11), $\alpha_s^4=\alpha$ or $\alpha_s=0.2923$. These considerations support the same detachment conjecture in the meson sector in §7.5.3.

That the Fermi constant G_F in (12.6.23) is a ratio between a large volume and a long relative time indicates that the weak interaction is related to the large scale, long time or low energy aspects of physics.

12.7. Possible Nonconservation of Angular Momentum

12.7.1. Theoretical Background of Possible J Nonconservation

The angular momentum $\underline{J}$ of an observable, spin ½ point particle in conventional form

$$\underline{J} = -i\underline{X} \otimes \frac{\partial}{\partial \underline{X}} + i\begin{pmatrix} \underline{\sigma} & \\ & \underline{\sigma} \end{pmatrix} \tag{12.7.1}$$

is a constant of motion, hence a conserved quantity. Therefore, the total angular momentum of an ensemble of such particles is also conserved.

However, a baryon is neither a point particle nor a detachable ensemble of such particles. Therefore, conservation of $\underline{J}$ in (12.7.1) cannot be applied to a baryon without reservation. $\underline{J}$ conservation also does not apply to the quarks that constitute the baryon because a quark is not observable in the sense implied by (12.7.1). For a slowly moving doublet baryon, however, §10.2.4 shows that (10.2.1a) can be reverted to a Dirac equation when the diquark coordinate x_I merges into the quark coordinate x_{II}. This merger reduces the present nonlocal description (9.3.11) to a local one so that (12.7.1) is applicable and $\underline{J}$ is conserved.

By reducing a baryon with extension into a point particle, a great amount of underlying physics leading to various observable baryon phenomena is irretrievably lost. However, the point particle approximation of a baryon can be valid in certain low energy interactions. For instance, the strong charge of a baryon may be considered to be concentrated at a point source in pion-nucleon scattering. Analogously, in Rutherford scattering, the proton can be regarded as having a point charge. In these cases, (12.7.1) can be applied and $\underline{J}$ is conserved.

In weak interactions, however, the gauge boson interacts differently with the differently flavored quarks, broadly speaking. Therefore, reduction of the baryon to a point particle cannot be made. This is evident in the introduction of a gauge fields in (7.1.4), where $\hat{O}^{a\dot{b}}$ operating in the relative space of the diquark and quark cannot be neglected in the ensuing calculations. Thus, the angular momentum $\underline{J}$ of (12.7.1) is not applicable to the baryon wave functions in (9.3.11), which depend upon both the laboratory coordinates X and the relative space coordinates x. Therefore, $\underline{J}$ needs not be conserved in neutron decay. This is supported by noting the following.

In the four possible spin combinations for the nucleons in (12.4.3), the total spin of the lepton pair is fixed, being zero for the Fermi decays and unity for the Gamow-Teller decays. However, (12.6.6-9) show that this total spin can also be unity for the Fermi decays and zero for the Gamow-Teller decays in violation of angular momentum conservation. Thus, a qualitative prediction is that angular momentum is not conserved in free neutron decay and hence in weak interactions in general.

12.7.2. Experimental Tests of $\underline{J}$ Conservation Involving Nucleons

$\underline{J}$ in (12.7.1) is conserved in muon decay which involves four spin ½ point particles.

As was mentioned in Sec. 12.1, (12.1.4) makes use of conservation of angular momentum. When combined with Coulomb correction functions, its predictions are relatively consistent with nuclear β-decay and free neutron decay data. Therefore, there is a prevalent view that angular momentum is conserved in such decays. Arguments against this view has been given in Sec. 12.1. The conclusion given at the end of §12.7.1 thus invalidates (12.1.4) by Jackson et al. and hence also the interpretations of the experimental results that ensue from it.

Already in their classical paper of 1956, Lee and Yang [L7] remarked that in weak interaction experiments up to that time, the baryon number, electric charge, energy and momentum are conserved. Conservation of angular momentum $\underline{J}$ and parity P as well as invariances under charge conjugation C and time reversal T had however not been established. Nonconservation of P and C was soon discovered and P violation has been extensively measured [S10 and references therein]. A small violation of T has also been detected and subjected to many experimental investigations [L6, S9 and references therein].

In contrast, no experiment dedicated to test conservation of $\underline{J}$ in nuclear β-decay or free neutron decay has been performed to my knowledge. In fact, no experiment exists that directly distinguishes Fermi from Gamow-Teller transitions in free neutron decay without making use of (12.1.3).

Therefore, specific tests on $\underline{J}$ conservation in such decays seem to be called for. Such a test is however not strictly a test of the present theory which holds for free neutron decay only. As was indicated below (12.1.4), the unknown effects of internucleon interactions intervene the theory and eventual experimental results. To this end, decays of free neutrons are needed and will give results of more fundamental importance. That this has not been done is due to the great technical difficulty of such an experiment.

In view of the wealth of raw data available on coincidental experiments with free, polarized neutrons, it may be possible to obtain some indication as to whether $\underline{J}$ is conserved in free neutron decay. No analysis along this line has been carried out to my knowledge. Important clues may be obtained by reviewing existing data.

Chapter 13

CP Violation in Kaon Decay and $\bar{B}^0$-B^0 Mixing [H20]

The present treatment differs from earlier ones in that the relative time between the two quarks in the kaon plays an essential role in accounting for these phenomena.

13.1. Earlier Phenomenology

The decays K_S^0, $K_L^0 \to 2\pi$, 3π have been considered using the time-dependent Schrödinger equation without specifying the Hamiltonian in connection with CP nonconservation [L5 §15.3-8]. The starting point is the ansatz to generalize (7.2.19) to the form [L5 (15.28)]

$$\left|\overline{K}^0\right\rangle = \exp(iS\Theta)CPT\left|K^0\right\rangle \tag{13.1.1}$$

where S denotes strangeness, CPT the conventional discrete operator and Θ an arbitrary phase angle. Under CPT invariance, (7.2.18) can be put in the form

$$\left|K_S^0\right\rangle = \frac{1}{\sqrt{2}}\begin{pmatrix}1+\varepsilon \\ 1-\varepsilon\end{pmatrix}, \qquad \left|K_L^0\right\rangle = \frac{1}{\sqrt{2}}\begin{pmatrix}1+\varepsilon \\ -(1-\varepsilon)\end{pmatrix} \tag{13.1.2}$$

where the upper row refers to K^0 and the low row to $\overline{K}^0$ and ε is a small, complex quantity [L5 (15.103)]. Using the measured [P1]

$$\begin{aligned} &m_{KL} - m_{KS} = 3.483\times 10^{-6}\ \text{eV} \\ &\Gamma(K_S^0 \to 2\pi) = 7.352\times 10^{-6}\ \text{ev} \approx 2(m_{KL} - m_{KS}) \end{aligned} \tag{13.1.3}$$

one finds the argument of $\varepsilon \approx 45°$ or $225°$ and the unitarity upper bound for $|\varepsilon|$;

$$\varepsilon \approx \pm|\varepsilon|(1+i)/\sqrt{2}, \qquad |\varepsilon| < 4.3\times 10^{-3} \tag{13.1.4}$$

Further, (13.1.1, 2) leads to

$$2\varepsilon \approx -i\Theta \tag{13.1.5}$$

so that the argument of $\Theta \approx -45°$ or $-225°$.

[L5 (15.105, 109, 113)] define the ratio of the semi-leptonic decay amplitudes

$$x = S_{fi}(\overline{K}^0 \to \pi^- L_s^+ \nu_L) / S_{fi}(K^0 \to \pi^- L_s^+ \nu_L) \tag{13.1.6a}$$

where *L* stands for the lepton species, as in (7.1.11-13), and *s* the lepton helicity. [L5 (15.116, 117)] give the ratios of the decay rates to first order in ε,

$$\frac{\Gamma(K_S^0 \to \pi^- L_s^+ \nu_L)}{\Gamma(K_S^0 \to \pi^+ L_{-s}^- \overline{\nu}_L)} = \left| \frac{1+\varepsilon+(1-\varepsilon)x}{(1+\varepsilon)x^* + (1-\varepsilon)} \right|^2 \cong 1 + 4\,\mathrm{Re}(\varepsilon) \cong \frac{\Gamma(K_L^0 \to \pi^- L_s^+ \nu_L)}{\Gamma(K_L^0 \to \pi^+ L_{-s}^- \overline{\nu}_L)} \tag{13.1.6b}$$

where x turns out to be small and has been dropped.

From the measured semi-leptonic decay ratios [P1], (13.1.6b, 4) yields

$$\mathrm{Re}\,\varepsilon = 1.612 \times 10^{-3}, \qquad |\varepsilon| \approx 2.28 \times 10^{-3} \tag{13.1.7}$$

Furthermore, [P1] gives the nonleptonic CP violating amplitude ratios

$$|\eta_{00}| = \sqrt{\frac{\Gamma(K_L^0 \to \pi^0 \pi^0)}{\Gamma(K_s^0 \to \pi^0 \pi^0)}} = 2.221 \times 10^{-3}, \quad |\eta_{+-}| = \sqrt{\frac{\Gamma(K_L^0 \to \pi^+ \pi^-)}{\Gamma(K_s^0 \to \pi^+ \pi^-)}} = 2.232 \times 10^{-3} \tag{13.1.8}$$

The numbers in (13.1.7) and (13.1.8) show that

$$|\varepsilon| \approx |\eta_{00}| \approx |\eta_{+-}| \tag{13.1.9}$$

This numerical agreement suggests that CP nonconservation for the semi-leptonic and nonleptonic decays can be characterized by one parameter ε. However, the above results say nothing about the nature of this CP violation.

13.2. Relative Energy and Time

The phase angle 45° in (13.1.4) will now be derived from the basic equations of motion (7.1.9) without relying on the data in (13.1.3). In the ansatz (13.1.1), the nature of the phase angle Θ is unknown. Here, it is naturally identified to be related to the product of the relative energy ω_K and the relative time x^0 in (3.1.9), as will be specified in (13.6.1) ff below.

In the absence of gauge field, (7.1.9) reverts to (2.4.3) which, after dropping the flavor indices, becomes (2.3.22) which in its turn goes over to (3.1.8) according to the steps of (3.1.1-7). Taking the trace of (3.1.8a) and dropping the vector meson component χ leads to

$$\left[a_m(1-a_m)(E_K^2 + \underline{K}^2) + \partial_0^2 + \Delta + i(1-2a_m)(E_K\partial_0 - \underline{K}\partial)\right]\chi_0(x) = (\Phi_m - M_m^2)\psi_0(x) \tag{13.2.1}$$

where a_m is given by (3.1.10a). Introducing the relative time via (3.1.9), (13.2.1) shows that the eigenvalue E_K is independent of ω_K. In the treatments that follow, the null relative energy condition $\omega_K=0$ of (5.7.1) has been used and $a_m=1/2$ of (5.7.2) effectively employed. With the association of Θ with $\omega_K x^0$ above, however, $\omega_K \neq 0$ and (5.7.1) has to be *relaxed* for the present application while retaining (5.7.2). For a pseudoscalar meson at rest, $\underline{K}$=0, (13.2.1) with (5.7.2) yields

$$\left(E_0^2/4+\partial_0^2+\Delta\right)\chi_0(x)=\left(\Phi_m-M_m^2\right)\psi_0(x) \tag{13.2.2}$$

Relative to the corresponding (3.2.1a), for which (3.1.9, 10a) have been used, there is an extra $\partial_0^2=\partial^2/\partial(x^0)^2$ term here.

In the absence of weak interaction, $g\to 0$ in (7.1.5) and K^0 and $\bar{K}^0$ are complex conjugate of each other (7.2.19) and are stable, physical states with the same mass given by (5.1.1). The phase angle Θ in (13.1.1), hence also the relative energy ω_K, drops out. Turning on the weak interaction igW_U or $\bar{W}_U gi$, K^0 and $\bar{K}^0$ are no longer physical states and Θ and $\omega_K \neq 0$ become small quatitites of the same first order as igW_U. The physical states are now K_S^0 and K_L^0 shown in (13.1.2) or (7.2.18) including the phase $exp(i\omega_K x^0)$ according to (3.1.9). Therefore, ∂_0 in (7.1.4) cannot be dropped but becomes $i\omega_K$ and is of the same order as the igW_U term there.

13.3. $K_S^0 \to 2\pi$ and 3π

Consider one of the two first order terms in (7.1.9a) for $\bar{K}^0\to\pi^0 W_U$ of (7.3.27b). Let the first operator in (7.1.9a) be of first order g included in (7.1.4-5) and the second operator be of zeroth order given by the last of (3.1.4). In (7.1.9a), $\chi_{(qr)}=\chi_{(32)}$ refers to $\bar{K}^0$ which by (7.2.18) becomes $K_S^0/\surd 2$. For this pseudoscalar meson at rest, the wave function is given by (3.1.1a) with the triplet $\underline{\chi}$=0, (3.1.5-6) with $\underline{K}$=0 and (3.1.9). This first order term now takes the form

$$\left(\delta^{a\dot{b}}\partial_0+i\tfrac{1}{4}g\sqrt{2}W_U^{a\dot{b}}(X)\right)\left(\tfrac{1}{2}\left(-\delta^{b\dot{e}}\partial_{X0}-\underline{\sigma}^{b\dot{e}}\underline{\partial}_X\right)-\underline{\sigma}^{b\dot{e}}\underline{\partial}\right)\frac{\chi_0(r)}{\sqrt{2}}\exp\left(-iE_0X^0+i\omega_0x^0\right) \tag{13.3.1}$$

With the degeneracy (7.2.21), (13.3.1) can be written as

$$\left(\delta^{a\dot{b}}i\omega_0+i\frac{1}{4}g\frac{1+i}{\sqrt{2}}\left(-\frac{Z^{a\dot{b}}(X)}{\cos\vartheta_W}\right)\right)\left(\frac{1}{2}\delta^{b\dot{e}}iE_0-\underline{\sigma}^{b\dot{e}}\underline{\partial}\right)\frac{\chi_0(r)}{\sqrt{2}}\exp\left(-iE_0X^0+i\omega_0x^0\right) \tag{13.3.2}$$

Since ω_0 is generated by the weak interaction g term, it must have the same phase in (13.3.2),

$$\omega_0=(1+i)\omega_{00},\qquad \omega_{00}=\text{real constant} \tag{13.3.3}$$

Turning to the first order term in the second operator in (7.1.9a) and repeat the above procedure. It is found that

$$\omega_0=-(1+i)\omega_{00} \tag{13.3.4}$$

These two relations are related to the two phases in (13.1.4) but without using the empirical data (13.1.3); they are the consequences of the necessary degeneracy (7.2.21). There is no conflict between (13.3.3) and (13.3.4) because they cancel out upon summing the two first order terms in (7.1.9a), as is reflected in (13.2.2) which contains no linear ∂_0 term.

Follow now §7.3.2-4 and obtain the first order decay amplitude $S_{fi}(K_S^0 \to 2\pi)$. In the source term (7.3.5a), the first term in the braces is replaced by (13.3.2) multiplied by a final state wave function $\chi^+{}_{0(22)}$:

$$\frac{ig_l}{4}\chi^+_{0(rp)\dot{e}a}(\lambda_l)_{ps}W_l^{a\dot{b}}\left(\partial_{ll}^{f\dot{e}}\chi_{0(sr)\dot{b}f}\right) \to \chi^+_{0(22)\dot{e}a}$$
$$\times\left(\delta^{ab}i\omega_0 + i\frac{1}{4}g\frac{1+i}{\sqrt{2}}\left(-\frac{Z^{ab}(X)}{\cos\vartheta_W}\right)\right)\left(\frac{1}{2}\delta^{b\dot{e}}iE_0 - \underline{\sigma}^{b\dot{e}}\underline{\partial}\right)\frac{\chi_0(r)}{\sqrt{2}}\exp\left(-iE_0X^0 + i\omega_0x^0\right) \tag{13.3.5}$$

The final state 2π comes from the decay of the Z boson via (7.7.2, 7) and the final state $\chi^+{}_{0(22)}$ represents a vacuum meson state π^0 given by (7.3.20) with $\psi \to \chi$. Consider the integral over the relative time x^0 in the source (7.3.5a) with the replacement (13.3.5),

$$\int_{T_1}^{T_2} dx^0 \exp\left(i\omega_0 x^0\right) = \int_{T_1}^{T_2} dx^0 \exp\left(i\omega_{00}x^0 - \omega_{00}x^0\right), \quad T_2 = -T_1 = T_0 \to \infty \tag{13.3.6}$$

where (13.3.3) has been consulted. In the surface term (7.3.4), the exponential $exp(i\omega_0 x^0)$ in (13.3.5) also enters but, in addition, also its complex conjugate $exp(-i\omega_0^* x^0)$ contained in $\chi^+{}_{0(23)}$ in (7.3.4). The integral over the relative time x^0 in the surface integral (7.3.4) now reads

$$\int_{T_1}^{T_2} dx^0 \exp\left(i\omega_0 x^0 - i\omega_0^* x^0\right) = \int_{T_1}^{T_2} dx^0 \exp\left(-2\omega_{00}x^0\right) \tag{13.3.7}$$

Equations (7.3.4) and (7.3.5) are sandwiched between the initial stae $|i = K_S^0>$ and final state $<f = 0, Z = 2\pi|$ as was mentioned beneath (7.3.13). The 0 that follows $<f=$ refers to the above-mentioned vacuum meson state π^0, as in (7.3.20). By (7.3.3-5, 13), $S_{fi}(K_S^0 \to 2\pi)$ is proportional to the ratio of (13.3.6) to (13.3.7) which vanishes for $T_0 \to \infty$ in (13.3.6);

$$\frac{\int_{T_1}^{T_2} dx^0 \exp\left(i\omega_{00}x^0 - \omega_{00}x^0\right)}{\int_{T_1}^{T_2} dx^0 \exp\left(-2\omega_{00}x^0\right)} = -(1+i)\frac{\exp\left((i-1)\omega_{00}T_2\right) - \exp\left((i-1)\omega_{00}T_1\right)}{\exp\left(-2\omega_{00}T_2\right) - \exp\left(-2\omega_{00}T_1\right)} \to 0 \tag{13.3.8}$$

This also holds if (13.3.3) is replaced by (13.3.4). Therefore, $K_S^0 \to 2\pi$ is forbidden to first order in igW_U. Even if this first order $S_{fi}(K_S^0 \to 2\pi)$ does not vanish, for instance by letting T_1, T_2 be finite such that (13.3.8) becomes of the magnitude of unity, it is expected to lead to a decay rate $\Gamma(K_S^0 \to 2\pi)$ of the same magnitude as $\Gamma(K^\pm \to 2\pi) \cong 1.1\times10^{-8}$ eV from phase space considerations. This rate is 668 times smaller than the observed rate in (13.1.3). This is "one of the remaining unsolved problems of the weak interaction" [L5 p640].

However, there is now a second order term ∂_0^2 in (13.2.2) operating on $exp(i\omega_0 x^0)$ in (13.3.5) and produces a term $-(\omega_0)^2= -i2(\omega_{00})^2$ via (13.3.3, 4). Let E_{00} be the K^0 mass in (5.1.1) and $E_0=E_{00}+\Delta E_{0S}$ in (13.2.2), the exponent in (13.3.5) will contain $-i\Delta E_{0S}X^0$ corresponding to the decay rate

$$\Gamma\left(K_S^0 \to 2\pi\right) = i\Delta E_{0S} = -4\omega_{00}^2 / E_{00} \tag{13.3.9}$$

where the lower sign in (5.1.1) is chosen. Note that the relative energy ω_{00} is a hidden variable but its square in (13.3.9) is visible. Although this decay rate comes from the second order ∂_0^2 term in (13.2.2), its amplitude is of first order in ω_0, hence of order g. In (13.3.5), the ratio of ω_0 to the g term that leads to the last mentioned $S_{fi}(K_S^0\to 2\pi)$ is not fixed or known. This allows $\Gamma(K_S^0\to 2\pi)$ to be >> $\Gamma(K^\pm\to 2\pi)$; it may be regarded that the nonvanishing $S_{fi}(K_S^0\to 2\pi)$ in the last paragraph is greatly amplified by the relative energy ω_{00}.

The factor $2 \approx \Gamma(K_S^0\to\pi^+\pi^-)/\Gamma(K_S^0\to 2\pi^0)$ [P1] comes from the factor $1/\sqrt{2}$ in front of π^0 in (2.4.18) that enters (7.7.2) via (7.7.7).

Instead of $\bar{K}^0\to\pi^0 W_U$ of (7.3.27b) considered above, $K^0\to \bar{W}_U\pi^0$ of (7.3.29) can be treated in the same way. The only differences are that $(1+i)\to(1-i)$ in (13.3.3, 4) and the upper sign in (5.1.1) is used when deriving the corresponding (13.3.9); the above results remain unchanged.

If the vacuum meson state π^0 assigned to $\chi^+{}_{0(22)}$ in (13.3.5) is replaced by a real final state π^0, $K_S^0\to 2\pi$ there goes over to $K_S^0\to 3\pi$. Because $\pi^\pm$ and π^0 form a triplet in the limit of SU(2) symmetry, they must have the same phase. Since $\pi^\pm$ cannot contain a phase factor with complex argument, $exp((i-1)\omega_{00}x^0)$, which would cause them to decay like $K_S^0\to 2\pi$ in (13.3.9), this final state π^0 can at most contain a phase factor of the form $exp(-i\omega_{00}x^0)$, similar to that for K_L^0 following (13.4.6) below. The $exp(-\omega_{00}x^0)$ factor in (13.3.6) remains unchanged and the ratio (13.3.8) remains 0; $K_S^0\to 3\pi$ is *forbidden*. However, if T_l is cut off from $-\infty$ in (13.3.6) and $\to$ finite $-T_S$, (13.3.8) becomes $2exp(-\omega_{00}T_S)$ and some $K_S^0\to 3\pi$ will be seen. This form is the same as that for the semi-leptonic decay in (13.5.4) below. The difference is that T_K in (13.5.4) given by (13.5.8) is small. Here, T_S is much larger and is estimated to be $\sim 3\times 10^{-15}$ sec if the small $\Gamma(K_S^0\to 3\pi)\approx 2.57\times 10^{-12}$ eV [P1] is to be accounted for.

13.4. $K_L^0\to 2\pi$, 3π and K_L^0- K_S^0 Mass Difference

The couplings $\bar{K}^0 W_U$ and $\bar{W}_U K^0$ of (7.3.27b) and the second of (7.3.29) are the same with respect to K_S^0 but not to K_L^0 according to (7.2.18). This leads to results mentioned near the end of Sec. 13.3 for K_S^0. For K_L^0, the W_U and $\bar{W}_U$ contributions to $K_L^0\to 2\pi$ needs be summed analogous to that the amplitudes of (7.3.27, 29) have been summed to arrive at (7.3.30, 31).

The first order (13.3.1) for K_S^0 can be taken over here for K_L^0 if its sign is changed, as is seen in (7.2.18). Take the hermitian adjoint of (7.1.9a) and consider the first order term corresponding to (13.3.1) for K_L^0,

$$\left(\delta^{b\dot{e}}\partial_0 - i\tfrac{1}{4}g\sqrt{2}\overline{W}_U^{b\dot{e}}(X)\right)\left(\tfrac{1}{2}\left(-\delta^{a\dot{b}}\partial_{X0} - \underline{\sigma}^{a\dot{b}}\partial_{\underline{X}}\right) - \underline{\sigma}^{a\dot{b}}\underline{\partial}\right)\frac{\chi_0(r)}{\sqrt{2}}\exp\left(-iE_0X^0 + i\omega_0 x^0\right) \tag{13.4.1}$$

Add this expression to the negative of (13.3.1) and work out the resulting expression using (7.2.21-22). The result shows that the imaginary part is of the form ig(real operator). Since $\partial_0 \rightarrow i\omega_0$ must have the same phase, analogous to that mentioned above (13.3.3), ω_0 must be real here. The summation removes the imaginary parts in the above (real operator). The expressions (13.3.3) and (13.3.4) are replaced by

$$\omega_0 = \omega_{00} \tag{13.4.2a}$$

$$\omega_0 = -\omega_{00} \tag{13.4.2b}$$

respectively, for $K_L^0 \rightarrow 2\pi$. The above (real operator) contains both W_6 and W_7.

The treatment of for $K_S^0 \rightarrow 2\pi$ in (13.3.3-5), using (13.4.2) instead, can be taken over and the ratio (13.3.8) is here replaced by

$$\frac{\int_{-T}^{T} dx^0 \exp\left(i\omega_{00}x^0\right)}{\int_{-T}^{T} dx^0 \exp\left(-i\omega_{00}x^0 + i\omega_{00}x^0\right)} = \frac{\sin(\omega_{00}T)}{\omega_{00}T} \rightarrow 0, \quad T = \frac{\tau_0}{2} \rightarrow \infty \tag{13.4.3}$$

where (7.3.16) has been noted. Thus, $K_L^0 \rightarrow 2\pi$, just like $K_S^0 \rightarrow 2\pi$, is also *forbidden* to first order in igW_U. This result agrees with the requirement of CP invariance [L5 (15.24)]. Being a first principles' theory, consequences of conservation laws, including CP conservation, are included in the equations of motion (7.1.8-9).

Turning to the second order term ∂_0^2 in (13.2.2) operating on $exp(i\omega_0 x^0)$ in (13.4.1) which produces a term $-(\omega_0)^2 = -(\omega_{00})^2$ via (13.4.2). Let E_{00} be the K^0 mass in (5.1.1) and $E_0 = E_{00} + \Delta E_{0L}$ in (13.2.2), the equivalent of (13.3.9) becomes the mass shift

$$\Delta E_{0L} = 2\omega_{00}^2 / E_{00} \tag{13.4.4}$$

when the upper sign in.in (5.1.1) is chosen. The square of the relative energy among the s and d quarks in the hidden space x is visible in the laboratory space X in form of the mass shift (13.4.4), just like it is in form of the decay rate (13.3.9). Again, the mass shift comes from the second order ∂_0^2 term in (13.2.2) but its amplitude is of first order in ω_0, hence of order g. Comparison of (13.4.4) to (13.3.9) yields

$$\Gamma\left(K_S^0 \rightarrow 2\pi\right) = 2\Delta E_{0L} \tag{13.4.5}$$

which is 5.25% smaller than data (13.1.3). This discrepancy has been used to modify the phase angle 45° in (13.1.4) to about 43.5° [P1, L5]. Here, this 45° cannot be changed due to the constraint (13.3.3, 4). This discrepancy cannot be accounted for in the present theory. Similar to the CP violation cases mentioned above, a finite T in (13.3.8) will render the first order $S_{fi}(K_S^0 \to 2\pi)$ mentioned below it to contribute and to reduce this discrepancy.

Using (13.1.3) for ΔE_{0L}, (13.4.4) gives the relative energy between the s and d quarks in neutral kaons,

$$\omega_{00} = \pm 29.44 \text{ eV} \tag{13.4.6}$$

The upper sign is used. The lower sign can also be used if it is accompanied by $x^0 \to -x^0$, as is evident from the phase factor $exp(i\omega_0 x^0)$ in (13.3.1), noting (13.3.3-4). This leads to that the Ts in (13.3.6), at the end of Sec. 13.3 and in (13.5.8) and (13.6.1) below also change sign.

If the vacuum meson state π^0 in (13.3.5) adapted for K_L^0 is changed to a real π^0, $K_L^0 \to 2\pi$, forbidden by (13.4.3) above, turns into $K_L^0 \to 3\pi$. This real final state π^0 must have a phase factor $exp(-i\omega_{00}x^0)$ which is to be inserted into the upper integral in (13.4.3) to make this ratio to become unity. This implies that any π^0 from K_L^0 decay will also have a mass shift analogous to (13.4.4). According to the last paragraph of Sec. 13.3, $\pi^\pm$ and π^0 have the same phase in the limit of SU(2) symmetry so that any $\pi^\pm$ from K_L^0 decay will also have a mass shift. With (13.4.6) and the π masses [P1], (13.4.4) yields the shifts

$$\Delta E_{\pi 0} = 1.284 \times 10^{-5} \text{ eV}, \qquad \Delta E_{\pi\pm} = 1.277 \times 10^{-5} \text{ eV} \tag{13.4.7}$$

Although these shifts are far less than the error margin 0.24 keV for the π masses and are not observable, it may signify that there exist *two different species of* π triplets with slightly different masses.

To achieve CP violation, let $T \to \infty$ in (13.4.3) be cut off and become some finite T_L, like the cutoff mentioned at the end of Sec. 13.3 for $\Gamma(K_S^0 \to 2\pi, 3\pi)$. For $T_L=0$, (13.4.3) becomes unity and $\Gamma(K_L^0 \to 2\pi)$, like $\Gamma(K_S^0 \to 2\pi)$ mentioned beneath (13.3.9), $\approx \Gamma(K^\pm \to 2\pi)$ from phase space considerations. This rate is much greater than data. To account for the mearsured $\Gamma(K_L^0 \to 2\pi)$, T_L is chosen such that (13.4.3) becomes of the magnitude Re$(\eta_{00}, \eta_{+-})\sqrt{668} \approx 0.0407$, where Re$(\eta_{00}, \eta_{+-})$ are given by (13.1.7-9) and 668 has been mentioned beneath (13.3.8). Thus, CP is correctly violated if

$$\frac{\sin(\omega_{00} T_L)}{\omega_{00} T_L} \approx 0.0407, \qquad T_L \approx \pm 0.1025, \quad \pm 0.226, \quad \pm 0.712 \text{ eV}^{-1} \tag{13.4.8}$$

where (13.4.6) has been used. The angles $\omega_{00} T_L$ are close to multiples of π. These relative times are very short, of the order of 10^{-16} sec. These values, like the finite T's mentioned in Sec. 13.3, cannot be predicted from the present theory and have to come outside of it.

13.5. Semi-leptonic Decay of K_L^0 and K_S^0

The amplitude for $\bar{K}^0 \to \pi^+ W^-$ is given by (7.3.27a) and for $K^0 \to \pi^- W^+$ by the first of (7.3.29). Subsequently, $W^- \to \pi^+ L^- \nu_L$ and $W^+ \to \pi L^+ \nu_L$, where $L=\mu$, e. But the amplitudes for $\bar{K}^0 \to \pi^- W^+$

and $K^0 \to \pi^+ W^-$ do not follow from the internal index combinations in (7.3.18-19) and hence do not appear in (7.3.26-29). These decays are therefore forbidden, in agreement with the selection rule $\Delta S = \Delta Q$ [L5 (15.112)]. This rule is a consequence of the present theory and has been verified by that x of (13.1.6a) is consistent with 0 [P1].

The amplitudes (7.3.27a, 29) assume the null relative energy condition (5.7.1). The rates of these decays have not been evaluated because the pions are relativistic and their wave functions unknown. Nevertheless, the forms of (7.3.27a) and the first of (7.3.29) are the same so that the decay rates $\Gamma(K^0 \to \pi^- L^+ \nu_L)$ and $\Gamma(\bar{K}^0 \to \pi^+ L^- \nu_L)$ are the same. By (7.2.18), $K_S{}^0$ and $K_L{}^0$ contain equal amount of $\bar{K}^0$ and K^0, they contribute about equally to these semi-leptonic decays. This is approximately verified by data [P1] and corresponds to the CP conserving part of these decays.

As was mentioned above (13.2.2), (5.7.1) has been relaxed here. Since the amplitudes for $\bar{K}^0 \to \pi^+ W^-$ and $\bar{K}^0 \to \pi^0 W_U$ have the same form according to (7.3.27), the developments (13.3.1-4) can with some modifications be taken over. The expression corresponding to (13.3.1) reads

$$\left(\delta^{ab}\partial_0 + i\tfrac{1}{4}g\sqrt{2}\left(W_1^{ab}(X) \pm iW_2^{ab}(X)\right)\right) \times\left(\frac{1}{2}\left(-\delta^{b\dot{e}}\partial_{X0} - \underline{\sigma}^{b\dot{e}}\underline{\partial}_X\right) - \underline{\sigma}^{b\dot{e}}\underline{\partial}\right)\frac{\chi_0(r)}{\sqrt{2}}\exp\left(-iE_0X^0 + i\omega_0 x^0\right) \tag{13.5.1}$$

where the degeneration (7.2.20) for $W_V{}^{\pm}$ together with (7.1.5b) have been used. $W_1(X) = W_2(X)$ here inasmuch as the both $W_I{}^{\pm}(X)$ have the same X dependence, so that the lower sign form of (13.5.1) turns to a form nearly the same as (13.3.2). Thus, (13.3.3) holds for $\bar{K}^0 \to \pi^+ W^-$. For $K^0 \to \pi^- W^+$, the upper sign of (13.5.1) lead to

$$\omega_0 = (1 - i)\omega_{00} \tag{13.5.2}$$

The phase factor considerations for $K_S{}^0 \to 3\pi$ in the last paragraph of Sec. 13.3 can be taken over here. The phase factor $exp(-i\omega_{00}x^0)$ for the final state π^0 there can also be used for the final state π^+ in $\bar{K}^0 \to \pi^+ W^-$ here. Such a factor is required for in $K_L{}^0 \to 3\pi$ mentioned beneath (13.4.6). Inserting this factor into (13.3.6) turns (13.3.8) into

$$\frac{\int_{T_1}^{T_2} dx^0 \exp\left(-\omega_{00}x^0\right)}{\int_{T_1}^{T_2} dx^0 \exp\left(-2\omega_{00}x^0\right)} = 2\frac{\exp(-\omega_{00}T_2) - \exp(-\omega_{00}T_1)}{\exp(-2\omega_{00}T_2) - \exp(-2\omega_{00}T_1)} \to 0, \quad T_2 = -T_1 = T_0 \to \infty \tag{13.5.3}$$

Analogous to that $K_S{}^0 \to 2\pi$ is forbidden by (13.3.8), the semi-leptonic decay $\bar{K}^0 \to \pi^+ W^- \to \pi^+ L^- \nu_L$ is also forbidden when the relative energy $\omega_{00} \neq 0$, contrary to observation. If $\omega_{00} = 0$ or the null relative energy condition (5.7.1) holds, (13.5.3) turns into $\infty/\infty \to 1$ and these semi-leptonic decays can take place, as was implied in the second paragraph of this section. These decays however conserve CP.

CP violation can be obtained in a way similar to that achieved in the last paragraph of Sec. 13.4 in which the limits of the relative time x^0 were not allowed to extend to $\pm\infty$. Let $T_2 = T_0 = \infty$ as in (13.5.3) and (13.3.6) but $T_1 = -T_K$ finite, (13.5.3) turns into

$$\frac{\int_{-T_K}^{\infty} dx^0 \exp\left(-\omega_{00} x^0\right)}{\int_{-T_K}^{\infty} dx^0 \exp\left(-2\omega_{00} x^0\right)} = 2\exp\left(-\omega_{00} T_K\right) \tag{13.5.4}$$

For $K^0 \to \pi^- W^+ \to \pi^- L^+ \nu_L$, (13.5.2) replaces (13.3.3). Let $-T_1 = T_0 = \infty$ as in (13.5.3) and (13.3.6) but T_2 be cut off at $-T_K$, the equivalent of (13.5.4) reads

$$\frac{\int_{-\infty}^{-T_K} dx^0 \exp\left(\omega_{00} x^0\right)}{\int_{-\infty}^{-T_K} dx^0 \exp\left(2\omega_{00} x^0\right)} = 2\exp\left(\omega_{00} T_K\right) \tag{13.5.5}$$

As was mentioned in the second paragraph of this section, $K_S{}^0$ and $K_L{}^0$ contain equal amount of K^0 and $\bar{K}^0$ and $\Gamma(K^0 \to \pi^- L^+ \nu_L) = \Gamma(\bar{K}^0 \to \pi^+ L^- \nu_L)$ for the dominating CP conserving part. This together with (13.5.4-5) give the expression corresponding to (13.1.6b)

$$\frac{\Gamma(K_S^0 \to \pi^- L_s^+ \nu_L)}{\Gamma(K_S^0 \to \pi^+ L_{-s}^- \bar{\nu}_L)} = \frac{\Gamma(K_L^0 \to \pi^- L_s^+ \nu_L)}{\Gamma(K_L^0 \to \pi^+ L_{-s}^- \bar{\nu}_L)} \approx \left|\frac{\exp\left(\omega_{00} T_K\right)}{\exp\left(-\omega_{00} T_K\right)}\right|^2 \cong 1 + 4\omega_{00} T_K \tag{13.5.6}$$

Comparison with (13.1.6b) gives the identification

$$\omega_{00} T_K = \mathrm{Re}(\varepsilon) \tag{13.5.7}$$

This together with (13.1.7) and the upper of (13.4.6) yields the cutoff

$$T_K \approx 5.5 \times 10^{-5}\ \mathrm{eV}^{-1} = 1.2 \times 10^{-11}\ \mathrm{s} \tag{13.5.8}$$

which is more than 10 times shorter than the $K_S{}^0$ decay time. Thus, by suitable choices of the limits of the relative times, the present theory reproduces the rather successful phenomenological (13.1.6b).

13.6. On the Origin of CP Violation in Neutral Kaon Decay

From the semi-leptonic decays in Sec. 13.5, the phenomenological phase angle Θ in (13.1.1) by (13.1.4-5) and (13.5.7) becomes

$$\Theta = i2\varepsilon \approx \pm i\sqrt{2}|\varepsilon|(1+i) = \pm i2\omega_{00} T_K \mp 2\omega_{00} T_K \tag{13.6.1}$$

Here, Θ is identified with the product of a relative energy and a relative time, both finite. For the CP violating $K_L^0 \to 2\pi$ in Sec. 13.4, the phase angle $\omega_{00} T_L$ in (13.4.8) via (13.4.3) associated with K_L^0 is real. This corresponds to that the angle Θ in (13.1.1) is also real for this case and is related to $\omega_{00} T_L$, also a product of a finite relative energy and a finite relative time.

Equations (13.5.4-5) show that it is the imaginary part of the relative energy ω_0 in (13.3.3) and (13.5.2) that causes (13.5.6) to deviate from unity and thereby causes CP violation in the semi-leptonic decays, which takes place when the relative time x^0 between the s and d quarks does not extend to both $+\infty$ and $-\infty$ but is cut off at one end.

This does not conflict with that $-\infty \leq x^0 \leq \infty$ in (7.4.6b) via (7.3.16) to generate the M_W mass. There, the actions in (7.4.3-4) involve stationary K^0 and $\bar{K}^0$ and not their decay so that (5.7.1) can and has been applied in that stage. The phase factor $exp(i\omega_0 x^0)$ here reduces to 1 there which allows for $-\infty \leq x^0 \leq \infty$, similar to that $\omega_{00}=0$ in (13.5.3) ff renders it to be $\infty/\infty \neq 0$.

For the CP violating $K_L^0 \to 2\pi$, the relative time x^0 also does not extend to both $+\infty$ and $-\infty$ but is cut off at both ends as is shown in (13.4.3) with $T \to T_L$ given in (13.4.8).

Summarizing, CP conservation is related to the phase angle $\omega_0 x^0$. The relative energy ω_0 gives rise to the mass shifts for K_L^0 in (13.4.4) and pions in (13.4.7) and to that the large $K_S^0 \to 2\pi$ decay rate in (13.3.9) is twice the K_L^0 mass shift in (13.4.4). These results are derived within the framework of the present theory.

The relative energy ω_0 is necessary but not sufficient to account for the CP violating $K_L^0 \to 2\pi$ in Sec. 13.4 and the semi-leptonic decays in Sec. 13.5. To achieve these CP violations, cutoffs need be put on the values of the relative time x^0 so that it cannot run from $-\infty$ to ∞. The values of these cutoffs, given in (13.4.8) and (13.5.8), respectively, lie outside the present theory.

The origin of such relative time cutoffs is not understood. How the kaons are produced may also enter here. An observation is that the relative time $|x^0| = |x_{II}^0 - x_I^0|$ must be shorter than twice the laboratory time $2X^0 = |x_{II}^0 + x_I^0|$ in (3.1.3a). Now this X^0 is limited by the finite decay time so that the relative time is also limited. Such cutoffs remind one of the cutoffs needed in loop momenta in quantum field theory, although no loop diagram enters here.

The CP violations here are not related to the CP violating phase in neutrino oscillation phenomenology [P1 Neutrino Mixing].

In this connection, it may be pointed out that the boundary condition of the wave functions χ and ψ in the basic equations (7.1.8-9), at $|x^0| \to \infty$, like T_0 and T in (13.3.6-7), (13.4.3) and (13.5.3), has been *assumed* to be the same as the corresponding ones (fixed) in the laboratory time $|X^0|$, as was pointed out in §6.1.1. The validity of this assumption has not been fully investigated and it is not clear whether this may impact upon the above relative time considerations.

13.7. $\bar{B}^0$- B^0 Mixing

The $\bar{B}^0$-B^0 mixing differs fundamentally from the $\bar{K}^0$-K^0 mixing considered above. The kaons and pions are members of an approximate SU(3) octet providing basis vectors of the *regular* representation of SU(3). They can be transformed into each other by suitable choice of the transformation $U_{3qs}(X)$ of (7.1.7). Their linear combinations K_S^0 and K_L^0 in (7.2.18) are also vectors in this octet space on par with the pion vectors and represent physical mesons suitable for describing some weak decays.

The *c* and *b* quarks are much heavier and the *D* and *B* mesons cannot meaningfully be accommodated in SU(4, 5) multiplets together with the kaons and pions, as was indicated above (2.4.5). In the limit of SU(3) symmetry, B^0 belongs to the triplet (B^+, B^0, $B_S{}^0$) providing basis vectors of the *first fundamental* representation of SU(3). But $\bar{B}^0$ belongs to the antitriplet (B^-, $\bar{B}^0$, $\bar{B}_S{}^0$) providing basis vectors of the *second fundamental* representation of SU(3) transforming differently [L2 (6.16)]. Thus, B^0 and $\bar{B}^0$ cannot be transformed into each other and linear combinations of them of the type (7.2.18) do not have definite transformation properties and hence are not members of any SU(n) multiplet. They remain as physical mesons in two different triplets. The *D* meson triplets behave analogously.

As in Sec. 13.2, the null relative energy condition (5.7.1) is also relaxed for B^0 and $\bar{B}^0$. The complex ω_0 in (13.3.3) is due to the degeneration (7.2.21) involving the complex neutral gauge boson W_U. Data [P1] however show that the semi-leptonic decays of B^0 and $\bar{B}^0$ proceed dominantly via charged gauge bosons $W^{\pm}\rightarrow$ charged leptons; the branching ratio of $B^0\rightarrow \bar{D}^0 Z \rightarrow \bar{D}^0(2K, 2\pi)$ is very small. Therefore, $\omega_0=\omega_{00}$=real as in (13.4.2) for K_L.

Therefore, a mass shift ΔE_{B0} equivalent to ΔE_{0L} in (13.4.4) also holds for B^0. For $\bar{B}^0$, the lower sign in (5.1.1) is chosen. The laboratory time X^0 dependent part of the B^0 and $\bar{B}^0$ wave functions is

$$\Psi_{B0}\left(X^0\right)=\exp\left[\left(-\frac{\Gamma_{B0}}{2}-iE_{00}-i\Delta E_{B0}\right)X^0\right]$$
$$\Psi_{\bar{B}0}\left(X^0\right)=\exp\left[\left(-\frac{\Gamma_{B0}}{2}-iE_{00}+i\Delta E_{B0}\right)X^0\right] \quad (13.7.1)$$

where E_{00} is the mass and Γ_{B0} the decay rate of B^0 and $\bar{B}^0$. The X^0 dependent part of the probability of mixed B^0 and $\bar{B}^0$ is

$$\left|\Psi_{B0}\left(X^0\right)\pm\Psi_{\bar{B}0}\left(X^0\right)\right|^2=\pm 2\left(\exp\left(-\Gamma_{B0}X^0\right)\right)\left(1+\cos\left(2\Delta E_{B0}X^0\right)\right)$$
$$\Delta E_{B0}=2\omega_{00}^2/E_{00} \quad (13.7.2)$$

It is proportional to the phenomenological probability for remaining in the original bottom state [K4 (6.9)]

$$P\left(B^0\rightarrow B^0\right)=P\left(\bar{B}^0\rightarrow\bar{B}^0\right)=\frac{1}{2}\exp(-\Gamma t)\left(1+\cos\left(\Delta m_d t\right)\right) \quad (13.7.3)$$

Here, $\Gamma=\Gamma_{B0}$, $t=X^0$ and the oscillation frequency $\Delta m_d=2\Delta E_{B0}=3.337\times10^{-4}$ eV [P1]. With the B^0 mass E_{00}=5.2796 GeV, the second of (13.7.2) gives the relative energy ω_{00}=663.66 eV between the *b* and *d* quarks. This value is 22.5 times greater than 29.44 eV in (13.4.6) for that between the *s* and *d* quarks in K^0. Note that the ratio between the B^0 and K^0 masses is 10.6, nearly half the above ratio.

The mass difference 3.337×10^{-4} eV is somewhat less than the B^0 decay rate $\Gamma_{B0}=4.43\times10^{-4}$ eV [P1], similar to that the K_L^0-K_S^0 mass difference is about half of the K_S^0 decay rate in (13.1.3). These mass differences, apart from their values, are outcomes of the present theory, irrespective CP violation. Analogously, CP violation in the $\bar{B}^0$-B^0 system is also attributed to relative energy and time between the *b* and *d* quarks. Such a treatment however requires the knowledge of the amplitudes of 5 specific decays [K4 §6.9] and is beyond the scope of this paper.

In passing, it may be noted that while mixings of *d*, *s* and *b* quarks take place, the *c* and *u* quarks with charge 2*e*/3 do not seem to mix, as $\bar{D}^0$-D^0 mixing is absent in [P1].

Chapter 14

QCD as High Energy Limit of the Present Theory [H21]

In this chapter, QCD will be derived from the present SSI in some high energy region. Quarks in mesons have two "colors" and quarks in baryons have in general three "colors."

14.1. Comparison to QCD

This has been discussed in Sec. 12.8 of the first edition of this book [H18] and will be worked out here.

Table 14.1. Key ingredients in QED, QCD and SSI (scalar strong interaction hadron theory) for comparison

Nonlocal theory Cannot be quantized	Loop diagrams Renormalization- -diff. gauges	Loop diagrams Renormalization	
At high energies, the quarks are nearly free. The different internal spaces for quarks in SSI provide a new degree of freedom similar to color in QCD, which can largely be taken over (this Chapter)	Asymtotic freedom- 1st order nonAbelian self coupling Feynman Rules:(FR) quark ≈ gluon ≈ Ghost-nonabelian self coupling	Feynman Rules:(FR) lepton photon	QUANTUM FIELD THEORY Higher energies, Higher orders in coupling constant
Predictive power: Similar to QCD's	Predictive power: Good	Predictive power: Highly accurate	
$A^l_{\mu\nu} = \partial_\mu A^l_\nu - \partial_\nu A^l_\mu$ $+ q\varepsilon^{lmn} A^m_\mu A^n_\nu$ A^l_μ = like "gluon"	$F^l_{\mu\nu} = \partial_\mu V^l_\nu - \partial_\nu V^l_\mu$ $+ gf^{lmn} V^m_\mu V^n_\nu$ V^l_μ = gluon	$F_{\mu\nu} = \partial_\mu A_\nu - \partial_\nu A_\mu$ A_μ = photon	
SSI Lagrangians ↕ Meson eq. of motion (akin to $\lambda\phi^4$ theory) Baryon eq. of motion	QCD Lagrangian (↑FR) does not yield useful eq. of motion	QED Lagrangian ↕ Dirac eq. (↑FR) Maxwell eq. (↑FR)	QUANTUM MECHANICS Low energies, 0th, 1st order in coupling constant
Predictive power: Limited but of basic nature, Ok presently	Predictive power: Nearly none	Predictive power: Firmly established	
Scalar Strong Int-SSI	QCD	QED	

Quantum Chromodynamics, QCD, is a quantum field theory for "colored" quarks based on the QCD Lagrangian [P1, P2]. The interquark force is of "color" vectorial nature. However, the equations of motion at the quantum mechanical level obtained from the QCD Lagrangian are in terms of unobservable "colored" quarks and are of no use at low energies. This theory can basically not account for low energy phenomena but has proven to be successful at high energies.

As is shown above, the present theory SSI can account, to a limited extent of varying accuracy, low energy hadronic phenomena of basic importance. The high energy end has been left out. The situation may be summarized in Table 14.1, which includes the established QED as reference.

The wave functions for mesons in (2.4.2) and for baryons in (9.3.11) have been solved for hadrons at rest. In motion, only nonrelativistic and extremely relativistic wave functions for pseudoscalar meson are approximately given in Sec. 5.7. More basically, the free hadron wave functions in (2.4.2) and (9.3.11) contain in addition to the laboratory coordinate X, also the relative coordinate x as well as the internal coordinates z and u. The latter ones have no correspondence in classical mechanics and the usual transition rule to quantum mechanics is insufficient. This is in tune with the fact that nonlocal theories can presently not be quantized.

14.2. Equations of Motion for Quarks at High Energies

The rest frame pseudoscalar meson is confined by the interquark potential (3.2.8a, 21) via the generalization (2.2.3),

$$V_{SA}(x_{II})V_{SB}(x_I) \to \Phi_m(x_I, x_{II}) \to \Phi_m(\underline{x}) = -\Phi_c(\underline{x}) + d_{m2}r^2 + d_{m0} \tag{14.2.1}$$

$$\Phi_c(r \to \infty) = \frac{g_s^4}{2} r \int_0^\infty dr' r'^2 \left|\psi_0(r')\right|^2 = \beta_{m0} r \tag{14.2.2}$$

$$\psi_{J0}(r) = \frac{1}{\sqrt{\Omega}} \left(\frac{d_h}{\pi}\right)^{3/4} \exp\left(-\frac{d_h}{2} r^2\right) \tag{14.2.3}$$

where (3.2.19) and (4.3.4a) have been consulted. The quarks are confined by the $d_{m2}r^2$ term in (14.2.1) to a size of about $r_0 \approx 3.78$ GeV^{-1} (4.6.1).

In experiments with high energies of tens to hundreds GeV, the quarks become very energetic and can overcome the confining $d_{m2}r^2 \approx (0.26\text{ GeV})^2$, using (5.2.2) and (3.2.21), for $r \approx r_0$ and Φ_c in (14.2.1) in a relatively large volume in space in which they may be considered as approximately *free*. Now, (2.1.1-4) with V_{SA}, $V_{SB} \to 0$ via the left member of (14.2.1) and the reverse of (2.2.1, 2) is approximately applicable. The numbers are such that this applicability also holds for quarks in excited mesons with an average $r \gg r_0$ to some extent.

Under such circumstances, the van der Waerden spinor form (2.3.11, 12) (see also §6.1.3) generalized from (C10), when transformed back to the usual Dirac bispinor form (A3) with (A5d) via the reverse of (C10) applied to quark A in (2.1.1), becomes

$$\left[-i\gamma^{\mu}\left(\frac{\partial}{\partial x_I^{\mu}}+iq_{op2}(z_I,z_{II})A_{\mu}(x_I)\right)+m_{1op2}(z_I,z_{II})\right]\psi_A(x_I)z_I^p=0 \qquad (14.2.4)$$

Similarly, (2.1.3) goes over to

$$\left[-i\gamma^{\mu}\left(\frac{\partial}{\partial x_{II}^{\mu}}+iq_{op2}(z_I,z_{II})A_{\mu}(x_{II})\right)+m_{1op2}(z_I,z_{II})\right]\psi_B(x_{II})z_{IIr}=0 \qquad (14.2.5)$$

Here,

$$m_{1op2}(z_I,z_{II})=2m_{1op}(z,u), \qquad q_{op2}(z_I,z_{II})=q_{op}(z)+q_{op}(u) \qquad (14.2.6)$$

with their right sides given by (2.3.26, 16) and (2.3.14, 16), respectively. These are generalizations of the mass operator $m_{1op}(z)$ and charge operator $q_{op}(z)$ in (2.3.11) given by (2.3.13, 14). z_I and z_{II} now appear symmetrically in the two operators in (14.2.6).

14.3. Internal Space Symmetry and Gauge Transformation

The internal degrees of freedom in form of the three internal coordinates z_I, z_{II} and z_{III} of Sec. 9.3 can play the same roles as the three colors in QCD. In the meson case, the two internal spaces z_I and z_{II} in (14.2.4, 5) can similarly be interpreted as that each quark has two colors. These internal coordinates z_I and z_{II} are not observables but are "hidden variables," mentioned at the end of Sec. 2.3. They are interchangeable in (14.2.4, 5) since m_{1op2} and q_{op2} therein are invariants under $z_I \leftrightarrow z_{II}$ according to (14.2.6). This provides a *new symmetry* equivalent to color symmetry in QCD. Noting this, the total quark wave function $\psi_A(x_I)z_I^p$ in (14.2.4) is generalized to a column matrix with two components, one with z_I the other z_{II}. Consequently, the U(1) gauge field A_μ must also be generalized to an SU(2) gauge field matrix. The so generalized (14.2.4, 5) read

$$\left[-i\gamma^{\mu}\left(\frac{\partial}{\partial x_I^{\mu}}+iq_{op2}(z_I,z_{II})\overline{\underline{\sigma}\,\underline{A}}_{\mu}(x_I)\right)+m_{1op2}(z_I,z_{II})\right]\Psi_A^p=0, \quad \Psi_A^p=\begin{pmatrix}\psi_A(x_I)z_I^p\\ \psi_A(x_I)z_{II}^p\end{pmatrix} \qquad (14.3.1)$$

$$\left[-i\gamma^{\mu}\left(\frac{\partial}{\partial x_{II}^{\mu}}-iq_{op2}(z_I,z_{II})\left\{\overline{\underline{\sigma}\,\underline{A}}_{\mu}(x_I)\right\}_{I\leftrightarrow II}\right)+m_{1op2}(z_I,z_{II})\right]\Psi_{Br}=0$$

$$\Psi_{Br}=\begin{pmatrix}\psi_B(x_{II})z_{IIr}\\ \psi_B(x_{II})z_{Ir}\end{pmatrix} \qquad (14.3.2)$$

observing the definitions

$$A=\begin{pmatrix} A_{11} & A_{12} \\ A_{21} & A_{22} \end{pmatrix}, \qquad \bar{A}=\begin{pmatrix} A_{11}z_I^p\partial/z_I^p & A_{12}z_I^p\partial/z_{II}^p \\ A_{21}z_{II}^p\partial/z_I^p & A_{22}z_{II}^p\partial/z_{II}^p \end{pmatrix} \tag{14.3.3}$$

The stepping operators of the from $z_I\partial/\partial z_{II}$ has been introduced earlier [H12] in connection with massive gauge bosons. As the $\bar{A}$ type of matrices in (14.3.1, 2) operates on z_I and z_{II},

$$\bar{A}^2=\begin{pmatrix} A_{11}z_I^p\partial/z_I^p & A_{12}z_I^p\partial/z_{II}^p \\ A_{21}z_{II}^p\partial/z_I^p & A_{22}z_{II}^p\partial/z_{II}^p \end{pmatrix}^2 = A\bar{A}=\overline{A^2}, \qquad \bar{A}^n = A^{n-1}\bar{A}=\overline{A^n} \tag{14.3.4}$$

because the second order derivatives of the form $\partial^2/\partial z_I^2$, $\partial^2/\partial z_I\partial z_{II}$ in (14.3.4) vanish. Therefore, all higher order derivatives in z_I and z_{II} also drop out. Also, $z_I\partial/\partial z_I$ and $z_{II}\partial/\partial z_{II}$ in $\bar{A}$ may be dropped without affecting the results.

Analogous to the usual field tensor [L5 (18.8)], define the gauge field tensor

$$\overline{\underline{\sigma A}_{\mu\nu}}(x_I)=\frac{\partial}{\partial x_I^\mu}\overline{\underline{\sigma A}_\mu}(x_I)-\frac{\partial}{\partial x_I^\nu}\overline{\underline{\sigma A}_\mu}(x_I)+iq_{op2}(z_I, z_{II})\left[\overline{\underline{\sigma A}_\mu}(x_I), \overline{\underline{\sigma A}_\nu}(x_I)\right] \tag{14.3.5}$$

Let

$$U_2(x_I)=\exp(i\underline{\sigma}\underline{\vartheta}(x_I)), \qquad \overline{U_2}(x_I)=\exp\left(i\overline{\underline{\sigma}\underline{\vartheta}}(x_I)\right) \tag{14.3.6}$$

Under the SU(2) gauge transformations

$$\Psi_A^p \to \Psi_A^{p\prime}=\begin{pmatrix} \psi_A(x_I)' z_I^p \\ \psi_A(x_I)' z_{II}^p \end{pmatrix}=\overline{U_2}(x_I)\Psi_A^p \tag{14.3.7a}$$

$$\overline{\underline{\sigma A}_\mu}(x_I)\to\overline{\underline{\sigma A}_\mu}(x_I)'=\overline{U_2}(x_I)\overline{\underline{\sigma A}_\mu}(x_I)\overline{U_2^{-1}}(x_I)-\frac{i}{q_{op2}(z_I, z_{II})}\overline{U_2}(x_I)\frac{\partial}{\partial x_I^\mu}\overline{U_2^{-1}}(x_I) \tag{14.3.7b}$$

(14.3.1, 5) are inv33ariant; these invariances are the same as the conventional ones without the z´s in (14.3.1, 5, 7a), noting that m_{1op2} and q_{op2} are invariant under $z_I \leftrightarrow z_{II}$ and can respectively be replaced by m_p and q_p. $\underline{\bar{A}}_\mu$ corresponds to the SU(2) gluons in QCD. There are only two degrees of freedom represented by z_I and z_{II} corresponding to two colors for quarks in a meson.

14.4. Derivation of QCD Lagrangian and Relation to Confinement in SSI

The quark Lagrangian density L_Q is obtained by multiplying (14.3.1) from the left by $\bar{\Psi}_{Ap}$ and integrating over the angles in z_I^p and z_{II}^p (2.3.6). Limiting to light quarks u, d and s, corresponding respectively to flavor $p=1$, 2 and 3, which have about the same quark mass m_p in Table 5.2, one obtains

$$\overline{\Psi}_{Ap} = \left(\overline{\psi}_A(x_I)z_{Ip},\ \overline{\psi}_A(x_I)z_{IIp}\right)$$

$$L_Q = \int dv_{z_I p} dv_{z_{II} p} \left\{ \overline{\Psi}_{Ap}\left[-i\gamma^\mu\left(\frac{\partial}{\partial x_I^\mu} + iq_p\overline{\underline{\sigma}\underline{A}_\mu}(x_I)\right) + m_p\right]\Psi_A^p \right\}$$

$$= C_N\left(\overline{\psi}_A(x_I),\ \overline{\psi}_A(x_I)\right)\left[-i\gamma^\mu\left(\frac{\partial}{\partial x_I^\mu} + iq_p\underline{\sigma}\underline{A}_\mu(x_I)\right) + m_p\right]\begin{pmatrix}\psi_A(x_I)\\ \psi_A(x_I)\end{pmatrix},\quad C_N = N_q^2\frac{\pi^6}{3}$$

(14.4.1)

Here, (2.3.9, 6b) have been employed and N_q is a constant in (2.3.9). The quark charge q_p becomes here an unrenormalized coupling constant.

The SU(2) "gluon" Lagrangian density L_G is similarly obtained

$$L_G = \int dv_{z_I p} dv_{z_{II} p} \left\{ z_{Kp}\left(-\frac{1}{2}\right)\mathrm{trace}\left[\overline{\underline{\sigma}\underline{A}_{\mu\nu}}(x_I)\overline{\underline{\sigma}\underline{A}_{\mu\nu}}(x_I)\right]z_K^p \right\}$$

$$= C_N\left(-\frac{1}{2}\right)\mathrm{trace}\left[\underline{\sigma}\underline{A}_{\mu\nu}(x_I)\underline{\sigma}\underline{A}_{\mu\nu}(x_I)\right] \tag{14.4.2}$$

where K runs from I to II. Note that quarks having different "colors" or z_K's have the same space time wave function in (14.4.1), as it should. Adding (14.4.1) and (14.4.2) leads to the total "two color" Lagragian density for $p=1$, 2 or 3.

$$L_Q + L_G = C_N L_{QCD2} \tag{14.4.3}$$

The conventional QCD Lagragian density L_{QCD2} [P1, L5 line below (18.8)] for two colors is thus recovered.

The antiquark equation (14.3.2) can be treated analogously leading to the same results.

Baryon consists of three quarks and makes use of three of (14.2.4) associated with three internal spaces z_I, z_{II} and z_{III} in (9.3.1) or three internal degrees of freedom or "colors." At rest, two quarks merge to form a diquark via (9.2.12) and (9.3.4) and there are only two "colors." The quark-diquark confinement potential (10.1.6a) is analogous to (14.2.1).

When interacting with another particle at higher energies, the quarks also become energetic and the diquark is expected to break up into two quarks so that there are three interquark distances instead of r. These three distances, like r in high energy mesons, are expected to be large so that the three quarks may be regarded as approximately *free* in some ranges of the three distances.

In this case, the above treatment of quarks in meson can be extended to apply to quarks in baryons. The Pauli matrices $\underline{\sigma}$ above is replaced by the Gell-Mann matrices $\underline{\lambda}$ and $\underline{\vartheta}$ has now eight components. The conventional L_{QCD3} [P1, L5 line below (18.8)] for three colors is recovered.

The whole development of L_{QCD2} and L_{QCD3}, including quantization, choice of gauges, renormalization, Feynman rules, asymptotic freedom [G6, P3], etc can be taken over. The anti-screening effect in asymptotic freedom has the strength q_p and corresponds to the electro-weak coupling g in (7.1.2b, 4). This effect is effective at large quark separations r caused by the high energies of the quarks in the experiments. At low energies, confinement is taken over by the scalar strong interaction confinement $d_{m2}r^2$ in (14.2.1) for mesons and $d_{b2}r^2$ in (10.1.6a) for baryons. Therefore, contrary to the mainstream conception of recent decades, *QCD is not a theory for strong interactions*. The strong quark-quark force is given by the scalar potentials Φ_m (2.2.5) and Φ_b (9.2.11).

The QCD running coupling constant α_S depends upon $\beta \propto 11C_2-2n_f$ [L5 (18.146)], where C_2 which is 3 for quarks in baryons but 2 in mesons and the number of massless quark flavors n_f is 2-5. β is thus 61-92% greater in high energy interactions involving baryons than that for mesons. This prediction should be *testable* against experiment designed to measure α_S in high energy mesons, which may not be easy to produce due to their relatively short lifetime.

In this way, QCD is reconciled with the scalar strong interaction hadron theory and complement each other; the former holds at high energies while the latter accounts for, so far to limited extent of basic nature, data at the low energy end of hadron theory. The intermediate energy range remains not covered.

14.5. On Exact and Broken Symmetry and Final Remarks

The known symmetries, C, P, T, and electro-weak SU(2) gauge, are all broken. Because they reside in space-time and isospace, the degrees of symmetry breaking can be measured. The SU(2) internal or "color" gauge symmetry here is however exact and cannot be broken. The associated gauge transformation act on two abstract, internal spaces z_I and z_{II}, which have been created artificially [H5 Sec. 5], Sec. 2.3 to accommodate different quark flavors. These two spaces are identical in structure and there is no quantity in the formalism that distinguishes them from each other, i.e., can break this $z_I \leftrightarrow z_{II}$ symmetry. Even if some such quantity will appear later, it cannot be measured to determine the degree of symmetry breaking because z_I and z_{II} are unobservable "hidden" variables mentioned in Sec. 14.3. Such a symmetry breaking would appear as non-existent. As the "gluons" in (14.3.1, 2) depend upon the unobservable quark coordinates x_I and x_{II} as well as z_I and z_{II}, they can also not be observed.

Chapters 3 and 10 further show that the bulk of hadron physics takes place in the relative space among the quarks. These physics come out of solutions to partial differential equations and cannot be adequately represented by parameters and structure functions introduced into local phenomenological models widely used. The relative time among the quarks, absent in these models, turns out to be a chief contributor to the new physics found in the present theory.

Returning to the low energy end, many of the present problems are computational. The wave functions of moving mesons in Sec. 5.7 need be further specified and the classical energy-momentum relation (5.7.32) needs be established for large meson momenta $\underline{K}$. The physical meaning of ∞/∞ of §7.5.4 needs be understood. The baryon sector has been only touched upon. The formulation of meson-meson (four quarks), meson-baryon (three quarks and a diquark) and baryon-baryon (two quarks and two diquarks) interaction problems should be of great interest to nuclear physics.

Chapter 15

Gravitation, Relative Energy and Dark Matter [H29-H33]

The standard model SM cannot be integrated with general relativity and cannot explain the interactions enter; the much weaker gravitational forces have been left out. In cosmic phenomena, however, these forces become important and must be included.

Recently, dark matter and dark energy were recognized to be inherent in SSI extended to include gravity [H29]; their origin is the invisibility or "darkness" of quarks. Many such dark phenomena could be accounted for [H30-33], as was mentioned in the introduction of [H33].

In these applications, the diquark and quark in proton in interstellar hydrogen gas are polarized by their ambient gravitations field. This will be treated in this chapter.

15.1. Equations of Motion for Diquark in Gravitational Field

Due to the small size of the nucleon, only the scalar or Newtonian component of an ambient gravitational field needs be incorporated into SSI, ignoring the tensorial components.

15.1.1. Equations of Motion for Quark in Gravitational Field

These are naturally obtained by adding a scalar gravitational potential next to the scalar strong interquark potentials in the equations of motion of a quark. Thus, (9.1.2) turns into [H31 (2.1), H30 A1]

$$\begin{aligned} &\partial_{II}^{d\dot{e}}\chi_{B\dot{e}}(x_{II})-i\left(V_{BC}(x_{II})+V_{BA}(x_{II})+V_{BG}(x_{II})\right)\psi_B^d(x_{II})=im_B\psi_B^d(x_{II}) \\ &\partial_{II\,\dot{e}f}\psi_B^f(x_{II})-i\left(V_{BC}(x_{II})+V_{BA}(x_{II})+V_{BG}(x_{II})\right)\chi_{B\dot{e}}(x_{II})=im_B\chi_{B\dot{e}}(x_{II}) \end{aligned} \tag{15.1.1}$$

where the first two V's are the scalar strong interquark potential like those mentioned below (2.1.2). V_{BG} is an ambient, perturbative gravitational potential [H32 (A1)]

$$V_{BG}(x_{II})=m_B\varepsilon_{II}, \qquad \varepsilon_{II}=\varepsilon_{II}\left(|\underline{x}_{II}|\right)=-\frac{GM_g}{|\underline{x}_{II}|} \tag{15.1.2}$$

Here, G is the gravitational constant. Taking the Milky Way as an example, M_g is its mass and $\underline{x}_{II}$ the distance vector between the center of this mass and quark B and may be of the magnitude of 100 ly (light year). ε_{II} is thus a small number of the magnitude of 10^{-6}.

The equations of motion for the quarks A and C (9.1.1, 3) have similarly been extended to include gravitation to yield

$$\partial_I^{a\dot{b}}\chi_{A\dot{b}}(x_I)-i(V_{AB}(x_I)+V_{AC}(x_I)+V_{AG}(x_I))\psi_A^a(x_I)=im_A\psi_A^a(x_I)$$
$$\partial_{I\dot{b}c}\psi_A^c(x_I)-i(V_{AB}(x_I)+V_{AC}(x_I)+V_{AG}(x_I))\chi_{A\dot{b}}(x_I)=im_A\chi_{A\dot{b}}(x_I) \qquad (15.1.3)$$

$$\partial_{III}^{g\dot{h}}\chi_{C\dot{h}}(x_{III})-i(V_{CA}(x_{III})+V_{CB}(x_{III})+V_{CG}(x_{III}))\psi_C^g(x_{III})=im_C\psi_C^g(x_{III})$$
$$\partial_{III\,\dot{h}k}\psi_C^k(x_{III})-i(V_{CA}(x_{III})+V_{CB}(x_{III})+V_{CG}(x_{III}))\chi_{C\dot{h}}(x_{III})=im_C\chi_{C\dot{h}}(x_{III}) \qquad (15.1.4)$$

15.1.2. Construction of Diquark Equation of Motion in Gravitational Field

The original equations of motion (9.3.9) for baryons have been constructed from the equations of motion of three quarks (9.1.1-2.3). For ground state baryons, two of the quarks have the same flavor and have been merged into a diquark leading to (9.3.11). In this process, the diquark equations of motion were sidestepped.

When gravitation is turned on, it affects the diquark and the remaining quark differently. Therefore, the diquark equations of motion need be written out explicitly.

Following the procedure of [H32 (A5), (A6)], multiply (15.1.3) by (15.1.4) and generalize the product wave functions into nonseparable diquark wave functions like those in (2.2.2-3). The result reads

$$\chi_{A\dot{b}}(x_I)\chi_{C\dot{h}}(x_{III})\to\chi_{AC\{\dot{b}\dot{h}\}}(x_I,x_{III}),\quad \psi_A^c(x_I)\psi_C^k(x_{III})\to\psi_{AC}^{\{ck\}}(x_I,x_{III}) \qquad (15.1.5)$$

$$V_{ABCG}^2(x_I,x_{III})=(V_{AB}(x_I)+V_{AC}(x_I)+V_{AG}(x_I))(V_{CA}(x_{III})+V_{CB}(x_{III})+V_{CG}(x_{III})) \qquad (15.1.6)$$

$$\partial_I^{a\dot{b}}\partial_{III}^{g\dot{h}}\chi_{AC\{\dot{b}\dot{h}\}}(x_I,x_{III})=-(V_{ABCG}^2(x_I,x_{III})+m_Am_C)\psi_{AC}^{\{ag\}}(x_I,x_{III})$$
$$\partial_{I\dot{b}c}\partial_{III\dot{h}k}\psi_{AC\{\dot{b}\dot{h}\}}(x_I,x_{III})=-(V_{ABCG}^2(x_I,x_{III})+m_Am_C)\chi_{AC\{\dot{b}\dot{h}\}}(x_I,x_{III}) \qquad (15.1.7)$$

In this process, mixed spinors possessing one dotted and one undotted indices transform like mesons, which are absent here, and are dropped, similar to the equivalent procedure in Sec. 9.2.

15.1.3. Equations of Motion for Diquark and Quark in Gravitational Field

Follow the procedure of [H32 (A5)] and move quark C at x_{III} towards quark A at x_I and let both quarks be merged into a diquark,

$$\chi_{AC\{\dot{b}\dot{h}\}}(x_I,x_{III})\to\chi_{A\{\dot{b}\dot{h}\}}(x_I),\quad \psi_{AC}^{\{ck\}}(x_I,x_{III})\to\psi_A^{\{ck\}}(x_I) \qquad (15.1.8)$$

In ground state nucleons, (15.1.7-8) describes the *uu* diquark in a proton or the *dd* diquark in a neutron. The remaining quark obeys the quark equation (15.1.1). In this merging process, V_{AC} and V_{CA} drop out and $V_{CB}=V_{AB}$ in (15.1.6). Since G in (15.1.2) is small, only terms linear in $V_{AG}=V_{CG}$ need be included in (15.1.6) so that

$$\begin{gathered} V_{ABCG}^{2}\left(x_{I}, x_{III}\right) \rightarrow V_{AB}^{2}\left(x_{I}\right)+2 V_{AB}\left(x_{I}\right) V_{AG}\left(x_{I}\right) \\ \square_{I} \square_{I} V_{AB}^{2}\left(x_{I}\right)=\frac{1}{4} g_{s}^{4}\left\{\begin{array}{l} \psi_{A}^{\{ag\}}\left(x_{I}\right) \chi_{A\{ag\}}\left(x_{I}\right)+\psi_{A}^{\{\dot{a}\dot{g}\}}\left(x_{I}\right) \chi_{A\{\dot{a}\dot{g}\}}\left(x_{I}\right) \\ +\psi_{B}^{\{eh\}}\left(x_{I}\right) \chi_{B\{eh\}}\left(x_{I}\right)+\psi_{B}^{\{\dot{e}\dot{h}\}}\left(x_{I}\right) \chi_{B\{\dot{e}\dot{h}\}}\left(x_{I}\right) \end{array}\right\} \end{gathered} \tag{15.1.9}$$

The last relation is (9.1.4a)×(9.1.4c) together with (15.1.5, 8). Equation (15.1.7) now becomes

$$\begin{aligned} \partial_{I}^{a\dot{b}} \partial_{I}^{g\dot{h}} \chi_{A\{\dot{b}\dot{h}\}}\left(x_{I}\right) &= -\left(V_{AB}^{2}\left(x_{I}\right)+2 V_{AB}\left(x_{I}\right) V_{AG}\left(x_{I}\right)+m_{A}^{2}\right) \psi_{A}^{\{ag\}}\left(x_{I}\right) \\ \partial_{I \dot{b} c} \partial_{I \dot{h} k} \psi_{A\{\dot{b}\dot{h}\}}\left(x_{I}\right) &= -\left(V_{AB}^{2}\left(x_{I}\right)+2 V_{AB}\left(x_{I}\right) V_{AG}\left(x_{I}\right)+m_{A}^{2}\right) \chi_{A\{\dot{b}\dot{h}\}} \end{aligned} \tag{15.1.10}$$

The quark equations (15.1.1) now become

$$\begin{aligned} \partial_{II}^{d\dot{e}} \chi_{B\dot{e}}\left(x_{II}\right) &= i\left(2 V_{BA}\left(x_{II}\right)+V_{BG}\left(x_{II}\right)+m_{B}\right) \psi_{B}^{d}\left(x_{II}\right) \\ \partial_{II \dot{e} f} \psi_{B}^{f}\left(x_{II}\right) &= i\left(2 V_{BA}\left(x_{II}\right)+V_{BG}\left(x_{II}\right)+m_{B}\right) \chi_{B\dot{e}}\left(x_{II}\right) \end{aligned} \tag{15.1.11}$$

15.1.4. Recovering Equations of Motion for Ground State Baryon

Following the steps that led to the nucleon wave equations in [H32 (A9)], multiplication of (15.1.10) by (15.1.11) leads analogously to

$$\begin{aligned} \partial_{I}^{a\dot{b}} \partial_{I}^{g\dot{h}} \partial_{II \dot{e} f} \chi_{\{\dot{b}\dot{h}\}}^{f}\left(x_{I}, x_{II}\right) &= -i\left(m_{A}^{2} m_{B}+\Phi_{b}\left(x_{I}, x_{II}\right)+\Phi_{G}\left(x_{I}, x_{II}\right)\right) \psi_{\dot{e}}^{\{ag\}}\left(x_{I}, x_{II}\right) \\ \partial_{I \dot{b} c} \partial_{I \dot{h} k} \partial_{II}^{d\dot{e}} \psi^{ck}{}_{\dot{e}}\left(x_{I}, x_{II}\right) &= -i\left(m_{A}^{2} m_{B}+\Phi_{b}\left(x_{I}, x_{II}\right)+\Phi_{G}\left(x_{I}, x_{II}\right)\right) \chi_{\dot{b}\dot{h}}{}^{d}\left(x_{I}, x_{II}\right) \end{aligned} \tag{15.1.12}$$

Multiplying the second of (15.1.9) by (9.1.4b) recovers (9.2.13b)

$$\square_{I} \square_{I} \square_{II} \Phi_{b}\left(x_{I}, x_{II}\right)=\frac{1}{4} g_{s}^{6}\left\{\chi_{\{\dot{b}\dot{h}\}}^{f}\left(x_{I}, x_{II}\right) \psi_{f}^{\{\dot{b}\dot{h}\}}\left(x_{I}, x_{II}\right)+c.c.\right\} \tag{15.1.13}$$

Here, g_s^2 is the strong quark-quark coupling constant,

$$\Phi_{b}\left(x_{I}, x_{II}\right)=2 V_{AB}^{2}\left(x_{I}\right) V_{BA}\left(x_{II}\right) \tag{15.1.14}$$

is the strong diquark-quark interaction potential and

$$\Phi_G(x_I, x_{II}) = 4V_{AG}(x_I)V_{AB}(x_I)V_{BA}(x_{II}) + V_{BG}(x_{II})V_{AB}^2(x_I) \quad (15.1.15)$$

is the correction to Φ_b in due to gravitation.

Turning to (15.1.12), leave the gravitational perturbation Φ_G aside for a moment, replace the quark mass term by quark mass operators, as in (9.3.8) and multiply the baryon wave functions by baryon internal functions, as in (9.3.6). These converts (15.1.12) to (9.3.16) which in the subsequent developments led to the radial equations for ground state baryons (10.2 12).

Thus, the baryon wave equations in Chapter 10 can also be derived via combining the diquark and quark equations in §15.1.3, as expected.

In specializing (15.1.12) to (10.2.12),

$$\Phi_b(x_I, x_{II}) \to \Phi_{bd}(r) = \Phi_b(r) \quad (15.1.16)$$

where Figure 12.1 has been noted. Therefore, (15.1.14) becomes (12.6.18) [H30 A22].

15.2. Gravitational Polarization of Diquark-Quark in Nucleon

The parameter regions considered here will be like those in interstellar medium away from the center of a galaxy like the Milky Way. This medium is dominated by rarefied, cold hydrogen gas with a density of 20-50 atoms/cm^3 and a temperature of 50-100 °K and has a pressure gradient and eventual centrifugal force acting on it that largely balance off the gravitational pull on this gas from the galactic center [W7 Milky Way]. Let the elastic collisions cross section between two such atoms be a disk of $4\pi a_0^2$ where a_0=0.53Å is the Bohr radius. Then, the magnitude of the mean free path of a test hydrogen atom is 10 AU and of the mean collision time 10 years.

15.2.1. Structure of Free Hydrogen Atom and Gravitational Polarization

The neutron characteristics in §12.6.4 can approximately be taken over for a free proton because both nucleons have nearly the same mass. The structure of a test hydrogen atom containing this proton is illustrated in Figure 15.1.

Place now this test atom with *uu-d* in Figure 15.1 in the above-mentioned interstellar medium in which a gas pressure gradient exists causing the galaxy to expand. This test atom will in time experience collisions with other atoms and will on the average move outwards toward larger $\underline{X}$. As the gas temperature is low, such collisions are mostly elastic. The atoms interact electromagnetically via their electrons. The accompanying forces are transmitted to the proton via Coulomb interaction. The proton is dragged along and also moves outwards. The heavier *uu-d* unit (see Table 5.2) experiences however a greater gravitational pull and may lag behind and end up to the left of $\underline{X}_H=\underline{X}_p$.

It is such lag or shift that gives rise to dark matter. This situation is illustrated in Figure 15.2; the quarks *uu-d* are polarized by the gravitational field, with the heavier *uu* diquark closer to the galaxy center. This will be treated in §15.2.2 below.

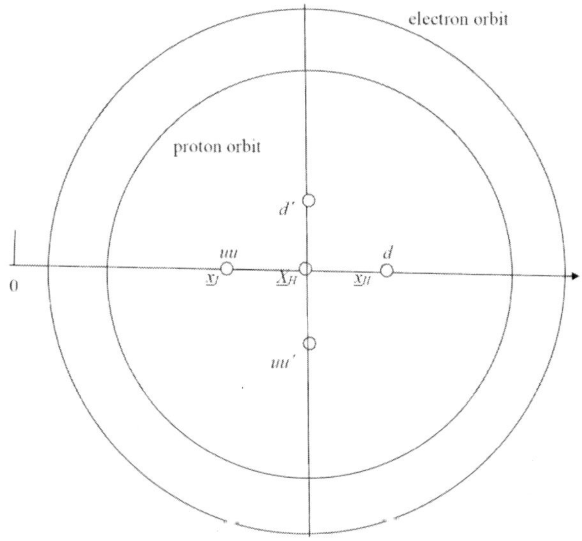

Figure 15.1. Schematic structure of a free, ground state hydrogen atom at rest in SSI. The large electron orbit has been scaled down to fit inside this figure. $\underline{X}_H$ denotes the coordinate of the center of this atom. It is also the center $\underline{X}_e$ of the electron charge cloud having a radius of 0.53Å (Bohr radius a_0, outer circle) as well as the center $\underline{X}_p$ of the proton charge cloud having a radius of 28.8 fm (proton Bohr radius a_{0p}, inner circle). $\underline{X}_H=\underline{X}_p=\underline{X}_e$. The small distance $r_a=|\underline{x}|=3.05$ fm (12.6.22), where $\underline{x}=\underline{x}_{II}-\underline{x}_I$ is the distance vector between the *uu* diquark and the *d* quark, has been scaled up for illustration. In the absence of gravitational field, $\underline{x}$ can form any angle with the horizontal $\underline{X}$ axis. Here, the angles 0° for *uu-d* and 270° for *uu´-d´* have been chosen for illustration. $\underline{X}_H$ lies in the middle of these four quarks. If a galaxy center is placed at $\underline{X}=0$, $\underline{X}_H$ will become $10^{3\text{-}4}$ ly and experience a gravitational field along $\underline{X}$, as do the quarks with the heavier *uu* diquark closer to the galaxy center.

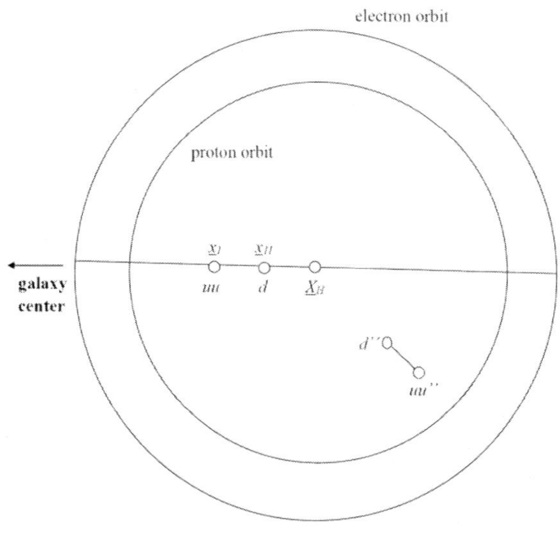

Figure 15.2. Schematic structure of the test hydrogen atom in Figure 15.1 after elastic collisions with other hydrogen atoms in interstellar medium. Gas pressure gradients causes $\underline{X}_H=\underline{X}_p$ to increase but the heavier *uu-d* quarks may lag behind and end up to the left of $\underline{X}_H=\underline{X}_p$; they have been shifted by the galaxy's gravitational field and dark matter is generated by this atom. In a subsequent collision, these quarks are dislocated again and may end up as *uu´´-d´´*; the polarization of the *uu-d* quarks before this collision as in Figure 15.1 is lost and so does the generated dark matter. But differential gravitational pull on *uu´´* and *d´´* will quickly cause it to return to a configuration parallel to *uu-d* and thereby restore the original polarization and the dark matter.

This polarization along the gravitational field can however be destroyed in the next collision which can cause the quarks to end up in new positions that settle down to, for instance, *uu''* and *d''* in Figure 15.2. In quasi-steady state, *uu''*, *d''* and the proton at $\underline{X}_H$ all lie on another straight line, as they did before the collision on the horizontal line. This will be seen in (15.3.2) ff below. However, the polarization of *uu* and *d* is now lost.

15.2.2. Persistency of Gravitational Polarization of Proton

At this stage, the gravitational field will act upon *uu''* and *d''* now at new, asymmetrical positions. If *uu''* and *d''* were free, classical particles, the gravitational forces acting upon them will pull them toward the galaxy center with the same acceleration and velocity (Galileo's Pisa experiment); the asymmetry persists and the earlier polarization remains lost.

But the *uu''* and *d'* quarks are not classical particles. The diquark *uu''* is described by (15.1.10) which can be put in the form

$$\begin{aligned} \partial_I^{a\dot{b}} \partial_I^{g\dot{h}} \chi_{A\{\dot{b}\dot{h}\}}(x_I) &= -\left(V_{AB}^2(x_I)(1+\Lambda_{Guu}(x_I)) + m_A^2\right)\psi_A^{\{ag\}}(x_I) \\ \partial_{I\dot{b}c} \partial_{I\dot{h}k} \psi_{A\{\dot{b}\dot{h}\}}(x_I) &= -\left(V_{AB}^2(x_I)(1+\Lambda_{Guu}(x_I)) + m_A^2\right)\chi_{A\{\dot{b}\dot{h}\}} \end{aligned} \tag{15.2.1a}$$

$$\Lambda_{Guu}(x_I) = 2V_{AG}(x_I)/V_{AB}(x_I) \tag{15.2.1b}$$

Similarly, the quark equations (15.1.11) for *d''* become

$$\begin{aligned} \partial_{II}^{d\dot{e}} \chi_{B\dot{e}}(x_{II}) &= i\left(2V_{BA}(x_{II})(1+\Lambda_{Gd}(x_{II})) + m_B\right)\psi_B^d(x_{II}) \\ \partial_{II\,\dot{e}f} \psi_B^f(x_{II}) &= i\left(2V_{BA}(x_{II})(1+\Lambda_{Gd}(x_{II})) + m_B\right)\chi_{B\dot{e}}(x_{II}) \end{aligned} \tag{15.2.2a}$$

$$\Lambda_{Gd}(x_{II}) = V_{BG}(x_{II})/2V_{BA}(x_{II}) \tag{15.2.2b}$$

Here, Δ_{Guu} represents the correction to the potential experienced by the diquark *uu''* due to the presence of gravitation. Analogously, Δ_{Gd} represents the corresponding correction for the quark *d''*.

With (12.6.18) and (15.1. 2), these corrections take the form

$$\Lambda_{Guu}(x_I) = \left(-\frac{GM_g}{|\underline{x}_I|} m_A\right)\left(\frac{2}{V_s(r)}\right) \tag{15.2.3}$$

$$\Lambda_{Gd}(x_{II}) = \left(-\frac{GM_g}{|\underline{x}_{II}|} m_B\right)\left(\frac{1}{2V_s(r)}\right) \tag{15.2.4}$$

Since the *u* quark mass $m_A \cong m_B$, the *d* quark mass, and $|\underline{x}_{II}| \cong |\underline{x}_I|$, these results show that the gravitational correction Δ_{Guu} of the potential experienced by the diquark *uu''* is four times greater than Δ_{Gd} for the d'' quark. Since the gravitational force acting on these quarks are gradients of these potentials, the uu'' diquark experiences a gravitational pulling force four times that by the d'' quark.

Putting these forces equal to mass×acceleration, the acceleration towards the galaxy center experienced by the diquark uu'' is twice that experienced by the quark d''. This situation differs from the classical mechanics model mentioned above (15.2.1) in which uu' and d' experience the same acceleration. Therefore, the diquark uu'' will move towards the galactic center faster than does the d'' quark in Figure 15.2. This uu''- d'' "rod" [H30 §A8] will be polarized by the gravitational field and return to an orientation same as that before the collision, i.e., that of the *uu-d* rod in Figure 15.2. In this orientation, the gravitational forces become aligned with the strong interquark force along the uu''- d'' rod and can neglected.

Thus, the gravitational polarization of this test proton persists, unaffected by collision, except for a short relaxation time.

15.2.3. Estimate of Relaxation Time

The uu''-d'' distance is the same as the *uu-d* rod length $r_a \approx 3.05$ fm (12.6.22) fixed by the strong interquark potential $V_s(r)$ in (12.6.18), shown in Figure 12.1. Gravitational force cannot change this length but can change the orientation of this uu''-d'' rod to that before the collision.

The time scale needed for such a change may be estimated quasi-classically as follows. From the end of §15.2.2, it is seen that the relative gravitational acceleration $\underline{a}_r$ between uu'' and d'' is the same as the acceleration $\underline{a}_{BG}$ of the d'' quark. It can be estimated from (15.1.2);

$$\underline{a}_r(\underline{x}_{II}) \approx \underline{a}_{BG}(\underline{x}_{II}) = -\frac{\partial V_{BG}(\underline{x}_{II})}{m_B \partial \underline{x}_{II}} = -\frac{GM_g}{|\underline{x}_{II}|^2} \approx 1.48 \times 10^{-10} \text{ m/s}^2 \qquad (15.2.5)$$

where the Milky Way mass $M_g \approx 10^{12} \times M_{SUN}$ and the galaxy radius $|\underline{x}_{II}| \approx 100$ kly (kilo light years).

This relative acceleration $\underline{a}_r$ is directed towards left and is parallel to the horizontal axis in Figure 15.2. It can be split up in a component $\underline{a}_{r1}$ parallel to $\underline{x}$, separating uu'' and d'', and a component $\underline{a}_{r2}$ perpendicular to it. $\underline{a}_{r1}$ will push this uu''-d'' rod towards left and upwards along $\underline{x}$. $\underline{a}_{r2}$ will tend to swing uu'' downwards towards the left in a circular movement and cause it to pass d'' until it ends up on its left side on a horizontal line. The original polarized *uu-d* rod orientation is recovered.

The distance covered by this movement is of the magnitude $\pi r_a \approx 9.6$ fm. Let the component $\underline{a}_{r2}$ be approximated by $\underline{a}_r/2$ which covers a distance of the magnitude of $a_r t_c^2/4$ where t_c is the time from collision. Equating these two distances provides an estimate

$$t_c \approx 0.04 \text{ sec} \qquad (15.2.6)$$

This time is negligible next to the mean collision time of 10 years mentioned above §15.2.1.

Thus, the *uu´´-d´´* rod will "immediately" after the collision change its orientation back to the original one and end up in the polarized configuration with *uu''* lying closer to the mass center of the galaxy, like the original *uu-d* rod in Figure 15.2.

15.3. Relative Energy between Quarks in Nucleon and Dark Matter

15.3.1. Relative Energy between Diquark and Quark in Proton as Dark Matter

In the above two sections, gravitational potential was introduced at the quark locations x_I and x_{II}. Via the transformation (3.1.3a), the x_I and x_{II} dependence of baryon wave functions has been replaced by dependence upon the visible laboratory coordinate X and the invisible relative coordinate x, as is shown in (10.1.1). Inserting (10.1.1) into the baryon equations of motion (10.1.2), it is seen that the rest frame time dependence of these functions can be written as

$$\exp(-iE_0X^0 + i\omega_0 x^0) = \exp\left[-ix_I^0\left(E_0(1-a_m)+\omega_0\right) - ix_{II}^0\left(a_m E_0 - \omega_0\right)\right] \tag{15.3.1}$$

where (3.1.3a) has been consulted. The right side of (15.3.1) shows that the baryon energy E_0 appears on the same level as does the relative energy, defined as $-\omega_0$, between the diquark and quark in this baryon.

Putting this baryon in a gravitational field, as in Figure 15.2, its mass E_0 is known to interact with a gravitational field observable in the laboratory space X. Therefore, ω_0 will also interact with this gravitational field, albeit unobservable or dark because ω_0 is associated with the invisible relative space x. This has to originate from the gravitational potentials V_{BG}, V_{AG} and V_{CG} introduced in (15.1.1-4). Both E_0 and ω_0 interact with the gravitational field. But only E_0 interacts with the electromagnetic field in laboratory space X and hence is visible while ω_0 in the "hidden" relative space x does not and therefore is invisible.

In a gravitational field, therefore, $\omega_0 \neq 0$. By (3.1.10a), the transformation constant $a_m \neq 1/2$. Therefore, (3.1.12) no longer holds in this chapter; the general (3.1.10a) has to be employed.

Thus, presence of a gravitational field alters the symmetrical configuration in Figure 15.1 where the proton center lies in the middle of the quark pairs. Gravitation will change the *uu-d* configuration in Figure 15.1 to that in Figure 15.2, where the same *uu-d* quarks no longer are placed symmetrically around the proton center but shifted, in this case to the left, closer to the galactic center corresponding to $a_m > 1/2$ and $-\omega_0 < 0$.

Consider the *uu-d* unit in F/igure 15.2, where $\underline{X}_H$, the location of the center of the hydrogen atom, is also the location $\underline{X}_p$ of the center of its proton cloud. Inserting (3.1.3a) into (3.1.10a) yields

$$a_m = \frac{1}{2} + \frac{\omega_0}{E_0} = \frac{\underline{X}_p - \underline{x}_I}{\underline{x}_{II} - \underline{x}_I}, \qquad R_D = \frac{-\omega_0}{E_0} = \frac{1}{2} - \frac{\underline{X}_p - \underline{x}_I}{\underline{x}_{II} - \underline{x}_I} = \frac{1}{2} - \frac{X_p - x_I}{r_a} \tag{15.3.2}$$

$$r_a = x_{II} - x_I = 3.05 \text{ fm}$$

where the three vectors $\underline{X}_p$, $\underline{x}_I$ and $\underline{x}_{II}$ all lie on the same straight line, as is shown in Figure 15.2. The average interquark distance r_a (12.6.22) is fixed by strong interquark interaction and is fairly rigid, unaffected by other forces.

As $-\omega_0$ is a constant in the invisible relative space,

negative relative energy $-\omega_0<0$ has been identified as "dark matter" and
positive relative energy $-\omega_0>0$ as PRE or "dark energy" [H33 (1.1-3)].
(15.3.3)

In a gravitational field, the energy of a proton is proportional to $-E_0<0$. The energy $-\omega_0<0$, identified as "dark matter," generated by this proton has the same sign and therefore causes this proton to be heavier than its mass E_0. The "dark energy" in this book refers to PRE which is produced in hydrogen atom in gravitational field (see §16.1.1 below). It tends to make the proton mass in it lighter or even negative. This "dark energy" is not to be confused with the dark energy, commonly seen in the literature, which stands for some unknown and invisible energy permeating throughout the universe and causes it to expand. R_D in (15.3.2) is the ratio between the unobservable or dark relative energy and the observable proton mass E_0. $R_D<0$ for dark matter and $R_D>0$ for PRE or dark energy.

$r_a>0$ in (15.3.2) and Figure 15.2 implies that the proton is polarized by the ambient gravitational field with the heavier diquark uu at $\underline{x}_I$ closer to the galaxy center than does the d quark at $\underline{x}_{II}$. This polarization can be destroyed by collision of the host hydrogen atom with other atoms, but is restored after a negligibly short time (15.2.6).

The dependence of a_m upon gravity via ω_0 in (15.3.2) implies that the transformation constant a_m in (3.1.3a) can no longer be chosen arbitrarily but has to be proportional to the proton-diquark separation $\underline{X}_p-\underline{x}_I$, as is seen in the first of (15.3.2). Conversely, the relative positions of the quarks and the proton cloud center will determine a_m hence also the dark relative energy $-\omega_0$. These positions may be altered by collisions experienced by the host hydrogen atom, as is illustrated by uu''-d'' in Figure 15.2. Such collisions are mainly of electromagnetic nature and will affect the amount of dark relative energy generated, as is implied above Figure 15.2. In this way, atomic physics affects PRE dark energy production.

15.3.2. Upper Limit of the Ratio Dark Matter/Ordinary Matter in Interstellar Hydrogen Gas

According to §15.3.1, when adding a gravitational field to Figure 15.1, both the proton centered at $\underline{X}_H$ and the quark unit uu-d at x_I and x_{II} will be affected. The gravitational force acting upon a quark B is the gradient of the potential V_{BG} jn (15.1.2). It is proportional to the quark mass m_B and $1/|\underline{x}_{II}|^2$. Similar expressions hold for the diquark at $\underline{x}_I$ and the proton at $\underline{X}_H$. Since these three large distances are nearly the same, the spatial dependence of these three forces is nearly the same. The three forces differ only by the different masses they act upon.

The mass of the quark unit uu-d is $2m_I+m_2\approx 1.98$ GeV according to Table 5.2. It is 2.1 times the proton mass $E_0\approx 0.938$ GeV. Therefore, the quark unit uu-d at x_I and x_{II} will be pulled by a gravitational force 2.1 times that experienced by the proton at $\underline{X}_H$, which is further held back by the pressure gradient in and eventual centrifugal force acting on this atom, as was mentioned above Figure 15.2. Consequently, the *uu-d* unit will lie closer to the galaxy center than does the proton cloud center, as is seen in Figure 15.2.

The magnitude of the left shift of the *uu-d* unit from the proton center due to $\omega_0 \neq 0$ or $a_m \neq 1/2$ is unknown. Present state of SSI is insufficient to provide such prediction.

However, there is a heuristic limit on such left shift if it is assumed that this *uu-d* unit has to reside inside the proton cloud having a radius of 28.8 fm given in the caption of Figure 15.1. Using (15.3.2) applied to the *uu-d* unit in Figure 15.2, it is seen that this requirement gives rise to an upper limit of dark matter/ordinary matter ratio $-R_D$

$$R_D = \frac{-\omega_0}{E_0} \geq \frac{1}{2} - \frac{X_p - x_l}{r_a} = \frac{1}{2} - \frac{28.8 \text{ fm}}{r_a} = -8.94 \tag{15.3.4}$$

The corresponding observed ratio, averaged over the universe, ≈ –5 [W7 dark matter] and lies near the middle of the no shift position in Figure 15.1 to that given by (15.3.4). Note however that in addition to hydrogen gas, stars, dust etc are also included as observable matter in this ratio. But in (15.3.4) only the mass of the hydrogen atom ≈ E_0 enters. Thus, data can only be regarded as roughly compatible with (15.3.4).

15.3.3. Properties of Negative Relative Energy as Dark Matter

Conventional conception of dark matter is that it is an unknown, invisible massive object. This is not the case for the dark matter, represented by the negative relative energy $-\omega_0<0$, generated in SSI above. Such dark matter cannot exist by itself; *it can only exist in cold, rarefied and hydrogen gas with pressure gradient in which the protons are polarized by and their uu-d quarks shifted in ambient gravitational field* (Figure 15.2).

In such gas, each hydrogen atom with a mass E_0 becomes $(1+|R_D|)E_0$ or on the average 5 times more massive gravitationally. This atom will now experience on the average 5 times stronger gravitational pull. This increase may be balanced off if this atom generates greater centrifugal force by moving faster around the galactic center, like that in the case of galaxy rotation curve [W7 dark matter].

The above-mentioned left shift of the *uu-d* quarks is expected to increase with the strength of the gravitational field, which is greater, as does the gas density and gas pressure gradient, near the galactic center. Therefore, more matter and still more dark matter are expected to exist in that region. Such regions are expected to exist in the early phases of the expansions of galaxies and the universe. No dark "energy" is created at this stage. These results are in agreement with current conception.

Note that (15.3.4) has been obtained in the environment mentioned in the beginning of Sec. 15.2. It fails in the rare cases involving inelastic or ionizing collisions in the hydrogen gas. It is also not valid in stars which consist of plasma but contain no hydrogen gas. On the earth, gas pressure and temperature are so high that the frequent interatom collisions destroy the dark matter eventually generated.

In helium, the simple two body, *uu* and *d*, problem here turns into a many body problem involving many quarks and relative spaces. This problem has not been investigated.

15.3.4. Applications

1. *Conventional Applications.* There is a large body of data that requires the presence of dark matter [W7 dark matter]. These include galaxy rotation curves considered in §15.3.3, velocity dispersions, gravitational lensing, etc. In galaxy clusters, the galaxies may play the role of stars and the intergalactic medium that of the interstellar medium above.
   The negative relative energies generated above may play the required roles of such dark matter.
2. *Model for Filament Formation.* Consider the following scenario. A cold, tenuous hydrogen gas cloud exists between two galaxy clusters. Consider a cylinder of this cloud. The gas near the cylinder surface will fall towards the cylinder axis. This scenario is similar to that on the left side of Figure 15.2, where the galaxy center is replaced by the cylinder axis. The gas will according to the mechanism explained in the caption of Figure 15.2 produce dark matter which tends to increase the fall speed. The gas along the cylinder axis will not produce any dark matter due to symmetry but will be compressed by the falling matter and dark matter and produce a radial pressure gradient. This cylinder then shrinks into a thin cylinder or tube consisting mostly of dark matter except for its core which now contains hydrogen gas with high density. Galaxies may be formed along this matter and dark matter tube, resembling a filament [R5]. The observed ratio of dark matter/visible matter of about 5 in such filaments is compatible to the upper limit (15.3.4).
3. *Star Production and Removal of Dark Matter.* In the above, dark matter can be created in hydrogen gas in the environment mentioned above §15.2.1. However, Stars are also formed from the same gas. When a hydrogen atom in this gas is used to build a new star, it gets ionized and becomes part of the hot plasma in this star. The dark matter generated by this atom is lost and the so-produced free proton can, contrary to the proton in a hydrogen atom, not generate any dark matter, as was mentioned at the end of §15.3.3.

Thus, star formation in a galaxy reduces its dark matter content. The amount of dark matter that contributes to e. g. the galaxy rotation curve is diminished by star formation. This galaxy will appear to expand faster.

Similarly, if the universe runs out of hydrogen gas, all dark matter and PRE will also vanish, except possibly in neutron stars and some other exotic objects.

15.4. On Removal of Gravitational Singularity in Collapsing Neutron Star

In this chapter so far, dark matter has been generated by protons in hydrogen atoms in gravitational field but not by free protons. Unlike proton, a neutron cannot form an atom. However, the neutron can generate dark matter in a different environment, a neutron star.

A neutron star with mass greater that the Tolman-Oppenheimer-Volkoff (TOV) limit M_{TOV} ~3 solar mass M_{SUN} becomes a black hole in which the star core collapses to a gravitational mass singularity according to general relativity [W7 black hole/§2.3]. The quark structure of the neutron has been ignored.

General relativity is a classical theory in which mass, length and mass density are continuous quantities that can be 0 and ∞; mass singularity in a black hole is allowed. But the smallest mass unit of baryonic matter is the proton mass, which comprises of three separate point-like quarks interacting strongly (Ch 9). It has extension (§12.6.4) so that mass density may not reach ∞ and no mass singularity may then exist. General relativity breaks down at small distances and high mass densities when applied to the real universe and has to be "cut off" at suitable distances from such 0 and ∞; quark structure of matter enters in such regions.

In dense stellar objects like the neutron star, gravitational forces are so strong and their gradients so large that quark structure of neutron likewise has to be taken into account.

15.4.1. Neutron Star Collapse Scenario

The mechanism of dark matter generation in neutron star can be illustrated in the following idealized scenario. A neutron star with mass $M_{NS}=M_{NSa}$, a critical mass, such that the quantum degeneracy pressure of the neutrons and the strong neutron-neutron repulsion precisely balance off the gravitational pressure. This star is on the verge of gravitational collapse. Let an external neutron arrive at the surface of this star. The star now becomes too heavy and a gravitational collapse starts. Conventionally, this collapse gives rise to a black hole and continues until the star ends up in a mass singularity at its center. However, in neutron stars and black holes, the gravitational forces are so strong and their gradients so large that the diquark-quark structure of the neutron may be affected. This scenario is illustrated in Figure 15.3.

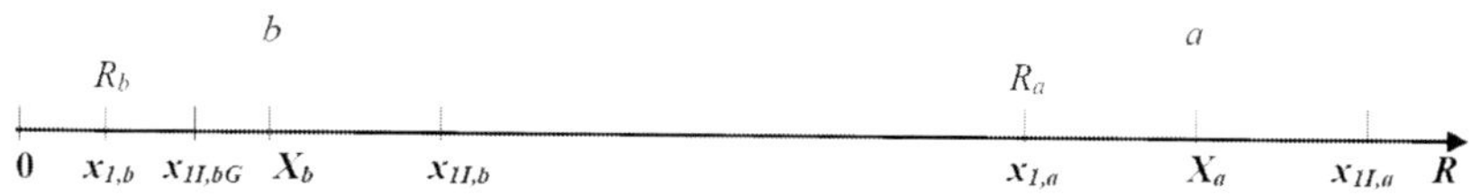

Figure 15.3. Illustration of the above idealized scenario. The horizontal line represents the radius R from the center of the neutron star at R=0. This star having a radius R_a and mass M_{NSa} is on the verge of gravitational collapse. An external neutron arrives at X_a on the surface of this star at $R=R_a=x_{I,a}$ in position a. $x_{I,a}$ is the coordinate of the diquark dd and $x_{II,a}$ that of the quark u in the neutron, The dd-u separation $x_{II,a}-x_{I,a}=r_a$=3.05 fm (12.6.22). The star now becomes too heavy and begins to collapse and shrink from R_a to R_b closer to the star center in position b. At first, this dd-u unit of the arriving neutron is simply shifted from a to b; X_a, $x_{II,a}$ and $x_{I,a}$ become X_b, $x_{II,b}$ and $x_{I,b}$, respectively. But the shrinkage of the star also causes r_a to shrink by a factor R_b/R_a. In this process, $x_{II,b}$ is shifted to $x_{II,bG}$ so that r_a=3.05 fm is reduced to $r_b=x_{II,bG}-x_{I,b}=r_a(R_b/R_a)<3.05$ fm at position b.

In Figure 15.3, an external neutron arrives on the surface of the above-mentioned neutron star at position a on the right part of the figure. The interquark distance is $x_{II,a}-x_{I,a}=r_a$=3.05 fm (12.6.22). This neutron has been polarized by the gravitational field of the star so that the diquark dd arrives first, closer to the star center, analogous to the proton polarization in §15.2.2. The neutron coordinate X_a lies in the middle of dd and u corresponding to a_m=1/2 and ω_0=0 (3.1.12), no dark matter is generated.

This neutron arrival causes the star to collapse gravitationally which is a continuous process. For illustration, let this process be approximated by two discrete steps. In the first step, the *dd-u* unit of the arriving neutron is simply shifted from *a* to *b*; X_a, $x_{II,a}$ and $x_{I,a}$ become X_b, $x_{II,b}$ and $x_{I,b}$, respectively. The diquark-quark distance $r_b=x_{II,b}-x_{I,b}=r_a$ remains unchanged.

In the second step, it is noted that the collapsing star has shrunk from R_a to R_b at position *b*. The arrived neutron is therefore similarly compressed by gravity so that r_a also shrinks to $r_b<r_a$. This is achieved by shifting the *u* quark at $x_{II,b}$ to $x_{II,bG}$ with the diquark *dd* at $x_{I,b}$ remaining on the surface of the star now with radius R_b in Figure 15.3 so that

$$r_a = x_{II,a} - x_{I,a} = x_{II,b} - x_{I,b} \rightarrow r_b = x_{II,bG} - x_{I,b} = r_a R_b / R_a \tag{15.4.1}$$

With this shrinkage of r_a to r_b, the *dd-u* unit is shifted to the left of the neutron at X_b in position *b* of Figure 15.3. This situation is analogous to that the *uu-d* unit has been shifted to the left of X_H by the gravitational field from the galaxy center in Figure 15.2, also explained in §15.3.2. The mass of the quark unit *dd-u* is now $2m_2+m_1$ and is still 2.1 times that of the neutron mass. Therefore, the quark unit *dd-u* at $x_{I,b}$ and $x_{II,bG}$ will be similarly pulled by a gravitational force 2.1 times that experienced by the neutron at X_b. Unlike $\underline{X}_H$ held back by the pressure gradient in Figure 15.2, this X_b is held back by the quantum degeneracy pressure of the neutrons and the strong neutron-neutron repulsion mentioned above.

Therefore, dark matter will likewise be generated by the neutron in Figure 15.3, similar to that generated by the proton in Figure 15.2. Note that the quark and the diquark are point particles in quantum theory and hence cannot be "spaghettified" here.

15.4.2. Possible Non-Collapse of Neutron Star and Absence of Singularity

Application of (3.1.3a), (3.1.10a), (15.4.1), and (15.3.4) to position *b* in Figure 15.3 yields

$$a_m = \frac{1}{2} + \frac{\omega_0}{E_0} = \frac{X_b - x_{I,b}}{x_{II,bG} - x_{I,b}} = \frac{1}{2}\frac{r_a}{r_b} = \frac{R_a}{2R_b}, \qquad R_D = -\frac{\omega_0}{E_0} = -\frac{R_a}{2}\left(\frac{1}{R_b} - \frac{1}{R_a}\right) \tag{15.4.2}$$

where $-\omega_0$ is the relative energy gained when the external neutron arriving at position *a* falls to position *b*. Since this $-\omega_0<0$, it represents dark matter according to (15.3.3).

In this fall, the gravitational energy E_G released is given by

$$\frac{E_G}{E_0} = \frac{R_{Scha}}{2}\left(\frac{1}{R_b} - \frac{1}{R_a}\right), \qquad R_{Scha} = 2GM_{NSa} \tag{15.4.3}$$

where *G* is the gravitational constant and R_{Scha} is the Schwarzschild radius of this collapsing star in Figure 15.3. When the star's radius

$$R_a = R_{Scha} \tag{15.4.4}$$

these two energies cancel each other;

$$E_G - \omega_0 = 0 \tag{15.4.5}$$

In other words, when the neutron star in Figure 15.3 with the critical mass M_{NSa} reaches a radius equal to its Schwarzschild radius R_{Scha}, the gravitational energy generated in the collapse of this star is exactly cancelled by the negative relative energy $-\omega_0<0$ produced due to the ensuing shrinkage of this star.

Thus, at the star center $R_b=0$, both energies become infinite but these both singularities cancel; no net mass singularity is created when (15.4.4) holds. Here, it is implicitly assumed that the gravitational pressure is so strong that it overcomes the strong interaction interquark potential Φ_b in the invisible relative space $\underline{x}$ shown in Figure 12.1.

But this result is based upon the two-step approximation above (15.4.1). In the actual, continuous shrinking process, the distance $X_b-x_{I,b}$ in Figure 15.3 has not been shown to remain constant $r_a/2$ in the second step. If X_b changes in Figure 15.3 in this process, then $-\omega_0$ will deviate from that in (15.4.2) so that the cancellation (15.4.5) no longer is exact; this leads to creation of singularity. Note also that when approaching the star center and R_b becomes of the size of the neutron of a few fm. For $R_a \sim 10$ km; $a_m=R_a/2R_b\approx\omega_0/E_0$ is a huge number $\sim 10^{18}$, far exceeding the upper limit of 9.44 in (15.3.4) for the proton case. This is due to that the requirement for the quarks to reside inside the proton cloud underlying (15.3.4) is absent in the neutron case.

However, (15.4.2) holds in the beginning of the collapse when R_a-R_b is a small shrinkage. In this case, (15.4.2, 5) hold; no net energy is produced in this small shrinkage. This star may not collapse. In this case, the fall of this external neutron actually gains no energy because $E_G-\omega_0=0$ for all R_b. This neutron therefore remains at position a and becomes "weightless." The anticipated collapse of the neutron star does not start and no mass singularity is created.

This is consistent with that SSI is a quantum theory not allowing such a singularity. This achieved by recognizing that baryons are not point particles but has quark structure absent in general relativity.

The radius R_a of the initial neutron star has been estimated by equating gravitational pressure to the pressure of the degenerate neutrons [R6 p161]

$$R_a = 0.0026 R_{Earth}\left(\frac{M_{SUN}}{M_{NSa}}\right)^{1/3} \tag{15.4.5}$$

which together with (15.4.3, 4) yields $R_a=R_{Scha}=10.8$ km and $M_{NSa}=3.6\ M_{SUN}$. This mass is consistent with the similarly estimated maximum mass 4.3 $\underline{M}_{SUN}$ [R6 p162] of a neutron star. It is somewhat higher than $M_{TOV}\sim 3\ M_{SUN}$ cited in the beginning of this section. However, estimates of M_{TOV} are uncertain and vary widely because *equations of state* for *extremely dense matter* are not well known and neutron-neutron repulsion and pressure in general relativity [R6 p162] are uncertain. Thus, the so-estimated star mass may be used on equal footing with those in the literature.

A possible scenario is as follows. As additional neutrons arrive at the star surface, a thin shell of weightless neutrons is added to the star at first. Let the mass of this shell be ΔM_{NSa}, the new Schwarzschild radius will be $R_{Scha\Delta}=(1+\Delta)R_{Scha}$ and the new star radius will be $R_{a\Delta}=(1+\Delta)^{1/3}R_a$, assuming that the neutron density in the shell is the same as that in the star.

Since $R_{Scha\Delta}>R_{a\Delta}$, a black hole is created. As a new neutron arrives at the new star surface with radius $R_{a\Delta}$, it will tend to fall inwards. This time, the gravitational energy (15.4.3) will slightly exceed the relative energy loss (15.4.2) and this new neutron tends to fall slowly. However, the pressure of the degenerate neutron gas in the shell is now unopposed by the weightless neutrons and this gas will therefore expand accompanied by a reduced density. If the expansion reaches a radius > $R_{Scha\Delta}$, the black hole is lost and this enlarged star will be a visible neutron star similar to the initial star in Figure 15.3. If the expansion stops just inside $R_{Scha\Delta}$, the created black hole persists and one arrives at a situation nearly the same as that on the right part of Figure 15.3 with R_a replaced by $R_{a\Delta}$ and (15.4.4) holds. This process may be repeated and more shells are added. It can in principle lead to a super-massive black hole. How the neutrons, part of them "weightless," are distributed inside such a black hole is unknown and needs not be known, inasmuch as they are inside its Schwarzschild radius and cannot be observed any way; there is no conflict with observation.

In this scenario, the neutrons in such a black hole fill it up to its Schwarzschild radius. Such a black hole may more suitably be called a "black neutron star." The above super-massive black hole may actually be a "super-massive black neutron star." Absence of mass singularity in such "black objects" does not contradict quantum mechanics and is consistent with the conjecture that an eventual future quantum gravity theory will not contain any singularity.

Chapter 16

Accelerating Expansion of the Universe and Positive Relative Energy [H33]

In the last chapter, the negative relative energy assigned to dark matter in (15.3.3) was treated in an interstellar medium mentioned above §15.2.1. Its counterpart, the positive relative energy PRE assigned to dark energy in (15.3.3) will be considered in this chapter.

16.1. Generation of Positive Relative Energy PRE or Dark Energy

16.1.1. Mechanism of Generation of PRE Dark Energy

The dark matter generated in Figure 15.2 depends upon two factors, the gravitational polarization of the *uu-d* unit according to §15.2.2 and the gravitational shift of this unit to the left of the proton at X_p mentioned above (15.3.2). When this shift $X_p - x_I > r_a/2 \approx 1.53$ fm in (15.3.2), relative energy $-\omega_0 < 0$; dark matter is generated according to (15.3.3).

Under certain circumstances, however, this *uu-d* unit may be shifted to the right of X_p, as is shown in Figure 16.1. In this case, $X_p - x_I < 0$ so that (15.3.2) yields $-\omega_0 > 0$; PRE dark energy is generated according to (15.3.3).

16.1.2. PRE Dark Energy and "Run Away" Hydrogen Atom

Return to Figure 15.2, the test hydrogen atom in the interstellar medium mentioned above §15.2.1 will migrate outwards due the pressure gradient. In time, it arrives at the outskirts of the galaxy. In that region, the gas pressure gradient, eventual centrifugal force and gravitational pull acting on this atom all become very small and nearly balance off each other so that the expansion of this galaxy nearly comes to a halt. In the absence of force acting on this hydrogen atom, its *uu-d* aggregate in Figure 15.2 will move back close to its normal position in a free hydrogen atom centered at $X_p = X_H$, as is seen in Figure 15.1.

Although the net outward movement of this test hydrogen atom and it's like may nearly vanish, they will still have some small random velocities corresponding at least to the cosmic microwave background average temperature in the universe ~ 2.8 ^0K. In time, this test hydrogen atom will experience a collision with another hydrogen atom that happens to be moving inward towards the galaxy center in Figure 16.1. The electron orbit of the test atom will then be slightly pushed to the left. This motion drags the proton at $X_H = X_p$ also to the left via Coulomb force. The *uu-d* aggregate, ~ 2.1 times heavier than the proton mass, lags behind so that it now lies to the right of $X_H = X_p$, as is shown in Figure 16.1.

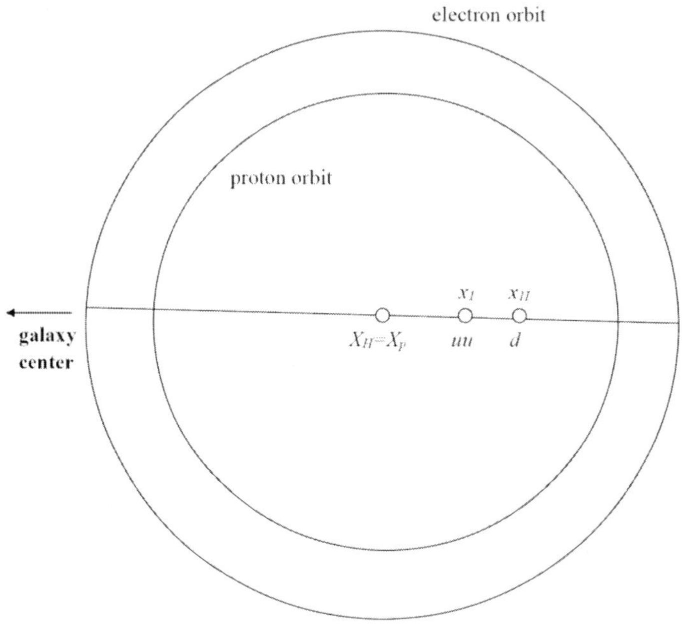

Figure 16.1. This figure is the same as Figure 15.2 with the *uu´´-d´´* quarks removed and the *uu-d* quarks moved from the left side of the center of the proton cloud at X_H=X_p to its right side. In this move, the dark matter generated in the test hydrogen atom in Figure 15.2 turns into PRE dark energy here.

According to §16.1.1, PRE dark energy is generated in this configuration. The gravitational attraction or pull of the dark matter in the test atom in §15.2.1 from the galactic center now turns into antigravity repulsion or push on the PRE dark energy produced, pushing this test atom outwards, towards the right of Figure 16.1. In the outward movement, this atom now is unopposed by any pressure gradient, contrary to the case in Figure 15.2.

Analogous to the case in §15.3.2, it is heuristically assumed that this *uu-d* aggregate has to reside inside the proton cloud having a radius of 28.8 fm. The quark coordinate x_{II} has to lie inside the proton orbit in Figure 16.1. With this requirement, (15.3.2, 4) become

$$R_D = \frac{-\omega_0}{E_0} = -a_m + \frac{1}{2} \leq \frac{28.8\,\text{fm}}{r_a} - \frac{1}{2} = 8.94 \tag{16.1.1}$$

which has the same magnitude as that in (15.3.4).

In this case, however, (16.1.1) does not lead to any limitation to the outward movement of this test hydrogen atom. When the *uu-d* aggregate approaches the proton cloud radius 28.8 fm to the right of X_H=X_p in Figure 16.1, it simply drags the proton cloud together with its orbiting electron along in its outward movement without violating (16.1.1). This time, the outward movement of this atom is unopposed, on the contrary assisted, by the small gas pressure gradient and centrifugal force eventually present. This test hydrogen atom will "*run away*" into the intergalactic void outside the galaxy.

16.2. SSI Model of the Universe

The "run away" mechanism in the expanding galaxy in the above section can however not be applied to the universe in the current ΛCDM model [W7]. Unlike galaxy, finite in size, this universe is infinite in extension and homogeneous and its expansion is driven by the assumed cosmological constant Λ permeating through it.

To show that this mechanism may be relevant to the accelerating expansion of the universe, it will instead be applied to the following model universe, illustrated in Figure 16.2.

From [W7], the radius of the observable universe is $R_{US} = 4.4\times10^{26}$ m. The mass of this universe is estimated from the average density $9.9\times!0^{-30}$ g/cm^3 of the universe and its volume and is $M_U = 3.53\times10^{54}$ kg. The test galaxy is taken to be a copy of the Milky Way in spherical shape. The radius is $R_{GS} = 100$ kly $= 9.46\times10^{20}$ m and the mass $M_G = 2.4\times10^{42}$ kg. This is about 3 times the mass of the Milky Way and reflects the modification of its disc form to sphere form here.

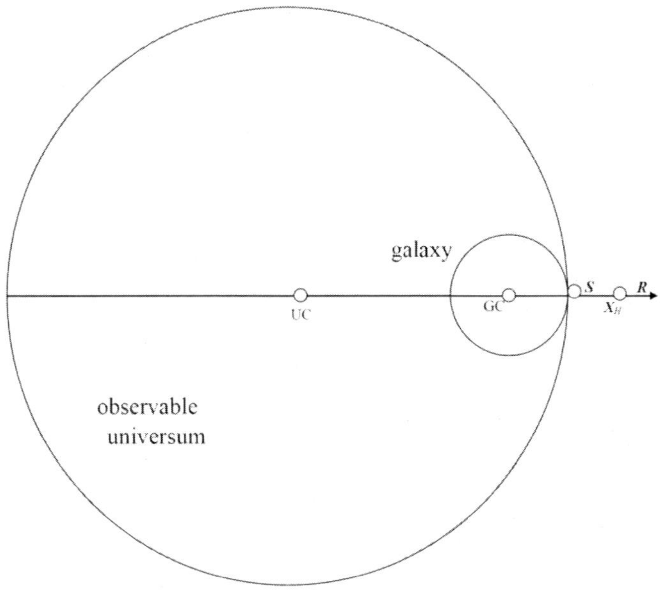

Figure 16.2. A hypothetical SSI model of the observable universe for illustration of the expansion of the outer parts of this universe. The large circle represents the observable universe as a sphere surrounded by vacuum. The actual boundary of this universe is not as sharp as is depicted but is somewhat diffuse. This universe is populated by galaxies with homogeneous distribution. The earth's position in it is unknown. The small circle represents a "test" galaxy like that in Figure 15.2 and is also a sphere lying in an outskirt of this universe. *UC* denotes the center of this universe and may eventually be associated with the big bang itself. *GC* is the center of the test galaxy. *S* denotes the point where the outer edges of both circles coincide. The distance of the test hydrogen atom at X_H from *S* is denoted by *R*.

In (15.3.3) ff, dark matter with relative energy $-\omega_0<0$ has the same negative sign as does the gravitational energy of the proton $\propto -E_0<0$ that generates it. Both add to make the proton heavier. Here, however, $-\omega_0>0$ has the opposite sign and overcomes the gravitational pull $\propto -E_0<0$ from the galaxy center to become antigravitational push instead.

This shows that dark matter and PRE dark energy are not foreign objects in SSI, like those in the ΛCDM model, but are generated in hydrogen gas in gravitational field and can vary and transform into each other dependent upon the positions of the *uu-d* aggregates relative to the centers of the proton clouds.

The present scenario is compatible with a current view that dark matter appears first and dark energy later.

16.3. Antigravity Motion of the Test Hydrogen Atom

16.3.1. Equation of Antigravity Motion

Anticipating greater velocities for the accelerated test hydrogen atom, a Lorentz boost is performed on the rest frame proton whereby the heuristic limit (16.1.1) is approximately modified to

$$R_D = \frac{-\omega_0}{\gamma E_0} \le \frac{28.8\,\mathrm{fm}}{\gamma r_a} - \frac{1}{2}, \qquad \gamma = 1/\sqrt{1 - v^2/c^2} \tag{16.3.1}$$

where v is the proton velocity. Note that for $v \neq 0$, $\omega_0 \to \omega_K \neq \omega_0$ in (3.1.9). But baryon has only been treated in the rest frame K=0 in this book. Even the classical the relation (5.7.32) has only been verified for slow mesons in §5.7.6.

Let the position X_H of the test hydrogen atom after the collision in §16.1.2 be $R(t)$ from S in Figure 16.2; t denotes the laboratory frame time X^0 and $R(0)$=0. This test hydrogen atom will in time experience another collision. Before this happens, the proton in this atom obeys the equation of motion

$$\frac{d}{dt} E_0 \gamma(t) v(t) = G\left[\frac{M_G}{(R_{GS} + R(t))^2} + \frac{M_U}{(R_{US} + R(t))^2}\right](-\omega_0 - E_0\gamma(t)), \quad v(t) = \frac{dR(t)}{dt} \tag{16.3.2}$$

Here, the identification (15.3.3) ff has been used in the inclusion of the relative energy $-\omega_0$ next to the proton energy $E_0\gamma$. The remarks below (16.3.1) renders that (16.3.2), hence also the ensuing results below, at best hold approximately for slow protons.

The right side of the first relation is the gravitational pulling force acting on this proton. For $-\omega_0$=0, this force $\propto -E_0$<0 and this proton will "freely fall" towards the galaxy center. If $-\omega_0$<0, it will add to $-E_0$ making the right side more negative by a factor of $|R_D|$<8.94 according to (15.3.4). Dark matter is generated according to (15.3.3) and causes the pulling force to become $|R_D|$ times stronger, considered in §15.3.1-3. Such gravitational pull is on the average largely balanced off by the pressure gradient in and centrifugal force of the hydrogen gas, as in Sec. 15.3. The gas still slowly expands outwards.

If $-\omega_0$>0 and is in addition greater than the proton mass E_0, $-\omega_0 - E_0$>0; the right side of (16.3.2) is now positive. The above gravitational pull turns into antigravity push. The above "free fall" of this proton toward the galaxy center is converted to "free rise" driving this proton away from the galaxy into the void outside it. The host atom is of the "run away" type considered in §16.1.2 with the quark configuration in Figure 16.1.

This result may provide the basic mechanism of the accelerating expansion of the universe.

16.3.2. Evolution of the Antigravity Run Away of the Test Atom

Collisions that lead to such run away hydrogen atoms mentioned above Sec. 16.2 must be strong enough. These are few due to the low gas density and temperature. Further, this run away property will be lost in a subsequent collision with another atom, similar to the loss of polarization due to collision illustrated in Figure 15.2.

On the other hand, once such a run away atom is created, it is expected to persist for a long time. Due to the accelerating outward movement, this atom will soon leave other atoms behind and rush into the void in Figure 16,2. Therefore, chance for this run away atom to collide again is small; it will have a long life and be very far away from its creation at S in Figure 16.2.

The acceleration in (16.3.2) is largely constant and decreases very slowly with increasing distance $R(t)$ from S in Figure 16.2, The velocity of this run away atom may soon become relativistic. At that point, the nonrelativistic limitation of (16.3.1) ff will enter in some unknown manner.

Initially, t is small, $R(t)$ can be neglected in (16.3.2) and $\gamma \cong 1$. Using the values given below Figure 16.2, (16.3.2) yields

$$dv(t)/dt = -a_{c0}(1+\omega_0/E_0), \quad a_{c0} = 1.396\times10^{-9}\ \text{m/s}^2 \tag{16.3.3}$$

$$v(t) = v(0) - a_{c0}(1+\omega_0/E_0)t, \quad R(t) = v(0)t - a_{c0}(1+\omega_0/E_0)t^2/2 \tag{16.3.4}$$

where $v(0)$ is the initial velocity of this test hydrogen atom at S in Figure 16.2. About 13% of the initial acceleration a_{c0} comes from the galaxy mass M_G and 87% from the mass M_U of the universe.

If (16.3.3-4) were applied to the test hydrogen atom in Sec. 15.3, a_{c0} needs be reduced by 87%. In the absence of relative energy, $-\omega_0 = 0$, (16.3.3) simply describes the "free fall" of this test atom towards the galaxy center. If dark matter is generated, $-\omega_0 < 0$, and this atom will fall faster.

The case $-\omega_0 - E_0 > 0$ is achieved by a strong collision of this test atom with another hydrogen atom that happens to be moving inward towards the galaxy center in Figure 16.1, as was considered in §16.1.2. The so-obtained antigravity rise may be introduced in a formal way by putting

$$-\omega = (1+\Delta)u(t)E_0 < \left(9.44 - \frac{\gamma(t)}{2}\right)E_0 \tag{16.3.5}$$

in (16.3.2). Here, $u(t)$ is a step function; $u(t<0) = 0$ and $u(t>0) = 1$ representing the onset of the collision that produces the shift of the uu-d unit to the right of X_p in Figure 16.1. This collision takes place at time $t = 0$. $1+\Delta$ is the amplitude of this step function and has to be > 1 to overcome the gravitational pull on the test hydrogen atom; $\Delta > 0$. The limit (16.3.1) is tentatively adopted on the right of (16.3.5). Inserting (16.3.5) into (16.3.2) yields

$$\frac{d}{dt}v(t) = G\left[\frac{M_G}{(R_{GS}+R(t))^2}+\frac{M_U}{(R_{US}+R(t))^2}\right]\left[\frac{(1+\Delta)}{\gamma(t)}-1\right], \quad \Delta+1<9.44-\frac{\gamma(t)}{2} \tag{16.3.6}$$

16.3.3. Computer Solutions of the Antigravity Rise

The initial velocity $v(0)$ of the test atom will be taken to be the mean thermal speed of hydrogen atoms corresponding to the average temperature of the universe of 2.8 ^0K mentioned in §16.1.2,

$$v(0) = 263\,\text{m/s} \tag{16.3.7}$$

The value of Δ signifies the strength of the collision and depends upon complicated atomic as well as strong forces in the relative space $\underline{x}$ and is beyond the scope of this book. Here, it will be regarded as a free parameter limited to $0 < \Delta < 7.4$ which is 0.54 inside the heuristic limit 7.94 from (16.3.1, 5).

The momentum exchange in such a collision that led to the creation of PRE is sufficiently energetic to move the charged clouds up to $a_{0p} = 28.8$ fm (see Figure 15.1 caption) away from the *uu-d* pair in some of such collisions so as to produce all allowed Δ values up to 7.4.

The nonlinear (16.3.6) with the initial conditions $R(t{=}0) = 0$, $v(t{=}0) = v(0)$ has been solved on computers at Uppsala University. Some results are given in Table 16.1.

This table shows that the position $R(t)$ of the test atom and its velocity $v(t)$ increase with time. For small t, these values follow the antigravity repulsion (16.3.4-5) closely. As $R(t)$ approaches first R_{GS} and then R_{US}, (16.3.6) shows that the acceleration a_c slows down. This is also reflected in Table 16.1. As $v(t)$ approaches the light speed, the present nonrelativistic treatment of the motion of the proton breaks down, as was mentioned below (16.3.2), and the results, marked by * in this table, are unreliable.

For $v(0) = 0$, (16.3.3-5) show that R, v and a_c are all proportional to Δ. With (16.3.1), (16.3.6) is seen to behave similarly for small v. These three sets of values in Table 1 then largely reduce to one multiplied by 3 different Δ values. Since $v(0)$ in (16.3.7) is small relative to $v(t)$ in general, results in Table 16.1 are not sensitive to $v(0)$ and are nearly independent of it for large Δ values.

For a collision that leads to $\Delta = 4.6$, which is close to the measured average ratio $|R_D| = 5$ for dark matter given below (15.3.4), the test hydrogen atom will reach a distance of 3×10^6 ly with a velocity of 1.8×10^7 m/s 10^8 years after its collision at S in Figure 16.2 provided that it did not collide with another atom.

As was shown beneath (16.3.5), $\Delta > 0$. Computer runs with $\Delta < 0$ leads to negative $v(t)$ and blueshift. The bulk of the random collisions will yield $\Delta < 0$ and these do not contribute to expansion. But sooner or later, a subsequent collision will produce $\Delta > 0$. Once this occurs, one of the colliding atoms will become of the "run away" type obeying (16.3.6) and starts to move outwards and leave the S region in Figure 16.2 and cannot back off. An analogy may be to push a "test ball" onto a road with a downward slope $\propto \Delta$; it will "roll away" and cannot back up.

Table 16.1. Some results from numerical integration of the equation of motion of the test hydrogen atom (16.3.6). Δ is defined in (16.3.5) and characterizes the surplus of the positive relative energy PRE generated in the test hydrogen atom after a sufficiently strong collision with another atom near S in the model of Figure 16.2. It is a free parameter here satisfying $0 < \Delta < 7.4$. R is the distance of this test hydrogen atom from S and v its speed at time t after the collision. a_c/a_{c0} is the acceleration $a_c = dv/dt$ of this test atom in (16.3.6) normalized to its initial value a_{c0} in (16.3.3) just after the collision. H_0 is the Hubble constant given in (16.5.1) and H the Hubble parameter calculated from (16.5.5) below. The * specifies that this entry is relativistic with $\gamma > 1.2$ and hence is not reliable

t (yr)	0	10^4	10^5	10^6	10^7	10^8	10^9	10^{10}
Δ=1.0								
R (ly)	0	1.61×10^{-2}	0.821	74.2	7.32×10^3	6.82×10^5	6.43×10^7	4.97×10^9
v(m/s)	263.3	703	4.66×10^3	4.43×10^4	4.38×10^5	4×10^6	3.83×10^7	2.38×10^8
a_c/a_{c0}	1.0	1.0	1.0	1.0	0.983	0.874	0.855	0.156*
H/H_0	1.0	2.67	17.7	167	1040	267	27.6	2.22*
Δ=4.6								
R (ly)	0	4.25×10^{-2}	3.46	338	3.33×10^4	3.05×10^6	2.85×10^8	8.85×10^9
v(m/s)	263.3	2290	2.05×10^4	2.03×10^5	1.98×10^6	1.8×10^7	1.64×10^8	2.95×10^8
a_c/a_{c0}	1.0	1.0	1.0	0.999	0.944	0.87	0.69	1.5×10^{-11}*
H/H_0	1.0	8.69	77.9	740	2020	273	26.7	1.55*
Δ=7.4								
R (ly)	0	6.31×10^{-2}	5.52	544	5.33×10^4	4.87×10^6	4.35×10^8	9.32×10^9
v(m/s)	263.3	3250	3.28×10^4	3.06×10^5	3.16×10^6	2.88×10^7	2.38×10^8	2.98×10^8
a_c/a_{c0}	1.0	1.0	1.0	0.999	0.926	0.867	0.474*	7.5×10^{-12}*
H/H_0	1.0	13.4	125	1180	2030	274	25.4*	1.48*

Δ is initiated by (16.3.7). At the outskirts of a galaxy on an outskirt of the universe, the electron and proton clouds and the center of the *uu-d* pair all lie at the center as in Figure 15.1, as was mentioned in the beginning of §16.1.2. Under such circumstances, a "run away" $\Delta > 0$ collision needs to move the electron and proton clouds only a few fm to the left of the *uu-d* pair to produce $\Delta \sim 1$. Equivalently, with the electron and proton clouds remain centered in Figure 16.1, its right half depicts this case. The heavier diquark-quark pair *uu-d* there "lags" behind relative to the charged clouds' motion towards left.

It is this "lag" that produces PRE, positive relative energy, which is repulsed by the antigravity turned gravitational force from the mass inside the large circle in Figure 16.2. The atom containing this *uu-d* pair, instead of "falling" towards the mass centers, will "rise" from them and moves away from them.

16.4. On Antigravity Expansion of the Model Universe

16.4.1. States of the Migrating Test Hydrogen Atom

Table 16.1 shows that the test hydrogen atom moves outwards from the galaxy and universe edge near S in the model universe in Figure 16.2 with nearly constant acceleration, dependent upon Δ, a measure of the strength of collision experienced by this atom near S. Its gravitational energy is positive on the right side of (16.3.2) where $-\omega_0>0$ is the PRE dark energy. The *uu-d* quark unit lies to the right of the proton at X_p in Figure 16.1.

Before this outward movement, i.e., before this atom suffered the collision, it is at S in Figure 16.2 where it is nearly free and its *uu-d* unit is largely centered at $X_p=X_H$, shown in Figure 15.1. Before migrating to this position, this atom was inside the universe and in the interstellar medium of the galaxy with its *uu-d* unit lying to the left of $X_p=X_H$ in Figure 15.2. $-\omega_0<0$ representing dark matter was generated by this atom in that position.

Thus, in SSI, dark matter and PRE dark energy are the same, differing only by sign. Dark matter can turn into PRE dark energy but not vice versa in the expanding universe scenario. This in agreement with the present view that dark matter comes first and prevail in the inner part of the universe. PRE dark energy comes later in the outskirts of galaxy or model universe.

16.4.2. On Applicability to Expanding Model Universe

The results in Table 16.1 together with the above considerations refer to a single test hydrogen atom. It is compatible with an acceleratingly expanding universe [P4]. If these results are to be applied to the accelerating expansion of the model universe of Figure 16.2, the following ad-hoc assumptions need made:

I. A sufficient percentage of the hydrogen atoms arriving at the outskirt of the observable universe indicated by the large circle in Figure 16.2 will become of the "run away" test atom type near S there. They obey (16.3.6) between collisions and persist for long times, as was mentioned in the beginning of §16.3.2.

II. All these atoms form hydrogen gas clouds in regions outside the large circle in Figure 16.2 and condense to galaxies in which some stars are created. Complications with respect to different generations of stars are disregarded.

III. The protons in these stars cannot be accelerated according to (16.3.6), as was pointed out above §15.3.4. These stars are assumed to be dragged along by the moving galaxies containing them via gravitational interaction and acquire the same speeds.

16.4.3. Scenarios of Accelerating Expansion of the Model Universe

1. With the assumptions I-III above, the velocity $v(t)$ increases with time t and with the distance $R(t)$ in Table 16.1 compatible with the observed accelerating expansion of the universe in time [P4] as well as with the distance from the observer (see Hubble's law in §16.5.1 below). These results arise from the generated PRE dark energy.
   In this SSI model universe, hydrogen gas "leaks" out at its boundary (large circle in Figure 16.2) via PRE dark energy generated there whereby the hydrogen gas pressure also diminishes. This will maintain the gas pressure gradient there and the leak can continue. A semi-steady state scenario of the expansion of the universe at the present time is reached.
2. The scenario in i) is derived from (16.3.6) and holds only for $R(t) << R_{US}$ because the newly created energy in the shell with thickness $R(t)$ outside the original universe (large circle in Figure 16.2) has not been taken into account. In time, this shell will be filled with the "run away" hydrogen atoms with PRE and part of them will collide with each other. As was mentioned below Table 16.1, the bulk of such random collisions

will yield $\Delta < 0$ so that the PRE carried by the participating atoms are lost. These atoms now return on the average to their normal state of a hydrogen atom. Only a small portion of collisions will produce new $\Delta > 0$ "run away" hydrogen atoms with PRE dark energy.

In this qualitative manner, the hydrogen atoms "leaked" out from the universe inside the large circle in Figure 16.2 are largely recovered in the shell. The universe with radius R_{US} in Figure 16.2 has now expanded into one with larger radius $R_{US}+R(t)$. This process is repeated as this model universe expands. This antigravity accelerating expansion itself slows down with increasing t and $R(t)$ according to (16.3.6).

3. Another scenario concerns the assumed form of (16.3.5). The collision of the test hydrogen atom with another atom mentioned above (16.1.1) causes the relative energy $-\omega_0$ to change its sign. This implies that $-\omega_0$, a constant in the relative space x, can depend upon the laboratory time coordinate $X^0 = t$. There is no conflict here as such gravitationally induced time dependence is negligibly weak relative to those normally associated with strong inter-quark forces. Such a time dependence was included in (16.3.5) in form of the step function $u(t)$ with a constant amplitude $1+\Delta$. This may be regarded to be a first order t dependence. To second order, a linear dependence in form of βt, where β is another unknown constant, may be added to the above step function and modify (16.3.5) to

$$-\omega = (1+\Delta)u(t)E_0 + \beta t \tag{16.4.1}$$

Inserting this into (16.3.2) renders the acceleration in (16.3.6) to increase with time instead of decreasing with time and enhances the rate of acceleration. The heuristic limit in (16.3.5-6) may then need be modified. Furthermore, as the expansion velocities approach the light speed, relativistic effects become important so that (16.3.2) no longer holds.

16.4.4. Application to PRE Dark Energy in Intergalactic Void

The mechanism of §16.4.2 1) for the expansion at the outskirts of the model universe can be taken over to apply to the outer edges of a galaxy. The hypothetical center UC of the universe in Figure 16.2 is replaced by the actual galaxy center. The analogously generated PRE dark energy in the gas near the outer boundary of this galaxy will "leak" into the space outside it. Such PRE loaded hydrogen gas can play the role of the conventional dark energy observed in the intergalactic void.

16.5. Relations to Hubble¨s Law

16.5.1. Estimate of Hubble's Parameter

Evidence of the expansion of the universe comes from Hubble's law

$$v_H(t) = H(t)D(t), \quad H(0) = H_0 = 2.28 \times 10^{-18}/\text{s} \tag{16.5.1}$$

where v_H denotes redshift velocities of stars in distant galaxies measured from the earth, D the earth to stars distances, $H(t)$ the Hubble parameter, and H_0 the measured Hubble constant. Differentiation of (16.5.1) yields

$$\begin{aligned} \frac{dv_H(t)}{dt} &= H(t)v_H(t) + \frac{dH(t)}{dt}D(t), \quad v_H(t) = \frac{dD(t)}{dt} \\ \frac{dH(t)}{dt} &= -H^2(t) + H(t)\frac{1}{v_H(t)}\frac{dv_H(t)}{dt} \end{aligned} \tag{16.5.2}$$

Let the earth be on a radius in Figure 16.2, closer to the boundary of the universe (large circle) than to its center UC. There is no loss of generality to choose this radius to be that ending at S in Figure 16.2. Let the distance from the earth to S be $R_{ES}(t)$ and the light emitting stars be located near $R(t)$, the position of the test hydrogen atom governed by (16.3.6). Then,

$$D(t) = R(t) + R_{ES}(t) \tag{16.5.3}$$

The Hubble constant H_0 in (16.5.1) cannot be derived from the present model because $R_{ES}(t)$ is unknown. Now $R_{ES}(t)$ lies inside the observable universe and changes with t slowly compared to $R(t)$ for a "run away" test atom accelerated via PRE dark energy near S in Figure 16.2.

With the assumptions I-III given in §16.4.2, differentiation of (16.5.3) together with the second of (16.5.2) and (16.3.2) leads approximately to

$$v(t) = v_H(t) \tag{16.5.4}$$

where the unknown $R_{ES}(t)$ drops out upon differentiation. Equations (16.5.4), (16.3.6) and the last of (16.5.2) leads to

$$\frac{dH(t)}{dt} = -H^2(t) + H(t)\frac{G}{v(t)}\left[\frac{M_G}{(R_{GS} + R(t))^2} + \frac{M_U}{(R_{US} + R(t))^2}\right]\left[\frac{1+\Delta}{\gamma(t)} - 1\right] \tag{16.5.5}$$

For small t, (16.3.6) can be replaced by (16.3.3-5) and (16.5.5) becomes

$$\frac{dH(t)}{dt} = -H^2(t) + H(t)\frac{\Delta a_{c0}}{v(0) + a_{c0}\Delta t} \tag{16.5.6}$$

For small Δ, the last term can be dropped and the solution is

$$H(t) = \frac{H_0}{1 + H_0 t} \tag{16.5.7}$$

which reduces to the second of (16.5.1) at $t=0$. This deceleration is extremely weak. A 1% reduction of $H(t)$ will take 1.4×10^8 years.

A linearized approximation, valid for small t, is achieved via $H^2(t)\rightarrow H_0H(t)$ in (16.5.6) which now yields

$$H(t)=H_0\left(1+\frac{\Delta a_{c0}t}{v(0)}\right)\exp(-\frac{H_0}{\Delta}t) \tag{16.5.8}$$

For Δ values in Table 16.1, $H_0/\Delta<<\Delta a_{c0}/v(0)$ and the exponential factor in (16.5.8) can be dropped. This is equivalent to putting the small decelerating term $-H^2(t)$ in (16.5.6) to 0. Equation (16.5.8) then becomes the same as the first of (16.3.4) using (16.3.5) if $H(t)$ and H_0 were replaced by $v(t)$ and $v(0)$, respectively. Thus, the Hubble parameter $H(t)$ increases with time at the same rate as does the accelerating expansion $v(t)$ in (16.3.4) for small t. As was mentioned below Table 16.1, this acceleration is qualitatively compatible with data [P4].

This increase is due to that the last term in (16.5.6) arising from PRE dark energy acceleration is positive and large compared to the decelerating $-H^2(t)$. This last term becomes large as $H(t)$ become greater at larger times; (16.5.8) then no longer holds and the nonlinear (16.5.5) has to be solved on computer.

The computer results in Table 16.1 show that $H(t)$ increases initially as in (16.5.8). At some intermediate time, the decelerating $-H^2(t)$ term becomes large enough to cancel out the last, accelerating term in (16.5.5) so that $H(t)$ reaches very large maxima there and then starts to decrease to smaller values at larger times, of the order of magnitude of $10^{8\text{-}9}$ years. At such large times, the test atom may have collided with other atoms so that the PRE dark energy gained via (16.5.5) was lost and the results in Table 16.1 no longer hold.

These results are based upon the identification (16.5.4) which in its turn depend upon the gross, ad-hoc assumptions 1)-3) in §16.4.3. Therefore, the $H(t)$ predictions in Table 16.1 can only be taken to be qualitative estimates that indicate the mechanism involved.

16.5.2. Hubble's Law as Complement to the SSI Universe Model

The Hubble law (16.5.1) is empirical and valid in the part of the observable universe containing the earth and the galaxies visible from it. This scenario is more realistic in this respect but does not include dark matter. This law cannot be derived from any first principles' theory without introducing additional concepts. The expansion mechanism is not clear; the mainstream candidate is the unidentified dark energy.

On the other hand, in the present SSI model in Figure 16.2, there is a center of the universe but no specified position of the earth. This model however includes dark matter and can be connected to the first principles' theory SSI [H27] partially verified by hadron data. The accelerating expansion mechanism is delineated. But the expansions predicted in this model cannot be connected to any observable data; the positions and velocities of atoms in neutral hydrogen gas cannot be measured as such.

Results from both of these approaches are compatible with the general conception of an acceleratingly expanding universe and *complement* each other. In the Hubble case, measurements can be made but no theory exists to account for them. In the SSI model of Figure 16.2, theory exists to explain the accelerating expansion, but no measurement can be made to verify it. The theoretical results can thus not confirm data directly because they refer to different environments.

Nevertheless, with the aid of the assumptions I-III in §16.4.2, the connection (16.5.4) could be set in a heuristic manner. This connection leads to qualitative compatibility between data and present theory under such circumstances for small velocities.

Another approximately mutually compatible scenario may be that evolution according to the SSI model took place long, perhaps 10^9-10^{10} years, ago. Evolution of such a universe may eventually have ended up in the present state of the observable universe in which Hubble's law (16.5.1) can be established.

16.6. Comparison to the Λcdm Scenario and Summary

16.6.1. Comparison to the ΛCDM Model

The present standard model of big bang cosmology ΛCDM [1 Lambda CDM] is based upon general relativity, a first principles' theory, augmented by additional concepts including Friedmann's scale factor and Cold Dark Matter. In the development of this subject, it is desirable to reduce the number such postulates introduced by hand and incorporate some of the aimed effects as natural outcome of a new such theory.

Table 16.2. Comparison of the ΛCDM model of the universe with the present SSI model

Model	ΛCDM	SSI
Foundation	General relativity and additional basic postulates	First principles' theory supported by hadron data. No additional basic postulate
Dark Matter	Assumed CDM, cold dark matter, WIMPs not found	As negative relative energy generated among quarks in inhomogeneous, cold hydrogen gas in gravitational field
Dark Energy	Difficulty with the cosmological constant problem	No dark energy. Only positive relative energy PRE in hydrogen gas in outskirts of observable universe yielding antigravity expansion
Distribution	Universe has no center, no boundary, supported by Hubble's law	Universe has an unobserved center and is bounded by surrounding vacuum into which it expands

As was mentioned in the caption of Figure 16.2, the present SSI scenario was originally constructed for illustration of the mechanisms for the generation of dark matter and the antigravity expansion of the universe via PRE dark energy and was not aimed at a model for the universe per se. It turned out however that this scenario covers several areas also considered in the current mainstream ΛCDM model. Therefore, a comparison of these two models in these areas listed in Table 16.2 may illuminate the pros and cons for both.

16.6.2. Summary

Negative relative energy between the diquark *uu* and the quark *d* in proton in cold, rarefied hydrogen gas plays the role of dark matter. Positive relative energy PRE dark energy between these quarks in such can lead to antigravity expansion of the universe.

Inside the universe, the amount of dark matter produced depends upon the gravitational force acting on the quarks in hydrogen gas opposed by the pressure gradients acting on the electrons in this gas. In a galaxy, such amount can prevent fast moving stars from escaping the galaxy and cause gravitational lensing. Star formation in this gas uses up the hydrogen atoms that create such dark matter and hence reduces the dark matter content in this galaxy. In intergalactic space, such dark matter can contribute to formation of filaments.

To account for the expansion of the universe, a hypothetical model of the universe is proposed. Near the outskirts of the observable universe, both the gas pressure gradient and gravitational force become very weak and the the hydrogen atoms become nearly free so that the amount of dark matter generated nearly vanishes. Random collisions between hydrogen atoms in this region can flip such a small amount of negative relative energy or dark matter into a small positive relative energy or PRE dark energy in hydrogen atom. Once such a sign change takes place, gravitational attraction switches into antigravity repulsion now unopposed by any pressure gradient. This leads to a "run away" hydrogen atom and provides the mechanism for an acceleratingly expanding universe.

A number of ad-hoc assumptions are needed to extend these results to apply to the model universe. The present theoretical expansion and the measured Hubble data are both compatible with the conception of an expanding universe and *complement* each other. But they *cannot verify* each other directly because the present model has been constructed for purposes different from those of the measurements. On the other hand, the present accelerating expansion mechanism of the universe is based upon a first principles' theory while Hubble's law cannot be derived from any such theory. However, these both approaches can under certain circumstances be shown to support each other qualitatively at small velocities.

Dark matter and PRE dark energy are not foreign objects like WIMPs and dark energy-cosmological constant but can only be created in cold, tenuous hydrogen gas in gravitational field. To achieve this, collisions among the hydrogen atoms must take place. Dark matter was created first and can eventually later evolve into PRE dark energy in the outskirts of the universe. The so-created dark constituents will disappear if the hydrogen atoms creating them become ionized as in stars or enter chemical compounds.

Appendices

Appendices A-C serve to introduce notations and present well-known results in forms that provide starting points of the present theory. For proof and further details, the reader is referred to the literature cited. Appendices D-F are reprints on this subject from the proceedings of the 9th, 7th and 6th international conferences on hadron spectroscopy. Appendices G is a recent paper on the epistemological and historical background underlying the present theory. Appendices H gives a brief account on how I, an outsider to the high energy physics community, has been received.

A. Notation and Dirac's Equation

Natural units are used; $h/2\pi = c = 1$. The unit of mass, energy, momentum, and the inverses of length and of time generally used is 10^9 electron volts or GeV. The fine structure constant is $\alpha = e^2/4\pi = 1/137.04$, where $-e$ is the electron charge. The action S is dimensionless. The notations of Schweber et al. [S1] will be used. The space time coordinate is denoted by the contravariant vector

$$X^{\mu} = \left(X^0, \underline{X}\right) = \left(X^0, X^k\right) = \left(X^0, X^1, X^2, X^3\right) \tag{A1a}$$

The metric tensor $g^{\mu\nu}=g_{\mu\nu}$ has the nonvanishing elements $g^{00} = g_{00} = 1$ and $g^{kl} = g_{kl} = -1$ for $k = l = 1, 2$ and 3. The associated covariant space time vector is given by

$$X_{\mu} = \left(X^0, -\underline{X}\right) = \left(X^0, -X^k\right) = g_{\mu\nu} X^{\nu} \tag{A1b}$$

Repeated Greek indices are summed over from 0 to 3. The corresponding gradients are

$$\partial_{X\mu} = \left(\partial/\partial X^0, \partial/\partial \underline{X}\right), \qquad \partial_X^{\mu} = \left(\partial/\partial X^0, -\partial/\partial \underline{X}\right) \tag{A2}$$

The Dirac equation for a spin ½ particle reads

$$\left(-i\gamma^{\mu}\partial_{X\mu} + m\right)\psi(X) = I_B \tag{A3}$$

where ψ is a column vector (ψ_ν) with $\nu = 1, 2, 3,$ and 4 and is called a bispinor or four-spinor in the terminology of Appendix B, m is the particle mass and

$$\gamma^0 = \begin{pmatrix} I & 0 \\ 0 & -I \end{pmatrix}, \quad \gamma^k = \begin{pmatrix} 0 & \sigma^k \\ -\sigma^k & 0 \end{pmatrix}$$

$$\sigma^1 = \begin{pmatrix} 0 & 1 \\ 1 & 0 \end{pmatrix}, \quad \sigma^2 = \begin{pmatrix} 0 & -i \\ i & 0 \end{pmatrix}, \quad \sigma^3 = \begin{pmatrix} 1 & 0 \\ 0 & -1 \end{pmatrix}, \quad I = \sigma^0 = \begin{pmatrix} 1 & 0 \\ 0 & 1 \end{pmatrix} \tag{A4}$$

I_B denotes the interaction term. If the particle is free or interacts with a pseudoscalar potential V_{PB}, or with a scalar potential V_{SB}, or with an electromagnetic potential A_μ, then

$$I_B = 0 \tag{A5a}$$

$$I_B = \gamma_5 V_{PB} \psi \tag{A5b}$$

$$I_B = V_{SB} \psi \tag{A5c}$$

$$I_B = -q_r \gamma^\mu A_\mu \psi \tag{A5d}$$

$$\gamma_5 = -i \begin{pmatrix} 0 & I \\ I & 0 \end{pmatrix} \tag{A6}$$

where q_r is the charge of the ψ field. If these potentials are generated by another spin ½ particle B with wave function $\psi_B = (\psi_{B\nu})$, then

$$\Box V_{PB} = g_s^2 \overline{\psi}_B \gamma_5 \psi_B \tag{A7a}$$

$$\Box V_{SB} = g_s^2 \overline{\psi}_B \psi_B \tag{A7b}$$

$$\overline{\psi} = \psi^+ \gamma^0, \qquad \psi^+ = \left(\psi_1^*, \psi_2^*, \psi_3^*, \psi_4^*\right) \tag{A7c}$$

$$\Box = \partial_{X\mu} \partial_X^\mu = \left(\partial / \partial X^0\right)^2 - \left(\partial / \partial \underline{X}\right)^2 \tag{A8}$$

where g_s^2 is the interaction coupling constant between the both particles and * denotes complex conjugation.

Equations (A3), (A5) and (A7) are invariant under the homogeneous Lorentz transformations [S1]

$$X^{\mu\prime} = L^{\mu}_{\ \nu} X^{\nu} \tag{A9}$$

where $L^{\mu}_{\ \nu}$ is required to conserve

$$s_X^2 = X_\mu{}' X^{\mu\prime} = X_\mu X^\mu = \left(X^0\right)^2 - \left(X^1\right)^2 - \left(X^2\right)^2 - \left(X^3\right)^2 \tag{A10}$$

This leads to

$$L_\nu^{\ \mu} L^{\nu}_{\ \lambda} = \delta^{\mu}_{\ \lambda} = \begin{pmatrix} 1 & \text{for } \mu = \lambda \\ 0 & \text{for } \mu \neq \lambda \end{pmatrix} \tag{A11}$$

Equation (A9) is the self representation of the Lorentz group and X^μ spans the smallest nontrivial tensorial representation space. The product of n X^μ's spans the 4^n dimensional tensorial representation space for the Lorentz group.

If (A9) is restricted to represent the proper Lorentz group L_p, then

$$L^0_{\ 0} > 0, \quad \det\left|L^{\mu}_{\ \nu}\right| = +1 \tag{A12}$$

L_p is characterized by six real parameters, three angles of rotations and boosts in three directions.

For a free particle (A3)-(A5a) have the solution

$$\left(\psi_\nu(X)\right) = \left(u_\nu\right)\exp\left(-iK_\mu X^\mu\right) \tag{A13a}$$

$$K_\mu = \left(E, -\underline{K}\right) \tag{A13b}$$

$$E = \pm\sqrt{m^2 + \underline{K}^2} \tag{A13c}$$

where E denotes the energy of the particle and $\underline{K}$ its momentum.

$$(u_\nu) = \begin{pmatrix} u_1 \\ u_2 \\ u_3 \\ u_4 \end{pmatrix} = N_D \begin{pmatrix} 1 & , & 0 \\ 0 & , & 1 \\ K^3/(E+m) & , & \left(K^1 - iK^2\right)/(E+m) \\ \left(K^1 + iK^2\right)/(E+m), & & -K^3/(E+m) \end{pmatrix} \quad \text{positive energy in (A13c)}$$

$$(u_\nu) = \begin{pmatrix} u_1 \\ u_2 \\ u_3 \\ u_4 \end{pmatrix} = N_D \begin{pmatrix} \left(-K^1 + iK^2\right)/(E+m), & & K^3/(E+m) \\ K^3/(E+m) & , & \left(K^1 + iK^2\right)/(E+m) \\ 0 & , & -1 \\ 1 & , & 0 \end{pmatrix} \quad \text{negative energy in (A13c)}$$

$$N_D = \sqrt{\frac{E+m}{2E\Omega}} \tag{A14}$$

are the four solutions for (u_ν) with the commas separating the spin up and spin down solutions. Ω is a large normalization volume. In the nonrelativistic limit $|\underline{K}| << E$, ψ_1 and ψ_2 are called the large components and ψ_3 and ψ_4 the small components.

In the extreme relativistic limit, $|\underline{K}| \approx E$ and m can be dropped. The four component (A3) with (A5a) decomposes into two decoupled two component equations

$$\gamma^\mu \partial_{X\mu} \psi_L = 0, \qquad \gamma^\mu \partial_{X\mu} \psi_R = 0 \tag{A15}$$

where ψ_L and ψ_R are left and right handed, respectively, and are given by

$$\psi_R = \tfrac{1}{2}(1 + i\gamma_5)\psi = \frac{1}{2}(\psi_1 + \psi_3)\begin{pmatrix}1\\0\\1\\0\end{pmatrix} + \frac{1}{2}(\psi_2 + \psi_4)\begin{pmatrix}0\\1\\0\\1\end{pmatrix} \tag{A16a}$$

$$\psi_L = \tfrac{1}{2}(1 - i\gamma_5)\psi = \frac{1}{2}(\psi_1 - \psi_3)\begin{pmatrix}1\\0\\-1\\0\end{pmatrix} + \frac{1}{2}(\psi_2 - \psi_4)\begin{pmatrix}0\\1\\0\\-1\end{pmatrix} \tag{A16b}$$

B. Spinors and Lorentz Invariance

The material in this appendix comes largely from [W1, L1, C1, R1]. That the Dirac equation (A3) with (A5a) is invariant under proper Lorentz transformations [D1, S1] suggests that there are other representations of the Lorentz group than the vectorial representation of (A9) and the tensorial representations of dimension 4^n mentioned below (A11). Such representations were first uncovered by van der Waerden in 1929 [W1] and are called spinorial representations. Basis vectors generating such representations are called spinors, a word coined by Ehrenfest [W1] shortly after the proposal of the Dirac equation in 1928.

Let two complex variables ψ_a, $a = 1, 2$ be defined in a two dimensional complex space and transform according to

$$\psi_a' = \psi_b s^b{}_a \tag{B1}$$

$$\det\left|s^b{}_a\right| = +1 \tag{B2}$$

ψ_a has two components and is called a two-spinor, to be distinguished from the four component bispinor or four-spinor to which the Dirac wave function ψ in (A3) belongs. More precisely, it is called an elementary spinor or a covariant spinor of first rank but will often be called a spinor for short. Dummy spinor indices *a, b,...* are summed over *1* and *2*. Let χ_c be another spinor transforming in the same way as ψ_a does in (B1). Making use of (B2), we find

$$\psi_1'\chi_2'-\psi_2'\chi_1'=\psi_1\chi_2-\psi_2\chi_1=\text{invariant} \tag{B3}$$

An analog of the antisymmetric ε tensors in tensor analysis in spinor analysis is the raising operator ε^{ab} with

$$\varepsilon^{12}=1, \qquad \varepsilon^{21}=-1, \qquad \varepsilon^{11}=\varepsilon^{22}=0 \tag{B4}$$

A contravariant spinor is defined as

$$\psi^a=\varepsilon^{ab}\psi_b \tag{B5a}$$

so that

$$\psi^1=\psi_2, \quad \psi^2=-\psi_1 \tag{B5b}$$

Conversely, the lowering operator is defined as

$$\varepsilon_{ba}=\varepsilon^{ab}, \qquad \varepsilon_{ab}\varepsilon^{ab}=-1 \quad \text{(no summation)} \tag{B6}$$

It converts a contravariant spinor to a covariant one

$$\psi_b=\varepsilon_{ba}\psi^a \tag{B7}$$

which also yields (B5b). The invariant (B3) now takes the form of the scalar product

$$\psi_a'\chi^{a\prime}=-\psi^{a\prime}\chi_a'=\psi_a\chi^a=-\psi^a\chi_a=\text{invariant} \tag{B8}$$

Raising the lower index and lowering the upper repeated index leads to a sign change.

By analogy to (B1),

$$\psi^{a\prime}=S^a_{\ b}\psi^b \tag{B9}$$

Forming the scalar product of (B1) and (B9) and noting (B8) leads to

$$\psi_a'\psi^{a\prime}=\psi_a s^a_{\ b}S^b_{\ c}\psi^c=\psi_a\psi^a \tag{B10}$$

whence

$$s^a_{\ b} S^b_{\ c} = \delta^a_{\ c} \tag{B11}$$

which relates the transformations (B1) and (B9). Here, the contraction operator $\delta^a_{\ c}=1$ for $a=c$ and 0 otherwise. Taking the determinant of (B10) and noting (B2), we obtain

$$\det\left|S^b_{\ c}\right| = +1 \tag{B12}$$

The complex conjugates of the spinors ψ_a and ψ^a are respectively denoted by $\psi_{\dot{a}}$ and $\psi^{\dot{a}}$ which are called dotted spinors. Since the spinor ψ_a and the transformation matrix $s^b_{\ a}$ are already complex, the forms of (B1)–(B12) hold also for the dotted spinors, which however transform genuinely differently;

$$\psi_{\dot{a}}' = \psi_{\dot{b}} s^{\dot{b}}_{\ \dot{a}}, \qquad \psi^{\dot{a}\prime} = S^{\dot{a}}_{\ \dot{b}} \psi^{\dot{b}} \tag{B13}$$

$$\det\left|s^{\dot{b}}_{\ \dot{a}}\right| = \det\left|S^{\dot{b}}_{\ \dot{a}}\right| = 1, \qquad s^{\dot{a}}_{\ \dot{b}} S^{\dot{b}}_{\ \dot{c}} = \delta^{\dot{a}}_{\ \dot{c}} \tag{B14}$$

$$\varepsilon^{\dot{1}\dot{2}} = 1, \quad \varepsilon^{\dot{2}\dot{1}} = -1, \quad \varepsilon^{\dot{1}\dot{1}} = \varepsilon^{\dot{2}\dot{2}} = 0, \quad \varepsilon_{\dot{b}\dot{a}} = \varepsilon^{\dot{a}\dot{b}}, \quad \varepsilon_{\dot{a}\dot{b}}\varepsilon^{\dot{a}\dot{b}} = -1 \ \text{(no summation)} \tag{B15}$$

$$\psi^{\dot{a}} = \varepsilon^{\dot{a}\dot{b}} \psi_{\dot{b}}, \qquad \psi_{\dot{a}} = \varepsilon_{\dot{a}\dot{b}} \psi^{\dot{b}}, \qquad \psi_{\dot{2}} = \psi^{\dot{1}}, \qquad \psi_{\dot{1}} = -\psi^{\dot{2}} \tag{B16}$$

$$\psi_{\dot{a}}' \chi^{\dot{a}\prime} = -\psi^{\dot{a}\prime} \chi_{\dot{a}}' = \psi_{\dot{a}} \chi^{\dot{a}} = -\psi^{\dot{a}} \chi_{\dot{a}} = \text{invariant} \tag{B17}$$

The last equation and (B8) provide the basic invariants in spinor analysis. The ε and δ matrices or spinors of second rank in (B4), (B11), (B14), and (B15) are invariant under the transformations (B1), (B9) and (B13), applied to each of the spinor indices.

The set of unimodular matrices $s^a_{\ b}$ in (B1) and (B2) forms a group and is a representation of the SL(2,C) group (Special($\approx$ unimodular or (B2)) Linear group of Complex dimension 2). So do also $S^a_{\ b}$, $s^a_{\ b}$, $S^{\dot{a}}_{\ \dot{b}}$, $s^{\dot{a}}_{\ \dot{b}}$ as can be inferred from (B11), (B13) and (B14). The group SL(2,C) is characterized by six real parameters; one relation (B2) holds between four complex numbers in $s^a_{\ b}$, just like the proper Lorentz group L_p in Appendix A is. Van der Waerden [W1] has pointed out that L_p is homomorphic to SL(2,C). The unimodularity condition (B2) has its origin in the conservation of the "length" s_X in (A10).

These representations of SL(2,C) contain genuine spinorial representations of the proper Lorentz group, in addition to the tensorial representations mentioned in Appendix A. They have the dimensionality $(2j+1)(2j'+1)$. The elements of the corresponding representation space are spinors (undotted) of order $2j$ and dotted spinors of order $2j'$ belonging to the Minkowski space [R1].

Representations with $j+j'=$ integer coincide with the tensorial representations of L_p in Appendix A. They are single valued, i.e., corresponding to any element of L_p there is only one transformation in a representation space of given dimensionality.

Representations with $j+j'=$ half integer are genuine spinorial representations of L_p not covered by tensorial representations. They are double valued, i.e., corresponding to any proper Lorentz transformation, there is a matrix representation as well as its negative. Therefore, any equation which is covariant under SL(2,C) transformations will be also covariant under L_p transformations.

Some results of spinor calculus are quoted below. The basic invariants of spinor calculus have been given by (B8) and (B17). Putting $\psi=\chi$ there, we find that the "value" of the spinor of first rank vanishes;

$$\psi^a\psi_a = -\psi_a\psi^a = 0, \qquad \psi^{\dot a}\psi_{\dot a} = -\psi_{\dot a}\psi^{\dot a} = 0 \tag{B18a}$$

Indeed, the "value" of any spinor of odd rank vanishes,

$$\psi^{\dot a bc}\psi_{\dot a bc} = -\psi_{\dot a bc}\psi^{\dot a bc} = 0 \tag{B18b}$$

Higher rank spinors can be formed by multiplying together spinors of first rank. For example,

$$w^{ab} = \psi^a\chi^b, \qquad w^{a\dot b}_{\ \ c} = \psi^a\chi_c\chi^{\dot b} \tag{B19}$$

The spinor

$$w_{ab....\dot c}^{\ \ \ \ \ \ \ \ d......\dot e} \tag{B20a}$$

is generally defined as a quantity transforming under SL(2,C) as the product of first rank spinors

$$\psi_a\chi_b.....\xi_{\dot c}\varphi^d......\eta^{\dot e} \tag{B20b}$$

While the positions of the spinors in (B20b) can be rearranged, the positions of any pair of undotted or dotted upper or lower indices in (B20a) cannot be interchanged. There exists, however, a subset of this spinor for which such an interchange is allowed. This subset is called a symmetric spinor. An interchange between a dotted index and an undotted index is however allowed, because the obey different transformation rules. The complex conjugate of a spinor of any rank is obtained by changing all dotted indices to undotted ones and vice versa.

The rank of a spinor can be lowered by means of the two types of invariant spinors ε and δ in (B4), (B6), (B11), (B14) and (B15). For example,

$$\varepsilon^{\dot a\dot b}w^{\dot c}_{e\dot a\dot b} = u^{\dot c}_e, \qquad \delta^a_{\ d}w^{dc}_{ba\dot e} = v^c_{b\dot e} \tag{B21}$$

Such contractions are often applied in the reduction of a higher dimensional representation space to lower dimensional invariant subspaces.

Any equation that can be written in tensor form is covariant under L_p. For instance, the Maxwell equation

$$\partial F^{\mu\nu} / \partial X^{\nu} = J^{\mu} \tag{B22}$$

is manifestly covariant under L_p, where $F^{\mu\nu}$ denotes the electromagnetic field tensor and J^{μ} the source current. Similarly, any equation that can be written in spinor form is manifestly covariant under SL(2,C) and hence also covariant under L_p. This will be shown explicitly for the following example.

Consider Dirac's equation in van der Waerden's [W2] spinor form (C10) below, put V_{PB} and q_r there to 0 for simplicity and use (B17). One can write

$$\partial_X^{a\dot{b}} \chi_{\dot{b}}(X) = -\partial^a_{X\dot{b}} \delta^{\dot{b}}_{\ \dot{c}} \chi^{\dot{c}}(X) = i(m + V_{SB}(X))\psi^a(X) \tag{B23a}$$

$$\partial_{X\dot{b}c} \psi^c(X) = \partial_{X\dot{b}c} \delta^c_{\ d} \psi^d(X) = i(m + V_{SB}(X))\chi_{\dot{b}}(X) \tag{B23b}$$

Perform proper Lorentz transformation L_p similar to (A9)

$$X^{\mu} \to X^{\mu\prime} = L^{\mu}_{p\nu} X^{\nu} \tag{B24}$$

The homomorphism between L_p and SL(2,C) enables a determination, up to a sign, of the corresponding genuine spinorial representations (B1) and (B9),

$$\psi_a{}'(X') = \psi_b(X) s^b_{\ a}, \qquad \psi^a{}'(X') = S^a_{\ b} \psi^b(X) \tag{B25}$$

and their complex conjugates (B13). Operating (B23a) by $S^d_{\ a}$ and (B23b) by $S^{\dot{a}}_{\ \dot{e}} \varepsilon^{\dot{e}\dot{b}}$ $S^a_{\ e}\varepsilon^{eb}$ and replacing the δ spinors by (B11) and (B14) leads to

$$-S^d_{\ a} \partial^a_{X\dot{b}} s^{\dot{b}}_{\ \dot{e}} S^{\dot{e}}_{\ \dot{c}} \chi^{\dot{c}}(X) = i\left(m + V_{SB}\left(\left(L^{\mu}_{\ \nu}\right)^{-1} X'\right)\right) S^d_{\ a} \psi^a(X) \tag{B26a}$$

$$S^{\dot{a}}_{\ \dot{e}} \partial^{\dot{e}}_{Xc} s^c_{\ b} S^b_{\ d} \psi^d(X) = i\left(m + V_{SB}\left(\left(L^{\mu}_{\ \nu}\right)^{-1} X'\right)\right) S^{\dot{a}}_{\ \dot{e}} \chi^{\dot{e}}(X) \tag{B26b}$$

Apply now (B1), (B9) and (B13) to (B26) and make the identifications

$$S^d_{\ a} \partial^a_{X\dot{b}} s^{\dot{b}}_{\ \dot{e}} = \partial'^d_{\ \dot{e}}, \qquad S^{\dot{a}}_{\ \dot{e}} \partial^{\dot{e}}_{Xc} s^c_{\ b} = \partial'^{\dot{a}}_{\ b} \tag{B27}$$

where the prime denotes differentiation with respect to $X^{\mu\prime}$. After another application of (B17) and (B16), we obtain

$$\partial'^{d\dot{e}}\chi'_{\dot{e}}(X')=i(m+V'_{SB}(X'))\psi'^{d}(X') \tag{B28a}$$

$$\partial'_{\dot{a}b}\psi'^{b}(X')=i(m+V'_{SB}(X'))\chi'_{\dot{a}}(X') \tag{B28b}$$

$$V'_{SB}(X')=V_{SB}\left(\left(L^{\mu}_{\ \nu}\right)^{-1}X'\right)=V_{SB}(X) \tag{B29}$$

Equation (B28) with (B29) has the same form as (B23) and covariance under SL(2,C) is demonstrated.

Under space inversion, invariance of the Dirac equation (A3) with (A5c) and (A7b) requires that the Dirac wave function transforms like [J1]

$$\psi'(X'^{0},\underline{X}')=\gamma^{0}\psi(X^{0},\underline{X}), \qquad X'^{0}=X^{0}, \qquad \underline{X}'=-\underline{X} \tag{B30}$$

Applying this relation to (C11) below leads to that

$$\chi_{\dot{a}}(X^{0},\underline{X})\leftrightarrow\psi^{a}(X^{0},-\underline{X}) \tag{B31}$$

under space inversion [W2].

C. Formulae Relating Spinors and Tensors

The material in this appendix is again largely gathered from [W1, L1, R1]. The spinor ψ_a is specified by two complex or four real quantities. Therefore, the product spinor $\psi_a\psi_{\dot{b}}$ is also determined by four real quantities. This spinor transforms as a mixed spinor of second rank $X_{\dot{b}a}$. Let

$$X_{\dot{b}a}=\begin{pmatrix} X^{0}+X^{3} & X^{1}-iX^{2} \\ X^{1}+iX^{2} & X^{0}-X^{3}\end{pmatrix}=\delta_{\dot{b}a}X^{0}+\underline{\sigma}_{\dot{b}a}\underline{X}$$

$$X^{b\dot{a}}=\begin{pmatrix} X^{0}-X^{3} & -X^{1}+iX^{2} \\ -X^{1}-iX^{2} & X^{0}+X^{3}\end{pmatrix}=\delta^{b\dot{a}}X^{0}-\underline{\sigma}^{b\dot{a}}\underline{X} \tag{C1a}$$

where the second relation follows from the first one. Equation (C1a) also contains only four real quantities, i.e., X^{μ} with μ=0-3. It further yields

$$\tfrac{1}{2}X_{\dot{b}a}X^{a\dot{b}}=(X^{0})^{2}-(\underline{X})^{2} \tag{C1b}$$

which is a Lorentz invariant. Therefore, (X^0, $\underline{X}$) is a vector, here assigned to the space-time vector. With this association, the spinor ψ_a above has the dimension (length)$^{1/2}$. $\delta_{\dot{b}a}$ and $\delta^{a\dot{b}}$ are defined as 1 for a=b and 0 otherwise. They are introduced for convenience and do not transform as spinors.

The Pauli matrices

$$\underline{\sigma}_{\dot{b}a} = \underline{\sigma}^{b\dot{a}} = \left[\begin{pmatrix} 0 & 1 \\ 1 & 0 \end{pmatrix}, \begin{pmatrix} 0 & -i \\ i & 0 \end{pmatrix}, \begin{pmatrix} 1 & 0 \\ 0 & -1 \end{pmatrix}\right] \tag{C2}$$

are classified as spin-tensors here. Since the positions of the undotted and dotted indices can be interchanged, the following convention will be followed in this book; *the first index is dotted* (*undotted*) *if it is a covariant* (*contravariant*) *index and refers to the rows of the matrices. The second index refers to the columns.* Corresponding to (C1), define

$$\partial_{X\dot{b}a} = -\delta_{\dot{b}a}\partial_{X0} + \underline{\sigma}_{\dot{b}a}\partial_{\underline{X}}, \qquad \partial_X^{b\dot{a}} = -\delta^{b\dot{a}}\partial_{X0} - \underline{\sigma}^{b\dot{a}}\partial_{\underline{X}} \tag{C3a}$$

$$\partial_{X0} = \partial / \partial X^0, \qquad \partial_{\underline{X}} = \partial / \partial \underline{X} \tag{C3b}$$

which are mixed gradient spinors of second rank.

Extending (C2) to

$$\sigma_{\mu\dot{b}a} = \sigma^{\mu b\dot{a}} = \left(\delta_{\dot{b}a}, \underline{\sigma}_{\dot{b}a}\right) = \left(\delta^{b\dot{a}}, \underline{\sigma}^{b\dot{a}}\right) \tag{C4}$$

the relations between the vector components (A1) and (A2) and the spinor components (C1a) and (C3a) are

$$\begin{aligned} &X_{\dot{b}a} = \sigma_{\mu\dot{b}a}X^{\mu}, \quad X^{b\dot{a}} = \sigma^{\mu b\dot{a}}X_{\mu}, \quad X^{\nu} = \tfrac{1}{2}\sigma^{\nu b\dot{a}}X_{\dot{a}b}, \quad X_{\nu} = \tfrac{1}{2}\sigma_{\nu\dot{b}a}X^{a\dot{b}} \\ &\partial_{X\dot{b}a} = -\sigma_{\mu\dot{b}a}\partial_X^{\mu}, \quad \partial_X^{b\dot{a}} = -\sigma^{\mu b\dot{a}}\partial_{X\mu}, \quad \partial_X^{\nu} = -\tfrac{1}{2}\sigma^{\nu b\dot{a}}\partial_{X\dot{a}b}, \quad \partial_{X\nu} = -\tfrac{1}{2}\sigma_{\nu\dot{b}a}\partial_X^{a\dot{b}} \end{aligned} \tag{C5}$$

Further,

$$\tfrac{1}{2}\partial_{X\dot{b}a}\partial_X^{a\dot{b}} = \Box, \qquad \tfrac{1}{2}\partial_{X\dot{b}a}y^{a\dot{b}} = \partial_{X\mu}y^{\mu} \tag{C6}$$

Application of the first of (C3a) to the second of (C1a) with X replaced by y yields

$$\partial_{Xba}y^{a\dot{c}} = \left(-\delta_{\dot{b}a}\partial_{X0} + \underline{\sigma}_{\dot{b}a}\partial_{\underline{X}}\right)\left(\delta^{a\dot{c}}y^0 - \underline{\sigma}^{a\dot{c}}\underline{y}\right)$$
$$= -\delta_{\dot{b}}{}^{\dot{c}}\partial_{X0}y^0 + \underline{\sigma}_{\dot{b}}{}^{\dot{c}}\left(\partial_{\underline{X}}y^0 + \partial_{X0}\underline{y}\right) - \delta_{\dot{b}}{}^{\dot{c}}\partial_{\underline{X}}\underline{y} - i\underline{\sigma}_{\dot{b}}{}^{\dot{c}}\left(\partial_{\underline{X}} \times \underline{y}\right) \tag{C7}$$

where the Dirac formula [D1]

$$\left(\underline{\sigma}\partial_{\underline{X}}\right)\left(\underline{\sigma}\,\underline{y}\right) = \partial_{\underline{X}}\underline{y} + i\underline{\sigma}\left(\partial_{\underline{X}} \times \underline{y}\right) \tag{C8}$$

has been employed. Here,

$$\delta_{\dot{b}a}\delta^{a\dot{c}} = \delta_{\dot{b}}{}^{\dot{c}}\begin{pmatrix} 1 & \text{for } b = c \\ 0 & \text{otherwise} \end{pmatrix}, \qquad \underline{\sigma}_{\dot{b}}{}^{\dot{c}} = \underline{\sigma}_{\dot{b}a}\delta^{a\dot{c}} = \delta_{\dot{b}a}\underline{\sigma}^{a\dot{c}} \tag{C9}$$

where b is the row number. $\delta^{a}{}_{c}$ and $\underline{\sigma}^{a}{}_{c}$ can be analogously constructed with a being the row number. These δ and $\underline{\sigma}$ and the corresponding ones with dotted indices have been introduced for convenience of notation. They do not transform as spinors, apart from the coincidence of the δ's with those in (B11) and (B14).

The Dirac equation (A3) and (A5b-d) can now be put in the spinor form [W2], like (B23)

$$\left(\partial_X^{a\dot{b}} + iq_r A^{a\dot{b}}\right)\chi_{\dot{b}} = i\left(m + V_{SB} - V_{PB}\right)\psi^a \tag{C10a}$$

$$\left(\partial_{X\dot{b}c} + iq_r A_{\dot{b}c}\right)\psi^c = i\left(m + V_{SB} + V_{PB}\right)\chi_{\dot{b}} \tag{C10b}$$

where (C4) and (C5) have been used. Here,

$$\chi_{\dot{1}} = \psi_1 + \psi_3, \qquad \chi_{\dot{2}} = \psi_2 + \psi_4, \qquad \psi^1 = \psi_1 - \psi_3, \qquad \psi^2 = \psi_2 - \psi_4 \tag{C11}$$

Inserting this expression into (A7) yields

$$\Box V_{PB} = \frac{i}{2}g_s^2\left(\psi_B^{b}\chi_{Bb} - \psi_B^{\dot{b}}\chi_{B\dot{b}}\right) \tag{C12a}$$

$$\Box V_{SB} = \frac{1}{2}g_s^2\left(\psi_B^{b}\chi_{Bb} + \psi_B^{\dot{b}}\chi_{B\dot{b}}\right) \tag{C12b}$$

Proper Lorentz invariance of (C10) with V_{PB}=0 as well as its invariance under space inversion have been demonstrated at the end of Appendix B. Using the same method, it is readily seen that the full (C10) and (C12) are also covariant under these transformations.

Putting m, V_{SB}, V_{PB} and q_r to 0 in (C10), it becomes

$$\partial_X^{a\dot{b}} \chi_{\dot{b}} = 0 \qquad (\chi_{\dot{b}} \text{ right handed}) \tag{C13a}$$

$$\partial_{X\dot{b}c} \psi^c = 0 \qquad (\psi^c \text{ left handed}) \tag{C13b}$$

which is the spinor form of the bispinor equations (A15) and (A16). The first one is sometimes called the Weyl equation and describes neutrinos.

D. Scalar Strong Interaction Hadron Theory - An Alternative to QCD

(Reprinted from *Hadron '01* [H1])

F. C. Hoh

Dragarbrunnsg. 9B, 75332 Uppsala and associated with Department of Radiation Sciences, Uppsala University, Box 535, SE-751 21 Uppsala, Sweden

Abstract

Reasons for not accepting QCD as the correct strong interaction theory given at Hadron '95 and Hadron '97 are expanded and made more precise. The scalar strong interaction hadron theory, recently presented in a book, provides an alternative to QCD. The motivation for and basic steps leading to this theory are outlined.

Introduction

On the theoretical side of this meeting, the contributions consist largely of the latest versions of phenomenological models, mostly on hadron spectra. These are but a tiny increment to the large body of such models already existing in the literature, or as some put it, on the "market." In his summary talk, Ted Barnes hinted at this situation by putting forth the formula: If there are n theorists, there are n+1 theories. Actually, the number n+1 is too small and may be replaced by αn, where $\alpha > 1$. This is due to the fact that the same theorist can have different models for different applications. Moreover, there may be several models for the same application area as he updates and improves his earlier models.

There are hundreds of such kinds of models with different assumptions, parameters, form factors, structure functions,... While these models work well within the relatively narrow application angle they are designed for, they provide little understanding of hadronic phenomena in any coherent fashion. This aspect together with the large number of such models makes it very difficult to extract from them eventual guidance to a correct hadron theory. In this respect, the above-mentioned models seem to differ from the models that preceded quantum mechanics. The atomic models of Bohr and Sommerfeld and the Rydberg formula played important roles in the development and verification of the Schrödinger theory.

The great freedom in constructing these models stems from the lack of a working first principles' hadron theory. The current strong interaction theory, quantum-chromodynamics(QCD), is nonperturbative at low energies and has not been able to provide useful predictions ever since it was proposed nearly 30 years ago. By contrast, 30 years after the appearance of the Maxwell equations, nearly all basic electromagnetic phenomena were explained. Similarly, 30 years after the publication of the Schrödinger-Dirac equations, most of the atomic phenomena were understood.

Furthermore, Dirac's book appeared already seven years after he published his equation and Schiff's text came out 23 years after the appearance of the Schrödinger equation. Still, there is no book covering QCD.

These circumstances indicate that QCD is not the correct strong interaction theory. Reasons for taking this standpoint have been given in Hadron '95 and Hadron '97[1]. This contribution is a further and more precise development of these references.

Quarks, Fermions, QCD, and Models

QCD as a hadron theory does not include two basic properties of quarks, namely, *property Q1: A quark cannot be observed alone* and *property Q2: A quark is always accompanied by an antiquark or two other quarks or a diquark.*

Prior to the quark hypothesis of 1963-64, a fermion is defined to be a lepton or a point particle having higher odd half-integer spin. Since the latter has not been observed, it is dropped for the present considerations. A fermion has two basic proper-ties, namely, *property F1: A fermion can exist freely and is described by Dirac's wave functions* and *property F2: In weakly interacting aggregates, fermions obey Pauli's exclusion principle.*

After the quark hypothesis, quarks were soon embraced into the fermion family. This inclusion is present in QCD and in chiral symmetry models for hadrons because at the times of the proposals of these theories, the nonobservation of free quarks or *property Q1* was not firmly established. Only afterwards was this *property Q1* accepted as an experimental fact.

Accordingly, a quark is not a fermion in the sense of *property F1.* Consequently, there is no reason that *property F2* should hold for quarks. With these observations, the color parts of QCD and chiral symmetry models are no longer needed. Further, quark wave functions like those of *property F1* appear in QCD and chiral symmetry models. According to quantum mechanics, these wave functions can be used to form expectation values of dynamical variables such as energy, momentum and position. But such formations would contradict *property Q1.* Therefore, these theories cannot be correct. Also, the concept of spontaneous symmetry breaking in chiral symmetry models is borrowed from solid state physics. But there is no reason why such a mechanism would apply in the totally different case of hadrons.

On par with the chiral symmetry models are the constituent quark models and the Bethe-Salpeter (BS) equation approach [2]. Although no quark wave function appears in the BS approach explicitly, they are present implicitly. This can be seen in the positronium case, which is described by a BS equation with 16 wave function components. The positronium can however disintegrate into a free electron and a free positron and the BS equation decomposes into two Dirac equations describing these free particles. But a meson cannot disintegrate into a free quark and a free antiquark. This difference prevents that the same BS formalism can be applied to a meson. Because of *properties Q1* and *Q2,* quarks in a meson have less degrees of freedom as do the constituents of positronium. Hence the number of meson wave function components should be less than 16(see eq. (3) ff below). Similarly, the number of baryon wave function components should be less than 64 (see last §).

The constituent quark models are more phenomenological in nature and have been the most successful ones. The interaction potential among the quarks are usually assumed to be of vector type in order to conform to QCD. In this connection, the spin-orbit terms in the potential have caused quite some controversy [3]. More importantly, confinement potential must be assumed to fit data.

Scalar Strong Interaction Hadron Theory

In view of the above considerations, alternatives to QCD are obviously called for. I am as surprised as I was at Hadron '95 [1] at that no voice on this issue has been heard also at this meeting. One such alternative was proposed in 1993 [4]. Since then, it has been developed in 10 papers which have recently been synthesized and amplified into a book [5].

The approach of this theory is to construct sets of differential equations for hadrons. These sets are then taken as basic postulates and are solved for various applications, just like that we solve the Maxwell and the Schrödinger-Dirac equations for different purposes and get results. They stand or fall with their ability to account for data.

To begin with, it is observed that the conventional form of the Dirac equation involving 4×4 γ matrices is not Lorentz invariant by inspection. van der Waerden [6] has transformed this equation into a set of manifestly Lorentz invariant two-spinor equations. Consider the meson case. Quark A at x_I and antiquark B at x_{II} interacting with each other via a massless scalar potential V_S are each described by a set of such two-spinor equations. For quark A, it reads

$$\partial_I^{a\dot{b}}\chi_{A\dot{b}}(x_I)-iV_{SB}(x_I)\psi_A^a(x_I)=im_A\psi_A^a(x_I)$$
$$\partial_{I\dot{b}c}\psi_A^c(x_I)-iV_{SB}(x_I)\chi_{A\dot{b}}(x_I)=im_A\chi_{A\dot{b}}(x_I)$$
$$\Box_I V_{SB}(x_I)=\tfrac{1}{2}g_s^2\left(\psi_B^c(x_I)\chi_{Bc}(x_I)+c.c.\right) \tag{1}$$

Here, a, b, c = 1, 2 and $\chi_{\dot{a}}=(\chi_a)^*$, $g_s^2/4\pi$ is the strong quark-quark coupling, I refers to x_I, and m_A is the mass of quark A. Both sets are multiplied together and the basic assumption of the present theory is the generalization of the product wave functions into nonseparable quantities according to

$$\chi_{A\dot{b}}(x_I)\chi_{Ba}(x_{II})\rightarrow\chi_{\dot{b}a}(x_I,x_{II}),, \qquad \psi_A^c(x_I)\psi_B^{\dot{a}}(x_{II})\rightarrow\psi^{c\dot{a}}(x_I,x_{II}) \tag{2a}$$

$$\chi_{A\dot{b}}(x_I)\psi_{B\dot{e}}(x_{II})\rightarrow\chi_{\dot{b}\dot{e}}(x_I,x_{II}), \qquad \psi_A^c(x_I)\chi_B^f(x_{II})\rightarrow\psi^{cf}(x_I,x_{II}) \tag{2b}$$

$$V_{SA}(x_{II})V_{SB}(x_I)\rightarrow\Phi_m(x_I,x_{II}) \tag{2c}$$

where Φ_m is the interquark potential. The right sides of (2a) contain mixed spinors of second rank and are assigned to represent mesons. The right sides of (2b) contain unmixed spinors and transform like diquarks. In the so-generalized equations, these last quantities and unpaired quarks are dropped to conform to *properties Q1* and *Q2*. The resulting meson wave equations read

$$
\begin{aligned}
&\partial_I^{a\dot{b}}\partial_{II}^{f\dot{e}}\chi_{\dot{b}f}(x_I,x_{II})-\left(M_m^2-\Phi_m(x_I,x_{II})\right)\psi^{a\dot{e}}(x_I,x_{II})=0\\
&\partial_{I\dot{b}c}\partial_{II\dot{e}d}\psi^{c\dot{e}}(x_I,x_{II})-\left(M_m^2-\Phi_m(x_I,x_{II})\right)\chi_{\dot{b}d}(x_I,x_{II})=0\\
&\Box_I\Box_{II}\Phi_m(x_I,x_{II})=-\tfrac{1}{2}g_s^4\,\mathrm{Re}\,\psi^{b\dot{a}}(x_I,x_{II})\chi_{\dot{a}b}^*(x_I,x_{II})
\end{aligned}
\tag{3}
$$

M_m turns out to be an eigenvalue equal to the average quark mass [5, §2.3.5]. It is obtained after having generalized the quark mass in (1) into a mass operator, similar to that employed in the Gell Mann-Okubo formula.

We note that there is no quark wave function in (3) so that *property Q1* is present. The two indices of the meson wave functions χ and ψ on the right sides of (2a) and in (3) show that a quark and an antiquark appear together in agreement with *property Q2*. On the other hand, *properties F1* and *F2* are absent. There are eight meson wave function components, half the number 16 for the corresponding BS amplitudes. Equations (3) consist of two coupled second order equations containing an interaction potential term that depends nonlinearly upon the meson wave functions.

Equations (3) provide the starting point from which all two quark meson phenomena are to be accounted for, similar to that the Schrödinger-Dirac equations are the basis for understanding all atomic phenomena. So far, (3) has been rather successful when compared to QCD.

A set of baryon wave equations has been analogously constructed. In ground state, a baryon consists of a quark and a diquark and is described by 12 wave function components, far less than 64 in the BS case. However, contact with data has hitherto been hampered by difficulties in solving the differential equations, which are much more complicated than those for the mesons. The present theory has so far only been applied to low energy data. It has not been worked out for application to high energy hadronic phenomena.

References

[1] Hoh, F. C., "QCD versus Spinor Strong Interaction Theory" in *Hadron '95 The 6th International Conference on Hadron Spectroscopy,* edited by M. C. Birse et al., World Scientific, 1995, pp. 368-370 and "On the Foundation of QCD and an Overview of the Spinor Strong Interaction Theory" in *Hadron Spectroscopy 7th International Conference,* edited by S-U. Chung et al., AIP Conference Proceedings 432, New York, 1997, pp. 181-184.

[2] Metsch, B., these proceedings.

[3] Barnes, T., these proceedings.

[4] Hoh, F. C., *Int. J. Theor. Phys.* 32 1111-1133 (1993).

[5] Hoh, F. C., *Two-Spinor Hadron Theory, http://www4.tsl.uu.se/~ho*h 2001.

[6] van der Waerden, B., *Göttinger Nachrichten* 100-109 (1929).

E. On the Foundation of QCD and an Overview of the Spinor Strong Interaction Theory

(Reprinted from *Hadron '97* [H1])

F. C. Hoh
Dragarbrunnsg. 9B, 75332 Uppsala, Sweden

Abstract

Based upon its predictive power as well as its theoretical foundation, it is reasoned that QCD is not the correct strong interaction theory for hadrons. The meson and baryon wave equations of the spinor strong interaction theory are presented. Contact of this theory with data is good for a number of basic issues at low energies. At high energies, this theory possesses properties similar to those of QCD.

Introduction

The material presented at this meeting has been rich. It reinforces and makes clearer our picture and the status of hadron theory that were present in the Hadron '95 conference two years ago in Manchester. This contribution can be considered as an updated and expanded version of a similar one to Hadron '95(1).

There are two distinct but incomplete approaches to account for data, dedicated largely to mesons so far, i.e., phenomenology and quantum chromo-dynamics (QCD).

In phenomenological models (2), some essential features of the Bethe-Salpeter equation and QCD are collected and certain inter-quark potentials are assumed. The models are mostly semi-relativistic and are separately constructed for application to specific low energy regions, where each of them is highly successful in accounting for data.

These models are rather independent of each other, pay no attention to gauge invariance considerations, cannot be derived from any first principles' formulation, such as QCD, and hence lack a self-consistent physical basis. We may at most hope that some of them may eventually constitute certain limits of a correct strong interaction theory, in the manner that the Rydberg formula preceded the Schroedinger theory.

QCD is a Lorentz and gauge invariant theory. It has been shown to work well in the high energy region in which perturbational calculations can be carried out. In fact, QCD has its origin in that region. For low energy phenomena, however, the QCD equations are largely non-perturbative and must be approximated (3) or solved numerically on a lattice (4). In the former case, QCD's relatively weak predictive power has deteriorated. For instance, $f_0(1510)$ and $\xi(2230)$ were strong glueball candidates in Hadron '95(5) two years ago but are no longer so at this meeting (3,6). Confinement, on the other hand, has not been proved theoretically.

It has been conjectured that these approximations may be too coarse and the issues need be resolved by lattice calculations. These have been carried out to some extent with much effort. They have however led to little physical understanding (4). The predictions can be made to fit a relatively small amount of data. Overall, they are not convincingly supported by data or have too large error margins or require greater computing capacity.

The present status of hadron theory is therefore highly unsatisfactory.

On the Foundation of QCD

An important underpinning of QCD is provided by the three-jet data from JADE experiments in 1979. One of the jets differed from the other two, could be associated with a spin one structure and was assigned to a jet spear-headed by a gluon. However, this underpinning is removed if the gluon is replaced by a diquark, which has a spin one part and is also not observable. This possibility has not been disproved to my knowledge.

On principle grounds, one may raise two debatable points, which also hold for some common phenomenological models. In the first place, why nature prefers a vector(gluon) force among the quarks and bypasses the more fundamental scalar and pseudoscalar forces? Second, why are the quarks described by Dirac's equation like any other observable fermion(a Newtonian particle in the spinless and low speed limit) is, in spite of the fact that they are not observable?

Conception and Description of a Particle

Our conception of a particle is in the simplest case a Newtonian particle, i.e., a point mass at some space-time point moving with a certain velocity, which depends upon this mass and the force acting on it. This is nearly automatically formed by our daily experiences and is so ancient and so ingrained in our minds that we are almost unconscious of it. This conception has been greatly dented by the rise of quantum mechanics, which attaches a wave property to the particle and renders its position and speed diffuse.

Nevertheless, this Newtonian conception remains with us intuitively and was taken over to apply to quarks, without paying much attention to whether quarks are observable or not. For some physicists, this may be construed as a slight oversight. Nature, however, is incapable of distinguishing an unintentional violation of her laws from an intentional one. She is relentless on such basic issues. If one particle is observable and another is not, they are to be described differently.

In QCD, this difference is provided by the hypothesis of colored quarks. I think that this hypothesis is a superficial one and serves only to "paper" over the non-observation of quarks. Further, quarks do not have to obey the spin-statistics theorem so that no color is needed in this regard. Beneath this "paper," QCD provides as a detailed description of quarks as that of an observable fermion. Such a detailed description is superfluous from the viewpoint of nature since it cannot be verified anyway. Nature is economical and concise; if a description can be dispensed with consistently, it will be.

Two Approaches to Construct a Physical Theory

During the first part of this century, two different approaches to the construction of basic physical theories were much debated on. In the first and older one, advocated by Eddington and

Einstein, one starts from basic and known physical concepts and general physical principles or postulates and builds up a mathematically self-consistent theory. This approach is largely based upon physical reasoning and is the common one. Thermodynamics, statistical mechanics and the theory of relativity were constructed in this way. The description of quarks in QCD and the Bethe-Salpeter equation also follow this approach in essence.

The second and newer one is associated with logical positivism, propounded by R. Carnap and others of the Vienna school in the 1920's. It downplays the significance of physical concepts and is more pragmatic. In practice, any self-consistent mathematical construction that leads to predictions that systematically account for data with sufficient coverage is a good theory. New mathematical entities entering the construction are subsequently associated with some physical concepts (words) which we may comprehend.

This approach is to a considerable degree guided by mathematic. It is in line with the Kantian thesis that "the thing-itself is unknowable." It is employed more seldom and only when we delve into regions where existing concepts fail and we can only rely on data and self-consistent mathematical representation. Older physical concepts are dropped if required by mathematical consistency. The Maxwell, Schroedinger and Dirac equations were constructed along this line.

Comparison to Earlier Theories

The mathematical formulation of the known basic disciplines, classical gravitation, classical electromagnetism, quantum mechanics, and quantum electrodynamics all began with differential equations. Integral formulations, i.e., Lagrangians, are later constructed from these equations. In QCD, however, one starts with a Langrangian; the differential equations derived from it are not useful since they contain open color.

Furthermore, a criterion of a good fundamental theory is its high degree of mathematical elegance. QCD does not appear to fulfil this criterion; its aesthetic level is much lower than those of the basic disciplines above.

On ground of its predictive power as well as its theoretical foundation according to the above, I think that QCD is not the correct strong interaction theory for hadrons and will in time be replaced by a correct such.

Overview of the Spinor Strong Interaction Theory

It is against earlier versions of such a background that the spinor strong interaction theory was proposed a few years ago (7) and subsequently developed (8). Its construction follows the second approach above (logical positivism) and makes full use of the invisibility of quarks.

This theory is based upon manipulations of van der Waerden's two component spinors which are right- and left-handed and hence suitable to represent relativistic fermions such as quarks and neutrinos. Dirac's equations in this spinor form for quarks interacting with each other via pseudoscalar and scalar forces are used to construct hadron wave equations. Afterwards, the quark and diquark wave functions are discarded so that the resulting hadron wave equations are much simpler than the QCD and the Bethe-Salpeter equations. These meson and baryon wave equations are Lorentz and gauge invariant and read

$$\partial_I^{a\dot{b}} \chi_{\dot{b}}^{f}(x_I, x_{II}) \partial_{II\, f\dot{e}} = (\Phi_P(x_I, x_{II}) - M_m^2) \psi_{\dot{e}}^{a}(x_I, x_{II})$$
$$\partial_{I\,\dot{c}b} \psi_{\dot{e}}^{b}(x_I, x_{II}) \partial_{II}^{\dot{e}d} = (\Phi_P(x_I, x_{II}) - M_m^2) \chi_{\dot{c}}^{d}(x_I, x_{II})$$
$$\Box_I \Box_{II} \Phi_P(x_I, x_{II}) = \tfrac{1}{2} g_A^2 g_B^2 \left[\psi_{\dot{b}}^{a}(x_{II}, x_I) \left(\chi_{\dot{a}}^{b}(x_{II}, x_I) \right)^* \right] \tag{1}$$

$$\partial_I^{a\dot{b}} \partial_I^{g\dot{h}} \chi_{\{\dot{b}\dot{h}\}}^{f}(I\ II) \partial_{II\, f\dot{e}} = -i(M_b^3 + \Phi_S(I\ II)) \psi^{\{ag\}}_{\dot{e}}(I\ II)$$
$$\partial_{I\,\dot{b}c} \partial_{I\,\dot{h}k} \psi^{\{ck\}}_{\dot{e}}(I\ II) \partial_{II}^{\dot{e}d} = -i(M_b^3 + \Phi_S(I\ II)) \chi_{\{\dot{b}\dot{h}\}}^{d}(I\ II)$$
$$\Box_I \Box_I \Box_{II} \Phi_S(I\ II) = \frac{1}{4} g_q^6 \left(\chi_{\{\dot{b}\dot{h}\}}^{f}(I\ II) \left(\psi^{\{bh\}}_{f}(I\ II) \right)^* + c.c. \right) \tag{2}$$

respectively. Here, ψ and χ are the hadron wave functions, x_I = I and x_{II} = II the quark coordinates(I for diquark in equation (2)), M the average quark mass, and g's strong pseudoscalar(meson) and scalar(baryon) coupling constants which can however be absorbed into ψ and χ. Two of the quarks in baryon is taken to form a diquark with respect to the strong force. In this way, the three-body problem of the baryon is reduced to a much simpler two body one.

The method by which equations (1) and (2) are constructed is heuristic and intuitive. Justification of these equations lies ultimately in their ability to account for data.

Equations (1) and (2) naturally lead to confinement and a new hadron classification scheme. The ground state hadron spectra fit well into this scheme, which leaves no unobserved states. Scalar mesons, much discussed in the literature, during Hadron '95(5) and at this conference, do not exist according to equation (1) because the quark are not confined. Equation (1) also largely successfully addresses the following basic problems: the ground state meson spectra, the U(1) problem, the absence of Higgs bosons, the Cabibbo and Weinberg angles, the conserved vector current hypothesis, and radiative decays of some open flavor vector mesons.

Internal functions $\xi(z)$ dependent upon internal coordinates $z=z_I$, z_{II} have been introduced into equations (1) and (2) via the substitutions ψ, χ->$\psi\xi(z)$, $\chi\xi(z)$. These functions contain flavor dependence and are needed to distinguish some members of different SU(3) multiplets. The M's are eigenvalues of the corresponding mass operator operating on $\xi(z)$. For electromagnetic interactions, $z=z_I$, z_{II}, z_{III}, has been introduced into equation (2) and may play the role of color in QCD. In the high energy region, equations (1) and (2) possess asymptotic freedom type of property and may therefore not contradict QCD results. No work has as yet been done in that region.

The spinor strong interaction theory is by no means free from problems. A basic problem has been the determination of integration constants which accompany these higher order equations (1) and (2) and the associated Lagrangians.

References

[1] Hoh, F. C., "QCD versus Spinor Strong Interaction Theory" in *Hadron '95, The 6th International Conference on Hadron Spectroscopy,* 1995, pp. 368-370.

[2] Barnes, T., Godfrey, S., Iachello, F., Metsch. B., these proceedings.

[3] Swanson, E. S., these proceedings.
[4] Michael, C., these proceedings.
[5] Pennington, M. R., "Hadron '95-Summary: Part I" in *Hadron '95, The 6th International Conference on Hadron Spectroscopy,* 1995, pp. 3-18.
[6] Shen, X., these proceedings.
[7] Hoh, F. C., *Int. J. Theor. Phys.* 32, 1111-1133 (1993), 33, 2325-2349 (1994).
[8] Hoh F. C., *Int. J. Mod. Phys.* A9, 365-381 (1994), *J. Phys.* G22, 85-98 (1996), *Int. J. Theor. Phys.* 33, 2351-2363 (1994), 36, 509-531 (1997), "Radiative Decay of Vector Meson V->P+Gamma in the Spinor Strong Interaction Theory," "The Spinor Strong Interaction Theory and Strong Decay of Heavy Vector Meson V->PP," "The Weinberg Angle and Pion Beta Decay in the Spinor Strong Interaction Theory," submitted.

F. QCD versus Spinor Strong Interaction Theory

(Reprinted from *Hadron '95* [H2])

F. C. Hoh

Dragarbrunnsg. 9B, Uppsala, Sweden

QCD is critically viewed in regard to predictive power, comparison to other basic disciplines and historical development. Reasons are given that it cannot be a good strong interaction theory. A brief introduction to the recently developed spinor strong interaction theory is presented. The large blocks of data successfully covered by it are pointed out.

1. Quantum Chromodynamics

As an outsider to the high energy physics community, I was struck, even surprised, by the passivity and uncritical attitude toward QCD at this meeting. There are staunch supporters of QCD. There are those who go along and say that QCD is a good strong interaction theory but has not yet reached the stage of making low energy predictions. But I heard no one actively voicing that QCD may be basically wrong and that alternative strong interaction theories ought to be sought.

This attitude is present in face of the fact that QCD, two decades after its proposal, can practically make no predictions on basic hadronic phenomena at low energies. Since QCD cannot be proven to be confining, there are no basic equations for hadrons. Therefore, hadron spectra and decay and other low energy phenomena cannot be predicted on a firm theoretical basis. Predictions in these areas are phenomenological and semi-relativistic and hence unreliable. If QCD is to be adhered to more strictly, complicated computer calculations are required to obtain even the simplest meson spectra approximately and sparsely. A prediction characteristic to QCD, the glueballs, has on the other hand not been confirmed by data. At higher energies, the non-Abelian gauge properties of QCD lead to asymptotic freedom and some success has been met.

The predictive power of QCD as a basic theory for strong interactions is orders of magnitude below those of equivalent basic disciplines, such as QED, C(lassical)ED, classical gravitation, and to some extent the standard model. At low energies and for simple configurations, the basic equations of these disciplines reduce to very simple forms that account for bulk of basic data with natural ease and elegance. Only at high energies or for complicated geometries do they exhibit calculational difficulties and their validity becomes questionable.

It has sometimes been argued that QCD differs from the above disciplines in that the coupling constant is large. However, this should not be an obstacle in treating stationary states such as meson spectra. For example, if the fine structure constant is allowed to be unity, the Schroedinger equation for a hydrogen atom still yields the same form of spectra although with different values. Difficulties arise first when higher order effects are considered. Another example is fluid mechanics, although it is not a basic discipline in the above sense. The governing equations are highly nonlinear but are still capable of producing stationary solutions to simple geometries rather easily.

That QCD, contrary to the other basic disciplines, claims some success at high energies but fails at low energies is possibly related to its development during the early 1970's, when existence of free quarks was not firmly rules out. Color was originally introduced to appease the spin statistics theorem applied to the delta++ baryon consisting of three u quarks. Later it was thought to offer a means for confinement as well. Around that time, a renormalizable non-Abelian gauge theory proved to be highly successful in the standard model. Impressed and supported by the great success of QED as a renormalizable gauge theory, QCD was composed to incorporate the above features for quarks. Not much attention was paid to low energy phenomena such as hadron spectra.

In the two decades that follow, non-existence of free quarks has been well established. The need for color drops out since the spin statistics theorem which holds for observable particles does not have to hold for non-observable quarks. Further, quark wave functions satisfying Dirac type of equations no longer need to appear in the theory. I believe that many physicists will agree that nature does not "play games" by offering us the elegant Dirac equation that describes observable particles, such as leptons, and at the same time also describe non-observable particles like quarks, irrespective color. In a sense, some basic motivations underlying QCD has been removed.

2. Spinor Strong Interaction Theory

The spinor strong interaction theory [1-4] has been developed in the above background. It follows the development of the above-mentioned disciplines, except for QCD, and emphasizes the low energy end. The theory is so named because it is based upon van der Waerden's two component spinors. These are either left or right-handed and hence suitable for description of quarks and leptons which are essentially relativistic. The commonly used Dirac four component bispinors are more suited for approaching the non-relativistic limit, but lead to cumbersome transportation of some gamma matrices when describing quarks and leptons.

Quarks obeying Dirac's equations are assumed to act upon each other via massless scalar forces. For quark-antiquark interaction, the force is pseudoscalar. The quark wave functions are generalized to include internal functions and the quark masses and charges to operators operating upon these internal functions. The so-generalized Dirac equations and associated massless interaction potential equations in spinor form are multiplied into the corresponding ones for the other quark or quarks. The resulting product wave functions and operators are subsequently generalized to non-separable quantities [1].

In the resulting hadron equations, the remaining quark wave functions are put to zero on account of that they have not been observed; they have been used as "scaffolding" in constructing the hadron equations and removed afterwards. Baryon is assumed to consist of a quark-diquark pair structure and the 64 components of its Bethe-Salpeter amplitude are reduced to 12. The usual 16 components of the meson Bethe-Salpeter amplitude are reduced to 8. The differential equations for the interaction potentials are of fourth and sixth orders which lead to linear and harmonic confinement for meson and baryons, respectively.

The so-obtained meson equations [1] have proved to be successful in classifying the known two quark mesons [3]. The ground state scalar and axial vector mesons are not confined and hence do not exist. The two quark pseudoscalar isosinglets such as eta/b are forbidden by U(1) gauge invariance considerations. For mesons without angular excitation, the basic meson equations can be reduced, without approximation, to radial equations like that for the hydrogen atom yielding a simple mass formula. Using a number of meson masses to fix the quark masses and as input, the remaining masses of unmixed mesons are mostly correctly predicted.

Lorentz and SU(2)XU(1) gauge invariances of the meson equations have been established [1, 2]. It is shown that the kaon doublet plays the role of the Higgs doublet in generating the masses of the gauge bosons, thus rendering the Higgs bosons unnecessary. The large body of rather successful results of leptonic inter*actions predicted by the standard model can thus be carried over to hold in the spinor strong interaction theory [4]. For semi-leptonic interactions, the standard model is far less successful. In the spinor strong interaction theory, however, no unknown Cabibbo angle is needed to account for the ratio of the kaon and pion rates of decay to muons. The equivalent Cabibbo angle is correctly predicted.

At high energies, the quark mass and interaction potential terms in the meson and baryon equations can be neglected. The non-separable hadron wave functions become now separable into nearly free quark wave functions while retaining non-Abelian gauge invariance in the meson case. This is similar to the asymptotic freedom of QCD.

3. Summary

A comparison of the predictive power of the over two decade old QCD to that of the newly developed spinor strong interaction theory so far show that the latter power is much greater and more natural than the former at the low energy end. At high energies, both theories lead to that quarks are nearly free but no work has yet been done employing the latter theory.

References

[1] F. C. Hoh, *Int. J. Theor. Phys.* 32, 1111 (1993), 33, 2325, 2351 (1994).

[2] F. C. Hoh, *Int. J. Mod. Phys.* A9, 365 (1994).

[3] F. C. Hoh, « Meson Classification and Spectra in the Spinor Strong Interaction Theory," *J. Phys.* G, to appear.

[4] F. C. Hoh, « Meson Lepton Interaction in the Spinor Strong Interaction Theory," submitted.

G. Epistemological and Historical Implications or Elementary Particle Theories
(Reprint of [H16])

F. C. Hoh

Abstract

The epistemological credo of Einstein is further developed and specified in greater detail for practical applications. The results are applied to quasi-historical creation processes of established physical theories and to current theories for elementary particles. The outcome of these applications is then considered from epistemological viewpoints. Reasons underlying the basic difficulties of the current mainstream particle theory, the standard model, are given. The steps in the creation of an alternative approach, the scalar strong interaction hadron theory, are delineated.

1. Introduction

The current main stream elementary particle theory is the standard model(SM) [1, 2] which includes quantum chromodynamics(QCD) and the electro-weak interaction model(EWM). Despite the claim that QCD's predictions agree with many accurate experiments [2], QCD cannot account for low energy hadronic data, such as those given by the Particle Data Group(PDG) [1]. In spite of the claim that EWM has been "wonderfully successful" [2], the Higgs boson, on which EWM hinges, has not been seen.

In view of these difficulties, an alternative to low energy QCD and EWM, the scalar strong interaction hadron theory (SSI) has been proposed [3-5]. This theory naturally accounts for many basic low energy hadronic phenomena that cannot be accounted for by QCD and EWM. The approach of SSI however drastically differs from that of SM and appears to be unfamiliar to most physicists.

To clarify this situation, therefore, EWM, QCD and SSI will be examined from two basic points of view. One of them is provided by epistemology or theory of knowledge, which in earlier centuries has been the main branch of philosophy but is presently much less dominant. Another one is given by the history of the creation of the established physical theories.

The epistemologies of interest are sketched in Appendix A. The teachings of these are generally accepted and are, is short, the common knowledge that theory needs be tested against experiment. But how this is practiced varies over a wide range of rigor. Allowing epistemology to bear upon the creation of physical theories will sharpen this practice. As the early Wittgenstein expressed: "The object of philosophy is the logical clarification of thoughts. Philosophy is not a theory but an activity. A philosophical work consists essentially of elucidations. The result of philosophy is not a number of philosophical propositions, but to make propositions clear."

In Sec. 2, Einstein's epistemological belief is further developed and specified in greater detail for practical applications. The results are then applied to creation processes of established physical theories from historical points of view in Sec. 3. In Sec. 4, the same procedure is carried out for EWM, QCD and SSI. The results of these studies are then discussed from epistemological viewpoints in Sec. 5. Sec. 6 gives the main conclusion of the present investigations. For reference, the epistemologies of interest are sketched in Appendix A. Appendix B presents difficulties of QCD. In Appendix C, the steps leading to SSI are given making use of Sec. 2-3.

2. Further Development of Einstein's Exposition

For the present investigations, the epistemologies mentioned in Appendix A need be specified in greater detail. Closest to the present application is Einstein's exposition in §A3, which will be the starting point. To obtain practical rules for application, the ideas of §A3 are extended and the results are represented in Figure 2.1 below. His statements Ea) in §A3, which is equivalent to LPb) in §A2, is expanded to *domain Data* and Eb) in §A3, which is equivalent to LPa) in §A2, to *domain Logic*. His *connection* between Ea) and Eb) is expanded to an intervening *domain Physics*. These domains are set up in order to avoid possible mix-up of mathematical and physical concepts.

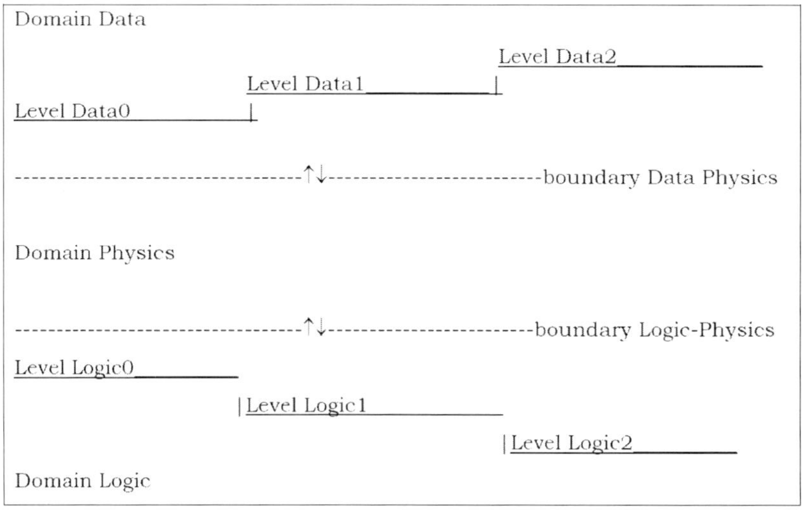

Figure 2.1. It shows the three domains separated by two boundaries. The ↑↓ signs indicate that the contents in domains Data and Logic can be moved across the boundaries Data-Physics and Logic-Physics, respectively, into domain Physics and be brought back from it. Roughly speaking, the vertical distance between two levels indicates the distance between measurement and basic theory. The horizontal axis is some measure of time since renaissance. The left, middle and right parts of this figure are further considered in §5.2, 5.3 and 5.4 below.

2.1. Domain Data

It consists of several levels Data0, Data1, Data2,... The highest level contains raw experimental data, which by a series of treatments, which can for instance include Monte-Carlo calculations, are converted to quantities on lower levels and finally to the lowest level Data0. This level contains data in form of quantities that can be identified with corresponding quantities on level Logic0 in §2.2 below when brought into domain Physics. Algebraical combinations of such quantities are also on this level. Examples of the content of level Data0 are coordinates of a particle, temperature of a substance, magnetic field, electric current density, mass and decay time of a hadron, and in general data given by PDG [1].

2.2. Domain Logic

It contains only logic and pure mathematics. Since Newton, such logical or *mathematical structures* have been differential equations for all known and established basic physical disciplines. For the sake of clarity, all symbols in domain Logic are attached by a prime ´ which denotes that these symbols are mathematical quantities. The definitions, statements, propositions, and equations need only be self-consistent and obey conventions of logic, but are otherwise free from any restraint. They are exact but have no physical meaning and belong to LPa) in §A2 and Eb) in §A3 below. This domain presently consists of three levels, Logic0, Logic1 and Logic2.

Level Logic0 contains mathematical structures(differential equations) whose variables, or some quantities formed algebraically from them, when brought into domain Physics, can all be associated with and tested against the corresponding data quantities from level Data0. Examples are Newton's equations, thermodynamical relations and Ampère's law which becomes on this level

$$\nabla' \times \underline{B}'(\underline{x}') = \underline{j}'(\underline{x}') \tag{2.1}$$

This mathematical structure states that a vector field $\underline{j}'$(not electric current density here) is defined as the curl of another vector field $\underline{B}'$ in a flat three dimensional space $\underline{x}'$.

Level Logic1 is more abstract. The mathematical structures(differential equations) therein will now be the source of the physics. Here, some *hidden dependent variables* which, after crossing the boundary Logic-Physics, have no corresponding quantities from level Data0 to identify with and compare to. Examples of such variables are the Schrödinger wave function ψ' and the metric tensor $g'_{\mu\nu}$ in general relativity. By mathematical manipulations the content on this level can be converted to that on level Logic0.

Level Logic2 is still more abstract. The mathematical structures (differential equations) therein will now be the source of the physics. However, in addition to hidden dependent variables, there are also some *hidden independent variables* and functions of them which, after crossing the boundary Logic-Physics, have no corresponding quantities from level Data0 to identify with and compare to. Examples of such variables are the relative space time between two quarks and coordinates in flavor space in SSI (see Appendix C). By mathematical manipulations, the content on level Logic2 can be converted to that on level Logic1 and, if necessary, subsequently to level Logic0.

2.3. Domain Physics

The contents or data on level Data0 are temporarily be brought across the boundary Data-Physics into domain Physics in Figure 2.1. Simultaneously, a *mathematical structure* on level Logic0 is also temporarily carried across the boundary Logic-Physics and thereby loses the primes ´ attached to the symbols therein and becomes a *theory* in domain Physics. The mathematical symbols in this theory are now intuitively assigned to various physical quantities. The theory has now physical meaning but is no longer exact. It is then worked out and tested against the corresponding data quantities in this domain. If the test is successful, the theory can be, but does not have to be, "right" (see §A4). If there is disagreement or conflict, the theory in domain Physics and hence also the corresponding mathematical structure in domain Logic need be changed and more experiments may be called for. The contents in domain Physics are then brought across the boundaries Data-Physics and Logic-Physics back to levels Data0 and Logic0, respectively.

It is also possible to bring the mathematical structures on levels Logic1 and Logic2 directly across the boundary Logic-Physics into domain Physics to becomes physical theories, which can then be reduced to theories corresponding to those on level Logic0. This reduction was done in domain Logic in §2.2. These both ways of reduction are equivalent but the latter is simpler conceptually because one has only to follow the rules of logic and can leave physics aside in the meantime.

2.4. Development of Physical Theories

The history of the development of physical theories shows that the creation of a new theory can be considered to proceed in the following stages in terms of activities in the three domains of §2.1-3.

- Stage I: *Recent data* This stage takes place in domain Data in which some new or recent data become available.
- Stage II: *Conflict* This stage takes place in domain Physics. The *Recent data* are brought across the boundary Data-Physics into domain Physics. Simultaneously, the associated *existing mathematical structure* in domain Logic, preferably reduced to level Logic0, is also carried over the boundary Logic-Physics into domain Physics to become the *existing theory*, which is then tested against the *Recent data*. A *Conflict* between the existing theory and the recent data arises. The existing theory is then returned into domain Logic to resume its role as the existing mathematical structure.
- Stage III: *Leap* This stage takes place in domain Logic. The *Recent data* in domain Physics in Stage II are taken across the boundary Logic-Physics to become a *recent mathematical requirement* in domain Logic. The *Conflict* in domain Physics becomes an *Inconsistency* in domain Logic between this recent mathematical requirement and the existing mathematical structure. A *Leap* or a change is then introduced into the existing mathematical structure to obtain a modified or *new mathematical structure* consistent with logical rules. This new mathematical structure may now be consistent with the recent mathematical requirement.
- Stage IV: *Hypothesis-Theory* The *Leap* made in domain Logic is brought across the boundary Logic-Physics to become a physical *Hypothesis* in domain Physics. The *new mathematical structure* becomes in this domain a *new theory* that may now agree with the *Recent data*.

If however there is still conflict, the above cycle or part of it is repeated. New experiments and new theories can be needed. The development of physical theories may be considered to consist of the chain D-P, L-P, L-P, D-P, D-L-P, and so on, where D-L-P stands for "activities in domain Data followed by activities in domain Logic followed by activities in domain Physics."

The leap made in Stage III takes place in domain Logic and has no physical meaning. It is therefore completely arbitrary, as long as logic is maintained, and can be done in an infinite number of ways. Such a leap or a guess cannot be derived in any way. The choice of the leap obviously takes into account the *Recent data* and is such that the new theory will hopefully remove the *Conflict* in Stage II or agree with new data. If there is no data that can guide the choice, the simplest form of the new mathematical structure may be chosen, as is indicated in Ed) ff of §A3 below.

The choice of new experiments is also in principle arbitrary but is largely aimed at testing the new theories. New technologies can also lead to new or more accurate experiments and thereby produce new or more accurate data. After these experiments, the content on level Data0 will be new *Recent data* which, upon crossing the boundary Data-Physics, tests the theory again.

3. Historical Survey of Physical Theories

3.1. Criteria in the Formation of New Physical Theories

The steps in §2.4 are now applied to the creation processes of established physical theories in §3.2 below. The result of this application shows that in the creation processes the following criteria CR1 and CR2 are satisfied.

CR1: Between Stages II and III,

a) the only new quantities crossing the boundary Logic-Physics into domain Logic are the *Recent data*, which become recent mathematical requirements to be satisfied by performing suitable leaps in the existing mathematical structure. In particular,
b) no physical quantities or concepts foreign to the existing theory in form of any physical hypothesis made in domain Physics make this crossing to become foreign mathematical symbols, relations and requirements that need be compatible with the existing mathematical structure in domain Logic.

CR2: The new theory satisfies the requirements of

a) pragmatism in §A1,
b) the original verifiability principle of logical positivism LPa) and LPb) in §A2 and c) Einstein's criteria Ec) and Ed) in §A3.

3.2. Historical Cases

In this subsection, the creation processes of the physical theories below are sketched in terms of the stages in §2.4. The criterion CR2 is considered to be satisfied in each of the following well-established cases. The criterion CR1 and the levels in domain Logic will be considered separately below.

1) Copernican universe ~1543

Recent data: Astronomical data were acquired for astrological purposes.

Conflict: Increasing number of geocentric models conflicted with each other and disagreed with data. Astronomers disagreed as to whether Venus and Mercury were inside or outside the orbit of the sun. The civil calendar had fallen seriously out of alignment with the sun's positions.

Leap-Hypothesis: The existing mathematical or logical structures are those pertaining to the various geocentric models. The recent mathematical or logical requirements originate in *Recent data*; CR1 is satisfied. The leap-hypothesis consists of new assignments of the roles of the heavenly bodies and the replacement of geocentric models by the heliocentric model so that the inconsistencies corresponding to the *Conflict* are removed. The new logical structure remains on level Logic0 because the quantities involved all have their counterparts on level Data0.

2) Newtonian Mechanics ~1687

Recent data: They were observations by Kepler and others.

Conflict: There was no existing theory in form of differential equations; hence there was no conflict.

Leap-Hypothesis: The definitions and assumptions, to which the mathematical structure of Newton's equations together with the inverse square law of gravity can be reduced to, are taken as the leaps. The new mathematical structures are differential equations and are on level Logic0 because the quantities involved therein, when moved across the boundary Logic-Physics into domain Physics, have all counterparts on level Data0. Since there was no conflict, CR1 does not apply.

3) Thermodynamics and Statistical Mechanics 1700's and late 1800's

Recent data: They were work on heat engines for the first topic. For the last topic, chemical and mechanical experiments brought down the caloric theory of heat so that the atomistic view of matter could regain ground.

Conflict: There were no viable existing theories in form of differential equations in these areas; hence there was no conflict.

Leap-Hypothesis: In thermodynamics, it is the impossibility to create perpetuum mobile. Although the concept of caloric was used, it did not cross the boundary Logic-Physics into domain Logic to become a recent mathematical requirement; CR1 is not violated in practice. The quantities in the equations of thermodynamics are obviously on level Logic0. For statistical mechanics, it is the atomic hypothesis and mechanical nature of heat. The quantities in the associated differential expressions can all be measured and are hence on level Logic0. Since there was no conflict, CR1 does not apply.

4) Electromagnetism ~1873

Recent data: They were data summarized by the laws of Coulomb, Ampère, and Faraday.

Conflict: Ampère's law disagreed with conservation of charge.

Leap-Hypothesis: The existing mathematical structures in domain Logic are the above three laws in form of differential equations (with prime ´ attached to the symbols), which may be considered to have been moved from domain Data via domain Physics into domain Logic. CR1 is therefore satisfied. Among these existing mathematical structures, Maxwell discovered an inconsistency corresponding to the *Conflict*. The hypothesis corresponding to the leap consists of adding a displacement current(derivative of the electric field with respect to time) to the Ampère law (2.1), whereby the inconsistency is removed. The quantities in Maxwell's equations are all measurable and the new mathematical structure is therefore on level Logic0.

Later developments showed that the electric and magnetic fields can be written as derivatives of a vector potential A_μ which in domain Logic satisfies

$$\left(\nabla'^2 - \frac{1}{c^2}\frac{\partial^2}{\partial t'^2}\right)A'_\mu(\underline{x}',t') = j'_\mu(\underline{x}',t') \tag{3.1}$$

where j_μ denotes the electric current density and c the speed of light. These equations are simpler but are of second order while the Maxwell equations are of first order. A_μ can however not be observed directly and hence do not have any counterpart on level Data0 and (3.1) is therefore assigned to level Logic1. The mathematical manipulation that converts A'_μ to the fields on level Logic0 is derivation.

5) Quanta 1900, 1905

Recent data: The black body radiation spectrum was accurately measured and fitted empirically to a formula, the Planck law.

Conflict: This spectrum could not be calculated from classical physics at that time, which could also not be modified to obtain this law.

Leap-Hypothesis: The established thermodynamics and Boltzmann's statistical mechanics can be brought across the boundary Logic-Physics to become the existing mathematical structures in domain Logic. Apart from that, only the Planck law is brought across the same boundary to become the recent mathematical requirement; CR1 is satisfied. The inconsistency between them corresponding to the *Conflict* is eliminated by introducing the leap $E'=h\nu'$ into the existing mathematical structures. The variables in Planck's law are all measurables and the new mathematical structures are therefore on level Logic0.

The physical meaning of $E=h\nu$ came in1905, when Einstein noticed that the entropies of low intensity monochromatic radiation and of an ideal gas varied in the same way with the volume and inferred that light behaves also like material particle.

6) Special relativity 1905

Recent data: Accurate measurements of the velocity of light c showed that it was the same in different inertial systems.

Conflict: c = constant was inconsistent with absolute time in Newtonian mechanics.

Leap-Hypothesis: The existing mathematical structure is that pertaining to Newtonian mechanics and Galileo transformations. Only c = constant is taken across the boundary Logic-Physics to become the recent mathematical requirement; CR1 is satisfied. The hypothesis corresponding to the leap consists of removal of the above absolute time concept and allow time to be different in different inertial systems. The inconsistency associated with the *Conflict* is now removed in the new mathematical structure pertaining to Lorentz transformations. This structure remains on level Logic0.

7) General relativity 1915

Recent data: They were accurate measurements showing that inertial and gravitational masses were equivalent.

Conflict: Lorentz transformations could not accommodate this equivalence.

Leap-Hypothesis: The existing mathematical structure is that pertaining to special relativity. The recent mathematical requirement originates in the equivalence of inertial and gravitational masses; CR1 is satisfied. The first leap consists of replacing Lorentz transformations, in which $g_{\mu\nu}$ are constants, by general nonlinear transformations $g_{\mu\nu}(x_\sigma)$ and thereby the inconsistency due to the *Conflict* is eliminated. This is followed by the leap in setting the Ricci tensor $R_{\lambda\nu}(g_{\mu\nu}(x_\sigma)$ and its derivatives up to second order) = 0, which is the simplest possible choice, in accordance with CR2c)Ed) ff in §A3, because there was no guidance from data. $g_{00}-1(g_{00}^{-1})$ is identified as the Newtonian gravitational potential, when it is weak, and hence does not have counterpart on level Data0; only the derivative of the gravitational potential is measurable and can appear on level Data0. The other components in $g_{\mu\nu}(x_\sigma)$, identified as the generalized gravitational potentials can analogously not be observed directly. The new mathematical structure and the leap are therefore on level Logic1. The mathematical manipulation that converts $g'_{\mu\nu}(x'_\sigma)$ to fields on level Logic0 is derivation, analogous to the conversion of A'_μ to electric and magnetic fields.

8) Quantum Mechanics 1923-26

Recent data: Compton(1923) confirmed that light wave behaves also like material particle.

Conflict: de Broglie (1924) pointed out that this would be inconsistent with that material particle were not considered as wave.

Leap-Hypothesis: Debye said that a wave equation is needed. Schrödinger followed this up and considered the table below, which refers to domain Physics [6]. Boxes 2 and 3 can be taken across the boundary Logic-Physics into domain Logic to become the existing mathematical structures. The content of *Recent data* is similarly brought across the same boundary to become the recent logical requirement; CR1 is obeyed. This requirement is fulfilled by the leap that creates the logical counterpart of box 1, which can be derived from box 2. Now an inconsistency corresponding to the *Conflict* arises and is removed by the leap creating box 4. Because the contents of box 1 and box 3 have the same form (Hamilton 1834), the form of box 4 is therefore the same as that of box 2. Since the material particle in classical mechanics is a scalar, let its wave function be a scalar function ψ. Replacing A_μ in box 2 by ψ and make use of p in box 3, the Schrödinger equation is obtained in box 4. These last steps take place in domain Physics but can also be considered to have taken place in domain Logic, analogous to the both alternatives mentioned at the end of §2.3. The Schrödinger equation is on level Logic1 because ψ' replaces A_μ' in (3.1).

	Particle Description	**Wave Description**
Light	*Box 1:* Eikonal equation of geo-metrical optics in a medium with refractive index n	*Box 2:* Wave equation (3.1) with no prime, $j_\mu=0$, light speed c replaced by $u=c/n$, and frequency ν
Material Particle	*Box 3:* Hamilton Jacobian equation with energy E, potential V, mass m, and momentum $p=(2m(E-V))^{1/2}$	*Box 4:* An analogous wave equation with wave length $\lambda=u/\nu=h/p$; the Schrödinger equation

The manipulation that converts ψ' to quantities on level Logic0 is the formation of expectation values.

9) Relativistic Quantum Mechanics 1928

Recent data: These were summarized by Schrödinger's equation and special relativity.

Conflict: Schrödinger's equation was inconsistent with special relativity.

Leap-Hypothesis: The Schrödinger equation is taken across the boundary Logic-Physics to become the existing mathematical structure. The same is done to Lorentz transformations which become the recent mathematical requirement; CR1 is satisfied. The inconsistency derived from the *Conflict* is eliminated by the leap that requires that the Schrödinger equation be modified to a new mathematical structure linear in momenta in order to conform to special relativity. The new mathematical structure is that pertaining to Dirac's equation (C1.2) and is similarly on level Logic1. The extra ψ' components are on the same level as ψ' in the previous case. The manipulation that converts ψ' to quantities on level Logic0 is the same as that in case 8).

10) Parity nonconservation 1956

Recent data: The $\tau(K_L)$ and $\vartheta(K_S)$ mesons were found to be the same meson but their decay products had different parities.

Conflict: These results were inconsistent with the view at that time that parity was always conserved.

Leap-Hypothesis: The existing mathematical structure is that pertaining to Dirac's equation or more generally quantum electrodynamics (QED) which conserves parity. The recent mathematical requirement is derived from *Recent data* so that CR1 is satisfied. It corresponds to nonconservation of parity. This inconsistency corresponding to *Conflict* is eliminated by the leap that removes the requirement of parity conservation in the existing mathematical structure when applied to weak interactions. The new mathematical structure later evolved into the Glashow-Salam-Weinberg (GSW) [7] model for electro-weak interactions. It is on level Logic1, similar to the previous case.

In summary, the criterion CR1, where applicable, is satisfied by all the above classical cases. The mathematical structures for classical physics in cases 1-6 are om level Logic0. Those for general relativity and quantum physics in cases 7-10 are on level Logic1.

4. EWM, QCD and SSI

The steps applied to the above ten cases are now also applied to the current main stream particle theories EWM and QCD and also to SSI.

4.1. EWM 1960's

Recent data: They were experimental results that follow §3.2.10) and the experimental verification of the $W^{\pm}$ and Z gauge bosons.

Conflict: The then existing GSW model did not allow finite masses of these gauge bosons.

Leap-Hypothesis: The existing mathematical structure is that pertaining to the GSW model. The recent mathematical requirement is derived from *Recent data* and CR1 is satisfied in this respect. According to the *Conflict*, it is inconsistent with the existing mathematical structure due to the finite masses of the gauge bosons. In §3.2, such inconsistencies have been overcome by leaps performed in the existing mathematical structure in domain Logic. In EWM, however, the hypotheses that the symmetry of vacuum is spontaneously broken and vacuum consists of

Higgs condensate are made in domain Physics. These are then brought across the boundary Logic-Physics to become additional recent mathematical requirements. Because these hypotheses contain concepts absent in the existing GSW structure and in *Recent data*, CR1b) is *violated.* Moreover, Higgs boson is not present on level Data0 because it has not been seen. Consequently, it also violates CR2b)LPb) and CR2c)Ec). Further, quark wave functions are put on par with lepton wave functions in the GSM model, contrary to the observation that "no free quark exists" in §4.3 below. Thus, it can be shown that the creation of the GSM model itself violates CR1. The new mathematical structure involved is on level Logic1, just like that for the case §3.2.10).

4.2. QCD Early 1970's

Recent data: Experiments on hadrons in the 1950's and 1960's led to the quark(fractionally charged spin ½ point particle) hypothesis. Nucleons were found to contain point-like objects, called partons, which could not be shown to be quarks. Although no free quark had been seen, its absence was not fully established experimentally at that time. Therefore, the interpretation was that "quarks are confined" which implied that quarks existed but were somehow confined(see §B3 below). It differs from that "no free quark exists" in §4.3 below. There was also a large amount of data on hadrons.

Conflict: The then existing QED could not account for quark confinement and other hadronic data.

Leap-Hypothesis: The existing mathematical structure is that pertaining to QED. However, the content of *Recent data* about quarks is not taken directly across the boundary Logic-Physics into domain Logic to become recent mathematical requirements, as in the cases of §3.2. Instead, this content is modified into the hypotheses that quarks come in 3 colors and interact with each other via gauge fields having 8 colors in domain Physics. These are then brought across the boundary Logic-Physics to become recent mathematical requirements and relations as are seen in (B1) below. Because these physical quantities and concepts are absent in the existing QED structure and in *Recent data*, CR1b) is *violated.* Further, these colored objects are not present on level Data0 because they cannot be observed. Therefore, they also violate CR2b)LPb) and CR2c)Ec). QCD also violates CR2a), CR2b)LPb) and CR2c)Ec) because QCD cannot account for low energy hadronic data in PDG [1]. The new mathematical structure involved is formally on level Logic1 but there are no straightforward mathematical manipulations that can convert this structure to level Logic0.

Additional difficulties of QCD are given in Appendix B.

4.3. SSI 1990's

Recent data: Data showed convincingly that "no free quark and no free diquark exist." This differed from the interpretation that "quarks are confined" in §4.2 above. There were also a huge amount of data on hadrons.

Conflict: The existing QED, in form of Bethe-Salpeter (BS) equation, could not account for confinement and other hadronic data.

Leap-Hypothesis: The existing mathematical structure is that pertaining to the BS equation The content of *Recent data* regarding quark and diquark, when taken across the boundary Logic-Physics into domain Logic, becomes the recent mathematical requirement that wave functions to be associated with quarks and diquarks cannot be present in the new mathematical structure. The construction of SSI is given in Appendix C and §C5 shows that CR1 is satisfied.

The inconsistency related to confinement in *Conflict* is removed in [3]. The new mathematical structure involved is on level Logic2.

Summarizing, the criteria CR1 are CR2 are satisfied by SSI but not by EWM and QCD. The mathematical structures of EWM and QCD are formally on level Logic1. For SSI, it is on level Logic2.

5. Interaction of Particle Theories with Epistemology

5.1. Hypotheses on Vacuum

Vacuum can carry gravitational and electromagnetic energies and waves and can yield particle-antiparticle pairs. In the late 1940's, vacuum was found to be slightly polarizable by electromagnetic fields and such effects are exactly calculated in QED. The virtual particles in QED are however *not new*, but have observable counterparts.

Contemporary hadron physicists believe that vacuum can also carry other types of *new, not observed* media. In EWM, vacuum is assumed to be a Higgs condensate. For color confinement in QCD, vacuum is assumed to be a perfect color dia-electric. These virtual media have however no observable counterparts and these two vacua hence differ from the QED vacuum in this respect.

Attempts to resort to vacuum as a means to explain physical phenomena are not new. Over a century ago, the "vacuum" at that time was thought to be filled by a universal ether in which light propagates and this view was widely accepted by physicists. It persisted in spite of the fact that Maxwell's theory of light does not require any ether but was finally brought down by special relativity.

Over two centuries ago, the then "vacuum" was analogously thought to contain a hypothetical weightless fluid known as caloric representing heat. This caloric hypothesis helped Carnot to arrive at his discoveries in thermodynamics and was widely accepted in the 1700's. But by the mid-1800's, many kinds of experiments showed that heat is a form of mechanical energy and the caloric concept had to be abandoned.

These earlier "vacua" however did not interfere with the mathematical formalisms of Huygens and Carnot. The difficulties were conceptual. The "vacua" in EWM and QCD also differ from these earlier ones in that they are specific and characterize the mathematical formalisms.

Nevertheless, this is some resemblance between these two "vacua" and the two earlier ones. The caloric concept held for more than a century. The history of ether was even longer. Judging from these time scales, the concepts of vacuum as Higgs condensate and color dia-electric may continue to prevail for some time to come. However, in a few years, when the Large Hadron Collider will deliver data, the existence of Higgs boson will face a decisive test.

5.2. Level Logic0

As was mentioned at the end of Sec. 3, the mathematical structures (differential equations) for physical theories up to about 1910 are on level Logic0. As was defined in §2.2, level Logic0 can be "seen" form level Data0 via domain Physics. The left part of Figure 2.1 concerns these levels. The concepts are therefore all familiar and "Gedanken" or thought experiments, so forcefully employed by Einstein and Bohr, could be performed. The results of algebraical manipulations on this level can likewise be "understood" in terms of known concepts.

5.3. Level Logic1 and Its Implications

The mathematical structures for general relativity and quantum physics are on level Logic1. Because level Logic1 is "hidden" from direct view from level Data0 across domain Physics, new degrees of freedom become possible. In quantum mechanics, such a freedom is expressed in form of the existence of an arbitrary local phase associated with a wave function which is a hidden dependent variable. This arbitrary phase in its turn necessitates a U(1) gauge field, identified as the electromagnetic field.

In addition, purely quantum mechanical effects having no counterparts on level Data0 before quantum mechanics, such as exchange effects, tunnelling, Bose-Einstein condensation, etc, emerge. These new physics comes from mathematical operations on level Logic1 and cannot be "understood," like we "understand" Newtonian mechanics, because the associated concepts are unrelated to the then known concepts on level Data0 (see §5.5 below). Words like "tunnelling"(osmosis or infiltration could as well be used instead) are names assigned to certain mathematical results, confirmed by data, so as to give us some feeling what they are like in terms of familiar concepts.

Einstein's standpoint, that quantum mechanics offers no useful point of departure for future development, was based upon the hypothesis of "spatial separability," a result of "Gedanken" experiment, applied to Schrödinger's ψ [8]. This viewpoint is untenable here; "Gedanken" experiments make use of familiar concepts on level Logic0 and cannot be reliably initiated from level Logic1. This hypothesis was introduced in domain Physics and hence violates CR1b).

The purely quantum mechanical results can only be accepted as new concepts that one "gets used to" them after some time.

5.4. Level Logic2 and Its Implications

This section concerns the right part of Figure 2.1 which commences in the 1990's. Level Logic2 is still farther away and more "hidden" from direct view from level Data0, as was predicted in Ed) ff of §A3. Therefore, still more freedoms are allowed on this level, as is evidenced by choices of the forms of quark-antiquark interaction, the mass operators and the meson internal or flavor functions in Appendix C. Here, the example set in §3.2.7) and the "inner perfection" criterion Ed) of §A3 come to aid.

The hidden independent variables on this level allow for new physics not obtainable on level Logic1. These include the relative space $\underline{x}$ and relative time x^0 between quarks(see (C5.1) below) which give rise to confinement and finite $W\pm$ and Z boson masses(without Higgs boson), respectively, in SSI considered in Appendix C.

The internal or flavor coordinates z_I, z_{II} in (C5.2-3) below can be considered to be on par with the "hidden" relative space coordinate x mentioned above. Thus, the mass operator $m_{2op}(z_I,z_{II})$ in (C5.3) may for instance be generalized to $m_{2op}(z_I,z_{II},x)$ such that Lorentz invariance is preserved. The internal or flavor space $z_Iz_{II}^*$, when real, and the relative space $\underline{x}$ between quarks are now coupled and this may lead to additional new physics. This may be related to that the masses of mesons with closed flavors ($z_Iz_{II}^*$ real) differ somewhat from the predictions in Table 5.5 of [5].

5.5. Physics Comes out of Mathematics

The results obtained from levels Logic1 and Logic2 cannot be "understood" at first. This is due to that we can only "understand" by referring back to familiar concepts. However, the physics that arises from mathematics on these two levels are associated with new, unknown concepts which can therefore not be "understood." A theorist's task is to provide a concise "account," not "explanation," of data, here using partial differential equations and their solutions. Whether the new concepts in the account can be "explained" or "understood" or not is of no concern in the beginning. Eventual "understanding" may come later when people get used to such new concepts because they work.

CR1 of §3.1 does not allow physical quantities or concepts outside the existing theory and *Recent data* in domain Physics to be "put into" domain Logic. From the new mathematical structure obtained in domain Logic, however, comes new physical concepts when this structure is brought into domain Physics to become a new theory. As V. Weisskopf has pointed out: physics comes out of mathematics.

Examples are time dilatation and Lorentz contraction on level Logic0, red shift, curved space time, quantum mechanical exchange effects and tunnelling, and Bose-Einstein condensation on level Logic1, and confinement and mass generation for the $W^{\pm}$ and Z gauge bosons (without Higgs boson) in SSI on level Logic2. Apart from those on level Logic0, these new concepts cannot be obtained by manipulations of the old concepts, such as "Gedanken" experiments or constructions of phenomenological models because these can only contain known, hence not new, concepts. The Bohr-Sommerfeld models and potential models for hadron spectra are examples.

The *Conflict* in Stage II of §2.4 is not resolved in that stage in domain Physics. It is resolved in Stage III, in which the *Conflict* turns into an *Inconsistency* that is eliminated by the *Leap.* This leap is the *turning point* in the stages of development in §2.4 and is of purely logical nature or some general principle because Stage III takes place in domain Logic.

In the cases of §4.1-2, however, physical quantities and concepts(Higgs bosons, colored objects) foreign to the existing theories are created in Stage II in domain Physics in form of hypotheses which are then "forced" into domain Logic in Stage III. This violates of CR1 of §3.1. These concepts have their origins in analogies with existing physical concepts in solid state physics and are basically old. In fact, any physical hypothesis created in this stage can invariably only contain known, hence old, physical concepts because these are the only ones we have at our disposal.

These specific, second guesses of nature fix beforehand the directions of subsequent developments in domain Logic in Stage III and thereby deprive nature of the possibility to take its own course through mathematical developments from a more "loose" and general new mathematical structure, observing CR1, as in the cases of §3.2. CR1 means that physical hypotheses cannot "move" in the direction from domain Physics in Stage II into domain Logic in Stage III to become leaps or additional recent mathematical requirements. If it is not heeded, the new mathematical structure will be forced to live with forms of old concepts that may thwart the emergence of genuinely new physics. This is also the case for phenomenological models which are therefore stop-gap theories having narrow, specific application angles.

The direction of "motion" is the opposite. It is the *Leap,* which is logical and not physical, made in Stage III in domain Logic that "moves" into domain Physics in Stage IV to be suitably interpreted as a physical *Hypothesis.*

5.6. Impact of Quark Physics on Our Conception of the Universe

Up to a century ago, people's daily experiences and concepts formed from them originated in the Newtonian world. Time was absolute, space Euclidean and physics continuous and deterministic. The parameter region in which this Newtonian conception of the universe holds were subsequently expanded by new experiments and this conception had to be modified in the new parameter regions.

Thus, at high speeds, the above space and time become relative and interconnected to become space-time according to special relativity. Considering the large masses of the heavenly bodies, the above space-time become connected to mass to become space-time-mass or "curved space-time" in accordance to general relativity. In the atomic region, the continuous and deterministic conceptions of the universe become discrete and statistical described by quantum mechanics.

The emergence of quarks and the theories to account for them again introduce new conceptions in the subnuclear region of parameters. The new feature is the "hidden relative space-time x" and "hidden complex flavor space z" (see §C5 and §C1 below) or shortly "hidden space" necessitated by that quarks are not observable individually. Such "hidden spaces," or synonymously "hyperspaces," are not limited to SSI here but have to be present in any realistic hadron theory containing quarks at different space-times so that the first line of (C5.1) below holds. There is at least one set of "hidden spaces" or "hyperspaces" associated with each hadron. Thus, *our conception of the universe now includes infinitely many such "hyperspaces," in which essential physics takes place.*

Conventionally, hadrons are conceived to have finite sizes in laboratory space. However, such sizes are inferred from experiments involving collisions and do not necessarily apply to a hadron not under interaction. Such a hadron is described by the wave equations (C5.2) or (C6.1) and (C5.1) applies. After having solved these equations and integrated over the "hyperspaces," the wave functions reduced to the exponential form in (C5.1) which describes a free point particle in laboratory space X^μ. This puts the hadron on equal footing with the lepton; the difference is that the hadron, but not the lepton, is accompanied by "hidden relative spaces."

Thus, *the four-dimensional space time X^μ we live in contains only vacuum and point particles and is "empty."* This conception is not new but has for instance been arrived at long ago by Buddhists in akin form.

Classical physical theories were largely constructed from observed data. Thus, Maxwell set out to put Faraday's experimental results in mathematical form which became part of his theory and Kepler's data played role in the formation of Newton's theory. The newer ones, such as those mentioned in §3.2-7), §3.2-8) and §4.3, were no longer constructed in that way but were "guessed mathematically," based upon earlier mathematical forms, hints from data, intuition, and the criteria of §A3Ec)-Ed) below.

The basic language of nature may be considered to be solutions to partial differential equations. New concepts derived from these equations represent the basic features of that part of nature pertaining to these equations and have no counterparts in the Newtonian world. This is why ordinary people, including some philosophers not familiar with the creation process of newer physical theories, find the new physics difficult to "understand."

Conclusion

Past experiences show that in the creation of a new physical theory, one does not put in physics, which invariably refer to known concepts, into new theories but relies on logic or some basic principles in the creation of the new mathematical structure. New physics and concepts then comes out of mathematics development from this structure.

These experiences in form of CR1 were not heeded in the creation processes leading to EWM and QCD, as was mentioned in §5.5. CR2 is also not fulfilled. Appendix B indicates further that difficulties of QCD are too fundamental to be overcome by modifications. From epistemological as well as historical viewpoints, the Higgs related part of EWM and low energy QCD therefore appear to be stop-gap theories to be replaced by a more correct theory, for which SSI may be a candidate.

Appendix A. Relevant Epistemologics

Ever since renaissance, scientists and philosophers have influenced each other. Copernicus and Galilei influenced Descartes, who in his turn influenced Newton who influenced Kant. Hume and Mach influenced Einstein who influenced the Vienna Circle. Many of the philosophers had scientific background or started off as scientists. On the whole, science had more impact upon epistemology than vice versa.

Four epistemologies of interest to the present investigations are sketched below for reference.

A1. Pragmatism [9]

"Pragmatism is a school of philosophy founded by Peirce (1877)... It is based on the principle that the usefulness, workability, and practicality of ideas and proposals are the criteria of their merit. Ideas borrow their meanings from their consequences and their truths from their verification.

Peirce's pragmatism is primarily a theory of meaning that emerged from his first-hand reflections on his own scientific work, in which the experimentalist understands a proposition as meaning that, if a prescribed experiment is performed, a stated experience will result. The method has two different uses: (1) It is a way of showing that when disputes permit no resolution, the difficulties are due to misuses of language, to subtle conceptual confusions. (2) The method may be employed for clarification. Consider what effects, that might conceivably have practical bearings, we conceive the object of our conception to have. Then our conception of these effects is the whole of our conception of the object."

Peirce' also introduced the term *retroduction*, which means the forming and accepting on probation of a hypothesis to explain surprising facts. This was once his main theme of pragmatism.

A2. Logical Positivism [9]

Logical Positivism comes out of the Vienna Circle (1923-38) founded by Schlick. Einstein (special relativity) had significant impact on it. Its members paid much attention, firstly, to the form of scientific theories, in the belief that the logical structure of any particular scientific theory could be specified quite apart from its content. Second, they formulated a "verifiability principle" or criterion of meaning, a claim that the meaningfulness of a proposition is grounded in experience and observation. In its negative form, the principle said that no statement could both be a statement about the world and have no method of verification attached to it. In other words, all *meaningful* discourse consists either of

LPa) the formal sentences of logic and mathematics or

LPb) the factual propositions of the special sciences. Any assertion that claims to be factual has meaning only if it is possible to say how it might be verified. Metaphysical assertions, coming under neither of the two classes, are meaningless.

Because this principle is by itself not verifiable, they could only recommend its use. During 1930-60, verifiability was replaced by a more tolerant version expressed in terms of testability or confirmability. The logical positivists continued to reformulate their criteria of factual meaningfulness. There are different versions; all of them are more lenient than the stringent original formulation.

A3. Einstein's Epistemological Credo [8]

Einstein saw on the one side

Ea) *the totality of sense*-experiences and

Eb) *the totality of concepts and propositions* on the other. The relations between the concepts and propositions among themselves and each other are of a logical nature and follow firmly laid down rules.

He wrote further: "The concepts and propositions get "meaning," viz., "content," only through their *connection* with sense-experiences. The connection of the latter with the former is purely intuitive, not itself of a logical nature. The degree of certainty with which this connection, viz., intuitive combination, can be undertaken, and nothing else, differentiates empty phantasy from scientific "truth." The system of concepts is a creation of man together with the rules of syntax, which constitute the structure of the conceptual systems. Although the conceptual systems are logically entirely arbitrary, they are bound by the aim to permit the most nearly possible certain (intuitive) and complete coordination with the totality of sense-experiences; secondly, they aim at greatest possible sparsity of their logically independent elements (basic concepts and axioms), i.e., undefined concepts and underived (postulated) propositions... A proposition is correct if, within a logical system, it is deduced according to the accepted logical rules. A system has truth-content according to the certainty and completeness of its coordination-possibility to the totality of experience. A correct proposition borrows its "truth" from the truth-content of the system to which it belongs. Judgement of the theory is based upon the both conventions:

Ec) "external confirmation." The theory must not contradict empirical facts even if its application can be quite delicate. For it is often, perhaps even always, possible to adhere to a general theoretical foundation by securing the adaptation of the theory to the facts by means of artificial additional assumptions...

Ed) "inner perfection." This is characterized by the "naturalness" or "logical simplicity" of the premises of the basic concepts and of the relations between these which are taken as a basis.

Among theories of equally "simple" foundation that one is to be taken as superior which most sharply delimits the qualities of systems in the abstract i.e., contains the most definite claims... We prize a theory more highly if, from the logical standpoint, it is not the result of an arbitrary choice among theories which, among themselves, are of equal value and analogously constructed... *in the choice of theories in the future will have to play an all the greater role the more the basic concepts and axioms distance themselves from what is directly observable, so that the confrontation of the implications of theory by the facts becomes constantly more difficult and more drawn out...* A theory is the more impressive in the greater the simplicity of its premises is, the more different to kinds of things it relates, and the more extended is its area of applicability."

A4. Feynman's Summary

Today's physicists follow the above epistemologies to varying degrees without thinking about them. These teachings have been summarized, among others, in Feynman's lectures:

> "One guesses a theory and computes its consequences. If the results disagree with experiment, this theory is wrong. If the results agree with experiment, it does not mean that this theory is right."

Appendix B. On the Foundation of QCD

Apart from the remarks in §4.2 that the creation of QCD does not satisfy CR1 and at least part of CR2, the following points show that the foundation of QCD is far from being firm.

B1. QCD at High Energies

That QCD is allegedly successful at high energies does not mean that it is right (§A4). Further, this allegation is not stringent. An often cited agreement with data comes from deep inelastic scattering experiments but the test is on the level of structure function, which contains assumptions so that the derived results are no longer firmly anchored in first principles.

The circumstance may be compared to that classical mechanics agrees with data at high angular momenta but breaks down at small angular momenta and has to be replaced by quantum mechanics. Somewhat similarly, QCD holds perturbatively at high energies but becomes nonperturbative around 1 GeV and cannot produce predictions without resorting to assumptions or phenomenological models. In the low energy region, QCD analogously needs be replaced by another theory; SSI may be a candidate. Such a theory, at higher energies, has to go over to a form that will yield results compatible to those of perturbative QCD; there may be an equivalent "correspondence principle" analogous to that taking quantum mechanics to classical mechanics.

B2. Experimental Evidences

An important underpinning of QCD is provided by the three jet data from the JADE experiments in 1979. One of the jets differed from the other two, could be associated with a spin one structure and was assigned to a jet spear-headed by a gluon. However, this underpinning is removed if the gluon is replaced by a diquark, which has a spin one and is also not observable. The diquark interpretation is consistent with the successful quark-diquark classification of baryon spectra.

Further, the predicted glueball has not been observed.

The so-called quark-gluon plasma experiments start with nucleons whose mutual interaction is scalar. In the plasma state, however, the interaction among quarks takes place via colored vector gauge fields. It is not clear how these two widely different types of interactions can "convert" into each other.

B3. QCD Action

In the notation of [1], the QCD Lagrangian reads

$$L_{QCD} = -\frac{1}{4} F_{\mu\nu}^{(a)} F^{\mu\nu(a)} + i \sum_q \overline{\psi}_q^i \gamma^\mu (D_\mu)_{ij} \psi_q^j - \sum_q m_q \overline{\psi}_q^i \psi_{qi} \tag{B1}$$

$$F_{\mu\nu}^{(a)} = \partial_\mu A_\nu^a - \partial_\nu A_\mu^a - g_s f_{abc} A_\mu^b A_\nu^c \tag{B2}$$

$$(D_\mu)_{ij} = \delta_{ij} \partial_\mu + i g_s \sum_a \frac{\lambda_{i,j}^a}{2} A_\mu^a \tag{B3}$$

where the $\psi_q^i(x)$ are the 4-component Dirac spinors associated with each quark field of (3) color i and flavor q, and $A_\mu^a(x)$ are the (8) Yang-Mills (gluon) fields.

As was mentioned in §2.2, the starting points of all established physical disciplines are all differential equations. These can subsequently be converted into action integrals. QCD, however, also breaks this rule in that it starts with an action integral with Lagrangian density

(B1). Equations of motion derived from the QCD action involve quantities on level Logic0 such as colored electric and magnetic fields that have no corresponding quantities on level Data0 and can hence not be measured.

That (B1) contains quark wave functions $\psi_q{}^i(x)$ reflects the view of *Recent data* in §4.2 that quarks exist but are somehow confined. Here, quarks are treated as if they can be observed, contrary to experience, because one can in principle form expectation values, on level Logic0, of dynamic variables using these $\psi_q{}^i(x)$ on level Logic1. Confinement may be regarded as a "papering over" via the attachment of three colors indices i to each $\psi_q(x)$. This is different from the *Recent data* for SSI in §4.3, where the interpretation "no free quark exists" is adopted. This is reflected in that the hadron wave equations (C5.2), (C4.5) and (C6.1) below contain no quark wave functions.

Practically, there are also no simple ways to obtain hadron wave functions from (B1-3) so that CR2a) is not fulfilled.

B4. Applicability of "Asymptotic Freedom" [10]

In QCD, phenomenological confinement is obtained if the vacuum is a perfect color dia-electric. This is allegedly supported by "asymptotic freedom." But this result was derived from an extension of QED(U(1), Abelian), which provides a tiny screening effect, to quarks belonging to an SU(n) multiplet(non-Abelian), which led to anti-screening. Now the charged leptons are directly observable point particles interacting via a U(1) gauge field in QED. The derivation cannot be simply taken over to apply to the not directly observable quarks. From this viewpoint, this "asymptotic freedom" provides no support to confinement.

Appendix C. SSI (Scalar Strong Interaction Hadron Theory)

The background leading to SSI [3, 4] has been given in [5]. Here, it is summarized taking Sec. 2 and §3.1 into consideration. Unless specified to be otherwise, the symbols and formulae below are taken to refer to hypothetical cases and are within domain Logic but with the primes ´ dropped for simplicity.

The physics mentioned below serve to aid in the choices of leaps which are in principle arbitrary and hence infinite in number on level Logic2, so that when the completed new mathematical structure is taken across the boundary Logic-Physics into domain Physics in Figure 2.1, it becomes a new theory that can be tested favorably against data from level Data0.

C1. Internal or Flavor Space

The Dirac equation in classical form reads

$$\gamma^{\mu} p_{\mu} + m = 0 \tag{C1.1}$$

where p_μ is the 4-momentum and m the mass of a particle. When going over to quantum mechanics, the momenta p_μ become operators operating on a wave function so that (C1.1) becomes the Dirac equation

$$\left(-i\gamma^{\mu}\partial_{X\mu}+m\right)\psi(X)=0 \tag{C1.2}$$

Now, both p_μ and m are measurable quantities and should be treated on equal footing. Therefore, m should also be generalized into an operator m_{op} operating on some function ξ. This conception originated in the early 1960's and hadron masses were regarded as expectation values of mass operators. This led to the successful classification of hadron masses by the Gell-Mann-Okubo formula [11]. Referring to quarks, (C1.2) is thus generalized to

$$\left(-i\gamma^{\mu}\partial_{X\mu}+m_{op}\right)\psi(X)\xi^{p}\left(z^{q}\right)=0 \tag{C1.3}$$

where the superscripts p and q designate quark flavor and z^q represents a complex internal or flavor space of dimension equal to the number of quark flavors under consideration. To begin with, let $p, q = 1, 2, 3$ which refer to the u, d, and s quarks, respectively. These z^q coordinates are not observable and hence are hidden independent variables on level Logic2. They constitute the basis vectors generating the first fundamental representation of the group of global SU(3) transformations. $\xi^p(z)$ transforms as z^p, but its form, as well as that of m_{op}, are arbitrary provided that

$$m_{op}\xi^{p}\left(z^{q}\right)=m_{p}\xi^{p}\left(z^{q}\right) \tag{C1.4}$$

where m_p is the mass of the quark with flavor p. Thus, (C1.2) can be replaced by (C1.3) and (C1.4).

Following the thesis Ed) of §A3, employed in §3.2-7), the simplest forms of the quantities in the eigenvalue equation (C1.4) are

$$\xi^{p}(z)=z^{p}, \qquad m_{op}=\sum\nolimits_{q} m_{q}\left(z^{q}\frac{\partial}{\partial z^{q}}+c.c\right) \tag{C1.5}$$

where m_{op} will be called a mass counting operator. These assumptions are analogous to the leap in the general relativity case of §3.2.7) and are in accordance with Ed) ff in §A3; the simplest forms are chosen in the absence of physical requirements.

C2. van der Waerden's Equations

Since the advance of special relativity, the basics equations of classical mechanics and electromagnetism have been written in invariant(tensor) forms which guarantee their Lorentz invariance. Dirac's equation (C1.2) is however not in such a form. This has remedied by van der Waerden [12] who rewrote this equation in the form

$$\partial_X^{a\dot{b}} \chi_{\dot{b}}(X) = im\psi^a(X), \qquad \partial_{X\dot{b}c}\psi^c(X) = im\chi_{\dot{b}}(X) \tag{C2.1}$$

where a and b are spinor indices running from 1 to 2 and ψ^a and $\chi_{\dot{b}}$ are two-spinors. (C2.1) is by its spinor form manifestly invariant under the SL(2,C) group of transformations, which include Lorentz transformations. The relations between the undotted and dotted spinors and Dirac's wave functions ψ_1, ψ_2, ψ_3, and ψ_4 in (C1.2) are

$$\begin{array}{lll} \text{Right handed :} & \chi_{\dot{1}} = \psi_1 + \psi_3, & \chi_{\dot{2}} = \psi_2 + \psi_4 \\ \text{Left handed :} & \psi^1 = \psi_1 - \psi_3, & \psi^2 = \psi_2 - \psi_4 \end{array} \tag{C2.2}$$

ψ_3 and ψ_4 are small components which vanish in the relativistic limit and (C1.2) is suitable when considering nonrelativistic problems. Quarks are however relativistic and the two-spinor form of the wave functions in (C2.2) is more natural.

Taking the complex conjugate of (C2.1) yields for the corresponding antiparticle,

$$\partial_X^{b\dot{a}} \chi_b(X) = im\psi^{\dot{a}}(X), \qquad \partial_{X\dot{c}b}\psi^{\dot{c}}(X) = im\chi_b(X) \tag{C2.3}$$

Noting (C1.4), the equivalent of (C1.3) becomes for a hypothetical quark

$$\partial_X^{a\dot{b}} \chi_{\dot{b}}(X)\xi^p(z^q) = im_{op}\psi^a(X)\xi^p(z^q), \qquad \partial_{X\dot{b}c}\psi^c(X)\xi^p(z^q) = im_{op}\chi_{\dot{b}}(X)\xi^p(z^q) \tag{C2.4}$$

$$\frac{\partial_X^{a\dot{b}} \chi_{\dot{b}}(X)}{\psi^a(X)} = i\frac{m_{op}\xi^p(z^q)}{\xi^p(z^q)} = im_p, \qquad \frac{\partial_{X\dot{b}c}\psi^c(X)}{\chi_{\dot{b}}(X)} = i\frac{m_{op}\xi^p(z^q)}{\xi^p(z^q)} = im_p \tag{C2.5}$$

The last line shows that the quark mass m_p is a separation constant between the space time coordinates X and the internal or flavor coordinates z^q.

For the corresponding antiquark, one takes the complex conjugate of (C2.4) to obtain

$$\partial_X^{b\dot{a}} \chi_b(X)\xi_p(z_q) = im_{op}\psi^{\dot{a}}(X)\xi_p(z_q), \qquad \partial_{X\dot{c}b}\psi^{\dot{c}}(X)\xi_p(z_q) = im_{op}\chi_b(X)\xi_p(z_q) \tag{C2.6}$$

$$z_q = (z^p)^* = (z_1, z_2, z_3) \tag{C2.7}$$

C3. Starting Equations

Under *Conflict* in §4.3, the BS equation was considered as the existing theory. Consider at first the meson case. Let the quark therein be labelled A and be located at x_I and the antiquark therein be labelled B and be located at x_{II}. The BS equation for a system of this type is of the form

$$\left(i\gamma_I^{\mu}\partial_{I\mu}-m_A\right)\left(i\gamma_{II}^{\nu}\partial_{II\nu}-m_B\right)\psi_{BS}\left(x_I,x_{II}\right)=\text{int eraction terms},\ \partial_{I\mu}=\frac{\partial}{\partial x_I^{\mu}},\ \partial_{II\nu}=\frac{\partial}{\partial x_{II}^{\nu}} \tag{C3.1}$$

The left side is obtained by multiplying the left side of (C1.2) applied to quark A by the same applied to antiquark B together with the generalization

$$\psi_A\left(x_I\right)\psi_B\left(x_{II}\right)\rightarrow\psi_{BS}\left(x_I,x_{II}\right) \tag{C3.2}$$

The BS equation (C3.1) has successfully applied to positronium but obviously fails for meson in which the quark-antiquark interaction is not electromagnetic. If the electron and positron have large enough energy, they are no longer bound and can hence be free. This is contrary to the meson case in which the quark and antiquark cannot be free. Therefore, the quark-antiquark interaction must be of another kind. Further, the BS amplitude (C3.2) has 16 components, far too many for application to mesons. This suggests that the form (C1.2) leading to (C3.1) does not provide a suitable starting point. As was pointed out below (C2.2), the van der Waerden form (C2.1) is more suited to represent quarks.

As to the choice of the quark-antiquark interaction, there are in principle infinite many possibilities. In the absence of physical requirements, the simplest form, namely scalar interaction, is chosen. This is entirely analogous to the reasoning underlying (C1.5) and the leap in §3.2.7) and is in accordance with Ed) ff in §A3. Further, such an interaction is suggested by the known scalar nucleon-nucleon strong interaction.

With these two departures from the BS equation, the present starting points are (C2.1) complemented by a scalar interaction term V and applied to quark A at x_I and (C2.3), after raising and lowering indices, analogously complemented and applied to antiquark B at x_{II}. Instead of (C3.1), one starts with

$$\partial_I^{a\dot{b}}\chi_{A\dot{b}}\left(x_I\right)-iV_B\left(x_I\right)\psi_A^a\left(x_I\right)=im_A\psi_A^a\left(x_I\right) \tag{C3.3a}$$

$$\partial_{I\dot{b}c}\psi_A^c\left(x_I\right)-iV_B\left(x_I\right)\chi_{A\dot{b}}\left(x_I\right)=im_A\chi_{A\dot{b}}\left(x_I\right) \tag{C3.3b}$$

$$\square_I V_B\left(x_I\right)=\tfrac{1}{2}g_s^2\left(\psi_B^b\left(x_I\right)\chi_{Bb}\left(x_I\right)+\psi_B^{\dot{b}}\left(x_I\right)\chi_{B\dot{b}}\left(x_I\right)\right) \tag{C3.3c}$$

$$\partial_{II\dot{e}f}\chi_B^f\left(x_{II}\right)-iV_A\left(x_{II}\right)\psi_{B\dot{e}}\left(x_{II}\right)=im_B\psi_{B\dot{e}}\left(x_{II}\right) \tag{C3.4a}$$

$$\partial_{II}^{d\dot{e}}\psi_{B\dot{e}}\left(x_{II}\right)-iV_A\left(x_{II}\right)\chi_B^d\left(x_{II}\right)=im_B\chi_B^d\left(x_{II}\right) \tag{C3.4b}$$

$$\square_{II}V_A\left(x_{II}\right)=\tfrac{1}{2}g_s^2\left(\psi_A^b\left(x_{II}\right)\chi_{Ab}\left(x_{II}\right)+\psi_A^{\dot{b}}\left(x_{II}\right)\chi_{A\dot{b}}\left(x_{II}\right)\right) \tag{C3.4c}$$

Here, g_s^2 is the scalar strong coupling constant for quark-antiquark or quark-quark interaction. The terms in (C3.3a, 3b) and (C3.4a, 4b) are grouped such that the left sides only contain operators in space time and the right sides contain the quark masses which refer to internal space, as is seen in (C1.4). Equations (C3.3c) and (C3.4c) are written such that the potentials are on the left side and wave functions on the right.

C4. Construction of Meson Wave Equations

Analogous to the formal construction of (C3.1), the left and right sides of (C3.3) are multiplied into the left and right sides, respectively, of (C3.4). There are 3×3=9 equations, in which the operators are placed to the left of the wave functions. Similar to (C3.2), the separable product wave functions are generalized into two-quark wave functions not separable in x_I and x_{II} according to

$$\chi_{A\dot{b}}(x_I)\chi_B^f(x_{II}) \to \chi_{\dot{b}}^f(x_I, x_{II}), \qquad \psi_A^c(x_I)\psi_{B\dot{e}}(x_{II}) \to \psi_{\dot{e}}^c(x_I, x_{II}) \tag{C4.1a}$$

$$\chi_{\dot{b}}^{*\dot{f}}(x_I, x_{II}) = \left(\chi_{\dot{b}}^f(x_I, x_{II})\right)^*, \qquad \chi \to \psi \tag{C4.1b}$$

$$\chi_{A\dot{b}}(x_I)\psi_{B\dot{e}}(x_{II}) \to \chi_{\dot{b}\dot{e}}(x_I, x_{II}) \tag{C4.2a}$$

$$\psi_A^c(x_I)\chi_B^f(x_{II}) \to \psi^{cf}(x_I, x_{II}) \tag{C4.2b}$$

$$V_A(x_{II})V_B(x_I) \to \Phi_m(x_I, x_{II}) \tag{C4.3}$$

The mixed spinor $\chi_{\dot{b}}^f$ of (C4.1a) has four components, which correspond to those of a conventional 4-vector. It is therefore decomposable into a singlet and a triplet, which can be assigned to the rest frame pseudoscalar and vector meson wave functions, respectively. The same holds for $\psi_{\dot{e}}^c$. The complex conjugates of the mixed spinors of second rank (C4.1b) are still mixed spinors and behave in the same way under SL(2,C) transformations.

χ and ψ on the left of (C4.2) can be transposed and this leads to that the right members of (C4.2) are symmetric spinors of second rank each having three components only. They can therefore not represent the pseudoscalar meson. In view of the indistinguishability of a quark and an antiquark inside a meson in the context mentioned at the end of Sec. 2.1 of Ch. 2 in [5], ψ^{cf} and $\chi_{\dot{b}\dot{e}}$ of (C4.2) are associated with a diquark or an antidiquark from the space time and transformation points of view. ψ^{cf} and $\chi_{\dot{b}\dot{e}}$ are put to zero here in accordance with that "no free diquark exists" under *Recent data* in §4.3.

The quark wave functions ψ and χ not paired off according to (C4.1) and (C4.2) are also put to zero, in accordance with that "no free quark exists" under *Recent data* in §4.3. This differs from the interpretation "quarks are confined" in §4.2 which led to the presence of quark wave functions in (B1). Accordingly, the unpaired V_A or V_B also vanishes by virtue of (C3.3c) and (C3.4c).

Applying (C4.1-3) to the 9 product equations and noting the above null results, 6 of them drop out. The three surviving equations arise from the products of (C3.3a) with (C3.4a), (C3.3b) with (C3.4b) and (C3.3c) with (C3.4c). The last product necessitates (C4.3) because the right side is no longer separable in x_I and x_{II} after application of (C4.1-2).

The result is the following three coupled meson wave equations,

$$\partial_I^{a\dot{b}}\partial_{II\dot{e}f}\chi_{\dot{b}}^{f}(x_I,x_{II})+(m_A m_B-\Phi_m(x_I,x_{II}))\psi_{\dot{e}}^{a}(x_I,x_{II})=0 \tag{C4.4a}$$

$$\partial_{I\dot{b}c}\partial_{II}^{d\dot{e}}\psi_{\dot{e}}^{c}(x_I,x_{II})+(m_A m_B-\Phi_m(x_I,x_{II}))\chi_{\dot{b}}^{d}(x_I,x_{II})=0 \tag{C4.4b}$$

$$\Box_I\Box_{II}\Phi_m(x_I,x_{II})=-\frac{g_s^4}{4}\left(\psi^{b\dot{a}}(x_I,x_{II})\chi_{\dot{a}b}^{*}(x_I,x_{II})+\psi^{*a\dot{b}}(x_I,x_{II})\chi_{\dot{b}a}(x_I,x_{II})\right) \tag{C4.5}$$

If the quark-antiquark interaction is chosen to be vector(gauge) instead of scalar, similar calculations show that no self-consistent set of meson wave equations like (C4.4-5) can be formed.

C5. Hidden Independent Variables, Level Logic2 and CR1

The quark and antiquark coordinates x_I and x_{II} are not observables. They are transformed into an observable laboratory coordinate X^μ for the meson and a relative coordinate x^μ according to

$$x^\mu=x_{II}^\mu-x_I^\mu,\qquad X^\mu=(1-a_m)x_I^\mu+a_m x_{II}^\mu$$
$$\chi_{\dot{b}}^{f}(x_I,x_{II})=\chi_{\dot{b}}^{f}(X,x)\rightarrow\chi_{\dot{b}}^{f}(x)\exp(iK_\mu X^\mu),\qquad \chi\rightarrow\psi \tag{C5.1}$$

when a_m is a constant and K_μ the 4-momentum of the meson. The arrow refers to cases separable in X and x. x^μ is also a hidden independent variable and belongs to level Logic2. It cannot be observed so that the requirement that the "no free quark exists" in §4.3 is fulfilled. If x^μ were observable, the quark and antiquark coordinates x_I and x_{II} would also be observable according to (C5.1), contrary to data.

Analogous to the transition of (C2.1) to (C2.4) and of (C2.3) to (C2.6), $m_A m_B$ in (C4.4) becomes an operator m_{2op} operating on an internal function $\xi^p{}_r$,

$$\partial_I^{a\dot{b}}\partial_{II\dot{e}f}\chi_{\dot{b}}^{f}(x_I,x_{II})\xi_r^p(z_I^q,z_{IIs})+(m_{2op}-\Phi_m(x_I,x_{II}))\psi_{\dot{e}}^{a}(x_I,x_{II})\xi_r^p(z_I^q,z_{IIs})=0 \tag{C5.2a}$$

$$\partial_{I\dot{b}c}\partial_{II}^{d\dot{e}}\psi_{\dot{e}}^{c}(x_I,x_{II})\xi_r^p(z_I^q,z_{IIs})+(m_{2op}-\Phi_m(x_I,x_{II}))\chi_{\dot{b}}^{d}(x_I,x_{II})\xi_r^p(z_I^q,z_{IIs})=0 \tag{C5.2b}$$

z_I and z_{II} are associated with the quark and antiquark, respectively, just like x_I and x_{II} do. They are hidden independent variables(§C1). Therefore, The meson wave equations (C5.2) and (C4.5) [5] are on level Logic2 of §2.2.

The choice of m_{2op} is, similar to (C1.5), of the simplest form and is

$$m_{2op}=m_{1op}m_{1op}^{*},\qquad m_{1op}=m_{1op}^{*}=\sum_q m_q\left(z_I^q\frac{\partial}{\partial z_I^q}+z_{II}^q\frac{\partial}{\partial z_{II}^q}+c.c\right) \tag{C5.3}$$

m_{op} in (C1.5) can be replaced by m_{1op} in (C5.3) without affecting (C1.4). This simple product form is approximate and needs be refined. The simplest choice of $\xi^{p}{}_{r}(z_I{}^{q}, z_{IIs})$ is analogously to combine the first of (C1.5) with (C2.7). Let $\xi^{p}{}_{r}$ be the octet part, to be associated with the octet mesons, in the decomposition $\underline{3}\times\underline{3}^{*}=\underline{1}+\underline{8}$, it then constitutes the basis vectors that generate the regular representation of the group of global SU(3) transformations.

The leaps here, i.e., departures from the BS equation (C3.1) in §4.3, originate in domain Logic. The introduction of the internal space z in §C1 is necessitated by the requirement that the particle mass and momenta, being both observables, should be put on equal footing. The use of (C2.1) is equivalent to the use of (C1.2). The choice of scalar interaction in (C3.3) and (C3.4) is the simplest one, following Ed) of §A3, and also takes place in domain Logic. In this domain, this leap can be considered as choosing (one of) the simplest form of coupling between the mathematical systems (C2.1) and (C2.3). The recent mathematical requirements obtained when the relevant content in *Recent Data* in §4.3 are taken across the boundary Logic-Physics, i.e., no free quark or diquark exists, are satisfied in (C5.2) and (C4.5). Thus, CR1 is fulfilled.

An alternative viewpoint is to discard the BS equation as an existing theory for hadrons. Then there is no conflict in §4.3 and CR1 does not apply, similar to the cases §3.2.3).

C6. Baryon Wave Equations

The above procedure can analogously be applied to baryons. Here, the problem is greatly simplified for ground state baryons which have been successfully classified by considering them to consist of a quark and a diquark. Let the subscript *II* refer to the diquark, the corresponding baryon wave equations read [3]

$$\begin{aligned}
&\partial_I^{a\dot b}\partial_I^{g\dot h}\partial_{II\dot e f}\,\chi^{f}_{\{\dot b\dot h\}}(x_I,x_{II})\xi^{\{ps\}q}(z_I^r,z_{II}^t)=-i\left(m_{3op}+\Phi_b(x_I,x_{II})\right)\psi^{\{ag\}}_{\dot e}(x_I,x_{II})\xi^{\{ps\}q}(z_I^r,z_{II}^t)\\
&\partial_{I\dot b c}\partial_{I\dot h k}\partial_{II}^{d\dot e}\,\psi^{\{ck\}}_{\dot e}(x_I,x_{II})\xi^{\{ps\}q}(z_I^r,z_{II}^t)=-i\left(m_{3op}+\Phi_b(x_I,x_{II})\right)\chi^{d}_{\{\dot b\dot h\}}(x_I,x_{II})\xi^{\{ps\}q}(z_I^r,z_{II}^t)\\
&\Box_I\Box_I\Box_{II}\,\Phi_b(x_I,x_{II})=\frac{1}{4}g_s^6\left\{\chi^{f}_{\{\dot b\dot h\}}(x_I,x_{II})\psi^{\{\dot b\dot h\}}_{f}(x_I,x_{II})+c.c.\right\}\\
&m_{3op}=\left(m_{1op}\right)^3
\end{aligned}\qquad\text{(C6.1)}$$

The simple product form of the last line is likewise approximate and needs be refined.

C7. Origin and Status of SSI

The quark wave functions in (C3.3-4) have been used as "scaffolding" in constructing the hadron wave equations (C5.2), (C4.5) and (C6.1) and are removed afterwards. It may seem that these equations have been arrived in ad-hoc ways. This is indeed the case. However, recall that all the operations in this Appendix take place in domain Logic and are completely free from restraint apart from self-consistency. Acceptance of these equations is solely based upon the test results. These results are obtained by mathematical manipulations of these equations on level Logic2 so that they can be moved to level Logic1, level Logic0 and finally across the boundary Logic-Physics in Figure 2.1 into domain Physics, where they become new theories and are tested by contents (PDG data) from level Data0. This is equivalent to the criteria Ec) of §A3, LPb) in §A2 and §A1.

If the tests are successful, it makes no difference how ad-hoc or odd the above construction processes of these equations may seem. In this case, one can in principle discard all the steps leading to (C4.5), (C5.2) and (C6.1) and imagine that they have been dreamt up or conferred on as revelation. This is not different from that students accept the Newton and Schrödinger equations because they have been successfully tested, irrespective of the ways these equations were arrived at.

Equations (C4.5), (C5.2) and (C6.1) for mesons and baryons, if right, play the same role as the one played by Dirac's equation for atoms. The strong interaction part resides largely in functions dependent upon the hidden independent variables, the relative space x and z_I and z_{II}, and is at first aimed at low energy phenomena not successfully covered by QCD. Introducing local phases into the X dependent part of the wave functions leads to massive $W\pm$ and Z gauge bosons without any Higgs boson.

Confinement arises naturally from (C4.5) and the third of (C6.1) as a result of their higher order nature. The role of Higgs bosons is taken over by the kaons or pions by virtue of the presence of the relative time x^0 among the quarks. Ground state meson spectra and some meson decay problems involving weak, electromagnetic and strong interactions have been rather successfully treated. Thus, the Dalitz slope parameters in $K\to 3\pi$ have been largely correctly predicted [5]. Further applications are presently hampered by mathematical complexities.

The rest frame ground state meson wave functions have been found in closed form but not the baryon wave functions due to mathematical complications associated with higher order differential equations. Assuming the existence of such functions, the baryon magnetic moments are largely correctly predicted. Further, angular momentum is found to be not conserved in free neutron decay [5]. Recently, this assumption has been substantiated and baryon wave functions have been obtained numerically as eigen solutions to these differential equations.

SSI has however not been treated at high energies. Also, quantization of SSI has not been investigated; the hidden independent variable aspects of SSI renders that the conventional procedures in quantizing nonlocal theories, which led to difficulties, need be reassessed.

References

[1] Particle Data Group 2004 Phys Lett B592, A short exposition of QCD and EWM is given there.
[2] Wilczek F 2005 *Nature* 433(no. 7023) 239.
[3] Hoh F C 1993 *Int J Theoretical Physics* 32 1111, 1994 ibid 33 2325.
[4] Hoh F C 1996 *J Physics* G22 85, 1999 *Int J Theoretical Physics* 38 2617.
[5] Hoh F C 2005 *Scalar Strong Interaction Hadron Theory.* It has been shown at http://www4.tsl.uu.se/~hoh and is now seen at http://web.telia.com/~u80001955.
[6] Goldstein H *Classical Mechanics* 1950 Addison-Wesley, p307-314.
[7] Glashow S 1961 *Nucl Phys* 22 579, Weinberg S 1967 *Phys Rev Lett* 19 1264 and Salam A 1968 in *Elementary Particle Physics, Nobel Symp*(ed Svartholm N) 8 367.
[8] "Einstein's autobiography" in *Albert Einstein-Philosopher-Scientist* 1949, Library of living Philosophers, ed. P. A. Schilpp.
[9] *Encyclopedia Britannica.*
[10] Gross D and Wilczek F 1973 *Phys Rev Lett* 30 1343, Politzer H 1973 ibid 30 1346.
[11] Okubo S 1962 *Prog Theor Phys* 27 949.
[12] van der Waerden B 1929 *Göttinger Nachrichten* 100.

H. "Quasi-White Book" on the Particle Physics Community (2010)

This appendix does not deal with physics itself but gives my observations and views on the particle theory community in regard to the present theory. Future science historians may find it to be of some interest.

The reactions to the scalar strong interaction hadron theory I received at meetings and visits to institutions range from avoidance to anger. The theory has been published in a series of papers in *Int. J. Theor. Phys.* except for an early one in *Int J Modern Phys. A* and another in *J. Phys. G.* The standard journals, including the last two journals lately have rejected them. The reason for rejection given by *Phys. Rev. D(PRD)* ranged from that it is too speculative and its wish to keep its readership to that there is no reason to provide any alternative to QCD. During 1992-2005, nine papers were submitted to and rejected by *PRD* and none was sent out to referee for review. Still, the Editor-in-Chief concludes that the hearing has been fair. *Nucl. Phys. B* said: "We choose not to publish your papers." *European Phys. J. C* defended QCD, considered a paper of mine as crackpot and asked me to refrain from submitting paper on scalar strong interaction hadron theory. Los Alamos' arXiv considered my book submission to be "inappropriate."

The nonacceptance may partly be due to that to penetrate the underlying ideas, procedures and work can require much time and effort, perhaps more than what the reviewers are willing to put down. But the following may be more important.

A science journalist recently wrote that all academic areas, including particle theory, are institutionalized so that anyone acts or even thinks differently from the mainstream becomes ostracized. My background is plasma physics at first. In 1992, I presented the early part of this theory to a professor in theoretical physics in Stockholm, whom I knew decades earlier. He said that particle physics is a closed society, outsiders are not let in. When I pointed out QCD's inability to account for low energy data to another professor there, he agreed but said that this is an "internal critique," implying that it is not for "outsiders" like me to interfere. This professor abandoned QCD because it could not account for the baryon magnetic moments and that the SSC (superconducting super collider) project was dropped by the US government. He went into astrophysical particles. I met his young successor, who works with neutrino models, in 2008 and showed him my last paper Appendix G above, he said that QCD is not to be tampered with too much. He further said that "it is like the church," implying, I guess, that QCD has an religious aura and the particle physicists have to tow the line in order not to be ostracized.

It seems that there is a diffuse international establishment on particle theory that tacitly and largely controls the main, relevant journals and research grants. The "official" theory is QCD and heresy is not allowed. A local professor said angrily that I threw "shit" at QCD. Another local professor said that I have been regarded as a heretic and did not allow me to give seminar on the present theory. But privately many admit that low energy QCD is wrong. A third local professor said that I, as a financially independent retiree, can afford to say this. But if a young particle physicist says this, it will not be good for his career. This and the overcrowding(article co-authored by hundreds of names) have contributed to that many formerly QCD physicist have switched to astro-particle physics, cosmology, supersymmetry, string theory, where theory cannot be checked by experiment, and to fields like condensed matter, biophysics, etc. This is a *unhealthy* situation. The task of particle theorists is foremost the accounting of the data given by the Particle Data Group and we should tackle it *first*, from a first principles' theory; the scalar strong interaction hadron theory is a candidate.

A 1979 paper in *Physica A* by Weinberg extolling the virtues of phenomenological Lagrangians appeared timely to the rescue of low energy QCD which turned out to be not solvable. Since then, a huge number of phenomenological models has been built; nearly every group or sometimes person has its own model. Piles of papers get published. Already in the 1960's, Wigner said that 70-80% of *Phys. Rev.* is either wrong or irrelevant. That percentage should be much higher now. Instead of searching for other first principles' theories, I think that paper has guided the development of particle theory in a short-sighted direction and hence greatly impeded real progress.

The spectacular successes of fission and fusion bombs have helped to propel high energy physics into big business, turning over big money and providing steady livelihood of large groups of people. Experimentalists like the Higgs, which calls for bigger machines and hence more money. A new theory that opposes QCD and does not need Higgs is bad news; it threatens future grants and stable funding. Scientific truth can wait, monthly payments cannot.

The early scientific idealism, which led to our present-day knowledge, can be swept away by "business" concerns. When I worked in plasma physics in the 1960's, I made a feasibility study of thermonuclear fusion upon a request. The efficiency was found to be way too low to be of interest. When I mentioned this to a respected colleague, he said: "Don't rock the boat." With some modification, it seems that this attitude may be taken over to particle physics, where jobs are more important for the bulk of practitioners.

Centuries ago, the then young physics was suppressed by the church, who's teachings were not to be challenged. It seems that modern particle theory as frontier of physics has itself grown big and old into an institution and plays some of the roles of the old church. If some future historian happens to look into this case, he may say that "history repeats itself." Well, not exactly, inquisition is out and websites are in.

I worked as an engineer and my work on the present theory has been carried out beside it and full time since retirement. I had free hands. Einstein did his early work in his spare time, and sometimes in his work during working time, and was completely unfettered. Such freedom is nowadays greatly curtailed in academic institutions where "business" considerations have partly turned academic freedom into academic constraint with strong peer pressure. In his autobiography, Einstein wrote: "That little frail plant (meaning some promising scientific idea) which apart from stimulation, mainly stands in need of freedom, without which it dies without exception." Incidentally, a sociologist recently remarked that Einstein is an "impossibility" today. He would not get any grant; a researcher nowadays depends upon outside network that support him.

Very basic new grounds are mostly broken and spearheaded by few individuals, not by the "masses," which almost by definition are followers. Galileo described his work by: "...like an eagle soaring high above....not 100 working horses but a full blod racing horse." This is so in spite of that new theories are often rejected for good reasons because most of them turn out to be not viable. A practical example is that only a tiny fraction of new ideas are worked out to patents, only a tiny fraction, 2-3%, of patents leads to products, and only a small fraction of them becomes commercial successes. Such small fractions exists analogously in scientific theories.

Under the editorship of David Finkelstein, the *International Journal of Theoretical Physic* had a distinguished editorial board and my papers were accepted. After his retirement around

2005, the new editor has switched to the now common peer review system. This system may work for papers working with the mainstream type of theories. It may however not work for entirely new, basic ground-breaking theories because most of the peers are in the mainstream and may not be capable to judge an approach completely deviating from the conventional one. Further, peer pressure will make the referee or editor to ask what may happen to him if he lets an "outsider" in? It is safer to consider my papers unsuitable, inappropriate, outside our scope… like the standard journals do. Not the least, the funding situation in the future may be adversely affected. Scientific advancement can wait, present power is what counts, as was the church's attitude in medieval times.

It will take some time for a drastically new approach to sink in. As Roosevelt observed; those who lead cannot be too far ahead of those who are led. Similarly, Schopenhauer wrote that people listen to those whom they know and are not too much "above" them. He also noted that all truths pass through three stages; ridiculed at first, then violently counteracted and finally accepted as self-evident. Hegel divides the development of a new idea into three stages, thesis, antithesis, and synthesis. The present theory is perhaps now in the second stages of these developments.

References

[A1] ATLAS, CMS Collaboration 2012 *Phys Lett* B716 1, 30.

[A2] Aoki S 1986 *Phys Rev Lett* 57 3136.

[A3] Adler S L 1969 *Phys Rev* 177 2426, Bell J S and Jackiw R *Nuovo Cim* 1969 A60 47.

[B1] Bég M A B and Ruegg H 1965 *J Math Phys* 6 677.

[B2] Blatt J M and Weisskopf V F 1979 *Theoretical Nuclear Physics* Springer, Appendix B.

[B3] Bebek C J et al. 1978 *Phys Rev* D17 1693.

[B4] Bjorken J D and Drell S D 1964 *Relativistic Quantum Mechanics* McGraw-Hill.

[B5] Bergström L 1990 in *Rare Decays of Light Mesons* Ed Mayer B, Frontiers, 161.

[B6] Belinfante F J 1953 *Phys Rev* 92 997.

[B7] Bethe H A and Salpeter E E 1957 in *Handbook der Physik* Springer, Vol. 35 §14, §1.

[B8] Burgess C and Moore G, 2007 *The Standard Model, A Primer* Cambridge Univ. Press.

[C1] Corson E M 1953 *Introduction to Tensors, Spinor and Relativistic Wave Equations* Blackie and Sons, Ch. 2.

[C2] Condon E U and Shortly G H1963 *Theory of Atomic Spectra* Cambridge Univ. Press, 76.

[C3] Carruthers P 1966 *Introduction to Unitary Symmetry* Interscience.

[C4] Coddington E A and Levinson N 1955 *Theory of Ordinary Differential Equations* McGraw-Hill.

[D1] Dirac P A M 1928 *Proc Roy Soc* A117 610.

[D2] Dally E B et al. 1977 *Phys Rev Lett* 39 1176, 1980 *Phys Rev Lett* 45 232.

[F1] Frank M and O'Donnell P J 1985 *Phys Lett* 159B 174.

[F2] Fierz M and Pauli W 1939 *Proc Roy Soc* A173 211.

[F3] Feynman R P, Kislinger M and Ravendal F 1971 *Phys Rev* D3 2706.

[G1] Goldstein H 1950 *Classical Mechanics* Addison-Wesley, Ch. 9.

[G2] Gell Mann M 1962 *Phys Rev* 125 1067.

[G3] Gell Mann M 1964 *Phys Rev Lett* 8 214.

[G4] Goldberg H 1980 *Phys Rev Lett* 44 363.

[G5] Gell Mann M, Sharp D and Wagner W G 1962 *Phys Rev Lett* 8 261.

[G6] Gross D and Wilczek F 1973 *Phys Rev Lett* 30 1343.

[H1] Hoh F C 2001 in *Hadron '01, The 9th Int Conference on Hadron Spectroscopy* Ed Amelin et al. AIP Conf Proc 619, 611 and 1997 in *Hadron '97, The 7th Int Conference on Hadron Spectroscopy* Ed Chung et al. AIP Conf Proc 432, 181.

[H2] Hoh F C 1995 in *Hadron '95, The 6th Int Conference on Hadron Spectroscopy* Ed Birse et al. World Scientific, 368.

[H3] Hurley W J 1974 *Phys Rev* D10 1185.

[H4] Huang K and Weldon H A 1975 *Phys Rev* D11 257.

[H5] Hoh F C 1993 *Int J Theoretical Physics* 32 1111.

[H6] Hoh F C 1996 *J Physics* G22 85.

[H7] Harai H 1976 1980 *Phys Lett* 60B 172.

[H8] Hoh F C 1994 *Int J Modern Physics* A9 365.

[H9] Hoh F C 1994 *Int J Theoretical Physics* 33 2351.

[H10] Hoh F C 1999 *Int J Theoretical Physics* 38 2647.

[H11] Hoh F C 1997 *Int J Theoretical Physics* 36 509.

[H12] Hoh F C 1998 *Int J Theoretical Physics* 37 1693.

[H13] Hoh F C 1999 *Int J Theoretical Physics* 38 2617.

[H14] Hoh F C 2000 *Int J Theoretical Physics* 39 1069.
[H15] Hoh F C 1994 *Int J Theoretical Physics* 33 2325.
[H16] Hoh F C 2007 *Int J Theoretical Physics* 46 269.
[H17] Hoh F C 2010 *Natural Science* 2 398 open access: http://www.scirp.org/journal/ns.
[H18] Hoh F C 2011 *Scalar Strong Interaction Hadron Theory* Nova Science Publishers, Hauppauge, New York.
[H19] Hoh F C 2010 *Natural Science* 2 929 open access: http://www.scirp.org/journal/ns.
[H20] Hoh F C 2012 *J Modern Physics* 3 1562 open access: http://www.scirp.org/journal/jmp.
[H21] Hoh F C 2013 *J Modern Physics* 4 1163 open access: http://www.scirp.org/journal/jmp.
[H22] Hoh F C 2014 *J Modern Physics* 5 995 open access: http://www.scirp.org/journal/jmp.
[H23] Hoh F C 2016 *J Modern Physics* 7 36 open access: http://www.scirp.org/journal/jmp.
[H24] Hoh F C 2016 *J Modern Physics* 7 1304 open access: http://www.scirp.org/journal/jmp.
[H25] Hoh F C 2017 *J Modern Physics* 8 1127 open access: http://www.scirp.org/journal/jmp.
[H26] Hoh F C 2018 *J Modern Physics* 9 584 open access: http://www.scirp.org/journal/jmp.
[H27] Hoh F C 2011 *Scalar Strong Interaction Hadron Theory* II Nova Science Publishers, Hauppauge, New York.
[H29] Hoh F C 2019 *J Modern Physics* 10 635 open access: https://doi.org/10.4236/jmp.2019.106045.
[H30] Hoh F C 2021 *Int. Astronomy and Astrophysics Research* 3 (3) 49 open access: https://www.journaliaarj.com/index.php/IAARJ/article/view/48.
[H31] Hoh F C 2019 *J Modern Physics* 10 1645 open access: https://doi.org/10.4236/jmp.2019.1014108.
[H32] Hoh F C 2020 *J Modern Physics* 11 967 open access: https://doi.org/10.4236/jmp.2020.117060.
[H33] Hoh F C 2021 *J Modern Physics* 12 139 open access: *10.4236/jmp.2021.123013.*
[J1] Jauch J M and Rohrlich F 1955 *Theory of Photons and Electrons* Addison-Wesley, 86 ff.
[J2] Jackson J D 1962 *Classical Electrodynamics* Wiley, §6.3.
[J3] Jackson J D, Treiman S B and Wyld Jr. H W 1957 *Phys Rev* 106 517.
[K1] Kemmer N 1938 *Proc Roy Soc* A166 127.
[K2] Kleima D 1965 *Nucl Phys* 70 577.
[K3] Källén G 1964 *Elementary Particle Physics* Addison-Wesley.
[K4] Kleinknecht K. 2003 *Uncovering CP violation: experimental clarification in the neutral K meson and B meson systems* Springer Tracts in Modern Physics, vol. 195.
[L1] Laporte O and Uhlenbeck G E 1931 *Phys Rev* 37 1380.
[L2] Lichtenberg D B 1978 *Unitary Symmetry and Elementary Particles* Academic Press.
[L3] Lichtenberg D B 1987 *Int J Modern Physics* A2 1669.
[L4] Ludwig W and Falter C 1988 *Symmetry in Physics* Springer.
[L5] Lee T D 1981 *Particle physics and an Introduction to Field Theory* Harwood Academic Publisher, Ch. 15, 21-22.
[L6] Lising L J et al. 2000 *Phys Rev* C62 055501.
[L7] Lee T D and Yang C N 1956 *Phys Rev* 104 254.
[M1] Mitra A N 1981 *Z Phys* C8 25, Nimai Singh N and Mitra A N 1988 *Phys Rev* D38 1454.
[N1] Ne'eman Y 1961 *Nucl Phys* 26 222.
[O1] Okubo S 1962 *Prog Theor Phys* 27 949.
[P1] Tanabashi M et al. 2018 (Particle Data Group), *Phys Rev D* 98, 010001. Some of the data used have appeared in earlier versions of PDG.
[P2] Peskin M L and Schroeder D V 1995 *An Introduction to Quantum Field Theory* Addison-Wesley.
[P3] Politzer H 1973 *Phys Rev Lett* 30 1346.
[P4] Peebles P J E and Ratra Bharat 2003 *Rev Mod Phys* 75 (2) 559.
[R1] Roman P 1960 *Theory of Elementary Particles* North Holland, Ch.1.
[R2] Raczka R and Fischer J 1966 *Comm Math Phys* 2 233.
[R3] van Royen R and Weisskopf V F 1967 *Nuovo Cim* A50 617.
[R4] Rose M L 1957 *Elementary Theory of Angular Momentum* Wiley, 34.
[R5] Riordan M and Schramm D N 1991 *Shadows of Creation: Dark Matter and the Structure of the Universe* W H Freeman & Co
[R6] Ryan S G and Norton A J 2010 *Stellar Evolution and Nucleosynthesis*, Cambridge Univ. Press.

[S1] Schweber S, Bethe H A and de Hoffman F 1955 *Mesons and Fields* Harper and Row, Vol. 1 Ch. 1 §2-4.
[S2] Schrödinger E 1926 *Ann d Physik* 79 361.
[S3] Salpeter E E and Bethe H A 1951 *Phys Rev* 84 1232.
[S4] Sharp R and von Baeyer H 1966 *J Math Phys* 7 1105.
[S5] Schiff L 1955 *Quantum Mechanics* McGraw-Hill.
[S6] Steinberger J 1949 *Phys Rev* 76 1180.
[S7] Sakurai J J 1969 *Currents and Mesons* Univ. Chicago Press.
[S8] Serebrov A P et al. 1998 *JETP* 86 1074.
[S9] Sromicki J et al. 1996 *Phys Rev* C53 932.
[S10] Schreckenbach K et al. 1995 *Phys Lett* B349 427.
[S11] Stratowa Chr et al. 1978 *Phys Rev* D18 3970.
[S12] Shay D 1968 *L Nuovo Cim* 53 1039.
[S13] Somalwar S V et al. 1992 *Phys Rev Lett* 68 2580.
[W1] van der Waerden B 1929 *Göttinger Nachrichten* 100.
[W2] van der Waerden B 1932 *Die Gruppentheoretsche Methode in der Quantenmechanik* Springer, 80 ff.
[W3] Weinberg S 1964 *Phys Rev* B133 1318.
[W4] Wick G C 1954 *Phys Rev* 96 1124.
[W5] Weinberg S 1975 *Phys Rev* D11 3583.
[W6] Wilczek F 2005 *Nature* 433 no. 7023 239.
[W7] Wikipedia (2020) https://en.wikipedia.org/wiki/Main_Page.
[Z1] Zweig G 1964 *CERN Report* Th. 401, 412 (unpublished).

About the Author

Fang Chao Hoh, PhD
Retired
Uppsala, Sweden
Email: hoh@telia.com

Born in Shanghai, China 1933
BSEE Royal Inst. Techn., Stockholm, Sweden, 1957
MS in Plasma Physics 1961, BSEE Royal Inst. Techn., Stockholm, Sweden
PhD in Plasma Physics 1963, BSEE Royal Inst. Techn., Stockholm, Sweden
Post doc U. Calif., San Diego, California, USA, 1963-64
Sr Research Scientist, Boeing Co. Seattle, Washington, USA, 1964-71
Zenith Radio Corp, Chicago, Illinois, USA, 1978-82
Engr. Ericsson Co., Stockholm, Sweden, 1983-98
Elementary particle physics research as retiree 1998-

Index

A

accelerating expansion, vii, ix, 273, 275, 277, 280, 281, 283, 284, 285
action, 2, 38, 39, 63, 64, 67, 81, 82, 83, 84, 85, 87, 88, 90, 91, 92, 102, 112, 125, 127, 129, 131, 135, 138, 140, 141, 142, 162, 164, 218, 224, 225, 227, 287, 326
amplitude, 38, 40, 41, 51, 61, 73, 75, 76, 77, 78, 95, 96, 98, 100, 101, 110, 112, 113, 127, 130, 131, 133, 137, 138, 139, 140, 153, 154, 155, 156, 189, 204, 222, 223, 227, 228, 234, 240, 242, 243, 244, 245, 277, 281, 308, 330
antigravity repulsion, 274, 278, 285
axial vector meson, 31, 32, 308

B

B^0-B^0 system, 250
baryon, vii, xi, 10, 11, 47, 65, 133, 169, 170, 171, 172, 173, 174, 175, 176, 177, 179, 180, 181, 182, 184, 185, 187, 188, 189, 192, 193, 196, 203, 204, 205, 206, 207, 208, 211, 212, 213, 214, 216, 218, 220, 225, 234, 235, 236, 255, 256, 259, 260, 264, 276, 299,301, 302, 304, 305, 307, 308, 326, 333, 334, 335
baryon octet, 212
baryon sector, xi, 218, 256
baryon wave functions, vii, 133, 175, 179, 182, 189, 192, 193, 203, 208, 212, 225, 236, 260, 264, 334
baryon, doublet ground state, 193
basic postulate, 3, 15, 176, 300

C

Cabibbo angle, 81, 116, 117, 118, 119, 161, 308
charge operator, 11, 12, 13, 211, 253
classical energy momentum, 188
classification, vii, 10, 12, 33, 36, 43, 45, 54, 55, 172, 203, 209, 210, 305, 308, 326, 328
confinement, xiii, 1, 3, 5, 31, 43, 44, 53, 68, 96, 130, 134, 151, 182, 185, 196, 199, 207, 254, 255, 300, 302, 305, 307, 308, 318, 319, 320, 321, 327, 334
- meson wave, 96
- quark confinement, 5, 318

coupling constant, xi, 5, 7, 66, 81, 87, 116, 117, 118, 126, 135, 139, 147, 160, 161, 225, 232, 234, 255, 256, 259, 288, 305, 307, 330
CP violation, vii, xi, 239, 240, 245, 247, 248, 250, 340

D

dark energy, ix, 2, 257, 265, 273, 274, 276, 280, 281, 283, 285
- positive relative energy PRE, 265, 273, 274, 276, 279, 280, 281, 282, 283, 284, 285

dark matter, vii, ix, 2, 257, 260, 261, 264, 265, 266, 267, 268, 269, 273, 274, 275, 276, 277, 278, 280, 283, 284, 285, 340
- properties, 266
- ratio to ordinary matter, 266

decay, xi, 55, 59, 63, 65, 68, 69, 72, 73, 75, 76, 77, 78, 79, 80, 81, 86, 87, 91, 93, 94, 95, 96, 97, 98, 99, 100, 101, 105, 107, 108, 110, 111, 112, 113, 114, 115, 116, 117, 119, 120, 124, 125, 127, 129, 137, 138, 139, 140, 141, 142, 145, 147, 148, 149, 150, 151, 153, 154, 155, 156, 157, 158, 159, 160, 161, 162, 164, 165, 166, 167, 207, 217, 218, 220, 221, 222, 223, 224, 225, 227, 228, 229, 231, 232, 234, 235, 236, 239, 240, 242, 243, 244, 245, 246, 247, 248, 249, 250, 306, 308, 311, 317, 334
- radiative decays, xi, 78, 305
- strong decay, vii, xi, 73, 147, 151, 160, 166, 306
- weak and strong decays, 73
- weak decay, vii, 81, 91, 97, 117, 160, 164, 249, 334

decay amplitude, 75, 76, 77, 78, 93, 95, 98, 99, 101, 108, 110, 111, 112, 127, 137, 138, 139, 140, 145, 153, 155, 156, 222, 223, 224, 227, 234, 239, 242
decay amplitudes, 93, 99, 101, 108, 111, 112, 140, 145, 224, 239
decay mechanism, 165, 218
decay rate, xi, 73, 77, 78, 79, 80, 112, 113, 114, 115, 116, 119, 120, 124, 147, 153, 157, 158, 159, 160, 161, 162, 167, 217, 224, 228, 229, 232, 234, 235, 240, 242, 243, 244, 246, 248, 249, 250
decay rates, xi, 73, 79, 80, 112, 116, 120, 147, 159, 160, 161, 224, 228, 234, 235, 240, 246
derivatives, 4, 44, 56, 63, 64, 131, 224, 254, 315, 316
- laboratory & relative space, vii, xiii, 16, 23, 24, 31, 32, 33, 39, 40, 43, 44, 46, 47, 53, 54, 56, 57, 62, 63, 66, 69, 72, 77, 78, 97, 98, 118, 128, 140, 144, 147, 154, 167, 180, 181, 182, 187, 192, 193, 196, 208, 222, 224, 225, 232, 234,

236, 244, 256, 264, 265, 266, 270, 278, 281, 311, 320, 322, 334
detachment of weak and electromagnetic coupling, 147
diquark, 9, 172, 173, 174, 176, 177, 179, 180, 187, 204, 206, 207, 211, 213, 219, 232, 233, 234, 235, 236, 255, 256, 257, 258, 259, 260, 261, 262, 263, 264, 265, 268, 269, 279, 285, 299, 301, 303, 304, 305, 308, 318, 326, 331, 333
diquark-quark, 174, 176, 177, 179, 211, 232, 234, 259, 260, 268, 269, 279
doublet, 11, 85, 128, 129, 170, 171, 179, 180, 182, 183, 186, 187, 188, 189, 190, 192, 193, 196, 197, 201, 202, 203, 209, 210, 211, 218, 234, 235, 308

E

equations of motion, xiii, 5, 10, 15, 23, 63, 81, 82, 84, 85, 91, 169, 172, 176, 177, 179, 203, 217, 218, 240, 244, 252, 257, 258, 264
excited doublet baryons, 193
excited meson, xi, 31, 43, 44, 50, 52, 53, 54, 64, 192, 193, 252

F

Fermi constant, 104, 110, 111, 117, 135, 139, 147, 235
first order system, 132, 193
flavor independence, 42, 43, 45, 47, 56
flavor or internal space, 26
free neutron decay, xiii, 218, 236, 237, 334

G

galaxy, 260, 261, 262, 263, 264, 265, 266, 267, 269, 273, 274, 275, 276, 277, 279, 280, 281, 285
gauge boson, xi, xiii, 1, 4, 26, 38, 64, 65, 68, 81, 82, 83, 90, 91, 92, 93, 94, 95, 96, 97, 98, 100, 101, 102, 103, 104, 105, 107, 108, 117, 119, 126, 127, 129, 130, 131, 134, 135, 138, 140, 141, 142, 143, 144, 148, 149, 152, 164, 165, 188, 219, 221, 224, 225, 226, 236, 249, 254, 308, 317, 321, 334
gauge boson action, 81, 91, 135, 164, 225
Glashow model, 86, 91, 92, 148
gravitation, vii, ix, 2, 26, 257, 258, 260, 262, 264, 304, 306
ground state, 2, 24, 26, 27, 29, 31, 32, 33, 34, 39, 42, 43, 45, 46, 47, 48, 49, 50, 57, 62, 64, 68, 70, 72, 73, 171, 175, 176, 186, 193, 203, 204, 211, 212, 232, 234, 258, 259, 260, 261, 301, 305, 308, 333, 334

H

heavy meson approximation, 59
Hidden variable, 16, 23, 26, 66, 72, 97, 131, 141, 243, 253
Higgs boson, xi, 1, 68, 81, 103, 104, 105, 125, 126, 127, 130, 131, 137, 140, 305, 308, 309, 318, 319, 320, 321, 334
higher spin wave equations, 3, 4
historical background, 287
hydrogen atom, 40, 44, 91, 260, 261, 264, 265, 266, 267, 273, 274, 275, 276, 277, 278, 279, 280, 281, 282, 285, 307, 308

I

impasse, xi, 151, 152, 153, 159, 161, 162, 166, 167
intermediate gauge boson, 81, 94, 97, 100, 140, 149, 152
internal or flavor, 8, 9, 14, 16, 82, 320, 328, 329
internal or flavor functions, 320
internal or flavor space, 8, 320, 328
internal space, 8, 10, 11, 14, 16, 26, 43, 46, 49, 177, 181, 208, 209, 253, 255, 256, 331, 333
intrabaryon potential, 170
intrameson potential, 28, 149
isotriplet, 46, 127, 129, 162

J

j=1/2, 201

K

Kaon decay, vii, 239, 247

L

labelling, 17
Lagrangians, 3, 32, 304, 305, 336
lepton action, 84, 85, 87, 90, 91, 92, 138, 141, 225
leptons, 1, 2, 4, 81, 84, 85, 92, 101, 105, 106, 137, 140, 144, 152, 224, 225, 249, 307, 327
Lorentz invariance, 4, 66, 91, 290, 297, 320, 328

M

magnetic moments, xi, 65, 70, 72, 175, 203, 216, 334, 335
mass, xi, xiii, 8, 10, 11, 12, 13, 14, 16, 18, 20, 24, 25, 26, 39, 41, 42, 43, 44, 45, 46, 47, 48, 49, 50, 51, 52, 53, 64, 67, 68, 72, 78, 80, 81, 82, 84, 85, 86, 88, 90, 91, 92, 96, 97, 98, 102, 103, 104, 105,

106, 107, 108, 111, 115, 117, 120, 125, 126, 127,128, 129, 130, 132, 135, 136, 138, 139, 140, 141, 150, 151, 159, 160, 173, 175, 176, 177, 178, 181, 192, 204, 208, 216, 224, 225, 226, 241, 243, 244, 245, 248, 249, 250, 253, 254, 257, 260, 262, 263, 264, 265, 266, 267, 268, 269, 270, 271, 273, 275, 276, 277, 279, 287, 288, 300, 301, 303, 305, 308, 311, 316, 320, 321, 322, 328, 329, 333
mass operator, 8, 10, 11, 12, 14, 16, 151, 173, 176, 208, 253, 260, 301, 305, 320, 328
meson action, 63, 64, 67, 82, 83, 88, 91, 92, 127, 135, 138, 224, 225
meson sector, xi, 203, 218, 235
meson wave functions, 9, 17, 19, 21, 23, 24, 25, 26, 29, 34, 38, 39, 40, 43, 54, 55, 56, 57, 58, 63, 80, 86, 91, 93, 96, 97, 105, 112, 114, 117, 118, 140, 147, 151, 162, 165, 188, 301, 331, 334
mesons, vii, xiii, 7, 9, 10, 15, 16, 18, 19, 20, 24, 26, 27, 29, 31, 32, 33, 34, 36, 39, 40, 41, 42, 43, 44, 45, 46, 47, 48, 49, 50, 51, 52, 53, 54, 55, 56, 57, 58, 59, 60, 61, 62, 63, 64, 65, 68, 69, 70, 73, 75, 77, 79, 81, 86, 92, 105, 112, 127, 137, 140, 141,142, 147, 148, 150, 151, 152, 154, 156, 157, 158, 159, 161, 165, 166, 167, 169, 170, 174, 177, 181, 185, 189, 190, 192, 193, 200, 203, 204, 209, 212, 233, 249, 251, 252, 255, 256, 258, 276, 300, 301, 302, 305, 308, 317, 320, 330, 333, 334, 339, 341
mixing, vii, xiii, 49, 239, 248, 250
muon, 85, 86, 92, 111, 125, 129, 137, 138, 139, 140, 225, 236
muon decay, 125, 129, 137, 138, 140, 225, 236

N

neutron, vii, xi, xiii, 11, 117, 178, 203, 204, 205, 207, 208, 217, 218, 220, 221, 222, 223, 224, 225, 226, 227, 231, 232, 233, 234, 236, 237, 259, 260, 267, 268, 269, 270, 271, 334
neutron decay, vii, xiii, 117, 207, 217, 218, 220, 225, 232, 234, 236, 237, 334
neutron star, 267, 268, 269, 270, 271
  super-massive black, 271
neutron, free decay, xiii, 218, 236, 237, 334
nonconservation of angular momentum, xiii
nonlocal, xi, xiii, 2, 9, 10, 26, 32, 81, 130, 135, 170, 235, 252, 334
nonlocal theory, xi, xiii, 2, 26, 81
nonminimal substitution, 219
nonrelativistic pseudoscalar, 55, 56, 156
normalization, vii, 12, 26, 31, 37, 38, 40, 51, 52, 64, 74, 80, 87, 97, 103, 106, 113, 114, 118, 135, 136, 143, 144, 180, 189, 192, 203, 225, 228, 234, 290
notations, xiii, 14, 19, 83, 175, 210, 287
null relative energy, 55, 131, 240, 246, 249
numerical solution, 5, 136

O

octet, 10, 18, 19, 21, 69, 127, 175, 212, 216, 248, 333
octet internal functions, 18
octet mesons, 127, 333
octet(s) or decuplet(s), 10, 11
orbitally excited, 42, 43, 52, 53

P

parity, meson wave function, 32
perturbation, 10, 70, 100, 148, 149, 165, 214, 260
phenomenological, 2, 5, 73, 110, 111, 218, 247, 249, 256, 298, 300, 302, 303, 306, 321, 326, 327, 336
Pion action, 140, 142
pion beta decay, 110, 145, 224, 225, 306
Pion beta decay, 306
positive relative energy, 265, 273, 279, 285
proton, 11, 40, 43, 72, 127, 161, 188, 216, 221, 222, 223, 228, 236, 257, 259, 260, 261, 262, 263, 264, 265, 266, 267, 268, 269, 270, 273, 274, 275, 276, 278, 279, 285
  gravitational polarization, 260, 262, 263, 273
pseudoscalar, 7, 8, 9, 19, 20, 32, 41, 42, 43, 44, 45, 46, 47, 48, 49, 55, 56, 57, 58, 62, 68, 69, 70, 72, 73, 75, 76, 77, 78, 79, 81, 88, 94, 95, 96, 97, 117, 127, 137, 140, 141, 147, 148, 149, 152, 154, 156, 157, 158, 160, 164, 165, 167, 193, 217, 241, 252, 288, 303, 304, 305, 307, 308, 331
pseudoscalar meson, 9, 19, 20, 32, 42, 44, 45, 46, 47, 48, 49, 55, 56, 57, 58, 62, 68, 70, 72, 75, 76, 77, 78, 79, 81, 88, 94, 95, 96, 97, 117, 127, 137, 140, 141, 147, 148, 149, 152, 154, 156, 157, 158, 160, 164, 165, 167, 241, 252, 331

Q

QCD Lagrangian, 1, 134, 135, 252, 254, 326
quantization, rudimentary, 75, 94, 221
quantum chromodynamics (QCD), vii, xi, xiii, 1, 2, 5, 7, 65, 134, 135, 251, 252, 253, 254, 255, 256, 298, 299, 300, 301, 302, 303, 304, 305, 306, 307, 308, 309, 317, 318, 319, 323, 325, 326, 327, 334, 335, 336
quark, ix, xiii, 5, 7, 8, 9, 10, 11, 12, 13, 14, 15, 16, 17, 18, 23, 24, 25, 26, 32, 41, 42, 43, 45, 46, 47, 48, 49, 50, 52, 53, 54, 55, 56, 58, 59, 63, 65, 66, 69, 73, 74, 77, 79, 81, 84, 86, 88, 91, 94, 97, 120,

127, 130, 135, 141, 147, 148, 149, 150, 160, 165, 166, 169, 170, 172, 173, 174, 175, 176, 177, 178, 179, 180, 181, 187, 188, 190, 204, 206, 207, 209, 211, 212, 213, 216, 218, 232, 233, 234, 235, 236, 252, 253, 254, 255, 256, 257, 258, 259, 260, 261, 262, 263, 264, 265, 268, 269, 270, 274, 277, 279, 281, 285, 299, 300, 301, 302, 304, 305, 307, 308, 318, 320, 322, 326, 327, 328, 329, 330, 331, 332, 333
quark-antiquark pair, 148, 160
quartet, 170, 171, 179, 180, 182, 183, 188, 190, 193, 196, 197, 199, 200, 201, 202, 210, 222

R

radial, 28, 29, 31, 33, 35, 36, 41, 44, 45, 55, 183, 184, 193, 197, 198, 200, 201, 202, 203, 204, 206, 207, 210, 211, 217, 231, 232, 234, 260, 267, 308
radially excited, 33, 34, 50, 51, 53, 54, 55, 186, 193
relative energy, vii, ix, xiii, 25, 55, 131, 143, 180, 240, 241, 243, 244, 245, 246, 248, 249, 250, 257, 264, 265, 266, 269, 270, 271, 273, 275, 276, 277, 281, 285
relative space, vii, xiii, 16, 23, 31, 33, 43, 44, 46, 47, 53, 54, 56, 57, 62, 63, 66, 78, 97, 98, 128, 140, 144, 154, 180, 181, 182, 187, 193, 196, 208, 224, 225, 232, 234, 236, 256, 264, 265, 266, 270, 278, 281, 311, 320, 322, 334
rest frame, 20, 25, 27, 32, 33, 39, 41, 42, 44, 56, 88, 102, 105, 118, 180, 182, 184, 192, 196, 252, 264, 276, 331, 334
running coupling constant, 135, 256

S

scalar, ix, xi, xiii, 1, 4, 7, 8, 9, 11, 12, 15, 31, 32, 38, 39, 87, 105, 115, 127, 147, 148, 149, 150, 153, 169, 176, 217, 218, 233, 251, 256, 257, 288, 291, 298, 300, 303, 304, 305, 307, 308, 309, 316, 326, 327, 330, 332, 333, 334, 335, 336, 340
scalar potential, 148, 150, 153, 256, 288, 300
second order perturbation, 100
singlet, 9, 19, 23, 25, 27, 32, 33, 43, 46, 49, 50, 51, 52, 55, 56, 57, 61, 68, 84, 97, 98, 101, 104, 105, 108, 127, 156, 165, 175, 180, 202, 208, 227, 331
space inversion, 15, 31, 32, 176, 295, 297
space time, 8, 9, 11, 13, 14, 15, 19, 20, 21, 43, 72, 82, 128, 130, 144, 147, 150, 170, 171, 172, 175, 177, 211, 222, 255, 287, 311, 321, 322, 329, 330, 331
spectra, vii, xi, xiii, 42, 45, 47, 48, 50, 55, 63, 68, 80, 172, 177, 192, 204, 234, 298, 305, 306, 307, 308, 321, 326, 334, 339
spinors, 4, 9, 15, 90, 105, 170, 171, 172, 183, 258, 290, 292, 293, 294, 295, 296, 297, 300, 304, 307, 326, 329, 331
SSI, ix, xi, 1, 2, 217, 218, 251, 252, 254, 257, 261, 266, 270, 275, 276, 280, 283, 284, 309, 311, 317, 318, 319, 320, 321, 322, 323, 326, 327, 333, 334
strong decay, vii, xi, 73, 147, 151, 160, 166, 306
strong interaction potential, 7, 43, 233
SU(2)×U(1), 38, 68, 82, 84, 86, 92
SU(3), 10, 11, 12, 16, 17, 18, 19, 20, 21, 49, 50, 68, 69, 81, 82, 83, 84, 85, 86, 87, 88, 89, 90, 91, 92, 102, 108, 129, 147, 162, 164, 174, 175, 176, 178, 220, 248, 249, 305, 328, 333
su(3) gauge fields, 87
SU(6) symmetry, 11, 18, 43
super-massive black neutron star, 271
superposition principle, vii, 37, 40, 43, 192, 193
symmetric quark postulate, 175, 179

T

tensor gauge field, 218, 219, 220, 221, 224, 226
tensor gauge fields, 218, 220, 224
triplet, 9, 11, 21, 23, 25, 27, 32, 34, 36, 42, 43, 46, 50, 51, 53, 54, 55, 56, 61, 98, 104, 105, 128, 139, 156, 162, 165, 180, 200, 202, 209, 227, 241, 243, 249, 331

U

U(1), 7, 38, 48, 66, 67, 68, 69, 73, 74, 81, 82, 85, 86, 125, 128, 147, 166, 219, 253, 305, 308, 320, 327
unified strong and electromagnetic coupling, 153, 154
universe, vii, ix, 1, 2, 265, 266, 267, 268, 273, 275, 277, 278, 279, 280, 281, 282, 283, 284, 285, 313, 322, 340
  filament formation, 267
  SSI model, 275, 280, 283, 284

V

vacuum meson state, 96, 97, 117, 129, 149, 152, 153, 242, 243, 245
variation, 64, 67, 82, 85, 103, 107, 108, 112, 128, 139, 140, 142, 164, 219, 225, 226
virtual, 86, 105, 108, 119, 124, 129, 140, 147, 149, 152, 153, 156, 160, 161, 165, 166, 167, 224, 225, 227, 319
V_S, 9, 233, 234, 263, 300

W

wave functions, vii, 5, 8, 9, 10, 11, 13, 17, 19, 21, 23, 24, 25, 26, 29, 31, 32, 34, 35, 37, 38, 39, 40, 42, 43, 44, 48, 50, 52, 53, 54, 55, 56, 57, 58, 63, 70, 72, 73, 77, 80, 83, 84, 85, 86, 88, 91, 93, 95, 96, 97, 98, 102, 105, 106, 108, 112, 114, 117, 118, 128, 130, 131, 133, 135, 136, 139, 140, 141, 142, 147, 148, 149, 151, 152, 154, 156, 162, 164, 165, 166, 170, 175, 179, 180, 182, 183, 185, 186, 187, 188, 189, 190, 192, 193, 196, 197, 198, 200, 201, 202, 203, 204, 205, 206, 207, 208, 212, 213, 216, 221, 223, 225, 227, 228, 231, 232, 234, 236, 246, 248, 249, 252, 256, 258, 299, 300, 301, 304, 305, 307, 308, 318, 322, 327, 329, 331, 333, 334
weak coupling constant, xi, 81, 87, 116, 117, 118, 234
weak decays, 81, 117, 249